BUSINESS COMMUNICATION

Process & Product

Brief Canadian Edition

Mary Ellen Guffey, Los Angeles Pierce College
Kathleen Rhodes, Durham College
Patricia Rogin, Durham College

Australia Canada Mexico Singapore Spain United Kingdom United States

Business Communication: Process and Product
Brief Canadian Edition

by Mary Ellen Guffey, Kathleen Rhodes,
and Patricia Rogin

Editorial Director and Publisher:
Evelyn Veitch

Executive Editor:
Chris Carson

Marketing Manager:
Cara Yarzab

Senior Developmental Editor:
Rebecca Rea

Production Editor:
Julie van Veen

Production Coordinator:
Helen Jager Locsin

Copy Editor and Proofreader:
Erin Moore

Creative Director:
Angela Cluer

Interior Design:
Liz Harasymczuk Design

Cover Design and Interior Design Modifications:
Katherine Strain

Cover Image:
Phil & Jim Bliss/The Stock Illustration Source

Compositor:
Tammy Gay

Indexer:
Jin Tan

Printer:
Transcontinental

Printed and bound in Canada
2 3 4 06 05 04 03

For more information contact Nelson, 1120 Birchmount Road, Scarborough, Ontario, M1K 5G4. Or you can visit our Internet site at http://www.nelson.com

National Library of Canada Cataloguing in Publication

Guffey, Mary Ellen

Business communication : process and product / Mary Ellen Guffey, Kathleen Rhodes, Patricia Rogin. — Brief Canadian ed.

Includes bibliographical references and index.
ISBN 0-17-622516-1

1. Business communication.
2. Business writing. I. Rhodes, Kathleen, 1951- II. Rogin, Patricia, 1958- III. Title.

HF5718.3.G82 2003 651.7
C2002-904457-X

Brief Contents

UNIT 1	**Communication Foundations**	**1**
CHAPTER 1	COMMUNICATING AT WORK	**2**
CHAPTER 2	COMMUNICATING IN TEAMS: LISTENING, NONVERBAL COMMUNICATION, COLLABORATION, AND MEETING SKILLS	**24**
CHAPTER 3	COMMUNICATING ACROSS CULTURES	**50**
UNIT 2	**The Writing Process**	**71**
CHAPTER 4	PREPARING TO WRITE BUSINESS MESSAGES	**72**
CHAPTER 5	ORGANIZING AND WRITING BUSINESS MESSAGES	**90**
CHAPTER 6	REVISING BUSINESS MESSAGES	**112**
UNIT 3	**Business Correspondence**	**129**
CHAPTER 7	ROUTINE LETTERS AND GOODWILL MESSAGES	**130**
CHAPTER 8	ROUTINE MEMOS AND E-MAIL MESSAGES	**162**
CHAPTER 9	PERSUASIVE AND SALES MESSAGES	**186**
CHAPTER 10	NEGATIVE MESSAGES	**212**
UNIT 4	**Reports and Proposals**	**237**
CHAPTER 11	REPORT PLANNING AND RESEARCH	**238**
CHAPTER 12	REPORT ORGANIZATION AND PRESENTATION	**268**
CHAPTER 13	TYPICAL BUSINESS REPORTS	**288**
CHAPTER 14	PROPOSALS AND FORMAL REPORTS	**308**

UNIT 5 **Presentations** 339

CHAPTER 15 SPEAKING SKILLS 340

CHAPTER 16 EMPLOYMENT COMMUNICATION 362

APPENDIX A C.L.U.E. COMPETENT LANGUAGE USAGE ESSENTIALS A-1

APPENDIX B DOCUMENTATION FORMATS B-1

KEY TO C.L.U.E. EXERCISES K-1

ENDNOTES E-1

ACKNOWLEDGMENTS ACK-1

INDEX I-1

Detailed Contents

UNIT 1 **Communication Foundations** **1**

CHAPTER 1 COMMUNICATING AT WORK **2**

Ensuring That You Succeed in the New Workplace 3

Career Coach: *Sharpening Your Skills for Critical Thinking, Problem Solving, and Decision Making* 6

Examining the Process of Communication 7

Overcoming Interpersonal Communication Barriers 9

Communicating in Organizations 10

Career Coach: *Practising Courteous and Responsible Cell Phone Use* 12

Improving the Flow of Information in Organizations 13

Tech Talk: *Tips for Controlling the E-Mail Monster* 14

Facing Increasing Ethical Challenges 16

Strengthening Your Communication Skills 18

Summary of Learning Objectives 18

Chapter Review 20

Critical Thinking 20

Activities 21

C.L.U.E. Review 1 22

CHAPTER 2 COMMUNICATING IN TEAMS: LISTENING, NONVERBAL COMMUNICATION, COLLABORATION, AND MEETING SKILLS **24**

Communicating in a Team-Oriented Workplace 25

Characteristics of Successful Teams 27

Checklist for Developing Team Effectiveness 28

Organizing Team-Based Written and Oral Presentations 29

Becoming an Effective Team Listener 31

Checklist for Improving Listening 34

Communicating Through Nonverbal Messages 34

Checklist of Techniques for Improving Nonverbal Communication Skills 38

Planning and Participating in Productive Meetings 38

Checklist for Planning and Participating in Productive Meetings 42

Using Groupware to Facilitate Meetings and Decision Making 43

Strengthening Your Teamwork Skills Now 44

Summary of Learning Objectives 44

Chapter Review 46

	Critical Thinking	46
	Activities	46
	C.L.U.E. Review 2	48
CHAPTER 3	COMMUNICATING ACROSS CULTURES	**50**
	The Increasing Importance of Multicultural Communication	51
	Tech Talk: *Being Multiculturally Correct on the Web*	52
	Understanding Culture	53
	Achieving Multicultural Sensitivity	57
	Improving Communication With Multicultural Audiences	59
	Written Messages	61
	Checklist for Improving Multicultural Sensitivity and Communication	62
	Capitalizing on Workforce Diversity	63
	Summary of Learning Objectives	66
	Chapter Review	67
	Critical Thinking	67
	Activities	68
	C.L.U.E. Review 3	70
UNIT 2	**The Writing Process**	**71**
CHAPTER 4	PREPARING TO WRITE BUSINESS MESSAGES	**72**
	Approaching the Writing Process Systematically	73
	Adapting and Altering the Process	74
	Analyzing the Task	75
	Anticipating the Audience	77
	Adapting to the Task and Audience	78
	Checklist for Adapting a Message to Its Audience	83
	Adapting to Legal Responsibilities	84
	Summary of Learning Objectives	85
	Chapter Review	87
	Critical Thinking	87
	Activities	87
	C.L.U.E. Review 4	89
CHAPTER 5	ORGANIZING AND WRITING BUSINESS MESSAGES	**90**
	Researching Data and Generating Ideas	91
	Organizing Data	93
	Organizing Ideas Into Patterns	97
	Composing the First Draft	99
	Drafting Meaningful Paragraphs	102
	Checklist for Composing Sentences and Paragraphs	105
	Summary of Learning Objectives	106
	Chapter Review	107
	Critical Thinking	107
	Activities	108
	C.L.U.E. Review 5	110

CHAPTER 6 REVISING BUSINESS MESSAGES **112**
Revising Messages 113
Revising for Vigour and Directness 116
Revising for Readability 117
Checklist for Revising Messages 119
Proofreading for the Finishing Touch 120
Career Coach: *The Canadian Spelling Dilemma* 121
How to Proofread Routine Documents 121
Evaluating the Product 122
Summary of Learning Objectives 123
Chapter Review 124
Critical Thinking 124
Activities 124
C.L.U.E. Review 6 126

UNIT 3 **Business Correspondence** **129**

CHAPTER 7 ROUTINE LETTERS AND GOODWILL MESSAGES **130**
Strategies for Routine Letters 131
Direct Request Letters 135
Placing Orders 136
Making Straightforward Claims 138
Checklist for Writing Direct Requests 139
Direct Reply Letters 140
Complying With Requests 140
Writing Letters of Recommendation 144
Granting Claims and Making Adjustments 146
Checklist for Writing Direct Replies 150
Writing Winning Goodwill Messages 151
Checklist for Writing Goodwill Messages 155
Summary of Learning Objectives 156
Chapter Review 157
Critical Thinking 157
Activities 157
C.L.U.E. Review 7 161

CHAPTER 8 ROUTINE MEMOS AND E-MAIL MESSAGES **162**
Writing Routine Memos and E-Mail Messages 163
Organization of Memos and E-Mail Messages 166
Using E-Mail Effectively 167
Procedure and Information Memos and E-Mail Messages 172
Request and Reply Memos and E-Mail Messages 173
Confirmation Memos and E-Mail Messages 176
Checklist for Writing Routine Memos and E-Mail Messages 176
Summary of Learning Objectives 178
Chapter Review 179

Critical Thinking 179
Activities 179
C.L.U.E. Review 8 184

CHAPTER 9 PERSUASIVE AND SALES MESSAGES **186**
Strategies for Making Persuasive Requests 187
Applying the 3-×-3 Writing Process to Persuasive Messages 187
Career Coach: *Seven Rules Every Persuader Should Know* 188
Blending the Components of a Persuasive Message 190
Writing Successful Persuasive Requests 193
Persuading Within Organizations 195
Complaint Letters: Requesting Adjustments and Making Claims 196
Checklist for Making Persuasive Requests 198
Planning and Composing Sales Messages 198
Checklist for Writing Sales Letters 204
Developing Persuasive Media Releases 204
Summary of Learning Objectives 205
Chapter Review 206
Critical Thinking 206
Activities 206
C.L.U.E. Review 9 210

CHAPTER 10 NEGATIVE MESSAGES **212**
Strategies for Breaking Bad News 213
Goals in Communicating Bad News 213
Avoiding Three Causes of Legal Problems 214
Developing Bad-News Messages 215
When to Use the Direct Pattern 218
Refusing Routine Requests 219
Checklist for Refusing Routine Requests 222
Sending Bad News to Customers 222
Checklist for Delivering Bad News to Customers 226
Managing Negative Organization News 227
Checklist for Managing Negative Organization News 229
Presenting Bad News in Other Cultures 229
Summary of Learning Objectives 230
Chapter Review 231
Critical Thinking 231
Activities 231
C.L.U.E. Review 10 236

UNIT 4 **Reports and Proposals** **237**

CHAPTER 11 REPORT PLANNING AND RESEARCH **238**
Understanding Report Basics 239
Applying the 3-×-3 Writing Process to Reports 244
Researching Secondary Data 250

Tech Talk: *Understanding Natural Language, Keyword, and Boolean Searching* 255
Generating Primary Data 256
Documenting Data 260
Summary of Learning Objectives 263
Chapter Review 264
Critical Thinking 264
Activities 264

CHAPTER 12 REPORT ORGANIZATION AND PRESENTATION **268**
Interpreting Data 269
Tabulating and Analyzing Responses 269
Drawing Conclusions in Reports 271
Writing Report Recommendations 273
Organizing Data 274
Providing Reader Cues 276
Illustrating Data With Graphics 278
Incorporating Graphics in Reports 282
Summary of Learning Objectives 283
Chapter Review 284
Critical Thinking 284
Activities 284

CHAPTER 13 TYPICAL BUSINESS REPORTS **288**
Writing Informational Reports 289
Typical Informational Reports 289
Checklist for Writing Informational Reports 294
Writing Analytical Reports 294
Checklist for Writing Analytical Reports 301
Summary of Learning Objectives 304
Chapter Review 305
Critical Thinking 305
Activities 305

CHAPTER 14 PROPOSALS AND FORMAL REPORTS **308**
Preparing Formal and Informal Proposals 309
Components of Informal Proposals 309
Special Components of Formal Proposals 311
Checklist for Writing Proposals 312
Career Coach: *Preparing an Effective Business Plan* 313
Writing Formal Reports 314
Components of Formal Reports 314
The Introduction 316
Components Following the Introduction 317
Final Writing Tips 318
Checklist for Preparing Formal Reports 332

Summary of Learning Objectives 334
Chapter Review 335
Critical Thinking 335
Activities 335

UNIT 5 **Presentations** **339**

CHAPTER 15 SPEAKING SKILLS **340**
Preparing an Effective Oral Presentation 341
Organizing the Content 342
Career Coach: *Nine Techniques for Gaining and Keeping Audience Attention* 343
Planning Visual Aids and Handouts 346
Designing an Electronic Presentation 347
Polishing Your Delivery 350
Career Coach: *How to Avoid Stage Fright* 351
Adapting to International and Cross-Cultural Audiences 353
Checklist for Preparing and Organizing Oral Presentations 354
Telephones and Voice Mail 355
Summary of Learning Objectives 358
Chapter Review 359
Critical Thinking 359
Activities 359

CHAPTER 16 EMPLOYMENT COMMUNICATION **362**
Preparing for Employment 363
The Persuasive Résumé 366
Arranging the Parts 367
Preparing for Computer Scanning 374
Faxing or E-Mailing Your Résumé 379
Checklist for Writing a Persuasive Résumé 379
Ethical Insights: *Are Inflated Résumés Worth the Risk?* 380
The Persuasive Letter of Application 382
Checklist for Writing a Persuasive Letter of Application 387
Follow-Up Letters and Other Employment Documents 387
Interviewing for Employment 390
Career Coach: *Answering Ten Frequently Asked Interview Questions* 392
Summary of Learning Objectives 394
Chapter Review 395
Critical Thinking 395
Activities 395

APPENDIX A C.L.U.E. COMPETENT LANGUAGE USAGE ESSENTIALS: A BUSINESS COMMUNICATOR'S GUIDE **A-1**
APPENDIX B DOCUMENTATION FORMATS **B-1**
KEY TO C.L.U.E. EXERCISES **K-1**

ENDNOTES **E-1**
ACKNOWLEDGMENTS **ACK-1**
INDEX **I-1**

Preface

At the urging of those who like the Third Canadian Edition of *Business Communication: Process and Product* but find that it contains more material than they can cover in their courses, we are pleased to present a brief edition of this bestselling text. In responding to customer needs, we didn't want to simply cut, but rather craft a brief text.

Business Communication: Process and Product, Brief Canadian Edition is ideal for one- or two-semester courses. We have remained true to Mary Ellen Guffey's 3-×-3 process. The content of the book has not been compromised in any way; instead, we have condensed the information to focus on key elements. Based on instructor feedback, much of the *nice to know* information such as the case studies and career track profiles has been removed to the Instructor's Web Site. In addition, the number of end-of-chapter activities has been reduced.

At the same time that we reduced some areas, we also updated existing content and even incorporated new material such as cell phone etiquette, effective e-mail usage, search engine data, and Web use.

In short…
We've listened to customer needs and exceeded expectations for a brief edition of *Process and Product.*

Appreciation for Support

We are indebted to many individuals for the enormous success of previous editions of *Business Communication: Process and Product.* Our heartfelt thanks go to the hundreds of thousands of instructors and students who have used this book and made it the premier business communication textbook in North America.

In producing this new Canadian edition, we are especially grateful to our friends at Thomson Nelson for their creative talent and expertise in converting ideas into practical applications. Our Nelson sales representatives, including Paul Saundercook and Bill More, amazed us with their ability to listen to customers and provide invaluable advice. Frank Killen and Marc Trudel shared constructive insights and experiences. Special accolades go to Cara Yarzab, whose thorough knowledge of the text proved invaluable; to Chris Carson, who listened and made crucial decisions; and to Rebecca Rea and Julie van Veen, who managed details and deadlines with efficiency and graciousness.

Nelson would like to thank those who reviewed *Business Communication: Process and Product* for their insightful comments: Sharon Brown, Sir Sandford Fleming College; Ausra Maria Karka, Humber College; Susan Lieberman, Grant MacEwan College; Deborah Meredith, University of British Columbia; Bruce Powell, Georgian College; Mark Rust, Sheridan College; Ron Slavik, Mohawk College; Alberta Smith, Algonquin College; Ted Spicer, Conestoga College; Tatiana N. Teslenko, University of British Columbia; and William G. Truscott, McMaster University.

In addition, the Durham College administration, faculty, and students provided exceptional support, academic perspective, and feedback as the book evolved. To them we are grateful.

Finally, we thank members of our families—George, Bryan, Tim, Emily, Howie, and Alison—whose understanding and encouragement fueled our efforts.

Mary Ellen Guffey
Kathleen Rhodes
Patricia Rogin

Support Package

A rich variety of instructional resources supplement and support *Business Communication: Process and Product, Brief Canadian Edition.* These materials give you excellent working tools to create a dynamic, exciting, and effective course.

For the Instructor:

Instructor's Manual (0176225250)
This comprehensive resource includes chapter synopses, teaching ideas, lecture enrichment material, classroom management techniques, answers for chapter review questions, suggested discussion guides for critical thinking questions, solution guides for case study questions and applications, and much more.

Printed Test Bank (0176225269)
Each chapter of the test bank contains between 60 and 150 tested questions. A special feature of this edition is the inclusion of feedback for the response to each question. Every chapter opens with a correlation table that identifies questions by chapter learning objective and by content: factual, conceptual, or application. Page references to the text ensure quick reference.

Computerized Testing Tools (0176225277)
All items from the printed test bank are available through this automated testing program. Create exams by selecting provided questions, modifying existing questions, and adding questions. It is provided free to adopters of the text.

Microsoft® PowerPoint® Presentation Slides (0176225285)
This comprehensive lecture system offers summaries, explanations, and illustrations of key chapter concepts, plus lecture enrichment material not included in the text. With PowerPoint® software, instructors can easily customize any slide to support their lectures.

Instructor's CD-ROM (0176415831)
Using key course resources is now easier than ever! The Instructor's CD-ROM combines popular text supplement material in one easy-to-use format. You'll have complete access to the Instructor's Manual (chapter outlines, bonus lecture material, before-and-after documents, and solutions to select chapter activities), PowerPoint® presentation slides, and the Test Bank.

Book-Specific Web Site **http://www.guffeybrief.nelson.com**
The book-specific Web site contains a link to Instructor Resources providing access to Mary Ellen Guffey's on-line newsletter, and electronic downloadable versions of the Instructor's Manual and PowerPoint® slides. The book-specific site also contains links to professional organizations, media resources, online writing labs, and much more! The site leader is Panteli Tritchew, Chair of Applied Communications, Kwantlen University College. Contact your local sales rep for a password to the Instructor Resources portion of the site.

Newsletters and Free Teaching Materials
Adopters are eligible to receive a free subscription to our twice-yearly newsletter, *Business Communication News.* It highlights current issues and news of interest in the business communication course as well as offering free teaching materials that may be ordered directly from the author. In addition, instructors may receive *The On-Line Guffey Report*, a monthly electronic newsletter sent directly to e-mail inboxes of instructors who sign up.

For the Student:

Student Web Site **http://www.guffeybrief.nelson.com**
This powerful site features chapter-by-chapter quizzes and Web links, career and job search information, Web media resources, online writing labs, and much more! The site leader is Panteli Tritchew, Chair of Applied Communications, Kwantlen University College.

Guffey Power Pack CD-ROM (0176415440)
Free with every new copy of the text, this CD-ROM is packed with material to enhance the learning experience: Interactive C.L.U.E. Self-tests, Grammar Review with Quizzes, Letter and Memo Writing Exercises, Critical Thinking Case Studies, and an Employment Interview Kit. Have fun using this dynamic CD-ROM study tool!

Nelson Guide to Web Research, 2003–2004 (0176223878)
Written by Grant Heckman, this useful guide contains everything the student needs to know about using the World Wide Web as a research tool. *The Nelson Guide to Web Research for Canadian Students* can be packaged with *Business Communication: Process and Product*, Brief Canadian Edition, at an affordable price.

UNIT 1

COMMUNICATION FOUNDATIONS

CHAPTER 1

Communicating at Work

CHAPTER 2

Communicating in Teams: Listening, Nonverbal Communication, Collaboration, and Meeting Skills

CHAPTER 3

Communicating Across Cultures

CHAPTER • 1 •

COMMUNICATING AT WORK

LEARNING OBJECTIVES

1 Identify changes in the workplace and the importance of communication skills.

2 Describe the process of communication.

3 Discuss barriers to interpersonal communication and the means of overcoming those barriers.

4 Analyze the functions and procedures of communication in organizations.

5 Assess the flow of communication in organizations, including barriers and methods for overcoming those barriers.

6 List the goals of ethical business communication and important tools for doing the right thing.

Ensuring That You Succeed in the New Workplace

1

Employees at many organizations are experiencing change and upheaval. In fact, the entire work world you are about to enter is changing dramatically. The kind of work you'll do, the tools you'll use, the form of management, the environment where you'll work, the people with whom you'll interact—all are undergoing a profound transformation. Many of the changes in this dynamic workplace revolve around processing and communicating information. As a result, the most successful players in this new world of work will be those with highly developed communication skills.

To become an effective communicator, though, you need more than a good book. You also need practice—with meaningful feedback. You need someone such as your instructor to tell you how to modify your responses so that you can improve. We've designed this book and its supplements to provide you and your instructor with principles, processes, products, and practice—everything necessary to make you a successful business communicator in today's dynamic workplace.

Yes, the workplace is undergoing profound changes. As a businessperson and especially as a business communicator, you will undoubtedly be affected by many transformations. Some of the most significant changes include global competition, flattened management hierarchies, and team-based projects. Other changes reflect our constantly evolving information technology, new work environments, a diverse workforce, and the emergence of a knowledge-based economy.

Heightened Global Competition

Communication is more complicated with people who have different religions, customs, and lifestyles.

Small, medium, and large companies increasingly find themselves competing in global rather than local markets. Improved systems of telecommunication, advanced forms of transportation, and saturated local markets—all of these developments have encouraged companies to move beyond familiar territories to emerging markets around the world.

Doing business in far-flung countries means dealing with people who are very different from you. They have different religions, engage in different customs, live different lifestyles, and rely on different approaches in business. Now add the complications of multiple time zones, vast distances between offices, and different languages. No wonder global communicators can blunder.[1]

Successful communication in these new markets requires developing new skills such as cultural knowledge and sensitivity, flexibility, patience, and tolerance. Because these are skills and traits that most of us need to polish, you will receive special communication training to help you deal with intercultural business transactions.

Flattened Management Hierarchies

Flatter organizations demand that every employee be a skilled communicator.

In response to intense global competition and other pressures, businesses have been cutting costs and flattening their management hierarchies for years. This flattening means that fewer layers of managers separate decision makers from line workers. In traditional companies, information flows through many levels of managers. In flat organizations, however, where the lines of communication are shorter, decision makers can react more quickly to market changes.

But today's flatter organizations also bring greater communication challenges. In the past, authoritarian and hierarchical management structures did not require that every employee be a skilled communicator. Managers simply passed along messages to the next level. Today, however, front-line employees as well as managers participate in decision making. Their input and commitment are necessary for their organizations to be successful in global markets. Moreover, everyone has become a writer and a communicator.[2] Administrative assistants no longer "clean up" their bosses' writing.

Expanded Team-Based Management

Along with flatter chains of command, companies are also turning to the concept of team-based operations. Nearly 80 percent of employers in all industries have adopted some form of quality circles or self-directed teams.

When companies form cross-functional teams, individuals must work together and share information. What's tough is that these individuals often don't share the same background, knowledge, or training. Some companies must hire communication coaches to help existing teams get along. They work on developing interpersonal, negotiation, and collaboration techniques. But companies would prefer to hire new workers who already possess these skills. That's why so many ads say "must possess good communication skills."

Innovative Communication Technologies

E-mail, voice mail, fax, videoconferencing, and the Web are revolutionizing the way we exchange information.

Because technology is completely revolutionizing the way we communicate, recruiters are also looking for people with good computer skills. We now exchange information and stay in touch through e-mail, fax, voice mail, two-way pagers, laptop computers, and satellite communications. Through teleconferencing and videoconferencing, we can conduct meetings with associates around the world. Interactive software enables dozens or even hundreds of users to collaborate on projects. Most businesspeople today rely on sophisticated presentation software.

We now make tremendous use of the Internet and the Web for collecting information, serving customers, and promoting products and services.

Just as companies are scrambling to use the Web most effectively, individual businesspeople are eagerly embracing the new technologies and revamping the way they communicate. Studies reveal that e-mail is the most often used means of communication. To use these new resources most effectively, you, as a skilled business communicator, must develop a tool kit of new communication skills. For example, you will want to know how to design documents for screen appeal, how to select the best medium for a message, and how to use online search tools efficiently.

New Work Environments

Global competition, restructuring, and mobile technologies are encouraging more flexible working arrangements.

As a result of global competition, restructuring, and the Internet, it's no surprise that we are also seeing dramatic changes in work environments. Thanks to mobile technologies, over one million Canadians now *telecommute*. They have flexible working arrangements so that they can work at home at least part of the time. Many workers live thousands of miles from the office, and others carry their work with them as they travel.[3]

Office workers are admittedly working in tighter quarters and under greater stress. Some are in open offices divided into small work cubicles, resulting in the need for new rules of office etiquette and civility. For example, instead of wandering into a cubicle, visitors should knock on the frame (they have no doors) to ask permission to enter.[4] Tight quarters, intense cost-cutting measures, demands for increased productivity, and the fast-paced world of information technology—all are creating stress for today's workers. Combined with new responsibilities of team problem solving, business communicators can expect to need interpersonal skills that deal with heightened levels of emotion. Especially important are listening to and empathizing with fellow employees. Equally significant is respecting others' periodic need for uninterrupted, focused work time.[5] And employees at home may face added communication challenges since staying connected with the office often requires exchanging more messages than if they were face to face with their colleagues.

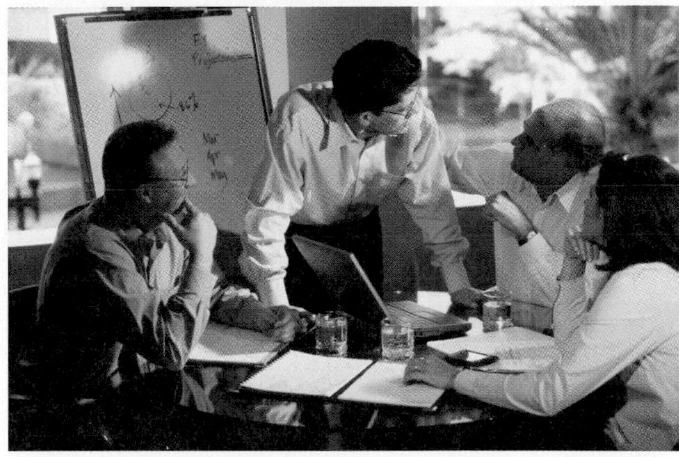

One unspoken benefit of teams is their role in making diversity more successful. Teams encourage members to get to know one another as they work together to solve problems.

Increasingly Diverse Workforce

Changes in today's work environments include more than new technology, team management, and different work routines. You can also expect to see hordes of new faces. No longer, say the experts, will the workplace be predominantly male or Anglo-oriented. With increasing multiculturalism, numbers of women in the labour force, and the number of employed young people (15–24) on the decline,[6] you can count on interacting with many coworkers who differ from you in race, ethnicity, gender, age, and many other ways.

Communicating with workers who differ in race, ethnicity, gender, and age requires new attitudes and skills.

Communicating in this diverse work environment requires new attitudes and skills. Acquiring these new employment skills is certainly worth the effort because of the benefits diversity brings to consumers, work teams, and business organizations. A diverse staff is better able to read trends and respond to the increasingly diverse customer base in local and world markets. In the workplace, diversity also makes good business sense. Teams made up of different people with different experiences are more likely to create the different products that consumers demand. Customers also want to deal with companies that respect their values. Learning to cooperate and communicate successfully with diverse coworkers should be a major priority for all businesspeople.

Thriving in the Age of Knowledge

Knowledge workers deal with symbols, such as words, figures, and data.

We're now witnessing the emergence of an advanced economy based on information and knowledge. Physical labour, raw materials, and capital are no longer the key ingredients in the creation of wealth. Knowledge workers engage in mind work. They deal with symbols: words, figures, data.

What does all this mean for you? As a future knowledge worker, you can expect to be generating, processing, and exchanging information. Whether you work in the new economy of dot-coms (Internet-based businesses) or the old economy of brick and mortar companies, three out of four jobs involve some form of mind work. Management and employees alike will be making decisions in such areas as product development, quality control, and customer satisfaction.

You will be asked to think critically. This means having opinions that are backed by reason and evidence. When your boss or team leader says, "What do you think we ought to do?" you want to be able to supply good ideas. The accompanying Career Coach box provides a five-point critical thinking plan to help you solve problems and make decisions. But having a plan is not enough. You also need chances to try out the plan and get feedback from colleagues and your boss (your instructor, for the time being). At the end of each chapter, you'll find activities and problems that will help you develop and apply your critical thinking skills.

CAREER COACH

SHARPENING YOUR SKILLS FOR CRITICAL THINKING, PROBLEM SOLVING, AND DECISION MAKING

Gone are the days when management expected workers to check their brains at the door and do only as told. As a knowledge worker, you'll be expected to use your brain in thinking critically. You'll be solving problems and making decisions. Much of this book is devoted to solving problems and communicating those decisions to management, fellow workers, clients, the government, and the public.

Faced with a problem or an issue, most of us do a lot of worrying before separating the issues or making a decision. All that worrying can become directed thinking by channeling it into the following procedure.

1. **Identify and clarify the problem.** Your first task is to recognize that a problem exists. Some problems are big and unmistakable, such as failure of an air-freight delivery service to get packages to customers on time. Other problems may be continuing annoyances, such as regularly running out of toner for an office copy machine. The first step in reaching a solution is pinpointing the problem area.
2. **Gather information.** Learn more about the problem situation. Look for possible causes and solutions. This step may mean checking files, calling suppliers, or brainstorming with fellow workers. For example, the air-freight delivery service would investigate the tracking systems of the commercial airlines carrying its packages to determine what went wrong.
3. **Evaluate the evidence.** Where did the information come from? Does it represent various points of view? What biases could be expected from each source? How accurate is the information gathered? Is it fact or opinion? For example, it is a fact that packages are missing; it is an opinion that they are merely lost and will turn up eventually.
4. **Consider alternatives and implications.** Draw conclusions from the gathered evidence and pose solutions. Then weigh the advantages and disadvantages of each alternative. What are the costs, benefits, and consequences? What are the obstacles, and how can they be handled? Most important, what solution best serves your goals and those of your organization? Here's where your creativity is especially important.
5. **Choose and implement the best alternative.** Select an alternative and put it into action. Then, follow through on your decision by monitoring the results of implementing your plan. The freight company decided to give its unhappy customers free delivery service to make up for the lost packages and downtime. Be sure to continue monitoring and adjusting the solution to ensure its effectiveness over time.

In the new world of work, you can look forward to being in constant training to acquire new skills that will help you keep up with improved technologies and procedures. You can also expect to be taking greater control of your career. Many workers today will not find nine-to-five jobs, lifetime security, predictable promotions, and even the conventional workplace, as you have learned earlier. Don't presume that companies will provide you with a clearly defined career path or planned developmental experiences. And don't wait for someone to "empower" you. You have to empower yourself.[7] To thrive in the new work world, you must be flexible and continually willing to learn new skills that supplement the strong foundation of basic skills you acquire in college or university.

Probably the most important foundation skill for knowledge workers in the new environment is the ability to communicate. This means being able to listen and to express your ideas effectively in writing and in speech. As you advance in your career, communication skills become even more important. The number one requirement for promotion to management is the ability to communicate.

Examining the Process of Communication

2

Since communication is a central factor in the emerging knowledge economy and a major consideration for anyone entering today's workforce, we need to look more closely at the total process of communication. Just what is communication? For our purposes, communication is the *transmission of information and meaning from one individual or group to another.* The crucial element in this definition is meaning. Communication has as its central objective the transmission of meaning. The process of communication is successful only when the receiver understands an idea as the sender intended it. Both parties must agree not only on the information transmitted but also on the meaning of that information. This entire book is devoted to one objective: teaching you the skills of communication so that you can transmit meaning along with information. How does an idea travel from one person to another? We engage in a sensitive process of communication that generally involves five steps that are discussed here and depicted in Figure 1.1.

Sender Has Idea

The communication process has five steps: idea formation, message encoding, message transmission, message decoding, and feedback.

The process of communication begins when the person with whom the message originates (the *sender*) has an idea. The form of the idea will be influenced by complex factors surrounding the sender: mood, frame of reference, background, culture, and physical makeup, as well as the context of the situation and many other factors. The way you greet people on campus, for example, depends a lot on how you feel, whom you are addressing, and what your culture has trained you to say.

The form of the idea, whether a simple greeting or a complex idea, is shaped by assumptions based on the sender's experiences. A manager sending a message to employees assumes they will be receptive, while direct mail advertisers assume that receivers will give only a quick glance to their message. Ability to accurately predict how a message will affect its receiver and skill in adapting that message to its receiver are key factors in successful communication.

Sender Encodes Idea in Message

The next step in the communication process involves *encoding.* This means converting the idea into words or gestures that will convey meaning. A major problem in communicating any message verbally is that words have different meanings for different people or at different times. When misunderstandings result from missed meanings, it's called *bypassing.* Recognizing how easy it is to be misunderstood, skilled communicators choose familiar words with concrete meanings on which both senders and receivers agree. In selecting proper symbols, senders must be alert to the receiver's communication skills, attitudes, background, experiences, and culture: How will the selected words affect the receiver? Because the sender initiates a communication transaction, he or she has primary responsibility for its success or failure. Choosing appropriate words or symbols is the first step.

Message Travels Over Channel

Channels are the media—computer, telephone, letter, fax, and so on—that transmit messages.

The medium over which the message is physically transmitted is the *channel.* Messages may be delivered by computer, telephone, letter, memorandum, report, announcement, picture, spoken word, fax, pager, Web-page or through some other channel. Because communication channels deliver both verbal and nonverbal messages, senders must choose the channel and shape the message carefully. A company may use its annual report, for example, as a channel to deliver many messages to

FIGURE 1.1 **The Communication Process**

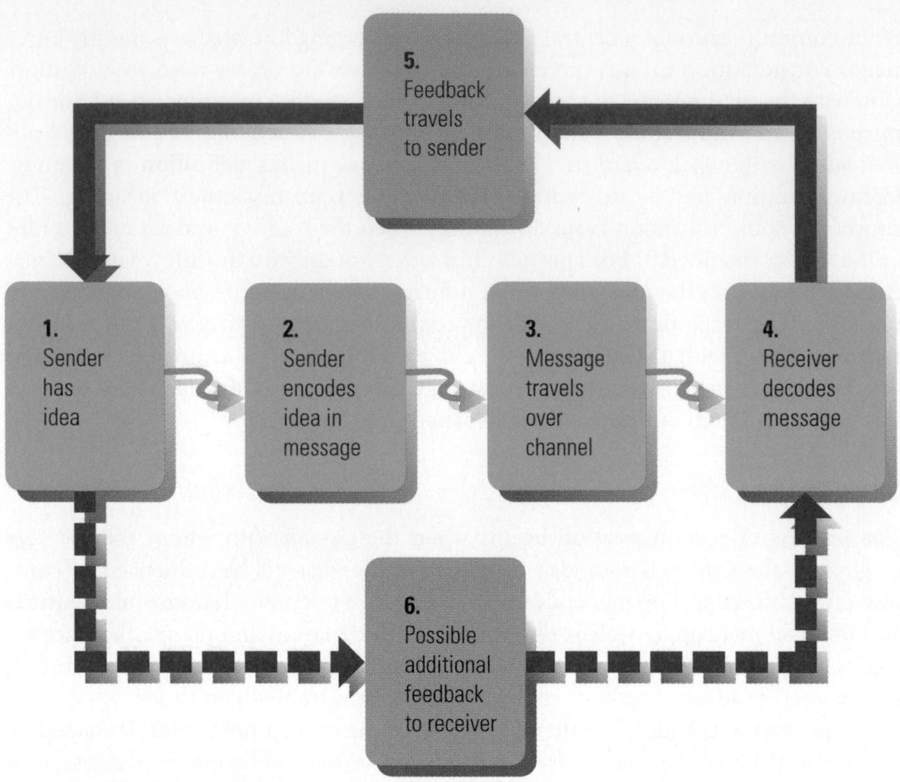

stockholders. The verbal message lies in the report's financial and organizational news. Nonverbal messages, though, are conveyed by the report's appearance (showy versus bland), layout (ample white space versus tightly packed columns of print), and tone (conversational versus formal).

Anything that interrupts the transmission of a message in the communication process is called *noise.* Channel noise ranges from static that disrupts a telephone conversation to typographical errors in a letter or e-mail message. Such errors damage the credibility of the sender. Channel noise might even include the annoyance a receiver feels when the sender chooses an improper medium for sending a message, such as announcing a loan rejection via postcard or firing an employee by e-mail.

Receiver Decodes Message

The individual for whom the message is intended is the *receiver.* Translating the message from its symbol form into meaning involves *decoding.* Only when the receiver understands the meaning intended by the sender (that is, successfully decodes the message) does communication take place. Such success, however, is difficult to achieve because no two people share the same life experiences and because many barriers can disrupt the process.

Decoding can be disrupted internally by the receiver's lack of attention to or bias against the sender. It can be disrupted externally by loud sounds or illegible words. Decoding can also be sidetracked by perceptual obstacles, such as misunderstood words or emotional reactions to certain terms. A memo that refers to all the women in an office as "girls," for example, may disturb its receivers so much that they fail to comprehend the total message.

Feedback Travels to Sender

The verbal and nonverbal responses of the receiver create *feedback*, a vital part of the communication process. Feedback helps the sender know that the message was received and understood. Although the receiver may respond with additional feedback to the sender (thus creating a new act of communication), we'll concentrate here on the initial message flowing to the receiver and the resulting feedback.

Asking questions encourages feedback that clarifies communication.

Senders can encourage feedback by asking questions such as, *Am I making myself clear?* and *Is there anything you don't understand?* Senders can further improve feedback by timing the delivery appropriately and by providing only as much information as the receiver can handle. Receivers can improve the process by paraphrasing the sender's message with comments such as, *Let me try to explain that in my own words.* The best feedback is descriptive rather than evaluative. An evaluative response is judgmental and doesn't tell the sender if the receiver actually understood the message.

Overcoming Interpersonal Communication Barriers

3

The communication process is successful only when the receiver understands the message as intended by the sender. It sounds quite simple. Yet, it's not. How many times have you thought that you delivered a clear message, only to learn later that your intentions were totally misunderstood? Most messages that we send reach their destination, but many are only partially understood.

Obstacles That Create Misunderstanding

You can improve your chances of communicating successfully by learning to recognize barriers that are known to disrupt the process. The most significant barriers for individuals are bypassing, frame of reference, lack of language skill, and distractions.

Barriers to successful communication include bypassing, differing frames of reference, lack of language or listening skills, emotional interference, and physical distractions.

Bypassing. One of the biggest barriers to clear communication involves words. Each of us attaches a little bundle of meanings to every word, and these meanings are not always similar. *Bypassing* happens when people miss each other with their meanings.[8] Bypassing can lead to major miscommunication because people assume that meanings are contained in words. Actually, meanings are in people. For communication to be successful, the receiver and sender must attach the same symbolic meanings to their words.

Differing Frames of Reference. Another barrier to clear communication is your *frame of reference*. Everything you see and feel in the world is translated through your individual frame of reference. Your unique frame is formed by a combination of your experiences, education, culture, expectations, personality, and many other elements. As a result, you bring your own biases and expectations to any communication situation. Because your frame of reference is totally different from everyone else's, you will never see things exactly as others do. Wise business communicators strive to prevent communication failure by being alert to both their own frames of reference and those of others.

Miscommunication often results when the sender's frame of reference differs markedly from the receiver's.

Lack of Language Skill. No matter how extraordinary the idea, it won't be understood or fully appreciated unless the communicators involved have good language skills. Each individual needs an adequate vocabulary, a command of basic punctuation and grammar, and skill in written and oral expression. Moreover, poor listening skills can prevent us from hearing oral messages clearly and thus responding properly.

Successful communication requires good oral and written language skills.

Distractions. Other barriers include emotional interference and physical distractions. Shaping an intelligent message is difficult when you're feeling joy, fear, resentment, hostility, sadness, or some other strong emotion. To reduce the influence of emotions on communication, both senders and receivers should focus on the content of the message and try to remain objective. Physical distractions such as faulty acoustics, noisy surroundings, or a poor telephone connection can disrupt oral communication. Similarly, sloppy appearance, poor printing, careless formatting, and typographical or spelling errors can disrupt written messages.

Overcoming the Obstacles

To overcome obstacles, communicators must anticipate problems in encoding, transmitting, and decoding.

Careful communicators can conquer barriers in a number of ways. Half the battle in communicating successfully is recognizing that the entire process is sensitive and susceptible to breakdown. Like a defensive driver anticipating problems on the road, a good communicator anticipates problems in encoding, transmitting, and decoding a message. Effective communicators also focus on the receiver's environment and frame of reference. They ask themselves questions such as, *How is that individual likely to react to my message?* or *Does the receiver know as much about the subject as I do?*

Misunderstandings are less likely if you arrange your ideas logically and use words precisely. But communicating is more than expressing yourself well. A large part of successful communication is listening. Management advisor Peter Drucker observed that "too many executives think they are wonderful with people because they talk well. They don't realize that being wonderful with people means listening well."[9]

Good communicators ask questions to stimulate feedback.

Overcoming interpersonal barriers often involves questioning your preconceptions. Successful communicators continually examine their personal assumptions, biases, and prejudices. The more you pay attention to subtleties and know "where you're coming from" when you encode and decode messages, the better you'll communicate.

Finally, effective communicators create an environment for useful feedback. In oral communication this means asking questions such as, *Do you understand?* and *What questions do you have?* as well as encouraging listeners to repeat instructions or paraphrase ideas. To a listener, it means providing feedback that describes rather than evaluates. And in written communication it means asking questions and providing access: *Do you have my telephone number in case you have questions?* or *Here's my e-mail address so that you can give me your response immediately.*

Communicating in Organizations

4

Until now, you've probably been thinking about the communication you do personally. But business communicators must also be concerned with the bigger picture, and that involves sharing information in organizations. Creating and exchanging knowledge are critical to fostering innovation, the key challenge in today's knowledge economy. On the job you'll be exchanging information by communicating internally and externally.

Internal and External Functions

Internal communication includes sharing ideas and messages with superiors, coworkers, and subordinates. When those messages must be written, you'll probably choose e-mail or a printed memorandum.

Some of the functions of internal communication are to issue and clarify procedures and policies, inform management of progress, persuade employees or management to make changes or improvements, coordinate activities, and evaluate and reward employees. External functions are to answer inquiries about products or services, persuade customers to buy products or services, clarify supplier specifications, issue credit, collect bills, respond to government agencies, and promote a positive image of the organization.

Internal communication often consists of e-mail, memos, and voice messages; external communication generally consists of letters.

In all of these tasks employees and managers use a number of communication skills: reading, listening, speaking, and writing. You probably realize that you need to improve these skills to the proficiency level required for success in today's knowledge society. This book and this course will provide you with practical advice on how to do just that.

Now, look back over the preceding discussion of internal and external functions of communication in organizations. Although there appear to be a large number of diverse business communication functions, they can be summarized in three simple categories: (1) to inform, (2) to persuade, and/or (3) to promote goodwill.

Organizational communication has three basic functions: to inform, to persuade, and/or to promote goodwill.

New Emphasis on Interactive and Mobile Communication

The flattening of organizations, coupled with the development of sophisticated information technology, has greatly changed the way we communicate internally and externally. We're seeing a major shift away from one-sided and rather slow forms of communication, such as memos and letters. More companies are seeking customer and employee input to learn ways to improve business.

To convey information to various audiences, organizations prefer more interactive, fast-results communication such as e-mail, voice mail, instant messaging, pagers, and cell phones. Cell phones have proliferated so rapidly that their careless use has become an annoyance in many public places. See the accompanying Career Coach box for tips on using this technological privilege courteously and responsibly.

Other forms of interactive communication involve intranets (company versions of the Internet), Web sites, video transmission, and videoconferencing. You'll be learning more about these forms of communication in subsequent chapters. Despite the range of interactive technologies, communicators are still working with two basic forms of communication: oral and written. Each has advantages and disadvantages.

Oral Communication. Nearly everyone agrees that the best way to exchange information is orally in face-to-face conversations or meetings. Oral communication has many advantages. For one thing, it minimizes misunderstandings because communicators can immediately ask questions to clarify uncertainties. For another, it enables communicators to see each other's facial expressions and hear voice inflections, further improving the process. Oral communication is also an efficient way to develop consensus when many people must be consulted. Finally, most of us enjoy face-to-face interpersonal communication because it's easy, feels warm and natural, and promotes friendships.

Oral communication minimizes miscommunication but provides no written record.

The main disadvantages of oral communication are that it produces no written record, sometimes wastes time, and may be inconvenient. When individuals meet face to face or speak on the telephone, someone's work has to be interrupted. And how many of us are able to limit a conversation to just business? Nevertheless, oral communication has many advantages. The forms and advantages of both oral and written communication are summarized in Figure 1.2.

Written Communication. Written communication is impersonal in the sense that two communicators cannot see or hear each other and cannot provide immediate feedback. Most forms of business communication—including e-mail,

CAREER COACH

PRACTISING COURTEOUS AND RESPONSIBLE CELL PHONE USE

Business communicators find cell phones to be enormously convenient and real time-savers. But rude users have generated a backlash of sorts. Most of us have experienced thoughtless and offensive cell phone behaviour. Although the cell phone industry vigorously opposes restrictive legislation, many major manufacturers admonish users to be courteous. Here are specific suggestions for using cell phones safely and responsibly:

- **Be courteous to those around you.** Don't force those near you to hear your business. Think first of those in close proximity instead of those on the other end of the phone. Apologize and make amends gracefully for occasional cell phone blunders.
- **Observe wireless-free quiet areas.** Don't allow your cell phone to ring in theatres, restaurants, museums, classrooms, important meetings, and similar places. Use the cell phone's silent/vibrating ring option. A majority of travellers prefer that cell phone conversations not be held on most forms of public transportation.
- **Speak in low, conversational tones.** Microphones on cell phones are quite sensitive, thus making it unnecessary to talk loudly. Avoid "cell yell."
- **Take only urgent calls.** Make full use of your cell phone's caller ID feature to screen incoming calls. Let voice mail take those calls that are not pressing.
- **Drive now, talk later.** Pull over if you must make a call. Talking while driving increases the chance of accidents fourfold, about the same as driving while intoxicated.

announcements, memos, faxes, letters, newsletters, reports, proposals, and manuals—fall into this category.

Written communication provides a permanent record but lacks immediate feedback.

Organizations rely on written communication for many reasons. It provides a permanent record, a necessity in these times of increasing litigation and extensive government regulation. Writing out an idea instead of delivering it orally enables communicators to develop an organized, well-considered message. Written documents are also convenient. They can be composed and read when the schedules of both communicators permit, and they can be reviewed if necessary.

Written messages have drawbacks, of course. They require careful preparation and sensitivity to audience and anticipated effects. Words spoken in conversation may soon be forgotten, but words committed to hard or soft copy become a public record—and a potentially embarrassing one.

Written messages demand good writing skills, which can be developed through training.

Another drawback to written messages is that they are more difficult to prepare. They demand good writing skills, and such skills are not inborn. But writing proficiency can be learned. Because as much as 90 percent of all business transactions may involve written messages and because writing skills are so important to your business success, you will be receiving special instruction in becoming a good writer and a good communicator.

Avoiding Information Overload and Productivity Meltdown

Although technology provides a myriad of communication channel choices, the sheer volume of messages is overwhelming many employees. Information overload and resulting productivity meltdown are becoming serious problems for workers

FIGURE 1.2 **Forms of Organizational Communication**

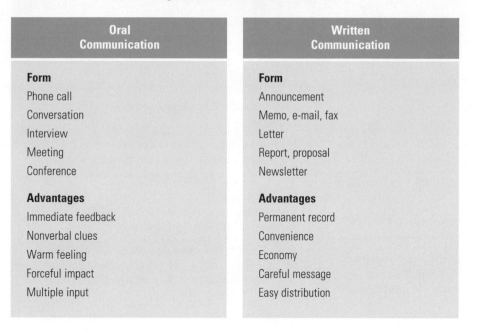

Oral Communication	Written Communication
Form	**Form**
Phone call	Announcement
Conversation	Memo, e-mail, fax
Interview	Letter
Meeting	Report, proposal
Conference	Newsletter
Advantages	**Advantages**
Immediate feedback	Permanent record
Nonverbal clues	Convenience
Warm feeling	Economy
Forceful impact	Careful message
Multiple input	Easy distribution

and their employers. While some software programs can now automatically sort messages into limited categories, one expert says that "human brainpower"—not new technology—is the key to managing e-mail overload.[11] Suggestions for controlling the e-mail monster are shown in the accompanying Tech Talk box.

The large volume of messages and communication channel choices overwhelms many workers.

Improving the Flow of Information in Organizations

5

Information within organizations flows through formal and informal communication channels. A free exchange of information helps organizations respond rapidly to changing markets, increase efficiency and productivity, build employee morale, serve the public, and take full advantage of the ideas of today's knowledge workers. However, barriers can obstruct the flow of communication.

Formal Channels

Formal channels of communication generally follow an organization's hierarchy of command. Information about policies and procedures originates with executives and flows down through managers to supervisors and finally to lower-level employees. Many organizations have formulated official communication policies that encourage regular open communication, suggest means for achieving it, and spell out responsibilities. Official information among workers typically flows through formal channels in three directions: downward, upward, and horizontally.

Formal communication channels follow an organization's chain of command.

Downward Flow. Information flowing downward generally moves from decision makers, including the CEO and managers, through the chain of command to workers. This information includes job plans, policies, and procedures. Managers also provide feedback about employee performance and instill a sense of mission in achieving the organization's goals.

Job plans, policies, instructions, feedback, and procedures flow downward from managers to employees.

TECH TALK

TIPS FOR CONTROLLING THE E-MAIL MONSTER

- Send only business messages that you would have sent in a memo format.
- Check your e-mail in-box only at specific times each day, say at 9 a.m. and again at 4 p.m.
- Print important memos to read during free time away from your desk.
- Avoid using the copy function and sending unnecessary replies.
- Pick up your incoming messages online, but answer them offline. Take time to think about your responses. Compose them on your word processor and upload them to your mail program, thus saving valuable network connection time.
- Practice e-mail triage: This means focusing on the most urgent messages first. Read the subject lines; then delete unwanted messages (spam) and those that require no response.
- Devise a logical storage system, and religiously move incoming mail into electronic folders.
- Subscribe only to listservs (automated mailing lists) in which you are really interested. (Some high-volume Internet listservs disgorge 30 or more messages a day.)[10]

One obstacle that can impede the downward flow of information is distortion resulting from long lines of communication. To improve communication and to compete more effectively, many of today's companies have "reengineered" themselves into smaller operating units and work teams. Rather than being bogged down with long communication chains, management speaks directly to team leaders, thus speeding up the entire process.[12] Management is also improving the downward flow of information through newsletters, announcements, meetings, videos, and company intranets. Instead of hoarding information at the top, today's managers recognize how essential it is to let workers know how well the company is doing and what new projects are planned.

Feedback from employees forms the upward flow of communication in most organizations.

Upward Flow. Information flowing upward provides feedback from nonmanagement employees to management. Subordinate employees describe progress in completing tasks, report roadblocks encountered, and suggest methods for improving efficiency. Channels for upward communication include phone messages, e-mail, memos, reports, departmental meetings, and suggestion systems. Ideally, the heaviest flow of information should be upward with information being fed steadily to decision makers.

A number of obstacles, however, can interrupt the upward flow of communication. Employees who distrust their employers are less likely to communicate openly. Employees cease trusting managers if they feel they are being tricked, manipulated, criticized, or treated unfairly. Unfortunately, in the current workplace, some employees no longer have a strong trusting attitude toward employers. Downsizing, cost-cutting measures, the tremendous influx of temporary workers, discrimination and harassment suits, outrageous compensation packages for chief executives, and many other factors often erode the feelings of trust and pride that employees once felt toward their employers and their jobs. Other obstacles include fear of reprisal for honest communication, lack of adequate communication skills, and differing frames of reference. Imperfect communication results when individuals are not using words or symbols with similar meanings, when they cannot express their ideas clearly, or when they come from different backgrounds.

To improve the upward flow of communication, some companies are (1) hiring communication coaches to train employees, (2) asking employees to report customer complaints, (3) encouraging regular meetings with staff, (4) providing a trusting, nonthreatening environment in which employees can comfortably share their observations and ideas with management, and (5) offering incentive programs that encourage employees to collect and share valuable feedback. Companies are also building trust by setting up hotlines for anonymous feedback to management and by installing ombudsman programs. An *ombudsman* is a mediator who hears employee complaints, investigates, and seeks to resolve problems fairly.

Horizontal Flow. Lateral channels transmit information horizontally among workers at the same level. These channels enable individuals to coordinate tasks, share information, solve problems, and resolve conflicts. Horizontal communication takes place through personal contact, telephone, e-mail, memos, voice mail, and meetings. Most traditional organizations have few established regular channels for the horizontal exchange of information. Reengineered companies with flattened hierarchies and team-based management, however, have discovered that when employees combine their knowledge with that of other employees, they can do their jobs better. Much of the information in these organizations is travelling horizontally between team members.[13]

Obstacles to the horizontal flow of communication, as well as to upward and downward flow, include poor communication skills, prejudice, ego involvement, and turf wars. Some employees avoid sharing information if doing so might endanger their status or chances for promotion within the organization. Competition within units and an uneven reward system may also prevent workers from freely sharing information.

To improve horizontal communication, companies are training and rewarding employees.

To improve horizontal communication, companies are (1) training employees in teamwork and communication techniques, (2) establishing reward systems based on team achievement rather than individual achievement, and (3) encouraging full participation in team functions. However, employees must also realize that they are personally responsible for making themselves heard, for really understanding what other people say, and for getting the information they need. Developing those business communication skills is exactly what this book and this course will do for you.

Informal Channels

Informal organizational communication transmits unofficial news through the grapevine.

Not all information within an organization travels through formal channels. Often, it travels in informal channels called the *grapevine.* These channels are usually based on social relationships in which individuals talk about work when they are having lunch, meeting at the water cooler, working out, golfing, or carpooling to work. Alert managers find the grapevine an excellent source of information about employee morale and problems. They have also used the grapevine as a "break it to them gently" device, planting "rumours," for example, of future layoffs or other changes.

Researchers studying communication flow within organizations know that the grapevine can be a major source of information. One study found that two-thirds of an employee's information comes from informal channels. Is this bad? Yes and no. The grapevine can be a fairly accurate and speedy source of organization information. However, grapevine information is often incomplete because it travels in headlines. When employees obtain most of their company news from the grapevine, it's a pretty sure bet that management is not releasing sufficient information through formal channels.

Employees prefer to receive vital company information through formal channels.

The truth is that most employees want to know what's going on. In fact, one study found that regardless of how much information organization members reported receiving, they wanted more.[14] Many companies today have moved away from a rigid authoritarian management structure in which only managers were privy to vital information, such as product success and profit figures. Employees who know the latest buzz feel like important members of the team.[15] Through formal lines of communication, smart companies are keeping employees informed. Thus, the grapevine is reduced to carrying gossip about who's dating whom and what restaurant is trendy for lunch.

Facing Increasing Ethical Challenges

6 The work world is indeed changing. One of the most remarkable changes involves ethics in the workplace. "Corporate accountability is emerging as the business issue of the 21st century" notes Anne Golden, president of the Conference Board of Canada.[16]

Ethical awareness grows as companies recognize that ethical practices make good business sense.

What caused this explosion of ethical awareness? According to one poll, many companies were primarily interested in incorporating ethics into their organizations because they wished to be more socially responsible.[17] Actually, however, many businesses simply recognized that ethical practices make good business sense. Ethical companies endure less litigation, less resentment, and less government regulation.[18] As a result, companies are adding ethics officers, hotlines, workshops, training programs, and codes of conduct.

Just what is ethical behaviour? According to Linda Crompton, president and chief executive officer of Citizen's Bank of Canada, "How well you stand up in a controversy—that's also what ethics are all about. People understand the effect of business on the environment or children in other countries."[19] Ethical behaviour involves four principles: honesty, integrity, fairness, and concern for others.

Five Common Ethical Traps

In making ethical decisions, business communicators commonly face five traps that can make arriving at the right decision more difficult.[20]

The False Necessity Trap. People act from the belief that they're doing what they must do. They convince themselves that they have no other choice, when in fact it's generally a matter of convenience or comfort. When people fall into the false necessity trap, they overestimate the cost of doing the right thing and underestimate the cost of failing to do so.[21]

The Doctrine-of-Relative-Filth Trap. Unethical actions sometimes look good when compared with the worse behaviour of others.

The Rationalization Trap. In falling into the rationalization trap, people try to explain away unethical actions by justifying them with excuses.

The Self-Deception Trap. People may persuade themselves that a lie is not really a lie. Self-deception is justifying our beliefs to ourselves by convincing ourselves to accept as true what is false or invalid. Self-deception can lead to unethical and possibly illegal behaviour.

The Ends-Justify-the-Means Trap. Taking unethical actions to accomplish a desirable goal is a common trap. Despite a worthy goal, the means of reaching it may be unethical.

Goals of Ethical Business Communication

Business communicators can minimize the danger of falling into ethical traps by setting specific ethical goals. Although the following goals hardly comprise a formal code of conduct, they will help business writers maintain a high ethical standard.

Telling the Truth. Half-truths, exaggerations, and deceptions constitute unethical communication. But conflicting loyalties in the workplace sometimes blur the line between right and wrong.

Labelling Opinions. Sensitive communicators know the difference between facts and opinions. Facts are verifiable and often are quantifiable; opinions are beliefs held with confidence but without substantiation. Stating opinions as if they were facts is unethical.

***Facts* are verifiable; *opinions* are beliefs held with conviction.**

Being Objective. Ethical business communicators recognize their own biases and strive to keep them from distorting a message. Honest reporting means presenting the whole picture and relating all facts fairly.

Communicating Clearly. Ethical business communicators feel an obligation to write clearly so that receivers understand easily and quickly. Many organizations, such as banks and insurance companies, have even created "Plain English" guidelines to ensure that policies, warranties, and contracts are written in language comprehensible to average readers. Plain English means short sentences, simple words, and clear organization. Communicators who intentionally obscure the meaning with complex sentences and ambiguous words are being unethical. A thin line, however, separates unethical communication from ethical communication. Some might argue that writers and speakers who deliver wordy, imprecise messages requiring additional correspondence or inquiry to clarify the meaning are acting unethically. However, the problem may be one of experience and skill rather than ethics. Such messages waste the time and resources of both senders and receivers. However, they are not unethical unless the intent is to deceive.

"Plain English" guidelines require simple, understandable language in policies, contracts, warranties, and other documents.

Giving Credit. As you probably know, using the written ideas of others without credit is called *plagiarism*. Ethical communicators give credit for ideas by (1) referring to originators' names within the text, (2) using quotation marks, and (3) documenting sources with endnotes, footnotes, or internal references. In school or on the job, stealing ideas or words from others is unethical.

Plagiarists use the ideas of others without giving credit.

Tools for Doing the Right Thing

In composing messages or engaging in other activities on the job, business communicators can't help being torn by conflicting loyalties. Acting ethically means doing the right thing given the circumstances. Each set of circumstances requires analyzing issues, evaluating choices, and acting responsibly.

Resolving ethical issues is never easy, but the task can be made less difficult if you know how to identify key issues. The following questions may be helpful.

Acting ethically means doing the right thing in the given situation.

- **Is the action you are considering legal?** No matter who asks you to do it or how important you feel the result will be, avoid anything that is prohibited by law.

Business communicators can help resolve ethical issues through self-examination.

- **How would you see the problem if you were on the opposite side?** Looking at all sides of an issue helps you gain perspective. By weighing both sides of an issue, you can arrive at a more equitable solution.
- **What are alternative solutions?** Consider all dimensions of other options. Would the alternative be more ethical? Under the circumstances, is the alternative feasible? Can another solution be implemented with a minimum of disruption and with a high degree of probable success?

Discussing an ethical problem with a coworker or colleague might lead to helpful alternatives.

- **Can you discuss the problem with someone whose advice you trust?** Talking about your dilemma with a coworker or with a colleague in your field might give you helpful insights and lead to possible alternatives.
- **How would you feel if your family, friends, employer, or coworkers learned of your action?** If the thought of revealing your action publicly disturbs you, your choice is probably not a wise one. Losing the faith of your friends or the confidence of your customers is not worth whatever short-term gains might be realized.

Perhaps the best advice in ethical matters is contained in the Golden Rule: Do unto others as you would have others do unto you. The ultimate solution to all ethics problems is treating others fairly and doing what is right to achieve what is good. In succeeding chapters you will find additional discussions of ethical questions as they relate to relevant topics.

Strengthening Your Communication Skills

You can improve your communication skills by making use of the model documents, practice exercises, procedures, tips, strategies, summaries, and checklists in this book.

You've just taken a brief look at the changing workplace, the process of communication, the flow of communication in organizations, and ethical challenges facing business communicators today. Each topic provided you not only with the latest information about an issue but also with tips and suggestions that will help you function successfully in the changing workplace. After all, it's not enough to know the problems; you also need to know some of the solutions. Our goal is to help you recognize the problems and also to equip you with techniques for overcoming the obstacles that others have faced.

Remember, communication skills are not inherent; they must be learned. Remember also to take advantage of the unique opportunity you now have. You have an expert who is willing to work with you to help improve your writing, speaking, and other communication skills. Many organizations pay thousands of dollars to communication coaches and trainers to teach employees the very skills that you are learning in this course. Your coach is your instructor. Get your money's worth! Pick his or her brains. With this book as your guide and your instructor as your coach, you will find that this course, as we mentioned earlier, could very well be the most important in your entire postsecondary curriculum.

Summary of Learning Objectives

1 **Identify changes in the workplace and the importance of communication skills.** The workplace has undergone profound changes, such as the emergence of heightened global competition, flattened management hierarchies, expanded team-based management, innovative communication technologies, new work environments, and an increasingly diverse workforce. In this dynamic workplace you can

expect to be a knowledge worker; that is, you will deal with words, figures, and data. The most important foundation skill for knowledge workers is the ability to communicate. You can improve your skills by studying the principles, processes, and products of communication as provided in this book and in this course.

2 **Describe the process of communication.** The sender encodes (selects) words or symbols to express an idea. The message is sent verbally over a channel (such as a letter, e-mail message, or telephone call) or is expressed nonverbally, perhaps with gestures or body language. "Noise"—such as loud sounds, misspelled words, or other distractions—may interfere with the transmission. The receiver decodes (interprets) the message and attempts to make sense of it. The receiver responds with feedback, informing the sender of the effectiveness of the message. The objective of communication is the transmission of meaning so that a receiver understands a message as intended by the sender.

3 **Discuss barriers to interpersonal communication and the means of overcoming those barriers.** *Bypassing* causes miscommunication because people have different meanings for the words they use. One's *frame of reference* creates a filter through which all ideas are screened, sometimes causing distortion and lack of objectivity. *Weak language skills* as well as *poor listening skills* impair communication efforts. *Emotional interference*—joy, fear, anger, and so forth—hampers the sending and receiving of messages. *Physical distractions*—noisy surroundings, faulty acoustics, and so forth—can disrupt oral communication. You can reduce or overcome many interpersonal communication barriers if you (a) realize that the communication process is imperfect, (b) adapt your message to the receiver, (c) improve your language and listening skills, (d) question your preconceptions, and (e) plan for feedback.

4 **Analyze the functions and procedures of communication in organizations.** Internal functions of communication include issuing and clarifying procedures and policies, informing management of progress, persuading others to make changes or improvements, and interacting with employees. External functions of communication include answering inquiries about products or services, persuading customers to buy products or services, clarifying supplier specifications, and so forth. Oral, face-to-face communication is most effective, but written communication is often more expedient. The volume of messages today is overwhelming many employees, who must institute techniques to control information overload and productivity meltdown.

5 **Assess the flow of communication in organizations including barriers and methods for overcoming those barriers.** Formal channels of communication follow an organization's hierarchy of command. Information flows downward from management to workers. Long lines of communication tend to distort information. Many organizations are improving the downward flow of communication through newsletters, announcements, meetings, videos, and company intranets. Information flows upward from employees to management, thus providing vital feedback for decision makers. Obstacles include mistrust, fear of reprisal for honest communication, lack of adequate communication skills, and differing frames of reference. To improve upward flow, companies are improving relations with staff, offering incentive programs that encourage employees to share valuable feedback, and investing in communication training programs. Horizontal communication is between workers at the same level. Obstacles include poor communication skills, prejudice, ego involvement, competition, and turf wars. Techniques for overcoming the obstacles include (a) training employees in communication and teamwork tech-

niques, (b) establishing reward systems, and (c) encouraging full participation in team functions. Informal channels of communication, such as the grapevine, deliver unofficial news—both personal and organizational—among friends and coworkers.

6 **List the goals of ethical business communication and important tools for doing the right thing.** Ethical business communicators strive to (a) tell the truth, (b) label opinions so that they are not confused with facts, (c) be objective and avoid distorting a message, (d) write clearly and avoid obscure language, and (e) give credit when using the ideas of others. When you face a difficult decision, the following questions serve as valuable tools in guiding you to do the right thing: (a) Is the action you are considering legal? (b) How would you see the problem if you were on the opposite side? (c) What are alternative solutions? (d) Can you discuss the problem with someone whose advice you trust? (e) How would you feel if your family, friends, employer, or coworkers learned of your action?

CHAPTER REVIEW

1. How are business communicators affected by the emergence of global competition, flattened management hierarchies, and expanded team-based management? (Obj. 1)
2. How are business communicators affected by the emergence of innovative communication technologies, new work environments, and an increasingly diverse workforce? (Obj. 1)
3. What are knowledge workers? Why are they hired? (Obj. 1)
4. Define *communication* and explain its most critical factor. (Obj. 2)
5. Describe the five steps in the process of communication. (Obj. 2)
6. List four barriers to interpersonal communication. Be prepared to discuss each. (Obj. 3)
7. Name five specific ways in which you can personally reduce barriers in your communication. (Obj. 3)
8. What are the three main functions of organizational communication? (Obj. 4)
9. What are the advantages of oral, face-to-face communication? (Obj. 4)
10. What are the advantages of written communication? (Obj. 4)
11. Within organizations how do formal and informal channels of communication differ? (Obj. 5)
12. Describe three directions in which communication flows within organizations and what barriers can obstruct each. (Obj. 5)
13. How can barriers to the free flow of information in organizations be reduced? (Obj. 5)
14. Discuss five thinking traps that block ethical behaviour. (Obj. 6)
15. When faced with a difficult ethical decision, what questions should you ask yourself? (Obj. 6)

CRITICAL THINKING

1. Why should business and professional students strive to improve their communication skills, and why is it difficult or impossible to do it on their own? (Obj. 1)
2. Recall a time when you experienced a problem as a result of poor communication. What were the causes of and possible remedies for the problem? (Objs. 2 and 3)
3. Some companies say that the more information they provide to employees, the more employees want. How would you respond to this complaint? (Objs. 4 and 5)
4. How would you describe the communication climate in an organization to which you belonged or for which you worked? (Objs. 4 and 5)

ACTIVITIES

1.1 Communication Assessment: How Do You Stack Up? (Objs. 2 and 3)

You know more about yourself than anyone else. That makes you the best person to assess your present communication skills. Take an honest look at your current skills and rank them using the following chart. How well you communicate will be an important factor in your future career—particularly if you are promoted into management, as many college graduates are. For each skill, circle the number from 1 (indicating low ability) to 5 (indicating high ability) that best reflects your perception of yourself.

Writing Skills	Low				High
1. Possess basic spelling, grammar, and punctuation skills	1	2	3	4	5
2. Am familiar with proper memo, letter, and report formats for business documents	1	2	3	4	5
3. Can analyze a writing problem and quickly outline a plan for solving the problem	1	2	3	4	5
4. Am able to organize data coherently and logically	1	2	3	4	5
5. Can evaluate a document to determine its probable success	1	2	3	4	5
Reading Skills	Low				High
1. Am familiar with specialized vocabulary in my field as well as general vocabulary	1	2	3	4	5
2. Can concentrate despite distractions	1	2	3	4	5
3. Am willing to look up definitions whenever necessary	1	2	3	4	5
4. Am able to move from recreational to serious reading	1	2	3	4	5
5. Can read and comprehend postsecondary-level material	1	2	3	4	5
Speaking Skills	Low				High
1. Feel at ease in speaking with friends	1	2	3	4	5
2. Feel at ease in speaking before a group of people	1	2	3	4	5
3. Can adapt my presentation to the audience	1	2	3	4	5
4. Am confident in pronouncing and using words correctly	1	2	3	4	5
5. Sense that I have credibility when I make a presentation	1	2	3	4	5
Listening Skills	Low				High
1. Spend at least half the time listening during conversations	1	2	3	4	5
2. Am able to concentrate on a speaker's words despite distractions	1	2	3	4	5
3. Can summarize a speaker's ideas and anticipate what's coming during pauses	1	2	3	4	5
4. Provide feedback, such as nodding, paraphrasing, and asking questions	1	2	3	4	5
5. Listen with the expectation of gaining new ideas and information	1	2	3	4	5

Now analyze your scores. Where are you strongest? Weakest? How do you think outsiders would rate you on these skills and traits? Are you satisfied with your present skills? The first step to improvement is recognition of a need. Put check marks next to the five traits you feel you should begin working on immediately.

1.2 E-Mail or Printed Memo: Getting to Know You (Objs. 1 and 2)

Send an e-mail or write a memo of introduction to your instructor. See Chapter 8 for tips on preparing an e-mail message. In your message include the following:

- **a.** Your reasons for taking this class
- **b.** Your career goals (both temporary and long-term)

c. A brief description of your employment, if any, and your favourite activities

d. An assessment and discussion of your current communication skills, including your strengths and weaknesses

e. A brief discussion of your familiarity with e-mail, the Internet, and other communication technologies

1.3 Want Ads: Analyzing Job Requirements (Obj. 1)

At the direction of your instructor, conduct a survey of print or electronic job advertisements in your field. Consult a large newspaper or visit the Guffey student Web site **<buscomm.nelson.com>**. At the Web site click on "Internship, Job-Search, and Résumé-Creation Information." Then select one of the links to job listings. Find five or more job listings in which you might be interested. If possible, print the results of your search. If you cannot print, make notes on what you found and how you found it. Study the skills requested. How often do the ads mention communication, teamwork, and computer skills? What tasks do the ads mention? Your instructor may ask you to submit your findings and/or report to the class.

1.4 Information Flow (Obj. 5)

Consider an organization to which you belong or a business where you've worked. How did members learn what was going on in the organization? What kind of information flowed through formal channels? What were those channels? What kind of information was delivered through informal channels? Was the grapevine as accurate as official channels? What barriers obstructed the flow of information? How could the flow be improved?

1.5 Communication Process: Analyzing the Process (Obj. 2)

Review the communication process and its barriers as described in the text. Now imagine that you are the human resources professional in an organization where you've worked and you wish to announce a new policy aimed at improving customer service. Examine the entire communication process from sender to feedback. How will the message be encoded? What assumptions must you make about your audience? How should you announce the new policy? How can you encourage feedback? What noise may interfere with transmission? What barriers should you expect? How can you overcome them? Your instructor may ask you to write a memo describing your responses to these questions.

1.6 Workplace Writing: Separating Myths From Facts (Obj. 1)

Today's knowledge workers are doing more writing on the job than ever before. Flattened management hierarchies, heightened global competition, expanded team-based management, and heavy reliance on e-mail have all contributed to more written messages.

Your Task. In teams discuss the following statements. Are they myths or facts?

a. Because I'm in a technical field, I'll work with numbers, not words.

b. Secretaries will clean up my writing problems.

c. Technical writers do most of the real writing on the job.

d. Computers can fix any of my writing mistakes.

e. I can use form letters for most messages.

1.7 Document Analysis: Barriers to Communication (Objs. 3, 4, and 5)

The following memo was actually written in a large business organization. Comment on its effectiveness, tone, and potential barriers to communication.

TO: All Department Personnel

SUBJECT: FRIDAY P.M. CLEAN-UP

Every Friday afternoon starting at 3 p.m. there is suppose to be a departmental clean-up. This practice will commence this Friday and continue until otherwise specified.

All CC162 employees will partake in this endeavour. This means not only cleaning his own area, but contributing to the cleaning of the complete department.

Thank you for your cooperation.

C.L.U.E. REVIEW 1

Each chapter includes an exercise based on Appendix A, "Competent Language Usage Essentials (C.L.U.E.)." This appendix is a business communicator's condensed guide to language usage, covering 54 of the most used, and abused, language elements. It also includes a list of 160 frequently misspelled words and a quick review of selected confusing words. The following exercise is packed with errors based on concepts and spelling words from the appendix. If you are rusty on these language essentials, spend some time studying the guidelines and examples in Appendix A. Then, test your skills with the chapter C.L.U.E. exercises. You will find the corrections for these exercises at the end of the appendix.

Remember, these exercises contain only usage and spelling words from Appendix A. On a separate sheet, edit the following sentences to correct faults in grammar, punctuation, spelling, and word use.

1. After he checked many statements our Accountant found the error in column 2 of the balance sheet.
2. Because Mr. Lockwoods business owned considerable property. We were serprised by it's lack of liquid assets.
3. The mortgage company checked all property titles separatly, however it found no discrepancies.
4. When Ms. Diaz finished the audit she wrote 3 letters. To appraise the owners of her findings.
5. Just between you and I whom do you think could have ordered all this stationary.
6. Assets and liabilities is what the 4 buyers want to see, consequently we are preparing this years statements.
7. Next spring my brother and myself plan to enroll in the following courses marketing english and history.
8. Dan felt that he had done good on the exam but he wants to do even better when it's given again next Fall.
9. Our records show that your end of the month balance was ninety-six dollars and 30 cents.
10. When the principle in the account grows to large we must make annual withdrawals.

CHAPTER • 2 •

COMMUNICATING IN TEAMS:
LISTENING, NONVERBAL COMMUNICATION, COLLABORATION, AND MEETING SKILLS

LEARNING OBJECTIVES

1 Discuss the importance of communicating in a team-oriented workplace and the four phases of team development.

2 Identify the characteristics of successful teams.

3 List techniques for organizing team-based written and oral presentations.

4 Explain how to become an effective team listener.

5 Analyze how information is transmitted through nonverbal messages and discuss how to improve nonverbal communication skills.

6 Discuss how to plan and participate in face-to-face and electronic meetings.

Communicating in a Team-Oriented Workplace

1

You will probably eventually find yourself working in some form of team-oriented environment. You may already be part of one or more teams. That's good, because experience on a team has become one of the top requests among recruiters looking over job candidates. To function effectively on a team, however, you'll need a number of skills. In this chapter you'll learn to polish your listening and nonverbal communication skills. You'll also study how to collaborate in team writing projects and how to participate in productive meetings.

Many organizations develop teams to compete globally, meet higher standards, and increase profits.

As organizations in the past decade were downsized, restructured, and reengineered, one reality became increasingly clear. Companies were expected to compete globally, meet higher standards, and increase profits—but often with fewer people and fewer resources.[1] Striving to meet these seemingly impossible goals, organizations began developing teams. As a study from Queen's University revealed, the key success factors for top manufacturing plants were that they value their workforce highly, delegate to work teams, and allocate resources to training.[2] In most models of future organizations, teams, not individuals, function as the primary performance unit.[3]

Why this emphasis on teams? Teams improve communication by sharing information within an organization. Because of their versatility, they do work that ordinary groups or single individuals could not accomplish. They make better use of resources. Teams increase productivity by delivering better quality goods and services and by developing improved processes. In the new world of work, it is important to be an autonomous, self-reliant decision maker, as well as a community-oriented team player.[4] Employees working in successful teams report improved job satisfaction, increased pride in their jobs, and higher self-esteem.[5] Best of all for organizations, effective teams solve problems more creatively and more efficiently.[6]

As you prepare for your business and professional career, you need to know more about how teams work. Primary concerns are the four phases of team development, the role of conflict, and the characteristics of successful teams.

The Four Phases of Team Development

Teams generally accomplish more than individuals can.

Teams may be formed to complete a single task or to function as permanent ongoing groups. Regardless of their function, successful teams normally go through four predictable phases, as identified by psychologist B. A. Tuckman: **forming**, **storming**, **norming**, and **performing**.[7] Some teams get lucky and move quickly from forming to performing. But most teams struggle through disruptive, although ultimately constructive, team-building stages.

Forming. During the first stage of team development, individuals get to know each other. They often are overly polite and feel a bit awkward. As they search for similarities and attempt to bond, they begin to develop trust in each other. Members will discuss fundamental topics such as why the team is necessary, who "owns" the team, whether membership is mandatory, how large the team should be, and what talents team members can contribute. The team leader functions primarily as a traffic director. Teams should resist the efforts of some members to sprint through the first stages and vault to the performing stage. Moving slowly through the stages is necessary in building a cohesive, productive unit.

Storming. During the second phase, members define their roles and responsibilities, decide how to reach their goals, and iron out the rules governing how they interact. Unfortunately, this stage often produces conflict, resulting in storming. A good team

FIGURE 2.1 **Why Teams Fail: Typical Problems, Symptoms, and Solutions**

Problem	Symptom	Solution
Confused goals	People don't know what they're supposed to do	Clarify team purpose and expected outcomes
Mismatched needs	People with private agendas are working at cross-purposes	Get hidden agendas on table by asking what people personally want from teaming
Unresolved roles	Team members are uncertain what their jobs are	Inform team members what is expected of them
Senseless procedures	Team is at the mercy of an employee handbook from hell	Throw away the book and develop procedures that make sense
Bad leadership	Leader is tentative, inconsistent, or foolish	Leader must learn to serve the team and keep its vision alive or give up role
Anti-team culture	Organization is not committed to the idea of teams	Team for the right reasons or don't team at all; never force people onto a team
Poor feedback	Performance is not being measured; team members are groping in the dark	Create system of free flow of useful information to and from all team members

Based on Harvey Robbins and Michael Finley, *Why Teams Don't Work: What Went Wrong and How to Make It Right* (Princeton, NJ: Peterson's/Pacesetter Books, 1995), pp. 14–15.

leader, however, should step in to set limits, control the chaos, and offer suggestions. The leader will be most successful if she or he acts like a coach rather than a cop. Teams composed of dissimilar personality types may take longer to progress through the storming phase. Tempers may flare, sleep may be lost, leaders may be deposed. However, most often the storm passes, and a cohesive team emerges.

In the norming stage, tensions subside, roles clarify, and information flows between team members.

Norming. Once the sun returns to the sky, teams enter the norming stage. Tension subsides, roles clarify, and information begins to flow between members. The group periodically checks its agenda to remind itself of its progress toward its goals. People are careful not to shake the hard-won camaraderie and formation of a single-minded team purpose. Formal leadership is unnecessary since everyone takes on leadership functions. Important data is shared with the entire group, and mutual interdependence becomes typical. The team begins to move smoothly in one direction. Members make sure that procedures are in place to resolve future conflicts.

Performing. In Tuckman's team growth model, some teams never reach the final stage of performing. Problems that may cause them to fail are shown in Figure 2.1. For those that survive the first three phases, however, the final stage is gratifying. Team members have established a pace and a shared language. They develop loyalty and a willingness to resolve all problems. A "can-do" mentality pervades as they progress toward their goal. Fights are clean, and team members continue working together without grudges. Best of all, information flows freely, deadlines are met, and production often exceeds expectations.

Characteristics of Successful Teams

The use of teams has been called the "solution" to many ills in the current workplace.[8] Someone even observed that as an acronym TEAM means "Together, Everyone Achieves More."[9] Yet, many teams do not work well together. In fact, some teams can actually increase frustration, lower productivity, and create employee dissatisfaction. Experts who have studied team workings and decisions have discovered that effective teams share some or all of the following characteristics.

Small, diverse teams often produce more creative solutions with broader applications than homogeneous teams.

Small Size, Diverse Makeup. For most functions the best teams range from 2 to 25 members, although 4 or 5 is optimum for many projects. Larger groups have trouble interacting constructively, much less agreeing on actions.[10] For the most creative decisions, teams generally have male and female members who differ in age, social background, training, and experience. Members should bring complementary skills to a team. Diverse teams can produce innovative solutions with broader applications than homogeneous teams can.

Agreement on Purpose. An effective team begins with a common purpose. Working from a general purpose to specific goals typically requires a huge investment of time and effort. Meaningful discussions, however, motivate team members to "buy into" the project.

Agreement on Procedures. The best teams develop procedures to guide them. They set up intermediate goals with deadlines. They assign roles and tasks, requiring all members to contribute equivalent amounts of real work. They decide how they will reach decisions using strategies such as majority votes, consensus, or authority rule with discussion. Procedures are continually evaluated to ensure movement toward attainment of the team's goals.

Ability to Confront Conflict. Poorly functioning teams avoid conflict, often preferring sulking, gossiping, or backstabbing. A better plan is to acknowledge conflict and address the root of the problem openly. Although it may feel emotionally risky, direct confrontation saves time and enhances team commitment in the long run. To be constructive, however, confrontation must be task oriented, not person oriented. An open airing of differences, in which all team members have a chance to speak their minds, should centre on strengths and weaknesses of the different positions and ideas—not on personalities. After hearing all sides, team members must negotiate a fair settlement, no matter how long it takes. The best decisions are based on consensus: all members agree.

Good teams exchange information freely and collaborate rather than compete.

Use of Good Communication Techniques. The best teams exchange information and contribute ideas freely in an informal environment. Team members speak clearly and concisely, avoiding generalities. They encourage feedback. Listeners become actively involved, read body language, and ask clarifying questions before responding. Tactful, constructive disagreement is encouraged. Although a team's task is taken seriously, successful teams are able to inject humour into their interactions.

Ability to Collaborate Rather than Compete. Effective team members are genuinely interested in achieving team goals instead of receiving individual recognition. They contribute ideas and feedback unselfishly. They monitor team progress, including what's going right, what's going wrong, and what to do about it. They celebrate individual and team accomplishments.

Shared Leadership. Effective teams often have no formal leader. Instead, leadership rotates to those with the appropriate expertise as the team evolves and moves from one phase to another. Many teams operate under a democratic approach. This approach can achieve buy-in to team decisions, boost morale, and create fewer hurt feelings and less resentment. But in times of crisis, a strong team member may need to step up as leader.

Checklist for Developing Team Effectiveness

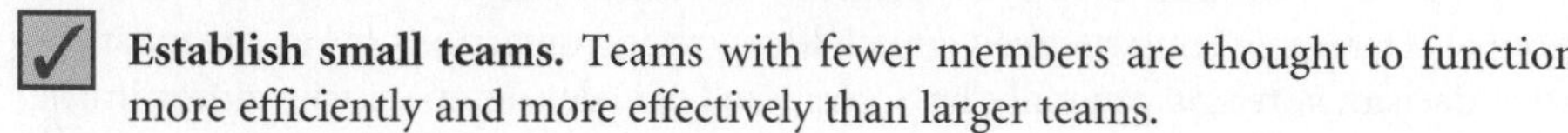

☑ **Establish small teams.** Teams with fewer members are thought to function more efficiently and more effectively than larger teams.

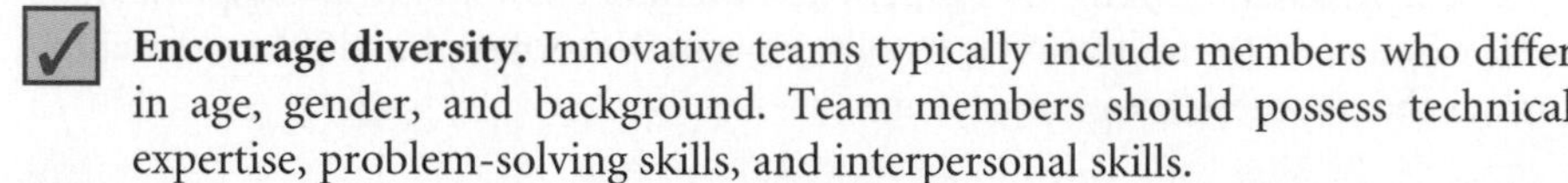

☑ **Encourage diversity.** Innovative teams typically include members who differ in age, gender, and background. Team members should possess technical expertise, problem-solving skills, and interpersonal skills.

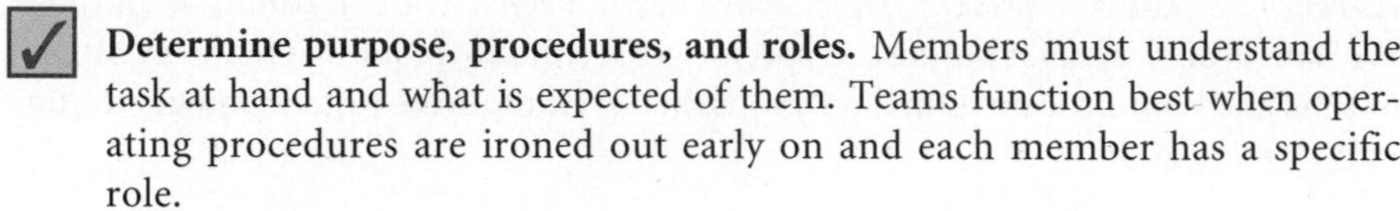

☑ **Determine purpose, procedures, and roles.** Members must understand the task at hand and what is expected of them. Teams function best when operating procedures are ironed out early on and each member has a specific role.

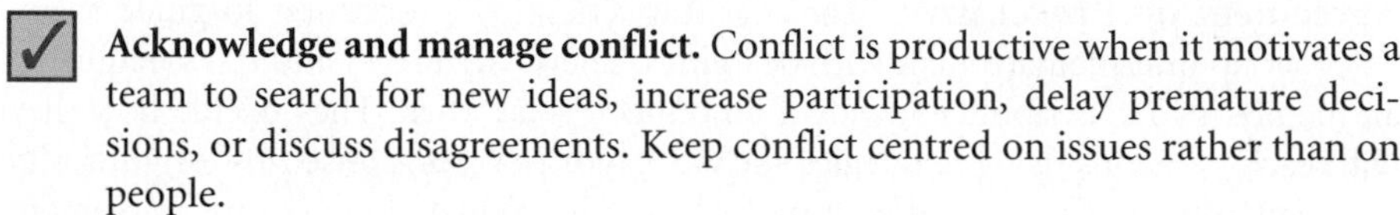

☑ **Acknowledge and manage conflict.** Conflict is productive when it motivates a team to search for new ideas, increase participation, delay premature decisions, or discuss disagreements. Keep conflict centred on issues rather than on people.

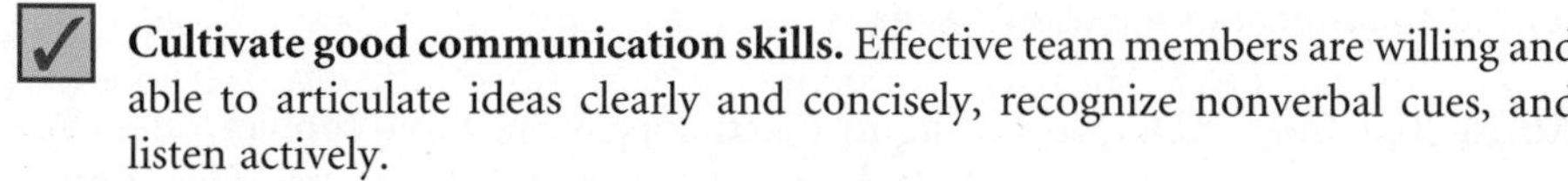

☑ **Cultivate good communication skills.** Effective team members are willing and able to articulate ideas clearly and concisely, recognize nonverbal cues, and listen actively.

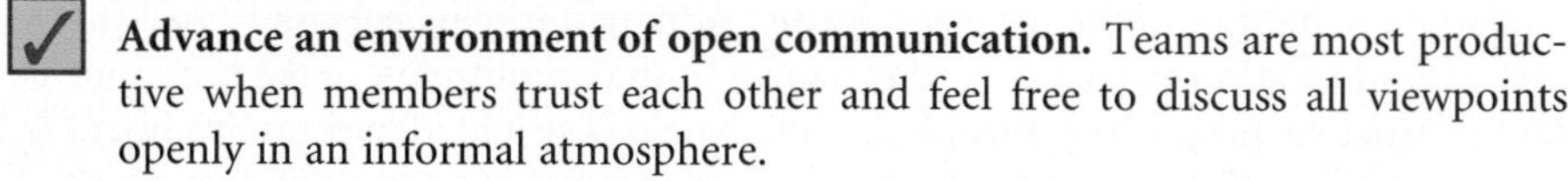

☑ **Advance an environment of open communication.** Teams are most productive when members trust each other and feel free to discuss all viewpoints openly in an informal atmosphere.

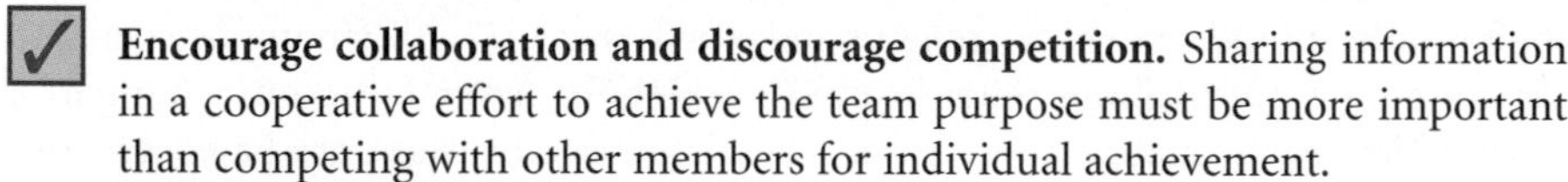

☑ **Encourage collaboration and discourage competition.** Sharing information in a cooperative effort to achieve the team purpose must be more important than competing with other members for individual achievement.

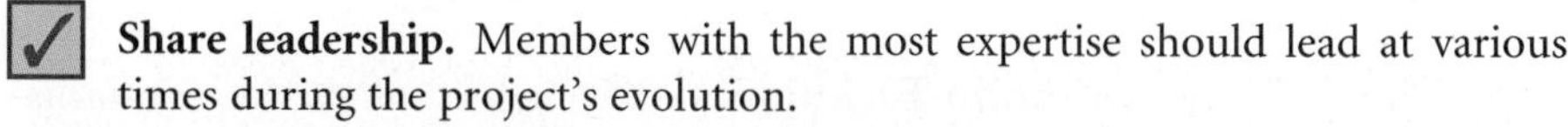

☑ **Share leadership.** Members with the most expertise should lead at various times during the project's evolution.

☑ **Create a sense of fairness in making decisions.** Effective teams resolve issues without forcing members into a win-lose situation.

☑ **Lighten up.** The most successful teams take their task seriously, but they are also able to laugh at themselves and interject humour to enliven team proceedings.

☑ **Continually assess performance.** Teams should establish checkpoints along the way to determine whether they are meeting their objectives and adjust procedures if progress is unsatisfactory.

Organizing Team-Based Written and Oral Presentations

3

Companies form teams for many reasons. The goal of some teams is an oral presentation to pitch a new product or to win a high-stakes contract. The goal of other teams is to investigate a problem and submit recommendations to decision makers in a report. The end product of any team is often a written report or an oral presentation.

Guidelines for Team Writing and Oral Presentations

Team projects proceed more smoothly when members agree on ground rules.

Whether your team's project produces written reports or oral presentations, you generally have considerable control over how the project is organized and completed. If you've been part of any team efforts before, you also know that such projects can be very frustrating—particularly when some team members don't carry their weight or when members cannot resolve conflict. On the other hand, team projects can be harmonious and productive when members establish ground rules and follow guidelines related to preparing, planning, collecting information for, organizing, rehearsing, and evaluating team projects.

Preparing to Work Together. Before you begin talking about a specific project, it's best to discuss some of the following issues in regard to how your group will function.

- Name a meeting leader to plan and conduct meetings, a recorder to keep a record of group decisions, and an evaluator to determine whether the group is on target and meeting its goals.
- Decide whether your team will be governed by consensus (everyone must agree), by majority rule, or by some other method.
- Compare schedules of team members in order to set up the best meeting times. Plan to meet often. Make team meetings a top priority. Avoid other responsibilities that might cause disruption during these meetings.
- Discuss the value of conflict. By bringing conflict into the open and encouraging discussion, your team can prevent personal resentment and group dysfunction. Confrontation can actually create better final products by promoting new ideas and avoiding groupthink. Conflict is most beneficial when team members are allowed to air their views fully and a closure process is in place.
- Discuss how you will deal with team members who are not pulling their share of the load.

Teams must decide whether they will be governed by consensus, by majority rule, or by some other method.

Planning the Document or Presentation. Once you've established ground rules, you're ready to discuss the final document or presentation. Be sure to keep a record of the following decisions your team makes.

- Establish the specific purpose for the document or presentation. Identify the main issues involved.
- Decide on the final format. For a report, determine what parts it will include, such as an executive summary, figures, and an appendix. For a presentation, decide on its parts, length, and graphics.
- Discuss the audience(s) for the product and what questions it would want answered in your report or oral presentation. If your report is persuasive, consider what appeals might achieve its purpose.

In planning a team document or presentation, develop a work plan, assign jobs, and set deadlines.

- Develop a work plan. Assign jobs. Set deadlines. If time is short, work backward from the due date. For oral presentations, build in time for content and creative development as well as for a series of rehearsals.
- For oral presentations, give each team member a written assignment that details his or her responsibilities for researching content, producing visuals, developing handout materials, building transitions between segments, and showing up for rehearsals.
- For written reports, decide how the final document will be composed: individuals working separately on assigned portions, one person writing the first draft, the entire group writing the complete document together, or some other method.

Unless facts are accurate, reports and presentations will fail.

Collecting Information. The following suggestions help teams generate and gather accurate information. Unless facts are accurate, the most beautiful report or the best high-powered presentation will fail.

- Brainstorm for ideas; consider cluster diagramming.
- Assign topics. Decide who will be responsible for gathering what information.
- Establish deadlines for collecting information.
- Discuss ways to ensure the accuracy of the information collected.

Organizing, Writing, and Revising. As the project progresses, your team may wish to modify some of its earlier decisions.

For team reports, assign one person to coordinate all the parts and make the style consistent.

- Review the proposed organization of your final document or presentation and adjust it if necessary.
- Compose the first draft of a written report or presentation. If separate team members are writing segments, they should use the same word processing and/or presentation graphics program to facilitate combining files.
- Meet to discuss and revise the draft(s) or rehearse the presentation.
- If individuals are working on separate parts of a written report, appoint one person (probably the best writer) to coordinate all the parts, striving for consistent style and format. Work for a uniform look and feel to the final product.
- For oral presentations, be sure each member builds a bridge to the next presenter's topic and launches it smoothly. Strive for logical connections between segments.

Editing, Rehearsing, and Evaluating. Before the presentation is made or the final document is submitted, complete the following steps.

One person should be responsible for finding and correcting errors.

- For a written report, give one person responsibility for finding and correcting grammatical and mechanical errors.
- For a written report, meet as a group to evaluate the final document. Does it fulfill its purpose and meet the needs of the audience? Successful group documents emerge from thoughtful preparation, clear definition of contributors' roles, commitment to a group-approved plan, and willingness to take responsibility for the final product.
- For oral presentations, assign one person the task of merging the various files, running a spell checker, and examining the entire presentation for consistency of design, format, and vocabulary.

- Schedule at least five rehearsals, say the experts.[11] Consider videotaping one of the rehearsals so that each presenter can critique his or her own performance.
- Schedule a dress rehearsal with an audience at least two days before the actual presentation. Practice fielding questions.

More information about writing business reports and making individual presentations appears in subsequent chapters of this book.

Becoming an Effective Team Listener

4

A vital part of every successful team is high-quality communication. And three quarters of high-quality communication involves listening.[12] In addition to helping you interact with teams, listening skills are important in getting along with colleagues, managers, family, and friends. Although our discussion centres on business and employment needs, many of the listening tips you learn will be equally effective in your personal life.

Most of us listen at only 25-percent efficiency.

Statistics report that 40 percent of an employee's day is spent listening and top executives spend more than 60 percent of their day listening.[13] Although executives and workers devote the bulk of their communication time to listening, research suggests that they're not very good at it. In fact, most of us are poor listeners. Some estimates indicate that only half of the oral messages heard in a day are completely understood. Experts say that we listen at only 25-percent efficiency. In other words, we ignore, forget, distort, or misunderstand 75 percent of everything we hear.

We are inefficient listeners because of lack of training, competing sounds, slowness of speech, and daydreaming.

Such listening inefficiency may result from several factors. Lack of training is one significant reason. Few schools give as much emphasis to listening as they do to the development of reading, speaking, and writing skills. In addition, our listening skills may be less than perfect because of the large number of competing sounds and stimuli in our lives that interfere with concentration. Finally, we are inefficient listeners because of the slowness of speech. While most speakers talk at about 150 words per minute, listeners can process oral communication at over 400 words per minute. This lag time causes daydreaming, which in turn reduces listening efficiency.

Examining the process of listening, as well as its barriers, may shed some light on ways to improve your listening efficiency and retention.

The Listening Process and Its Barriers

The four stages of listening are perception, interpretation, evaluation, and action.

Listening takes place in four stages—perception, interpretation, evaluation, and action—as illustrated in Figure 2.2. Barriers, however, can obstruct the listening process. These barriers may be mental or physical.

Perception. The listening process begins when you hear sounds and concentrate on them. The conscious act of listening begins when you focus on the sounds around you and select those you choose to hear. You tune in when you (1) sense that the message is important, (2) are interested in the topic, or (3) are in the mood to listen. Perception is reduced by impaired hearing, noisy surroundings, inattention, and pseudolistening. *Pseudolistening* occurs when listeners "fake" it. They look as if they are listening, but their minds are wandering far off.

Interpretation. Once you have focused your attention on a sound or message, you begin to interpret, or decode, it. As described in Chapter 1, interpretation of a message is coloured by your cultural, educational, and social frames of reference. The meanings

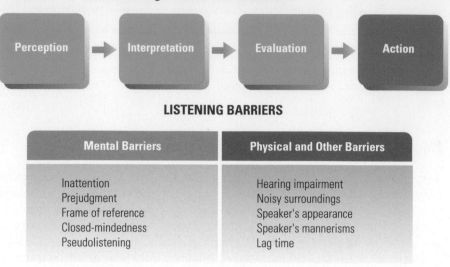

FIGURE 2.2 **The Listening Process and Its Barriers**

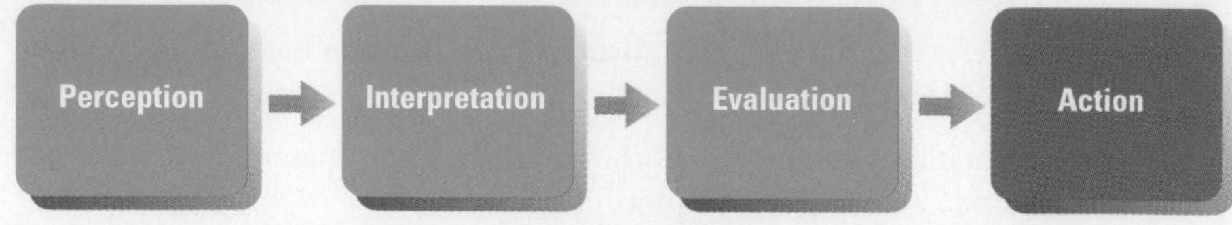

LISTENING BARRIERS

Mental Barriers	Physical and Other Barriers
Inattention	Hearing impairment
Prejudgment	Noisy surroundings
Frame of reference	Speaker's appearance
Closed-mindedness	Speaker's mannerisms
Pseudolistening	Lag time

you attach to the speaker's words are filtered through your expectations and total life experiences. Thus, your interpretation of the speaker's meaning may be quite different from what the speaker intended because your frame of reference is different.

Evaluation involves separating fact from opinion and judging messages objectively.

Evaluation. After interpreting the meaning of a message, you analyze its merit and draw conclusions. To do this, you attempt to separate fact from opinion. Good listeners try to be objective, and they avoid prejudging the message. The appearance and mannerisms of the speaker can also affect a listener's evaluation of a message. Thus, to evaluate a message accurately and objectively, you should (1) consider all the information, (2) be aware of your own biases, and (3) avoid jumping to hasty conclusions.

Action. Responding to a message may involve storing the message in memory for future use, reacting with a physical response (a frown, a smile, a laugh), or supplying feedback to the speaker. Listener feedback is essential because it helps clarify the message so that it can be decoded accurately. Feedback also helps the speaker to find out whether the message is getting through clearly. In one-to-one conversation, of course, no clear distinction exists between the roles of listener and speaker—you give or receive feedback as your role alternates.

Tips for Better Team Listening

Team listening is more challenging because information is often exchanged casually. It may be disorganized, unclear, and cluttered with extraneous facts. Moreover, team members are often friends. Because they are familiar with one another, they may not be as polite and respectful as they are with strangers. Friends tend to interrupt, jump to conclusions, and take each other for granted. Team members cannot do this, despite their familiarity with each other. They must remember that their job is to listen carefully and to understand what is being said so that they can do their work well. The following suggestions can help you improve your listening effectiveness—both as a team member and as a business communicator in general.

Control External and Internal Distractions. Move to an area where you can hear without conflicting noises or conversations. Block out surrounding physical distractions. Internally, try to focus totally on the speaker. If other projects are on your mind, put them on the back burner temporarily. When you are emotionally charged, whether angry or extremely happy, it's a good idea to postpone any serious listening.

Team efforts require listening with an open mind, observing nonverbal cues, and interpreting the feelings of the speaker.

Become Actively Involved. Show that you are listening closely by leaning forward and maintaining eye contact with the speaker. Don't fidget or try to complete another task at the same time you are listening. Listen to more than the spoken words. How are they said? What implied meaning, reasoning, and feelings do you hear behind the spoken words? Does the speaker's body language (eye contact, posture, movements) support or contradict the main message?

Identify Important Facts. Team members may intersperse critical information with casual conversation. Unrelated topics pop up—ball scores, a customer's weird request, a computer glitch. Your task is to select what's important and register it mentally. What step is next in your project? Who does what? What is your role?

Don't Interrupt. While someone else has the floor, don't interrupt with a quick reply or opinion. And don't show nonverbal disagreement such as negative head shaking, rolling eyes, sarcastic snorting, or audible sighs. Good team members let speakers have their say. Interruptions are not only impolite, but they also prevent you from hearing the speaker's complete thought. Listeners who interrupt with their opinions sidetrack discussions and cause hard feelings.

Ask Clarifying Questions. Good team members wait for the proper moment and then ask questions that do not attack the speaker. Instead of saying, "But I don't understand how you can say that," a good listener seeks clarification with questions such as, "Please help me understand by explaining more about...." Because questions can put you in the driver's seat, think about them in advance. Use open questions (those without set answers) to draw out feelings, motivations, ideas, and suggestions. Use closed fact-finding questions to identify key factors in a discussion.[14] And, by the way, don't ask a question unless you are ready to be quiet and listen to the answer.

Paraphrasing means rephrasing the speaker's ideas in your own words.

Paraphrase to Increase Understanding. To make sure you understand a speaker, rephrase and summarize a message in your own words. Be objective and nonjudgmental. Remember that your goal is to understand what the speaker has said—not to show how mindless the speaker's words sound when parroted. Remember, too, that the rest of the team will also benefit from a clear summary of what was said.

Take Advantage of Lag Time. While you are waiting for a speaker's next idea, use the time to review what the speaker is saying. Separate the central idea, key points, and details. Sometimes you may have to supply the organization. You can also use lag time to silently rephrase and summarize the speaker's message in your own words. Most important, keep your mind focused on the speaker and his or her ideas—not on all the other work waiting for you.

Take Notes to Ensure Retention. Don't trust your memory. If you have a hallway conversation with a team member and don't have a pencil handy, make a mental note of the important items. Then write them down as soon as possible. Even with seemingly easily remembered facts or instructions, jot them down to ease your mind and also to be sure you understand them correctly. Two weeks later, you'll be glad that you did. Be sure you have a good place to store notes of various projects, such as in file folders, notebooks, or computer files.

Checklist for Improving Listening

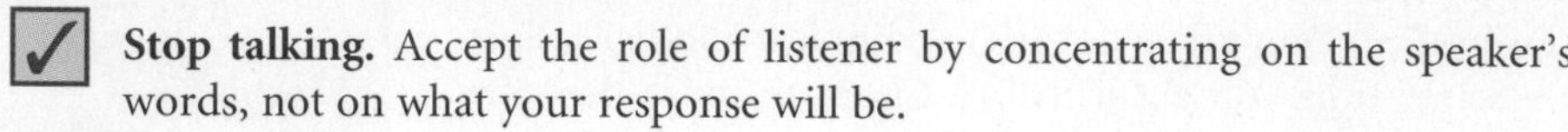
Stop talking. Accept the role of listener by concentrating on the speaker's words, not on what your response will be.

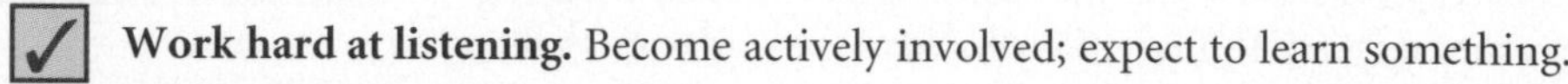
Work hard at listening. Become actively involved; expect to learn something.

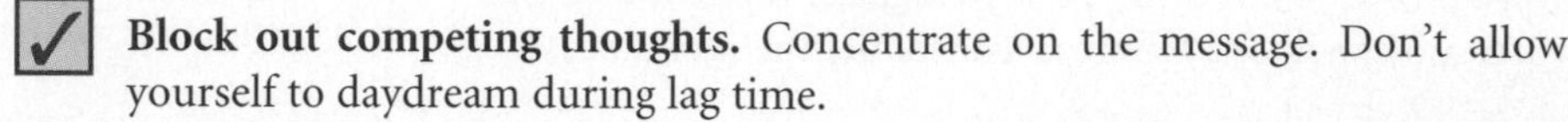
Block out competing thoughts. Concentrate on the message. Don't allow yourself to daydream during lag time.

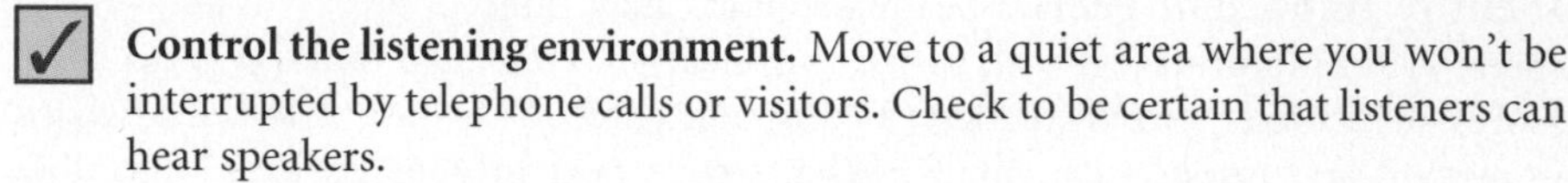
Control the listening environment. Move to a quiet area where you won't be interrupted by telephone calls or visitors. Check to be certain that listeners can hear speakers.

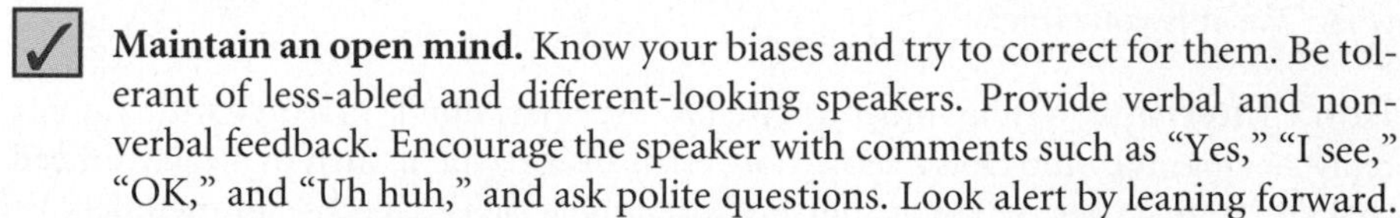
Maintain an open mind. Know your biases and try to correct for them. Be tolerant of less-abled and different-looking speakers. Provide verbal and nonverbal feedback. Encourage the speaker with comments such as "Yes," "I see," "OK," and "Uh huh," and ask polite questions. Look alert by leaning forward.

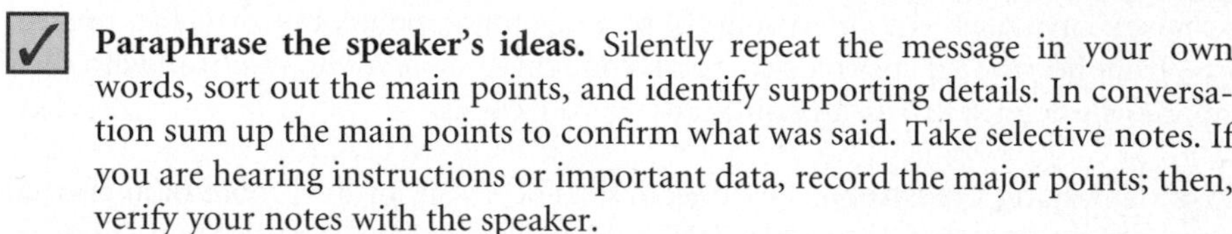
Paraphrase the speaker's ideas. Silently repeat the message in your own words, sort out the main points, and identify supporting details. In conversation sum up the main points to confirm what was said. Take selective notes. If you are hearing instructions or important data, record the major points; then, verify your notes with the speaker.

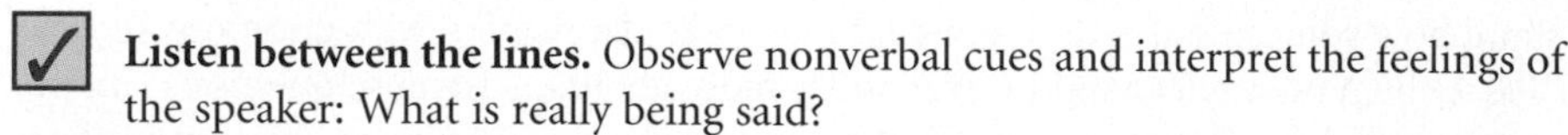
Listen between the lines. Observe nonverbal cues and interpret the feelings of the speaker: What is really being said?

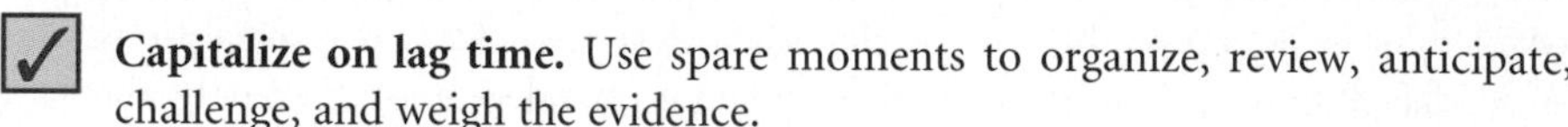
Capitalize on lag time. Use spare moments to organize, review, anticipate, challenge, and weigh the evidence.

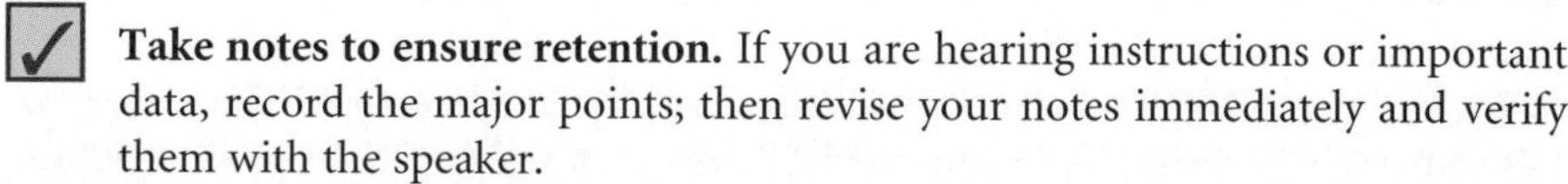
Take notes to ensure retention. If you are hearing instructions or important data, record the major points; then revise your notes immediately and verify them with the speaker.

Communicating Through Nonverbal Messages

Understanding often involves more than merely listening to the spoken words. Nonverbal cues, in fact, can speak louder than words. Eye contact, facial expression, body movements, space, time, distance, appearance—all of these nonverbal cues influence the way the message is interpreted, or decoded, by the receiver.

Nonverbal communication includes all unwritten and unspoken messages, both intentional and unintentional. These "silent signals" exert a strong influence on the

FIGURE 2.3 **Olympic Games staff working with international visitors were trained in what to say and how to gesture. This illustration shows several examples.**

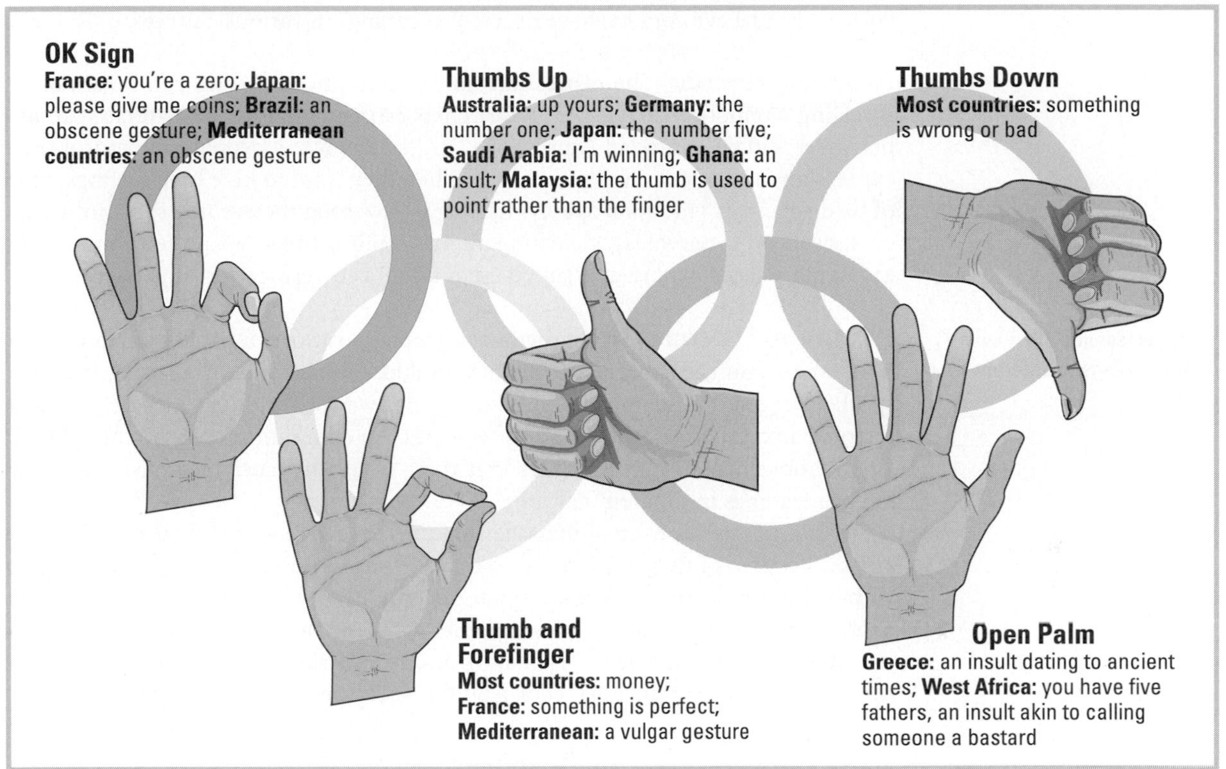

receiver. Yet, interpreting them is by no means a science. Does a downward glance indicate modesty, embarrassment, or fatigue? Does a constant stare reflect coldness, insensitivity, or dullness? Messages are especially difficult to decipher when the verbal and nonverbal codes contradict each other.

OK Sign
France: you're a zero; **Japan:** please give me coins; **Brazil:** an obscene gesture; **Mediterranean countries:** an obscene gesture
Thumbs Up
Australia: up yours; **Germany:** the number one; **Japan:** the number five; **Saudi Arabia:** I'm winning; **Ghana:** an insult; **Malaysia:** the thumb is used to point rather than the finger
Thumbs Down
Most countries: something is wrong or bad
Thumb and Forefinger
Most countries: money; **France:** something is perfect; **Mediterranean:** a vulgar gesture
Open Palm
Greece: an insult dating to ancient times; **West Africa:** you have five fathers, an insult akin to calling someone a bastard

Nonverbal ommunication includes all unwritten and unspoken messages, both intentional and unintentional.

As numerous studies indicate, when verbal and nonverbal messages conflict, receivers put more faith in the nonverbal cues. Successful communicators recognize the power of nonverbal messages. While it's unwise to attach arbitrary meanings to specific gestures or actions, some of the cues broadcast by body language are helpful in interpreting the general feelings and attitudes of the sender. For example, body language can suggest defensiveness, cooperation, nervousness, frustration, weakness, and power.

When verbal and nonverbal messages clash, receivers tend to believe the nonverbal messages.

Listeners are understandably confused when a speaker's nonverbal cues contradict the verbal message. Let's look more closely at the powerful effect eye contact, facial expressions, posture, and gestures have on communication.

Eye Contact. Communicators consider the eyes to be the most accurate predictor of a speaker's true feelings and attitudes. Most of us cannot look another person straight in the eyes and lie. As a result, we tend to believe people who look directly at us. We have less confidence in and actually distrust those who cannot maintain eye contact. Sustained eye contact suggests trust and admiration; brief eye contact signifies fear or stress. Prolonged eye contact, however, can be intrusive and intimidating.

Eye contact, facial expressions, and posture and gestures can all convey meaning.

Good eye contact enables the message sender to determine whether a receiver is paying attention, showing respect, responding favourably, or feeling distress. From the receiver's perspective, good eye contact reveals the speaker's sincerity, confidence, and truthfulness. Since eye contact is a learned skill, however, you must be respectful of people who do not maintain it. You must also remember that nonverbal cues, including eye contact, have different meanings in various cultures.

Facial Expression. The expression on a communicator's face can be almost as revealing of emotion as the eyes. Researchers estimate that the human face can display over 250 000 different expressions.[15] Although a few people can control these expressions and maintain a "poker face" when they want to hide their feelings, most of us display our emotions openly. Raising or lowering the eyebrows, squinting the eyes, swallowing nervously, clenching the jaw, smiling broadly—these voluntary and involuntary facial expressions supplement or entirely replace verbal messages.

Nonverbal messages often have different meanings in different cultures.

Posture and Gestures. An individual's general posture can convey anything from high status and self-confidence to shyness and submissiveness. Leaning toward a speaker suggests attraction and interest; pulling away or shrinking back denotes fear, distrust, anxiety, or disgust. Similarly, gestures can communicate entire thoughts via simple movements. But remember that these nonverbal cues may have vastly different meanings in different cultures.

Tuning in on nonverbal messages requires an awareness of their existence and an appreciation of their importance. To take stock of how effective you are in nonverbal communication, ask a classmate to critique your use of eye contact, facial expressions, and body movements. Another way to analyze your nonverbal style is to videotape yourself making a presentation and study your performance. This way you can make sure your nonverbal cues send the same message as your words.

How Time, Space, and Territory Send Silent Messages

In addition to nonverbal messages transmitted by your body, three external elements convey information in the communication process: time, space, and distance.

People convey meaning in how they structure and organize time and how they order the space around themselves.

Time. How we structure and use time tells observers about our personality and attitudes. For example, when someone gives a visitor a prolonged interview, she signals her respect for, interest in, and approval of the visitor or the topic to be discussed. By sharing her valuable time, she sends a clear nonverbal message. Likewise, when an individual twice arrives late for a team meeting, it could mean that the team assignment is unimportant to him, that the meeting has low priority, that he is a self-centred person, or that he has little self-discipline. These are assumptions that may be made. In other cultures and regions, though, punctuality is viewed differently.

The way an office is arranged can send nonverbal messages about the openness of its occupant.

Space. How we arrange things in the space around us tells something about ourselves and our objectives. Whether the space is a dorm room, an office, or a department, people reveal themselves in the design and grouping of furniture within that space. Generally, the more formal the arrangement, the more formal and closed the communication environment.

Territory. Each of us has certain areas that we feel are our own territory, whether it's a specific spot or just the space around us. We all maintain zones of privacy in which we feel comfortable. Figure 2.4 categorizes the four zones of social interaction among North Americans, as formulated by anthropologist Edward T. Hall.

FIGURE 2.4 **Four Space Zones for Social Interaction**

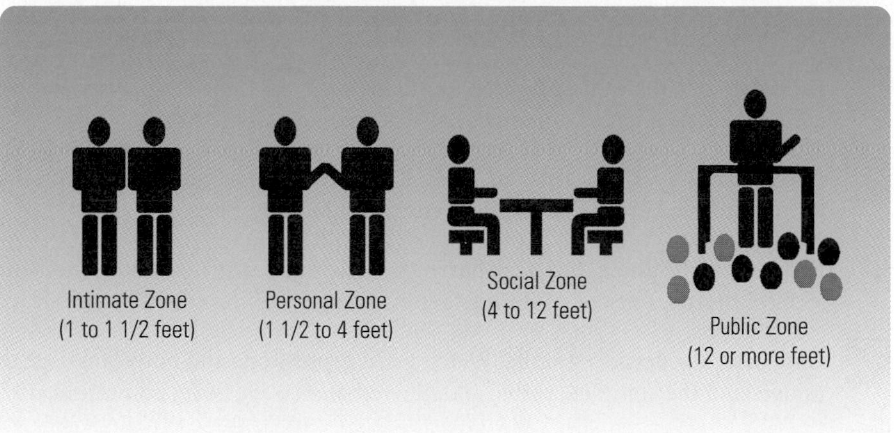

How Appearance Sends Silent Messages

The physical appearance of a business document, as well as the personal appearance of an individual, transmits immediate and important nonverbal messages.

Your appearance and the appearance of your documents convey nonverbal meanings.

Appearance of Business Documents. The way a letter, memo, or report looks can have either a positive or a negative effect on the receiver. Envelopes, through their postage, stationery, and printing, can suggest routine, important, or junk mail. Among the worst offenders are e-mail messages.

Although they seem like conversation, e-mails are business documents that create a permanent record and often a bad impression. Sending an e-mail message full of errors conveys a damaging nonverbal message. The sender may immediately doubt the credibility of the sender. Letters and reports can look neat, professional, well organized, and attractive—or just the opposite. Sloppy, hurriedly written documents convey negative nonverbal messages regarding both the content and the sender. In succeeding chapters you'll learn how to create documents that send positive nonverbal messages through their appearance, format, organization, readability, and correctness.

Appearance of People. The way you look—your clothing, grooming, and posture—sends an instant nonverbal message. Based on what they see, viewers make quick judgments about your status, credibility, personality, and potential. Businesspeople who look the part are more likely to be successful in working with teams, other colleagues, and customers.

Try to invest in conservative, professional-looking clothing and accessories; quality is much more important than quantity. Avoid flashy garments, clunky jewellery, garish makeup, and overpowering colognes. Pay attention to good grooming, including a neat hairstyle, body cleanliness, polished shoes, and clean nails. Project confidence in your posture both standing and sitting. The current trend is toward casual dress at work. Be aware that casual clothes change the image you project and may also affect your work style.

The cues we send nonverbally are probably more important than those we send verbally.

Nonverbal communication can outweigh words in the way it influences how team members and other colleagues perceive us. You can harness the power of silent messages by reviewing the tips in the following checklist.

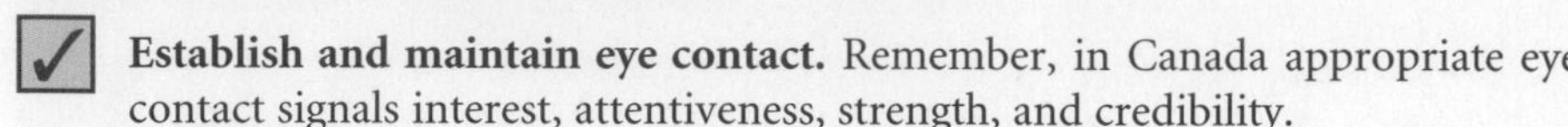

Checklist of Techniques for Improving Nonverbal Communication Skills

- ✓ **Establish and maintain eye contact.** Remember, in Canada appropriate eye contact signals interest, attentiveness, strength, and credibility.
- ✓ **Use posture to show interest.** Encourage communication interaction by leaning forward, sitting or standing erect, and looking alert.
- ✓ **Reduce or eliminate physical barriers.** Move out from behind a desk or lectern; shorten lines of communication; arrange meeting chairs in a circle.
- ✓ **Improve your decoding skills.** Watch facial expressions and body language to understand the complete verbal and nonverbal message being communicated.
- ✓ **Probe for more information.** When you perceive nonverbal cues that contradict verbal meanings, politely seek additional clues (*I'm not sure I understand, Please tell me more about …* , or *Do you mean that …*).
- ✓ **Avoid assigning nonverbal meanings out of context.** Make nonverbal assessments only when you understand a situation or a culture.
- ✓ **Associate with people from diverse cultures.** Learn about other cultures to widen your knowledge and tolerance of intercultural nonverbal messages.
- ✓ **Appreciate the power of appearance.** Keep in mind that the appearance of your business documents, your business space, and yourself send immediate positive or negative messages to receivers.
- ✓ **Observe yourself on videotape.** Ensure that your verbal and nonverbal messages are in sync by taping and evaluating yourself making a presentation.
- ✓ **Enlist friends and family.** Ask them to monitor your conscious and unconscious body movements and gestures to help you become a more effective communicator.

Planning and Participating in Productive Meetings

6 As businesses become more team oriented and management becomes more participatory, people are attending more meetings than ever. One survey of managers found that they were devoting as many as two days a week to various gatherings.[16] Yet, meetings are almost universally disliked. Typical comments include "We have too many of them," "They don't accomplish anything," and "What a waste of time!" In spite of employee reluctance and despite terrific advances in communication and team technology, face-to-face meetings are not going to disappear. So, get used to them. Meetings are here to stay. Our task, then, as business communicators, is to learn how to make them efficient, satisfying, and productive.

Meetings, by the way, consist of three or more individuals who gather to pool information, solicit feedback, clarify policy, seek consensus, and solve problems. But meetings have another important purpose for you. They represent opportunities. Because they are a prime tool for developing staff, they are career-critical. At meet-

ings judgments are formed and careers are made. Therefore, instead of treating them as thieves of your valuable time, try to see them as golden opportunities to demonstrate your leadership, communication, and problem-solving skills. So that you can make the most of these opportunities, here are techniques for planning and conducting successful meetings.

Because you can expect to attend many meetings, learn to make them efficient, satisfying, and productive.

Deciding Whether a Meeting Is Necessary

No meeting should be called unless the topic is important, can't wait, or requires an exchange of ideas. If the flow of information is strictly one-way and no immediate feedback will result, then don't schedule a meeting. For example, if people are merely being advised or informed, send an e-mail, memo, or letter. Leave a telephone or voice mail message, but don't call a costly meeting. Remember, the real expense of a meeting is the lost productivity of all the people attending. To decide whether the purpose of the meeting is valid, it's a good idea to consult the key people who will be attending. Ask them what outcomes are desired and how to achieve those goals. This consultation also sets a collaborative tone and encourages full participation.

Call meetings only when necessary, and invite only key people.

Selecting Participants

The number of meeting participants is determined by the purpose of the meeting, as shown in Figure 2.5. If the meeting purpose is motivational, such as an awards cere-

FIGURE 2.5 **Meeting Purpose and Number of Participants**

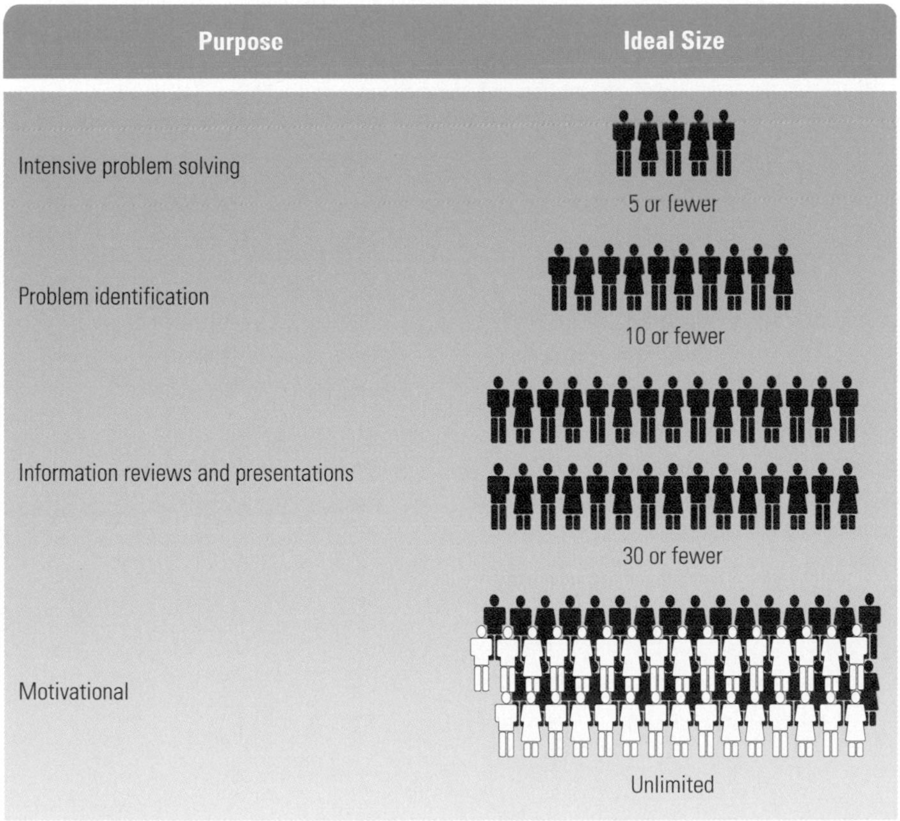

Purpose	Ideal Size
Intensive problem solving	5 or fewer
Problem identification	10 or fewer
Information reviews and presentations	30 or fewer
Motivational	Unlimited

mony, then the number of participants is unlimited. But to make decisions, according to studies at 3M Corporation, the best number is five or fewer participants.[17] Ideally, those attending should be people who will make the decision and people with information necessary to make the decision. Also attending should be people who will be responsible for implementing the decision and representatives of groups who will benefit from the decision.

Distributing Advance Information

Pass out a meeting agenda showing topics to be discussed and other information.

At least two days in advance of a meeting, distribute an agenda of topics to be discussed. Also include any reports or materials that participants should read in

FIGURE 2.6 **Typical Meeting Agenda**

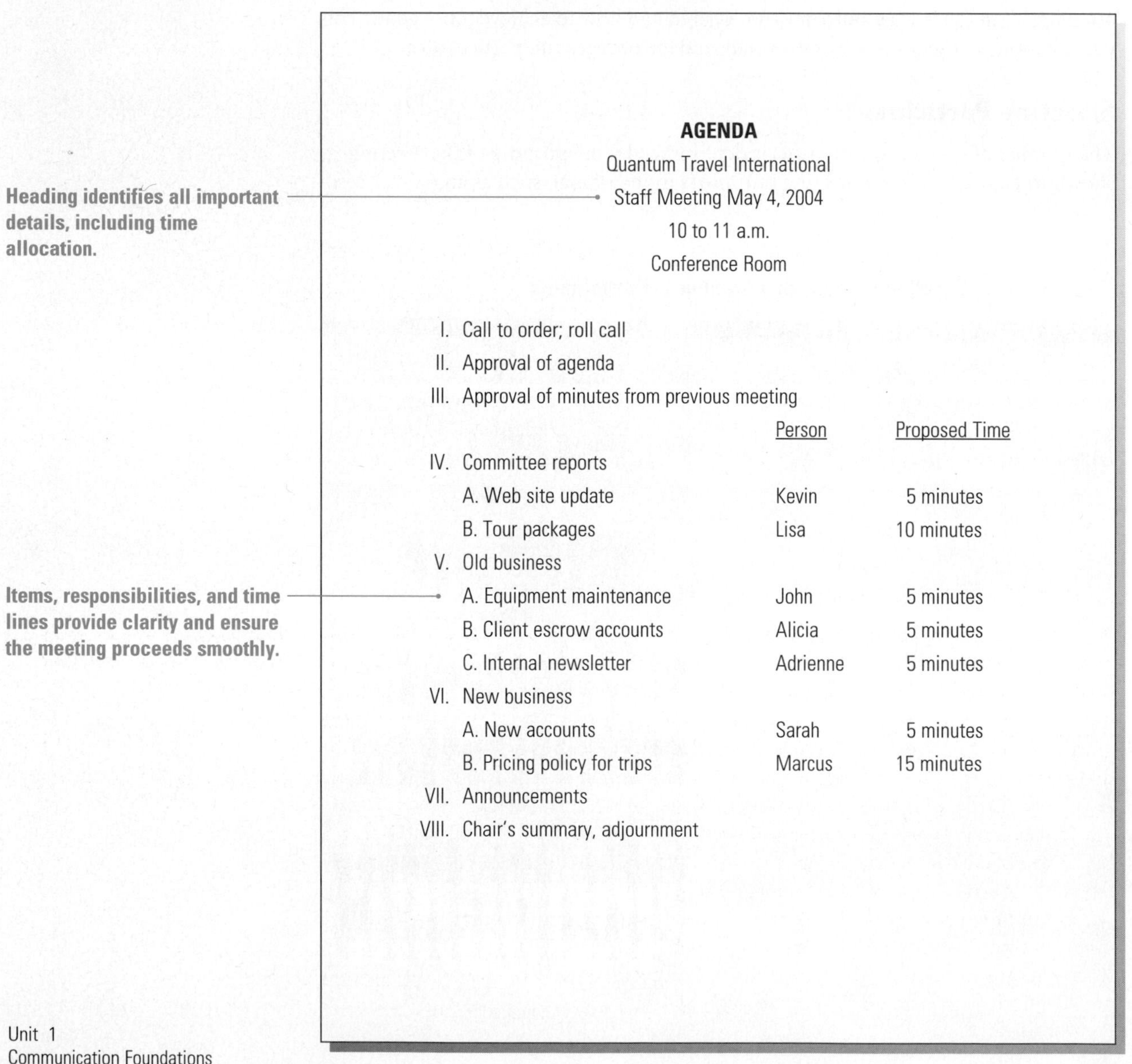

AGENDA
Quantum Travel International
Staff Meeting May 4, 2004
10 to 11 a.m.
Conference Room

		Person	Proposed Time
I.	Call to order; roll call		
II.	Approval of agenda		
III.	Approval of minutes from previous meeting		
IV.	Committee reports		
	A. Web site update	Kevin	5 minutes
	B. Tour packages	Lisa	10 minutes
V.	Old business		
	A. Equipment maintenance	John	5 minutes
	B. Client escrow accounts	Alicia	5 minutes
	C. Internal newsletter	Adrienne	5 minutes
VI.	New business		
	A. New accounts	Sarah	5 minutes
	B. Pricing policy for trips	Marcus	15 minutes
VII.	Announcements		
VIII.	Chair's summary, adjournment		

Heading identifies all important details, including time allocation.
Items, responsibilities, and time lines provide clarity and ensure the meeting proceeds smoothly.

advance. For continuing groups, you might also include a copy of the minutes of the previous meeting. To keep meetings productive, limit the number of agenda items. Remember, the narrower the focus, the greater the chances for success. A good agenda, as illustrated in Figure 2.6, covers the following information:

- Date and place of meeting
- Start time and end time
- Brief description of each topic, in order of priority, including the names of individuals who are responsible for performing some action
- Proposed allotment of time for each topic
- Any pre-meeting preparation expected of participants

Getting the Meeting Started

Start meetings on time and open with a brief introduction.

To avoid wasting time and irritating attendees, always start meetings on time—even if some participants are missing. Waiting for latecomers causes resentment and sets a bad precedent. For the same reasons, don't give a quick recap to anyone who arrives late. At the appointed time, open the meeting with a three- to five-minute introduction that includes the following:

- Goal and length of the meeting
- Background of topics or problems
- Possible solutions and constraints
- Tentative agenda
- Ground rules to be followed

A typical set of ground rules might include arriving on time, communicating openly, being supportive, listening carefully, participating fully, confronting conflict frankly, following the agenda, and adhering to Robert's Rules of Order. At this point, ask whether participants agree with you thus far. The next step is to assign one attendee to take minutes and one to act as a recorder. The recorder stands at a flipchart or whiteboard and lists the main ideas being discussed and agreements reached.

Moving the Meeting Along

Keep the meeting moving by avoiding issues that sidetrack the group.

After the preliminaries, the leader should say as little as possible. Like a talk show host, an effective leader makes "sure that each panel member gets some air time while no one member steals the show."[18] Remember that the purpose of a meeting is to exchange views, not to hear one person, even the leader, do all the talking. If the group has one member who monopolizes, the leader might say, "Thanks, Kurt, for that perspective, but please hold your next point while we hear how Ann would respond to that." This technique also encourages quieter participants to speak up.

To avoid allowing digressions to sidetrack the group, try generating a "Parking Lot" list. This is a list of important but divergent issues that should be discussed at a later time. Another way to handle digressions is to say, "We are getting off track here. Forgive me for pressing on, but I need to bring us back to the central issue of...."[19] It's important to adhere to the agenda and the time schedule. Equally important, when the group seems to have reached a consensus, is to summarize the group's position and check to see whether everyone agrees.

Dealing With Conflict

Before reaching decisions, most groups go through a "storming" or conflict stage. Conflict is natural and even desirable, but it can cause awkwardness and uneasiness. In meetings, conflict typically develops when people feel unheard or misunderstood. If two people are in conflict, the best approach is to encourage each to make a complete case while group members give their full attention. Let each one question the other. Then, the leader should summarize what was said, and the group should offer comments. The group may modify a recommendation or suggest alternatives before reaching consensus on a direction to follow.

Ending With a Plan

End the meeting with a summary of accomplishments.

End the meeting at the agreed time. The leader should summarize what has been decided, who is going to do what, and by what time. It may be necessary to ask people to volunteer to take responsibility for completing action items agreed to in the meeting. No one should leave the meeting without full understanding of what was accomplished. One effective technique that encourages full participation is "once around the table." Everyone is asked to summarize briefly his or her interpretation of what was decided and what happens next. Of course, this closure technique works best with smaller groups. The leader should conclude by asking the group to set a time for the next meeting. He or she should also assure the group that a report will follow and thank participants for attending.

Following Up Actively

Follow up by reminding participants of their assigned tasks.

If minutes were taken, they should be distributed within a couple of days after the meeting. It is up to the leader to see that what was decided at the meeting is accomplished. The leader may need to call people to remind them of their assignments and also to volunteer to help them if necessary.

Meetings are a necessary evil for today's team-oriented workplace. The following checklist can help you use them effectively and perhaps accelerate your career.

Checklist for Planning and Participating in Productive Meetings

Before the Meeting

Consider alternatives. Unless a topic is important and pressing, avoid calling a meeting. Perhaps an e-mail message, telephone call, or announcement would serve the purpose as well.

Invite the right people. To make decisions, invite those people who have information and authority to make the decision and implement it.

Distribute an agenda. Prepare and distribute an agenda that includes the date and place of the meeting, the starting and ending time, a brief description of each topic, the names of people responsible for any action, and a proposed time allotment for each topic.

During the Meeting

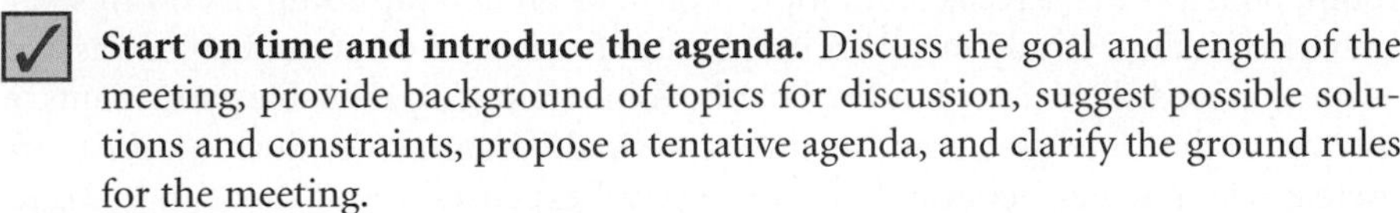

Start on time and introduce the agenda. Discuss the goal and length of the meeting, provide background of topics for discussion, suggest possible solutions and constraints, propose a tentative agenda, and clarify the ground rules for the meeting.

Appoint a secretary and a recorder. Ask one attendee to make a record of the proceedings, and ask another person to record discussion topics on a flipchart or whiteboard.

Encourage balanced participation. Strive to be sure that all participants' views are heard and that no one monopolizes the discussion. Avoid digressions by steering the group back to the topics on the agenda.

Confront conflict frankly. If people disagree, encourage each to explain his or her position completely. Then, restate each position and ask for group comments. The group may modify a recommendation or suggest alternatives before agreeing on a plan of action.

Summarize along the way. When the group seems to reach a consensus, summarize and see whether everyone agrees.

Ending the Meeting and Following Up

Review meeting decisions. At the end of the meeting, summarize what has been decided, discuss action items, and establish a schedule for completion.

Distribute minutes of meeting. A few days after the meeting, arrange to have the recorder or scribe distribute the minutes.

Remind people of action items. Follow up by calling people to see whether they are completing the actions recommended at the meeting.

Using Groupware to Facilitate Meetings and Decision Making

Groupware (sometimes called *teamware*) is a generic term for software designed to facilitate group activities. The term refers to the constantly evolving project management technologies that help groups exchange information, collaborate in, and reach consensus. For example, groupware is helpful in planning and managing focus groups, executive retreats, strategic planning sessions, product development meetings, team-building seminars, and other meetings and training programs. Groupware is also effective when members of organizations must work together to solve problems, write mission statements, and develop proposals. Two common groupware options include videoconferencing and e-mail meetings.[20]

Groupware **is a collection of computer tools to facilitate meetings and decision making.**

Videoconferencing. Although *videoconferencing* generally refers to technologies primarily associated with viewing and *teleconferencing* refers to technologies primarily associated with speaking, often the terms are used interchangeably. Both technologies enable individuals to conduct meetings without getting together face to face.

Videoconferencing and teleconferencing enable individuals to meet without coming together face to face.

Images in videoconferencing may be viewed on a large screen in a conference room, on television screens in multiple rooms, or on desktop computers with small cameras installed. Group members may be able to see documents and objects as well as notes recorded on electronic live boards. Some technologies enable participants to interact at the same time even when they are in different places. Such meetings are increasingly popular because they reduce travel expenses, travel time, and fatigue. Nevertheless, saving money is not among the top reasons for using videoconferencing, which are to "enhance customer service, train the workforce, and obtain instant access for crisis management."[21] Successful Canadian companies such as Bell and Telus are actively involved in videoconferencing.

E-mail meetings allow individuals to respond at different times.

E-Mail Meetings. Participants can exchange words and data, but not pictures, in e-mail meetings. These meetings are usually unmediated; that is, they function without the services of a facilitator to direct the exchange of information. E-mail meetings enable participants to respond at different times, thus erasing time constraints for global team members. E-mail meetings can increase participation by avoiding the dominance of overly vocal or very powerful team members. E-mail meetings also reduce writing inhibitions and decrease transmission time when circulating documents. However, e-mail meetings may suffer from excessive informality, lack of confidentiality, and lack of assurance that participants will read the messages.

Strengthening Your Teamwork Skills Now

At one time or another in your current or future job and certainly in your academic career, you will be working on a team. It may be a temporary team created to complete one specific task, such as developing a new product or completing a project. It could be a permanent team with a continuing function, such as overseeing a complete line of products. In your personal life you could be a committee member or part of the governing body for a volunteer organization, a social group, or a housing group. Most certainly, however, in your professional life you will be part of a team effort.

Teamwork skills need to be studied, modeled, nurtured, and practised.

Teamwork skills need to be studied, modeled, nurtured, and practised. You've just taken a look at the inner workings of teams, including the four phases of team development, the role of conflict, the characteristics of successful teams, listening skills, nonverbal communication skills, and participating in productive meetings. In this book, in this course, and throughout your career, you will have opportunities to work with teams. Begin to analyze their dynamics. Who has the power and why? Who are the most successful team members and why? What would make a team function more effectively? How can you improve your teamwork skills?

Remember, job recruiters consider team skills among the most important requirements for many of today's jobs. You can become the number one candidate for your dream job by developing team skills and acquiring experience now.

Summary of Learning Objectives

1 **Discuss the importance of communicating in a team-oriented workplace and four phases of team development.** Because they can be more productive and effective than individuals, many organizations are forming teams. Teams typically go through four stages of development. In the *forming* stage, they get to know each other and discuss general topics. In the second stage, *storming*, they define their

roles, goals, and governing procedures. Tempers may flare as conflict erupts. Once team members work through this stage, they enter the *norming* stage in which tension subsides, roles clarify, and information begins to flow. Finally, in the *performing* stage, teams develop loyalty and progress toward their goals. Conflict that centres on issues can generate new ideas and help the group progress toward consensus.

2 **Identify the characteristics of successful teams.** The most effective teams are usually small and diverse; that is, they are made up of people representing different ages, genders, and backgrounds. Successful teams agree on their purpose and procedures. They are able to channel conflict into constructive discussion and reach consensus. They encourage open communication, listen actively, provide feedback, and have fun. Members are able to collaborate rather than compete, and leadership is often a shared responsibility depending on the situation and expertise required.

3 **List techniques for organizing team-based written and oral presentations.** In preparing to work together, teams should limit their size, name a meeting leader, and decide whether they wish to make decisions by consensus, majority rule, or some other method. They should work out their schedules, discuss the value of conflict, and decide how to deal with team members who do not do their share. They should decide on the purpose, form, and procedures for preparing the final document or presentation. They must brainstorm for ideas, assign topics, establish deadlines, and discuss how to ensure information accuracy. In composing the first draft of a report or presentation, they should use the same software and meet to discuss drafts and rehearsals. For written reports one person should probably compose the final draft, and the group should evaluate it. For group presentations they need to work for consistency of design, format, and vocabulary. At least five rehearsals, one of which should be videotaped, will enhance the final presentation.

4 **Explain how to become an effective team listener.** Team members (as well as others) can become better listeners by controlling external and internal distractions, becoming actively involved, and identifying important facts. Good listeners do not interrupt speakers who have the floor. They ask clarifying questions at appropriate times, and they paraphrase to ensure that they understand what the speaker has said. While waiting for the speaker's next idea, good listeners analyze the speaker's central idea, key points, and details. To enhance memory and retention, effective listeners take notes or record important points as reminders for future reference or action.

5 **Analyze how information is transmitted through nonverbal messages and discuss how to improve nonverbal communication skills.** Nonverbal messages are sent by our eyes, face, and body. For example, sustained eye contact indicates trust or admiration; brief eye contact may signify fear or stress. Expressions on a communicator's face can supplement or entirely replace verbal messages. Posture can indicate status, confidence, shyness, or submissiveness. Gestures also send nonverbal messages, many of which are culture dependent. Moreover, how a communicator uses time, space, and territory sends messages that require no words. The amount of space we need for social interaction can be another means of sending messages nonverbally. Communicators may improve their nonverbal communication skills by maintaining eye contact, looking alert, eliminating physical barriers that separate them from their listeners, and improving their comprehension of nonverbal signals. They should evaluate nonverbal messages only in context, seek feedback, associate with diverse people, recognize the power of appearance, see themselves on videotape, and ask friends and family to monitor their body language.

6 Discuss how to plan and participate in face-to-face and electronic meetings. Call a meeting only when urgent two-way communication is necessary. Limit participants to those directly involved. Distribute an agenda in advance, start the meeting on time, and keep the discussion on track. Confront conflict openly by letting each person present his or her views fully before having the group decide which direction to take. End the meeting on time and summarize what was accomplished. Follow up by distributing minutes of the meeting and verifying that action items are being accomplished. *Groupware* is a collection of computer tools that facilitate meetings and decision making. Among groupware options are teleconferencing and e-mail meetings, both of which allow individuals to discuss topics although team members may be geographically dispersed.

CHAPTER REVIEW

1. Why can diverse teams be more effective than homogeneous teams? (Obj. 2)
2. Why are team decisions based on consensus better than decisions reached by majority rule? (Obj. 2)
3. In times of team crisis, is it better to have shared leadership or one leader? (Obj. 2)
4. What is the best way to set team deadlines when time is short to complete a project? (Obj. 3)
5. In completing a team-written report, should all team members work together to write the report? Why or why not? (Obj. 3)
6. Workers spend what percentage of their communication time listening? What percentage do executives spend? (Obj. 4)
7. Define *lag time.* (Obj. 4)
8. Describe the four elements in the listening process. (Obj. 4)
9. Define *nonverbal communication.* (Obj. 5)
10. When verbal and nonverbal messages disagree, which message does the receiver consider more truthful? Give an example. (Obj. 5)
11. How does good eye contact help a speaker/sender? How does it benefit a listener/receiver? (Obj. 5)
12. What is the ideal size for a problem-solving meeting, and who should be invited? (Obj. 6)

CRITICAL THINKING

1. How would you compare the advantages and disadvantages of teams in today's workplace? (Objs. 1, 2, and 3)
2. How are listening skills important to employees, supervisors, and executives? Who should have the best listening skills? (Obj. 4)
3. What arguments could you give for or against the idea that body language is a science with principles that can be interpreted accurately by specialists? (Obj. 5)
4. "If you can't orchestrate a meeting, then you are of little use to an organization." How would you comment on this statement? (Obj. 6)

ACTIVITIES

2.1 Team Formation and Discussion (Objs. 1, 2, and 3)

Team

In groups of four or five, conduct a team discussion using one of the topics below. Appoint a team leader and a recorder. Discuss a topic for ten minutes (or as long as your instructor directs). Then as a group, draft an outline of the major points discussed and the decision your team reached. Your instructor may ask you to report your decisions to the class or prepare a group memo describing your team's discussion and decision.

a. Should an employee be allowed to sell products such as Avon items or Girl Guide cookies at work?

b. Should an employee be allowed to send personal e-mail messages during breaks or lunch hours? How about using company computers after hours to prepare a college report? What if your supervisor gives her permission but asks you to keep quiet about it?

c. Should companies have the right to monitor e-mail messages sent by employees? If so, is it necessary for an organization to inform the employees of its policy?

2.2 Web Detectives (Objs. 1 and 2)

Web | Team

Assume your employer has asked you to investigate competitors' Web sites and report what you find. Team up with another class member. Select any two competing companies (say, Coke and PepsiCo. or Nike and Reebok). Examine their Web sites and compare what you find. What services do they offer? How easy is it to navigate each site? How attractive is the format? Is one site clearly better than the other? Why? As a team, report your findings in a memo to your instructor.

2.3 Bad Listening Habits (Obj. 4)

Concentrate for three days on your listening habits in class and on the job. What bad habits do you detect? Be prepared to discuss five bad habits and specific ways you could improve your listening skills. Your instructor may ask you to report your analysis in a memo.

2.4 Body Language (Obj. 5)

What attitudes do the following body movements suggest to you? Do these movements always mean the same thing? What part does context play in your interpretations?

a. Whistling, wringing hands

b. Bowed posture, twiddling thumbs

c. Steepled hands, sprawling sitting position

d. Rubbing hand through hair

e. Open hands, unbuttoned coat

f. Wringing hands, tugging ears

2.5 Document Appearance (Obj. 5)

Select a business letter and envelope that you have received at home or work. Analyze their appearance and the nonverbal messages they send. Consider the amount of postage, method of delivery, correctness of address, kind of stationery, typeface(s), format, and neatness. What assumptions did you make when you saw the envelope? How about the letter itself?

2.6 Gender Differences (Obj. 5)

Many researchers in the field of nonverbal communication report that women are better at accurately interpreting nonverbal signals than are men. Conduct a class survey. On a scale of 1 (low) to 5 (high), how would you rank men in general on their ability to interpret the meaning of eye, voice, face, and body signals? Then rank women in general. Tabulate the class votes. Why do you think gender differences exist in the decoding of nonverbal signals?

2.7 Planning a Meeting (Obj. 6)

Assume that the next meeting of your student organization will discuss preparations for a career day in the spring. The group will hear reports from committees working on speakers, business recruiters, publicity, reservations of campus space, setup of booths, and any other matters you can think of. As president of your organization, prepare an agenda for the meeting. Compose your introductory remarks to open the meeting. Your instructor may ask you to submit these two documents or use them in staging an actual meeting in class.

2.8 Analyzing a Meeting (Obj. 6)

Attend a structured meeting of a college, social, business, or other organization. Compare the manner in which the meeting is conducted with the suggestions presented in this chapter. Why did the meeting succeed or fail? Prepare a memo for your instructor or be ready to discuss your findings in class.

2.9 Searching the Web for Videoconferencing Data (Obj. 6)

Web

Your boss wants to find a way to reduce travel costs of staff members. He asks you to investigate videoconferencing technology. The first place you turn for research is the Web, and you discover that a surprising number of organizations offer videoconferencing services at their Web sites. Search for two organizations that provide information about videoconferencing technology, its applications, and costs. What services do they provide? How much does it cost to make a point-to-point conference call or to set up an entire in-house system? Gather preliminary data and condense it into a one-page memo (your boss doesn't like to read long memos).

C.L.U.E. REVIEW 2

On a separate sheet edit the following sentences to correct faults in grammar, punctuation, spelling, and word use.

1. If swimming is especialy good for you're figure how do you explain whales.
2. Although you may be on the right track you can get run over if you just set there.
3. Ellen and myself examined all simular accounts on a case by case basis.
4. Although both reports was wrote by Jeff and I, they carried the bosses signature.
5. The Vice President said, "Meetings are places where minutes may be kept but hours are lost."
6. At least fourteen patience were admitted after the accident, however, only four required treatment.
7. If the company is sold about one hundred and fifty employees will be out-of-work.
8. The meeting is scheduled for 4:00 p.m. consaquently Melissa and myself may be a little late.
9. Did you know that forty-five percent of canadians have visited disneyland or disney world.
10. I have allready checked the Web but I visited only one Government cite.

CHAPTER • 3 •

COMMUNICATING ACROSS CULTURES

LEARNING OBJECTIVES

1 Discuss three significant trends related to the increasing importance of multicultural communication.

2 Define *culture*. Describe five significant characteristics of culture, and compare and contrast five key dimensions of culture.

3 Explain the relationship between ethnocentrism, tolerance, and stereotypes in achieving multicultural sensitivity.

4 Illustrate how to improve nonverbal and oral communication in multicultural environments.

5 Illustrate how to improve written messages in multicultural environments.

6 Explain the challenge of capitalizing on workforce diversity, including its dividends and its divisiveness. List tips for improving harmony and communication among diverse workplace audiences.

The Increasing Importance of Multicultural Communication

1

The impact of the "tom tom drums of the global village," as predicted by Canadian Marshall McLuhan, is increasingly becoming a reality. National and even local businesses find that their markets frequently extend across borders. Especially in North America, this movement toward global markets has swelled to a torrent. To better compete, many organizations form multinational alliances. Some alliances work, and others may not. Those that flourish have generally confronted and overcome many obstacles.

Learning more about how culture affects behaviour helps you reduce friction and misunderstandings.

Some of the most significant obstacles involve misunderstandings and contrary views resulting from multicultural differences. In your current or future work, you may find that your employers, fellow workers, or clients are from other countries. You may travel abroad for your employer or on your own. Learning more about the powerful effect that culture has on behaviour will help you reduce friction and misunderstanding in your dealings with people from other cultures. Before examining strategies for helping you surmount intercultural obstacles, let's take a closer look at three significant trends: (1) globalization of markets, (2) technological advancements, and (3) a multicultural workforce.

Globalization of Markets

Doing business beyond our borders is now commonplace. Procter & Gamble is selling disposable diapers in Asia; Rubbermaid would like to see its plastic products in all European kitchens; and Unilever promotes its detergents around the world. Not only are market borders blurring, but acquisitions, mergers, and alliances are obscuring the nationality of many companies.

National boundaries mean less as businesses expand through mergers, alliances, and acquisitions.

As markets expand, national boundaries and national allegiance mean less and less. When the German manufacturer Daimler-Benz, makers of Mercedes luxury cars, merged with Chrysler, one executive commented: "There are no German and American companies. There are only successful and unsuccessful companies."[1]

North American companies in global markets must adapt to other cultures.

To be successful in this interdependent global village, North American companies are increasingly finding it necessary to adapt to other cultures. In Europe, Rubbermaid met resistance when it offered products in neutral blues and almond, favourite North American colours. Southern Europeans prefer red, while customers in Holland want white.[2] To sell its laundry products in Europe, Unilever learned that Germans demand a product that's gentle on lakes and rivers. Spaniards wanted cheaper products that get shirts white and soft. And Greeks preferred small packages that were cheap and easy to carry home.[3]

What's caused this rush toward globalization of markets and blurring of national identities? One significant factor is the passage of favourable trade agreements. The General Agreement on Tariffs and Trade (GATT) promotes open trade globally, while the North American Free Trade Agreement (NAFTA) expands free trade among Canada, the United States, and Mexico. NAFTA created the largest and richest free-trade region on earth.[4] The opening of Eastern Europe and the shift away from communism in Russia have also fueled the progress toward expanding world markets.

Favourable trade agreements and the growth of the middle class fuel the expansion of global markets.

Another important factor in the new global market is the explosive growth of the middle class. Parts of the world formerly considered underdeveloped now boast robust middle classes. And these consumers crave everything from cola to cellular phones. But probably the most important factor in the rise of the global market is the development of new transportation and information technologies.

TECH TALK

BEING MULTICULTURALLY CORRECT ON THE WEB

Early Web sites were almost always in English and meant for North Americans. But as online access grows around the world, multinational companies are taking a second look at their sites. Sony Music Entertainment, Inc., for example, now boasts 13 country-specific Web sites. French fans can see which Sony artists are "en tournée" in Nice; and German fans can see which Sony records topped the local album charts "diese woche." United Parcel Service, Inc., allows customers in 13 European countries to track packages in their native languages. And Reebok considers its multilingual Web presence a necessity in expanding its global sales and marketing. What should companies do when they decide to go global on the Web?

- **Learn the local lingo.** Other countries have developed their own Web jargon and iconography. *Home page* is "page d'accueil" (welcome page) in French and "pagina inicial" (initial page) in Spanish. Experts warn against simply translating English words page by page.
- **Check icons.** North American Web surfers easily recognize the mailbox, but in Europe a more universal icon would be an envelope. Test images with local residents.
- **Relax restrictions on consistency.** Allow flexibility to meet local tastes. For example, McDonald's main site greets visitors with the golden arches and a Ronald McDonald–red background. The Japanese site, though, complements the McDonald's red and gold with pinks and browns, which are more pleasing in their culture.
- **Keep the message simple.** Whether in English or the local language, use simple, easily translated words. Avoid slang, jargon, acronyms, or ambiguous expressions.
- **Develop the site together.** The best foreign Web sites for multinational companies are developed when domestic and foreign webmasters work together. Start early and build rapport, recommends Judy Newby, a McDonald's webmaster.[5]

Technological Advancements

Advancements in transportation and information technologies contribute to global interconnectivity.

Amazing new transportation and information technologies are major contributors to the development of our global interconnectivity. Equally significant in creating the global village are incredible advancements in communication technologies. The Internet now permits instantaneous oral and written communication across time zones and continents. Moreover, the Web is emerging as a vital business tool. Companies depend on the Web to sell products, provide technical support, offer customer service, investigate the competition, and link directly to suppliers. Many multinational companies are now establishing country-specific Web sites, as discussed in the Tech Talk box.

Companies use the Web to sell products, provide support, offer service, investigate the competition, and link to suppliers.

Internal Web networks called *intranets* streamline business processes and improve access to critical company information. Through intranets employees have access to information that formerly had to be printed, such as a company phone book, training manuals, job postings, employee newsletters, sales figures, price lists, and even confidential reports, which can be password-protected. The Internet and the Web are changing the way we do business and the way we communicate. These advancements in communication and transportation have made markets more accessible and the world of business more efficient and more globally interdependent.

Multicultural Workforce

As world commerce mingles more and more, another trend gives cross-cultural communication increasing importance. People are on the move. Lured by the prospects of peace, prosperity, education, or a fresh start, persons from many cultures are moving to countries promising to fulfil their dreams. For generations the two most popular destinations have been the United States and Canada.

With increases in immigration, foreign-born persons are an ever-growing portion of the Canadian population. By 2005, according to Statistics Canada, the proportion of "visible minorities" will rise to 16 percent of the national population, from 12 percent in 1996. By 2016, the number will rise to 20 percent. A new level of diversity is being added to Canada, and the regional metropolises of Toronto, Vancouver, and Montreal are largely multicultural and multiracial.[6]

Immigration makes cross-cultural communication skills increasingly necessary.

This influx of immigrants is reshaping Canadian society. While Americans have traditionally supported the "melting pot" approach to ethnic groups, Canada has often been compared to a mosaic. In 1971, Canada became the first country in the world to adopt a multiculturalism policy. In 1988, it passed the Canadian Multiculturalism Act, which provides "specific direction to the federal government to work toward achieving equality in the economic, social, cultural and political life of the country."[7] Individuals are invited to join the nation and still retain their cultural identities, complete with traditions, languages, and customs. Unofficially, Canada is a land of many languages, although by law its languages are French and English. In British Columbia, for example, drivers' licence tests are available in English, French, Chinese, and Punjabi, and Nunavut's primary language of government is Inuktitut, with secondary services available in English as required. Instead of being the exception, cultural diversity is increasingly the norm. As we seek to accommodate multiethnic neighbourhoods, multinational companies, and a multicultural workforce, we can expect some changes to happen smoothly. Other changes will involve conflict and resentment, especially for people losing their positions of power and privilege. Learning how to manage multicultural conflict is an important part of the education of any business communicator.

Understanding Culture

2

Every country or region within a country has a unique common heritage, joint experience, or shared learning. This shared background produces the culture of a region, country, or society. For our purposes, *culture* may be defined as the complex system of values, traits, morals, and customs shared by a society. Culture teaches people how to behave, and it conditions their reactions.

Anthropologists Edward T. Hall and Mildred Reed Hall suggested that culture is "a system for creating, sending, storing, and processing information." Society programs men and women to act differently. Gender, race, age, religion, and many other factors affect our behaviour and cause us to behave in certain patterns.

People from one culture may have difficulty getting through to those from another culture, because individuals do not always behave as expected. People are further differentiated by their environments. For example, work cultures differ remarkably from one organization to another. When people conditioned to work in casual surroundings are placed in work cultures that are more formal and regimented, they may experience culture shock.

The important thing to remember is that culture is a powerful operating force that conditions the way we think and behave. As thinking individuals, we are extraordinarily flexible and are capable of phenomenal change. The purpose of this chapter is to broaden your view of culture and open your mind to flexible attitudes so that you can avoid frustration when cultural adjustment is necessary.

Characteristics of Culture

Understanding basic characteristics of culture helps us make adjustments and accommodations.

Culture is shaped by attitudes learned in childhood and later internalized in adulthood. As we enter this current period of globalization and multiculturalism, we should expect to make adjustments and adopt new attitudes. Adjustment and accommodation will be easier if we understand some basic characteristics of culture.

Culture Is Learned. Rules, values, and attitudes of a culture are not inherent. They are learned and passed down from generation to generation. For example, in many Middle Eastern and some Asian cultures, same-sex people may walk hand-in-hand in the street, but opposite-sex people may not do so. In Arab cultures conversations are often held in close proximity, sometimes nose to nose. But in Western cultures if a person stands too close, one may react as if violated. Cultural rules of behaviour learned from your family and society are conditioned from early childhood.

Cultures Are Inherently Logical. The rules in any culture originated to reinforce that culture's values and beliefs. They act as normative forces. For example, in Japan the original Barbie doll was a failure for many reasons, one of which was her toothy smile.[8] Japan is a country where women cover their mouths with their hands when they laugh so as not to expose their teeth. Exposing one's teeth is not only immodest but also aggressive. Although current cultural behaviour may sometimes seem silly and illogical, nearly all serious rules and values originate in deep-seated beliefs. Rules about exposing teeth or how close to stand are linked to values about sexuality, aggression, modesty, and respect. Acknowledging the inherent logic of a culture is extremely important when learning to accept behaviour that differs from one's own cultural behaviour.

Culture determines our sense of who we are and our sense of community.

Culture Is the Basis of Self-Identity and Community. Culture is the basis for how we tell the world who we are and what we believe. People build their identities through cultural overlays to their primary culture. North Americans, for example, make choices in education, career, place of employment, and life partner. Each of these choices brings with it a set of rules, manners, ceremonies, beliefs, language, and values. They add to one's total cultural outlook, and they represent major expressions of a person's self-identity.

Culture Combines the Visible and Invisible. To outsiders, the way we act—those things that we do in daily life and work—are the most visible parts of our culture. In Japan, for instance, harmony with the environment is important. Thus, when attending a flower show, a woman would wear a dress with pastel rather than primary colours to avoid detracting from the beauty of the flowers. And in India people avoid stepping on ants or insects because they believe in reincarnation and are careful about all forms of life.[9] These practices are outward symbols of deeper values that are invisible but that pervade everything we think and do.

Attitudes, behaviours, and beliefs in a culture change as a result of migration, disasters, and wars.

Culture Is Dynamic. Over time, cultures will change. Changes are caused by advancements in technology and communication, as discussed earlier. Change is also caused by events such as migration, natural disasters, and wars. Attitudes, behaviours, and beliefs change in open societies more quickly than in closed societies.

Dimensions of Culture

The more you know about culture in general and your own culture in particular, the better able you will be to adapt to a multicultural perspective. The diverse Canadian society is really a group of cultures. Canada also has several regional subcultures: West Coast Canadians have a different way of thinking and a different spirit from Central and East Coast Canadians; Canadians who live on the Prairies are distinct from those in Ontario, as are Quebecois and Newfoundlanders.[10]

Canadians, it appears, now feel more different from Americans than they did a decade ago. As Michael Adams observes in his book *Sex in the Snow*,

> despite tribal differences, French and English Canadians have far more in common with each other in terms of values than either group has with the Americans (however offensive this observation might be to political ideologues of the "distinct society").... Canadians are not revolutionaries; they are rebels and reformers. And in spite of our growing intimacy with American commerce and culture, Canada remains a distinct society on the northern half of the North American continent.[11]

"The core virtues that Canadians have traditionally embraced—open-minded tolerance for other points of view; belief in a measure of equity between the advantaged and the less-so; a history built on negotiation rather than coercion—are still very much alive above the 49th parallel."[12]

Though Canadians may have a unique identity, we will always feel the impact of our southern neighbours. Former Prime Minister Pierre Trudeau once described sharing a border with the United States as being similar to sleeping with an elephant: "No matter how friendly or even tempered is the beast, if I may call it that," he said, "one is affected by every twitch and grunt."[13]

In our limited space in this book, it's impossible to cover fully the infinite facets of culture. But we can outline some key dimensions of culture and look at them from different views.

So that you will better understand your culture and how it contrasts with other cultures, we will describe five key dimensions of culture: context, individualism, formality, communication style, and time orientation.

Context. Context is probably the most important cultural dimension and also the most difficult to define. It's a concept developed by cultural anthropologist Edward T. Hall. In his model, context refers to the stimuli, environment, or ambience surrounding an event. Communicators in low-context cultures (such as those in North America, Scandinavia, and Germany) depend little on the context of a situation to convey their meaning. They assume that listeners know very little and must be told practically everything. In high-context cultures (such as those in Japan, China, and Arab countries), the listener is already "contexted" and does not need to be given much background information.[14] Figure 3.1 provides a continuum of low- and high-context countries and summarizes important differences between them.

Low-context cultures (North America, Western Europe) depend less on the environment of a situation to convey meaning than do high-context cultures (such as those in Japan, China, and Arab countries).

Individualism. An attitude of independence and freedom from control characterizes individualism. Members of low-context cultures, particularly Western cultures, tend to value individualism. They believe that initiative and self-assertion result in personal achievement. They believe in individual action and personal responsibility, and they desire a large degree of freedom in their personal lives. According to Professor Usha George of the University of Toronto, Western cultures tend to be more individualistic and vocal than other cultures.[15]

Members of high-context cultures are more collectivist. They emphasize membership in organizations, groups, and teams; they encourage acceptance of group values, duties, and decisions. They typically resist independence because it fosters competition and confrontation instead of consensus. In group-oriented cultures like many

FIGURE 3.1 **Comparing Low- to High-Context Cultures**

Low Context	High Context
Tends to prefer direct verbal interaction	Tends to prefer indirect verbal interaction
Tends to understand meaning at one level only	Tends to understand meanings embedded at many sociocultural levels
Is generally less proficient in reading nonverbal cues	Is generally more proficient in reading nonverbal cues
Values individualism	Values group membership
Relies more on logic	Relies more on context and feeling
Employs linear logic	Employs spiral logic
Says *no* directly	Talks around point; avoids saying *no*
Communicates in highly structured (contexted) messages, provides details, stresses literal meanings, gives authority to written information	Communicates in simple, ambiguous, noncontexted messages; understands visual messages readily

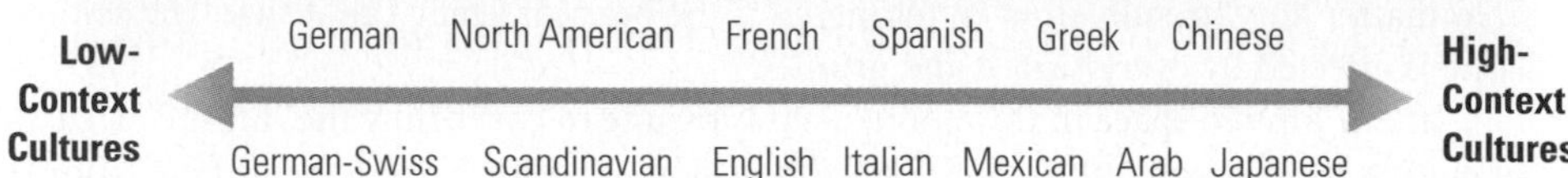

Asian societies, for example, self-assertion and individual decision making are discouraged. Business decisions are often made by all who have competence in the matter under discussion. Similarly, in China managers also focus on the group rather than on the individual, preferring a "consultative" management style to an autocratic style.[16]

Many cultures, of course, are quite complex and cannot be characterized as totally individualistic or group oriented.

Tradition, ceremony, and social rules are more important in some cultures.

Formality. Members of some cultures place less emphasis on tradition, ceremony, and social rules than do members of other cultures. While Canadians tend to be generally reserved and formal in their business dealings,[17] levels of formality vary across the country. In Quebec, where etiquette and politeness are considered very important, first names and informal greetings are generally not used and modes of dress are more conservative than in the rest of Canada.[18] In other parts of Canada, business dress may be more casual and business acquaintances are soon on a first-name basis. While French Canadians may be more formal in business settings, they may also have a tendency to be less reserved—gesturing more expansively, requiring less personal space, and engaging in more touching—than English Canadians.[19] Directness and a tendency to come right to the point often characterize a lack of formality in business. In many cases, lack of directness is thought to be a waste of time—another valuable commodity in Western cultures.

This informality and directness may be confusing abroad. In Mexico, for instance, a typical business meeting begins with handshakes, coffee, and an expansive conversation about the weather, sports, and other light topics.[20] In Japan signing documents and exchanging business cards are important rituals. In Europe first names are never used without invitation. In Arab, South American, and Asian cultures, a feeling of friendship and kinship must be established before business can be transacted.

In Western cultures people are more relaxed about social status and appearance of power.[21] Deference is not generally paid to individuals merely because of their wealth, position, seniority, or age. In many Asian cultures, however, these characteristics are important and must be respected.

Communication Style. People in low- and high-context cultures tend to communicate differently with words. To North Americans and Germans, words are very important, especially in contracts and negotiations. People in high-context cultures, on the other hand, place more emphasis on the surrounding context than on the words describing a negotiation. A Greek sees a contract as a formal statement announcing the intention to build a business for the future. The Japanese treat contracts as statements of intention, and they assume changes will be made as a project develops. Mexicans treat contracts as artistic exercises of what might be accomplished in an ideal world. They do not expect contracts to apply consistently in the real world. An Arab may be insulted by merely mentioning a contract; a man's word is more binding.[22]

Words are used differently by people in low- and high-context cultures.

Canadians tend to take words literally, while Latins enjoy plays on words; Arabs and South Americans sometimes speak with extravagant or poetic figures of speech that may be misinterpreted if taken literally. Nigerians prefer a quiet, clear form of expression, and Germans tend to be direct but understated.[23]

In communication style Canadians value honesty,[24] are suspicious of evasiveness, and distrust people who might have a "hidden agenda" or who "play their cards too close to the chest."[25] Canadians and Americans also tend to be uncomfortable with silence and impatient with delays. Some Asian businesspeople have learned that the longer they drag out negotiations, the more concessions impatient North Americans are likely to make.

North Americans value a direct communication style.

Western cultures have developed languages that use letters describing the sounds of words. But Asian languages are based on pictographical characters representing the meanings of words. Asian language characters are much more complex than the Western alphabet; therefore, Asians are said to have a higher competence in the discrimination of visual patterns.

Time Orientation. Punctuality is an important Western value. Although French-speaking Canadians tend to have a more casual attitude toward time than do English-speaking Canadians, individual francophone businesspeople vary.[26] Most Canadians correlate time with productivity, efficiency, and money. Keeping people waiting for business appointments wastes time and is also rude. In other cultures time may be perceived as an unlimited and never-ending resource to be enjoyed.

North Americans tend to correlate time with productivity, efficiency, and money.

Achieving Multicultural Sensitivity

3

Being aware of your own culture and how it contrasts with others is an important first step in achieving multicultural sensitivity. Another step involves recognizing barriers to multicultural accommodation and striving to overcome them. Some of these barriers occur quite naturally and require conscious effort to surmount. By becoming multiculturally competent your personal life will be more satisfying and your work life will be more productive, gratifying, and effective. According to international banker Wing Morse, "many business talks go sour because of poor understanding of non-verbal communication cues."[27]

Avoiding Ethnocentrism

The belief in the superiority of one's own race is known as ethnocentrism, a natural attitude inherent in all cultures. If you were raised in Canada, many of the dimensions of culture described previously probably seem "right" to you.

Ethnocentrism causes us to judge others by our own values. As Professor Usha George points out, "We all try to interpret the world through our own cultural lens."[28] We expect others to react as we would, and they expect us to behave as they would. Misunderstandings naturally result. Ethnocentric reactions can be reduced through knowledge of other cultures and development of increased multicultural sensitivity.

Bridging the Gap

Because culture is learned, you can learn new attitudes and behaviours through training.

Developing cultural competence often involves changing attitudes. Remember that culture is learned. Through exposure to other cultures and through training, such as you are receiving in this course, you can learn new attitudes and behaviours that help bridge gaps between cultures.

Tolerance. One desirable attitude in achieving multicultural sensitivity is that of tolerance. Closed-minded people cannot look beyond their own ethnocentrism. But as global markets expand and as our own society becomes increasingly multiethnic, tolerance becomes especially significant. Some job descriptions now include statements such as "Must be able to interact with ethnically diverse personnel."

***Empathy,* which means trying to see the world through another's eyes, helps you be more tolerant and less judgmental.**

To improve tolerance, you'll want to practice empathy. This means trying to see the world through another's eyes. It means being less judgmental and more eager to seek common ground. Accepting cultural differences and adapting to them with tolerance and empathy often results in a harmonious compromise.

Saving Face. In business transactions Westerners often assume that economic factors are the primary motivators of people. It's wise to remember, though, that strong cultural influences are also at work. *Saving face,* for example, is important in many parts of the world. Face refers to the image a person holds in his or her social network. Positive comments raise a person's social standing, but negative comments lower it. People in low-context cultures are less concerned with face.

Patience. Being tolerant also involves patience. International banker Wing Morse notes that North Americans have little tolerance for silence and often jump in to take control of the conversation. Koreans, on the other hand, tend to take their time to think about a question before they share their thoughts. Wing relates, "I'd be sitting in a management staff meeting biting my tongue without saying another word, waiting up to 30 seconds to a minute until somebody responded to my questions."[29] Remaining silent is another means of exhibiting tolerance. In Asian cultures people deliberately use periods of silence for reflection and contemplation.

About Stereotypes, Prototypes, Prejudices, and Generalizations

Most experts recognize that it is impossible to talk about cultures without using mental categories, representations, and generalizations to describe groups. These categories are sometimes considered *stereotypes.* Because the term *stereotype* has a negative meaning, intercultural authors Varner and Beamer suggest that we distinguish between *stereotype* and *prototype.*

A *stereotype* is an oversimplified behavioural pattern applied uncritically to groups. The term was used originally by printers to describe identical type set in two frames, hence *stereo type.* Stereotypes are fixed and rigid. Although they may be exaggerated and overgeneralized beliefs when applied to groups of people, stereotypes are not always entirely false.[30] Often they contain a grain of truth. When a stereotype develops into a rigid attitude and when it's based on erroneous beliefs or preconceptions, then it should be called a *prejudice.*

Stereotypes are oversimplified behavioural patterns applied uncritically to groups; _prototypes_ describe general characteristics that are dynamic and may change.

Varner and Beamer recommend the use of the term *prototype* to describe "mental representations based on general characteristics that are not fixed and rigid, but rather are open to new definitions."[31] Prototypes, then, are dynamic and change with fresh experience. Prototypes based on objective observations usually have a considerable amount of truth in them. That's why they can be helpful in studying culture. For example, Latin businesspeople often talk about their families before getting down to business. This prototype is generally accurate, but it may not universally apply and it may change over time.

Some people object to making any generalizations about cultures whatever. Yet, it is wise to remember that whenever we are confronted with something new and unfamiliar, we naturally strive to categorize the data in order to make sense out of it. In categorizing these new data, we are making generalizations. In fact, science itself would be impossible without generalizations, for what are scientific laws but valid generalizations? Being able to draw generalizations from masses of data is a sign of intelligence and learning. Unfounded generalizations about people and cultures, of course, can lead to bias and prejudice. But for our purposes, when we discuss cultures, it's important to be able to make generalizations and describe cultural prototypes.

Being able to draw valid generalizations is necessary for learning and education.

Improving Communication With Multicultural Audiences

4

Thus far we've discussed the increasing importance of multicultural sensitivity as a result of globalization of markets, increasing migration, and technological advancements. We've described characteristics and dimensions of cultures, and we've talked about avoiding ethnocentrism. Remember, the key to future business success may very well lie in finding ways to work harmoniously with people from different cultures.

Business success may depend on working harmoniously with people from different cultures.

Adapting Messages to Multicultural Audiences

As business communicators, we need to pay special attention to specific areas of communication to enhance the effectiveness of multicultural messages. To minimize the chance of misunderstanding, we'll look more closely at nonverbal communication, oral messages, and written messages.

Nonverbal Communication. Verbal skills in another culture can generally be mastered if one studies hard enough. But nonverbal skills are much more difficult to learn. Nonverbal behaviour includes areas such as eye contact, facial expression, posture, gestures, and the use of time, space, and territory. The messages sent by body language and the way we arrange time and space have always been open to interpretation. Deciphering nonverbal communication is difficult for people who are culturally similar, and it is even more troublesome when cultures differ.

Understanding nonverbal communication is difficult when people are from different cultures.

In Western cultures, for example, people perceive silence as a negative trait. It suggests rejection, unhappiness, depression, regret, embarrassment, or ignorance. However, the Japanese admire silence and consider it a key to success. Silence is equated with wisdom.

Gestures can create different reactions in multicultural environments.

Although nonverbal behaviour is ambiguous within cultures and even more problematic between cultures, it nevertheless conveys meaning. If you've ever had to talk with someone who does not share your language, you probably learned quickly to use gestures to convey basic messages. Since gestures can create very different reactions in different cultures, one must be careful in using and interpreting them.

As businesspeople increasingly interact with their counterparts from other cultures, they will become more aware of these differences. Some behaviours are easy to warn against, such as touching people from the Middle East with the left hand (because it is considered unclean and is used for personal hygiene). We're also warned not to touch anyone's head (even children) in Thailand, as the head is considered sacred. Numerous lists of cultural dos and don'ts have been compiled. However, learning all the nuances of nonverbal behaviour in other cultures is impossible, and such lists are merely the tip of the cultural iceberg.

Associating with people from different cultures broadens multicultural competence.

Although we can't ever hope to understand fully the nuances of meaning transmitted by nonverbal behaviour in various cultures, we can grow more tolerant, more flexible, and eventually, more competent. An important part of achieving nonverbal competence is becoming more aware of our own nonverbal behaviours and their meanings. Much of our nonverbal behaviour is learned in early childhood from our families and from society, and it is largely unconscious. Once we become more aware of the meaning of our own gestures, posture, eye gaze, and so on, we will become more alert and more sensitive to variations in other cultures. Striving to associate with people from different cultures can further broaden our multicultural competence.

Keep your gestures to a minimum or follow the lead of native businesspeople.

From a practical standpoint, when interacting with businesspeople in other cultures, it's always wise to follow their lead. If they avoid intense eye contact, don't stare. If no one is putting his or her elbows on a table, don't be the first to do so. Until you are knowledgeable about the meaning of gestures, it's probably a good idea to keep yours to a minimum. Learning the words for *please*, *yes*, and *thank you* is even better than relying on gestures.[32] Achieving multicultural competence in regard to nonverbal behaviour may never be totally attained, but sensitivity, nonjudgmentalism, and tolerance go a long way toward improving interactions.

When English is a second language, don't assume that speakers understand everything you say.

Oral Messages. Although it's best to speak a foreign language fluently, many of us lack that skill. Fortunately, global business transactions are often conducted in English, though the level of proficiency may be limited among those for whom it is a second language. Canadians abroad make a big mistake in thinking that people who speak English always understand what is being said. Comprehension can be fairly superficial. The following suggestions are helpful for situations in which one or both communicators may be using English as a second language.

Use simple English and avoid puns, sports references, slang, and jargon when communicating with people for whom English is a second language.

- **Learn foreign phrases.** In conversations, even when English is used, foreign nationals appreciate it when you learn greetings and a few phrases in their language.
- **Use simple English.** Speak in short sentences (under 15 words), and try to stick to the 3000 to 4000 most common English words. For example, use *old* rather than *obsolete* and *rich* rather than *luxurious* or *sumptuous*. Eliminate puns, sports and military references, slang, and jargon (special business terms). Be especially alert to idiomatic expressions that can't be translated, such as *burn the midnight oil* and *under the weather*.

- **Speak slowly and enunciate clearly.** Avoid fast speech, but don't raise your voice. Overpunctuate with pauses and full stops. Always write numbers for all to see.
- **Observe eye messages.** Be alert to a glazed expression or wandering eyes—these tell you the listener is lost.
- **Encourage accurate feedback.** Ask probing questions and encourage the listener to paraphrase what you say. Don't assume that a yes, a nod, or a smile indicates comprehension.
- **Check frequently for comprehension.** Avoid waiting until you finish a long explanation to request feedback. Instead, make one point at a time, pausing to check for comprehension. Don't proceed to B until A has been grasped.
- **Accept blame.** If a misunderstanding results, graciously accept the blame for not making your meaning clear.
- **Listen without interrupting.** Curb your desire to finish sentences or to fill out ideas for the speaker. Keep in mind that Westerners abroad are often accused of listening too little and talking too much.
- **Remember to smile!** Roger Axtell, international behaviour expert, calls the smile the single most understood and most useful form of communication in either personal or business transactions.[33]
- **Follow up in writing.** After conversations or oral negotiations, confirm the results and agreements with follow-up letters. For proposals and contracts, engage a translator to prepare copies in the local language.

To improve communication when English is a second language, speak slowly, enunciate clearly, observe eye messages, encourage feedback, check for comprehension, accept blame, don't interrupt, remember to smile, and follow up important conversations in writing.

Written Messages

5

In sending letters and other documents to businesspeople in other cultures, try to adapt your writing style and tone appropriately. For example, in cultures where formality and tradition are important, be scrupulously polite. Don't even think of sharing the latest joke. Humour translates very poorly and can cause misunderstanding and negative reactions. Familiarize yourself with accepted channels of communication. Are letters, e-mail, and faxes common? Would a direct or indirect organizational pattern be more effective? The following suggestions, coupled with the earlier guidelines, can help you prepare successful written messages for multicultural audiences.

- **Adopt local formats.** Learn how documents are formatted and addressed in the intended reader's country. Use local formats and styles.
- **Use short sentences and short paragraphs.** Sentences with fewer than 15 words and paragraphs with fewer than seven lines are most readable.
- **Avoid ambiguous expressions.** Include relative pronouns (*that, which, who*) for clarity in introducing clauses. Stay away from contractions (especially ones like *Here's the problem*). Avoid idioms (*once in a blue moon*), slang (*my presentation really bombed*), acronyms (*ASAP* for *as soon as possible*), abbreviations (*DBA* for *doing business as*), jargon (*input, bottom line*), and sports references (*play ball, slam dunk, ballpark figure*). Use action-specific verbs (*purchase a printer* rather than *get a printer*).
- **Strive for clarity.** Avoid words that have many meanings (the word *light* has 18 different meanings!). If necessary, clarify words that may be confusing. Replace

To improve written messages, adopt local formats, use short sentences and short paragraphs, avoid ambiguous expression, strive for clarity, use correct grammar, cite numbers carefully, and accommodate readers in organization, tone, and style.

two-word verbs with clear single words (*return* instead of *bring back*; *delay* instead of *put off*; *maintain* instead of *keep up*).

- **Use correct grammar.** Be careful of misplaced modifiers, dangling participles, and sentence fragments. Use conventional punctuation.
- **Cite numbers carefully.** For international trade it's a good idea to learn and use the metric system. In citing numbers use figures (*15*) instead of spelling them out (*fifteen*). Always convert dollar figures into local currency. Avoid using figures to express the month of the year.
- **Accommodate the reader in organization, tone, and style.** Organize your message to appeal to the reader. If flowery tone, formal salutations, indirectness, references to family and the seasons, or unconditional apologies are expected, strive to accommodate.

Making the effort to communicate with sensitivity across cultures pays big dividends. "Much of the world wants to like us," says businessperson and international consultant Kevin Chambers. "When we take the time to learn about others, many will bend over backward to do business with us."[34] The following checklist summarizes suggestions for improving communication with multicultural audiences.

Checklist for Improving Multicultural Sensitivity and Communication

Study your own culture. Learn about your customs, biases, and views and how they differ from those in other societies. This knowledge can help you better understand, appreciate, and accept the values and behaviour of other cultures.

Learn about other cultures. Education can help you alter cultural misconceptions, reduce fears, and minimize misunderstandings. Knowledge of other cultures opens your eyes and teaches you to expect differences. Such knowledge also enriches your life.

Curb ethnocentrism. Avoid judging others by your personal views. Get over the view that the other cultures are incorrect, defective, or primitive. Try to develop an open mindset.

Avoid judgmentalism. Strive to accept other behaviour as different, rather than as right or wrong. Try not to be defensive in justifying your culture. Strive for objectivity.

Look beyond stereotypes. Remember that individuals are often unlike their cultural stereotype, so forget preconceptions and probe beneath the surface.

Seek common ground. When cultures clash, look for solutions that respect both cultures. Be flexible in developing compromises.

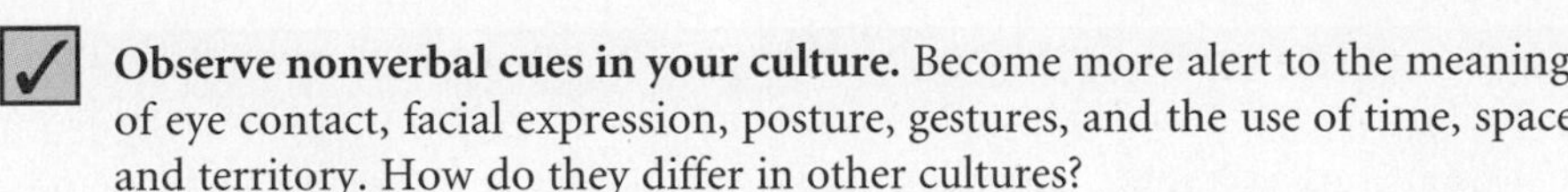

Observe nonverbal cues in your culture. Become more alert to the meanings of eye contact, facial expression, posture, gestures, and the use of time, space, and territory. How do they differ in other cultures?

Use plain English. Speak and write in short sentences using simple words and standard English. Eliminate puns, slang, jargon, acronyms, abbreviations, and any words that cannot be translated easily.

Encourage accurate feedback. In conversations ask probing questions and listen attentively without interrupting. Don't assume that a *yes* or a smile indicates assent or comprehension.

Adapt to local preferences. Shape your writing to reflect the reader's document styles, if appropriate. Express currency in local figures. Write out months of the year for clarity.

Capitalizing on Workforce Diversity

6

At the same time that Canadian businesspeople are interacting with people from around the world, the domestic workforce is becoming more diverse. This diversity has many dimensions—race, ethnicity, age, religion, gender, national origin, physical ability, and countless other qualities. No longer, say the experts, will the workplace be predominantly Anglo-oriented or male. According to Statistics Canada, women and minorities will significantly outnumber white males entering the workforce in the new millennium, and by 2005, more than 15 percent of the workforce will be 55 years or older.[35] And because of technological advances, more physically challenged people are joining the workforce.

Dividends of Diversity

A diverse workforce benefits consumers, work teams, and business organizations.

As society and the workforce become more diverse, successful interaction and communication among the various identity groups brings distinct challenges and dividends in three areas. Jeffery Lipton, president of Alberta's NOVA Corporation, says "If you don't have a culturally diverse organization, you can't win in business. Valuing diversity means acknowledging that everyone is different—in their education, their experience, their culture—and knowing how to use that diversity to an organization's advantage is the only way to be 'number one.'"[36]

Consumers. A diverse staff is better able to read trends and respond to the increasingly diverse customer base in local and world markets. Diverse consumers now want specialized goods and services tailored to their needs. Teams made up of different people with different experiences are better able to create the different products that these markets require. Consumers also want to deal with companies that respect their values.

Work Teams. As you learned in Chapter 2, employees today work in teams. Team members with different backgrounds may come up with more creative and effective problem-solving techniques than homogeneous teams. As J. P. Bryan, former presi-

Presentations in an intercultural setting, especially to an audience that uses English infrequently, require sensitivity. Wise speakers use simple language, speak slowly, watch for eye messages, and encourage frequent feedback.

dent and CEO of Gulf Canada Resources, asserts, "Teamwork is not reducing the person with the greatest ability to the lowest common denominator; it is elevating him to the position where he can exercise his talents to the fullest."[37]

Business Organizations. Companies that set aside time and resources to cultivate and capitalize on diversity will suffer fewer discrimination lawsuits, fewer union clashes, and less government regulatory action. Most important, though, is the growing realization among organizations that diversity is a critical bottom-line business strategy to improve employee relationships and to increase productivity. Developing a diverse staff that can work together cooperatively is one of the biggest challenges facing business organizations today.

Divisiveness of Diversity

Diversity can cause divisiveness, discontent, and clashes.

The *glass ceiling* is an invisible barrier of attitudes, prejudices, and "old boy networks" that blocks women from reaching important positions.

Diversity can be a positive force within organizations. But all too often it can also cause divisiveness, discontent, and clashes. Many of the identity groups, the so-called workforce "disenfranchised," have legitimate gripes.

Women complain of the *glass ceiling,* that invisible barrier of attitudes, prejudices, and "old boy networks" blocking them from reaching important corporate positions. However, more American women than Canadian women believe these obstacles exist in their workplace. Although women make up nearly half of the workforce, they hold only 11 to 12 percent of senior management jobs at major brokerage firms. Seventy percent of American women believe lack of mentors is holding them back while 57 percent of Canadian women perceive that to be a problem.[38] Some women feel that they are the victims of sexual harassment, unequal wages, sexism, and even their style of communication. On the other hand, men, too, have gender issues. One manager described gender discrimination in his office: "My boss was a woman and was very verbal about the opportunities for women to advance in my company. I have often felt she gave much more attention to the women in the office than the men."[39]

Older employees feel that the deck is stacked in favour of younger employees. Minorities complain that they are discriminated against in hiring, retention, wages, and promotions. Physically challenged individuals feel that their limitations should not hold them back, and they fear that their potential is often prejudged. Individuals with different religions feel uncomfortable working alongside each other.

Tips for Improving Communication Among Diverse Workplace Audiences

Integrating all this diversity into one seamless workforce is a formidable task and a vital one. Harnessed effectively, diversity can enhance productivity and propel a company to success well into this century. Mismanaged, it can become a tremendous drain on a company's time and resources. How companies deal with diversity will make all the difference in how they compete in an increasingly global environment. And that means that organizations must do more than just pay lip service to these issues. Harmony and acceptance do not happen automatically when people who are dissimilar work together. The following suggestions can help you and your organization find ways to improve communication and interaction.

A diverse workforce may reduce productivity unless trained to value differences.

- **Seek training.** Awareness-raising sessions may be helpful, especially if an organization is experiencing problems in managing diversity. Spend time reading and learning about workforce diversity and how it can benefit organizations. Look upon diversity as an opportunity, not a threat. Cross-cultural communication, team building, and conflict resolution are skills that can be learned in diversity training programs.
- **Understand the value of differences.** Diversity makes an organization innovative and creative. Sameness fosters an absence of critical thinking called "groupthink," which you learned about in Chapter 2. Diversity in problem-solving groups encourages independent and creative thinking.
- **Don't expect conformity.** Gone are the days when businesses could say, "This is our culture. Conform or leave."[40] Paul Fireman, CEO of Reebok, stresses seeking people who have new and different stories to tell. "And then you have to make real room for them, you have to learn to listen, to listen closely, to their stories. It accomplishes next to nothing to employ those who are different from us if the condition of their employment is that they become the same as us. For it is their differences that enrich us, expand us, provide us the competitive edge."[41]
- **Create zero tolerance for bias and stereotypes.** Cultural patterns exist in every identity group, but applying these patterns to individuals results in stereotyping. Assuming that people are good athletes, poor at math, good hockey players, or insensitive based on ethnic or gender identity fails to admit the immense differences in people in each group. Check your own use of stereotypes and labels. Don't tell sexist or ethnic jokes at meetings. Avoid slang, abbreviations, and jargon that imply stereotypes. Challenge others' biases politely but firmly.

Challenge others' biases and stereotypes politely but firmly.

- **Learn about your cultural self.** Begin to think of yourself as a product of your culture, and understand that your culture is just one among many. Try to stand outside and look at yourself. Do you see any reflex reactions and automatic thought patterns that are a result of your upbringing? These may be invisible to you until challenged by difference. Remember, your culture was designed to help you succeed and survive in a certain environment. Be sure to keep what works and yet be ready to adapt as environments change.

- **Make fewer assumptions.** Be careful of seemingly insignificant, innocent workplace assumptions. For example, don't assume that everyone wants to observe the holidays with a Christmas party and a decorated tree. Celebrating only Christian holidays in December and January excludes those who honour Hanukkah, Kwanza, and the Chinese New Year. Moreover, in workplace discussions don't assume that everyone is married or wants to be or is even heterosexual, for that matter. For invitations, avoid phrases such as *managers and their wives. Spouses or partners* is more inclusive. Valuing diversity means making fewer assumptions that everyone is like you or wants to be like you.

In times of conflict, look for areas of agreement and build on similarities.

- **Build on similarities.** Look for areas where you and others not like you can agree or at least share opinions. Be prepared to consider issues from many perspectives, all of which may be valid. Accept that there is room for different points of view to coexist peacefully. Although you can always find differences, it's much harder to find similarities. Look for common ground in shared experiences, mutual goals, and similar values. Concentrate on your objective even when you may disagree on how to reach it.[42]

Summary of Learning Objectives

1 **Discuss three significant trends related to the increasing importance of multicultural communication.** Three trends are working together to crystallize the growing need for developing multicultural sensitivities and improved communication techniques. First, the globalization of markets means that you can expect to be doing business with people from around the world. Second, technological advancements in transportation and information are making the world smaller and more intertwined. Third, more and more immigrants from other cultures are settling in Canada, thus changing the complexion of the workforce. Successful interaction requires awareness, tolerance, and accommodation.

2 **Define *culture*. Describe five significant characteristics of culture, and compare and contrast five key dimensions of culture.** Culture is the complex system of values, traits, morals, and customs shared by a society. Like a computer, each of us is shaped by the operating system of our culture. Some of the significant characteristics of culture include the following: (1) culture is learned, (2) cultures are inherently logical, (3) culture is the basis of self-identity and community, (4) culture combines the visible and invisible, and (5) culture is dynamic. Members of low-context cultures (such as those in North America, Scandinavia, and Germany) depend on words to express meaning, while people in high-context cultures (such as those in Japan, China, and Arab countries) rely more on context (social setting, a person's history, status, and position) to communicate meaning. Other key dimensions of culture include individualism, degree of formality, communication style, and time orientation.

3 **Explain the relationship between ethnocentrism, tolerance, and stereotypes in achieving multicultural sensitivity.** *Ethnocentrism* refers to a feeling that the culture you belong to is superior to all others and holds all truths. To function effectively in a global economy, we must develop knowledge of and tolerance for other cultures. We also need to move beyond stereotypes, which are oversimplified behavioural patterns applied uncritically to groups. To achieve multicultural sensitivity, we should discover and value individual personal qualities.

4 **Illustrate how to improve nonverbal and oral communication in multicultural environments.** We can minimize nonverbal miscommunication by recognizing that meanings conveyed by eye contact, posture, and gestures are largely culture dependent. Nonverbal messages are also sent by the use of time, space, and territory. Becoming aware of your own nonverbal behaviour and what it conveys is the first step in broadening your multicultural competence. In improving oral messages, you can learn foreign phrases, use simple English, speak slowly and enunciate clearly, observe eye messages, encourage accurate feedback, check for comprehension, accept blame, listen without interrupting, smile, and follow up important conversations in writing.

5 **Illustrate how to improve written messages in multicultural environments.** To improve written messages, adopt local formats, use short sentences and short paragraphs, avoid ambiguous expressions, strive for clarity, use correct grammar, and cite numbers carefully. Also try to accommodate the reader in organization, tone, and style.

6 **Explain the challenge of capitalizing on workforce diversity, including its dividends and its divisiveness. List tips for improving harmony and communication among diverse workplace audiences.** Having a diverse workforce can benefit consumers, work teams, and business organizations. However, diversity can also cause divisiveness among various identity groups. To promote harmony and communication, many organizations develop diversity training programs. As an individual, you must understand and accept the value of differences. Don't expect conformity, and create zero tolerance for bias and stereotypes. Learn about your cultural self, make fewer assumptions, and seek common ground when disagreements arise.

CHAPTER REVIEW

1. Why is it increasingly important for businesspeople to develop multicultural communication skills? (Obj. 1)
2. How is culture like a computer? (Obj. 2)
3. What is culture and how is culture learned? (Obj. 2)
4. Describe five major dimensions of culture. (Obj. 2)
5. Briefly, contrast high- and low-context cultures. (Obj. 2)
6. What is *ethnocentrism*? (Obj. 3)
7. What is a *stereotype*? Give original examples. (Obj. 3)
8. Name three processes that are effective in achieving competence in dealing with nonverbal messages in other cultures. (Obj. 4)
9. Describe five specific ways in which you can improve oral communication with someone from another culture. (Obj. 4)
10. Describe five specific ways in which you can improve written communication with someone from another culture. (Obj. 5)
11. Name three groups who benefit from workforce diversity and explain why. (Obj. 6)
12. Explain five strategies for improving communication among diverse workplace audiences. (Obj. 6)

CRITICAL THINKING

1. Since English is often considered the "language of business," why should Canadians bother to learn about other languages and cultures? (Objs. 1, 2, and 6)
2. If the rules, values, and attitudes of a culture are learned, can they be unlearned? Explain. (Obj. 2)
3. Some economists argue that the statement that "diversity is an economic asset" is an unproved and perhaps unprovable assertion. Should social responsibility or market forces determine whether an organization strives to create a diverse workforce? Why? (Obj. 6)

ACTIVITIES

3.1 Global Economy (Obj. 1)

It is an inescapable fact that our economy is becoming much more like the European and Asian economies, entirely tied to global trade. Read your local newspapers for a week and peruse national news magazines (*Maclean's*, *Canadian Business*, and so forth) for articles that support this assertion. Your instructor may ask you to (a) report on many articles or (b) select one article to summarize. Report your findings orally or in a memo to your instructor. This topic could be expanded into a long report for Chapter 13 or 14.

3.2 Interpreting Multicultural Proverbs (Objs. 2 and 3)

Proverbs, which tell truths with metaphors and simplicity, often reveal fundamental values held by a culture. Discuss the following proverbs and explain how they relate to some of the cultural values you studied in this chapter. What additional proverbs can you cite and what do they mean?

Japanese proverbs

The pheasant would have lived but for its cry.
The nail that sticks up gets pounded down.
To say nothing is a flower.

North American proverbs

The squeaking wheel gets the oil.
A stitch in time saves nine.
A bird in the hand is worth two in the bush.
A man's home is his castle.

German proverbs

No one is either rich or poor who has not helped himself to be so.
He who is afraid of doing too much always does too little.

3.3 Negotiating Traps (Objs. 2, 3, 4, and 5)

Discuss the causes and implications of the following common mistakes made by Westerners in their negotiations with people from other cultures.

a. Assuming that a final agreement is set in stone

b. Lacking patience and insisting that matters progress more quickly than the pace preferred by the locals

c. Thinking that an interpreter is always completely accurate

d. Believing that individuals who speak English understand every nuance of your meaning

e. Ignoring or misunderstanding the significance of rank

3.4 Learning About Other Cultures: Multicultural Panel (Objs. 1–6)

Team

Locate two or three students from other countries (possibly members of your class or international students on campus) who could report on differences between their cultures and Western culture. In addition to context, individualism, formality, communication style, and time, consider such topics as the importance of family and gender roles. Study attitudes toward education, clothing, leisure time, and work. You may want to try some questions such as these:

a. What behaviour or practices shocked you when you first arrived?

b. What are some things visitors should or shouldn't do in your country?

c. What is your educational system like?

d. What do you consider a proper greeting for a friend? For a teacher? For your boss?

e. What could we say or do to increase your comfort in social or business settings?

Conduct a panel discussion. You may wish to develop a chart.

3.5 Designing a Cell Phone Manual for Low- and High-Context Cultures (Obj. 2)

Critical Thinking

Sometime in the early part of this century, many are predicting that China will emerge as the world's largest consumer of electronics products.[43] Well aware of this prediction, Siemens AG, a German cellular telephone manufacturer, is preparing to sell its popular German model to the Chinese. To develop the cell phone user manual, it conducted focus groups with Chinese and German consumers. The traditional German manual was translated into Chinese, and both German and Chinese focus groups were given nine tasks to perform using the same manual.

The focus groups produced contrasting results. When Chinese users first approach a manual, they want to see basic operations illustrated in colour on single pages with pictures. They reported having "no patience" to learn functions they might not use. They also noted that they learned to use the phone by asking friends, but if they had a problem they would never admit it to a friend. The Germans, on the other hand, wanted a manual that would present a clear but detailed overview of all the phone functions, not just basic operations. They thought that it would be useful in the long run to know all the different functions. The Germans read the words in the manual carefully, sometimes complaining when sentences were illogical or contradictory.

The Chinese preferred the "help" key to the printed manual. One said, "It gives you a very foolish feeling to use the phone at the same time you use the manual. It is ridiculous." The Chinese requested a videotape to show operations, and they also recommended that the size of the characters in the manual correlate with the importance of the information.

Based on your knowledge of high- and low-context cultures, how do the reactions of these focus groups reflect cultural expectations? If you were the researcher in this study, would you suggest to Siemens that a totally different user manual be developed for the Chinese market? What design recommendations would you make regarding the Chinese manual?

3.6 Analyzing a Problem International Letter (Obj. 5)

Study the following letter[44] to be sent by a North American firm to a potential supplier in another country. Identify specific weaknesses that may cause trouble for multicultural readers.

Dear Madeleine:

Because of the on-again/off-again haggling with one of our subcontractors, we have been putting off writing to you. We were royally turned off by their shoddy merchandise, the excuses they made up, and the way they put down some of our customers. Since we have our good name to keep up, we have decided to take the bull by the horns and see if you would be interested in bidding on the contract for spare parts.

By playing ball with us, your products are sure to score big. So please give it your best shot and fire off your price list ASAP. We'll need it by 3/8 if you are to be in the running.

Yours,

3.7 Talking Turkey: Avoiding Ambiguous Expressions (Obj. 5)

When a German firm received a message from a Canadian firm saying that it was "time to talk turkey," it was puzzled but decided to reply in Turkish, as requested. Assume you are a businessperson engaged in exporting and importing. As such, you are in constant communication with suppliers and customers around the world. In messages sent abroad, what kinds of ambiguous expressions should you avoid? In teams or individually, list three to five original examples of idioms, slang, acronyms, sports references, abbreviations, jargon, and two-word verbs.

3.8 Diversity Role-Playing: Hey, We're All Clones! (Obj. 6)

Reebok International, the athletic footwear and apparel company, swelled from a $12-million-a-year company to a $3-billion footwear powerhouse in less than a decade. "When we were growing very, very fast, all we did was bring another friend into work the next day," recalls Sharon Cohen, Reebok vice president. "Everybody hired nine of their friends. Well, it happened that nine white people hired nine of their friends, so guess what? They were white, all about the same age. And then we looked up and said, 'Wait a minute. We don't like the way it looks here.'"[45] Assume you are a manager for a successful, fast-growing company like Reebok. One day you look around and notice that everyone looks alike. Pair off with a classmate to role-play a discussion in which you strive to convince another manager that your organization would be better if it were more diverse. The other manager (your classmate), however, is satisfied with the status quo. Suggest advantages for diversifying the staff. The opposing manager argues for homogeneity.

3.9 Locating Diversity Training Consultants (Obj. 6)

Web

Management thought it was doing the right thing in diversifying its staff. But now signs of friction are appearing. Staff meetings are longer, and conflicts have arisen in solving problems. Some of the new people say they aren't taken seriously and that they are expected to blend in and become just like everybody else. A discrimination suit was filed in one department. CEO William Somers asks you, a human resources officer, to present suggestions for overcoming this staff problem. Make a list of several suggestions, based on what you have learned in this chapter. In addition, go to the Web and locate three individuals, teams, or firms who you think might be possibilities for developing a diversity training program for your company. Prepare a memo or an e-mail to Mr. Somers outlining your suggestions and listing your recommendations for possible diversity training consultants. Describe the areas of expertise of each potential consultant.

3.10 Searching International Newspapers for Business News (Objs. 1–6)

Web

Using the Guffey student Web Site **<buscomm.nelson.com>**, click on "Research Tools" and "U.S. and World Newspapers." You'll find English editions of international newspapers from such countries as Ethiopia, Japan, Thailand, China, the Philippines, Sri Lanka, Egypt, South Africa, Israel, Hong Kong, Turkey, South Korea, Zambia, Russia, Turkey, and many others. Assume that your company seeks to expand its markets overseas. Your boss asks you to check three newspapers (your choice) every week to keep track of business-related events. She's interested in a variety of subjects and is always intrigued by whatever you uncover. Select three to five articles to summarize in a memo to your boss, Susan Plutsky. Include a short description of each newspaper.

C.L.U.E. REVIEW 3

On a separate sheet edit the following sentences to correct faults in grammar, punctuation, spelling, and word use.

1. To avoid embarassing any employee the personell manager and myself has decided to talk personal to each individual.
2. 3 assistants were sent on a search and destroy mission in a conscience effort to remove at least fifteen thousand old documents from the files.
3. Electronic mail, now used by ¾ of Canadas largest companys transmits messages quick and cheap.
4. An article entitled whats new with managers appeared in maclean's which is read by millions of Canadians.
5. Your account is now sixty days overdue consequently we have only 1 alternative left.
6. The marketing managers itinirary listed the following three destinations moncton thunder bay and calgary.
7. Each of the beautifully-printed books available at pickwick book company have been reduced to thirty dollars.
8. We reccommend therefor that a committee study our mail procedures for a 3 week period, and submit a report of it's findings.
9. Their going to visit there relatives in lethbridge alberta over the victoria day holiday.
10. The hotel can acommodate three hundred convention guests but it has parking facilities for only one hundred cars.

UNIT 2

THE WRITING PROCESS

CHAPTER 4

Preparing to Write Business Messages

CHAPTER 5

Organizing and Writing Business Messages

CHAPTER 6

Revising Business Messages

CHAPTER • 4 •

PREPARING TO WRITE BUSINESS MESSAGES

LEARNING OBJECTIVES

1 Describe three basic elements that distinguish business writing and summarize the three phases of the 3-×-3 writing process.

2 Explain how the writing process may be altered and how it is affected by team projects and technology.

3 Clarify what is involved in analyzing a writing task and selecting a communication channel.

4 Describe anticipating and profiling the audience for a message.

5 Specify six writing techniques that help communicators adapt messages to the task and audience.

6 Explain why four areas of communication hold legal responsibilities for writers.

Approaching the Writing Process Systematically

1

Preparing and writing any business message—whether a letter, an e-mail memo, or a sales presentation—is easier when the writer or presenter has a systematic plan to follow.

The Basics of Business Writing

Business writing is purposeful, economical, and reader oriented.

Business writing differs from other writing you may have done. Secondary or post-secondary school compositions and term papers may have required you to describe your feelings, display your knowledge, and meet a minimum word count. Business writing, however, has different goals. In preparing business messages and oral presentations, you'll find that your writing needs to be:

- **Purposeful.** You will be writing to solve problems and convey information. You will have a definite purpose to fulfil in each message.
- **Economical.** You will try to present ideas clearly but concisely. Length is not rewarded.
- **Reader oriented.** You will concentrate on looking at a problem from the reader's perspective instead of seeing it from your own.

Business writers seek to *express* rather than to *impress*.

These distinctions actually ease the writer's task. In writing most business documents, you won't be searching your imagination for creative topic ideas. You won't be stretching your ideas to make them appear longer. Conciseness is what counts in business. Furthermore, you won't be trying to dazzle readers with your extensive knowledge, powerful vocabulary, or graceful phrasing. The goal in business writing is to *express* rather than to *impress*. You will be striving to get your ideas across naturally, simply, and clearly.

In many ways business writing is easier than academic writing, yet it still requires hard work, especially from beginners. But following a process, studying models, and practising the craft can make nearly anyone a successful business writer and speaker. This book provides all three components: process, products (models), and practice. First, you'll focus on the process of writing business messages.

The 3-×-3 Writing Process for Business Messages and Oral Presentations

The phases of the 3-×-3 writing process are prewriting, writing, and revising.

This book divides the writing process into three distinct phases: prewriting, writing, and revising. As shown in Figure 4.1, each phase is further divided into three major activities. The 3-×-3 process provides a systematic plan for developing all your business communications from simple memos and informational reports to corporate proposals and oral presentations.

The time spent on each phase varies with the deadline, purpose, and audience for the message. The first phase (prewriting) prepares you to write and involves analyzing, anticipating, and adapting.

Collecting data, organizing it, and composing a first draft make up the second phase of the writing process.

The second phase (writing) involves researching, organizing, and then composing the message. Equipped with a plan, you're ready to compose the first draft.

The third phase of the process (revising) involves revising, proofreading, and evaluating your letter. After writing the first draft, you'll revise the message for clarity, conciseness, tone, and readability. You'll proofread carefully to ensure correct spelling, grammar, punctuation, and format. Finally, you'll evaluate the message to see whether it accomplishes your goal.

FIGURE 4.1 **The 3-×-3 Writing Process**

In the writing process, revising requires the most time.

Although our diagram of the writing process shows the three phases equally, the time you spend on each varies. One expert gives these rough estimates for scheduling a project: 25 percent worrying and planning (Phase 1), 25 percent writing (Phase 2), 45 percent revising, and 5 percent proofreading (Phase 3). These are rough guides, yet you can see that good writers spend most of their time revising. Much depends, of course, on your project, its importance, and your familiarity with it. What's critical to remember, though, is that revising is a major component of the writing process.

This process may seem a bit complicated for the daily messages and oral presentations that many businesspeople prepare. Does this same process apply to memos and short letters? And how do collaborators and modern computer technologies affect the process?

Adapting and Altering the Process

2

Although good writers proceed through each phase of the writing process, some steps may be compressed for short, routine messages. Brief, everyday documents enlist the 3-×-3 process, but many of the steps are performed quickly, without prolonged deliberation. For example, prewriting may take the form of a few moments of reflection. The writing phase may consist of looking in the files quickly, jotting a few notes in the margin of the original document, and composing at your computer. Revising might consist of reading a printout, double-checking the spelling and grammar, and making a few changes. Longer, more involved documents—such as persuasive memos, sales letters, management reports, proposals, and résumés—require more attention to all parts of the process.

Steps in the writing process may be rearranged, shortened, or repeated.

One other point about the 3-×-3 writing process needs clarification. It may appear that you perform one step and progress to the next, always following the same order. Most business writing, however, is not that rigid. Although writers perform the tasks described, the steps may be rearranged, abbreviated, or repeated. Some writers revise every sentence and paragraph as they go. Many find that new ideas occur after they've begun to write, causing them to back up, alter the organization, and rethink their plan. You should expect to follow the 3-×-3 process closely as you begin developing your business communication skills. With experience, though, you'll become like other good writers and presenters who alter, compress, and rearrange the steps as needed.

Working With Teams. At one time or another, you can expect to collaborate on a project. Collaborative composition is especially necessary for (1) big tasks, (2) items with short deadlines, and (3) team projects that require the expertise or consensus of many people. Businesspeople sometimes collaborate on short documents, such as memos, letters, information briefs, procedures, and policies. But more often, teams work together on big documents and presentations.

Team-written documents and presentations are standard in most organizations because collaboration has many advantages. Most important, collaboration produces a better product. Many heads are better than one. In addition, team members and organizations benefit from team processes. Working together helps socialize members. They learn more about the organization's values and procedures. They are able to break down functional barriers, and they improve both formal and informal chains of communication. Additionally, they "buy into" a project when they are part of its development. Members of effective teams are often more eager to implement their recommendations.

Team-written documents and presentations produce better products.

In preparing big projects, teams may not actually function together for each phase of the writing process. Typically, team members gather at the beginning to brainstorm. They iron out answers to questions about purpose, audience, content, organization, and design of their document or presentation. They develop procedures for team functioning, as you learned in Chapter 2. Then, they often assign segments of the project to individual members. Thus, teams work together closely in Phase 1 (prewriting) of the writing process. However, members generally work separately in Phase 2 (writing), when they conduct research, organize their findings, and compose a first draft. During Phase 3 (revising) teams may work together to synthesize their drafts and offer suggestions for revision. They might assign one person the task of preparing the final document and another the job of proofreading. The revision and evaluation phase might be repeated several times before the final product is ready for presentation.

Working With Technology. The composition process—whether you are writing a business document, preparing an oral presentation, or creating a Web page—is further affected by today's amazing computer tools. Software exists to help you generate ideas, conduct research electronically, and organize facts into outlines. In fact, many phases of the writing process—such as keyboarding, revision, and collaboration—are simplified and supported by word-processing programs.

Computer technology helps you generate ideas, conduct research, and organize facts.

Analyzing the Task

3

Whether you're writing with a team, composing by yourself, or preparing an oral presentation, the product of your efforts can be improved by following the steps described in the 3-×-3 writing process. Not only are you more likely to get your message across, but you'll feel less anxious and your writing will progress more quickly. The remainder of this chapter concentrates on the prewriting phase of composition: analyzing, anticipating, and adapting.

In analyzing the composition task, you'll first need to identify the purpose of the message and select the best channel or form in which to deliver it.

Identifying Your Purpose. As you begin to compose a message, ask yourself two important questions: (1) Why am I sending this message? and (2) What do I hope to achieve? Your responses will determine how you organize and present your information.

Your message may have primary and secondary purposes. For academic work, your primary purpose may be merely to complete the assignment; secondary purposes might be to make yourself look good and to get a good grade. The primary purposes for sending

Most business communication has both primary purposes (to inform or persuade) and secondary purposes (to promote goodwill).

business messages are typically to inform and to persuade. A secondary purpose is to promote goodwill: you and your organization want to look good in the eyes of your audience.

Most business messages do nothing more than *inform*. They explain procedures, announce meetings, answer questions, and transmit findings. Some business messages, however, are meant to *persuade*. These messages sell products, convince managers, motivate employees, and win over customers. Informative messages are developed differently than persuasive messages.

Choosing the best channel depends on the importance of the message, the feedback required, the need for a permanent record, the cost, and the degree of formality needed.

Selecting the Best Channel. After identifying the purpose of your message, you need to select the most appropriate communication channel. As you learned in Chapter 1, some information is most efficiently and effectively delivered orally. Other messages should be written, and still others are best delivered electronically. Whether to set up a meeting, send a message by e-mail, or write a report depends on some of the following factors:

- Importance of the message
- Amount and speed of feedback required
- Necessity of a permanent record

FIGURE 4.2 **Choosing Communication Channels**

Channel	Best Use
Face-to-face conversation	When you want to be persuasive, deliver bad news, or share a personal message.
Telephone call	When you need to deliver or gather information quickly, when nonverbal cues are unimportant, and when you cannot meet in person.
Voice-mail message	When you wish to leave important or routine information that the receiver can respond to when convenient.
Fax	When your message must cross time zones or international boundaries, when a written record is significant, or when speed is important.
E-mail	When you need feedback but not immediately. Lack of security makes it problematic for personal, emotional, or private messages. Effective for communicating with a large, dispersed audience.
Face-to-face group meeting	When group decisions and consensus are important. Inefficient for merely distributing information.
Videoconference	When group consensus and interaction are important but members are geographically dispersed.
Memo	When you want a written record to clearly explain policies, discuss procedures, or collect information within an organization.
Letter	When you need a written record of correspondence with customers, the government, suppliers, or others outside an organization.
Report or proposal	When you are delivering considerable data internally or externally.

- Cost of the channel
- Degree of formality desired

The foregoing factors could help you decide which of the channels shown in Figure 4.2 is most appropriate for delivering a message.

Anticipating the Audience

4

Some messages miss the mark. A good writer anticipates the audience for a message: What is the reader like? How will that reader react to the message? Although you can't always know exactly who the reader is, you can imagine some characteristics of the reader. Writers of direct-mail sales letters have a general idea of the audience they wish to target. Picturing a typical reader is important in guiding what you write. By profiling your audience and shaping a message to respond to that profile, you are more likely to achieve your communication goals.

Profiling the Audience. Visualizing your audience is a pivotal step in the writing process. The questions in Figure 4.3 will help you profile your audience. How much time you devote to answering these questions depends greatly on your message and its context. No matter how short your message, though, spend some time thinking about the audience so that you can tailor your words to your readers or listeners. "The most often unasked question in business and professional communication," claims a writing expert, "is as simple as it is important: Have I thought enough about my audience?"[1]

Responding to the Profile. Anticipating your audience helps you make decisions about shaping the message. You'll discover what kind of language is appropriate, whether you're free to use specialized technical terms, whether you should explain everything, and so on. You'll decide whether your tone should be formal or informal, and you'll select the most desirable channel. Imagining whether the receiver is likely to be neutral, positive, or negative will help you determine how to organize your message.

By profiling your audience before you write, you can identify the appropriate tone, language, and channel.

Another result of profiling your audience will be knowing whether a secondary audience is possible. If so, you'll provide more background information and be more

FIGURE 4.3 **Asking the Right Questions to Profile Your Audience**

Primary Audience	Secondary Audience
Who is my primary reader or listener? What is my personal and professional relationship with that person? What position does the individual hold in the organization? How much does that person know about the subject? What do I know about that person's education, beliefs, culture, and attitudes? Should I expect a neutral, positive, or negative response to my message?	Who might see this message after the primary audience? How do these people differ from the primary audience?

specific in identifying items than would be necessary for the primary audience only. Analyzing the task and anticipating the audience assists you in adapting your message so that it will accomplish what you intend.

Adapting to the Task and Audience

5 After analyzing your purpose and anticipating your audience, you must convey your purpose to that audience. Adaptation is the process of creating a message that suits your audience.

One important aspect of adaptation is tone. Conveyed largely by the words in a message, tone reflects how a receiver feels upon reading or hearing a message. For example, think how you would react to these statements:

You must return the form by 5 p.m.

Would you please return the form by 5 p.m.

Ways to adapt to the audience include choosing the right words and tone, spotlighting reader benefits, cultivating a "you" attitude, and using sensitive, courteous language.

The wording of the first message establishes an aggressive or negative tone—few people like being told what to do. The second message is reworded in a friendlier, more positive manner. Poorly chosen words may sound demeaning, condescending, discourteous, pretentious, or demanding. Notice in the Tilley Endurables letter in Figure 4.4 that the writer achieves a courteous and warm tone. The letter responds to a customer's concern about the changing merchandise mix available in Tilley's catalogues. The customer also wanted to receive fewer catalogues. The writer explains the company's expanded merchandise line and reassures the customer that Tilley has not abandoned its emphasis on classic styles.

Skilled communicators create a positive tone in their messages by using a number of adaptive techniques, some of which are unconscious. These include spotlighting receiver benefits, cultivating a *you* attitude, and avoiding gender, racial, age, and disability bias. Additional adaptive techniques include being courteous, using familiar words, and choosing precise words.

Empathic communicators envision the receiver and focus on benefits to that person.

Spotlighting Receiver Benefits. Focusing on the audience is a fundamental guideline for business communicators. A communication consultant gives this solid advice to his business clients: "Always stress the benefit to the readers of whatever it is you're trying to get them to do. If you can show them how you're going to save them frustration or help them meet their goals, you have the makings of a powerful message."[2]

The most successful messages are receiver-focused.

Adapting your message to the receiver's needs means putting yourself in that person's shoes. It's called empathy. Empathic senders think about how a receiver will decode a message. They try to give something to the receiver, solve the receiver's problems, save the receiver money, or just understand the feelings and position of that person. Which of the following messages are more appealing to the receiver?

Sender-Focused	**Receiver-Focused**
To enable us to update our stockholder records, we ask that the enclosed card be returned.	So that you may promptly receive dividend cheques and information related to your shares, please return the enclosed card.
Our warranty becomes effective only when we receive an owner's registration.	Your warranty begins working for you as soon as you return your owner's registration.

FIGURE 4.4 **Customer Response Letter**

February 23, 2004

Mrs. Elaine Hough
2175 Edenwood Road
Brandon, MB R7A 6A9

Dear Mrs. Hough:

Your letter was a strong endorsement of our belief that we made the right choice when we devoted our company to comfort, ease of care, durability, and a smart appearance — and that it's still the right choice.

It's true we've made changes. In the past few years, with the markets soft and tastes changing, we reexamined our merchandise with a view to continuing to serve valued customers while introducing ourselves to new ones. We decided we want to give you more choices for more occasions.

Our commitment to the classics hasn't weakened, as I hope you'd agree, having seen recent catalogues. But we've defined "classic" more inclusively than in the past. We're using new fabrics, new colours, a more relaxed fit. There's more imagination in our product mix now, but the hats, pants, vests, jackets, and other basics for which you've relied on us are still here. You may not find each one in every catalogue, and you may notice the new products more than those you've seen before. The classics are still here, and the selection will be growing.

I've arranged to send you just the four catalogues a year you wanted. I hope you'll keep an eye out for them. I think that, more and more, you'll be able to come to us for the styles you want.

Sincerely,

Lise Andrews

Lise Andrews
Customer Service

Tilley Endurables Inc., 900 Don Mills Road, Don Mills, Ontario M3C 1V6 • Telephone (416) 441-6141 • Fax (416) 444-3860

Opens response to inquiry by agreeing with customer

Explains evolving merchandise line from company's and reader's view

Uses conversational language to convey warmth and sincerity

Emphasizes areas of agreement

Concludes by giving customer what she wants and promoting future business

Cultivating the "You" View. Notice how many of the previous receiver-focused messages included the word *you.* In concentrating on receiver benefits, skilled communicators naturally develop the "you" view. They emphasize second-person pronouns (*you, your*) instead of first-person pronouns (*I/we, us, our*). Whether your goal is to inform, persuade, or promote goodwill, the catchiest words you can use are *you* and *your.* Compare the following examples.

Effective communicators develop the "you" view in a sincere, not manipulative or critical, tone.

"I/We" View	**"You" View**
I have scheduled your vacation to begin May 1.	You may begin your vacation May 1.

We have shipped your order by UPS, and we are sure it will arrive in time for the sales promotion January 15.	Your order will be delivered by UPS in time for your sales promotion January 15.

To see whether you're really concentrating on the reader, try using the "empathy index." In one of your messages, count all the second-person references. Then, count all the first-person references. Your empathy index is low if the *I*'s and *we*'s outnumber the *you*'s and *your*'s.

But the use of *you* is more than merely a numbers game. Second-person pronouns can be overused and misused. Readers appreciate genuine interest; on the other hand, they resent obvious attempts at manipulation. Some sales messages, for example, are guilty of overkill when they include *you* dozens of times in a direct mail promotion. Furthermore, the word can sometimes create the wrong impression. Consider this statement: *You cannot return merchandise until you receive written approval. You* appears twice, but the reader feels singled out for criticism. In the following version the message is less personal and more positive: *Customers may return merchandise with written approval.* In short, avoid using *you* for general statements that suggest blame and could cause ill will.

In recognizing the value of the *you* attitude, however, writers do not have to sterilize their writing and totally avoid any first-person pronouns or words that show their feelings. Skilled communicators are able to convey sincerity, warmth, and enthusiasm by the words they choose. Don't be afraid to use phrases such as *I'm happy* or *We're delighted,* if you truly are.

When speaking face to face, communicators show sincerity and warmth with nonverbal cues such as a smile and pleasant voice tone. In letters, memos, and e-mail messages, however, only expressive words and phrases can show these feelings. These phrases suggest hidden messages that say to readers and customers *You are important, I hear you, and I'm honestly trying to please you.*

Using Bias-Free Language. In adapting a message to its audience, be sure your language is sensitive and bias-free. Few writers set out to be offensive. Sometimes, though, we all say things that we never thought might be hurtful. The real problem is that we don't think about the words that stereotype groups of people, such as *the boys in the mail room* or *the girls in the front office.* Be cautious about expressions that might be biased in terms of gender, race, ethnicity, age, and disability.[3]

Avoiding Gender Bias. You can defuse gender time bombs by replacing words that exclude or stereotype people (sometimes called *sexist language*) with neutral, inclusive expressions. The following examples show how sexist terms and phrases can be replaced with neutral ones.

Gender Biased	**Improved**
female doctor, woman lawyer, cleaning woman	doctor, lawyer, cleaner
waiter/waitress, authoress, stewardess	server, author, cabin attendant
mankind, man-hour, man-made	humanity, working hours, artificial
office girls	office workers
the doctor ... he	doctors ... they
the teacher ... she	teachers ... they
executives and their wives	executives and their spouses or partners

foreman, flag-man, workman	lead worker, flagger, worker
businessman, salesman	businessperson, sales representative
Each worker had his picture taken.	Each worker had a picture taken. Each worker had his or her picture taken. All workers had their pictures taken.

Generally, you can avoid gender-biased language by leaving out the words *man* or *woman*, by using plural nouns and pronouns, or by changing to a gender-free word (*person* or *representative*).

Avoiding Racial or Ethnic Bias. You need to indicate racial or ethnic identification only if the context demands it.

Racially or Ethnically Biased	**Improved**
An Indian accountant was hired.	An accountant was hired.
James Lee, a Native Canadian, applied.	James Lee applied.

Avoiding Age Bias. Again, specify age only if it is relevant, and avoid expressions that are demeaning or subjective.

Age Biased	**Improved**
The law applied to old people.	The law applied to people over 65.
Sally Kay, 55, was transferred.	Sally Kay was transferred.
a spry old gentleman	a man
a little old lady	a woman

Avoiding Disability Bias. Unless relevant, do not refer to an individual's disability. When necessary, use terms that do not stigmatize individuals with disabilities.

Sensitive communicators avoid gender, racial or ethnic, and disability biases.

Disability Biased	**Improved**
afflicted with, suffering from, crippled by	has
defect, disease	condition
confined to a wheelchair	uses a wheelchair

The preceding examples have given you a quick look at a few problem expressions. The real key to bias-free communication, though, lies in your awareness and commitment. Always be on the lookout to be sure that your messages do not exclude, stereotype, or offend people.

Expressing Yourself Positively. Certain negative words create ill will because they appear to blame or accuse readers. For example, opening a letter to a customer with *You claim that* ... suggests that you don't believe the customer. Other loaded words that can get you in trouble are *complaint, criticism, defective, failed, mistake,* and *neglected.* Often the writer is unconscious of the effect of these words. To avoid angry reactions, restrict negative words and try to find positive ways to express ideas. You provide more options to the reader when you tell what can be done instead of what can't be done.

Positive language creates goodwill and gives more options to readers.

Negative	**Positive**
You failed to include your credit card number, so we can't mail your order.	We'll mail your order as soon as we receive your credit card number.

Negative expressions can often be rephrased to sound positive.

Your letter of May 2 claims that you returned a defective headset.	Your May 2 letter describes a headset you returned.
You cannot park in Lot H until April 1.	You may park in Lot H starting April 1.

Being Courteous. Maintaining a courteous tone involves not just guarding against rudeness but also avoiding words that sound demanding or preachy. Expressions like *you should, you must,* and *you have to* cause people to instinctively react with "Oh, yeah?" One remedy is to turn these demands into rhetorical questions that begin with *Will you please....* Giving reasons for a request also softens the tone.

Less Courteous	More Courteous
You must complete this report before Friday.	Will you please complete the report by Friday.
You should organize a car pool in this department.	Organizing a car pool will reduce your transportation costs and help preserve the environment.

Even when you are justifiably angry, courteous language is the best way to achieve your objectives.

Even when you feel justified in displaying anger, remember that losing your temper or being sarcastic will seldom accomplish your goals as a business communicator to inform, to persuade, and to create goodwill. When you are irritated, frustrated, or infuriated, keep cool and try to defuse the situation. Concentrate on the real problem. What must be done to solve it?

You May Be Thinking This	Better to Say This
This is the second time I've written. Can't you get anything right?	Please credit my account for $843. My latest statement shows that the error noted in my letter of June 2 has not been corrected.
Am I the only one who can read the operating manual?	Let's review the operating manual together so that you can get your documents to print correctly next time.

The simpler the language, the better.

Simplifying Your Language. In adapting your message to your audience, whenever possible use short, familiar words that you think they will recognize. Don't, however, avoid a more complex word that conveys your idea efficiently and is appropriate for the audience. Your goal is to avoid pompous and pretentious language. Instead, use "GO" words. If you mean *begin,* don't say *commence* or *initiate.* If you mean *give,* don't write *render.*[4] By substituting everyday, familiar words for unfamiliar ones, as shown here, you help your audience comprehend your ideas quickly.

Unfamiliar	Familiar
commensurate	equal
conceptualization	idea
interrogate	question
materialize	appear
remunerate	pay
terminate	end

At the same time, be selective in your use of jargon. *Jargon* describes technical or specialized terms within a field. These terms enable insiders to communicate complex ideas briefly, but to outsiders they mean nothing. Human resources professionals, for example, know precisely what's meant by *cafeteria plan* (a benefits option program), but most of us would be thinking about lunch. Geologists refer to *plate tectonics*, and physicians discuss *metastatic carcinomas*. But these terms mean little to most of us. Use specialized language only when the audience will understand it. And don't forget to consider secondary audiences: Will those potential readers understand any technical terms used?

Using familiar but precise words helps receivers understand.

Using Precise, Vigorous Words. Strong verbs and concrete nouns give readers more information and keep them interested. Don't overlook the thesaurus (or the thesaurus program on your computer) for expanding your word choices and vocabulary. Whenever possible, use specific words as shown here.

Imprecise, Dull	More Precise
a gain in profits a jump in profits	a 23-percent hike in profits
it takes memory	it requires 32 megabytes of RAM
to think about	to identify, diagnose, analyze to probe, examine, inspect

By reviewing the tips in the following checklist, you can master the steps of writing preparation. As you review these tips, remember the three basics of prewriting: analyzing, anticipating, and adapting.

Checklist for Adapting a Message to Its Audience

- ✓ **Identify the message purpose.** Ask yourself why you are communicating and what you hope to achieve. Look for primary and secondary purposes.
- ✓ **Select the most appropriate form.** Determine whether you need a permanent record or whether the message is too sensitive to put in writing.
- ✓ **Profile the audience.** Identify your relationship with the reader and your knowledge about that individual or group. Assess how much the receiver knows about the subject.
- ✓ **Focus on reader benefits.** Phrase your statements from the readers' viewpoint, not your own. Concentrate on the "you" view (*Your order will arrive, You can enjoy, Your ideas count*).
- ✓ **Avoid gender and racial bias.** Use bias-free words (*businessperson* instead of *businessman*; *working hours* instead of *man-hours*). Omit ethnic identification unless the context demands it.
- ✓ **Avoid age and disability bias.** Include age only if relevant. Avoid potentially demeaning expressions (*spry old gentleman*), and use terms that do not stigmatize disabled people (*he is disabled* instead of *he is a cripple* or *he has a handicap*).
- ✓ **Express ideas positively rather than negatively.** Instead of *Your order can't be shipped before June 1*, say *Your order can be shipped June 1*.

 **Use short, familiar words.** Use technical terms and big words only if they are appropriate for the audience (*end* not *terminate, required* not *mandatory*).

 **Search for precise, vigorous words.** Use a thesaurus if necessary to find strong verbs and concrete nouns (*announces* instead of *says, brokerage* instead of *business*).

Adapting to Legal Responsibilities

One of your primary responsibilities in writing for an organization or for yourself is to avoid language that may land you in court. In our current business environment, lawsuits abound, many of which centre on the use and abuse of language. You can protect yourself and avoid litigation by knowing what's legal and by adapting your language accordingly. Be especially careful when communicating in the following four areas: investments, safety, marketing, and human resources. Because these information areas generate the most lawsuits, we will examine them more closely.[5]

Investment Information

Careful communicators should familiarize themselves with information in four information areas: investments, safety, marketing, and human resources.

Writers describing the sale of stocks or financial services must follow specific laws written to protect investors. Any messages—including letters, newsletters, and pamphlets—must be free from misleading information, exaggerations, or half-truths. Experienced financial writers know that careless language and even poor timing may provoke litigation.

Safety Information

Warnings on dangerous products must be written especially clearly.

Writers describing potentially dangerous products worry not only about protecting people from physical harm but also about being sued. Although there are far fewer product liability cases filed in Canada than in the U.S.,[6] litigation arising from these cases is an active area of tort law (tort law involves compensating those who have been injured by the wrongdoing of others[7]). Under the law of product liability, a manufacturer is responsible to those injured by a product whose defect is caused by either the manufacturing process or the product's design.[8] Manufacturers are also obligated to warn consumers of any risks in their products. These warnings must do more than suggest danger; they must also clearly tell people how to use the product safely. In writing warnings, concentrate on major points. Omit anything that is not critical. In the work area describe a potential problem and tell how to solve it. For example, *Lead dust is harmful and gets on your clothes. Change your clothes before leaving work.*

Clearly written safety messages use easy-to-understand words, such as *doctor* instead of *physician*, *clean* instead of *sanitary*, and *burn* instead of *incinerate.* Technical terms are defined. For example *Asbestos is a carcinogen* (*something that causes cancer*).[9] Effective safety messages also include highlighting techniques, such as using headings and bullets. In coming chapters you'll learn more about these techniques for improving readability.

Marketing Information

Sales and marketing messages are illegal if they falsely advertise prices, performance capability, quality, or other product characteristics. Marketing messages must not deceive the buyer in any way. According to Canada's Competition Bureau, "misleading advertising occurs when representation is made to the public that is materially misleading." If the consumer purchases the product or service based on the advertising, it is material. To determine whether an advertisement is misleading, the courts consider the "general impression" it conveys as well as the literal meaning.[10] Sellers of services must also be cautious about the language they use to describe what they will do. Letters, reports, and proposals that describe services to be performed are interpreted as contracts in court. Therefore, language must not promise more than intended. Here are some dangerous words (and recommended alternatives) that have created misunderstandings leading to lawsuits.[11]

Sales and marketing messages must not make claims that can't be verified.

Dangerous Word	Court Interpretation	Recommended Alternative
inspect	to examine critically, to investigate and test officially, to scrutinize	to review, to study, to tour the facility
determine	to come to a decision, to decide, to resolve	to evaluate, to assess, to analyze

Human Resources Information

The vast number of lawsuits relating to employment makes this a treacherous area for business communicators. In evaluating employees in the workplace, avoid making unsubstantiated negative comments. It's also unwise to assess traits (*she is unreliable*) because they require subjective judgment. Concentrate instead on specific incidents (*in the last month she missed four workdays and was late three times*).

Defamation lawsuits have become so common that some companies no longer provide letters of recommendation for former employees. To be safe, give recommendations only when the former employee authorizes the recommendation and when you can say something positive. Stick to job-related information.

The safest employment recommendations contain positive, job-related information.

Statements in employee handbooks also require careful wording, because a court might rule that such statements are "implied contracts." Companies are warned to avoid promissory phrases in writing job advertisements, application forms, and offer letters. Phrases that suggest permanent employment and guaranteed job security can be interpreted as contracts.[12]

In adapting messages to meet today's litigious business environment, be sensitive to the rights of others and to your own rights. The key elements in this adaptation process are awareness of laws, sensitivity to interpretations, and careful use of language.

Summary of Learning Objectives

1 **Describe three basic elements that distinguish business writing and summarize the three phases of the 3-×-3 writing process.** Business writing differs from academic writing in that it strives to solve business problems, it is economical, and it is reader oriented. Phase 1 of the writing process (prewriting) involves analyzing the message, anticipating the audience, and considering ways to adapt the message to the audience. Phase 2 (writing) involves researching the topic, organizing the material, and composing the message. Phase 3 (revising) includes proofreading and evaluating the message.

2 **Explain how the writing process may be altered and how it is affected by team projects and technology.** The writing process may be compressed for short messages; steps in the process may be rearranged. Team writing, which is necessary for large projects or when wide expertise is required, alters the writing process. Teams often work together in brainstorming and working out their procedures and assignments. Then individual members write their portions of the report or presentation during Phase 2. During Phase 3 (revising), teams may work together to combine their drafts. Technology assists writers with word processing, revision, and collaboration tools.

3 **Clarify what is involved in analyzing a writing task and selecting a communication channel.** Communicators must decide why they are delivering a message and what they hope to achieve. Although many messages only inform, some must also persuade. After identifying the purpose of a message, communicators must choose the most appropriate channel. That choice depends on the importance of the message, the amount and speed of feedback required, the need for a permanent record, the cost of the channel, and the degree of formality desired.

4 **Describe anticipating and profiling the audience for a message.** A good communicator tries to envision the audience for a message. What does the receiver know about the topic? How well does the receiver know the sender? What is known about the receiver's education, beliefs, culture, and attitudes? Will the response to the message be positive, neutral, or negative? Is the secondary audience different from the primary audience?

5 **Specify six writing techniques that help communicators adapt messages to the task and audience.** Skilled communicators strive to (a) spotlight reader benefits, (b) look at a message from the receiver's perspective (the "you" view), (c) use sensitive language that avoids gender, racial, ethnic, and disability biases, (d) state ideas positively, (e) show courtesy, and (f) use short, familiar, and precise words.

6 **Explain why four areas of communication hold legal responsibilities for writers.** Actions and language in four information areas generate the most lawsuits: investments, safety, marketing, and human resources. In writing about investments, communicators must avoid misleading information, exaggerations, and half-truths. Safety information, including warnings, must tell people clearly how to use a product safely and motivate them to do so. In addition to being honest, marketing information must not promise more than intended. Finally, communicators in the area of human resources must use careful wording (particularly in employment recommendations and employee handbooks) to avoid potential lawsuits.

CHAPTER REVIEW

1. Name three ways in which business writing differs from other writing. (Obj. 1)
2. Describe the components in each stage of the 3-×-3 writing process. (Obj. 1)
3. List five factors to consider when selecting a communication channel. (Obj. 3)
4. Why should you "profile" your audience before composing a message? (Obj. 4)
5. What is *empathy*, and how does it apply to business writing? (Obj. 5)
6. Discuss the effects of first- and second-person pronouns. (Obj. 5)
7. What is gender-biased language? Give examples. (Obj. 5)
8. What is *jargon*, and when is it appropriate for business writing? (Obj. 5)
9. What's wrong with using words such as *commence*, *mandate*, and *interrogate*? (Obj. 5)
10. What four information areas generate the most lawsuits? (Obj. 6)
11. How can business communicators protect themselves against litigation? (Obj. 6)

CRITICAL THINKING

1. Business communicators are encouraged to profile or "visualize" the audience for their message. How is this possible if you don't really know the people who will receive a sales letter or who will hear your business presentation? (Obj. 4)
2. How can the 3-×-3 writing process help the writer of a business report as well as the writer of an oral presentation? (Obj. 1)
3. If adapting your tone to the receiving audience and developing reader benefits are so important, why do we see so much writing that does not reflect these suggestions? (Objs. 3 to 5)
4. Discuss the following statement: "The English language is a landmine—it is filled with terms that are easily misinterpreted as derogatory and others that are blatantly insulting.... Being fair and objective is not enough; employers must also appear to be so."[13] (Obj. 5)

ACTIVITIES

4.1 Document for Analysis (Obj. 5)

Discuss the following memo, which is based on an actual document sent to employees. How could you apply what you learned in this chapter to improving this memo?

TO: All Employees Using HP 5000 Computers

It has recently come to my attention that a computer security problem exists within our organization. I understand that the problem is twofold in nature:

a. You have been sharing computer passwords.
b. You are using automatic log-on procedures.

Henceforth, you are prohibited from sharing passwords for security reasons that should be axiomatic. We also must forbid you to use automatic log-on files because they empower anyone to have access to our entire computer system and all company data.

Enclosed please find a form that you must sign and return to the aforementioned individual, indicating your acknowledgment of and acquiescence to the procedures described here. Any computer user whose signed form is not returned will have his personal password invalidated.

4.2 Selecting Communication Channels (Obj. 3)

Using Figure 4.2, suggest the best communication channels for the following messages. Assume that all channels shown are available. Be prepared to explain your choices.

a. As department manager, you wish to inform four department members of a training session scheduled for three weeks from now.
b. As assistant to the vice president, you are to investigate the possibility of developing internship programs with several nearby colleges and universities.
c. You wish to send price quotes for a number of your products in response to a request from a potential customer in Taiwan.
d. You must respond to a notice from the Canada Customs and Revenue Agency insisting that you did not pay the correct amount for last quarter's employer's taxes.
e. As a manager, you must inform an employee that continued tardiness is jeopardizing her job.

4.3 Analyzing Audiences (Obj. 4)

Using the questions in Figure 4.3, write a brief analysis of the audience for each of the following communication tasks.

- **a.** Your letter of application for a job advertised in your local newspaper. Your qualifications match the job description.
- **b.** An e-mail memo to your boss persuading her to allow you to attend a computer class that will require you to leave work early two days a week for ten weeks.
- **c.** An unsolicited sales letter promoting life insurance to a targeted group of executives.
- **d.** A letter from the municipal water department explaining that the tap water may taste and smell bad; however, it poses no threats to health.
- **e.** A letter from a credit card organization refusing credit to an applicant.

4.4 Reader Benefits and the "You" View (Obj. 5)

Revise the following sentences to emphasize the reader's perspective and the "you" view.

- **a.** To prevent us from possibly losing large sums of money, our bank now requires verification of any large cheque presented for immediate payment.
- **b.** We take pride in announcing a new schedule of low-cost flights to Halifax.
- **c.** So that we may bring our customer records up to date and eliminate the expense of duplicate mailings, we are asking you to complete the enclosed card.
- **d.** For just $300 per person, we have arranged a three-day trip to Las Vegas that includes deluxe accommodations, the "City Lights" show, and selected meals.
- **e.** I give my permission for you to attend the two-day workshop.

4.5 Language Bias (Obj. 5)

Revise the following sentences to eliminate gender, racial, age, and disability stereotypes.

- **a.** Any applicant for the position of fireman must submit a medical report signed by his physician.
- **b.** We hired Todd Shimoyama, a Japanese Canadian, for the position of communications coordinator.
- **c.** Because she is confined to a wheelchair, we look for restaurants without stairs.
- **d.** Every employee is entitled to see his personnel file.
- **e.** Some restaurants have a special menu for old people.

4.6 Positive Expression (Obj. 5)

Revise the following statements to make them more positive.

- **a.** If you fail to pass the examination, you will not qualify.
- **b.** In the message you left at our Web site, you claim that you returned a defective headset.
- **c.** Although you apparently failed to read the operator's manual, we are sending you a replacement blade for your food processor. Next time read page 18 carefully so that you will know how to attach this blade.
- **d.** We can't process your application because you neglected to insert your social insurance number.
- **e.** Construction cannot begin until the building plans are approved.

4.7 Courteous Expression (Obj. 5)

Revise the following messages to show greater courtesy.

- **a.** You must sign and return this form immediately.
- **b.** This is the last time I'm writing to try to get you to record my January 6 payment of $500 to my account. Anyone who can read can see from the attached documents that I've tried to explain this to you before.
- **c.** As manager of your department, you will have to get your employees to use the correct forms.
- **d.** To the Staff: Can't anyone around here read instructions? Page 12 of the operating manual for our copy machine very clearly describes how to remove jammed paper. But I'm the only one who ever does it, and I've had it! No more copies will be made until you learn how to remove jammed paper.
- **e.** If you had listened to our agent more carefully, you would know that your policy does not cover accidents outside Canada.

4.8 Familiar Words (Obj. 5)

Revise the following sentences to avoid unfamiliar words.

- **a.** Pursuant to your invitation, we will interrogate our manager.
- **b.** To expedite ratification of this agreement, we urge you to vote in the affirmative.
- **c.** In a dialogue with the manager, I learned that you plan to terminate our agreement.
- **d.** Did the steering problem materialize subsequent to our recall effort?

e. Once we ascertain how much it costs, we can initiate the project.

4.9 Precise Words (Obj. 5)

From the choices in parentheses, select the most precise, vigorous words.

a. If you find yourself (having, engaged in, juggling) many tasks, find ways to remind yourself of them.

b. He is (connected to, associated with, employed by) the Dana Corporation.

c. We plan to (acknowledge, publicize, applaud) the work of exemplary employees.

d. The splendid report has (a lot of, many, a warehouse of) facts.

e. All the managers thought the new software was (good, nice, helpful).

For the following sentences, provide more precise alternatives for the italicized words.

f. If necessary, we will (a) *drop* overtime hours in order to (b) *fix* the budget.

g. The CEO (a) *said* that only (b) *the right kind of* applicants should apply.

h. After (a) *reading* the report, I decided it was (b) *bad*.

i. Jenny said the movie was (a) *different*, but her remarks weren't very (b) *clear* to us.

j. I'm (a) *going* to Grande Prairie tomorrow, and I plan to (b) *find out* the real problem.

4.10 Legal Language (Obj. 6)

To avoid possible litigation, revise the italicized words in the following sentences taken from proposals.

a. We will *inspect* the building plans before construction begins.

b. Our goal is to *assure* completion of the project on schedule.

c. We will *determine* the amount of stress for each supporting column.

C.L.U.E. REVIEW 4

On a separate sheet edit the following sentences to correct faults in grammar, punctuation, spelling, and word use.

1. If I was you I would schedule the conference for one of these cities Ottawa Kingston or Montreal.
2. The committees next meeting is scheduled for May fifth at three p.m., and should last about two hours.
3. Were not asking you to altar the figures, we are asking you to check there accuracy.
4. Will you please fax me a list of our independant contractors names and addresses?
5. The vacation calender fills up quick for the Summer months, therefore you should make your plans early.
6. After the inspector issues the waver we will be able to procede with the architects plan.
7. If we can't give out neccessary information what is the point in us answering the telephone.
8. Every new employee will receive their orientation packet, and be told about their parking priviledges.
9. About eighty-five percent of all new entrants into the workforce in the 1990s is expected to be: women, minorities and immigrants.
10. Our Vice President in the Human Resources Development Department asked the Manager and I to come to her office at three-thirty p.m.

CHAPTER • 5 •

ORGANIZING AND WRITING BUSINESS MESSAGES

LEARNING OBJECTIVES

1 Contrast formal and informal methods for researching data and generating ideas.

2 Specify how to organize data into lists and alphanumeric or decimal outlines.

3 Compare direct and indirect patterns for organizing ideas.

4 Discuss composing the first draft of a message, focusing on techniques for creating effective sentences.

5 Define a paragraph and describe three classic paragraph plans and techniques for composing meaningful paragraphs.

Researching Data and Generating Ideas

1

Business communicators face daily challenges that require data collection, idea generation, and concept organization. These activities are part of the second phase of the writing process, which includes researching, organizing, and composing.

No smart businessperson would begin writing a message before collecting all the needed information. We call this collection process *research*, a rather formal-sounding term. For simple documents, though, the procedure can be quite informal. Research is necessary before beginning to write because the information you collect helps shape the message. Discovering significant data after a message is half completed often means starting over and reorganizing. To avoid frustration and inaccurate messages, collect information that answers a primary question:

Before writing, conduct formal or informal research to collect or generate necessary data.

- *What does the receiver need to know about this topic?*

When the message involves action, search for answers to secondary questions:

- *What is the receiver to do?*
- *How is the receiver to do it?*
- *When must the receiver do it?*
- *What will happen if the receiver doesn't do it?*

Whenever your communication problem requires more information than you have in your head or at your fingertips, you must conduct research. This research may be formal or informal.

Formal Research Methods

Long reports and complex business problems generally require some use of formal research methods. To conduct formal research, you could:

Formal research may involve searching libraries and electronic databases or investigating primary sources (interviews, surveys, and experimentation).

- **Search manually.** You'll find helpful background and supplementary information through manual searching of resources in public and institutional libraries. These traditional sources include periodical indexes for lists of newspaper, magazine, and journal articles, along with the card catalogue for books. Other manual sources are book indexes, encyclopedias, reference books, handbooks, dictionaries, directories, and almanacs.
- **Access electronically.** Like other facets of life, the research process has been changed considerably by the computer. Much of the printed material just described is now available from the Internet, databases, or compact discs that can be accessed by computer. Institutional and public libraries subscribe to retrieval services that permit you to access thousands of bibliographic or full-text databases.
- **Investigate primary sources.** To develop firsthand, primary information for a project, go directly to the source. For example, you could conduct interviews or surveys, put together questionnaires, or organize focus groups. Formal research includes scientific sampling methods that enable investigators to make accurate judgments and valid predictions.

Good sources of primary information are interviews, surveys, questionnaires, and focus groups.

- **Experiment scientifically.** Another source of primary data is experimentation. Instead of merely asking for the target audience's opinion, scientific researchers present choices with controlled variables.

Informal Research and Idea Generation

Most routine tasks—such as composing e-mail messages, memos, letters, informational reports, and oral presentations—require data that you can collect informally. For some projects, though, you rely more on your own ideas instead of—or in addition to—researching existing facts. Here are some techniques for collecting informal data and for generating ideas:

- **Look in the files.** Before asking others for help, see what you can find yourself. For many routine messages you can often find previous documents to help you with content and format.
- **Talk with your boss.** Get information from the individual making the assignment. What does that person know about the topic? What slant should be taken? What other sources would he or she suggest?
- **Interview the target audience.** Consider talking with individuals at whom the message is aimed. They can provide clarifying information that tells you what they want to know and how you should shape your remarks.
- **Conduct an informal survey.** Gather helpful information via questionnaires or telephone surveys. In preparing a memo report predicting the success of a proposed fitness centre, for example, circulate a questionnaire asking for employee reactions.
- **Brainstorm for ideas.** Alone or with others, discuss ideas for the writing task at hand, and record at least a dozen ideas without judging them. Small groups are especially fruitful in brainstorming because people spin ideas off one another.
- **Develop a cluster diagram.** Prepare a cluster diagram (discussed in the next section) to help you generate and organize ideas. Clustering allows your mind to open up and free associate.

Collecting Information and Generating Ideas on the Job

Let's follow Susanne Tully to see how she collected data and generated ideas for two projects at Liz Claiborne, the women's clothing manufacturer. One of Susanne's tasks is simple, and one is complex.

Writing an Informational E-Mail Memo. Susanne's first task is to write an informational memo that describes a photo contest sponsored by Liz Claiborne. For this memo Susanne began by brainstorming with her staff, other employees, and her boss to decide on a photo contest theme. She consulted the files to see who had won prizes in last year's contest and double-checked with management to ensure that the prize money remained the same. Then she made the following quick scratch list outlining the points she wanted to cover in her memo.

Photo Contest E-Mail Memo

1. Announce theme; give examples
2. Encourage all employees to participate
3. Review prizes; name last year's winner
4. Limit: one entry each
5. Details in November; call Rosemary for more info

Many business messages require only simple data-collection and idea-generation techniques.

Preparing a Recruitment Brochure. Susanne's second project, though, demanded both formal and informal research, along with considerable creativity. She needed to produce a recruitment brochure that explained career opportunities for postsecondary graduates at Liz Claiborne. She had definite objectives for the brochure: it should be colourful, exciting, concise, lightweight and easily updated. Moreover, she wanted the brochure to promote Liz Claiborne, describing its progressive benefits, community involvement, career potential, and corporate values program (called "Priorities").

Some of her thoughts about this big project are shown in the cluster diagram in Figure 5.1. Cluster diagramming sparks our creativity; it encourages ideas to spill forth because the process is unrestricted. From the jumble of ideas in the initial cluster diagram, main categories—usually three to five—are extracted. At this point some people are ready to make an outline; others need further visualization, such as a set of subclusters, shown in Figure 5.2. Notice that four major categories (Purpose, Content, Development, and Form) were extracted from the initial diagram. These categories then became the hub of related ideas. This set of subclusters forms the basis for an outline, to be discussed shortly.

To collect data for this project, Susanne employed both formal and informal research methods. She studied recruiting brochures from other companies. She talked with students to ask what information they sought in a brochure. She conducted more formal research among the numerous division presidents and executives within her company to learn what really went on in all the departments, such as Information Systems, Operations Management, Production, and Design. She also had to learn the specific educational and personality requirements for careers in those areas. Working with an outside consultant, she prepared a questionnaire, which was used in personal interviews with company executives. The interviews included some open-ended questions, such as "How did you start with the company?" It also contained more specific questions about the number of employees in their departments, intended career paths, degree requirements, personality traits desired, and so forth. Organizing the mass of data collected was the next task.

More complex projects may require both formal and informal research.

Organizing Data

2

Writers of well-organized messages group similar ideas together so that readers can see relationships and follow arguments.

The process of organization may begin before you collect data or occur simultaneously with data collection. For complex projects, organization may be ongoing. Regardless of when organization occurs, its primary goals are grouping and patterning. Well-organized messages group similar items together; ideas follow a sequence that helps the reader understand relationships and accept the writer's views. Unorganized messages proceed free-form, jumping from one thought to another. Such messages fail to emphasize important points. Puzzled readers can't see how the pieces fit together, and they become frustrated and irritated. Many communication experts regard poor organization as the greatest failing of business writers. Two simple techniques can help you organize data: the scratch list and the outline.

Listing and Outlining

In developing simple messages, some writers make a quick scratch list of the topics they wish to cover. Writers often jot this scratch list in the margin of the letter or memo to which they are responding—and the majority of business messages are written in response to other documents. These writers then compose a message at their computers directly from the scratch list.

FIGURE 5.1 **Using Cluster Diagram to Generate Ideas for Liz Claiborne College Recruiting Brochure**

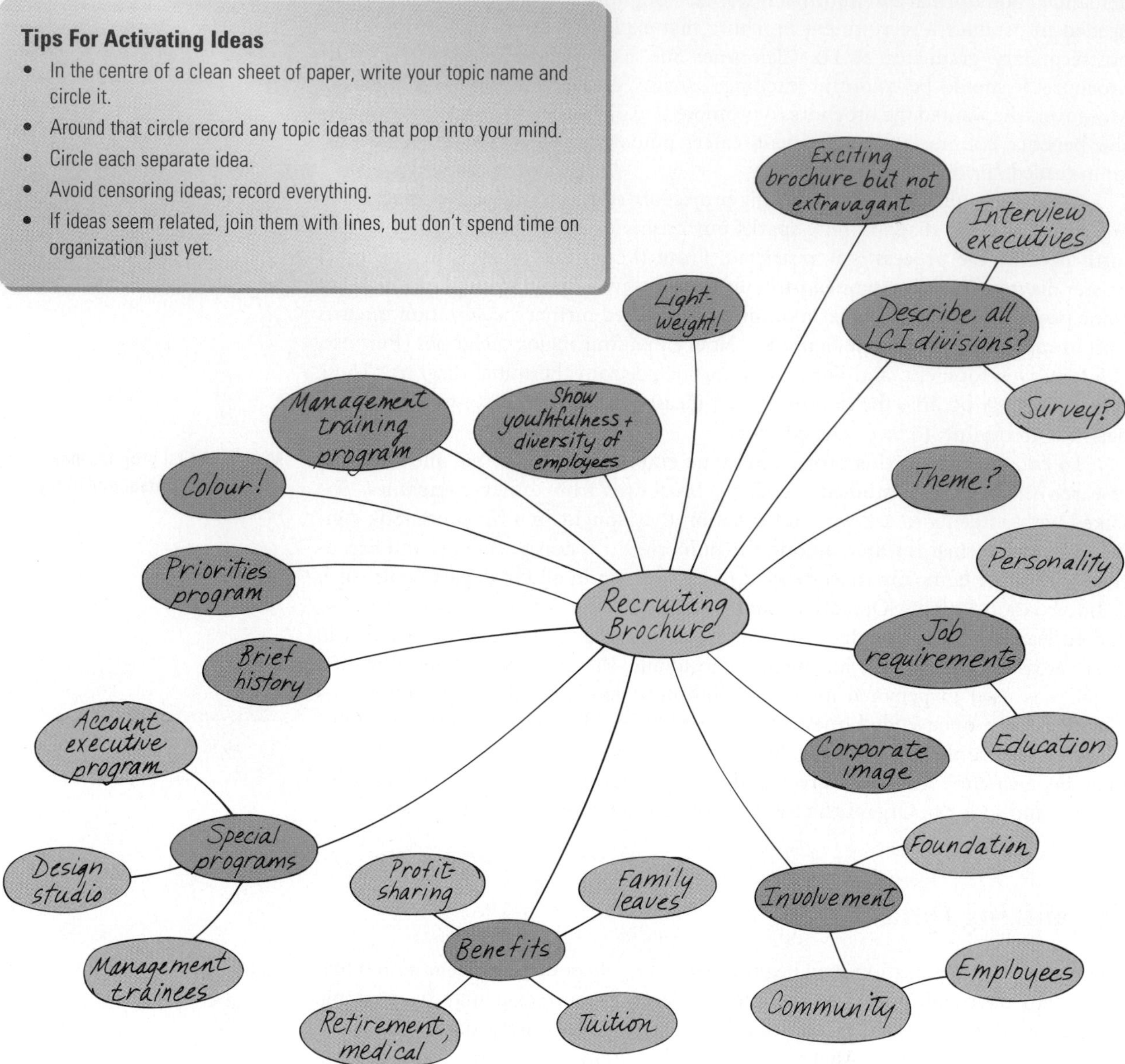

Alphanumeric outlines show major and minor ideas; decimal outlines show how ideas relate to one another.

Most writers, though, need to organize their ideas—especially if the project is complex—into a hierarchy, such as an outline. The beauty of preparing an outline is that it gives you a chance to organize your thinking before you get bogged down in word choice and sentence structure.[1] Figure 5.3 shows two outline formats: alphanumeric and decimal. The familiar alphanumeric format uses Roman numerals, letters, and numbers to show major and minor ideas. The decimal format has the advantage of showing how every item at every level relates to the whole. Both outlining formats force you to focus on the topic, identify major ideas, and support those ideas with details, illustrations, or evidence. Many computer outlining programs now on the market make the mechanics of the process much easier.

FIGURE 5.2 **Organizing Ideas From Cluster Diagram Into Subclusters**

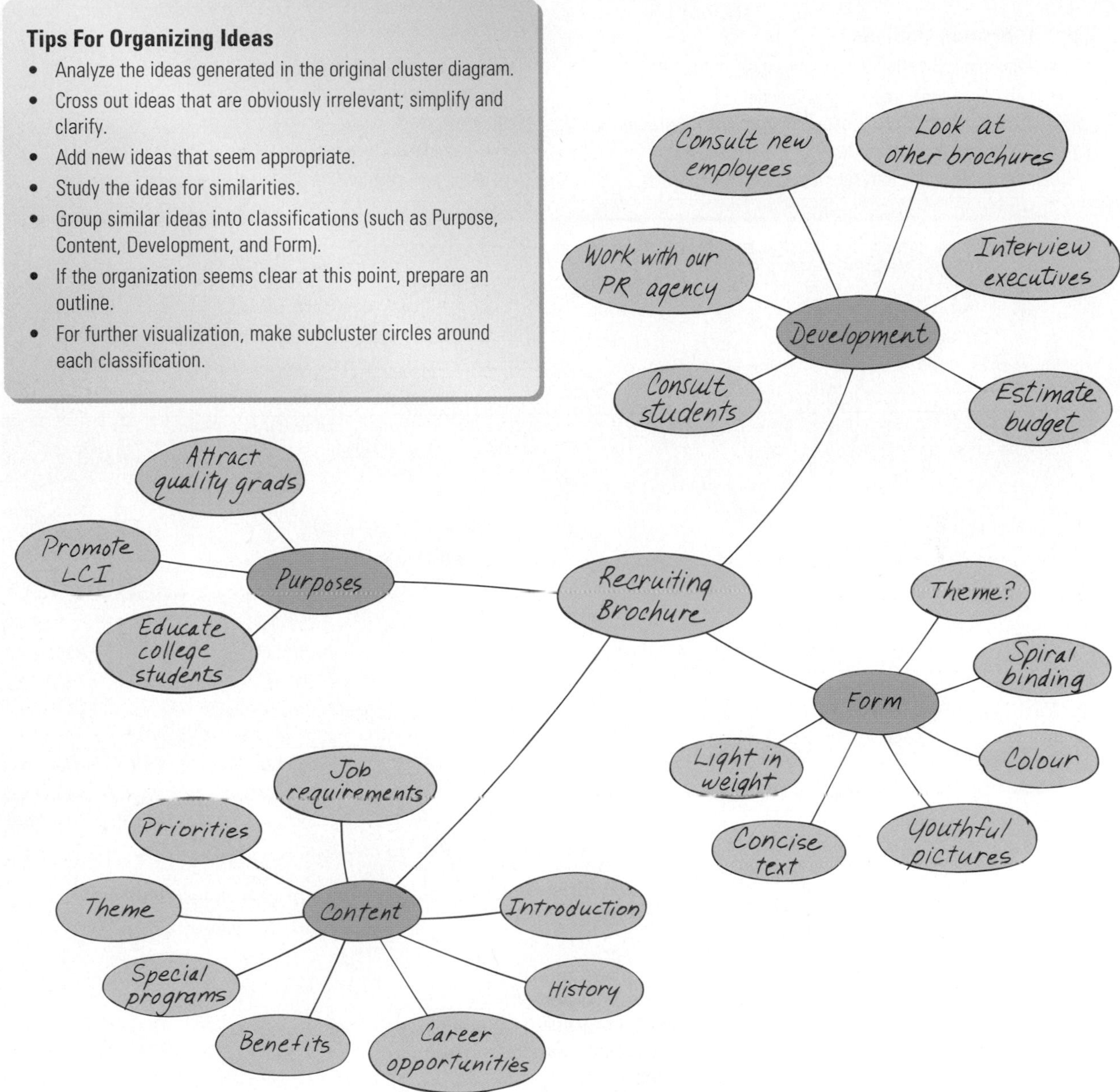

Tips For Organizing Ideas
Analyze the ideas generated in the original cluster diagram.
Cross out ideas that are obviously irrelevant; simplify and clarify.
Add new ideas that seem appropriate.
Study the ideas for similarities.
Group similar ideas into classifications (such as Purpose, Content, Development, and Form).
If the organization seems clear at this point, prepare an outline.
For further visualization, make subcluster circles around each classification.
Recruiting Brochure
Development
Consult new employees
Look at other brochures
Work with our PR agency
Interview executives
Consult students
Estimate budget
Purposes
Attract quality grads
Promote LCI
Educate college students
Form
Theme?
Spiral binding
Colour
Light in weight
Concise text
Youthful pictures
Content
Job requirements
Priorities
Theme
Introduction
Special programs
History
Benefits
Career opportunities

The hardest part of outlining is grouping ideas into components or categories—ideally three to five in number. These major categories will also become the major headings in your report. If you have more than five components, look for ways to combine smaller segments into broader topics. The preceding example shows how a portion of the Liz Claiborne brochure subcluster (Figure 5.2) can be organized into an alphanumeric outline.

I. Introduction
   A. Brief history of Liz Claiborne
      1. Founding, Fortune 500 status
      2. Product lines

FIGURE 5.3 **Two Outlining Formats**

Tips For Making Outlines

- Define the main topic (purpose of message) in the title.
- Divide the main topic into major components or classifications (preferably three to five). If necessary, combine small components into one larger category.
- Break the components into subpoints.
- Don't put a single item under a major component; if you have only one subpoint, integrate it with the main item above it or reorganize.
- Strive to make each component exclusive (no overlapping).
- Use details, illustrations, and evidence to support subpoints.

Format for Alphanumeric Outline

Title: Major Idea, Purpose

I. First major component
   A. First subpoint
      1. Detail, illustration, evidence
      2. Detail, illustration, evidence
   B. Second subpoint
      1.
      2.
II. Second major component
   A. First subpoint
      1.
      2.
   B. Second subpoint
      1.
      2.
III. Third major component
   A.
      1.
      2.
   B.
      1.
      2.

(This method is simple and familiar.)

Format for Decimal Outline

Title: Major Idea, Purpose

1.0 First major component
   1.1 First subpoint
      1.1.1 Detail, illustration, evidence
      1.1.2 Detail, illustration, evidence
   1.2 Second subpoint
      1.2.1
      1.2.2
2.0 Second major component
   2.1 First subpoint
      2.1.1
      2.1.2
   2.2 Second subpoint
      2.2.1
      2.2.2
3.0 Third major component
   3.1
      3.1.1
      3.1.2
   3.2
      3.2.1
      3.2.2

(This method relates every item to the overall outline.)

   B. Corporate environment
      1. System of values: "Priorities"
      2. Team spirit; corporate image
II. Career opportunities
   A. Operations management
      1. Traffic
      2. International trade and corporate customs
      3. Distribution
   B. Accounting and finance
      1. General accounting
      2. Internal audit
      3. Treasury and risk management
   C. Special opportunities
      1. Management training program
      2. Account executive sales training program
      3. Design studio

FIGURE 5.4 **Typical Major Components in Business Outlines**

Letter or Memo	Procedure	Informational Report	Analytical Report	Proposal
I. Opening	I. Step 1	I. Introduction	I. Introduction/ problems	I. Introduction
II. Body	II. Step 2	II. Facts	II. Facts/findings	II. Proposed solutions
III. Close	III. Step 3	III. Summary	III. Conclusions	III. Staffing
	IV. Step 4		IV. Recommendations (if requested)	IV. Schedule, cost
				V. Authorization

Notice that each major category is divided into at least two subcategories, which in turn are fleshed out with examples, details, statistics, case histories, and other data. In moving from major point to subpoint, progress from large abstract concepts to small concrete ideas. And further subdivide each subpoint with more specific illustrations if you desire. Determine the appropriate amount of detail by considering what your audience (primary and secondary) already knows about the topic and how much persuading you must do.

Every major category in an outline should have at least two subcategories.

How you group ideas into components depends on your topic and your channel of communication. The finished Liz Claiborne recruitment brochure required careful editing so that each component fit into the page layout. Business documents, on the other hand, do not have rigid page constraints. They usually contain typical components arranged in traditional patterns, as shown in Figure 5.4.

Thus far, you've seen how to collect information, generate ideas, and prepare an outline. How you order the information in your outline, though, depends on what pattern or strategy you choose.

Organizing Ideas Into Patterns

3

Two organizational patterns provide plans of action for typical business messages: the direct pattern and the indirect pattern. The primary difference between the two patterns is where the main idea is placed. In the direct pattern the main idea comes first, followed by details, explanation, or evidence. In the indirect pattern the main idea follows the details, explanation, and evidence. The pattern you select is determined by how you expect the audience to react to the message, as shown in Figure 5.5.

Business messages typically follow either (1) the direct pattern, with the main idea first, or (2) the indirect pattern, with the main idea following explanation and evidence.

The Direct Pattern for Receptive Audiences

In preparing to write any message, you need to anticipate the audience's reaction to your ideas and frame your message accordingly. When you expect the reader to be pleased, mildly interested, or, at worst, neutral—use the direct pattern. That is, put your main point—the purpose of your message—in the first or second sentence. Compare the direct and indirect patterns in the following memo openings. Notice how long it takes to get to the main idea in the indirect opening.

FIGURE 5.5 **Audience Response Determines Pattern of Organization**

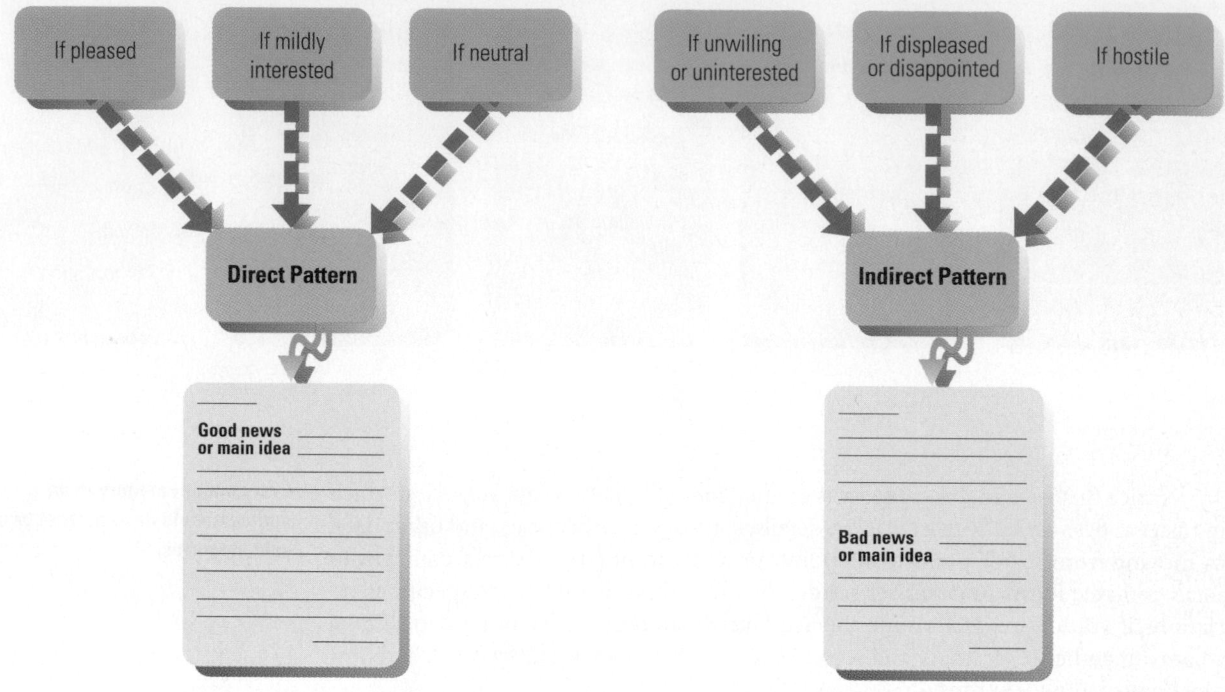

Indirect Opening
Our company has been concerned with attracting better-qualified prospective job candidates. For this reason, the Management Council has been gathering information about an internship program for college students. After considerable investigation, we have voted to begin a pilot program starting next fall.

Direct Opening
The Management Council has voted to begin a college internship pilot program next fall.

Frontloading saves the reader time, establishes the proper frame of mind, and prevents frustration.

Explanations and details should follow the direct opening. What's important is getting to the main idea quickly. This direct method, also called frontloading, has at least three advantages:

- **Saves the reader's time.** Many of today's businesspeople can devote only a few moments to each message. Messages that take too long to get to the point may lose their readers along the way.
- **Sets a proper frame of mind.** Learning the purpose up front helps the reader put the subsequent details and explanations in perspective. Without a clear opening, the reader may be thinking, "Why am I being told this?"
- **Prevents frustration.** Readers forced to struggle through excessive verbiage before reaching the main idea become frustrated. They resent the writer. Poorly organized messages create a negative impression of the writer.

This frontloading technique works best with audiences that are likely to be receptive to or at least not disagree with what you have to say. Typical business messages that follow the direct pattern include routine requests and responses, orders and acknowledgments, nonsensitive memos, e-mail messages, informational reports, and informational oral presentations. All these tasks have one element in common: none has a sensitive subject that will upset the reader.

The Indirect Pattern for Unreceptive Audiences

When you expect the audience to be uninterested, unwilling, displeased, or perhaps even hostile, the indirect pattern is more appropriate. In this pattern you don't reveal the main idea until after you have offered explanation and evidence. This approach works well with three kinds of messages: (1) bad news, (2) ideas that require persuasion, and (3) sensitive news, especially when being transmitted to superiors. The indirect pattern has these benefits:

- **Respects the feelings of the audience.** Bad news is always painful, but the trauma can be lessened when the receiver is prepared for it.
- **Ensures a fair hearing.** Messages that may upset the reader are more likely to be read when the main idea is delayed. Beginning immediately with a piece of bad news or a persuasive request, for example, may cause the receiver to stop reading or listening.
- **Minimizes the negative reaction.** A reader's overall reaction to a negative message is generally improved if the news is delivered gently.

The indirect pattern respects the feelings of the audience, facilitates a fair hearing, and minimizes a negative reaction.

Typical business messages that could be developed indirectly include letters and memos that refuse requests, deny claims, and disapprove credit. Persuasive requests, sales letters, sensitive messages, and some reports and oral presentations also benefit from the indirect strategy. You'll learn more about how to use the indirect pattern in Chapters 9 and 10.

In summary, business messages may be organized directly, with the main idea first, or indirectly, with the main idea delayed. Although these two patterns cover many communication problems, they should be considered neither universal nor inviolate. Every business transaction is distinct. Some messages are mixed: part good news, part bad; part goodwill, part persuasion. In upcoming chapters you'll practise applying the direct and indirect patterns in typical situations. Then, you'll have the skills and confidence to evaluate communication problems and vary these patterns depending on the goals you wish to achieve.

Composing the First Draft

4

Once you've researched your topic, organized the data, and selected a pattern of organization, you're ready to begin composing. Communicators who haven't completed the preparatory work often suffer from writer's block and sit staring at a piece of paper or at the computer screen. It's difficult to get started without organized ideas and a plan. Composition is also easier if you have a quiet environment in which to concentrate. Businesspeople with messages to compose set aside a given time and allow no calls, visitors, or other interruptions. This is a good technique for students as well.

As you begin composing, keep in mind that you are writing the first draft, not the final copy. Experts suggest that you write quickly (*sprint writing*). Get your thoughts down now and refine them in later versions.[2] As you take up each idea, imagine that you are talking to the reader. Don't let yourself get bogged down. If you can't think of the right word, insert a substitute or type "find perfect word later."[3] Sprint writing works especially well for those composing on a computer because it's

When composing the first draft, write quickly and save revision for later.

simple to make changes at any point of the composition process. If you are handwriting the first draft, double-space so that you have room for changes.

Creating Effective Sentences

As you create your first draft, you'll be working at the sentence level of composition. Although you've used sentences all your life, you may be unaware of how they can be shaped and arranged to express your ideas most effectively. First, let's review some basic sentence elements.

- Complete sentences have subjects and verbs and make sense.

Clauses have subjects and verbs, but phrases do not.

- Clauses and phrases, the key building blocks of sentences, are related groups of words. Clauses have subjects and verbs; phrases do not.

Independent clauses may stand alone; dependent clauses may not.

- Clauses may be divided into two groups: independent and dependent. Independent clauses are grammatically complete. Dependent clauses depend for their meaning on independent clauses. Dependent clauses are often introduced by words such as *if, when, because,* and *as.*

By learning to distinguish phrases, independent clauses, and dependent clauses, you'll be able to punctuate sentences correctly and avoid three basic sentence faults: the fragment, the run-on sentence, and the comma splice. In Appendix A, we examine these writing problems in greater detail. For now, however, let's look at some ways to make your sentences more readable.

Effective sentences are short and stress important ideas.

Using Short Sentences. Because your goal is to communicate clearly, you're better off limiting your sentences to about 20 or fewer words. The American Press Institute reports that reader comprehension drops off markedly as sentences become longer.[4] Thus, in crafting your sentences, think about the relationship between sentence length and comprehension:

Sentences of 20 or fewer words have the most impact.

Sentence Length	Comprehension Rate
8 words	100%
15 words	90%
20 words	80%
28 words	50%

Instead of stringing together clauses with *and, but,* and *however,* break some of those complex sentences into separate segments. Business readers want to grasp ideas immediately. They can do that best when thoughts are separated into short sentences. On the other hand, too many monotonous short sentences will sound "grammar schoolish" and may bore or even annoy the reader. Strive for a balance between longer sentences and shorter ones. Your computer probably can point out long sentences and give you an average sentence length.

Emphasizing Important Ideas. You can stress prominent ideas in three ways. The first is to place an important idea at the beginning of a sentence. Notice how the following sentence obscures the date of the meeting by burying it: *All production and administrative personnel will meet May 23, at which time we will announce a new plan of salary incentives.* To emphasize the date, start the sentence with it: *On May 23 all personnel will meet ...* A secondary position of importance is the end of a sentence: *All personnel will meet to discuss salary incentives on May 23.* Remember this guideline when composing paragraphs as well; put the main idea at the start and then follow up with supporting material.

A second way to emphasize an important idea is to be sure that it acts as the subject in a sentence. Notice the difference between the sentences *Michelle wrote the environmental report* and *The environmental report was written by Michelle.* Michelle receives the emphasis in the first version; the report receives it in the second.

A third way to emphasize an idea is to place it in a short sentence. Important ideas can get lost when enveloped by numerous competing words. How quickly can you grasp the important idea in this sentence? *This announcement is to inform all employees and guests that the hotel's restaurant will be closed Thanksgiving Day, although we do plan to resume restaurant services Tuesday at 7 a.m.* To give impact to the main idea, present it in a short sentence: *The hotel's restaurant will be closed Thanksgiving Day.* Then, provide explanations and details.

Using the Active Voice. In the active voice the subject performs the action: *Brandon selected new computers.* In the passive voice the subject receives the action: *New computers were selected by Brandon.* Passive-voice sentences de-emphasize the performer of the action. The performer is in a phrase (*by Brandon*) or is totally absent *(New computers were selected).* If you suspect that a verb is passive but you're not sure, try the "by whom?" test: *New computers were selected* [*by whom?*]. If you can fill in the performer of the action, the sentence is probably passive. What difference does it make if the verb is active or passive? Active-voice sentences are more direct because they reveal the performer immediately. They're easier to understand and shorter. Most business writing should be in the active voice.

Active-voice sentences are direct and easy to understand.

Using the Passive Voice Selectively. Although we prefer active verbs in business writing, passive verbs are useful in certain instances. For example, when the performer is unknown or insignificant, use the passive voice: *Drug tests are given to all applicants.* Who performs the drug tests is unimportant. You can also use the passive voice to tactfully deflect attention away from the people involved: *Three totals were calculated incorrectly.* Notice that this sentence stresses the problem while concealing the person who committed the error.

Passive-voice sentences are useful for tact and to direct attention to actions instead of people.

Avoiding Dangling and Misplaced Modifiers. For clarity, modifiers must be close to the words they describe or limit. A modifier dangles when the word or phrase it describes is missing from its sentence. A modifier is misplaced when the word or phrase it describes is not close enough to be clear. In both instances, the solution is to position the modifier closer to the word(s) it describes or limits. Introductory verbal phrases are particularly dangerous; be sure to follow them immediately with the words they can logically describe or modify.

Dangling Modifier	**Improved**
To win the lottery, a ticket must be purchased. (*The introductory verbal phrase must be followed by a logical subject.*)	To win the lottery, you must purchase a ticket.

Try this trick for detecting and remedying these dangling modifiers. Ask the question *who?* or *what?* after any introductory phrase. The words immediately following should tell the reader *who* or *what* is performing the action. Try the "who?" test on the previous dangler.

Misplaced Modifier	**Improved**
Seeing his error too late, the envelope was immediately resealed by Mark. (*Did the envelope see the error?*)	Seeing his error too late, Mark immediately resealed the envelope.
A wart appeared on my left hand that I want removed. (*Is the left hand to be removed?*)	A wart that I want removed appeared on my left hand.

Drafting Meaningful Paragraphs

5

From composing sentences, we progress to paragraphs. A paragraph is one or more sentences designated as a separate thought group. To avoid muddled paragraphs, writers must recognize basic paragraph elements, conventional sentence patterns, and ways to organize sentences into one of three classic paragraph patterns. They must also be able to polish their paragraphs by linking sentences and using transitional expressions.

Effective paragraphs focus on one topic, link ideas to build coherence, and use transitional devices to enhance coherence.

Discussing One Topic. Well-constructed paragraphs discuss only one topic. They reveal the primary idea in a main sentence that usually, but not always, appears first. Other ideas, connected logically with transitional expressions (verbal road signs), support or illustrate that idea.

Organizing Sentences Into Paragraphs. Paragraphs are generally composed of three kinds of sentences:[5]

- **Main sentence:** expresses the primary idea of the paragraph.
- **Supporting sentence:** illustrates, explains, or strengthens the primary idea.
- **Limiting sentence:** opposes the primary idea by suggesting a negative or contrasting thought; may precede or follow the main sentence.

These sentences may be arranged in three classic paragraph plans: direct, pivoting, and indirect.

The direct paragraph pattern is appropriate when defining, classifying, illustrating, or describing.

Using the Direct Paragraph Plan. Paragraphs arranged in the direct plan begin with the main sentence, followed by supporting sentences. Most business messages use this paragraph plan because it clarifies the subject immediately. This plan is useful whenever you must define (a new product or procedure), classify (parts of a whole), illustrate (an idea), or describe (a process). Simply start with the main sentence; then strengthen and amplify that idea with supporting ideas, as shown here:

Main Sentence	A social audit is a report on the social performance of a company.
Supporting Sentences	Such a report may be conducted by the company itself or by outsiders who evaluate the company's efforts to produce safe products, engage in socially responsible activities, and protect the environment. Many companies publish the results of their social audits in their annual reports. Commitment to the environment and social responsibility has been a core value for Vancouver City Savings Credit Union (VanCity) since 1993. The company conducts social audits to combine measures of financial return, social responsibility, and environmental performance.[6]

You can alter the direct plan by adding a limiting sentence if necessary. Be sure, though, that you follow with sentences that return to the main idea and support it, as shown here:

Main Sentence	Flexible work scheduling could immediately increase productivity and enhance employee satisfaction in our entire organization.
Limiting Sentence	Such scheduling, however, is impossible for all employees.
Supporting Sentences	Managers would be required to maintain their regular hours. For many other employees, though, flexible scheduling permits extra time to manage family responsibilities. Feeling less stress, employees are able to focus their attention better at work; hence, they become more relaxed and more productive.

Using the Pivoting Paragraph Plan. Paragraphs arranged in the pivoting plan start with a limiting sentence that offers a contrasting or negative idea before delivering the main sentence. Notice in the following example how two limiting sentences about drawbacks to military careers open the paragraph; only then do the main and supporting sentences describing rewards in military service appear. The pivoting plan is especially useful for comparing and contrasting ideas. In using the pivoting plan, be sure you emphasize the turn in direction with an obvious *but* or *however*.

The pivoting paragraph pattern is appropriate when comparing and contrasting.

Limiting Sentences	Military careers are certainly not for everyone. Many are in remote countries where harsh climates, health hazards, security risks, and other discomforts exist.
Main Sentence	However, military careers offer special rewards for the special people who qualify.
Supporting Sentences	Military employees enjoy the pride and satisfaction of representing their country abroad. They relish frequent travel, enriching cultural and social experiences in living abroad, and action-oriented work.

Using the Indirect Paragraph Plan. Paragraphs arranged in the indirect plan start with the supporting sentences and conclude with the main sentence. This useful plan enables you to build a rationale, a foundation of reasons, before hitting the audience with a big idea—possibly one that is bad news. It enables you to explain your reasons and then in the final sentence draw a conclusion from them. In the following example the vice president of a large accounting firm begins by describing the trend toward casual dress and concludes with a recommendation that his firm change its dress code. This indirect plan works well for describing causes followed by an effect.

The indirect paragraph pattern is appropriate when delivering bad news or when persuasion is necessary.

Supporting Sentences	According to a recent poll, more than half of all white-collar workers are now dressing casually at work. Many high-tech engineers and professional specialists have given up suits and ties, favouring khakis and sweaters instead. In our own business our consultants say they stand out like "sore thumbs" because they are attired in traditional buttoned-down styles, while the business people they visit are usually wearing comfortable, casual clothing.

Main Sentence Therefore, I recommend that we establish an optional "business casual" policy allowing consultants to dress casually, if they wish, as they perform their duties both in and out of the office.

You'll learn more techniques for implementing direct and indirect writing strategies when you prepare letters, memos, e-mail messages, reports, and oral presentations in subsequent chapters.

Coherent paragraphs link ideas by sustaining the main idea, using pronouns, dovetailing sentences, and using transitional expressions.

Linking Ideas to Build Coherence. Paragraphs are coherent when ideas are linked, that is, when one idea leads logically to the next. Well-written paragraphs take the reader through a number of steps. When the author skips from Step 1 to Step 3 and forgets Step 2, the reader is lost. You can use several techniques to keep the reader in step with your ideas.

Sustaining the Key Idea. This involves simply repeating a key expression or using a similar one. For example:

> Our philosophy holds that every customer is really a guest. All new employees to our theme parks are trained to treat *guests* as *VIPs.* These *VIPs* are never told what they can or cannot do.

Notice how the repetition of *guest* and *VIP* connects ideas.

Using pronouns strategically helps build coherence and continuity.

Using Pronouns. Familiar pronouns, such as *we, they, he, she,* and *it,* help build continuity, as do demonstrative pronouns, such as *this, that, these,* and *those.* These words confirm that something under discussion is still being discussed. For example:

> All new park employees receive a two-week orientation. They learn that every staffer has a vital role in preparing for the show. This training includes how to maintain enthusiasm.

Be careful with *this, that, these,* and *those,* however. These words usually need a noun with them to make their meaning absolutely clear. In the last example notice how confusing *this* becomes if the word *training* is omitted.

Dovetailing sentences means connecting ending and beginning ideas.

Dovetailing Sentences. Sentences are "dovetailed" when an idea at the end of one connects with an idea at the beginning of the next. For example:

> New hosts and hostesses learn about the theme park and its *facilities.* These *facilities* include telephones, food services, washrooms, and attractions, as well as the location of *offices.* Knowledge of administrative *offices* and internal workings of the company, such as who's who in administration, ensures that staffers will be able to *serve guests* fully. *Serving guests,* of course, is our number one priority.

Dovetailing of sentences is especially helpful with dense, difficult topics. This technique, however, should not be overused.

Transitional expressions help readers anticipate what's coming, reduce uncertainty, and speed comprehension.

Using Transitional Expressions to Build Coherence. Transitional expressions are another excellent device for achieving paragraph coherence. These words, some of which are shown in Figure 5.6, act as verbal road signs to readers and listeners. Transitional expressions enable the receiver to anticipate what's coming, to reduce uncertainty, and to speed up comprehension. They signal that a train of thought is moving forward, being developed, possibly detouring, or ending. Transitions are especially helpful in persuasive writing.

FIGURE 5.6 **Transitional Expressions to Build Coherence**

To Add or Strengthen	To Show Time or Order	To Clarify	To Show Cause and Effect	To Contradict	To Contrast
additionally	after	for example	accordingly	actually	as opposed to
again	before	for instance	as a result	but	at the same time
also	earlier	I mean	consequently	however	by contrast
besides	finally	in other words	for this reason	in fact	conversely
likewise	first	that is	so	instead	on the contrary
moreover	meanwhile	this means	therefore	rather	on the other hand
further	next	thus	thus	still	
furthermore	now	to put it another way	under the circumstances	though	
	previously			yet	

As Figure 5.6 shows, transitions can add or strengthen a thought, show time or order, clarify ideas, show cause and effect, contradict thoughts, and contrast ideas. Thus, you must be careful to select the best transition for your purpose. Look back at the examples of direct, pivoted, and indirect paragraphs to see how transitional expressions and other devices build paragraph coherence. Remember that coherence in communication rarely happens spontaneously; it requires effort and skill.

Composing Short Paragraphs. Although no rule regulates the length of paragraphs, business writers recognize the value of short paragraphs. Paragraphs with fewer than eight lines look inviting and readable, whereas long, solid chunks of print appear formidable. If a topic can't be covered in fewer than eight printed lines (not sentences), consider breaking it up into smaller segments.

Paragraphs with fewer than eight lines are inviting and readable.

The following checklist summarizes the key points of writing a first draft.

Checklist for Composing Sentences and Paragraphs

For Effective Sentences

 **Use short sentences.** Keep in mind that sentences with fewer than 20 words are easier to read. Use longer sentences occasionally, but rely primarily on short sentences.

 **Emphasize important ideas.** Place main ideas at the beginning of short sentences for emphasis.

 **Apply active and passive verbs carefully.** Use active verbs (*She sent the e-mail* instead of *The e-mail was sent by her*) most frequently; they immediately identify the doer. Use passive verbs to be tactful, to emphasize an action, or to conceal the performer.

 **Eliminate misplaced modifiers.** Be sure that introductory verbal phrases are followed by the words that can logically be modified. To check the placement of modifiers, ask *who?* or *what?* after such phrases.

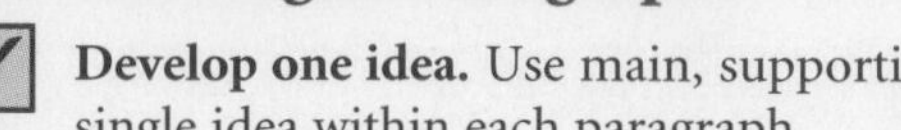

For Meaningful Paragraphs

- ✓ **Develop one idea.** Use main, supporting, and limiting sentences to develop a single idea within each paragraph.
- ✓ **Use the direct plan.** Start most paragraphs with the main sentence followed by supporting sentences. This direct plan is useful in defining, classifying, illustrating, and describing.
- ✓ **Use the pivoting plan.** To compare and contrast ideas, start with a limiting sentence; then, present the main sentence followed by supporting sentences.
- ✓ **Use the indirect plan.** To explain reasons or causes first, start with supporting sentences. Build to the conclusion with the main sentence at the end of the paragraph.
- ✓ **Build coherence by linking sentences.** Hold ideas together by repeating key words, using pronouns, and dovetailing sentences (beginning one sentence with an idea from the end of the previous sentence).
- ✓ **Provide road signs with transitional expressions.** Use verbal signals to help the audience know where the idea is going. Words like *moreover, accordingly, as a result,* and *thus* function as idea pointers.
- ✓ **Limit paragraph length.** Remember that paragraphs with fewer than eight printed lines look inviting. Consider breaking up longer paragraphs if necessary.

Summary of Learning Objectives

1 **Contrast formal and informal methods for researching data and generating ideas.** Formal research for long reports and complex problems may involve searching library data manually or electronically, as well as conducting interviews, surveys, focus groups, and experiments. Informal research for routine tasks may include looking in company files, talking with your boss, interviewing the target audience, conducting informal surveys, brainstorming for ideas, and cluster diagramming.

2 **Specify how to organize data into lists and alphanumeric or decimal outlines.** One method for organizing data in simple messages is to list the main topics to be discussed. Organizing more complex messages usually requires an outline. To prepare an outline, divide the main topic into three to five major components. Break the components into subpoints consisting of details, illustrations, and evidence. For an alphanumeric outline arrange items using Roman numerals (I, II), capital letters (A, B), and numbers (1, 2). For a decimal outline show the ordering of ideas with decimals (1., 1.1, 1.1.1).

3 **Compare direct and indirect patterns for organizing ideas.** The direct pattern places the main idea first. This pattern is useful when audiences will be pleased, mildly interested, or neutral. It saves the reader's time, sets the proper frame of mind, and prevents reader frustration. The indirect pattern places the main idea after explanations. This pattern is useful for audiences that will be unwilling, displeased, or hostile. It respects the feelings of the audience, encourages a fair hearing, and minimizes negative reactions.

4 **Discuss composing the first draft of a message, focusing on techniques for creating effective sentences.** Compose the first draft of a message in a quiet environment where you won't be interrupted. Compose quickly, preferably at a computer. Plan to revise. As you compose, remember that sentences are most effective when they are short (under 20 words). A main idea may be emphasized by making it the sentence subject, placing it first, and removing competing ideas. Effective sentences use active verbs, although passive verbs may be necessary for tact or de-emphasis. Effective sentences avoid dangling and misplaced modifiers.

5 **Define a paragraph and describe three classic paragraph plans and techniques for composing meaningful paragraphs.** A paragraph consists of one or more sentences designated as a separate thought group. Typical paragraphs follow one of three plans. Direct paragraphs (main sentence followed by supporting sentences) are useful to define, classify, illustrate, and describe. Pivoting paragraphs (limiting sentence followed by main sentence and supporting sentences) are useful to compare and contrast. Indirect paragraphs (supporting sentences followed by main sentence) build a rationale and foundation of ideas before presenting the main idea. Paragraphs may be improved through the use of coherence techniques and transitional expressions.

CHAPTER REVIEW

1. How does a writer "brainstorm"? (Obj. 1)
2. What is a cluster diagram, and when might it be useful? (Obj. 1)
3. Describe an alphanumeric outline. (Obj. 2)
4. What is the relationship between the major categories in an outline and those in a report written from the outline? (Obj. 2)
5. Distinguish between the direct and indirect patterns of organization for typical business messages. (Obj. 3)
6. Why should most messages be "frontloaded"? (Obj. 3)
7. List some business messages that should be frontloaded and some that should not be frontloaded. (Obj. 3)
8. Why should writers plan for revision? How can they do it? (Obj. 4)
9. Distinguish an independent clause from a dependent clause. Give examples. (Obj. 4)
10. Name three ways to emphasize important ideas in sentences. (Obj. 4)
11. Distinguish between active-voice sentences and passive-voice sentences. Give examples. (Obj. 4)
12. Give an original example of a dangling or misplaced modifier. Why are introductory verbal phrases dangerous? (Obj. 4)
13. Describe three kinds of sentences used to develop ideas in paragraphs. (Obj. 5)
14. Describe three paragraph plans. Identify the uses for each. (Obj. 5)
15. What is coherence, and how is it achieved? (Obj. 5)

CRITICAL THINKING

1. Why is cluster diagramming considered an intuitive process while outlining is considered an analytical process? (Obj. 1)
2. Why is audience analysis so important in choosing the direct or indirect pattern of organization for a business message? (Obj. 3)
3. In what ways do you imagine that writing on the job differs from the writing you do in your academic studies? Consider process as well as product. (Obj. 1)
4. Why are short sentences and short paragraphs appropriate for business communication? (Obj. 4)

ACTIVITIES

5.1 Document for Analysis (Objs. 3, 4 and 5)

First, read the following memo to see whether you can understand what the writer requests from all Western Division employees. Then, discuss why this memo is so hard to read. How long are the sentences? How many passive-voice constructions can you locate? How effective is the paragraphing? Can you spot four dangling or misplaced modifiers? In the next activity you'll improve the organization of this message.

TO: All Western Division Employees

[1]Personal computers and all the software to support these computers are appearing on many desks of Western Division employees. [2]After giving the matter considerable attention, it has been determined by the Systems Development Department (SDD) that more control should be exerted in coordinating the purchase of hardware and software to improve compatibility throughout the division so that a library of resources may be developed. [3]Therefore, a plan has been developed by SDD that should be followed in making all future equipment selections and purchases. [4]To make the best possible choice, SDD should be contacted as you begin your search because questions about personal computers, word processing programs, hardware, and software can be answered by our knowledgeable staff, who can also provide you with invaluable assistance in making the best choice for your needs at the best possible cost.

[5]After your computer and its software arrive, all your future software purchases should be channeled through SDD. [6]To actually make your initial purchase, a written proposal and a purchase request form must be presented to SDD for approval. [7]A need for the purchase must be established; benefits that you expect to derive resulting from its purchase must be analyzed and presented, and an itemized statement of all costs must be submitted. [8]By following these new procedures, coordinated purchasing benefits will be realized by all employees. [9]I may be reached at X466 if you have any questions.

5.2 Organizing Data (Obj. 2)

Use either a cluster diagram or an outline to organize the garbled message in Activity 5.1. Beyond the opening and closing of the message, what are the three main points the writer is trying to make? Should this message use the direct pattern or the indirect pattern? Your instructor may ask you to discuss how this entire message could be revised or to actually rewrite it.

5.3 Collaborative Brainstorming (Obj. 1)

In teams of four or five, analyze a problem on your campus such as the following: unavailable classes, unrealistic degree/diploma requirements, lack of student intern programs, poor parking facilities, inadequate registration process, lack of diversity among students on campus, and so forth. Use brainstorming techniques to generate ideas that clarify the problem and explore its solutions. Each team member should prepare a cluster diagram to record the ideas generated. Either individually or as a team, organize the ideas into an outline with three to five main points and numerous subpoints. Assume that your ideas will become part of a letter to be sent to an appropriate campus official or to your campus newspaper discussing the problem and your solution.

5.4 Individual Brainstorming (Objs. 1 and 2)

Critical Thinking

Analyze a problem that exists where you work or go to school, such as long lines at the copy or fax machines, overuse of express mail services, understaffing during peak customer service hours, poor scheduling of employees, inferior or inflexible benefit package, outdated office or other equipment, or one of the campus problems discussed in Activity 5.3. Select a problem about which you have some knowledge. Assume your boss or department chair wants you to submit a short report analyzing the problem. Prepare a cluster diagram to develop ideas. Then, organize the ideas into an outline with three to five main points and numerous subpoints.

5.5 Outlining (Obj. 2)

The following topics will be part of a report that a consultant is submitting to a group of investors who requested information about starting a new radio station in Fredericton, New Brunswick. Arrange the topics into a coherent alphanumeric outline. Clue: the items are already in the right order.

Problem: determining program format for new radio station CFSD-FM

Background: current radio formats available to listeners in Fredericton

Background: demographics of target area (population, age, sex, income)

Survey results: music preferences

Survey finds that top two favourites are easy listening and soft rock

Next two favourites are country and rock

Other kinds of music mentioned in survey: classical, jazz

Survey results: newscast preferences

News emphasis: respondents prefer primarily national news but with some local items

Respondents say yes to news but only short, hourly newscasts

Analysis of findings: discussion of all findings in greater detail

Recommendations: hybrid format combining easy listening and soft rock

Recommendations: news in 3- to 5-minute newscasts hourly; cover national news but include local flavour

We recommend starting new station immediately.

5.6 Collaborative Letter (Objs. 3–5)

Team

Divide into teams of three to five people who have similar majors. Work together to compose an inquiry letter requesting career information from someone in your field. Include questions about technical and general courses to take, possible starting salaries, good companies to apply to, technical skills required, necessary interpersonal skills, computer tools currently used, and tips for getting started in the field. Although this is a small project, your team can work more harmoniously if you apply some of the suggestions from Chapter 2. For example, appoint a meeting leader, recorder, and evaluator.

Your instructor may vary this project by asking teams to compose group letters to campus administrators discussing problems on campus; to newspaper editors reacting to news items or editorial positions; or to local, provincial, or federal elected officials discussing policies that you support or oppose.

5.7 Sentence Elements (Obj. 4)

In the following sentences underscore and identify dependent clauses (DC), independent clauses (IC), and phrases (P). Circle subjects and verbs in clauses.

a. We watched a television commercial, and the food looked delicious.

b. Although it looks delicious, the food in commercials often is inedible.

c. Food stylists use amazing techniques to create vivid colours and textures.

d. When viewers see ice cream, they probably are looking at a mixture of lard, powdered sugar, and food colouring.

e. For each plate of food filmed, stylists have typically prepared 20 plates.

5.8 Sentence Length (Obj. 4)

Break the following sentences into shorter sentences. Use appropriate transitional expressions.

a. If firms have a substantial investment in original research or development of new products, they should consider protecting those products with patents, although all patents eventually expire and what were once trade secrets can become common knowledge in the industry.

b. As soon as consumers recognize a name associated with a product or service, that name is entitled to legal protection as a trademark; in fact, consumers may even create a trademark where none existed or create a second trademark by using a nickname as a source indicator, such as the name "Coke," which was legally protected even before it had ever been used by the company.

c. Although no magic formula exists for picking a good trademark name, firms should avoid picking the first name that pops into someone's head; moreover, they should be aware that unique and arbitrary marks are best, while descriptive terms such as "car" or "TV repair" are useless, and surnames and geographic names are weak because they lack distinction and exclusivity.

5.9 Active and Passive Voice (Obj. 4)

In the following sentences convert passive-voice verbs to active-voice verbs. Add subjects if necessary. Be prepared to discuss which sentence version is more effective.

a. A decision to focus on customer service was made by the board.

b. First, the product line was examined to determine if it met customers' needs.

c. In the past, products had been built to the company's internal expectations of market needs.

d. When it was realized that changes were in order, a new product line was designed.

e. After just-in-time inventory procedures were introduced, our inventories were cut in half.

Now convert active-voice verbs to passive-voice verbs, and be prepared to discuss which sentence version is more effective.

f. We cannot authorize repair of your VCR since you have allowed the warranty period to expire.

g. I cannot give you a cash refund for merchandise that you purchased over 60 days ago.

h. Valley Golf Course does not accept players who are not members.

i. You must submit all reports by Friday at 5 p.m.

j. Joan added the two columns instead of subtracting them, thus producing the incorrect total.

5.10 Dangling and Misplaced Modifiers (Obj. 4)

Remedy any dangling or misplaced modifiers in the following sentences. Add subjects as needed, but retain the introductory phrases. Mark "C" if correct.

a. To stay in touch with customers, telephone contacts were encouraged among all sales reps.

b. By making sales reps a part of product design, a great deal of money was saved.

c. Acting as president, the contract was immediately signed by Rachel.

d. Noxious fumes made the office workers sick coming from the storage tanks of a nearby paint manufacturer.

e. Using available evidence, it becomes apparent that the court has been deceived by the witness.

5.11 Transitional Expressions (Obj. 5)

Add transitional expressions to the following sentences to improve the flow of ideas (coherence).

a. Computer style checkers rank somewhere between artificial intelligence and artificial ignorance. They are like clever children: smart but not wise. Business writers should be fully aware of the limitations and the usefulness of style checkers.

b. Our computerized file includes all customer data. It provides space for name, address, and other vital information. It has an area for comments, a feature that comes in handy and helps us keep our records up-to-date.

c. No one likes to turn out poor products. We began highlighting recurring problems. Employees make a special effort to be more careful in doing their work right the first time. It doesn't have to be returned to them for corrections.

d. In-depth employment interviews may be structured or unstructured. Structured interviews have little flexibility. All candidates are asked the same questions in the same order. Unstructured interviews allow a free-flowing conversation. Topics are prepared for discussion by the interviewer.

e. Fringe benefits consist of life, health, and dental insurance. Some fringe benefits might include paid vacations and sick pay. Other fringe benefits include holidays, funeral leave, and emergency leave. Paid lunch, rest periods, tuition reimbursement, and child care are also sometimes provided.

5.12 Paragraph Organization (Obj. 5)

The following poorly written paragraphs follow the indirect plan. Locate the main sentence in each paragraph. Then revise each paragraph so that it is organized directly. Improve coherence by using the techniques described in this chapter.

a. Many of our customers limp through their business despite problems with their disk drives, printers, and peripherals. We cannot service their disk drives, printers, and peripherals. These customers are unable to go without this equipment long enough for the repair. We've learned that there are two times when we can get to that equipment. We can do our repairs in the middle of the night or on Sunday. All of our staff of technicians now works every Sunday. Please authorize additional budget for my department to hire technicians for night and weekend service hours.

b. Air express is one of the ways SturdyBilt power mowers and chainsaws may be delivered. Air express promises two-day delivery but at a considerable cost. The cheapest method is for retailers to pick up shipments themselves at our nearest distribution centre. We have distribution centres in Regina, Winnipeg, and Thunder Bay. Another option involves having our trucks deliver the shipment from our distribution centre to the retailer's door for an additional fee. These are the options SturdyBilt provides for the retailers purchasing our products.

C.L.U.E. REVIEW 5

Edit the following sentences to correct faults in grammar, punctuation, spelling, and word use.

1. Although, we formally used a neighbourhood printer for all our print jobs we are now saving almost five hundred dollars a month by using desktop publishing.
2. Powerful softwear however cannot garantee a good final product.
3. To develop a better sense of design we collected desireable samples from: books, magazines, brochures, and newsletters.
4. We noticed that, poorly-designed projects often was filled with cluttered layouts, incompatible typefaces, and to many typefaces.
5. Our layout design are usually formal but ocasionally we use an informal layout design which is shown in figure six.
6. We usually prefer a black and white design; because colour printing is much more costly.
7. Expensive colour printing jobs are sent to foreign countries, for example china Italy and Japan.

8. Jeffreys article which he entitled "The Shaping of a corporate image" was excepted for publication in "the journal of communication."

9. Every employee will persenally receive a copy of his Performance Evaluation which the President said will be the principle basis for promotion.

10. We will print three hundred and fifty copies of the newsletter, to be sent to whomever is currently listed in our database.

CHAPTER • 6 •

REVISING BUSINESS MESSAGES

LEARNING OBJECTIVES

1 Identify revision techniques that make a document clear, conversational, and concise.

2 Describe revision tactics that make a document vigorous and direct.

3 Discuss revision strategies that improve readability.

4 List problem areas that good proofreaders examine carefully.

5 Compare the proofreading of routine and complex documents.

6 Evaluate a message to judge its success.

Revising Messages

1

The final phase of the 3-×-3 writing process focuses on revising, proofreading, and evaluating. Revising means improving the content and sentence structure of your message. Proofreading involves correcting its grammar, spelling, punctuation, format, and mechanics. Evaluating is the process of analyzing whether your message achieved its purpose. Many businesspeople realize that their ideas are worth little unless they can be communicated effectively to fellow workers and to management. In the communication process the techniques of revision can often mean the difference between the acceptance or rejection of ideas.

While the composition process differs for individuals and situations, this final phase should occupy a significant share of the total time you spend on a message. As you learned earlier, some experts recommend devoting about half the total composition time to revising and proofreading.[1]

Rarely is the first or even second version of a message satisfactory. The revision stage is your chance to make sure your message says what you mean. Many professional writers compose the first draft quickly without worrying about language, precision, or correctness. Then they revise and polish extensively. Other writers, however, prefer to revise as they go—particularly for shorter business documents.

Important messages—such as those you send to management or to customers or turn in to instructors for grades—deserve careful revision and proofreading. When you finish a first draft, plan for a cooling-off period. Put the document aside and return to it after a break, preferably after 24 hours or longer.[2]

Whether you revise immediately or after a break, you'll want to examine your message critically. You should be especially concerned with ways to improve its clarity, conciseness, vigour, and readability.

Keeping It Clear

One of the first revision tasks is assessing the clarity of your message. A clear message is one that is immediately understood. To achieve clarity, resist the urge to show off or be fancy. Remember that your goal is not to impress an instructor. Instead, the goal of business writing is to *express*, not *impress*. This involves two simple rules: (1) keep it simple and (2) keep it conversational.

Why do some communicators fail to craft simple, direct messages? For several reasons:

- Untrained executives and professionals worry that plain messages don't sound important.
- Subordinates fear that plain talk won't impress the boss.
- Unskilled writers create foggy messages because they've not learned how to communicate clearly.
- Unethical writers intentionally obscure a message to hide the truth.

Whatever the cause, you can eliminate the fog by applying the familiar KISS formula: Keep It Short and Simple! One way to achieve clear writing is to use active-voice sentences that avoid foggy, indirect, and pompous language.

To achieve clarity, remember to KISS—Keep It Short and Simple!

Foggy	**Clear**
Employees have not been made sufficiently aware of the potentially adverse consequences involved regarding these chemicals.	Warn your employees about these chemicals.

Keeping It Conversational

Clarity is further enhanced by language that sounds like conversation. This doesn't mean that your letters and memos should be chatty or familiar. Rather, you should strive to sound professional, yet not artificial or formal. This means avoiding legal terminology, technical words, and third-person constructions. Business messages should sound warm, friendly, and conversational—not stuffy and formal.[3] To sound friendly, include occasional contractions and first-person pronouns. This warmth is appropriate in all but the most formal business reports. You can determine whether your writing is conversational by trying the kitchen test. If it wouldn't sound natural in your kitchen, it probably needs revision. Note how the following formal sentence was revised to pass the kitchen test.

Formal	Conversational
As per your verbal instruction, steps will be undertaken immediately to investigate your billing problem.	At your suggestion I'm investigating your billing immediately.

Keeping It Concise

Main points are easier to understand in concise messages.

Another revision task is making certain that a message makes its point in the fewest possible words. This stage may be more time-consuming than actually writing the letter. In explaining a five-page letter to a friend, Winston Churchill once said, "I would have written you a short letter, but I didn't have the time."[4]

Messages without flabby phrases and redundancies are easier to comprehend and more emphatic because main points stand out. Efficient messages also save the reader valuable time.

Short messages require more effort than long, flabby ones.

Many busy executives today won't read wordy reports. Chairman Martin Kallen, of Monsanto Europe, complained that reports were too long, too frequent, and too unread. He then decreed that all writing be more concise, and he refused to read any report that was not summarized in two or fewer pages.[5]

But concise writing is not easy. To turn out slim sentences and lean messages, you do not have to be brusque, rude, or simple-minded. Instead, you must take time in the revision stage to "trim the fat." And before you can do that, you must learn to recognize it. Locating and excising wordiness involves (1) removing opening fillers, (2) eliminating redundancies, (3) reducing compound prepositions, and (4) purging empty words.

Removing Opening Fillers. Openers like *there is* and *it is* fill in sentences but generally add no meaning. These fillers reveal writers spinning their wheels until deciding where the sentence is going. Train yourself to question these constructions. About 75 percent of sentence-opening fillers can be eliminated, almost always resulting in more emphatic and more efficient sentences.

Wordy	There are three things I want you to do.
Concise	I want you to do three things.
Wordy	It is important to start meetings on time.
Concise	Starting meetings on time is important.

Eliminating Redundancies. Expressions that repeat meaning or include unnecessary words are redundant. To say *unexpected surprise* is like saying "surprise surprise" because *unexpected* carries the same meaning as *surprise.* Excessive adjectives, adverbs, and phrases often create redundancies and wordiness. The following list represents a tiny segment of the large number of redundancies appearing in business writing today. What word in each expression creates the redundancy?

Redundancies convey a meaning more than once.

Redundancies to Avoid

advance warning	few in number	positively certain
basic fundamentals	free and clear	potential opportunity
collect together	great majority	proposed plan
consensus of opinion	integral part	refer back
contributing factor	last and final	serious interest
dollar amount	midway between	true facts
each and every	past history	visible to the eye
end result	perfectly clear	unexpected surprise
exactly identical	personal opinion	

Reducing Compound Prepositions. Single words can often replace wordy prepositional phrases. In the following examples notice how the shorter forms say the same thing but more efficiently.

Wordy Compound Preposition	Shorter Form
as to whether	whether
at a later date	later
at such time, at which time	when
at this point in time	now
by means of, in accordance with	by
despite the fact that	although
due to the fact that, inasmuch as	because
for the amount of	for
in advance of, prior to	before
in view of the fact that	because
subsequent to	after
the manner in which	how
until such time as	until

Purging Empty Words. Familiar phrases roll off the tongue easily, but many contain expendable parts. Be alert to these empty words and phrases: *case, degree, the fact that, factor, instance, nature,* and *quality.* Notice how much better the following sentences sound when we remove all the empty words:

Many familiar phrases contain empty words.

~~In the case of~~ *The Halifax Gazette* ~~the newspaper~~ improved its readability.

Because ~~of the degree~~ of active participation by our sales reps, profits soared.

We are aware ~~of the fact~~ that many managers need assistance.

Also avoid saying the obvious. In the following examples notice how many unnecessary words we can omit through revision:

Good writers avoid saying what is obvious.

~~When it arrived,~~ I cashed your cheque immediately. (*Announcing the cheque's arrival is unnecessary. That fact is assumed in its cashing.*)

~~We need printer cartridges; therefore,~~ please send me two dozen laser cartridges. (*The first clause is obvious.*)

Finally, look carefully at clauses beginning with *that, which,* and *who.* They can often be shortened without loss of clarity. Search for phrases, such as *it appears that.* Such phrases can be reduced to a single adjective or adverb, such as *apparently.*

> successful
> Changing the name of a company ~~that is successful~~ is always risky.
> ^

> All employees ~~who are among those~~ completing the course will be reimbursed.

> final
> Our proposal, ~~which was~~ slightly altered ~~in its final form~~, won approval.
> ^

Revising for Vigour and Directness

2

Much business writing has been criticized as lifeless, cautious, and "really, really boring."[6] This boredom results not so much from content as from wordiness and dull, trite expressions. An Edmonton lawyer, David C. Elliott, has capitalized on the legalese of the judicial system by proposing a "Gobbledygook Fee Scale" in his "Model Plain Language Act." For example, using *above-referenced* involves a $100 fee; *herein,* $125; *pursuant to,* $100; and *witnesseth,* $200. If used more than ten times in a document, the fines are tripled.[7] You've already studied ways to improve clarity and conciseness. You can also reduce wordiness and improve vigour by (1) kicking the noun habit and (2) dumping trite business phrases.

Much business writing is plagued by wordiness and triteness.

Kicking the Noun Habit

Overusing noun phrases lengthens sentences, saps verbs, and muddies the message.

Some writers become addicted to nouns, needlessly transforming verbs into nouns (*we make a recommendation of* instead of *we recommend*). This bad habit increases sentence length, drains verb strength, slows the reader, and muddies the thought. Notice how efficient, clean, and forceful the verbs below sound compared with their noun phrase counterparts.

Wordy Noun Phrase	Verb
conduct a discussion of	discuss
create a reduction in	reduce
engage in the preparation of	prepare
give consideration to	consider
make a discovery of	discover
make an assumption of	assume
perform an analysis of	analyze
reach a conclusion about	conclude
take action on	act

Dumping Trite Business Phrases

Avoid trite expressions that are overused in business writing.

To sound "businesslike," many writers repeat the same stale expressions that other writers have used over the years. Your writing will sound fresher and more vigorous if you eliminate these phrases or find more original ways to convey the idea.

Trite Phrase	Improved Version
as per your request	as you request
pursuant to your request	at your request
enclosed please find	enclosed is

every effort will be made	we'll try
in accordance with your wishes	as you wish
in receipt of	have received
please do not hesitate to	please
thank you in advance	thank you
under separate cover	separately
with reference to	about

Revising for Readability

3

To help receivers anticipate and comprehend ideas quickly, two special writing techniques are helpful: (1) parallelism, which involves balanced writing, and (2) highlighting, which makes important points more visible. And to ensure that your document is readable, consider applying the Fog Index, a readability measure described later.

Developing Parallelism

Parallelism means matching nouns with nouns, verbs with verbs, phrases with phrases, and so on.

As you revise, be certain that you express similar ideas in balanced or parallel construction. For example, the phrase *clearly, concisely, and correctly* is parallel because all the words end in *-ly*. To express the list as *clearly, concisely, and with correctness* is jarring because the last item is not what the receiver expects. Instead of an adverb, the series ends with a noun. To achieve parallelism, match nouns with nouns, verbs with verbs, phrases with phrases, and clauses with clauses. Avoid mixing active-voice verbs with passive-voice verbs.

Not Parallel	Improved
The policy affected all vendors, suppliers, and those involved with consulting.	The policy affected all vendors, suppliers, and consultants. (*Series matches nouns.*)

Be alert to a list or series of items; the use of *and* or *or* should signal you to check for balanced construction. When elements cannot be balanced fluently, consider revising to subordinate or separate the items.

Not Parallel	Improved
Foreign service employees must be able to communicate rapidly, concisely, and be flexible in handling diverse responsibilities.	Foreign service employees must be able to communicate rapidly and concisely; they must also be flexible in handling diverse responsibilities.

Applying Graphic Highlighting

Graphic devices such as lists, bullets, headings, and white space spotlight important ideas.

One of the best ways to improve comprehension is through graphic highlighting techniques. Spotlight important items by setting them off with

- Letters, such as (a), (b), and (c), within the text
- Numerals, such as 1, 2, and 3, listed vertically
- Bullets—black squares, raised periods, or other figures
- Headings
- Capital letters, underscores, boldface, and italics

Ideas formerly buried within sentences or paragraphs stand out when targeted with one of these techniques. Readers not only understand your message more rapidly and easily but also consider you efficient and well organized. In the following sentence notice how highlighting with letters makes the three items more visible and emphatic.

Without Highlighting
Chez Hélène attracts upscale customers by featuring quality fashions, personalized service, and a generous return policy.

Highlighted With Letters
Chez Hélène attracts upscale customers by featuring (a) quality fashions, (b) personalized service, and (c) a generous return policy.

If you have the space and wish to create even greater visual impact, you can list items vertically. Capitalize the word at the beginning of each line. Don't add end punctuation unless the statements are complete sentences. And be sure to use parallel construction whenever you itemize ideas. In the following examples, each item in the bulleted list follows an adjective/noun sequence. In the numbered list, each item begins with a verb. Notice, too, that we use bullets when items have no particular order or importance. Numbers, however, are better to show a definite sequence.

Lists offset from the text and introduced with bullets have a strong visual impact.

Highlighted With Bullets
Chez Hélène attracts upscale customers by featuring the following:
- Quality fashions
- Personalized service
- Generous return policy

Numbers for Sequence
Chez Hélène advises recruiters to follow these steps in hiring applicants:
1. Examine application
2. Interview applicant
3. Check references

Headings help writers to organize information and enable readers to absorb important ideas.

Headings are another choice for highlighting information. They force the writer to organize carefully so that similar data are grouped together. And they help the reader separate major ideas from details. Moreover, headings enable a busy reader to skim familiar or less important information. They also provide a quick preview or review. Although headings appear more often in reports, they are equally helpful in complex letters and memos. Here, they informally summarize items within a message:

Highlighted With Headings
Chez Hélène focuses on the following areas in the employment process:
- **Attracting applicants.** We advertise for qualified applicants, and we also encourage current employees to recommend good people.
- **Interviewing applicants.** Our specialized interviews include simulated customer encounters as well as scrutiny by supervisors.
- **Checking references.** We investigate every applicant thoroughly, including conversations with former employers and all listed references.

To highlight individual words, use CAPITAL letters, underlining, **bold** type, or *italics*. Be careful with these techniques, though, because they SHOUT at the reader. Consider how the reader will react.

The following chapters supply additional ideas for grouping and spotlighting data. Although highlighting techniques can improve comprehension, they can also clutter a message if overdone. Many of these techniques also require more space, so use them judiciously.

Measuring Readability

Experts have developed methods for measuring how easy, or difficult, a message is to read. Probably the best known is Robert Gunning's Fog Index, which measures long words and sentence length to determine readability. Most word processing software packages have tools to measure readability.

Readability formulas like the Fog Index are based on word and sentence lengths.

The foggier a message, the higher its reading level. Based on actual literacy levels of Canadians, plain-language experts believe Grades 7 to 9 should be the target reading level for material aimed at the general public. Only writing geared to specialized audiences should be at the Grade 10 level or above. By occasionally calculating the Fog Index of your writing, you can ensure that you stay within the appropriate range. Remember that long words—those over two syllables—and long sentences make your writing foggy.

Readability formulas, however, don't always tell the full story. Although they provide a rough estimate, those based solely on word and sentence counts fail to measure meaningfulness. Even short words (such as *skew*, *onus*, and *wane*) can cause trouble if readers don't recognize them. More important than length are a word's familiarity and meaningfulness to the reader. In Chapter 3 you learned to adapt your writing to the audience by selecting familiar words. Other techniques that can improve readability include well-organized paragraphs, transitions to connect ideas, headings, and lists.

The task of revision, summarized in the following checklist, is hard work. It demands objectivity and a willingness to cut, cut, cut. Though painful, the process is also gratifying. It's a great feeling when you realize your finished message is clear, concise, and readable.

Checklist for Revising Messages

- ✓ **Keep the message simple.** Express ideas directly. Don't show off or use fancy language.
- ✓ **Be conversational.** Include occasional contractions (*hasn't, don't*) and first-person pronouns (*I/we*). Use natural-sounding language.
- ✓ **Avoid opening fillers.** Omit sentence fillers such as *there is* and *it is* to produce more direct expression.
- ✓ **Shun redundancies.** Eliminate words that repeat meanings, such as *mutual cooperation.* Watch for repetitious adjectives, adverbs, and phrases.
- ✓ **Tighten your writing.** Check phrases that include *case, degree, the fact that, factor,* and other words and phrases that unnecessarily increase wordiness. Avoid saying the obvious.
- ✓ **Don't convert verbs to nouns.** Keep your writing vigorous by avoiding the noun habit (*analyze* not *make an analysis of*).
- ✓ **Avoid trite phrases.** Keep your writing fresh, direct, and contemporary by skipping such expressions as *enclosed please find* and *pursuant to your request.*

In some ways business communicators can learn to improve the readability of their messages by emulating magazine articles. Magazine writers enhance comprehension by writing concisely, using short sentences, controlling paragraph length, including headings, and developing parallelism (expressing similar ideas in similar grammatical constructions).

 **Strive for parallelism.** Help receivers anticipate and comprehend your message by using balanced writing (*planning, drafting, and constructing* not *planning, drafting, and construction*).

 **Highlight important ideas.** Use graphic techniques such as letters, numerals, bullets, headings, capital letters, underlining, boldface, and italics to spotlight ideas and organization.

 **Test readability.** Check your writing occasionally to identify its reading level. Remember that short, familiar words and short sentences help readers comprehend.

Proofreading for the Finishing Touch

4

Once you have the message in its final form, it's time to proofread it. Don't proofread earlier because you may waste time checking items that eventually are changed or omitted.

Proofreading before a document is completed is generally a waste of time.

What to Watch for in Proofreading

Careful proofreaders check for problems in these areas:

- **Spelling.** Now's the time to consult the dictionary. Is *recommend* spelled with one or two *c*'s? Do you mean *affect* or *effect*? Use your computer spell checker, but don't rely on it totally. Remember that most spell checkers use American instead of Canadian spelling. To learn more about the Canadian spelling dilemma, refer to the accompanying Career Coach.
- **Grammar**. Locate sentence subjects; do their verbs agree with them? Do pronouns agree with their antecedents? Review the C.L.U.E. principles in Appendix A if necessary. Use your computer's grammar checker, but be suspicious.

CAREER COACH

THE CANADIAN SPELLING DILEMMA

An order-in-council, dated 12 June 1890, stated that "in all official documents, in the Canada Gazette, and in the Dominion Statutes, the English practice of *-our* endings shall be followed." However, times have changed and much uncertainty exists about what form of spelling to use.

The federal government has produced a helpful manual, *The Canadian Style*,[8] which provides guidance in matters of usage and style. According to *The Canadian Style*, spelling is a major problem in English, not only because of the various rules but also because of differences between the United Kingdom and the United States. Canadian spelling fluctuates between the two, and as Mark Orkin states, "To this day, there is no clearly established Canadian standard."[9]

Editing Canadian English, by the Editors' Association of Canada (Douglas & McIntyre, 1987), also recognizes the spelling dilemma. Ruth Chernia, the association's professional development chair, describes the association's typically Canadian noncommittal stance: "Sometimes it's British and sometimes it's American and sometimes it's our own version of the way things work."[10]

The Nelson Canadian Dictionary of the English Language (1997) acknowledges the distinct nature of Canadian spelling as an "erratic blend of U.S. and British usages." To the British and Europeans, we often sound like Americans, and to the Americans, we spell like the British. The use of *-our* in *honour* and *colour*, the *-re* in *centre* and *metre*, and the doubling of the *l* in words such as *cancelled* and *traveller* reflect British influence. But we are very inconsistent: we cash a *cheque* and order from a *catalogue*; we fly in an *airplane* (not the British *aeroplane*) and we repair a flat *tire* (as opposed to the British *tyre*). Adding to this confusion, to make words such as *beau* and *bureau* plural, many Canadians use the French form of adding –x (*beaux* and *bureaux*) rather than adding *–s*.

- **Punctuation**. Make sure that introductory clauses are followed by commas. In compound sentences put commas before coordinating conjunctions (*and, or, but, nor*). Double-check your use of semicolons and colons.
- **Names and numbers.** Compare all names and numbers with their sources because inaccuracies are not immediately visible. Especially verify the spelling of the names of individuals receiving the message. Most of us immediately dislike someone who misspells our name.
- **Format.** Be sure that your document looks balanced on the page. If you indent paragraphs, be certain that all are indented.

How to Proofread Routine Documents

Most routine documents require a light proofreading. You may be working with a handwritten or a printed copy or on your computer screen. If you wish to print a copy, make it a rough draft (don't print it on letterhead stationery). In time, you may be able to produce a "first-time-final" message, but beginning writers seldom do.

Routine documents need a light proofreading.

For handwritten or printed messages, read the entire document. Watch for all of the items just described. **Use standard proofreading marks, as shown on the inside front cover, to indicate changes.**

For computer messages you can read the document on the screen, preferably in WYSIWYG mode (what you see is what you get). Use the down arrow to reveal one line at a time, thus focusing your attention at the bottom of the screen. A safer proof-

For both routine and complex documents, it's best to proofread from a printed copy, not on a computer screen.

reading method, however, is reading from a printed copy. You're more likely to find errors and to observe the tone.

How to Proofread Complex Documents

Long, complex, or important documents demand more careful proofreading using the following techniques:

- Print a copy, preferably double-spaced, and set it aside for at least a day. You'll be more alert after a breather.
- Allow adequate time to proofread carefully. A common excuse for sloppy proofreading is lack of time.
- Be prepared to find errors. Psychologically, we don't expect to find errors, and we don't want to find them. You can overcome this obstacle by anticipating errors and congratulating, not criticizing, yourself each time you find one.
- Read the message at least twice—once for word meanings and once for grammar/mechanics. For very long documents (book chapters and long articles or reports), read a third time to verify consistency in formatting.
- Reduce your reading speed. Concentrate on individual words rather than ideas.
- For documents that must be perfect, have someone read the message aloud. Spell names and difficult words, note capitalization, and read punctuation.
- Use standard proofreading marks to indicate changes.

Complex documents should be proofread at least twice.

Your computer word processing program may include a style or grammar checker. These programs generally analyze aspects of your writing style, including readability level and use of passive voice, trite expressions, split infinitives, and wordy expressions. Some of them use sophisticated technology (and a lot of computer memory) to identify significant errors. In addition to finding spelling and typographical errors, some programs will also find subject–verb lack of agreement, word misuse, spacing irregularities, punctuation problems, and many other faults.

Evaluating the Product

6

As part of applying finishing touches, take a moment to evaluate your writing. How successful will this message be? Does it say what you want it to? Will it achieve your purpose? How will you know if it succeeds?

As you learned in Chapter 1, the best way to judge the success of your communication is through feedback. Thus, you should encourage the receiver to respond to your message. This feedback will tell you how to modify future efforts to improve your communication technique.

A good way to evaluate messages is through feedback.

Your instructor will also be evaluating some of your writing. Although any criticism can be painful, try not to be defensive. Look on these comments as valuable advice tailored to your specific writing weaknesses—and strengths. Many businesses today spend thousands of dollars bringing in communication consultants to improve employee writing skills. You're getting the same training in this course. Take advantage of this chance—one of the few you may have—to improve your skills. The best way to improve your skills, of course, is through instruction, practice, and evaluation.

Your instructor and this book provide you with the three keys to success: instruction, practice materials, and evaluation.

In this class you have all three elements: instruction in the writing process (summarized in Figure 6.1), practice materials, and someone willing to guide and evaluate your efforts. Those three elements are the reasons that this book and this course may be the most valuable in your entire curriculum.

FIGURE 6.1 **The Complete 3-×-3 Writing Process**

1 PREWRITING

Analyze: Define your purpose. Select the most appropriate form (channel). Visualize the audience.

Anticipate: Put yourself in the reader's position and predict his or her reaction to this message.

Adapt: Consider ways to shape the message to benefit the reader, using his or her language.

WRITING

Research: Collect data formally and informally. Generate ideas by brainstorming and clustering.

Organize: Group ideas into a list or an outline. Select direct or indirect strategy.

Compose: Write first draft, preferably with a good word processing program.

REVISING

Revise: Revise for clarity, tone, conciseness, and vigour. Revise to improve readability.

Proofread: Proofread to verify spelling, grammar, punctuation, and format. Check for overall appearance.

Evaluate: Ask yourself whether the final product will achieve its purpose.

Summary of Learning Objectives

1 **Identify revision techniques that make a document clear, conversational, and concise.** Clear documents use active-voice sentences and simple words and avoid negative expressions. Clarity is further enhanced by language that sounds like conversation, including occasional contractions and first-person pronouns (*I/we*). Conciseness can be achieved by excluding opening fillers (*There are*), redundancies (*basic essentials*), and compound prepositions (*by means of*).

2 **Describe revision tactics that make a document vigorous and direct.** Writers can achieve vigour in messages by revising wordy phrases that needlessly convert verbs into nouns. For example, instead of *we conducted a discussion of,* write *we discussed.* To make writing more direct, good writers replace trite business phrases, such as *please do not hesitate to,* with similar expressions, such as *please.*

3 **Discuss revision strategies that improve readability.** One revision technique that improves readability is the use of balanced constructions (*parallelism*). For example, *collecting, analyzing, and illustrating data* is balanced and easy to read. *Collecting, analysis of, and illustration of data* is more difficult to read because it is unbalanced. Parallelism involves matching nouns with nouns, verbs with verbs, phrases with phrases, and clauses with clauses. Another technique that improves readability is graphic highlighting. It incorporates devices such as lettered items, numerals, bullets, headings, capital letters, underlining, italics, and bold print to highlight and order ideas. A readability scale, such as the Fog Index, is helpful in measuring how easy or difficult a document is to read.

4 **List problem areas that good proofreaders examine carefully.** Proofreaders must be especially alert to these problem areas: spelling, grammar, punctuation, names, numbers, and document format.

5 **Compare the proofreading of routine and complex documents.** Routine documents may be proofread immediately after completion. They may be read line by line on the computer screen or, better yet, from a printed draft copy. More complex documents, however, should be proofread after a breather. To do a good job, you must read from a printed copy, allow adequate time, reduce your reading speed, and read the document at least three times—for word meanings, for grammar/mechanics, and for formatting.

6 **Evaluate a message to judge its success.** Encourage feedback from the receiver so that you can determine whether your communication achieved its goal. Try to welcome any advice from your instructor on how to improve your writing skills. Both techniques contribute to helping you evaluate the success of a message.

CHAPTER REVIEW

1. Approximately how much of the total composition time should be spent revising, proofreading, and evaluating? (Obj. 1)
2. What is the KISS method? In what three ways can it apply to business writing? (Obj. 1)
3. What is a redundancy? Give an example. Why should writers avoid redundancies? (Obj. 1)
4. Why should communicators avoid openings such as *there is*? (Obj. 1)
5. What shorter forms could be substituted for the expressions *by means of, despite the fact that*, and *at this point in time*? (Obj. 1)
6. Why should a writer avoid the opening *This memo is to inform you that our next committee meeting is Friday*? (Obj. 1)
7. Why should a writer avoid an expression such as *We hope you will give consideration to our proposal*? (Obj. 2)
8. What's wrong with businesslike expressions such as *enclosed please find* and *as per your request*? (Obj. 2)
9. Discuss five ways to highlight important ideas. (Obj. 3)
10. What two characteristics increase the Fog Index of written matter? (Obj. 3)
11. What is parallelism, and how can you achieve it? (Obj. 3)
12. Name five specific items to check in proofreading. Be ready to discuss methods you find useful in spotting these errors. (Obj. 4)
13. In proofreading, what major psychological problem do you face in finding errors? How can you overcome this barrier? (Obj. 4)
14. List four or more techniques for proofreading complex documents. (Obj. 5)
15. How can you overcome defensiveness when your writing is criticized constructively? (Obj. 6)

CRITICAL THINKING

1. Why is it difficult to recommend a specific process that all writers can follow in composition? (Obj. 1)
2. Would you agree or disagree with the following statement by writing expert William Zinsser? "Plain talk will not be easily achieved in corporate America. Too much vanity is on the line." (Objs. 1 and 2)
3. To be conversational, should business writing be exactly as we talk? Support your opinion. (Obj. 1)
4. Why should the proofreading process for routine documents differ from that for complex documents? (Objs. 4 and 5)

ACTIVITIES

6.1 Document for Analysis (Objs. 1 and 3)

Revise the following memo to improve its clarity, conciseness, vigour, and readability. How many wordy constructions can you spot?

TO: All Management

This memo is addressed to all members of management to advise you that once a year we like to remind management of our policy in relation to the matter of business attire. In this policy there is a recommendation that all employees should wear clothing that promotes a businesslike atmosphere and meets requirements of safety.

Employees who work in offices and who, as part of their jobs, meet the public and other outsiders should dress in a professional manner, including coat, tie, suit, dress, and so forth. In areas of industrial applications, supervisors may prohibit loose clothing (shirttails, ties, cuffs) that could become entangled in machinery that moves.

Where it is necessary, footwear should provide protection against heavy objects or sharp edges at the level of the floor. In the manufacturing and warehousing areas, prohibited footwear includes the following: shoes that are open toe, sandals, shoes made of canvas or nylon, tennis shoes, spiked heels, and heels higher than 1 1/2 inches.

Each and every manager has the responsibility for the determination of suitable business attire, and employees should be informed of what is required.

6.2 Document for Analysis (Objs. 4 and 5)

Use proofreading marks (see inside front cover) to indicate needed corrections in the following letter. Check spelling, typos, grammar, punctuation, names and numbers, and format.

Dear Ms. Willis,

We appreciate you interest in employe leasing through Dominion Staff Network. Our programs and our service has proved to be powerful management tools for business owners, like you.

Our seventeen year history, Ms. Williams, provide the local service and national strength neccesary to offer the best employee leasing programs available, we save business owners time, and money, employee hassles and employer liability.

Your employees' will receive health care benifits, retirement plan choices and a national credit union. As a small business owner you can eliminate personel administration. Which involves alot of goverment paperwork today.

Whether you have one or 1,000 employees and offer no benefits to a full-benefits package employee leasing will get you back to the basics of running your business more profitably. I will call you to arrange a time to meet, and talk about your specific needs.

Cordially,

6.3 Interview (Objs. 1–6)

To learn more about on-the-job writing, interview someone—preferably in your field of study. Ask questions such as these: *What kind of writing do you do? What kind of planning do you do before writing? Where do you get information? Do you brainstorm? Make lists? Do you compose with pen and paper, a computer, or a dictating machine? How long does it take you to compose a routine one- or two-page memo or letter? Do you revise? How often? Do you have a preferred method for proofreading? When you have questions about grammar and mechanics, what or whom do you consult? Does anyone read your drafts and make suggestions? Can you describe your entire composition process? Do you ever work with others to produce a document? How does this process work? What makes writing easier or harder for you? Have your writing methods and skills changed since you left school?* Your instructor may ask you to present your findings orally or in a written report.

6.4 Clarity (Obj. 1)

Revise the following sentences to make them direct, simple, and conversational.

a. As per your written instruction, we will undertake the task of studying your investment program.

b. A request that we are making to managers is that they not spend all their time in their departments and instead visit other departments one hour a month.

c. We in management are of the opinion that employees have not been made sufficiently aware of the problem of computer security.

d. Our organization is honoured to have the pleasure of extending a welcome to you as a new customer.

e. Please be advised that it is our intention to make every effort to deliver your order by the date of your request, December 1.

6.5 Conciseness (Obj. 1)

Suggest shorter forms for the following expressions.

a. at this point in time

b. in reference to

c. in regard to

d. without further delay

e. on an annual basis

6.6 Conciseness (Obj. 1)

Revise and shorten the following sentences.

a. There are three people who volunteered for the new team.

b. As per your suggestion, we will not attempt to make alterations or changes in the proposal at this point in time.

c. Because of the fact that his visit was an unexpected surprise, we were totally unprepared to make a presentation of profit and loss figures.

d. It is perfectly clear that meetings held on a weekly basis are most effective.

e. Despite our supposition that the bill appeared erroneous, we sent a cheque in the amount of $250.

6.7 Vigour (Obj. 2)

Revise the following sentences to reduce noun conversions, trite expressions, and other wordiness.

a. We must make the assumption that you wish to be transferred.

b. Please give consideration to our latest proposal, despite the fact that it comes into conflict with the original plan.

c. The committee reached the conclusion that a great majority of students had a preference for mail-in registration.

d. Please conduct an investigation of employee turnover in that department for the period of June through August.

e. After we engage in the preparation of a report, our recommendations will be presented in their final form before the Executive Committee.

6.8 Parallelism (Obj. 3)

Revise the following sentences to improve parallelism. If elements cannot be balanced fluently, use appropriate subordination.

a. Your goal should be to write business messages that are concise, clear, and written with courteousness.

b. Ensuring equal opportunities, the removal of barriers, and elimination of age discrimination are our objectives.

c. Ms. Thomas tries to read all e-mail messages daily, but responses may not be made until the following day.

d. Last year Mr. Li wrote letters and was giving presentations to promote investment in his business.

e. Because of its air-conditioning and since it is light and attractive, I prefer this office.

6.9 Highlighting (Obj. 3)

Revise the following statements using the suggested highlighting techniques. Improve parallel construction and reduce wordiness if necessary.

a. Revise using letters, such as (a) and (b), within the sentence.

The benefits for employees that our organization offers include annual vacations of two weeks, insurance for group life, provision for insurance coverage of medical expenses for the family, and a private retirement fund.

b. Revise using a vertical list with bullets.

The Canadian Automobile Association makes a provision of the following tips for safe driving. You should start your drive well rested. You should wear sunglasses in bright sunshine. To provide exercise breaks, plan to stop every two hours. Be sure not to drink alcohol or take cold and allergy medications before you drive.

c. Revise using a vertical list with numbers.

Our lawyer made a recommendation that we take several steps to avoid litigation in regard to sexual harassment. The first step we should take involves establishing an unequivocal written statement prohibiting sexual harassment within our organization. The second thing we should do is make sure training sessions are held for supervisors regarding a proper work environment. Finally, some kind of procedure for employees to lodge complaints is necessary. This procedure should include investigation of complaints.

6.10 Proofreading (Objs. 4 and 5)

Use proofreading marks (see inside front cover) to mark spelling, grammar, punc-tuation, capitalization, and other errors in the following sentences.

a. To be elligible for this job, you must: (1) Be a Canadian citizen, (2) Be able to pass a through back ground investigation, and (3) Be available for world wide assignment.

b. Some businesses view "quality" as a focus of the organization rather then as a atribute of goods or services.

c. Its easy to get caught up in internal problems, and to overlook customers needs.

d. Incidently we expect both the ceo and the president to give there speechs before noon.

e. This is to inform you that wordiness destroys clarity therefore learn to cut the fat from your writing.

C.L.U.E. REVIEW 6

Edit the following sentences to correct faults in grammar, punctuation, spelling, and word use.

1. Business documents must be written clear to insure that readers comprehend the message quick.
2. We expect Mayor Wilson to visit the premier in an attempt to increase the cities share of Provincial funding.
3. The caller could have been him but we don't know for sure. Since he didn't leave his name.
4. The survey was sited in an article entitled "Whats new in softwear, however I can't locate it now.
5. All three of our companys auditors—Jim Lucus, Doreen Delgado, and Brad Kirby—critisized there accounting procedures.
6. Anyone of the auditors are authorized to procede with an independant action, however, only a member of the management counsel can alter policy.

7. Because our printer has been broke everyday this week; were looking at new models.
8. Have you all ready ordered the following? a dictionary a reference manual and a style book.
9. In the morning Mrs Williams ordinarilly opens the office, in the evening Mr Williams usualy closes it.
10. When you travel in england and ireland I advice you to charge purchases to your visa credit card.

UNIT 3

BUSINESS CORRESPONDENCE

CHAPTER 7

Routine Letters and Goodwill Messages

CHAPTER 8

Routine Memos and E-Mail Messages

CHAPTER 9

Persuasive and Sales Messages

CHAPTER 10

Negative Messages

CHAPTER • 7 •

ROUTINE LETTERS AND GOODWILL MESSAGES

LEARNING OBJECTIVES

1. List three characteristics of good letters and describe the direct pattern for organizing letters.
2. Write letters requesting information and action.
3. Write letters placing orders.
4. Write letters making claims.
5. Write letters complying with requests.
6. Write letters of recommendation.
7. Write letters granting claims and making adjustments.
8. Write goodwill messages.

Strategies for Routine Letters

1

Although e-mail is incredibly successful for internal and external communication, many important messages still require written letters. Business letters are important when a permanent record is required, when formality is necessary, and when a message is sensitive and requires an organized, well-considered presentation. In this book we'll divide letters into three groups: (1) routine letters communicating straightforward requests, replies, and goodwill messages; (2) persuasive messages including sales pitches; and (3) negative messages delivering refusals and bad news.

Routine letters to outsiders encourage product feedback, project a favourable company image, and promote future business.

This chapter concentrates on routine, straightforward letters through which we conduct everyday business and convey goodwill to outsiders. Such letters go to suppliers, government agencies, other businesses, and, most importantly, customers. The letters to customers receive a high priority because these messages encourage product feedback, project a favourable image of the company, and promote future business.

This chapter teaches you what turns readers on. You'll study the characteristics of good letters, techniques for organizing direct requests and responses, and ways to apply the 3-×-3 writing process. You'll learn how to write six specific kinds of direct letters, along with special goodwill messages. Finally, you'll study how to modify letters to accommodate other cultures.

Characteristics of Good Letters

Although routine letters deliver straightforward facts, they don't have to sound and look dull or mechanical. At least three characteristics distinguish good business letters: clear content, a tone of goodwill, and correct form.

Clear letters feature short sentences and paragraphs, transitional expressions, familiar words, and active-voice verbs.

Clear Content. A clearly written letter separates ideas into paragraphs, uses short sentences and paragraphs, and guides the reader through the ideas with transitional expressions. Moreover, a clear letter uses familiar words and active-voice verbs. In other words, it incorporates the writing techniques you studied in Chapters 4, 5, and 6.

But many business letters are not written well. As many as one third of business letters do nothing more than seek clarification of earlier correspondence. Clear letters avoid this problem by answering all the reader's questions or concerns so that no further correspondence is necessary. Clear letters also speak the language of the receiver.

Letters achieve a tone of goodwill by emphasizing a "you" view and reader benefits.

A Tone of Goodwill. Good letters, however, have to do more than deliver clear messages; they also must build goodwill. Goodwill is a positive feeling the reader has toward an individual or an organization. By analyzing your audience and adapting your message to the reader, your letters can establish an overall tone of goodwill.

To achieve goodwill, look for ways to present the message from the reader's perspective. In other words, emphasize the "you" view and point out benefits to the reader. In addition, be sensitive to words that might suggest gender, racial, age, or disability bias. Finally, frame your ideas positively because they will sound more pleasing and will give more information than negative constructions.

Appropriate letter formats send silent but positive messages.

Correct Form. A business letter conveys silent messages beyond that of its printed words. The letter's appearance and format reflect the writer's carefulness and experience. A short letter bunched at the top of a sheet of paper, for example, looks as if it was prepared in a hurry or by an amateur.

For your letters to make a good impression, you need to select an appropriate format. Figure 7.1 illustrates the modified block style and explains how to format

FIGURE 7.1 **Business Letter Formatting (Modified Block)**

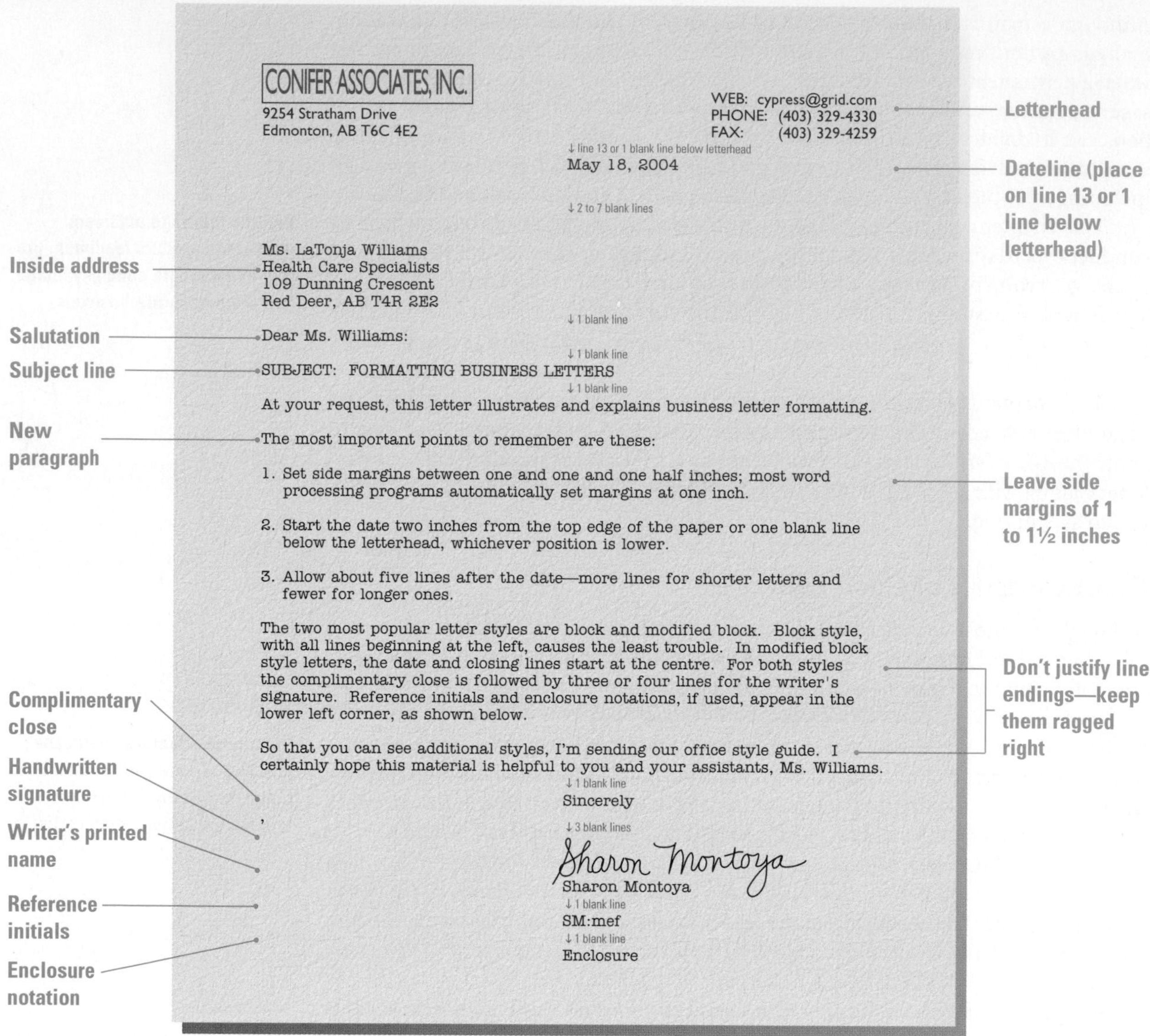
CONIFER ASSOCIATES, INC.
9254 Stratham Drive
Edmonton, AB T6C 4E2

WEB: cypress@grid.com
PHONE: (403) 329-4330
FAX: (403) 329-4259

May 18, 2004

Ms. LaTonja Williams
Health Care Specialists
109 Dunning Crescent
Red Deer, AB T4R 2E2

Dear Ms. Williams:

SUBJECT: FORMATTING BUSINESS LETTERS

At your request, this letter illustrates and explains business letter formatting.

The most important points to remember are these:

1. Set side margins between one and one and one half inches; most word processing programs automatically set margins at one inch.

2. Start the date two inches from the top edge of the paper or one blank line below the letterhead, whichever position is lower.

3. Allow about five lines after the date—more lines for shorter letters and fewer for longer ones.

The two most popular letter styles are block and modified block. Block style, with all lines beginning at the left, causes the least trouble. In modified block style letters, the date and closing lines start at the centre. For both styles the complimentary close is followed by three or four lines for the writer's signature. Reference initials and enclosure notations, if used, appear in the lower left corner, as shown below.

So that you can see additional styles, I'm sending our office style guide. I certainly hope this material is helpful to you and your assistants, Ms. Williams.

Sincerely

Sharon Montoya

Sharon Montoya

SM:mef

Enclosure

business letters. Figure 7.2 illustrates the block style and provides more information about formatting. Study Figures 7.1 and 7.2 for more tips on making your letters look professional.

Using the Direct Pattern for Routine Letters

Most business messages are routine requests or routine responses.

The everyday transactions of a business consist mainly of routine requests and responses. Such letters should be reader-centred and focus on the needs and expectations of the receiver. Because you expect the reader's response to be positive or neutral, you won't need special techniques to be convincing, to soften bad news, or to be tactful. Thus, in composing routine letters, you can organize your message into three parts:

FIGURE 7.2 **Block Letter Styles**

Block style
Open punctuation

Letterhead

*island*graphics
893 Dillingham Boulevard, Vancouver, BC V5A 1B1

↓ line 13 or 1 blank line below letterhead

Dateline

September 13, 2004

↓ 1 to 9 blank lines

Inside address

Mr. T. M. Wilson, President
Visual Concept Enterprises
2166 Ocean Forest Drive
Surrey, BC V3A 7K2

↓ 1 blank line

Salutation

Dear Mr. Wilson

↓ 1 blank line

Subject line

SUBJECT: BLOCK LETTER STYLE

↓ 1 blank line

Body

This letter illustrates block letter style, about which you asked. All typed lines begin at the left margin. The date is usually placed two inches from the top edge of the paper or two lines below the last line of the letterhead, whichever position is lower.

This letter also shows open punctuation. No colon follows the salutation, and no comma follows the complimentary close. Although this punctuation style is efficient, we find that most of our customers prefer to include punctuation after the salutation and the complimentary close.

If a subject line is included, it appears two lines below the salutation. The word *SUBJECT* is optional. Most readers will recognize a statement in this position as the subject without an identifying label. The complimentary close appears two lines below the end of the last paragraph.

↓ 1 blank line

Complimentary close

Sincerely

↓ 3 blank lines

Signature block

Mark H. Wong
Graphics Designer

↓ 1 blank line

MHW:pil

- **Opening:** a statement that announces the purpose immediately
- **Body:** details that explain the purpose
- **Closing:** a request for action or a courteous conclusion

Everyday business messages "frontload" by presenting the main idea or purpose immediately.

Frontloading in the Opening. You should begin everyday messages in a straightforward manner by frontloading the main idea. State immediately why you are writing so that the reader can anticipate and comprehend what follows. Remember, every time a reader begins a message, he or she is thinking, "Why was this sent to me?" "What am I to do?"

Some writers make the mistake of organizing a message as if they were telling a story.[1] They start at the beginning and follow the same sequence in which they thought through the problem. This means reviewing the background, discussing the reasons for action, and then requesting an action. Most business letters, though, are better written "backwards." Start with the action desired or the main idea. Don't get bogged down in introductory material, history, justifications, or old-fashioned "business" language.[2] Instead, reveal your purpose immediately. Compare the following indirect and direct openers to see the differences:

Indirect Opening	**Direct Opening**
Our company is experiencing difficulty in retaining employees. We also need help in screening job applicants. Our current testing program is unsatisfactory. I understand that you offer employee testing materials, and I have a number of questions to ask.	Please answer the following questions about your personnel testing materials.

Most simple requests should open immediately with a statement of purpose (*Please answer these questions about ....*). Occasionally, however, complex requests may require a sentence or two of explanation or background before the purpose is revealed. What you want to avoid, though, is delaying the purpose of the letter beyond the first paragraph.

The body explains the purpose for writing, perhaps using graphic devices to highlight important ideas.

Explaining in the Body. After a direct opening that tells the reader why you are writing, present details that explain your request or response. This is where your planning pays off, allowing you to structure the information for maximum clarity and readability. Here you should consider using some graphic devices to highlight the details: a numbered or bulleted list, headings, columns, or boldface or italic type.

If you have considerable information, you'll want to develop each idea in a separate paragraph with effective transitions to connect them. The important thing to remember is to keep similar ideas together. The biggest problem in business writing is poor organization, and the body of a letter is where that failure becomes apparent.

The closing courteously specifies what the receiver is to do.

Being Specific and Courteous in the Closing. In the last paragraph of direct letters, readers look for action information: schedules, deadlines, activities to be completed. Thus, at this point, you should specify what you want the reader to do. If appropriate, include an end date—a date for completion of the action. If possible, give reasons for establishing the deadline. Research shows that people want to know why they should do something—even if the reasons seem obvious. Moreover, people want to be treated courteously (*Please answer these questions before April 1, when we must make a final decision*), not bossed around (*Send this information immediately*).

Applying the 3-×-3 Writing Process to Routine Letters

Although routine letters may be short and straightforward, they benefit from attention to the composition process. "If you force yourself to think through what you want to say and to whom you want to say it," observed a communication consultant in *Business Week*, "the writing task becomes infinitely easier."[3] Here's a quick review of the 3-×-3 writing process to help you think through its application to routine letters.

Before writing routine letters, make yourself analyze your purpose and anticipate the response.

Analysis, Anticipation, and Adaptation. Before writing, spend a few moments analyzing your task and audience. Your key goals here are (1) determining your purpose, (2) anticipating the reaction of your audience, and (3) visualizing the audience.

Research, Organization, and Composition. Collect information and make a list of the points you wish to cover. For short messages such as an answer to a customer's inquiry, jot your notes down on the document you are answering. For longer documents that require formal research, use a cluster diagram or the outlining techniques discussed in Chapter 5. When business letters carry information that won't upset the receiver, you can organize them in the direct manner described earlier. And be sure to plan for revision. A writer can seldom turn out an excellent message on the first attempt. For easier revision, keyboard your message on your computer.

Revision, Proofreading, and Evaluation. When you finish the first draft, revise for clarity. The receiver should not have to read the message twice to grasp its meaning. Proofread for correctness. Check for punctuation irregularities, typos, misspelled words, or other mechanical problems. Always take time to examine the words highlighted by your spell checker. Finally, evaluate your product. Before any letter leaves your desk, always reread it and put yourself in the shoes of the reader and ask yourself, "How would I feel if I were receiving it?"

Direct Request Letters

2

Many of your routine business letters will fall into one of three categories: (1) asking for information or action, (2) placing orders for products, or (3) making a claim requiring an adjustment when something has gone wrong. In this section you'll learn how to write good letters for each of these circumstances. Before you write any letter, though, consider its costs in terms of your time and workload. Whenever possible, don't write! Instead of asking for information, could you find it yourself? Would a telephone call, an e-mail message, or a brief visit to a coworker solve the problem quickly? If not, use the direct pattern to present your request efficiently.

Requesting Information and Action

The majority of your business letters will request information or action. For these routine messages, put the main idea first. If your request involves several questions, you could open with a polite request, such as *Will you please answer the following questions about your payroll service.* Note that although this request sounds like a question, it's actually a disguised command. Since you expect an action rather than a reply, punctuate this polite command with a period instead of a question mark.

A direct letter may open with a question or a polite request.

Clarifying Requests. In the letter body, explain your purpose and provide details. If you have questions, express them in parallel form so that you balance them gram-

Questions in a direct letter should be parallel (balanced grammatically).

matically. To elicit the most information, pose open-ended questions (*What computer lock-down device can you recommend?*) instead of yes-or-no questions (*Do you carry computer lock-down devices?*). If you are asking someone to do something, be sure your tone is polite. When possible, focus on benefits to the reader (*To ensure that you receive the exact sweater you want, send us your colour choice*). In the closing tell the reader courteously what is to be done. If a date is important, set an end date to take action and explain why. Some careless writers end request letters simply with *Thank you,* forcing the reader to review the contents to determine what is expected and when. You can save the reader time by spelling out the action to be taken. Avoid other overused endings such as *Thank you for your cooperation* (trite) and *If you have any questions, do not hesitate to call me* (suggests that you didn't make yourself clear).

Direct request letters maintain a courteous tone, spell out what needs to be done, and focus on reader benefits.

Showing Appreciation. It's always appropriate to show appreciation, but try to do so in a fresh and efficient manner. For example, you could hook your thanks to the end date (*Thanks for returning the questionnaire before May 5, when we will begin tabulation*). You might connect your appreciation to a statement developing reader benefits (*We are grateful for the information you will provide because it will help us serve you better*). Or you could describe briefly how the information will help you (*I appreciate this information that will enable me to ...*). When possible, make it easy for the reader to comply with your request (*Here's my e-mail address so that you can reach me quickly*).

A direct request letter, written by office manager Melanie Marshall, shown in Figure 7.3, begins directly. The opening sentence introduces the purpose immediately so that the reader quickly knows why the letter was sent. Melanie then provides background information. Most important, she organizes all her requests into specific questions. Study the 3-×-3 writing process outlined in Figure 7.3 to see the plan Melanie followed in writing her letter.

Placing Orders

3

You may occasionally need to write a letter that orders supplies, merchandise, or services. Generally, such purchases are made by telephone, catalogue order form, fax, or Web page. Sometimes, however, you may not have a telephone number, order form, or Web address—only a street address. To order items by letter, supply the same information that an order blank would require. In the opening let the reader know immediately that this is a purchase authorization and not merely an information inquiry. Instead of *I saw a number of interesting items in your catalogue,* begin directly with order language such as *Please send me by Purolator the following items from your fall merchandise catalogue.*

Letters placing orders specify items or services, quantities, dates, prices, and payment method.

If you're ordering many items, list them vertically in the body of your letter. Include as much specific data as possible: quantity, order number, complete description, unit price, and total price. Show the total amount, and figure the tax and shipping costs if possible. The more information you provide, the less likely that a mistake will be made.

In the closing tell how you plan to pay for the merchandise. Enclose a cheque, provide a credit card number, or ask to be billed. Many business organizations have credit agreements with their regular suppliers that enable them to send goods without prior payment. In addition to payment information, tell when the merchandise should be sent and express appreciation. The following letter from the human resources department of a business illustrates the pattern of an order letter.

FIGURE 7.3 **Direct Request Letter**

The Three Phases of the Writing Process

Analyze: The purpose of this letter is to gain specific data about devices to lock down computer equipment.

Anticipate: The audience is expected to be a busy but receptive customer service representative.

Adapt: Because the reader will probably react positively to this inquiry, the direct pattern is best.

Research: Determine how much equipment must be locked down and what questions must be answered. Learn name of receiver.

Organize: Open with general inquiry about security devices. In the body give details; arrange any questions logically. Close by courteously providing a specific deadline.

Compose: Draft the first copy on a computer.

Revise: Improve the clarity by grouping similar ideas together. Improve readability by listing and numbering questions. Eliminate wordiness.

Proofread: Look for typos and spelling errors. Check punctuation and placement. Indent the second line of all listed items for a clean look.

Evaluate: Is this message attractive and easily comprehended?

---

inner Circle graphics

32 Horchoy Road, Dartmouth, N3 B2Y 2H5

(902) 488-3310 phone (902) 488-3319 fax

February 5, 2004

Ms. Sue Ivorson, Customer Service
Micro Supplies and Software
P.O. Box 862
Montreal, QC G5B 2G6

Dear Ms. Ivorson: — **Addresses receiver by name**

Please provide information and recommendations regarding security equipment to prevent the theft of office computers, keyboards, monitors, and printers. — **Introduces purpose immediately**

Our office now has 18 computer workstations and 6 printers that we must secure to desks or counters. Answers to the following questions will help us select the best devices for our purpose. — **Explains need for information**

1. What device would you recommend that can secure a workstation consisting of a computer, monitor, and keyboard?

2. What expertise and equipment are required to install and remove the security device?

3. How much is each device? Do you offer quantity discounts, and if so, how much?

Groups open-ended questions into list for quick comprehension and best feedback

Your response before February 15 will help us meet an April 1 deadline from our insurance company for securing this equipment. — **Courteously provides end date and reason**

Sincerely,

Melanie Marshall

Melanie Marshall
Office Manager

Opens directly with authorization for purchase, method of delivery, and catalogue source

Please send by Priority Post the following items from your summer catalogue.*

Uses columns to make quantity, catalogue number, description, and price stand out

Quantity	Catalogue #	Description	Price
250	No. OG-18	Payroll greeting cards	$102.50
250	No. OG-22	Payroll card envelopes	21.95
100	No. OM-01	Performance greeting cards	80.00
	Subtotal		$204.45
	GST at 7%		14.31
	PST at 8% (ON)		16.36
	Shipping		24.00
	Total		$259.12

Calculates totals to prevent possible mistakes

Expresses appreciation and tells when items are expected. Identifies method of payment

My company would appreciate receiving these cards immediately since we are starting an employee recognition program February 12. Enclosed is our cheque for $259.12. If additional charges are necessary, please contact me.

Making Straightforward Claims

4

In business many things can go wrong—promised shipments are late, warranted goods fail, or service is disappointing. When you as a customer must write to identify or correct a wrong, the letter is called a *claim.* Straightforward claims are those to which you expect the receiver to agree readily. But even these claims often require a letter. While your first action may be a telephone call or a visit to submit your claim, you may not be satisfied with the result. Written claims are often taken more seriously, and they also establish a record of what happened. Straightforward claims use a direct approach. Claims that require persuasion are presented in Chapter 9.

Most businesses today honestly want to please their customers. In today's competitive business environment, "it's important for companies to proactively meet—then surpass—customer expectations."[4] Particularly in today's high-speed market, one bad experience can permanently alienate a customer; consequently, managing customer experience is of crucial importance.[5]

Claim letters open with a clear problem statement, support the claim with specifics, and close with a statement of goodwill.

Opening Directly. When you, as a customer, have a legitimate claim, you can expect a positive response from a company. Smart businesses today want to hear from their customers. That's why you should open a claim letter with a clear statement of the problem or with the action you want the receiver to take. You might expect a replacement, a refund, a new order, credit to your account, correction of a billing error, free repairs, free inspection, or cancellation of an order. When the remedy is obvious, state it immediately (*Please send us 24 Royal hot-air popcorn poppers to replace the 24 hot-oil poppers sent in error with our order shipped January 4*). When the remedy is less obvious, you might ask for a change in policy or procedure or simply for an explanation (*Because three of our employees with confirmed reservations were refused rooms September 16 in your hotel, would you please clarify your policy regarding reservations and late arrivals*).

* Some unformatted letters and memos such as that shown here will appear in this textbook. They illustrate content rather than form. Documents that illustrate form are shown in figures, such as Figure 7.3.

Explaining. In the body of a claim letter, explain the problem and justify your request. Provide the necessary details so that the difficulty can be corrected without further correspondence. Avoid becoming angry or trying to fix blame. Bear in mind that the person reading your letter is seldom responsible for the problem. Instead, state the facts logically, objectively, and unemotionally; let the reader decide on the causes. Include copies of all pertinent documents such as invoices, sales slips, catalogue descriptions, and repair records. (By the way, be sure to send copies and NOT your originals, which could be lost.) When service is involved, cite names of individuals spoken to and dates of calls. Assume that a company honestly wants to satisfy its customers—because most do. When an alternative remedy exists, spell it out (*If you are unable to send 24 Royal hot-air popcorn poppers immediately, please credit our account now and notify us when they become available*).

Providing details without getting angry improves the effectiveness of a claim letter.

Concluding. Conclude a claim letter with a courteous statement that promotes goodwill and expresses a desire for continued relations. If appropriate, include an end date (*We realize that mistakes in ordering and shipping sometimes occur. Because we've enjoyed your prompt service in the past, we hope that you will be able to send us the hot-air poppers by January 15*). Finally, in making claims, act promptly. Delaying claims makes them appear less important. Delayed claims are also more difficult to verify. By taking the time to put your claim in writing, you indicate your seriousness. A written claim starts a record of the problem, should later action be necessary. Be sure to keep a copy of your letter.

Written claims submitted promptly are taken more seriously than delayed ones.

Figure 7.4 shows a first draft of a hostile claim that vents the writer's anger but accomplishes little else. Its tone is belligerent, and it assumes that the company intentionally mischarged the customer. Furthermore, it fails to tell the reader how to remedy the problem. The revision tempers the tone, describes the problem objectively, and provides facts and figures. Most important, it specifies exactly what the customer wants done.

To sum up, use the direct pattern with the main idea first when you expect little resistance to letters making requests. The following checklist reviews the direct strategy for information and action requests, orders, and adjustments.

Checklist for Writing Direct Requests

Information or Action Request Letters

- ✓ **Open by stating the main idea.** To elicit information, ask a question or issue a polite command (*Will you please answer the following questions....*).
- ✓ **Explain and justify the request.** In seeking information, use open-ended questions structured in parallel, balanced form.
- ✓ **Request action in the closing.** Express appreciation, and set an end date if appropriate. Avoid clichés (*Thank you for your cooperation*).

Order Letters

- ✓ **Open by authorizing the purchase.** Use order language (*Please send me ...*), designate the delivery method, and state your information source (such as a catalogue, advertisement, or magazine article).

 **List items in the body.** Include quantity, order number, description, unit price, extension, tax, shipping, and total costs.

 **Close with the payment data.** Tell how you are paying and when you expect delivery. Express appreciation.

Claim Letters

 **Begin with the purpose.** Present a clear statement of the problem or the action requested—such as a refund, replacement, credit, explanation, or correction of error.

 **Explain objectively.** In the body tell the specifics of the claim. Provide copies of necessary documents.

 **End by requesting action.** Include an end date if important. Add a pleasant, forward-looking statement. Keep a copy of the letter.

Direct Reply Letters

When you can respond favourably to requests, use the direct pattern.

Occasionally, you will receive requests for information or action. In these cases your first task is deciding whether to comply. If the decision is favourable, your letter should let the reader know immediately by using the direct pattern and frontloading the good news.

This section focuses on routine reply letters in three situations: (1) complying with requests for information or action, (2) writing letters of recommendation, and (3) granting claims and making adjustments.

Complying With Requests

5

Often, your messages will respond favourably to requests for information or action. In complying with such requests, you'll want to apply the same direct pattern you used in making requests.

Letters responding to requests may open with a subject line to identify the topic immediately.

The opening of a direct reply letter might contain a subject line, which helps the reader recognize the topic immediately. Usually appearing one blank line below the salutation, the subject line refers in abbreviated form to previous correspondence and/or summarizes a message (*Subject: Your Letter of August 5 About Award Programs*). It often omits articles (*a, an, the*), is not a complete sentence, and does not end with a period. Knowledgeable business communicators use a subject line to refer to earlier correspondence so that in the first sentence, the most emphatic spot in a letter, they are free to emphasize the main idea.

Opening Directly. In the first sentence of a direct reply letter, deliver the information the reader wants. Avoid wordy, drawn-out openings such as *I have before me your letter of August 5, in which you request information about....* More forceful and more efficient is an opener that answers the inquiry (*Here is the information you wanted about ...*). When agreeing to a request, announce the good news promptly (*Yes, I will be happy to speak to your class on the topic of ...*).

In the body of your reply, supply explanations and additional information. Because a letter written on company stationery is considered a legally binding con-

FIGURE 7.4 **Direct Claim Letter**

First Draft

Dear Premier Quality Systems, Inc.:

You call yourselves Premier Quality, but all I'm getting from your service is garbage! I'm furious that you have your salespeople slip in unwanted service warranties to boost your sales.

When I bought my Panatronic VCR from PQS, Inc., in August, I specifically told the salesperson that I did NOT want a three-year service warranty. But there it is on my VISA statement this month! You people have obviously billed me for a service I did not authorize. I refuse to pay this charge.

How can you hope to stay in business with such fraudulent practices? I was expecting to return this month and look at CD players, but you can be sure I'll find an honest dealer this time.

Sincerely,

Sounds angry; jumps to conclusions

Forgets that mistakes happen

Fails to suggest solution

Revision

2352 Hall Avenue
Windsor, ON N8X 2L9
September 3, 2004

Personal business letter style

Mr. Sam Lee, Customer Service
Premier Quality Systems, Inc.
41 Bricker Avenue
Waterloo, ON N2L 3B6

Dear Mr. Lee:

Please credit my VISA account, No. 0000-0046-2198-9421, to correct an erroneous charge of $299.

States simply and clearly what to do

On August 8 I purchased a Panatronic VCR from PQS, Inc. Although the salesperson discussed a three-year extended warranty with me, I decided against purchasing that service for $299. However, when my credit card statement arrived this month, I noticed an extra $299 charge from PQS, Inc. I suspect that this charge represents the warranty I declined.

Explains objectively what went wrong

Doesn't blame or accuse

Enclosed is a copy of my sales invoice along with my VISA statement on which I circled the charge. Please authorize a credit immediately and send a copy of the transaction to me at the above address.

Documents facts

I'm enjoying all the features of my Panatronic VCR and would like to be shopping at PQS for a CD player shortly.

Suggests continued business once problem is resolved

Uses friendly tone

Sincerely,

Keith Mayer

Keith Mayer

Enclosure

tract, be sure to check facts and figures carefully. If a policy or procedure needs authorization, seek approval from a supervisor or executive before writing the letter.

Responding to customer inquiries provides a good opportunity to promote your business.

Arranging Information Logically. When answering a group of questions or providing considerable data, arrange the information logically and make it readable by using lists, tables, headings, boldface, italics, or other graphic devices. When customers or prospective customers inquire about products or services, your response should do more than merely supply answers. You'll also want to promote your organization and products. Often, companies have particular products and services they want to spotlight. Thus, when a customer writes about one product, provide helpful information that satisfies the inquiry, but consider introducing another product as well. Be sure to present the promotional material with attention to the "you" view and to reader benefits (*You can use our standardized tests to free you from time-consuming employment screening*). You'll learn more about special techniques for developing sales and persuasive messages in Chapter 9.

In concluding, make sure you are cordial and personal. Refer to the information provided or to its use. If further action is required, describe the procedure and help the reader with specifics (*The Ministry of Consumer Affairs publishes a number of helpful booklets. Its Web address is ...*).

Illustrating Reply Letters. In replying to a customer's request for information, the writer in Figure 7.5 begins with a subject line that immediately identifies the topic and refers to previous correspondence. She uses the first sentence to present the most important information. Then she itemizes her list of responses to the customer's questions. If she had written these responses in paragraph form, they would have been less emphatic and more difficult to read. She goes on to describe and promote the product, being careful to show how it would benefit the customer. And she concludes by referring specifically to pages in an enclosed pamphlet and providing a number for the customer's response.

A direct reply letter, shown in Figure 7.6, responds to a request from a teacher and Raptors fan. The opening announces the letter's purpose immediately and also establishes rapport with the reader by thanking him for his support in the previous season. The body of the letter includes a bulleted list and an explanation of the information being sent. Notice how the writer invites future business by offering an "exclusive advanced booking opportunity." The cordial, personalized closing concludes a direct reply letter that is sure to build goodwill and promote future business while delivering the information sought.

In mixed-news messages the good news should precede the bad.

Treating Mixed Messages. The direct pattern is also appropriate for messages that are mostly good news but may have some negative elements. For example, a return policy has time limits; an airfare may contain holiday restrictions; a speaker can come but not at the time requested; an appliance can be repaired but not replaced. When the message is mixed, emphasize the good news by presenting it first (*Yes, I would be delighted to address your marketing class on the topic of ...*). Then, explain why a problem exists (*My schedule for the week of October 10 takes me to Calgary and Edmonton, where I am ...*). Present the bad news in the middle (*Although I cannot meet with your class at that time, perhaps we can schedule a date during the week of ...*). End the message cordially by returning to the good news (*Thanks for the invitation. I'm looking forward to arranging a date in October when I can talk with your students about careers in marketing*).

Your goal is to present the negative news clearly without letting it become the focus of the message. Thus, you want to spend more time talking about the good

FIGURE 7.5 **Customer Reply Letter**

1 PREWRITING

Analyze: The purpose of this letter is to provide helpful information and to promote company products.

Anticipate: The reader is the intelligent owner of a small business who needs help with personnel administration.

Adapt: Because the reader requested this data, she will be receptive. Use the direct pattern.

2 WRITING

Research: Gather facts to answer the business owner's questions. Consult brochures and pamphlets.

Organize: Prepare a scratch outline. Plan for a fast, direct opening. Use bulleted answers to the business owner's three questions.

Compose: Write the first draft on a computer. Strive for short sentences and paragraphs.

3 REVISING

Revise: Eliminate jargon and wordiness. Look for ways to explain how the product fits the reader's needs. Revise for "you" view.

Proofread: Double-check the form of numbers (*July 15, page 6, 8 to 5 PST*).

Evaluate: Does this letter answer the customer's questions and encourage an order?

Office Headquarters, Inc.
777 Raymer Road
Kelowna, BC V1W 1H7
www.OHQ.ca

July 15, 2004

Mr. Jeffrey M. White
White-Rather Enterprises
220 Telford Court
Leduc, AB T9E 5M6

Dear Mr. White:

SUBJECT: YOUR JULY 12 INQUIRY ABOUT PERSONNEL SOFTWARE — **Identifies previous correspondence and subject**

Puts most important information first — Yes, we do offer personnel record-keeping software specially designed for small businesses like yours. Here are answers to your three questions about this software:

Lists answers to sender's questions in order asked / **Emphasizes "you" view**

1. Our Personnel Manager software provides standard employee forms so that you are always in compliance with current government regulations.

2. You receive an interviewer's guide for structured employee interviews, as well as a scripted format for checking references by telephone.

3. Yes, you can update your employees' records easily without the need for additional software, hardware, or training.

This software was specially designed to provide you with expert forms for interviewing, verifying references, recording attendance, evaluating performance, and tracking the status of your employees. We even provide you with step-by-step instructions and suggested procedures. You can treat your employees as if you had a professional human resources specialist on your staff. — **Links sales promotion to reader benefits**

Helps reader find information by citing pages — On page 6 of the enclosed pamphlet you can read about our Personnel Manager software. To receive a preview copy or to ask questions about its use, just call 1-800-354-5500. Our specialists are eager to help you weekdays from 8 to 5 PST. If you prefer, visit our Web site to receive more information or to place an order. — **Makes it easy to respond**

Sincerely,

Amy Villanueva

Amy Villanueva
Senior Marketing Representative

Enclosure

FIGURE 7.6 **Direct Reply from Toronto Raptors**

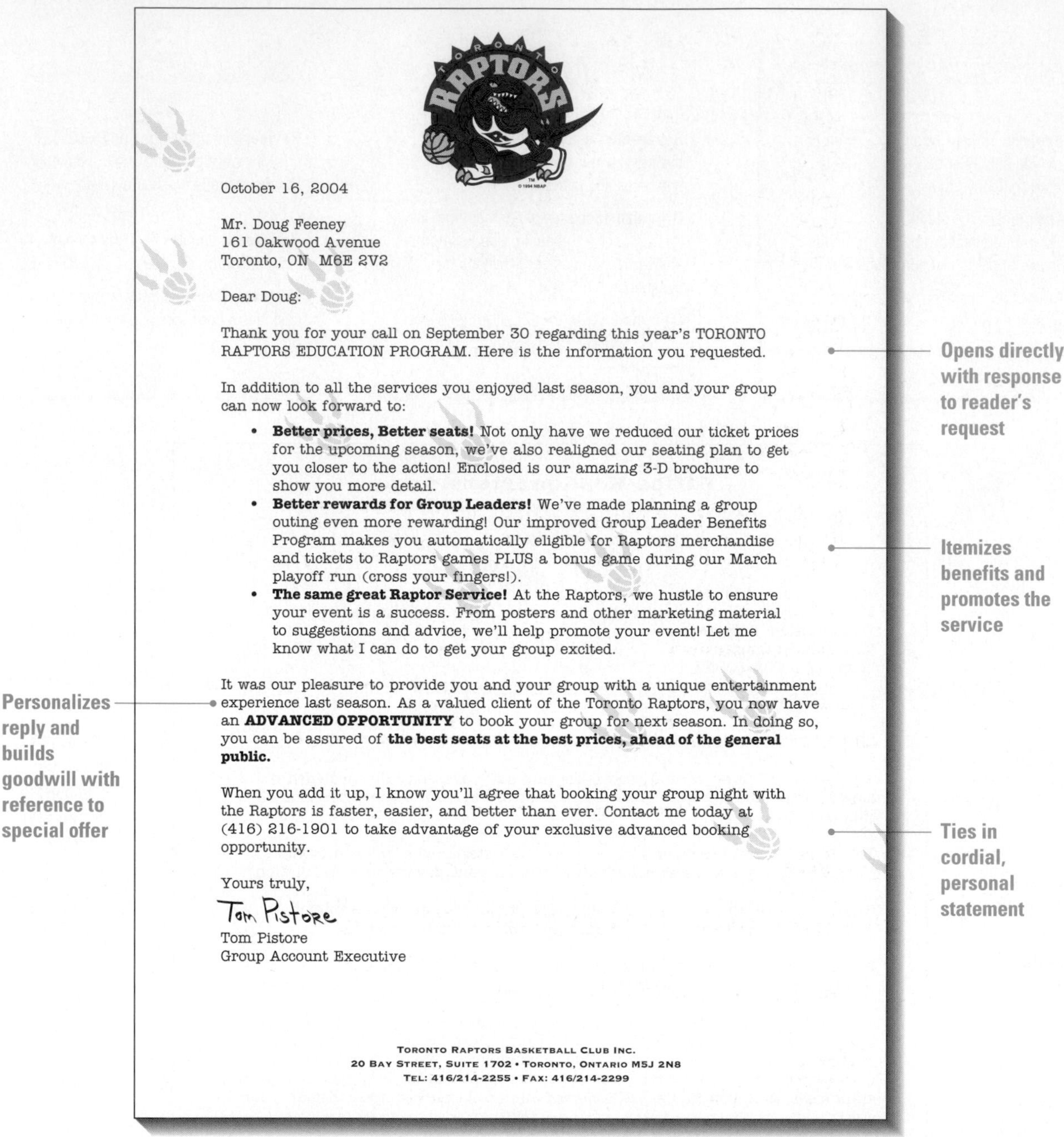

news. And by placing the bad news in the middle of the letter, you de-emphasize it. You'll learn other techniques for presenting bad news in Chapter 10.

TORONTO RAPTORS
October 16, 2004

Mr. Doug Feeney
161 Oakwood Avenue
Toronto, ON M6E 2V2

Dear Doug:

Thank you for your call on September 30 regarding this year's TORONTO RAPTORS EDUCATION PROGRAM. Here is the information you requested.

In addition to all the services you enjoyed last season, you and your group can now look forward to:

- **Better prices, Better seats!** Not only have we reduced our ticket prices for the upcoming season, we've also realigned our seating plan to get you closer to the action! Enclosed is our amazing 3-D brochure to show you more detail.
- **Better rewards for Group Leaders!** We've made planning a group outing even more rewarding! Our improved Group Leader Benefits Program makes you automatically eligible for Raptors merchandise and tickets to Raptors games PLUS a bonus game during our March playoff run (cross your fingers!).
- **The same great Raptor Service!** At the Raptors, we hustle to ensure your event is a success. From posters and other marketing material to suggestions and advice, we'll help promote your event! Let me know what I can do to get your group excited.

It was our pleasure to provide you and your group with a unique entertainment experience last season. As a valued client of the Toronto Raptors, you now have an **ADVANCED OPPORTUNITY** to book your group for next season. In doing so, you can be assured of **the best seats at the best prices, ahead of the general public.**

When you add it up, I know you'll agree that booking your group night with the Raptors is faster, easier, and better than ever. Contact me today at (416) 216-1901 to take advantage of your exclusive advanced booking opportunity.

Yours truly,

Tom Pistore

Tom Pistore
Group Account Executive

TORONTO RAPTORS BASKETBALL CLUB INC.
20 BAY STREET, SUITE 1702 • TORONTO, ONTARIO M5J 2N8
TEL: 416/214-2255 • FAX: 416/214-2299
Opens directly with response to reader's request
Itemizes benefits and promotes the service
Personalizes reply and builds goodwill with reference to special offer
Ties in cordial, personal statement

6 Writing Letters of Recommendation

Letters of recommendation may be written to nominate people for awards and for membership in organizations. More frequently, though, they are written to evaluate present or former employees. The central concern in these messages is honesty. Thus, we should avoid exaggerating or distorting a candidate's qualifications to cover up weaknesses or to destroy the person's chances. Ethically and legally, we have a duty to the candidate as well as to other employers to describe that person truthfully and objectively. We don't, however, have to endorse everyone who asks. Since recommendations are generally voluntary, we can—and should—resist writing letters for individuals we can't truthfully support. Ask these people to find other recommenders who know them better.

Well-written recommendations do help match candidates with jobs. Hiring companies learn more about a candidate's skills and potential. As a result, they are able to place a candidate properly. Therefore, you should learn to write such letters because you will surely be expected to do so in your future career.

Letters of recommendation present honest, objective evaluations of individuals and help match candidates to jobs.

Opening. Begin with the name of the candidate and the position sought, if it is known. State that your remarks are confidential, and suggest that you are writing at the request of the applicant. Describe your relationship with the candidate, as shown here:

> Ms. Cindy Robertson, whom your organization is considering for the position of media trainer, requested that I submit confidential information on her behalf. Ms. Robertson worked under my supervision for the past two years in our Video Training Centre.

The opening establishes the reason for writing and the relationship of the writer.

Letters that recommend individuals for awards may open with more supportive statements, such as *I'm very pleased to nominate Robert Walsh for the Employee-of-the-Month award. For the past sixteen months, Mr. Walsh served as staff accountant in my division. During that time he distinguished himself by ...*

Body. Describe the applicant's job performance and potential. Employers are particularly interested in such traits as communication skills, organizational skills, people skills, ability to work within a team, ability to work independently, honesty, dependability, ambition, loyalty, and initiative. In describing these traits, be sure to back them up with evidence. One of the biggest weaknesses in letters of recommendation is that writers tend to make global, nonspecific statements[6] (*He was careful and accurate* versus *He completed eight financial statements monthly with about 99-percent accuracy*). Employers prefer definite, task-related descriptions:

The body of a letter of recommendation should describe the candidate's job performance and potential in specific terms.

> As a training development specialist, Ms. Robertson demonstrated superior organizational and interpersonal skills. She started as a Specialist I, writing scripts for interactive video modules. After six months she was promoted to team leader. In that role she supervised five employees who wrote, produced, evaluated, revised, and installed 14 computer/videodisc training courses over a period of eighteen months.

A good recommendation describes general qualities ("organizational and interpersonal skills") backed up by specific evidence that illustrates those qualities.

Be especially careful to support any negative comments with verification (not *He was slower than other customer service reps* but *He answered 25 calls an hour, while most service reps average 40 calls an hour*). In reporting deficiencies, be sure to describe behaviour (*Her last two reports were late and had to be rewritten by her supervisor*) rather than evaluate it (*She is unreliable and her reports are careless*).

Conclusion. In the final paragraph, offer an overall evaluation. Tell how you would rank this person in relation to others in similar positions. Many managers add a statement indicating whether they would rehire the applicant. If you are strongly supportive, summarize the candidate's best qualities. In the closing you might also offer to answer questions by telephone. Such a statement, though, could suggest that the candidate has weak skills and that you will make damaging statements orally but not in print. Here's how our sample letter might close:

The closing of a recommendation presents an overall ranking and may provide an offer to supply more information by telephone.

Ms. Robertson is one of the most productive employees I have supervised. I would rank her in the top 10 percent of all the media specialists with whom I have worked. Were she to return to Regina, we would be pleased to rehire her. If you need additional information, call me at (306) 440-3019.

General letters of recommendation, written when the candidate has no specific position in mind, often begin with the salutation TO PROSPECTIVE EMPLOYERS. More specific recommendations, to support applications to known positions, address an individual. When the addressee's name is unknown, consider using the simplified letter format, shown in Figure 7.7, which avoids a salutation.

The letter shown in Figure 7.7 illustrates a complete employment letter of recommendation and shows a summary of writing tips. After naming the applicant and the position sought, the letter describes the applicant's present duties. Instead of merely naming positive qualities (*he is personable, possesses superior people skills, works well with a team, is creative,* and *shows initiative*), these attributes are demonstrated with specific examples and details.

Granting Claims and Making Adjustments

7

Businesses generally respond favourably to claims because of legal constraints and the desire to maintain customer goodwill.

Even the best-run and best-loved businesses occasionally receive claims or complaints from consumers. Most businesses grant claims and make adjustments promptly—they replace merchandise, refund money, extend discounts, send coupons, and repair goods. Businesses make favourable adjustments to legitimate claims for two reasons. First, consumers are protected by both federal and provincial legislation[7] for recovery of damages. Second, and more obviously, most organizations genuinely want to satisfy their customers and retain their business.

Customer goodwill and retention have an important effect on profits. Studies have shown that the most profitable companies have the lowest rate of both employee and customer turnover. When customers are unhappy, they don't return. A staggering 91 percent of disgruntled customers swear they will never do business again with a company that does not resolve their complaint.[8] What's worse, today's unhappy customers are wired; they have the Web on which to broadcast their protests to the world. In fact, Web pages launched by angry consumers or former employees have taken aim at a wide range of companies including BMW, Apple Computer, and Burger King.[9] Small wonder that businesses are increasingly concerned with improving customer service and listening to what customers are saying.

Wise organizations value complaints not only as a chance to retain customers but also as a significant source of feedback. Comments from complainers often provide more useful information than expensive customer surveys and focus groups.

Favourable responses to customer claims follow the *direct* pattern; unfavourable responses follow the *indirect* pattern.

In responding to customer claims, you must first decide whether to grant the claim. Unless the claim is obviously fraudulent or represents an excessive sum, you'll probably grant it. When you say yes, your adjustment letter will be good news to the reader, so you'll want to use the direct pattern. When your response is no, the indirect pattern might be more appropriate. Chapter 10 discusses the indirect pattern for conveying negative news.

Adjustment letters seek to right wrongs, regain customer confidence, and promote further business.

You'll have three goals in adjustment letters:

- Rectifying the wrong, if one exists
- Regaining the confidence of the customer
- Promoting further business

FIGURE 7.7 **Employment Recommendation Letter**

Tips for Writing Letters of Recommendation

- Respond only to written requests.
- Identify the purpose and confidentiality of the message.
- Establish your relationship with the applicant.
- Describe the length of employment and job duties, if relevant.
- Provide specific examples of the applicant's professional and personal skills.
- Avoid vague and ambiguous statements.
- Compare the applicant with others in his or her field.
- Offer an overall rating of the applicant.
- Stick to the truth.
- Summarize the significant attributes of the applicant.
- Draw a conclusion regarding the recommendation.

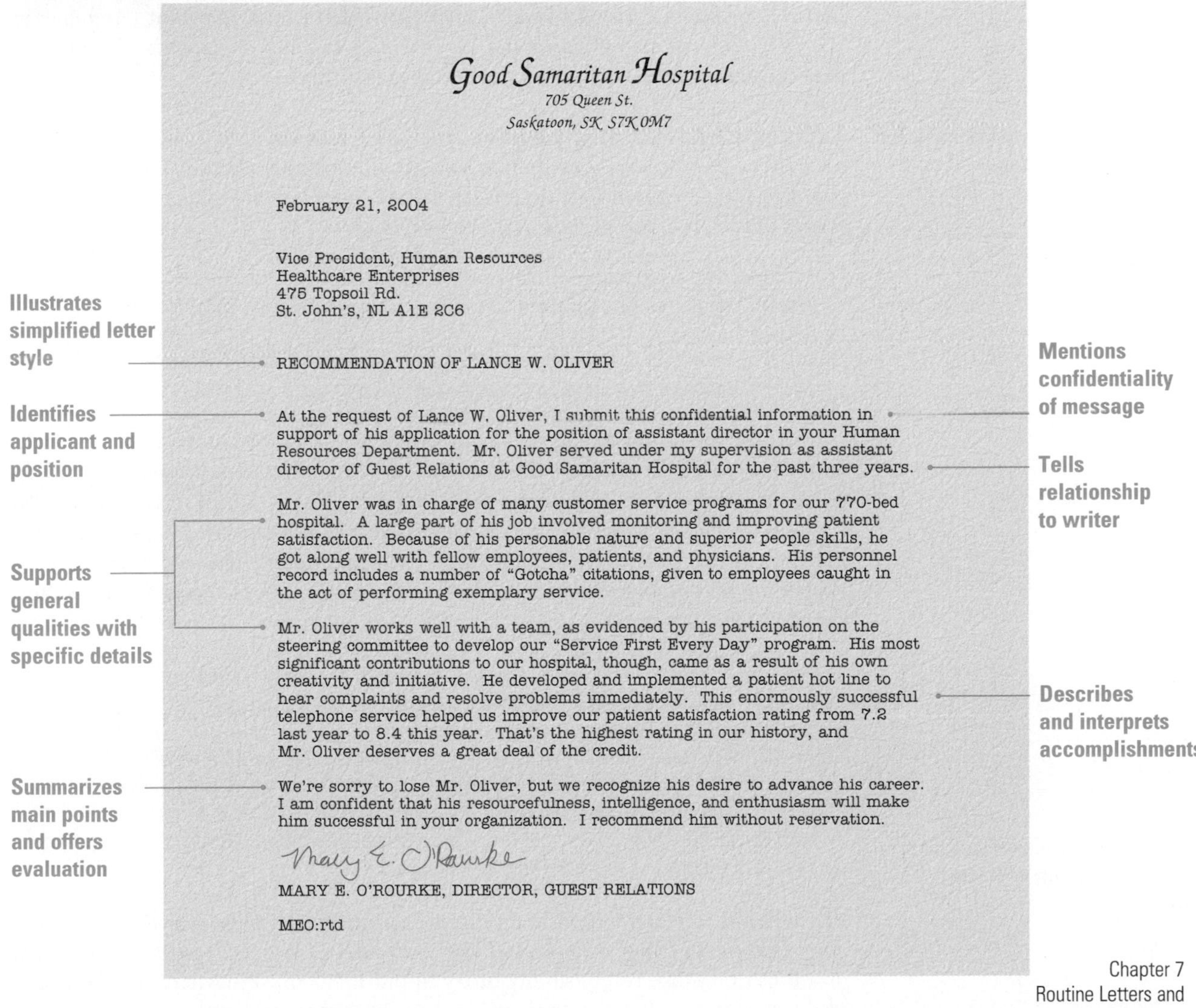

Good Samaritan Hospital
705 Queen St.
Saskatoon, SK S7K 0M7

February 21, 2004

Vice President, Human Resources
Healthcare Enterprises
475 Topsoil Rd.
St. John's, NL A1E 2C6

RECOMMENDATION OF LANCE W. OLIVER

At the request of Lance W. Oliver, I submit this confidential information in support of his application for the position of assistant director in your Human Resources Department. Mr. Oliver served under my supervision as assistant director of Guest Relations at Good Samaritan Hospital for the past three years.

Mr. Oliver was in charge of many customer service programs for our 770-bed hospital. A large part of his job involved monitoring and improving patient satisfaction. Because of his personable nature and superior people skills, he got along well with fellow employees, patients, and physicians. His personnel record includes a number of "Gotcha" citations, given to employees caught in the act of performing exemplary service.

Mr. Oliver works well with a team, as evidenced by his participation on the steering committee to develop our "Service First Every Day" program. His most significant contributions to our hospital, though, came as a result of his own creativity and initiative. He developed and implemented a patient hot line to hear complaints and resolve problems immediately. This enormously successful telephone service helped us improve our patient satisfaction rating from 7.2 last year to 8.4 this year. That's the highest rating in our history, and Mr. Oliver deserves a great deal of the credit.

We're sorry to lose Mr. Oliver, but we recognize his desire to advance his career. I am confident that his resourcefulness, intelligence, and enthusiasm will make him successful in your organization. I recommend him without reservation.

Mary E. O'Rourke

MARY E. O'ROURKE, DIRECTOR, GUEST RELATIONS

MEO:rtd

Illustrates simplified letter style
Identifies applicant and position
Supports general qualities with specific details
Summarizes main points and offers evaluation
Mentions confidentiality of message
Tells relationship to writer
Describes and interprets accomplishments

Opening sentences tell the good news quickly.

Opening With the Good News. The opening of a positive adjustment letter should approve the customer's claim immediately. Notice how quickly the following openers announce the good news:

> You're right! We agree that the warranty on your Diamond Standard Model UC600 dishwasher should be extended for six months.
>
> The enclosed $250 refund cheque demonstrates our desire to satisfy our customers and earn their confidence.

Occasionally, customers merely want to lodge a complaint and know that something is being done about it. Here's the opening from a bank responding to such a complaint:

> We agree with you completely. Some of our customers have recently spent too much time "on hold" while waiting to speak to a customer service representative. These delays are unacceptable, and we are taking strong measures to eliminate them.

In making an adjustment, avoid sounding resentful or grudging. Once you decide to grant a claim, do so willingly. Remember that a primary goal in adjustments is retaining customer loyalty. Statements that sound reluctant (*Although we generally refuse to extend warranties, we're willing to make an exception in this case*) may cause greater dissatisfaction than no response at all.

Explain what caused the problem and the measures taken to avoid future recurrence.

Explaining the Reasons. In the body of an adjustment letter, your goal is to win back the confidence of the customer. You can do this by explaining what caused the problem (if you know) or by describing the measures you are taking to avoid recurrences of the problem, such as in the following:

> In preparing our products, we take special care to see that they are wholesome and free of foreign matter. Approved spraying procedures in the field control insects when necessary during the growing season. Our processing plants use screens, air curtains, ultraviolet lights, and other devices to exclude insects. Moreover, we inspect and clean every product to ensure that insects are not present.

Notice that this explanation does not admit error. Many companies sidestep the issue of responsibility because they feel that such an admission damages their credibility or might even encourage legal action. Others admit errors indirectly (*Oversights may sometimes occur*) or even directly (*Once in a while a product that is less than perfect goes out*). The major focus of attention, however, should be on explaining how you are working to prevent the recurrence of the problem, as illustrated in the following:

> Waiting "on hold" is as unacceptable to us as it is to you. This delay was brought about when we installed a new automated system. Unfortunately, it took longer than we expected to implement the system and to train our people in their new roles. We are now taking strong measures to eliminate the problem. We have made a significant investment in new technology that will free our customer representatives from routine calls so that they can help you with those banking needs that require personal attention. We are also rerouting calls and modifying the way they are handled.

Explain what went wrong without admitting liability or making excuses.

When an explanation poses no threat of admitting liability, provide details. But don't make your explanation sound like an excuse. Customers resent it when organizations don't take responsibility or try to put the blame elsewhere. The tone of a response is extremely important, and customers expect sincerity.

Should You Apologize? Another sticky issue is whether to apologize. Studies of adjustment letters received by consumers show that a majority do contain apologies, either in the opening or in the closing.[10] Many business writing experts, however, advise against apologies, contending that they are counterproductive and merely remind the customer of unpleasantness related to the claim. However, if it seems natural to you to apologize, do so. People like to hear apologies. It raises their self-esteem and shows the humility of the writer.[11] Don't, however, fall back on the familiar phrase, "I'm sorry for any inconvenience we may have caused." It sounds mechanical and insincere. Instead, try something like this: *We understand the frustration our delay has caused you. We're sorry you didn't receive better service,* or *You're right to be disappointed.* If you feel that an apology is appropriate, do it early and briefly. Remember that the primary focus of your letter is on (1) how you are complying with the request, (2) how the problem occurred, and (3) how you are working to prevent its recurrence.

Apologize if it seems natural and appropriate.

Focus on complying with request, explaining reasons, and preventing recurrence.

The language of adjustment letters must be particularly sensitive, since customers are already upset. Here are some don'ts:

- Don't use negative words (*trouble, regret, misunderstanding, fault, error, inconvenience, you claim*).
- Don't blame customers—even when they may be at fault.
- Don't blame individuals or departments within your organization; it's unprofessional.
- Don't make unrealistic promises; you can't guarantee that the situation will never recur.

To regain the confidence of your reader, consider including resale information. Describe a product's features and any special applications that might appeal to the reader. Promote a new product if it seems appropriate.

Closing an Adjustment Letter. To close an adjustment letter, assume that the problem has been resolved and that future business will continue. You might express appreciation that the reader wrote, extend thanks for past business, refer to your desire to be of service, or mention a new product. Here are some effective adjustment letter closings for various purposes:

Close with appreciation, thanks for past business, and expression of desire to be of service.

> You were most helpful in informing us of this situation and permitting us to correct it. We appreciate your thoughtfulness in writing to us.
>
> Thanks for writing. Your satisfaction is important to us. We hope that this refund cheque convinces you that service to our customers is our number one priority. Our goal is to earn your confidence and continue to justify that confidence with quality products and excellent service.

The adjustment letter in Figure 7.8 offers to replace dead rose bushes. It's very possible that grower error caused the plants to die, yet the letter doesn't blame the customer. Notice, too, how resale information and sales promotion material are introduced without seeming pushy. Most important, the tone of the letter suggests that the company is in the customer's corner and wants to do what is right.

Although the direct pattern works for many requests and replies, it obviously won't work for every situation. With more practice and experience, you'll be able to alter the pattern and apply the writing process to other communication problems. The following checklist summarizes the process of writing direct replies.

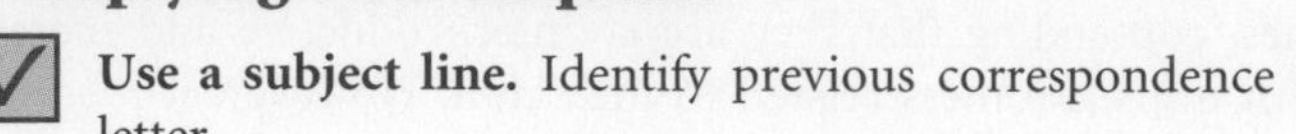

Checklist for Writing Direct Replies

Complying With Requests

- ✓ **Use a subject line.** Identify previous correspondence and the topic of this letter.

- ✓ **Open directly.** In the first sentence deliver the information the reader wants (*Yes, I can meet with your class* or *Here is the information you requested*). If the message is mixed, present the best news first.

- ✓ **Provide explanations and additional information in the body.** Arrange this information logically, perhaps using a list, headings, or columns. For prospective customers, build your company image and promote your products.

- ✓ **End with a cordial, personalized statement.** If further action is required, tell the reader how to proceed and give helpful details.

Writing Letters of Recommendation

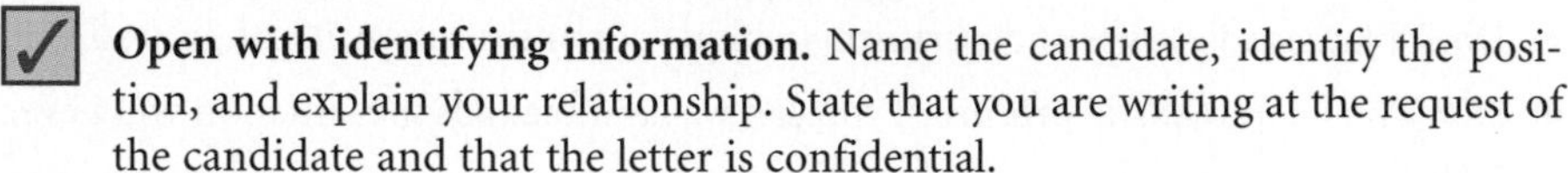

- ✓ **Open with identifying information.** Name the candidate, identify the position, and explain your relationship. State that you are writing at the request of the candidate and that the letter is confidential.

- ✓ **Add supporting statements in the body.** Describe the applicant's present duties, job performance, skills, and potential. Back up general qualities with specific evidence. Verify any negative statements.

- ✓ **Close with an overall ranking of the candidate.** (*Of all the people I have known in this position, Jim ranks ...*). Offer to supply more information by telephone.

Granting Claims and Adjustments

- ✓ **Open with approval.** Comply with the customer's claim immediately. Avoid sounding grudging or reluctant.

- ✓ **Win back the customer's confidence in the body.** Explain the cause of the problem or describe your ongoing efforts to avoid such difficulties. Focus on your efforts to satisfy customers. If you apologize, do so early and briefly. Avoid negative words, accusations, and unrealistic promises. Consider including resale and sales promotion information.

- ✓ **Close positively.** Express appreciation to the customer for writing, extend thanks for past business, anticipate continued patronage, refer to your desire to be of service, and/or mention a new product if it seems appropriate.

FIGURE 7.8 **Adjustment Letter**

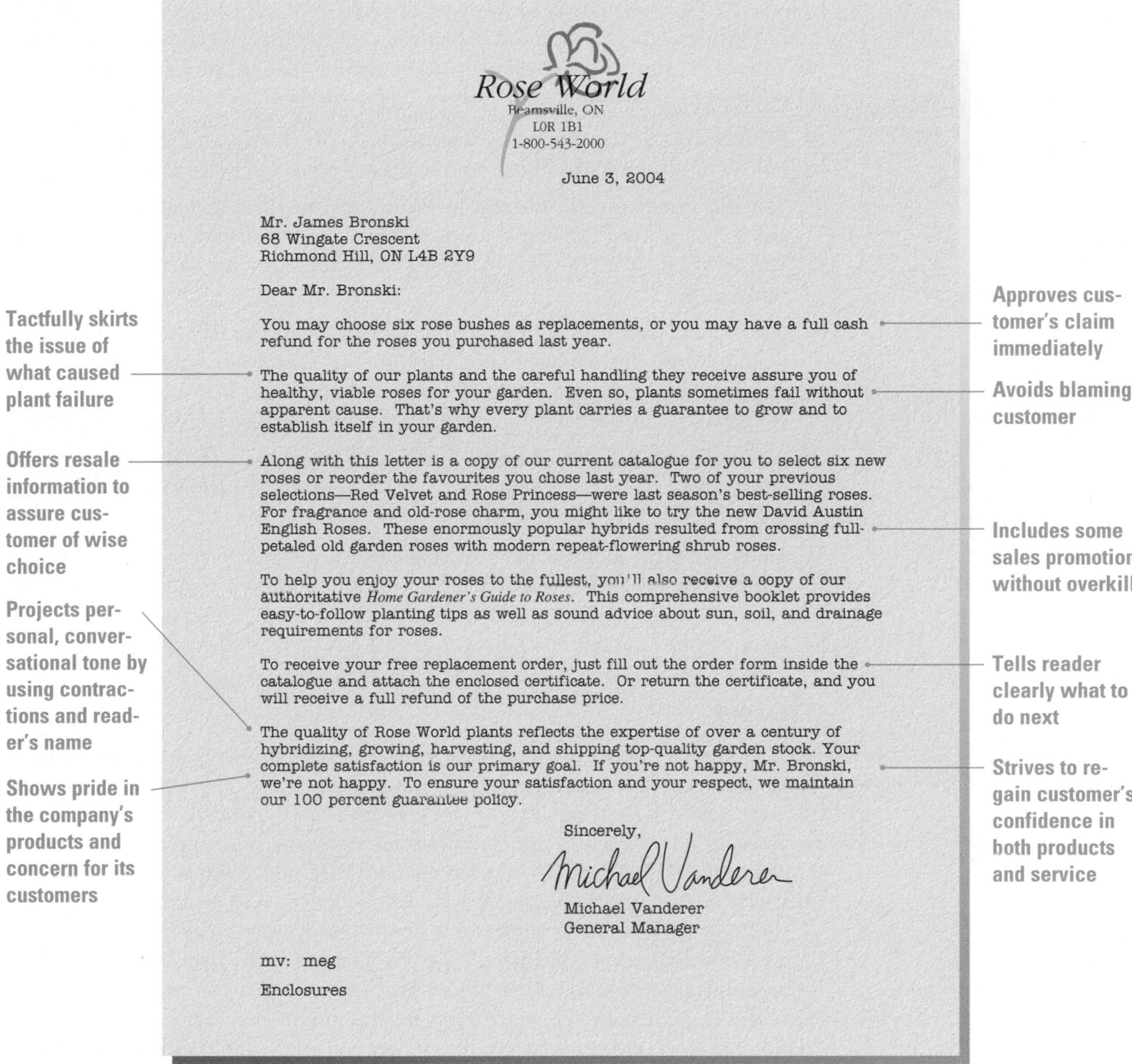

Rose World
Beamsville, ON
L0R 1B1
1-800-543-2000

June 3, 2004

Mr. James Bronski
68 Wingate Crescent
Richmond Hill, ON L4B 2Y9

Dear Mr. Bronski:

You may choose six rose bushes as replacements, or you may have a full cash refund for the roses you purchased last year.

The quality of our plants and the careful handling they receive assure you of healthy, viable roses for your garden. Even so, plants sometimes fail without apparent cause. That's why every plant carries a guarantee to grow and to establish itself in your garden.

Along with this letter is a copy of our current catalogue for you to select six new roses or reorder the favourites you chose last year. Two of your previous selections—Red Velvet and Rose Princess—were last season's best-selling roses. For fragrance and old-rose charm, you might like to try the new David Austin English Roses. These enormously popular hybrids resulted from crossing full-petaled old garden roses with modern repeat-flowering shrub roses.

To help you enjoy your roses to the fullest, you'll also receive a copy of our authoritative *Home Gardener's Guide to Roses*. This comprehensive booklet provides easy-to-follow planting tips as well as sound advice about sun, soil, and drainage requirements for roses.

To receive your free replacement order, just fill out the order form inside the catalogue and attach the enclosed certificate. Or return the certificate, and you will receive a full refund of the purchase price.

The quality of Rose World plants reflects the expertise of over a century of hybridizing, growing, harvesting, and shipping top-quality garden stock. Your complete satisfaction is our primary goal. If you're not happy, Mr. Bronski, we're not happy. To ensure your satisfaction and your respect, we maintain our 100 percent guarantee policy.

Sincerely,

Michael Vanderer

Michael Vanderer
General Manager

mv: meg

Enclosures

Tactfully skirts the issue of what caused plant failure
Offers resale information to assure customer of wise choice
Projects personal, conversational tone by using contractions and reader's name
Shows pride in the company's products and concern for its customers
Approves customer's claim immediately
Avoids blaming customer
Includes some sales promotion without overkill
Tells reader clearly what to do next
Strives to regain customer's confidence in both products and service

Writing Winning Goodwill Messages

8

Goodwill messages, which include thanks, recognition, and sympathy, seem to intimidate many communicators. Finding the right words to express feelings is sometimes more difficult than writing ordinary business documents. Writers tend to procrastinate when it comes to goodwill messages, or else they send a ready-made card or pick up the telephone. Remember, though, that the personal sentiments of the sender are always more expressive and more meaningful to readers than are printed cards or oral messages. Taking the time to write gives more importance to our well-wishing. Notes also provide a record that can be reread, savoured, and treasured.

In expressing thanks, recognition, or sympathy, you should always do so promptly. These messages are easier to write when the situation is fresh in your mind. They also mean more to the recipient. And don't forget that a prompt thank-you note carries the hidden message that you care and that you consider the event to be important. The best goodwill messages—whether thanks, congratulations, praise, or sympathy—concentrate on the five Ss. These goodwill messages are

- **Selfless.** Be sure to focus the message solely on the receiver, not the sender. Don't talk about yourself; avoid such comments as *I remember when I ...*
- **Specific.** Personalize the message by mentioning specific incidents or characteristics of the receiver. Telling a colleague *Great speech* is much less effective than *Great story about McDonald's marketing in Moscow.* Take care to verify names and other facts.
- **Sincere.** Let your words show genuine feelings. Rehearse in your mind how you would express the message orally. Then use that conversational language in your writing. Avoid pretentious, formal, or flowery language (*It gives me great pleasure to extend felicitations on the occasion of your firm's 20th anniversary*).
- **Spontaneous.** Keep the message fresh and enthusiastic. Avoid canned phrases (*Congratulations on your promotion, Good luck in the future*). Strive for directness and naturalness, not creative brilliance.
- **Short.** Although goodwill messages can be as long as needed, try to accomplish your purpose in only a few sentences. What's most important is remembering an individual. Such caring does not require documentation or wordiness. Individuals and business organizations often use special note cards or stationery for brief messages.

Thanks

When someone has done you a favour or when an action merits praise, you need to extend thanks or show appreciation. Letters of appreciation may be written to customers for their orders, to hosts and hostesses for their hospitality, to individuals for kindnesses performed, and especially to customers who complain. After all, complainers are actually providing you with "free consulting reports from the field." Complainers who feel that they were listened to often become the greatest promoters of an organization.[12]

Because the receiver will be pleased to hear from you, you can open directly with the purpose of your message. The letter in Figure 7.9 thanks a speaker who addressed a group of marketing professionals. Although such thank-you notes can be quite short, this one is a little longer because the writer wants to lend importance to the receiver's efforts. Notice that every sentence relates to the receiver and offers enthusiastic praise. And, by using the receiver's name along with contractions and positive words, the writer makes the letter sound warm and conversational.

Written notes that show appreciation and express thanks are significant to their receivers. In expressing thanks, you generally write a short note on special notepaper or heavy card stock. The following messages provide models for expressing thanks for a gift, for a favour, and for hospitality.

To Express Thanks for a Gift

Thanks, Laura, to you and the other members of the department for honouring me with the elegant Waterford crystal vase at the party celebrating my twentieth anniversary with the company.

The height and shape of the vase are perfect to hold roses and other bouquets from my garden. Each time I fill it, I'll remember your thoughtfulness in choosing this lovely gift for me.

FIGURE 7.9 **Thank-You Letter for a Favour**

1 PREWRITING

Analyze: The purpose is to express appreciation to a business executive for presenting a talk before professionals.

Anticipate: The reader will be more interested in personalized comments than in general statements showing gratitude.

Adapt: Because the reader will be pleased, use the direct pattern.

2 WRITING

Research: Consult notes taken during the talk.

Organize: Open directly by giving the reason for writing. Express enthusiastic and sincere thanks. In the body provide specifics. Refer to facts and highlights in the talk. Supply sufficient detail to support your sincere compliments. Conclude with appreciation. Be warm and friendly.

Compose: Write the first draft.

3 REVISING

Revise: Revise for tone and warmth. Use the reader's name. Include concrete detail but do it concisely. Avoid sounding gushy or phony.

Proofread: Check the spelling of the receiver's name; verify facts. Check the spelling of *gratitude, patience, advice, persistence,* and *grateful.*

Evaluate: Does this letter convey sincere thanks?

Hamilton–Wentworth Chapter
North American Marketing Association
484 Mountain Park Drive
Hamilton, ON L8V 4X2

March 20, 2004

Mr. Elliott P. Tarkanian
Marketing Manager
Toys "R" Us, Inc.
2777 Langstaff Avenue
Thornhill, ON L3T 3M8

Dear Elliott:

You have our sincere gratitude for providing the Hamilton–Wentworth chapter of the NAMA with one of the best presentations our group has ever heard. — **Tells purpose and delivers praise**

Your description of the battle Toys "R" Us waged to begin marketing products in Japan was a genuine eye-opener for many of us. Nine years of preparation establishing connections and securing permissions seems an eternity, but obviously such persistence and patience pay off. We now understand better the need to learn local customs and nurture relationships when dealing in Japan. — **Personalizes the message by using specifics rather than generalities**

In addition to your good advice, we particularly enjoyed your sense of humour and jokes—as you must have recognized from the uproarious laughter. What a great routine you do on faulty translations! — **Spotlights the reader's talents**

We're grateful, Elliott, for the entertaining and instructive evening you provided our marketing professionals. Thanks! — **Concludes with compliments and thanks**

Cordially,

Timothy W. Ellison

Timothy W. Ellison
Program Chair, NAMA

TWE:grw

To Send Thanks for a Favour
I sincerely appreciate your filling in for me last week when I was too ill to attend the planning committee meeting for the spring exhibition.

Without your participation much of my preparatory work would have been lost. It's comforting to know that competent and generous individuals like you are part of our team, Mark. Moreover, it's my very good fortune to be able to count you as a friend. I'm grateful to you.

To Extend Thanks for Hospitality
Jeffrey and I want you to know how much we enjoyed the dinner party for our department that you hosted Saturday evening. Your charming home and warm hospitality, along with the lovely dinner and sinfully delicious chocolate dessert, combined to create a truly memorable evening.

Most of all, though, we appreciate your kindness in cultivating togetherness in our department. Thanks, Jennifer, for being such a special person.

Response

Take the time to respond to any goodwill message you may receive.

Should you respond when you receive a congratulatory note or a written pat on the back? By all means! These messages are attempts to connect personally; they are efforts to reach out, to form professional and/or personal bonds. Failing to respond to notes of congratulations and most other goodwill messages is like failing to say "You're welcome" when someone says "Thank you." Responding to such messages is simply the right thing to do. Do avoid, though, minimizing your achievements with comments that suggest you don't really deserve the praise or that the sender is exaggerating your good qualities.

To Answer a Congratulatory Note
Thanks for your kind words regarding my award, and thanks, too, for sending me the newspaper clipping. I truly appreciate your thoughtfulness and best wishes.

To Respond to a Pat on the Back
Your note about my work made me feel good. I'm grateful for your thoughtfulness.

Sympathy

Sympathy notes should refer to the misfortune sensitively and offer assistance.

Most of us can bear misfortune and grief more easily when we know that others care. Notes expressing sympathy, though, are probably more difficult to write than any other kind of message. Commercial "In sympathy" cards make the task easier—but they are far less meaningful. Grieving friends want to know what you think—not what professional card writers think. To help you get started, you can always glance through cards expressing sympathy. They will supply ideas about the kinds of thoughts you might wish to convey in your own words. In writing a sympathy note, (1) refer to the death or misfortune sensitively, using words that show you understand what a crushing blow it is; (2) in the case of a death, praise the deceased in a personal way; (3) offer assistance without going into excessive detail; and (4) end on a reassuring, forward-looking note. Sympathy messages may be typed, although handwriting seems more personal. In either case, use notepaper or personal stationery.

To Express Condolences

Mentions the loss tactfully and recognizes good qualities of the deceased

We are deeply saddened, Gayle, to learn of the death of your husband. Bill's kind nature and friendly spirit endeared him to all who knew him. He will be missed.

Although words seem empty in expressing our grief, we want you to know that your friends at QuadCom extend their profound sympathy to you. If we may help you or lighten your load in any way, you have but to call.

Assures receiver of your concern. Offers assistance

We know that the treasured memories of your many happy years together, along with the support of your family and many friends, will provide strength and comfort in the months ahead.

Concludes on positive, reassuring note

Checklist for Writing Goodwill Messages

General Guidelines: The Five Ss

- ✓ **Be selfless.** Discuss the receiver, not the sender.
- ✓ **Be specific.** Instead of generic statements (*You did a good job*), include special details (*Your marketing strategy to target key customers proved to be outstanding*).
- ✓ **Be sincere.** Show your honest feelings with conversational, unpretentious language (*We're all very proud of your award*).
- ✓ **Be spontaneous.** Strive to make the message natural, fresh, and direct. Avoid canned phrases (*If I may be of service, please do not hesitate*...).
- ✓ **Keep the message short.** Remember that, although they may be as long as needed, most goodwill messages are fairly short.

Giving Thanks

- ✓ **Cover three points in gift thank-you cards.** (1) Identify the gift, (2) tell why you appreciate it, and (3) explain how you will use it.
- ✓ **Be sincere in sending thanks for a favour.** Tell what the favour means to you. Avoid superlatives and gushiness. Maintain credibility with sincere, simple statements.
- ✓ **Offer praise in expressing thanks for hospitality.** Compliment, as appropriate, the (1) fine food, (2) charming surroundings, (3) warm hospitality, (4) excellent host and hostess, and (5) good company.

Answering Congratulatory Messages

- ✓ **Respond to congratulations.** Send a brief note expressing your appreciation. Tell how good the message made you feel.
- ✓ **Accept praise gracefully.** Don't make belittling comments (*I'm not really all that good!*) to reduce awkwardness or embarrassment.

Extending Sympathy

- ✓ **Refer to the loss or tragedy directly but sensitively.** In the first sentence mention the loss and your personal reaction.
- ✓ **For deaths, praise the deceased.** Describe positive personal characteristics (*Howard was a forceful but caring leader*).

 **Offer assistance.** Suggest your availability, especially if you can do something specific.

 **End on a reassuring, positive note.** Perhaps refer to the strength the receiver finds in friends, family, colleagues, or religion.

Summary of Learning Objectives

1 **List three characteristics of good letters, and describe the direct pattern for organizing letters.** Good letters are characterized by clear content, a tone of goodwill, and correct form. Letters carrying positive or neutral messages should be organized directly. That means introducing the main idea (the purpose for writing) immediately in the opening. The body of the letter explains and gives details. Letters that make requests close by telling what action is desired and establishing a deadline (end date) for that action.

2 **Write letters requesting information and action.** The opening immediately states the purpose of the letter, perhaps asking a question. The body explains and justifies the request. The closing tells the reader courteously what to do and shows appreciation.

3 **Write letters placing orders.** The opening introduces the order and authorizes a purchase (*Please send me the following items ...*). The body lists the desired items including quantity, order number, description, unit price, and total price. The closing describes the method of payment, tells when the merchandise should be sent, and expresses appreciation.

4 **Write letters making claims.** The opening describes the problem clearly or tells what action is to be taken. The body explains and justifies the request without anger or emotion. The closing, which might include an end date, describes the desired action.

5 **Write letters complying with requests.** A subject line identifies previous correspondence, while the opening immediately delivers the good news. The body explains and provides additional information. The closing is cordial and personalized.

6 **Write letters of recommendation.** The opening identifies the candidate, the position, your relationship, and the confidentiality of the letter. The body describes the candidate's job duties, performance, skills, and potential. The closing provides an overall ranking of the candidate and offers to give additional information by telephone.

7 **Write letters granting claims and making adjustments.** The opening immediately grants the claim without sounding grudging. To regain the confidence of the customer, the body may explain what went wrong and how the problem will be rectified. However, it may avoid accepting responsibility for any problems. The closing expresses appreciation, extends thanks for past business, refers to a desire to be of service, and/or mentions a new product. An apology is optional.

8 **Write goodwill messages.** Goodwill messages deliver thanks, praise, or sympathy. They should be selfless, specific, sincere, spontaneous, and short. Gift thank-yous should identify the gift, tell why you appreciate it, and explain

how you will use it. Thank-yous for favours should tell, without gushing, what they mean to you. Expressions of sympathy should mention the loss tactfully; recognize good qualities in the deceased (in the case of a death); offer assistance; and conclude on a positive, reassuring note.

CHAPTER REVIEW

1. What is goodwill? Briefly describe five ways to develop goodwill in a letter. (Obj. 1)
2. Why is it best to write most business letters "backwards"? (Obj. 1)
3. What kind of questions elicit the most information? Give an example. (Obj. 2)
4. Why is the direct letter strategy appropriate for most business messages? (Obj. 2)
5. For order letters what information goes in the opening? In the body? In the closing? (Obj. 3)
6. What is a claim? (Obj. 4)
7. Why are most companies today particularly interested in listening to customers? (Obj. 4)
8. In complying with requests, why is it especially important that all facts are correct on letters written on company stationery? (Obj. 5)
9. When answering many questions for a customer, how can the information be grouped to improve readability? (Obj. 5)
10. What information should the opening of a letter of recommendation contain? (Obj. 6)
11. What is an appropriate salutation for a letter of recommendation when the candidate has no specific position in mind? (Obj. 6)
12. What are a writer's three goals for adjustment letters? (Obj. 7)
13. Name four things to avoid in adjustment letters. (Obj. 7)
14. Name five characteristics of goodwill messages. (Obj. 8)

CRITICAL THINKING

1. What's wrong with using the indirect pattern for writing routine requests and replies? If in the end the reader understands the message, why make a big fuss over the organization? (Obj. 1)
2. Is it insensitive to include resale or sales promotion information in an adjustment letter? (Obj. 7)
3. Why is it important to regain the confidence of a customer in an adjustment letter? How can it be done? (Obj. 7)

ACTIVITIES

7.1 Direct Openings (Objs. 1–8)

Revise the following openings so that they are more direct. Add information if necessary.

a. Please allow me to introduce myself. I am Todd Thompson, and I am the assistant manager of Body Trends, a fitness equipment centre in Dorval. My manager has asked me to make inquiry about the upright and semi-recumbent cycling machines that we saw advertised in the June issue of *Your Health* magazine. I have a number of questions.

b. Pursuant to your letter of January 15, I am writing in regard to your inquiry about whether or not we offer our European-style patio umbrella in colours. This unique umbrella receives a number of inquiries. Its 10-foot canopy protects you when the sun is directly overhead, but it also swivels and tilts to virtually any angle for continuous sun protection all day long. It comes in two colours: off white and forest green.

c. Your letter of March 21, which was originally sent to *Mountain Bike Action*, has been referred to my desk for response. In your letter you inquire about the mountain bike featured on the cover of the magazine in April. That particular bike is a Series 70 Paramount and is manufactured by Schwinn.

7.2 Subject Lines (Objs. 1–8)

Write efficient subject lines for each of the messages in Activity 7.1. Add dates and other information if necessary.

7.3 Document for Analysis: Information Request (Obj. 2)

Analyze the following letter. List its weaknesses. If your instructor directs, revise the letter.

Dear Sir:

I am a new member of the Corporate Travel Department of my company, QuadCom, and I have been assigned the task of writing to you to inquire about our next sales meeting. We would like to find a resort with conference facilities, which is why I am writing to the Vancouver Hilton.

We are interested in banquet facilities where we can all be together, but we will also need at least four smaller meeting rooms. Each of these rooms should accommodate about 75. We hope to arrange our conference August 4 through August 9, and we expect about 250 sales associates. Most of our associates will be flying in so I'm interested in what airport is closest and transportation to and from the airport.

Does the Vancouver Hilton have public address systems in the meeting rooms? How about audio-visual equipment and computer facilities for presentations? Thank you for any information you can provide.

Sincerely,

7.4 Document for Analysis: Claim Request (Obj. 4)

Analyze the following letter. List its weaknesses. If your instructor directs, revise the letter.

Dear Service Manager Kent Fowler:

This is to inform you that you can't have it both ways. Either you provide customers with cars with full gas tanks or you don't. And if you don't, you shouldn't charge them when they return with empty tanks!

In view of the fact that I picked up a car in Fredericton August 22 with an empty tank, I had to fill it immediately. Then I drove it until August 25. When I returned to Wolfville, I naturally let the tank go nearly empty, since that is the way I received the car in Fredericton.

But your attendant in Wolfville charged me to fill the tank—$26.50 (premium gasoline at premium prices)! Although I explained to him that I had received it with an empty tank, he kept telling me that company policy required that he charge for a fill-up. My total bill came to $266.50, which, you must agree, is a lot of money for a rental period of only three days. I have the signed rental agreement and a receipt showing that I paid the full amount and that it included $26.50 for a gas fill-up when I returned the car.

Inasmuch as my company is a new customer and inasmuch as we had hoped to use your agency for our future car rentals because of your competitive rates, I trust that you will give this matter your prompt attention.

Disappointedly yours,

7.5 Document for Analysis: Favourable Adjustment (Obj. 7)

Analyze the following letter. List its weaknesses. If your instructor directs, revise the letter.

Dear Mr. Yoder:

I have before me your letter in which you complain about a missing shipment. May I suggest that it is very difficult for us to deliver merchandise when we have been given an erroneous address.

Our investigators made an investigation of your problem shipment and arrived at the determination that it was sent immediately after we received the order. According to the shipper's records, it was delivered to the warehouse address given on your stationery: 3590 University Avenue, Toronto, Ontario M5X 7V7. Unfortunately, no one at that address would accept delivery, so the shipment was returned to us. I see from your current stationery that your company has a new address: 2293 Bay Street, Toronto, Ontario M5V 7J3. With the proper address, we probably could have delivered this shipment.

When an order cannot be delivered, we usually try to verify the shipping address by telephoning the customer. Apparently, we could not find you.

Although we feel that it is entirely appropriate and right to charge you shipping and restocking fees, as is our standard practice on returned goods, in this instance we will waive those fees. We hope this second shipment finally catches up with you.

Sincerely,

7.6 Information Request: Backpacking Cuisine (Obj. 2)

Assume that you are Benjamin Spring, manager of a health spa and also an ardent backpacker. You are organizing a group of hikers for a wilderness trip to northern Manitoba. One item that must be provided is freeze-dried food for the three-week trip. You are unhappy with the taste and quality of backpacking food products currently available. You expect to have a group of hikers who are older, affluent, and natural-food enthusiasts. Some are concerned about products containing preservatives, sugar, and additives. Others are on diets restricting cholesterol, fat, and salt.

You heard that Outfitters, Inc., offers a new line of freeze-dried products. You want to know what it offers and whether it has sufficient variety to serve all the needs of your group. You need to know where its products can be purchased and what the cost range is. You'd also like to try a few of its items before placing a large order. You are interested in how it produces the food products and what kinds of ingredients it uses. If you have any items left over, you wonder how long they can be kept and still be usable. Write an inquiry letter to Tia Osborne, Outfitters, Inc., 2380 Westside Drive, Vancouver, BC V6P 1W8.

7.7 Information Request: Online Microbrewery (Obj. 2)

Play the part of brewmaster Carol Fischer, owner of Crystal Ale Microbrewery, 147 Ruby Line, St. John's, NF A1G 1P9. Your Crystal Ale beers have won local taste awards. However, sales are dismal, perhaps because your beer is pricier than mass-produced beers and because you have a meagre advertising and sales budget.

Then you hear about MicroBeer On-Line, a service that sells microbrewed beer via the World Wide Web. When you visit the Web site, you find descriptions of beer from many microbreweries, along with ratings for each beer. An order page enables customers to order beer directly from the Web site.

You wonder whether you might sell your beer via MicroBeer On-Line, but you're not exactly sure how the service works. For example, who writes the product descriptions, and who rates the beer? Furthermore, because you offer some seasonal varieties of Crystal Ale, you are concerned about being able to change the selection of beer offered on the service. Of course, you also need to know the specifics of working with MicroBeer On-Line. For example, how much does it cost to sell online? In addition, since Crystal Ale badly needs customers, you would like to know how many customers Crystal Ale might gain through MicroBeer On-Line. You have many questions! You could e-mail Mr. Fahlk, but you prefer a paper copy as a permanent record of the correspondence. Write a letter to Peter Fahlk, Webmaster, MicroBeer On-Line, 22050 Ontario Street, Lennoxville, QC J1M 1Z7. Provide an end date and a logical reason for it.

7.8 Order Letter: Office Supplies to Go (Obj. 3)

You are Hector Rivera, Manager, Lasertronics, Inc., 627 Nordstrum Road, Lethbridge, AB T1R 3L5. You want to order some items from an office supply catalogue, but your catalogue is one year old and you have lost the order form. Because you're in a hurry, you decide to place a fax order. Rather than write for a new catalogue, you decide to take a chance and order items from the old catalogue, realizing that prices may be somewhat different. You want three Panasonic electric pencil sharpeners, Item 22-A, at $19.95 each. You want one steel desktop organizer, 60 inches long, Item No. 23-K. Its price is $117.50. Order two Roll-a-Flex files for 2- by 4-inch cards at $14.50 each. This is Item 23-G. The next item is No. 29-H, file folders, box of 100, letter size, at $5.29. You need ten boxes. You would like to be invoiced for this purchase, and you prefer UPS delivery. Even though the prices may be somewhat higher, you decide to list the prices shown in your catalogue so that you have an idea of what the total order will cost. Write a letter to Monarch Discount Office Furniture, 2890 Monarch Road, Lethbridge, AB T1K 1L6. Between the date and the inside address, type TRANSMITTED BY FAX.

7.9 Claim Letter: Deep Desk Disappointment (Obj. 4)

Assume that you are Monica Keil, President, Keil Consulting Services, 9802 Founders Drive, Antigonish, NS B2G 1C0. Since your consulting firm was doing very well, you decided to splurge and purchase a fine executive desk for your own office. You ordered an expensive desk described as "North American white oak embellished with hand-inlaid walnut cross-banding." Although you would not ordinarily purchase large, expensive items by mail, you were impressed by the description of this desk and by the money-back guarantee promised in the catalogue.

When the desk arrived, you knew that you had made a mistake. The wood finish was rough, the grain looked splotchy, and many of the drawers would not pull out easily. The advertisement had promised "full suspension, silent ball-bearing drawer slides." You are disappointed with the desk and decide to send it back, taking advantage of the money-back guarantee. You want your money refunded. You're not sure whether the freight charges can be refunded, but it's worth a try. Supply any details needed. Write a letter to Rodney Harding, Sales Manager, Harbourview Wood Products, 49 Harbourview Drive, Sydney, NS B1S 2A8.

7.10 Claim Letter: The Real Thing (Obj. 4)

Select a product or service that has disappointed you. Write a claim letter requesting a refund, replacement, explanation, or whatever seems reasonable. Generally, such letters are addressed to customer service departments. For claims about food products, be sure to include bar-code identification from the package, if possible. Your instructor may ask you to actually mail this letter. Remember that smart companies want to know what their customers think, especially if a product could be improved. Give your ideas for improvement. When you receive a response, share it with your class.

7.11 Request Response: Backpacking Cuisine (Obj. 5)

As Tia Osborne, owner of Outfitters, Inc., producer of freeze-dried backpacking foods, answer the inquiry of Benjamin Spring (described in Activity 7.6). You are eager to have Mr. Spring sample your new all-natural line of products containing no preservatives, sugar, or additives. You want him to know that you started this company two years ago after you found yourself making custom meals for discerning backpackers who rejected typical camping fare. Some of your menu items are excellent for individuals on restricted diets. Some dinners are cholesterol-, fat-, and salt-free, but he'll have to look at your list to see for himself.

You will send him your complete list of dinner items and the suggested retail prices. You will also send him a sample "Saturday Night on the Trail," a four-course meal that comes with fruit candies and elegant appetizers. All your food products are made from choice ingredients in sanitary kitchens that you personally supervise. They are flash frozen in a new vacuum process that you patented. Although your dried foods are meant to last for years, you don't recommend that they be kept beyond 18 months because they may deteriorate. This could happen if a package were punctured or if the products became overheated. Your products are currently available at Glen Elm Sports Centre, 14003 12th Avenue S, Regina, SK S4N 0M6. Large orders may be placed directly with you. You offer a 5-percent discount on direct orders. Write a response to Benjamin Spring, 2631 28th Avenue, Regina, SK S4S 6X3.

7.12 Request Response: MicroBeer On-Line (Obj. 5)

As Peter Fahlk, webmaster for MicroBeer On-Line, respond to a letter from a potential customer, microbrewer Carol Fischer (see Activity 7.7). In addition to answering Ms. Fischer's questions, you hope to gain her company, Crystal Ale Microbrewery, as a new customer by highlighting the benefits of MicroBeer On-Line. Of course, you want to clarify for Ms. Fischer that MicroBeer On-Line doesn't brew beer; it simply advertises and collects orders on its Web site. Orders are then forwarded to microbrewers, who fill the orders, ship the product to the consumer, and fork over 4 percent of online sales receipts to MicroBeer. (The fee of 4 percent of sales is well under the amount allocated for advertising in most company budgets.)

Although you can't predict how many customers each brewer will gain through MicroBeer On-Line, you do know that the service reaches thousands of consumers a day, 365 days a year, 24 hours a day. Small brewers appreciate MicroBeer On-Line because it brings in orders while brewers concentrate on brewing their specialty beers. Furthermore, by cutting out middlemen and reducing distribution costs, MicroBeer On-Line enables brewers to maintain reasonable beer prices. Consumers particularly appreciate MicroBeer's product write-ups and beer ratings by Ted Groebles, a well-known brewmaster. However, since Groebles is able to review only a reasonable number of beers at a time, MicroBeer limits its service to 50 breweries and about 250 beers. Brewers may sell up to five beers on the service, and the beers may change seasonally.

It is very inexpensive for MicroBeer to run its Web site; the cost of setting up the Web site was less than the cost of four half-page ads in a major newspaper. Gaining new customers, however, hasn't been easy, so MicroBeer now offers short-term contracts to brewers new to the service. Brewers may call you personally at (709) 756-1456 for more information.

Write to Carol Fischer, Crystal Ale Microbrewery, 147 Ruby Line, St. John's, NF A1G 1P9. Answer the questions in her inquiry (Activity 7.7). Along with your reply, send her your brochure, "MicroBeer On-Line."

7.13 Letter of Recommendation: Recommending Yourself (Obj. 6)

You are about to leave your present job. When you ask your boss for a letter of recommendation, to your surprise he tells you to write it yourself and then have him sign it. Actually, this is not an unusual practice today. Many businesspeople find that employees are very perceptive and accurate when they evaluate themselves. Use specifics from a current or previous job. Describe your duties and skills. Be sure to support general characteristics with specific examples.

7.14 Claim Response: Deep Desk Disappointment (Obj. 7)

As Rodney Harding, sales manager, Harbourview Wood Products, it is your job to reply to customer claims, and today you must respond to Monica Keil, President, Keil Consulting Services, 9802 Founders Drive, Antigonish, NS B2G 1C0 (described in Activity 7.9). You are disappointed that she is returning the executive desk (Invoice No. 3499), but your policy is to comply with customer wishes. If she doesn't want to keep the desk, you will certainly return the purchase price plus shipping charges. On occasion, desks are damaged in shipping, and this may explain the marred finish and the sticking drawers.

You want Ms. Keil to give Harbourview Wood Products another chance. After all, your office furniture and other wood products are made from the finest hand-selected woods by master artisans. Since she is apparently furnishing her office, send her another catalogue and invite her to look at the traditional conference desk on page 10-E. This is available with a matching credenza, file cabinets, and accessories. She might be interested in your furniture-leasing plan, which can produce substantial savings. You promise that you will personally examine any furniture she may order in the future. Write her a letter granting her claim.

7.15 Thanks for a Favour: The Century's Biggest Change in Job Finding (Obj. 8)

Team

Your business communication class was fortunate to have author Joyce Lain Kennedy speak to you. She has written many books, including *Electronic Job Search Revolution, Hook Up, Get Hired!*, and *Electronic Résumé Revolution.* Ms. Kennedy talked about writing a scannable résumé, using keywords to help employers hire you, keeping yourself visible in databases on the Internet, and finding online classified ads. The class especially liked hearing the many examples of real people who had found jobs on the Internet. Ms. Kennedy shared many suggestions from human resources people, and she described how large and small employers are using computers to read résumés and track employees. You know that she did not come to plug her books, but when she left, most class members wanted to head straight for a bookstore to get some of them. Her talk was a big hit. Individually or in small groups, draft a thank-you letter to Joyce Lain Kennedy, P.O. Box 3502, Madeira Park, BC V0N 2H0.

7.16 Thanks for the Hospitality: Holiday Entertaining (Obj. 8)

Write a thank-you letter to your boss (supervisor, manager, vice president, president, or chief executive officer) or to the head of an organization to which you belong. Assume that you and other members of your staff or organization were entertained at an elegant dinner during the winter holiday season. Include specific details that will make your letter personal and sincere.

7.17 Responding to Good Wishes: Saying Thank You (Obj. 8)

Write a short note thanking a friend who sent you good wishes when you recently completed your degree.

7.18 Extending Sympathy: To a Spouse (Obj. 8)

Imagine that a coworker was killed in an automobile accident. Write a letter of sympathy to his or her spouse.

C.L.U.E. REVIEW 7

Edit the following sentences to correct faults in grammar, punctuation, spelling, and word use.

1. The extrordinary increase in sales is related to us placing the staff on a commission basis and the increase also effected our stock value.
2. She acts as if she was the only person who ever received a complement about their business writing.
3. Karen is interested in working for the department of foreign affairs. Since she is hopping to travel.
4. Major Hawkins whom I think will be elected has all ready served three consecative terms as a member of the oshawa city counsel.
5. After Mr. Freeman and him returned from lunch the customer's were handled more quick.
6. Our new employees cafeteria, which opened six months ago has a salad bar that everyone definitly likes.
7. On Tuesday Ms Adams can see you at two p.m., on Wednesday she has a full skedule.
8. His determination courage and sincerity could not be denied however his methods were often questioned.
9. After you have checked the matter farther report to the CEO and I.
10. Mr. Garcia and her advised me not to dessert my employer at this time. Although they were quite sympathetic to my personel problems.

CHAPTER • 8 •

ROUTINE MEMOS AND E-MAIL MESSAGES

LEARNING OBJECTIVES

1. Discuss the characteristics of and writing process for successful routine memos and e-mail messages.
2. Analyze the organization of memos and e-mail messages.
3. Explain how to use e-mail effectively, including practices, netiquette, and formatting.
4. Write information and procedure memos and e-mail messages.
5. Write request and reply memos and e-mail messages.
6. Write confirmation memos and e-mail messages.

Writing Routine Memos and E-Mail Messages

1

In most organizations today an amazing change has taken place in internal communication. In the past, written messages from insiders took the form of hard copy memorandums, but recently e-mail has become the communication channel of choice. Canada Post reports a 10- to 15-percent drop in the number of letters mailed in Canada,[1] and it expects the volume of letters it handles to decline by 700 million pieces per year within the next five years.[2] Small wonder. It costs only about $1 to send 19 e-mail messages,[3] and they arrive almost instantaneously.

E-mail has become the primary channel for internal communication.

Developing skill in writing memos and e-mail brings you two important benefits. First, well-written documents are likely to achieve their goals. Second, such documents enhance your image within the organization. Individuals identified as competent, professional writers are noticed and rewarded; most often, they are the ones promoted into management positions.

This chapter concentrates on routine memos and e-mail messages. These straightforward messages open with the main idea first because their topics are not sensitive and require little persuasion. You'll study the characteristics, writing process, organization, and forms for preparing procedure, information, request, reply, and confirmation memos.

Characteristics of Successful Memos and E-Mail Messages

Because memos and e-mail messages are standard forms of communication within most organizations, they will probably become your most common business communication medium. These indispensable messages inform employees, request data, supply responses, confirm decisions, and give directions. Good memos and e-mail messages generally share certain characteristics.

Routine memos inform employees, request data, give responses, confirm decisions, and provide directions.

Date, To, From, Subject Headings. Memos and e-mail messages contain guide-word headings as shown in Figure 8.1. These headings help readers immediately identify the date, origin, destination, and purpose of a message.

Single Topic. Good memos and e-mail messages generally discuss only one topic. Notice that Figure 8.1 considers only one topic. Limiting the topic helps the receiver act on the subject and file it appropriately.

Effective memos contain guide-word headings, focus on a single topic, are concise and conversational, and use graphic highlighting.

Conversational Tone. The tone of memos and e-mail messages is expected to be conversational because the communicators are usually familiar with one another. This means using occasional contractions (*I'm, you'll*), ordinary words, and first-person pronouns (*I/we*). Yet, the tone should also be professional. E-mail is so fast and so easy to use that some writers have been seduced into an "astonishing lack of professionalism."[4] Although warm and friendly, e-mail messages should not be emotional. They should never include remarks that would not be said to the face of an individual.

Conciseness. As functional forms of communication, routine memos and e-mail messages contain only what's necessary to convey meaning and be courteous. Often, they require less background explanation and less attention to goodwill efforts than do letters to outsiders. Be particularly alert to eliminating wordiness. Avoid opening fillers (*there is, it is*), long lead-ins (*I am writing this memo to inform you that*), and wordy phrases (*because of the fact that*).

FIGURE 8.1

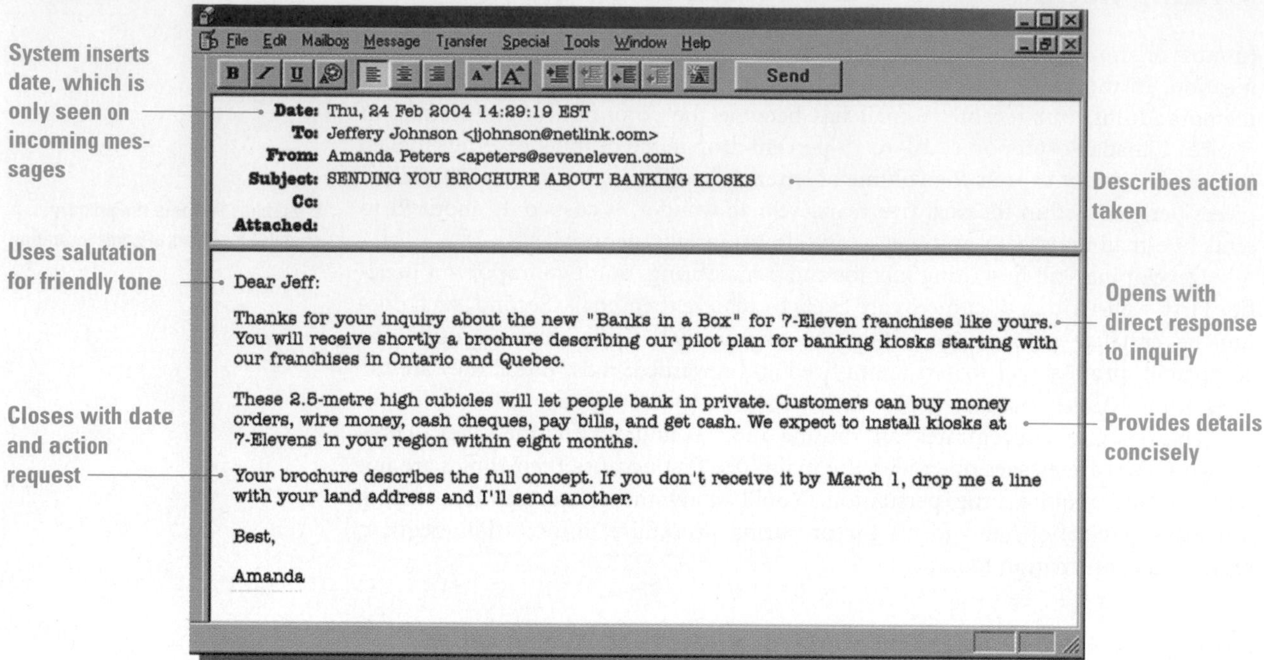

File Edit Mailbox Message Transfer Special Tools Window Help
Send
Date: Thu, 24 Feb 2004 14:29:19 EST
To: Jeffery Johnson <jjohnson@netlink.com>
From: Amanda Peters <apeters@seveneleven.com>
Subject: SENDING YOU BROCHURE ABOUT BANKING KIOSKS
Cc:
Attached:
Dear Jeff:
Thanks for your inquiry about the new "Banks in a Box" for 7-Eleven franchises like yours. You will receive shortly a brochure describing our pilot plan for banking kiosks starting with our franchises in Ontario and Quebec.
These 2.5-metre high cubicles will let people bank in private. Customers can buy money orders, wire money, cash cheques, pay bills, and get cash. We expect to install kiosks at 7-Elevens in your region within eight months.
Your brochure describes the full concept. If you don't receive it by March 1, drop me a line with your land address and I'll send another.
Best,
Amanda
System inserts date, which is only seen on incoming messages
Uses salutation for friendly tone
Closes with date and action request
Describes action taken
Opens with direct response to inquiry
Provides details concisely

Graphic highlighting includes numbered and bulleted lists and headings.

Graphic Highlighting. To make important ideas stand out and to improve readability, memo and e-mail writers make liberal use of graphic highlighting techniques. The content of many printed memos is enhanced by numbered or bulleted items, headings, tables, and other techniques you studied in Chapter 6. Some e-mail programs may not transmit italics, bolding, or double sets of columns. However, you can improve readability with good paragraphing, bullet or asterisk points, and side headings, especially for longer messages. Readers hate to scroll through screen after screen of solid writing. Although businesses have fallen in love with e-mail, users are less and less tolerant of writers who fail to follow writing conventions. They won't tolerate unattractive, unintelligible, and "impenetrable data dumps."[5]

Writing Process

Businesspeople are writing more messages than ever before.

"One of the most amazing features of the information revolution," says one technology vice president, is that the "momentum has turned back to the written word."[6] Businesspeople are writing more messages than ever before, and many of them are memos and e-mail. Like letters, good memos require careful preparation. Although they often seem routine, memos and e-mail messages may travel farther than you expect.

A systematic plan helps you write more quickly and more effectively.

Careful writing takes time—especially at first. By following a systematic plan and practising your skill, however, you can speed up your efforts and greatly improve the product. Bear in mind, moreover, that the effort you make to improve your communication skills can pay big dividends. Frequently, your speaking and writing abilities determine how much influence you'll have in your organization. As with other writing tasks, memo writing follows the familiar three-phase writing process.

Analysis, Anticipation, and Adaptation. In Phase 1 (prewriting) you'll need to spend some time analyzing your task. It's amazing how many of us are ready to put our pens to paper or computers into gear before engaging our minds. Ask yourself three important questions:

- **Do I really need to write this memo or e-mail?** A phone call or a quick visit to a nearby coworker might solve the problem —and save the time and expense of a written message. On the other hand, some written messages are needed to provide a permanent record. Another decision is whether to write a hard-copy memo or send an electronic one. Many offices are moving toward a *paperless workplace.*
- **Why am I writing?** Know why you are writing and what you hope to achieve. This will help you recognize what the important points are and where to place them.
- **How will the reader react?** Visualize the reader and the effect your message will have. Consider ways to shape the message to benefit the reader.

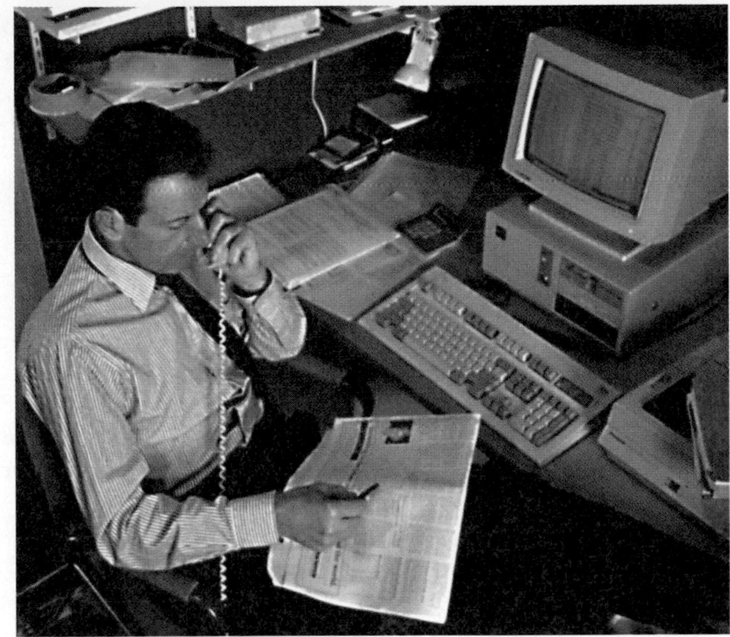

Technology allows increasing numbers of employees to work at home and telecommute to the office. As a result, more and more messages—especially memos—need to be written to keep the lines of communication open between remote employees and the office.

Research, Organization, and Composition. In Phase 2 (writing) you'll first want to check the files, gather documentation, and prepare your message. Make an outline of the points you wish to cover. For short messages you can jot down notes on the document you are answering. Be sure to prepare for revision, because excellence is rarely achieved on the first effort.

Analyzing the purpose of a message helps determine whether a permanent record is required.

Revision, Proofreading, and Evaluation. Careful and caring writers revise their messages, proofread the final copy, and make an effort to evaluate the success of their communication.

- **Revise for clarity.** Viewed from the receiver's perspective, are the ideas clear? Do they need more explanation? If the memo is passed on to others, will they need further explanation? Consider having a colleague critique your message if it is an important one.
- **Proofread for correctness.** Are the sentences complete and punctuated properly? Did you overlook any typos or misspelled words? Remember to use your spell checker and grammar checker to proofread your message before sending it.
- **Plan for feedback.** How will you know if this message is successful? You can improve feedback by asking questions (such as *Do you agree with these suggestions?*) and by making it easy for the receiver to respond.

Organization of Memos and E-Mail Messages

2

Whether hard-copy or electronic, routine memos generally contain four parts: (1) a subject line that summarizes the message, (2) an opening that reveals the main idea immediately, (3) a body that explains and justifies the main idea, and (4) an action closing. Remember that routine messages deliver good news or standard information.

Direct memos and e-mails contain a SUBJECT line, an opener stating the main idea, a body with explanation and justification, and an action closing.

Subject Line. In e-mails and memos a subject line is mandatory. The subject line should summarize the central idea. It provides quick identification for the reader and for filing. As you learned in Chapter 7, the subject line is usually written in an abbreviated style, often without articles (*a, an, the*). It need not be a complete sentence, and it does not end with a period. E-mail subject lines are particularly important, since meaningless ones may cause readers to delete the message without ever opening it. Good subject lines, such as the following, are specific, eye-catching, and talking (contain a verb form):

SUBJECT: Enhancing Our Messaging Capabilities (rather than *New Software*)

SUBJECT: Staff Meeting to Discuss Summer Vacation Schedules (rather than *Meeting*)

Most direct memos convey nonsensitive information and thus frontload the main idea in the opening.

Opening. Most memos and e-mails cover nonsensitive information that can be handled in a straightforward manner. Begin by frontloading; that is, reveal the main idea immediately. Even though the purpose of the memo or e-mail is summarized in the subject line, that purpose should be restated—and amplified—in the first sentence. Some readers skip the subject line and plunge right into the first sentence. Notice how the following indirect memo openers can be improved by frontloading.

Indirect Opening	Direct Opening
For the past six months the Human Resources Development Department has been considering changes in our employees' benefit plan.	Please review the following proposal regarding employees' benefits, and let me know by May 20 if you approve these changes.
As you may know, employees in Document Production have been complaining about eye fatigue as a result of the overhead fluorescent lighting in their centre.	If you agree, I'll order six high-intensity task desk lamps at $189 each for use in the Document Production Centre.

Body. The body provides more information about the reason for writing. It explains and discusses the subject logically. Design your data for easy comprehension by using numbered lists, headings, tables, and other graphic highlighting techniques. Compare the following versions of the same message. Observe how the graphic devices of columns, headings, and white space make the main points easy to comprehend.

Hard-to-Read Paragraph Version

Effective immediately are the following air travel guidelines. Between now and December 31, only account executives may take company-approved trips. These individuals will be allowed to take a maximum of two trips, and they are to travel economy or budget class only.

Improved Version With Graphic Highlighting

Effective immediately are the following air travel guidelines:

- Who may travel: Account executives only
- How many trips: A maximum of two trips
- By when: Between now and December 31
- Air class: Economy or budget class only

Closing. Generally end with (1) action information, dates, or deadlines; (2) a summary of the message; or (3) a closing thought. Here again the value of thinking through the message before actually writing it becomes apparent. This is where readers look for deadlines and action language.

Memos should close with (1) action information including dates and deadlines, (2) a summary, or (3) a closing thought.

In more complex messages a summary of main points may be an appropriate closing. If no action request is made and a closing summary is unnecessary, you might end with a simple concluding thought. Although you needn't close messages to coworkers with goodwill statements such as those found in letters to customers or clients, some closing thought is often necessary to prevent a feeling of abruptness. Closings can show gratitude or encourage feedback. Other closings look forward to what's next. As with routine letters, avoid trite expressions. Overused endings sound mechanical and insincere.

Putting It All Together. Now let's put it all together. An e-mail message, see Figure 8.2, was sent by Matt Barnes, marketing manager, to his supervisor Debbie Pickett. Notice that it opens directly. Both the subject line and the first sentence explain the purpose for writing. Bullets and headings emphasize the actions necessary to solve the database problems. The message ends with a deadline and refers to the next action to be taken.

Using E-Mail Effectively

3

Early e-mail users were encouraged to "ignore stylistic and grammatical considerations." They thought that "words on the fly," as e-mail messages were considered, required little editing or proofing. Correspondents used emoticons (such as sideways happy faces) to express their emotions. And some e-mail today is still quick and dirty. But as this communication channel matures, messages are becoming more proper and more professional. Today, the average e-mail message may remain in the company's computer system for up to five years. And in some instances the only impression a person has of the e-mail writer is from a transmitted message.

Wise e-mail business communicators are also learning its dangers. They know that their messages can travel (intentionally or unintentionally) long distances. A quickly drafted note may end up in the boss's mailbox or be forwarded to an adversary's box.

Smart E-Mail Practices

Despite its dangers and limitations, e-mail is increasingly the channel of choice for sending many business messages. Because e-mail has become a mainstream channel of communication, it is important to take the time to organize your thoughts, compose carefully, and be concerned with correct grammar and punctuation.

FIGURE 8.2 **Information E-Mail Message**

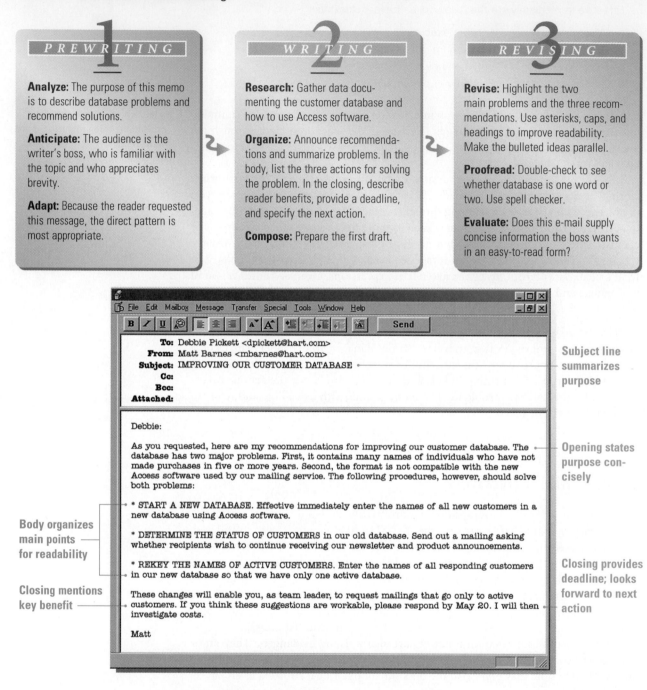

1 PREWRITING

Analyze: The purpose of this memo is to describe database problems and recommend solutions.

Anticipate: The audience is the writer's boss, who is familiar with the topic and who appreciates brevity.

Adapt: Because the reader requested this message, the direct pattern is most appropriate.

2 WRITING

Research: Gather data documenting the customer database and how to use Access software.

Organize: Announce recommendations and summarize problems. In the body, list the three actions for solving the problem. In the closing, describe reader benefits, provide a deadline, and specify the next action.

Compose: Prepare the first draft.

3 REVISING

Revise: Highlight the two main problems and the three recommendations. Use asterisks, caps, and headings to improve readability. Make the bulleted ideas parallel.

Proofread: Double-check to see whether database is one word or two. Use spell checker.

Evaluate: Does this e-mail supply concise information the boss wants in an easy-to-read form?

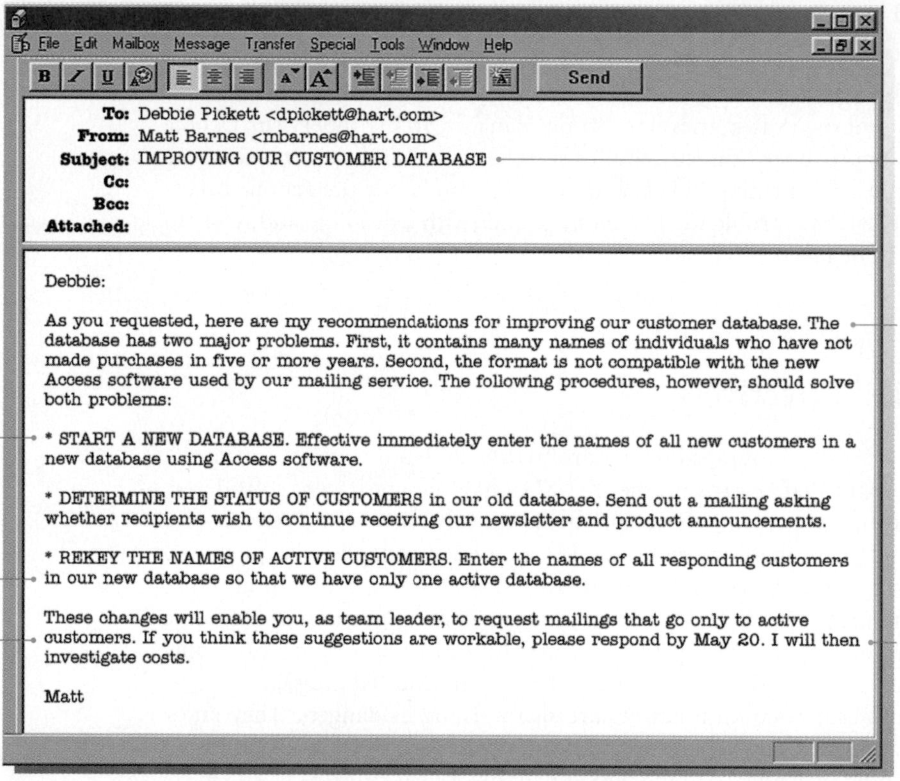

File Edit Mailbox Message Transfer Special Tools Window Help

Send

To: Debbie Pickett <dpickett@hart.com>
From: Matt Barnes <mbarnes@hart.com>
Subject: IMPROVING OUR CUSTOMER DATABASE
Cc:
Bcc:
Attached:

Debbie:

As you requested, here are my recommendations for improving our customer database. The database has two major problems. First, it contains many names of individuals who have not made purchases in five or more years. Second, the format is not compatible with the new Access software used by our mailing service. The following procedures, however, should solve both problems:

* START A NEW DATABASE. Effective immediately enter the names of all new customers in a new database using Access software.

* DETERMINE THE STATUS OF CUSTOMERS in our old database. Send out a mailing asking whether recipients wish to continue receiving our newsletter and product announcements.

* REKEY THE NAMES OF ACTIVE CUSTOMERS. Enter the names of all responding customers in our new database so that we have only one active database.

These changes will enable you, as team leader, to request mailings that go only to active customers. If you think these suggestions are workable, please respond by May 20. I will then investigate costs.

Matt

Subject line summarizes purpose

Opening states purpose concisely

Body organizes main points for readability

Closing mentions key benefit

Closing provides deadline; looks forward to next action

Getting Started

- **Compose offline.** Instead of dashing off hasty messages, consider using your word processing program to write offline. Then upload your message to the e-mail network.
- **Get the address right.** E-mail addresses are often complex, often illogical, and always unforgiving. Omit one character or misread the letter *l* for the number *1*,

and your message bounces. Solution: Use your electronic address book for people you write frequently. And double-check every address that you key in manually. Also be sure that you don't reply to a group of receivers when you intend to answer only one.

- **Avoid misleading subject lines.** With an abundance of spam (junk mail) clogging most inboxes, make sure your subject line is relevant and helpful. Generic tags like *Hello* and *Great Deal* may cause your message to be deleted before it is opened.

Content, Tone, and Correctness

Although e-mail seems as casual as a telephone call, it's not. Because it produces a permanent record, think carefully about what you say and how you say it.

- **Be concise.** Don't burden readers with unnecessary information. Remember that monitors are small and typefaces are often difficult to read. Organize your ideas tightly.

- **Don't send anything you wouldn't want published.** Because e-mail seems like a telephone call or a person-to-person conversation, writers sometimes send sensitive, confidential, inflammatory, or potentially embarrassing messages. Beware! E-mail creates a permanent record that often does not go away even when deleted. And every message is a corporate communication that can be used against you or your employer. Don't write anything that you wouldn't want your boss, your family, or a judge to read.

- **Don't use e-mail to avoid contact.** E-mail is inappropriate for breaking bad news or for resolving arguments. For example, it's improper to fire a person by e-mail. It's also not a good channel for dealing with conflict with supervisors, subordinates, or others. If there's any possibility of hurt feelings, pick up the telephone or pay the person a visit.

- **Never respond when you're angry.** Always allow some time to cool off before shooting off a response to an upsetting message. You often come up with different and better alternatives after thinking about what was said. If possible, iron out differences in person.

- **Care about correctness.** People are judged by their writing, whether electronic or paper-based. Sloppy e-mail messages (with missing apostrophes, haphazard spelling, and stream-of-consciousness writing) make readers work too hard. They resent not only the information but also the writer.

- **Resist humour and tongue-in-cheek comments.** Without the nonverbal cues conveyed by your face and your voice, humour can easily be misunderstood.

Netiquette

Although e-mail is a new communication technology, a number of rules of polite online interaction are emerging.

- **Limit any tendency to send blanket copies.** Send copies only to people who really need to see a message. It is unnecessary to document every business decision and action with an electronic paper trail.

- **Consider using identifying labels.** When appropriate, add one of the following labels to the subject line: ACTION (action required, please respond); FYI (for your information, no response needed); RE (this is a reply to another message); URGENT (please respond immediately).
- **Use capital letters only for emphasis or for titles.** Avoid writing entire messages in all caps, which is like SHOUTING.
- **Announce attachments.** If you're sending a lengthy attachment, tell your receiver. You might also ask what format is preferred.
- **Don't forward without permission.** Obtain approval before forwarding a message.

Other Smart E-mail Practices

Depending on your message and audience, the following tips promote effective electronic communication.

- **Use design to improve readability of longer messages.** When a message requires several screens, help the reader with headings, bulleted listings, side headings, and perhaps an introductory summary that describes what will follow. Although these techniques lengthen a message, they shorten reading time.
- **Consider cultural differences.** When using this borderless tool, be especially clear and precise in your language. Remember that figurative clichés (*pull up stakes, playing second fiddle*), sports references (*hit a home run, play by the rules*), and slang (*cool, stoked*) cause confusion abroad.
- **Don't use company computers for personal matters.** Unless your company specifically allows it, never use you employer's computers for personal messages, personal shopping, or entertainment.
- **Assume that all e-mail is monitored.** Employers legally have the right to monitor e-mail, and many do.
- **Double-check before hitting the *Send* button.** Have you included everything? Avoid the necessity of sending a second message, which makes you look disorganized. Use spell-check and reread for fluency before sending.

Formatting E-Mail Messages

Because e-mail is a developing communication channel, its formatting and usage conventions are still fluid. Users and authorities do not always agree on what's appropriate for salutations and closings, for instance. The following suggestions, however, can guide you in formatting most e-mail messages, but always check with your organization to observe its practices.

Guidewords. Following the guideword *To*, some writers insert just the recipient's electronic address, such as *mlammers@accountpro.com*, as shown in Figure 8.3. By including full names in the *To* and *From* slots, both receivers and senders are better able to identify the message. By the way, the order of *To, From, Date, Subject,* and other guidewords varies depending on your e-mail program and whether you are sending or receiving the message.

Most e-mail programs automatically add the current date after *Date*. On the *Cc* line (which stands for *carbon* or *courtesy copy*) you can type the address of anyone who

FIGURE 8.3 **E-Mail Request**

Tips for E-Mail Formatting

- After *To,* type the receiver's electronic address. If you include the receiver's name, enclose the address in angle brackets.
- After *From,* type your name and electronic address, if your program does not insert it automatically.
- After *Subject,* provide a clear description of your message.
- Insert the addresses of anyone receiving carbon or blind copies.
- Include a salutation (such as *Dear Marilyn; Hi, Marilyn;* or *Greetings*) or weave the receiver's name into the first line (see Figure 8.5). Some writers omit a salutation.
- Set your line length for no more than 80 characters. If you expect your message to be forwarded, set it for 60 characters.
- Use word-wrap rather than pressing *Enter* at line ends.
- Double-space (press *Enter*) between paragraphs.
- Do not type in all caps or in all lowercase letters.
- Include a complimentary close, your name, and your address if you wish.

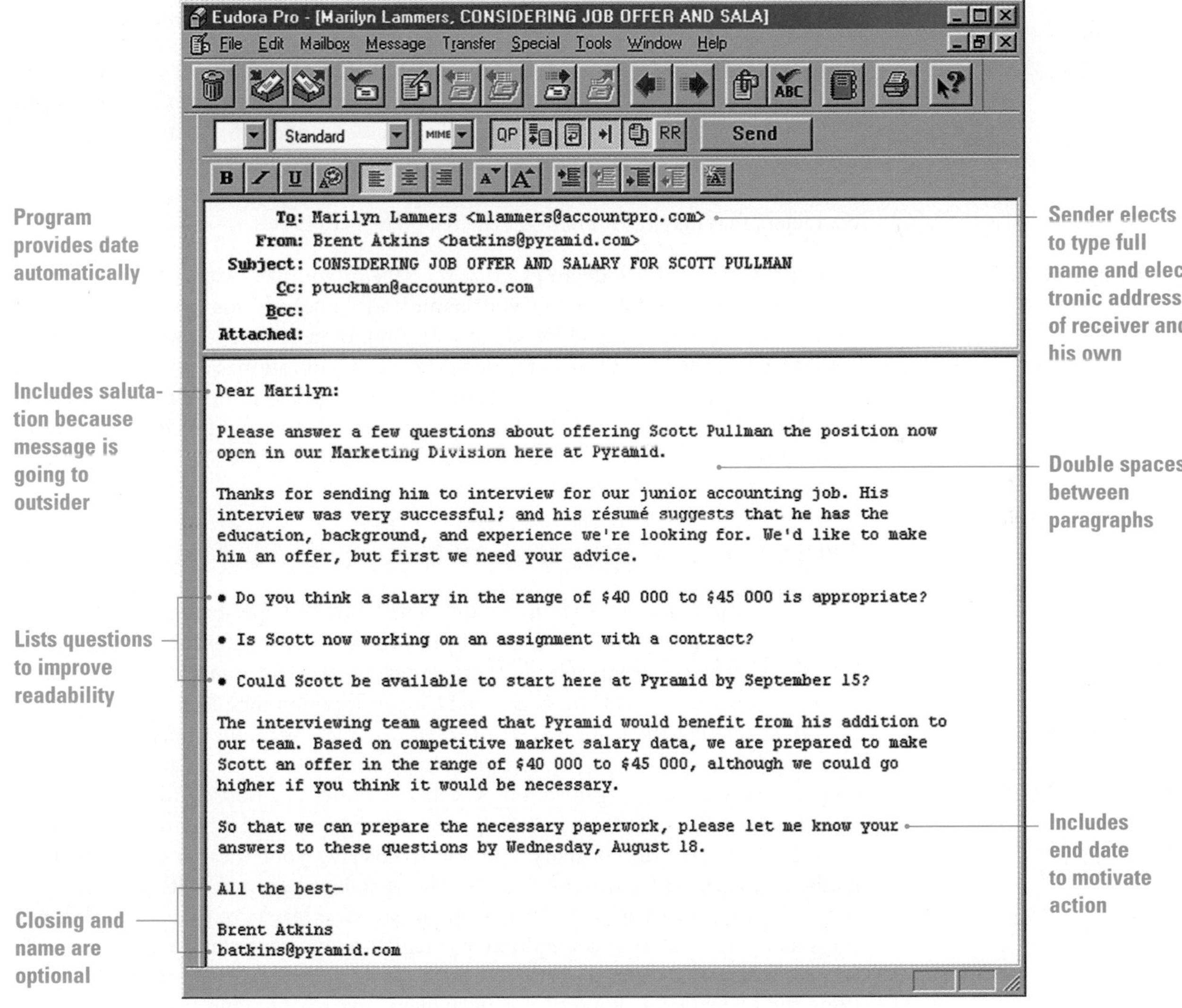

Eudora Pro - [Marilyn Lammers, CONSIDERING JOB OFFER AND SALA]

File Edit Mailbox Message Transfer Special Tools Window Help

Standard Send

To: Marilyn Lammers <mlammers@accountpro.com>
From: Brent Atkins <batkins@pyramid.com>
Subject: CONSIDERING JOB OFFER AND SALARY FOR SCOTT PULLMAN
Cc: ptuckman@accountpro.com
Bcc:
Attached:

Dear Marilyn:

Please answer a few questions about offering Scott Pullman the position now open in our Marketing Division here at Pyramid.

Thanks for sending him to interview for our junior accounting job. His interview was very successful; and his résumé suggests that he has the education, background, and experience we're looking for. We'd like to make him an offer, but first we need your advice.

- Do you think a salary in the range of $40 000 to $45 000 is appropriate?
- Is Scott now working on an assignment with a contract?
- Could Scott be available to start here at Pyramid by September 15?

The interviewing team agreed that Pyramid would benefit from his addition to our team. Based on competitive market salary data, we are prepared to make Scott an offer in the range of $40 000 to $45 000, although we could go higher if you think it would be necessary.

So that we can prepare the necessary paperwork, please let me know your answers to these questions by Wednesday, August 18.

All the best—

Brent Atkins
batkins@pyramid.com

Program provides date automatically
Sender elects to type full name and electronic address of receiver and his own
Includes salutation because message is going to outsider
Double spaces between paragraphs
Lists questions to improve readability
Includes end date to motivate action
Closing and name are optional

The positions of *To, From, Date,* and *Subject* vary depending on your e-mail program.

is to receive a copy of the message. Remember, though, to send copies only to those people directly involved with the message. Most e-mail programs also include a line for *Bcc* (*blind carbon copy*). This sends a copy without the addressee's knowledge. Sending blind copies, however, is dangerous because you just might make an address error, and the addressee could learn of the intended *bcc.* On the subject line, identify the subject of the memo. Be sure to include enough information to be clear and compelling.

Salutations for e-mail messages are optional, and practice is as yet unsettled.

Salutation. What to do about a salutation is sticky. Many writers omit a salutation because they consider the message a memo. In the past, hard-copy memos were sent only to company insiders, and salutations were omitted. However, many e-mail messages now go to outsiders, and omitting a salutation seems curt and unfriendly. Thus, if you think it is appropriate, include a salutation. Including a salutation is also a visual cue to where the message begins. Many messages are transmitted or forwarded with such long headers that finding the beginning of the message can be difficult. A salutation helps, as shown in Figure 8.3. Other writers do not use a salutation; instead, they use the name of the recipient in the first sentence.

Body. The body of an e-mail message should be typed with upper- and lowercase characters—never in all uppercase or all lowercase characters. Cover just one topic, and try to keep the total message under three screens in length. To assist you, many e-mail programs have basic text-editing features, such as cut, copy, paste, and word-wrap. However, avoid boldface and italics because they create a string of control characters that may cause chaos on the recipient's computer.

Closing lines may include the writer's name, title, and organization.

Closing Lines. Conclude an external message, if you like, with a closing such as *Cheers* or *All the best* followed by your name and e-mail address (because some systems do not transmit your address automatically). If the recipient is unlikely to know you, it's not a bad idea to include your title and organization. Some veteran e-mail users include a signature file with identifying information embellished with keyboard art. Use restraint, however, because signature files take up precious bandwidth (Internet capacity).

Procedure and Information Memos and E-Mail Messages

4

Procedure and information memos typically flow downward and convey clear information about daily operations.

Business communicators write many different kinds of paper-based and electronic messages to conduct the operations of organizations. This chapter focuses on routine messages that can be grouped in three categories: (1) procedure and information messages, (2) request and reply messages, and (3) confirmation messages.

Most internal messages describe procedures and distribute information. These messages typically flow downward from management to employees and relate to the daily operation of an organization. When the topics are nonsensitive, follow the overall memo plan: clear subject line, direct opening, concise explanation, and action closing. They have one primary function: conveying your idea so clearly that no further explanation (return message, telephone call, or personal visit) is necessary.

In writing information and procedure memos, be careful of tone. Today's managers and team leaders seek employee participation and cooperation, but they can't achieve that rapport if they sound like dictators or autocrats. Avoid making accusations and fixing blame. Rather, explain changes, give reasons, and suggest benefits to the reader. Assume that employees want to contribute to the success of the organization and to their own achievement. Remember, too, that saying something negatively (*Don't park in Lot A*) is generally less helpful than saying it positively (*Park in Lot B until Lot A is repaired*).

Information memos use the straightforward approach in supplying details about organization activities, services, and actions. The following memo describes four child-care options. Notice how the information was designed for maximum visual impact and readability. Imagine how it would have looked if it had been presented in one or two big paragraphs.

Effective Memo

MEMO TO: Staff

Members of your employee council have met with representatives from management in considering the following four options to provide child care.

- *On-site day-care centres.* This option accommodates employees' children on the premises. Weekly rates would be competitive with local day-care facilities. This option is most costly but is worth pursuing, particularly if local facilities are deficient.
- *Off-site centres in conjunction with other local employers.* We are looking into the possibility of developing central facilities to be shared with nearby firms.
- *Neighbourhood child-care centres.* We would contract with local centres to buy open slots for employees' children, perhaps at a discount.
- *Sick-child services.* This plan would provide employees with alternatives to missing work when children are ill. We are investigating sick-child programs at local hospitals and services that send workers to employees' homes to look after sick children.

As soon as we gather more information about these options, we will pass that data along to you.

Straightforward opening immediately sets forth the purpose from the reader's viewpoint.

Since these items reflect no particular order, they are bulleted to present a slightly cleaner appearance than a numbered list.

Ends with forward-looking statement. No action is required.

Request and Reply Memos and E-Mail Messages

In requesting routine information or action within an organization, the direct approach works best. Generally, this means asking for information or making the request without first providing elaborate explanations and justifications. Remember that readers are usually thinking, "Why me? Why am I receiving this?" Readers can understand the explanation better once they know what you are requesting.

5

Request and reply memos follow the direct pattern in seeking or providing information.

If you are seeking answers to questions, you have two options for opening the memo: (1) ask the most important question first, followed by an explanation and then the other questions, or (2) use a polite command.

In the body of the memo, you can explain and justify your request or reply. When many questions must be asked, list them, being careful to phrase them similarly. Be courteous and friendly. In the closing include an end date (with a reason, if possible) to promote a quick response. For simple requests some writers encourage their readers to jot responses directly on the request memo. In answering e-mail messages, writers may request a quick reply.

The request shown below seeks information from managers about the use of temporary office workers. It begins with a polite command followed by numbered questions. Notice that the writer develops reader benefits by describing how the data collected will be used to help the reader. Notice, too, the effort to promote the feeling that the writer is part of a team working with employees to achieve their common goals.

MEMO TO: Department Managers

Opens with polite command → Please answer the questions listed below about the use of temporary help in your department.

Explains the purpose concisely → With your ideas we plan to develop a policy that will help us improve the process of budgeting, selecting, and hiring temporaries.

1. What is the average number of temporary office workers you employ each month?

Lists parallel questions for easy reading and comprehension →

2. What is the average length of a temporary worker's assignment in your department?

3. What specific job skills are you generally seeking in your temporaries?

4. What temporary agencies are you now using?

Includes end date, along with reason and reader benefit → By replying before January 20, you will have direct input into the new policy, which we will be developing at the end of the month. This improved policy will help you fill your temporary employment needs more quickly and more efficiently.

Overused and long-winded openers bore readers and waste their time.

Writers sometimes fall into bad habits in answering memos. Here are some trite and long-winded openers that are best avoided:

In response to your message of the 15th ... (*States the obvious*)

Thank you for your memo of the 15th in which you ... (*Suggests the writer can think of nothing more original*)

Pursuant to your request of the 15th ... (*Sounds old-fashioned*)

This is to inform you that ... (*Delays getting to the point*)

Direct opening statements can also be cheerful and emphatic.

Instead of falling into the trap of using one of the preceding shopworn openings, start directly by responding to the writer's request. If you agree to the request, show your cheerful compliance immediately. Consider these good-news openers:

Yes, we will be glad to ... (*Sends message of approval by opening with "Yes"*)

Here are answers to the questions you asked about ... (*Sounds straightforward, businesslike, and professional*)

You're right in seeking advice about ... (*Opens with two words that every reader enjoys seeing and hearing*)

After a direct and empathic opener, provide the information requested in a logical and coherent order. If you're answering a number of questions, arrange your answers in the order of the questions. In the favourable reply shown in Figure 8.4, information describing dates, speakers, and topics is listed in columns with headings. Although it requires more space than the paragraph format, this arrangement vastly improves readability and comprehension.

In providing additional data, use familiar words, short sentences, short paragraphs, and active-voice verbs. When alternatives exist, make them clear. Consider

FIGURE 8.4 **Reply Memo**

Tips for Formatting Hard-Copy Memos

- Set one tab to line up all entries evenly after SUBJECT.
- Leave two blank lines between SUBJECT line and first line of memo text.
- Single-space all but the shortest memos. Double-space between paragraphs.
- For memos printed on plain paper, leave a top margin of 2 inches for full-page memos and 1 inch for half-page memos.
- Use $1\frac{1}{4}$-inch side margins.
- If a memo requires two pages, use a second-page heading that includes the addressee's name, page number, and date.
- Handwrite your initials after your typed name.

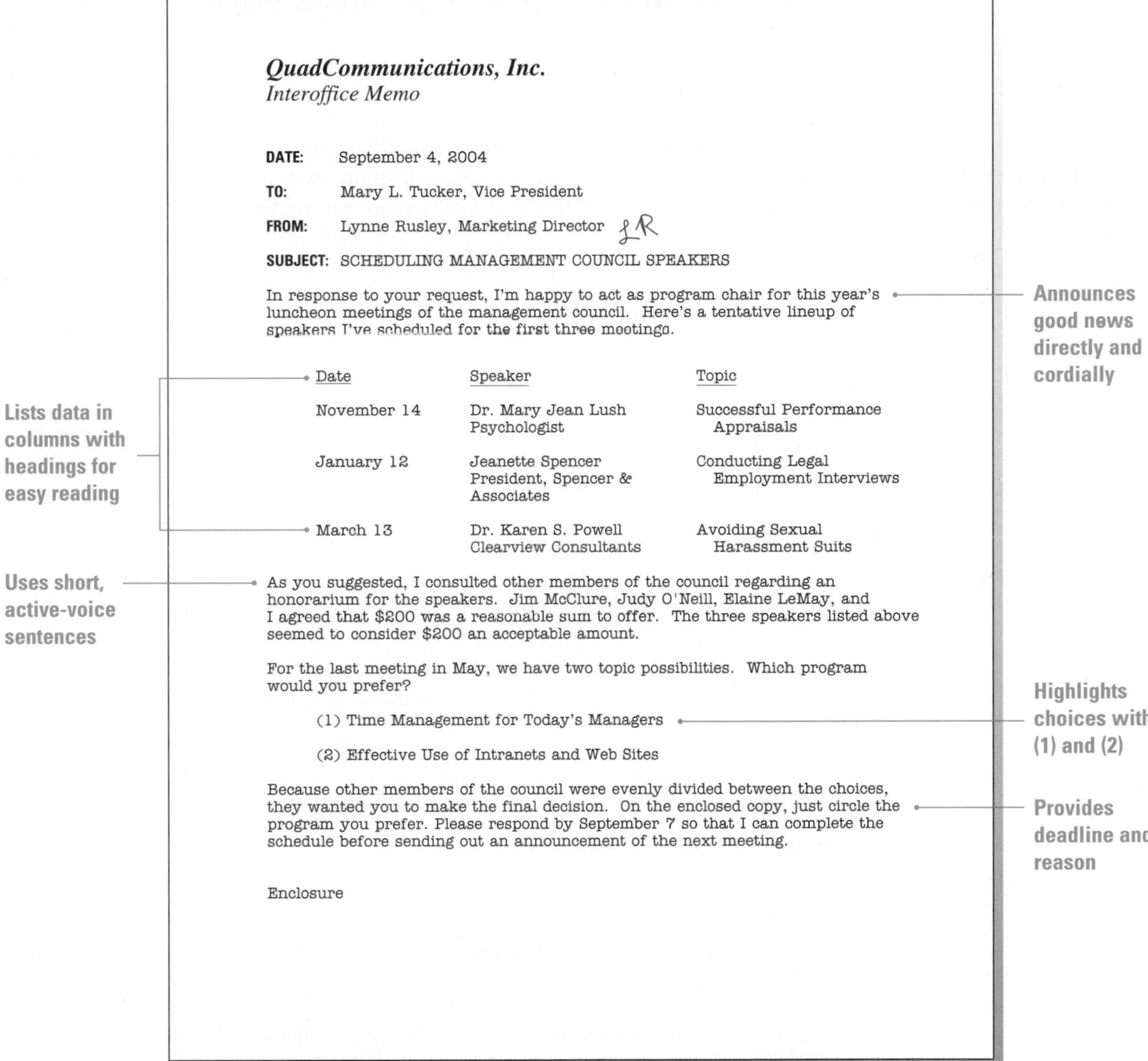

QuadCommunications, Inc.
Interoffice Memo

DATE: September 4, 2004

TO: Mary L. Tucker, Vice President

FROM: Lynne Rusley, Marketing Director LR

SUBJECT: SCHEDULING MANAGEMENT COUNCIL SPEAKERS

In response to your request, I'm happy to act as program chair for this year's luncheon meetings of the management council. Here's a tentative lineup of speakers I've scheduled for the first three meetings.

Date	Speaker	Topic
November 14	Dr. Mary Jean Lush Psychologist	Successful Performance Appraisals
January 12	Jeanette Spencer President, Spencer & Associates	Conducting Legal Employment Interviews
March 13	Dr. Karen S. Powell Clearview Consultants	Avoiding Sexual Harassment Suits

As you suggested, I consulted other members of the council regarding an honorarium for the speakers. Jim McClure, Judy O'Neill, Elaine LeMay, and I agreed that $200 was a reasonable sum to offer. The three speakers listed above seemed to consider $200 an acceptable amount.

For the last meeting in May, we have two topic possibilities. Which program would you prefer?

(1) Time Management for Today's Managers

(2) Effective Use of Intranets and Web Sites

Because other members of the council were evenly divided between the choices, they wanted you to make the final decision. On the enclosed copy, just circle the program you prefer. Please respond by September 7 so that I can complete the schedule before sending out an announcement of the next meeting.

Enclosure

Announces good news directly and cordially
Lists data in columns with headings for easy reading
Uses short, active-voice sentences
Highlights choices with (1) and (2)
Provides deadline and reason

using graphic highlighting techniques, as shown in Figure 8.4, for both the speakers' schedules and the two program choices offered further along in the letter. Imagine how much more effort would be required to read and understand the letter without the speaker list or the numbered choices.

If further action is required, be specific in spelling it out. What may be crystal clear to you (because you have been thinking about the problem) is not always immediately apparent to a reader with limited time and interest. Figure 8.4 not only illustrates a readable, well-organized reply memo, it also reviews formatting tips.

Confirmation Memos and E-Mail Messages

6

Confirmation memos provide a permanent record of oral discussions, decisions, and directives.

Confirmation memos—also called *to-file reports* or *incident reports*—record oral decisions, directives, and discussions. They create a concise, permanent record that could be important in the future. Because individuals may forget, alter, or retract oral commitments, it's wise to establish a written record of significant happenings. Such records are unnecessary, of course, for minor events. The confirmation e-mail message shown in Figure 8.5 reviews the significant points of a sales agreement discussed in a telephone conversation. When you write to confirm an oral agreement, remember these tips:

- Include names and titles of involved individuals.
- Itemize major issues or points concisely.
- Request feedback regarding unclear or inaccurate points.

Another type of confirmation memo simply verifies receipt of materials or a change of schedule. It is brief and often kept on file to explain your role in a project.

Confirmation memos can save employees from being misunderstood or blamed unfairly.

Some critics complain that too many "cover-your-tail" memos are written, thus creating excessive and unnecessary paperwork.[7] However, legitimate memos that confirm and clarify events have saved many thoughtful workers from being misunderstood or blamed unfairly.

Sometimes taken lightly, office memos and e-mail messages, like other business documents, should be written carefully. Once they leave the author's hands, they are essentially published. They can't be retrieved, corrected, or revised. Review the following checklist for tips in writing memos that accomplish what you intend.

Checklist for Writing Routine Memos and E-Mail Messages

Subject Line

✓ **Summarize the central idea.** Make the subject line read like a newspaper headline—brief but clear.

✓ **Use an abbreviated style.** Omit articles (*a, an, the*), and do not try to make the subject line a complete sentence. Omit an ending period.

Opening

✓ **State the purpose for writing.** Include the same information that's in the subject line, but expand it.

FIGURE 8.5 **Confirmation E-Mail**

Eudora Pro - [Lincoln Jones, CONFIRMATION OF CONVERSATION A]

File Edit Mailbox Message Transfer Special Tools Window Help

Standard MIME QP RR Send

To: Lincoln Jones <ljones@quatro.com>
From: Gwendolyn Hester <ghester@quatro.com>
Subject: CONFIRMATION OF CONVERSATION ABOUT SOFTWARE SALES AGREEMENT
Cc: <ktibbets@akron.net>, <rwolcott@quatro.com>
Bcc:
Attached:

Thanks, Lincoln, for talking with me Friday, August 1, about how your unit would market our software products at national trade shows. This e-mail message confirms our conversation and the four specific points on which we agreed:

1. David Williams, the chief product manager for my unit, will supply you with product descriptions, ad mats, catalogue tear sheets, and current price lists.

2. You will receive a 15 percent commission on all orders you generate from trade shows.

3. You will allow us three hours to demonstrate our new products at your September field staff meeting in Winnipeg.

4. This new arrangement is a six-month test to determine how much additional sales revenue your staff can generate for our software products.

We are confident that this new arrangement will be profitable for both of our divisions, and we look forward to using this new sales arrangement. If you agree that this message accurately reflects our conversation, please reply immediately with your agreement.

Gwen

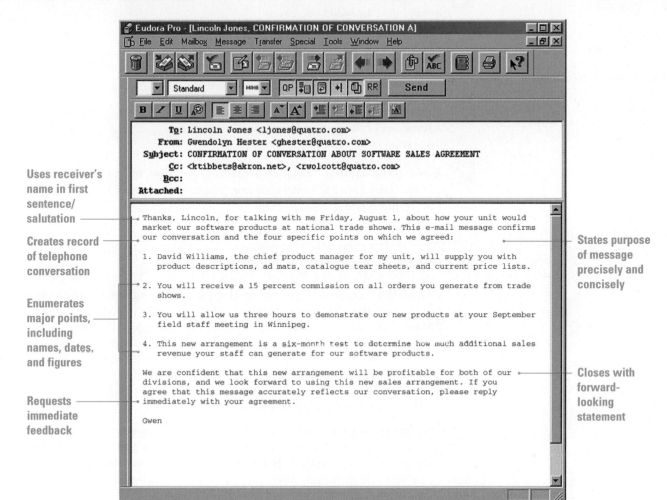

Uses receiver's name in first sentence/ salutation

Creates record of telephone conversation

Enumerates major points, including names, dates, and figures

Requests immediate feedback

States purpose of message precisely and concisely

Closes with forward-looking statement

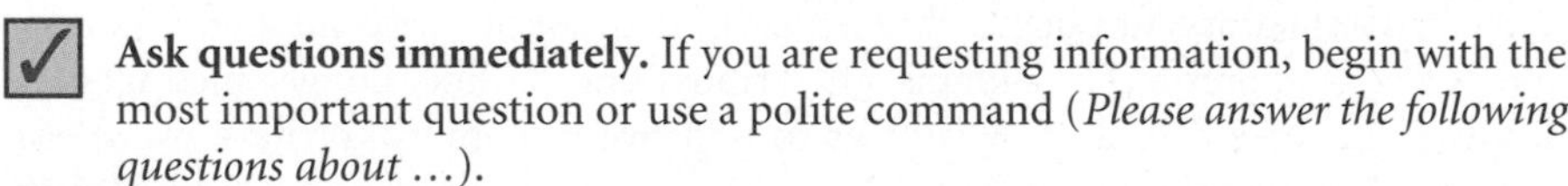

Ask questions immediately. If you are requesting information, begin with the most important question or use a polite command (*Please answer the following questions about …*).

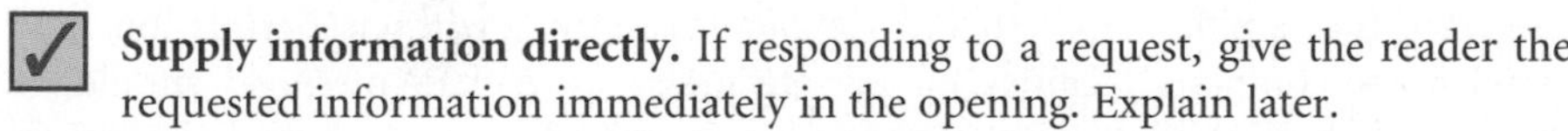

Supply information directly. If responding to a request, give the reader the requested information immediately in the opening. Explain later.

Body

Explain details. Arrange information logically. For complex topics use separate paragraphs developed coherently.

Enhance readability. Use short sentences, short paragraphs, and parallel construction for similar ideas.

Supply graphic highlighting. Provide bulleted and/or numbered lists, tables, or other graphic devices to improve readability and comprehension.

 **Be cautious.** Remember that memos and e-mail messages often travel far beyond their intended audiences.

Closing

 **Request action.** If appropriate, state specifically what you want the reader to do. Include a deadline, with reasons, if possible.

 **Summarize the memo or provide a closing thought.** For long memos provide a summary of the important points. If neither an action request nor a summary is necessary, end with a closing thought.

 **Avoid cliché endings.** Use fresh remarks rather than overused expressions such as *If you have additional questions, please do not hesitate to call* or *Thank you for your cooperation.*

Summary of Learning Objectives

1 **Discuss the characteristics of and writing process for successful memos and e-mail messages.** Successful memos and e-mails begin with DATE, TO, FROM, and SUBJECT and generally cover just one topic. They are written conversationally and concisely. Their content often can be highlighted with numbered or bulleted lists, headings, and tables. Before writing, determine whether you really must write. If you must, analyze your purpose and audience. Collect information, prepare an outline, and compose the first draft on a word processor. Revise for clarity and correctness. Encourage feedback from the reader.

2 **Analyze the organization of memos and e-mail messages.** The subject line summarizes the central idea, while the opening repeats that idea and amplifies it. The body explains and provides more information. The closing includes (a) action information, dates, and deadlines; (b) a summary of the memo; and/or (c) a closing thought.

3 **Explain how to use e-mail effectively, including practices, netiquette, and formatting.** Careful e-mail users do not transmit sensitive, confidential, inflammatory, or potentially embarrassing messages. Each message is concise and correctly addressed. It contains a descriptive subject line. Longer messages use headings, bulleted lists, and summaries to improve readability. Writers are careful about spelling, grammar, and usage. Courteous writers respond if requested, identify messages that are information only, avoid forwarding without permission, and avoid using company facilities for private messages. E-mail messages should be single-spaced with double-spacing between paragraphs. Salutations and closings are optional.

4 **Write information and procedure memos and e-mail messages.** Messages delivering information or outlining procedures follow the direct memo plan with the main idea stated immediately. Ideas must be explained so clearly that no further explanation is necessary. The tone of the memo should encourage cooperation.

5 **Write request and reply memos and e-mail messages.** Messages requesting action or information open with a specific request, followed by details. Memos that reply to requests open with information the reader most wants

to learn. The body contains details, and the closing may summarize the important points or look forward to a subsequent event or action.

6 **Write confirmation memos and e-mail messages.** Sometimes called "to-file reports" or "incident reports," confirmation messages create a permanent record of oral decisions, directives, and discussions. They should include names and titles of involved individuals, major issues discussed, and a request for approval by the receiver.

CHAPTER REVIEW

1. Name five characteristics of successful memos and e-mail messages. (Obj. 1)
2. What is graphic highlighting, and why is it particularly useful in memos and e-mail messages? (Obj. 1)
3. Briefly describe the writing process for memos and e-mail messages. (Obj. 1)
4. What three questions should you ask yourself before writing a memo or e-mail message? (Obj. 1)
5. Name three ways to close a memo or e-mail message. (Obj. 2)
6. What are some of the dangers for users of e-mail? (Obj. 3)
7. Suggest at least ten pointers that you could give to a first-time e-mail user. (Obj. 3)
8. Name at least five rules of e-mail etiquette that show respect for others. (Obj. 3)
9. What are three possibilities in handling the salutation for an e-mail message? (Obj. 3)
10. What tone should managers avoid in writing procedure or information memos and e-mail messages? (Obj. 4)
11. Why should writers of information memos and e-mail messages strive to express ideas positively instead of negatively? (Obj. 4)
12. Should a request memo or e-mail message open immediately with the request or with an explanation? Why? (Obj. 5)
13. What's wrong with a message opener such as *This is to inform you that ...*? (Obj. 5)
14. What is a confirmation memo or e-mail message? What other names could it be given? (Obj. 6)
15. What three elements should most confirmation memos and e-mail messages include? (Obj. 6)

CRITICAL THINKING

1. How can the writer of a business memo or an e-mail message develop a conversational tone and still be professional? Why do e-mail writers sometimes forget to be professional? (Objs. 1–3)
2. What factors would help you decide whether to write a memo, send an e-mail, make a telephone call, leave a voice-mail message, or deliver a message in person? (Objs. 1 and 2)
3. Why are lawyers and technology experts warning companies to store, organize, and manage computer data, including e-mail, with sharper diligence? (Obj. 3)
4. Discuss the ramifications of the following statement: Once a memo or any other document leaves your hands, you have essentially published it. (Objs. 2–6)

ACTIVITIES

8.1 Openers for Memos and E-Mail Messages (Objs. 1–3)

Revise the following memo openers so that they are more direct.

a. At the meeting of the management council last Thursday, you mentioned a very interesting study that you conducted last year. It reported data regarding employee turnover, and you said that it revealed some intriguing findings. Please send me a copy of your study.

b. I appreciate your asking me for my ideas on processing data electronically. In the nearly 15 years since EDI (electronic data interchange) was first introduced, large companies have always wanted their smaller suppliers to use it. But now with Internet-based systems, it's much more usable and less expensive. I've worked out six suggestions for how your company can switch to Internet-based EDI. They are discussed below.

c. I have before me your memo of the 16th in which you request permission to attend the Web Site Design Seminar sponsored by Presentation Planners. As I understand it, this is a two-day seminar scheduled for February 25 and 26. Your reasons for attending were well-stated and convincing. You have my permission to attend.

d. As you are aware, the document specialists in our department have been unhappy about their chairs and their inability to adjust the back height. The chairs are uncomfortable and cause back fatigue. As a result, I looked into the possibility of purchasing new adjustable chairs that I think will be just right for these employees. New chairs have been ordered for all these employees. The new chairs should be arriving in about three weeks.

8.2 Subject Lines (Objs. 1–3)

Write effective subject lines for the messages represented by the openings in Activity 8.1.

8.3 Graphic Highlighting Techniques (Objs. 1 and 3)

Revise the following hard-to-read paragraphs. Include an introductory statement or a title before presenting the data in bulleted or numbered lists.

a. A recent survey of car buyers uncovered some very interesting information about what electronic options they really wanted in new cars. Some technology visionaries have been saying that car buyers wanted a lot of fancy electronic gadgets, but the survey showed that only 5.1 percent, for example, wanted a trip computer. Most car buyers mentioned cruise control (79.1 percent). A total of 61.1 percent said that they wanted antilock brakes. A smaller percentage (50.5 percent) wanted keyless entry. Farther down the list we found that buyers wanted CD players (34.1 percent).

b. Our employee leasing program has proven to be an efficient management tool for business owners because we take care of everything. Our program will handle your payroll preparation. Moreover, benefits for employees are covered. We also know what a chore calculating worker's compensation premiums can be, so we do that for you. And we make all the necessary provincial and federal reports that are required today.

c. We are concerned about your safety in using our automated teller machines (ATMs) at night, so we think you should consider the following tips. Users of ATMs are encouraged to look around—especially at night—before using the service. If you notice anything suspicious, the use of another ATM is recommended. Or you could come back later. Another suggestion that we give our customers involves counting your cash. Be sure that the cash you receive is put away quickly. Don't count it as soon as you get it. It's better to check it in the safety of your car or at home. Also, why not take a friend with you if you must use an ATM at night? We also suggest that you park in a well-lighted area as close to the actual location of the ATM as possible.

8.4 Document for Analysis: Procedure Memo (Obj. 4)

Analyze the following memo. List its weaknesses. If your instructor directs, revise the memo.

DATE: Current

TO: Staff Members

FROM: Randy Eastman, Manager

SUBJECT: TIME MANAGEMENT SUGGESTIONS

Recently I had the pleasure of attending an excellent time management seminar in which we managers were told about some interesting strategies for managing the glut of information from which we all suffer. Since many of you have been complaining about all the time you spend on e-mail and voice mail, I thought I would send you some of the best pointers we were given. These might help you increase your productivity and decrease your frustration.

When it comes to e-mail, we were urged to practise e-mail "triage." This means glancing through all incoming mail quickly and separating the messages you need to answer immediately, as well as determining which messages can wait and which ones can be deleted. Generally, you can do this by checking subject lines and the names of senders. To cut down on the amount of time you spend on your e-mail, you should check e-mail messages only once or twice each day and at specific times so that you develop a routine. This simple practice can save you a lot of wasted time. Another technique involves time management but also courtesy. Be sure to respond briefly to all important e-mails, even if you can say only that you are looking into a matter.

When it comes to voice mail, check it at least three times a day. This prevents "message bump"—having the same person call you several times with the same request. Another idea for saving time with voice mail is to try skipping to the beep when you want to leave a message. Hit the star or pound key on your phone.

By the way, we need a volunteer to attend a conference on preventing violence in the workplace. Thank you for your cooperation.

8.5 Document for Analysis: Request Memo (Obj. 5)

Analyze the following memo. List its weaknesses. If your instructor directs, revise it.

DATE: Current

TO: All Employees

FROM: Elizabeth Mendoza, Human Resources

SUBJECT: NEW HOLIDAY PLAN

In the past we've offered all employees 11 holidays (starting with New Year's Day in January and proceeding through Christmas Day the following December). Other companies offer similar holiday schedules.

In addition, we've given all employees one floating holiday. As you know, we've determined that day by a company-wide vote. As a result, all employees had the same day off. Now, however, management is considering a new plan that we feel would be better. This new plan involves a floating holiday that each individual employee may decide for herself or himself. We've given it considerable thought and decided that such a plan could definitely work. We would allow each employee to choose a day that he or she wants. Of course, we would have to issue certain restrictions. Selections would have to be subject to our staffing needs within individual departments. For example, if everyone wanted the same day, we could not allow everyone to take it. In that case, we would allow the employee with the most seniority to have the day off.

Before we institute the new plan, though, we wanted to see what employees thought about this. Is it better to continue our current company-wide uniform floating holiday? Or should we try an individual floating holiday? Please let us know what you think as soon as possible.

8.6 Document for Analysis: Confirmation E-Mail (Obj. 6)

Analyze the following e-mail message. List its weaknesses. If your instructor directs, revise it.

To: WilliamMorrison@commercial.com

From: TracyAnnPhillips@aol.com

Subject: COMMERCIALS

It was good to talk to you on the telephone yesterday after exchanging letters with you and after reading so much about Bermuda. I was very interested in learning about the commercials you want me to write.
As I understand it, Mr. Morrison, you want a total of 240 one-minute radio commercials. These commercials are intended to rejuvenate the slumping tourist industry in Bermuda. You said that these commercials would be broadcast from March 30 through June 30. You said these commercials would be played on three radio stations. These stations are in five major cities on the East Coast. The commercials would be aimed at morning and evening drive time, for drivers who are listening to their radios, and the campaign would be called "Radio Bermuda."

I am sure I can do as you suggested in reminding listeners that Bermuda is less than three hours away. You expect me to bring to these commercials the colour and character of the island. You want me to highlight the attractions and the civility of Bermuda, at least as much as can be done in one-minute radio commercials. In my notes I wrote that you also mentioned that I should include references to tree frogs and royal palm trees. Another item you suggested that I include in some of the commercials was special Bermuda food, such as delicacies like shark on toast, conch fritters, and mussel stew.

I wanted to be sure to write these points down so that we both agreed on what we said in our telephone conversation. I am eager to begin working on these commercials immediately, but I would feel better if you looked over these points to see if I have it right. I look forward to working with you.

8.7 Information Memo: What I Do on the Job (Obj. 4)

Some employees have remarked to the boss that they are working more than other employees. Your boss has decided to study the matter by collecting memos from everyone. He asks you to write a memo describing your current duties and the skills required for your position. If some jobs are found to be overly demanding, your boss may redistribute job tasks or hire additional employees. Based on your own work or personal experience, write a well-organized memo describing your duties, the time you spend on each task, and the skills needed for what you do. Provide enough details to make a clear record of your job. Use actual names and describe actual tasks. Report to the head of the organization. The organization could be a campus club or committee on which you serve. Don't make your memo a list of complaints. Just describe what you do in an objective tone. And by the way, your boss appreciates brevity. Keep your memo under one page.

8.8 Information Memo: Retirement Questions (Obj. 4)

Team

The following memo was assigned by a writing consultant as an exercise to train your team in writing skills. In small groups discuss its weaknesses and then compose, either individually or as a team, an improved version.

DATE: Current

TO: All Employees

FROM: Mark Grist, Employee Benefits Division

SUBJECT: RETIREMENT

We are aware that many employees do not have sufficient information that relates to the prospect of their retirement. Many employees who are approaching retirement age have come to this office with specific questions about their retirement. It would be much easier for us to answer all these questions at once, and that is what we will try to do.

We would like to answer your questions at a series of retirement planning sessions in the company conference room. The first meeting is September 6. We will start at 4 p.m., which means that the company is giving you one hour of released time to attend this important session. We will meet from 4 to 6 p.m. when we will stop for dinner. We will begin again at 7 p.m. and finish at 8 p.m.

We have arranged for three speakers. They are: our company benefits supervisor, a financial planner, and a psychologist who treats retirees who have mental problems. The three sessions are planned for: September 6, October 4, and November 1.

8.9 Information Memo or E-Mail: Wilderness Retreat (Obj. 4)

E-Mail

Assume you are Mark Peters, president of a small printing operation employing 25 workers. On Friday, June 7, your print shop employees will join you at an expense-paid, one-day retreat that you hope will improve teamwork among the workers. The retreat will be led by Wilderness Retreats, which offers companies outdoor team training designed to build employee trust, teamwork, and loyalty. Employees will meet at work at 8 a.m., and a Wilderness Retreats van will pick them up and take them to a nearby provincial park. Employees will spend the day on team-building activities, including a map-reading exercise that will require employee teams to find their way through a wooded area to a "home base." The retreat will provide a catered picnic lunch and time for socializing. The group will return to work by 4 p.m. Since the print shop will be closed during the retreat, you consider the retreat a work day and expect all employees to attend. Employees should dress casually. They'll be outside most of the day. Write a memo to employees announcing the retreat.

8.10 Procedure Memo: Ticket-Free Parking (Obj. 4)

Assume that you are Tran Crozier, director of the Human Resources Division of IBM at Markham, Ontario. Both day- and swing-shift employees need to be reminded of the parking guidelines. Day-shift employees must park in Lots A and B in their assigned spaces. If they have not registered their cars and received their white stickers, the cars will be ticketed.

Day-shift employees are forbidden to park at the curb. Swing-shift employees may park at the curb before 3:30 p.m. Moreover, after 3:30 p.m., swing-shift employees may park in any empty space—except those marked Tandem, Handicapped, Van Pool, Car Pool, or Management. Day-shift employees may loan their spaces to other employees if they know they will not be using the space.

One serious problem is lack of registration (as evidenced by white stickers). Registration is done by Employee Relations. Any car without a sticker will be ticketed. To encourage registration, Employee Relations will be in the cafeteria May 12 and 13 from 11:30 a.m. to 1:30 p.m. and from 3 p.m. to 5 p.m. to take applications and issue white parking stickers.

Write a memo to employees that reviews the parking guidelines and encourages them to get their cars registered. Use itemization techniques and strive for a tone that fosters a sense of cooperation rather than resentment.

8.11 Request Memo or E-Mail: Smokers vs. Nonsmokers (Obj. 5)

E-Mail

As Lindsay English, director of human resources, write a memo to all department managers of General Wheat, a large foods company. The City of Toronto has mandated that employees "shall adopt, implement, and maintain a written smoking policy which shall contain a prohibition against smoking in restrooms and infirmaries." Employers must also "maintain a nonsmoking area of not less than two thirds of the seating capacity in cafeterias, lunchrooms, and employee lounges, and make efforts to work out disputes between smokers and nonsmokers." Make this announcement to your department managers. Tell the managers that you want them to set up departmental committees to mediate any smoking conflicts before the complaints surface. Explain why this is a good policy.

8.12 Reply Memo or E-Mail: Enforcing Smoking Ban (Obj. 5)

E-Mail

You are Bruni Comenic, manager of accounting services for General Wheat, responding to Ms. English's memo in the preceding activity. You could have called Ms. English, but you prefer to have a permanent record of this message. You are having difficulty enforcing the smoking ban in restrooms. Only one men's room serves your floor, and 9 of your 27 male employees are smokers. You have already received complaints, and you see no way to enforce the ban in the restrooms. You have also noticed that smokers are taking longer breaks than other employees. Smokers complain that they need more time because they must walk to an outside area. Smokers are especially unhappy when the weather is cold, rainy, or snowy. Moreover, smokers huddle near the building entrances, thus creating a negative impression for customers and visitors. Your committee members can find no solutions; in fact, they have become polarized in their meetings to date. You need help from a higher authority. Appeal to Ms. English for solutions. Perhaps she should visit your department.

8.13 Reply Memo or E-Mail: What's New at the P.O.? (Obj. 5)

E-Mail | Web

As Leticia Lawrence, assume that you work for MagicMedia, Inc., a large software manufacturer. The office manager, Patricia Wildey, asks you to seek two kinds of information from Canada Post. First, she wants to learn exactly how envelopes should be addressed according to Canada Post guidelines. Second, she wants to know how MagicMedia, Inc., can get involved in Canada Post's Literacy Awards. The easiest way to obtain both sets of information is by visiting the Canada Post Web site **<www.canadapost.ca>**. If that is impossible, go to a local office. Write a one-page memo summarizing your findings.

8.14 Reply Memo: Rescheduling Interviews (Obj. 5)

Your boss, Fred Knox, had scheduled three appointments to interview applicants for an accounting position. All of these appointments were for Friday, October 7. However, he now must travel to Halifax on that weekend. He asks you to reschedule all the appointments for one week later. He also wants a brief summary of the background of each candidate.

You call each person and arrange these times. Paul Scheffel, who has been an accountant for 15 years with Bechtel Corporation, agreed to come at 10:30 a.m. Mark Cunningham, who is a CPA and a consultant to many companies, will come at 11:30. Geraldine Simpson, who has a B.A. degree and eight years of experience in payroll accounting, will come at 9:30 a.m. You're wondering whether Mr. Knox forgot to include Don Stastry, operations personnel officer, in these interviews. Mr. Stastry usually is part of the selection process. Write a memo to Mr. Knox including all the vital information he needs.

8.15 Request Memo or E-Mail: Dress-Down Day for Us? (Obj. 5)

According to a poll funded by Levi Strauss & Co., more than half of all white-collar workers now can dress casually at work. The dress-down trend reflects larger changes in work patterns. Top-down management is less prevalent, and more people work at home or have flexible hours.

Play the role of Thomas Marshall, CEO of Marshall & Associates, a sedate accountancy firm. You have had some inquiries from your accountants and other employees about the possibility of dressing casually—not all the time, but occasionally. You decide to ask a few key people what they think about establishing a casual-dress day. It sounds like a good idea, especially if it makes people feel more at ease in the office. But you worry that it might look unprofessional and encourage sloppy work and horsing around. Moreover, you are concerned about what people might wear, such as shorts, tank tops, T-shirts with slogans, baseball caps, and dirty athletic clothes. Would a dress-down policy make the office atmosphere less professional? Perhaps a written dress code will be necessary if a casual-dress policy is allowed.

To solicit feedback, you write the same memo to two partners and your office manager. Ask for their opinions, but do so with specific questions. Be sure to include an end date so that you can decide on a course of action before the next management council meeting. Address the same memo or e-mail to Mary E. Leslie **<mel@marsh.com>**, Sam W. Miller **<sam@marsh.com>**, and Jonathon Galston **<jon@marsh.com>**.[8]

8.16 Reply E-Mail: Dress-Down Discussion and Decision (Obj. 5)

Team | Critical Thinking | E-Mail

Casual dress in professional offices seems to be increasingly common. Get together in groups to discuss a suitable response to the request made in Activity 8.15. Should the accountancy firm allow employees one dress-down day a week? Why or why not? If you decide to recommend a dress-down day, consider whether a dress code is appropriate. Give reasons. Then decide whether a dress down day would affect the professional environment of the office. You can tell from the CEO's words that he favours a limited dress-down program. But your team should make up its own mind. Once you reach consensus, respond to the boss either in individual memos or a team-written memo. Be sure to answer the questions and issues raised in Activity 8.15. Your reply memo should go to CEO Thomas Marshall **<tmarshall@marsh.com>**.

8.17 Confirmation Memo or E-Mail: Looking Over the Employee's Shoulder (Obj. 6)

E-Mail

At lunch one day you had a stimulating discussion with Barbara Wilson, your company lawyer, about e-mail privacy. You brought up the topic because you will be attending a conference shortly on Internet uses and abuses, and you will be serving on a panel discussing e-mail privacy. As you recall, Ms. Wilson emphasized the fact that the employer owns the workplace. She said, "It owns the desks, machines, stationery, computers, and everything else. Employees have no legal right to use the employer's property for personal business."

Equally important, however, is the recognition of a right to privacy, even in the workplace. "If an employee can demonstrate that the employer violated his or her reasonable expectation of privacy," said Ms. Wilson, "then he or she can hold the employer liable for that violation." You also remember a rather startling comment. Ms. Wilson said that an employer may listen to or read only as much of a communication as is necessary for the employer to determine whether it is personal or business. You wonder if you remembered this conversation accurately. Since one of the topics your panel will discuss is whether employers may monitor e-mail, you decide to write to Ms. Wilson to confirm what she said.[9]

C.L.U.E. REVIEW 8

Edit the following sentences to correct all language faults, including grammar, punctuation, spelling, and word use.

1. Mr. Krikorian always tries however to wear a tie and shirt that has complimentary colours.
2. The house of commons committee on trade and commerce are holding hearings in twenty-one city's.
3. Consumer buying and spending for the past 5 years, is being studied by a Federal team of analysts.
4. Because we recommend that students bring there own supplies; the total expense for the trip should be a miner amount.
5. Wasn't it Mr Cohen not Ms Lyons who asked for a tuition waver.
6. As soon as we can verify the figures either my sales manager or myself will call you, nevertheless, you must continue to disperse payroll funds.
7. Our human resources department which was formerly in room 35 has moved it's offices to room 5.
8. We have arranged interviews on the following dates, Wednesday at 330 pm Thursday at 1030 am and Friday at 415 pm.
9. The Bay News our local newspaper featured as its principle article a story entitled, Smarter E-Mail is here.
10. Every one on the payroll, which includes all dispatchers and supervisors were cautioned to maintain careful records everyday.

CHAPTER • 9 •

PERSUASIVE AND SALES MESSAGES

LEARNING OBJECTIVES

1 Apply the 3-×-3 writing process to persuasive messages.

2 Explain the components of a persuasive message.

3 Request favours and action effectively.

4 Write convincing persuasive messages within organizations.

5 Request adjustments and make claims successfully.

6 Compose successful sales messages.

7 Describe the basic elements included in effective media releases.

Strategies for Making Persuasive Requests

Successful persuasion results from a reasonable request and a well-presented argument.

The ability to persuade is one of life's important skills. Persuading means using argument or discussion to change an individual's beliefs or actions. Persuasion, of course, is a very important part of any business that sells goods or services. And selling online is even more challenging than other forms of persuasion due to the technology barrier that must be overcome. However, many of the techniques that may be used are similar to those you will use in persuasion at home, at school, and on the job.

Doubtless you've had to be persuasive to convert others to your views or to motivate them to do what you want. The outcome of such efforts depends largely on the reasonableness of your request, your credibility, and the ability to make your request attractive to the receiver. In this chapter you will learn many techniques and strategies to help you be successful in any persuasive effort.

When you think that your listener or reader is inclined to agree with your request, you can start directly with the main idea. But when the receiver is likely to resist, don't reveal the purpose too quickly. Ideas that require persuasion often benefit from a slow approach that includes ample preparation.

You must gain attention and move to logical reasons supporting your request. This indirect pattern is effective when you must persuade people to grant you favours, accept your recommendations, make adjustments in your favour, or grant your claims.

Effective sales messages reflect thorough product knowledge, writer credibility, and specific reader benefits.

The same is true for sales messages. Instead of making a sales pitch immediately, smart communicators prepare a foundation by developing credibility and linking their requests to benefits for the receiver. In persuasive messages other than sales, you must know precisely what you want the receiver to think or do. You must also anticipate what appeals to make or "buttons to push" to motivate action. Achieving these goals in both written and oral messages requires special attention to the initial steps in the process.

Applying the 3-×-3 Writing Process to Persuasive Messages

1

Persuasion means changing people's views, and that's a difficult task. Pulling it off demands planning and perception. The 3-×-3 writing process provides you with a helpful structure for laying a foundation for persuasion. Of particular importance here are (1) analyzing the purpose, (2) adapting to the audience, (3) collecting information, and (4) organizing the message.

Persuasive messages require careful analysis of the purpose for writing.

Analyzing the Purpose. The purpose of a persuasive message is to convert the receiver to your ideas or to motivate action. A message without a clear purpose is doomed. Not only must you know what your purpose is and what response you want, but you must know these things when you start writing a letter or planning a presentation. Too often, ineffective communicators reach the end of a message before discovering exactly what they want the receiver to do. Then they must start over, giving the request a different "spin" or emphasis. Because your purpose establishes the strategy of the message, determine it first.

By identifying your purpose up front, you can shape the message to point toward it. This planning effort saves considerable rewriting time and produces the most successful persuasive messages.

CAREER COACH

SEVEN RULES EVERY PERSUADER SHOULD KNOW

Successful businesspeople create persuasive memos, letters, reports, and presentations that get the results they want. Yet, their approaches are all different. Some persuaders are gentle, leading readers by the hand to the targeted recommendation. Others are brisk and authoritative. Some are objective, examining both sides of an issue like a judge deciding a difficult case. Some move slowly and carefully toward a proposal, while others erupt like a volcano in their eagerness to announce a recommendation.

Because of the immense number of variables involved, no single all-purpose strategy works for every persuasive situation. You wouldn't, for example, use the same techniques in asking for a raise from a stern supervisor as you would use in persuading a close friend to see a movie of your choice. Different situations and different goals require different techniques. The following seven rules suggest various strategies—depending on your individual need.

- **Consider whether your views will create problems for your audience.** If your views make trouble for the audience, think of ways to include the receivers in your recommendation if possible. Whatever your strategy, be tactful and empathic.
- **Don't offer new ideas, directives, or recommendations for change until your audience is prepared for them.** Receivers are threatened by anything that upsets their values or interests. The greater the change you suggest, the more slowly you should proceed.
- **Select a strategy that supports your credibility.** If you have great credibility with your audience, you can proceed directly. If not, you might want to establish that credibility first. *Given* credibility results from position or reputation, such as that of the boss of an organization or a highly regarded scientist. *Acquired* credibility is earned.

  To acquire credibility, successful persuaders often identify themselves, early in the message, with the goals and interests of the audience (*As a small business owner myself* . . .). Another way to acquire credibility is to mention evidence or ideas that support the audience's existing views (*We agree that small business owners need more government assistance*). Finally, you can acquire credibility by citing authorities who rate highly with your audience (*Richard Love, recently named Small Businessperson of the Year, supports this proposal*).
- **If your audience disagrees with your ideas or is uncertain about them, present both sides of the argument.** You might think that you would be most successful by revealing only one side of an issue—your side, of course. But persuasion doesn't work that way. You'll be more successful—particularly if the audience is unfriendly or uncertain—by disclosing *all* sides of an argument. This approach suggests that you are objective. It also helps the receiver remember your view by showing the pros and cons in relation to one another.
- **Win respect by making your opinion or recommendation clear.** Although you should be truthful in presenting both sides of an argument, don't be shy in supporting your conclusions or final proposals. You will, naturally, have definite views and should persuade your audience to accept them. The two-sided strategy is a means to an end, but it does not mean compromising your argument. Be decisive and make specific recommendations.
- **Place your strongest points strategically.** Some experts argue that if your audience is deeply concerned with your subject, you can afford to begin with your weakest points. Because of its commitment, the audience will stay with you until you reach the strongest points at the end of your argument.

  For an unmotivated audience, begin with your strongest points to get them interested. Other experts feel that a supportive audience should receive the main ideas or recommendations immediately, to avoid wasting time. Whichever position you choose, don't bury your recommendation, strongest facts, or main idea in the middle of your argument.
- **Don't count on changing attitudes by offering information alone.** "If customers knew the truth about our costs, they would not object to our prices," some companies reason. Well, don't bet on it. Companies have pumped huge sums into advertising and public relations

(continued)

campaigns that provided facts alone. Such efforts often fail because learning something new (that is, increasing the knowledge of the audience) is rarely an effective way to change attitudes. Researchers have found that presentations of facts alone may strengthen opinions—but primarily for people who already agree with the persuader. The added information reassures them and provides ammunition for defending themselves in discussions with others.

Adapting to the Audience. While you're considering the purpose of a persuasive message, you also need to concentrate on the receiver. How can you adapt your request to that individual so that your message is heard? A persuasive message is equally futile unless it meets the needs of its audience. In a broad sense, you'll be seeking to show how your request helps the receiver achieve some of life's major goals or fulfils key needs: money, power, comfort, confidence, importance, friends, peace of mind, and recognition, to name a few.

Effective persuasive messages focus on audience needs or goals.

On a more practical level, you want to show how your request solves a problem, achieves a personal or work objective, or just makes life easier for your audience.

To adapt your request to the receiver, consider these questions that receivers will very likely be asking themselves:

Why should I?	Says who?
What's in it for me?	What's in it for you?

Adapting to your audience means being ready to answer these questions. It means learning about audience members and analyzing why they might resist your proposal. It means searching for ways to connect your purpose with their needs. If completed before you begin writing, such analysis goes a long way toward overcoming resistance and achieving your goal. The accompanying Career Coach box presents additional strategies that can make you a successful persuader.

Researching and Organizing Data. Once you've analyzed the audience and considered how to adapt your message to its needs, you're ready to collect data and organize it. You might brainstorm and prepare cluster diagrams to provide a rough outline of ideas.

The next step is organizing your data. Suppose you have already decided that your request will meet with resistance. Thus, you decide not to open directly with your request. Instead, you use the four-part indirect pattern, listed below and shown graphically in Figure 9.1:

- Gain attention
- Build interest
- Reduce resistance
- Motivate action

The key components of a persuasive request are gaining attention, showing the worth of the proposal, overcoming resistance, and motivating action.

FIGURE 9.1 **Four-Part Indirect Pattern for Persuasion**

Gaining Attention	Building Interest	Reducing Resistance	Motivating Action
Free offer	Rational appeals	Testimonials	Gift
Promise	Emotional appeals	Satisfied users	Incentive
Question	Dual appeals	Guarantee	Limited offer
Quotation	Product description	Warranty	Deadline
Proverb	Reader benefits	Free trial	Guarantee
Product feature	Cold facts mixed with warm feelings	Sample	Repetition of selling feature
Testimonial		Performance tests	
Startling statement		Polls, awards	
Action setting			

Blending the Components of a Persuasive Message

2

Although the indirect pattern appears to contain separate steps, successful persuasive messages actually blend these steps into a seamless whole. However, the sequence of the components may change depending on the situation and the emphasis. Regardless of where they are placed, the key elements in persuasive requests are (1) gaining the audience's attention, (2) convincing them that your proposal is worthy, (3) overcoming resistance, and (4) motivating action.

Successful openers to persuasive requests are brief, targeted, and interesting.

Gaining Attention. To grab attention, the opening statement in a persuasive request should be brief, relevant, and engaging. When only mild persuasion is necessary, the opener can be low-key and factual. If, however, your request is substantial and you anticipate strong resistance, provide a thoughtful, provocative opening. The following examples suggest possibilities.

- **Problem description.** In a recommendation to hire temporary employees: *Last month legal division staff members were forced to work 120 overtime hours, costing us $6000 and causing considerable employee unhappiness.* With this opener you've presented a capsule of the problem your proposal will help solve.
- **Unexpected statement.** In a memo to encourage employees to attend an optional sensitivity seminar: *Men and women draw the line at decidedly different places in identifying what behaviour constitutes sexual harassment.* Note how this opener gets readers thinking immediately.
- **Reader benefit.** In a proposal offering writing workshops to an organization: *For every letter or memo your employees can avoid writing, your organization saves $78.50.* Companies are always looking for ways to cut costs, and this opener promises significant savings.
- **Compliment.** In a letter inviting a business executive to speak: *Because our members admire your success and value your managerial expertise, they want you to be our speaker.* In offering praise or compliments, however, be careful to avoid obvious flattery.
- **Related fact.** In a memo encouraging employees to start car pooling: *A car pool is defined as two or more persons who travel to work in one car at least once a week.* An

interesting, relevant, and perhaps unknown fact sets the scene for the interest-building section that follows.

- **Stimulating question.** In a plea for funds to support environmental causes: *What do Mike Bullard, the Sequoia redwood tree, and the spotted owl have in common?* Readers will be curious to find the answer to this intriguing question.

Building Interest. After capturing attention, a persuasive request must retain that attention and convince the audience that the request is reasonable. To justify your request, be prepared to invest in a few paragraphs of explanation. Persuasive requests are likely to be longer than direct requests because the audience must be convinced rather than simply instructed. You can build interest and conviction through the use of the following:

- Facts, statistics
- Examples
- Expert opinion
- Specific details
- Direct benefits
- Indirect benefits

Showing how your request can benefit the audience directly or indirectly is a key factor in persuasion. One direct benefit is a tax write-off for the contribution. An indirect benefit comes from feeling good about helping the college and knowing that students will benefit from the gift. Nearly all charities rely in large part on indirect benefits—the selflessness of givers—to promote their causes.

The body of a persuasive request may require several paragraphs to build interest and reduce resistance.

Reducing Resistance. One of the biggest mistakes in persuasive requests is the failure to anticipate and offset audience resistance. How will the receiver object to your request? In brainstorming for clues, try *What if?* scenarios. For each *What if?* scenario, you need a counterargument.

Unless you anticipate resistance, you give the receiver an easy opportunity to dismiss your request. Countering this resistance is important, but you must do it with finesse. You can minimize objections by presenting your counterarguments in sentences that emphasize benefits. However, don't spend too much time on counterarguments, thus making them overly important. Finally, avoid bringing up objections that may never have occurred to the receiver in the first place.

Persuasive requests reduce resistance by addressing *What if?* questions and establishing credibility.

Another factor that reduces resistance is credibility. Receivers are less resistant if your request is reasonable and if you are believable. When the receiver does not know you, you may have to establish your expertise, refer to your credentials, or demonstrate your competence. Even when you are known, you may have to establish your knowledge in a given area. Some charities establish their credibility by displaying on their stationery the names of prominent people who serve on their boards. The credibility of speakers making presentations is usually outlined by someone who introduces them.

Motivating Action. After gaining attention, building interest, and reducing resistance, you'll want to inspire the receiver to act. This is where your planning pays dividends. Knowing exactly what action you favour before you start to write enables you to point your arguments toward this important final paragraph. Here you will make your recommendation as specifically and confidently as possible—without seeming pushy. Compare the following closings for a persuasive memo recommending training seminars in communication skills.

Persuasive requests motivate action by specifying exactly what should be done.

Too General
We are certain we can develop a series of training sessions that will improve the communication skills of your employees.

Too Timid
If you agree that our training proposal has merit, perhaps we could begin the series in June.

Too Pushy
Because we're convinced that you will want to begin improving the skills of your employees immediately, we've scheduled your series to begin in June.

Effective
You will see decided improvement in the communication skills of your employees. Please call me at 439-2201 by May 1 to give your approval so that training sessions may start in June, as we discussed.

Note how the last opening suggests a specific and easy-to-follow action. Figure 9.2 summarizes techniques for overcoming resistance and crafting successful persuasive messages.

Being Persuasive but Ethical

Ethical business communicators maintain credibility and respect by being honest, fair, and objective.

Business communicators may be tempted to make their persuasion even more forceful by fudging on the facts, exaggerating a point, omitting something crucial, or providing deceptive emphasis. Consider the case of a manager who sought to persuade employees to accept a change in insurance benefits. His memo emphasized a small perk (easier handling of claims) but de-emphasized a major reduction in total coverage. Some readers missed the main point—as the manager intended. Others recognized the deception, however, and before long the manager's credibility was lost. A persuader is effective only when he or she is trusted. If receivers suspect that they are being manipulated or misled, or if they find any part of the argument untruthful, the total argument often fails. Persuaders can also fall into traps of logic without even being aware of it. Avoid the common logical fallacies of circular reasoning, begging the question, post hoc (after, thus, because).

FIGURE 9.2 **Components of a Persuasive Message**

Gaining Attention	Building Interest	Reducing Resistance	Motivating Action
Summary of problem	Facts, figures	Anticipate objections	Describe specific request
Unexpected statement	Expert opinion	Offer counterarguments	Sound confident
Reader benefit	Examples	Play *What if?* scenarios	Make action easy to take
Compliment	Specific details	Establish credibility	Offer incentive
Related fact	Direct benefits	Demonstrate competence	Don't provide excuses
Stimulating question	Indirect benefits	Show value of proposal	Repeat main benefit

Persuasion becomes unethical when facts are distorted, overlooked, or manipulated with an intent to deceive. Of course, persuaders naturally want to put forth their strongest case. But that argument must be based on truth, objectivity, and fairness.

In prompting ethical and truthful persuasion, two factors act as powerful motivators. The first is the desire to preserve your reputation and credibility. Once lost, a good name is difficult to regain. An equally important force prompting ethical behaviour, though, is your opinion of yourself.

Writing Successful Persuasive Requests

3

Convincing someone to change a belief or to perform an action when that individual is reluctant requires planning and skill—and sometimes a little luck. When the request is in writing, rather than face to face, the task is even more difficult. The indirect pattern, though, can help you shape effective persuasive appeals that (1) request favours and action, (2) persuade within organizations, and (3) request adjustments and make claims.

Requesting Favours and Actions

Persuading someone to do something that largely benefits you is not easy. Fortunately, many individuals and companies are willing to grant requests for time, money, information, special privileges, and cooperation. They grant these favours for a variety of reasons. They may just happen to be interested in your project, or they may see goodwill potential for themselves. Often, though, they comply because they see that others will benefit from the request. Professionals sometimes feel obligated to contribute their time or expertise to "pay their dues."

Shaping direct and indirect appeals is an important part of the persuasive process.

You may find that you have few direct benefits to offer in your persuasion. Instead, you'll be focusing on indirect benefits, as the writer does in Figure 9.3. In asking a manager to speak before a marketing meeting, the writer has little to offer as a direct benefit other than a $300 honorarium. But indirectly, the writer offers enticements such as an enthusiastic audience and a chance to help other companies solve overseas marketing problems. This persuasive request appeals primarily to the reader's desire to serve his profession—although a receptive audience and an opportunity to talk about one's successes have a certain ego appeal as well. Together, these appeals—professional, egoistic, monetary—make a persuasive argument convincing and effective.

An offer to work as an intern, at no cost to a company, would seem to require little persuasion. Actually, though, companies hesitate to participate in internship programs because student interns require supervision, desk space, and equipment. They also pose an insurance liability threat.

In Figure 9.4 college student Melanie Harris seeks to persuade Software Enterprises to accept her as an intern. In the analysis process before writing, Melanie thought long and hard about what benefits she could offer the reader and how she could present them strategically. She decided that the offer of a trained college student's free labour was her strongest benefit. Thus, she opens with it, as well as mentioning the same benefit in the letter body and in the closing. After opening with the main audience benefit, she introduces the actual request (*Could you use the part-time services of a college senior ...?*).

In the interest section, Melanie tells why she is making the request and describes its value in terms of direct and indirect benefits. Notice how she transforms obstacles (lack of equipment or desk space) into helpful suggestions about how her ser-

FIGURE 9.3 **Persuasive Favour Request**

1 PREWRITING

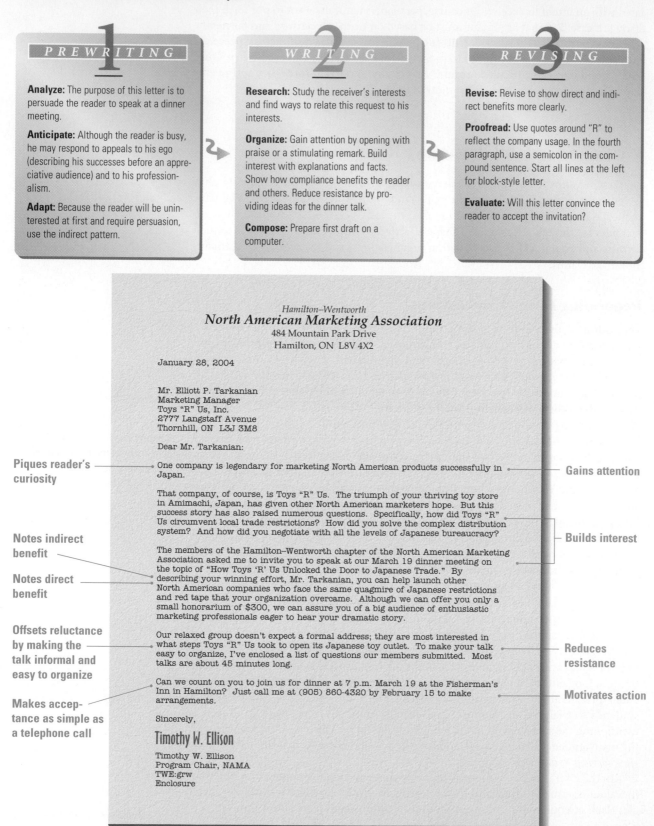

Analyze: The purpose of this letter is to persuade the reader to speak at a dinner meeting.

Anticipate: Although the reader is busy, he may respond to appeals to his ego (describing his successes before an appreciative audience) and to his professionalism.

Adapt: Because the reader will be uninterested at first and require persuasion, use the indirect pattern.

2 WRITING

Research: Study the receiver's interests and find ways to relate this request to his interests.

Organize: Gain attention by opening with praise or a stimulating remark. Build interest with explanations and facts. Show how compliance benefits the reader and others. Reduce resistance by providing ideas for the dinner talk.

Compose: Prepare first draft on a computer.

3 REVISING

Revise: Revise to show direct and indirect benefits more clearly.

Proofread: Use quotes around "R" to reflect the company usage. In the fourth paragraph, use a semicolon in the compound sentence. Start all lines at the left for block-style letter.

Evaluate: Will this letter convince the reader to accept the invitation?

Hamilton–Wentworth
North American Marketing Association
484 Mountain Park Drive
Hamilton, ON L8V 4X2

January 28, 2004

Mr. Elliott P. Tarkanian
Marketing Manager
Toys "R" Us, Inc.
2777 Langstaff Avenue
Thornhill, ON L3J 3M8

Dear Mr. Tarkanian:

One company is legendary for marketing North American products successfully in Japan.
[Piques reader's curiosity] [Gains attention]

That company, of course, is Toys "R" Us. The triumph of your thriving toy store in Amimachi, Japan, has given other North American marketers hope. But this success story has also raised numerous questions. Specifically, how did Toys "R" Us circumvent local trade restrictions? How did you solve the complex distribution system? And how did you negotiate with all the levels of Japanese bureaucracy?
[Builds interest]

The members of the Hamilton–Wentworth chapter of the North American Marketing Association asked me to invite you to speak at our March 19 dinner meeting on the topic of "How Toys 'R' Us Unlocked the Door to Japanese Trade." By describing your winning effort, Mr. Tarkanian, you can help launch other North American companies who face the same quagmire of Japanese restrictions and red tape that your organization overcame. Although we can offer you only a small honorarium of $300, we can assure you of a big audience of enthusiastic marketing professionals eager to hear your dramatic story.
[Notes indirect benefit] [Notes direct benefit]

Our relaxed group doesn't expect a formal address; they are most interested in what steps Toys "R" Us took to open its Japanese toy outlet. To make your talk easy to organize, I've enclosed a list of questions our members submitted. Most talks are about 45 minutes long.
[Offsets reluctance by making the talk informal and easy to organize] [Reduces resistance]

Can we count on you to join us for dinner at 7 p.m. March 19 at the Fisherman's Inn in Hamilton? Just call me at (905) 860-4320 by February 15 to make arrangements.
[Makes acceptance as simple as a telephone call] [Motivates action]

Sincerely,

Timothy W. Ellison

Timothy W. Ellison
Program Chair, NAMA
TWE:grw
Enclosure

FIGURE 9.4 **Persuasive Action Request**

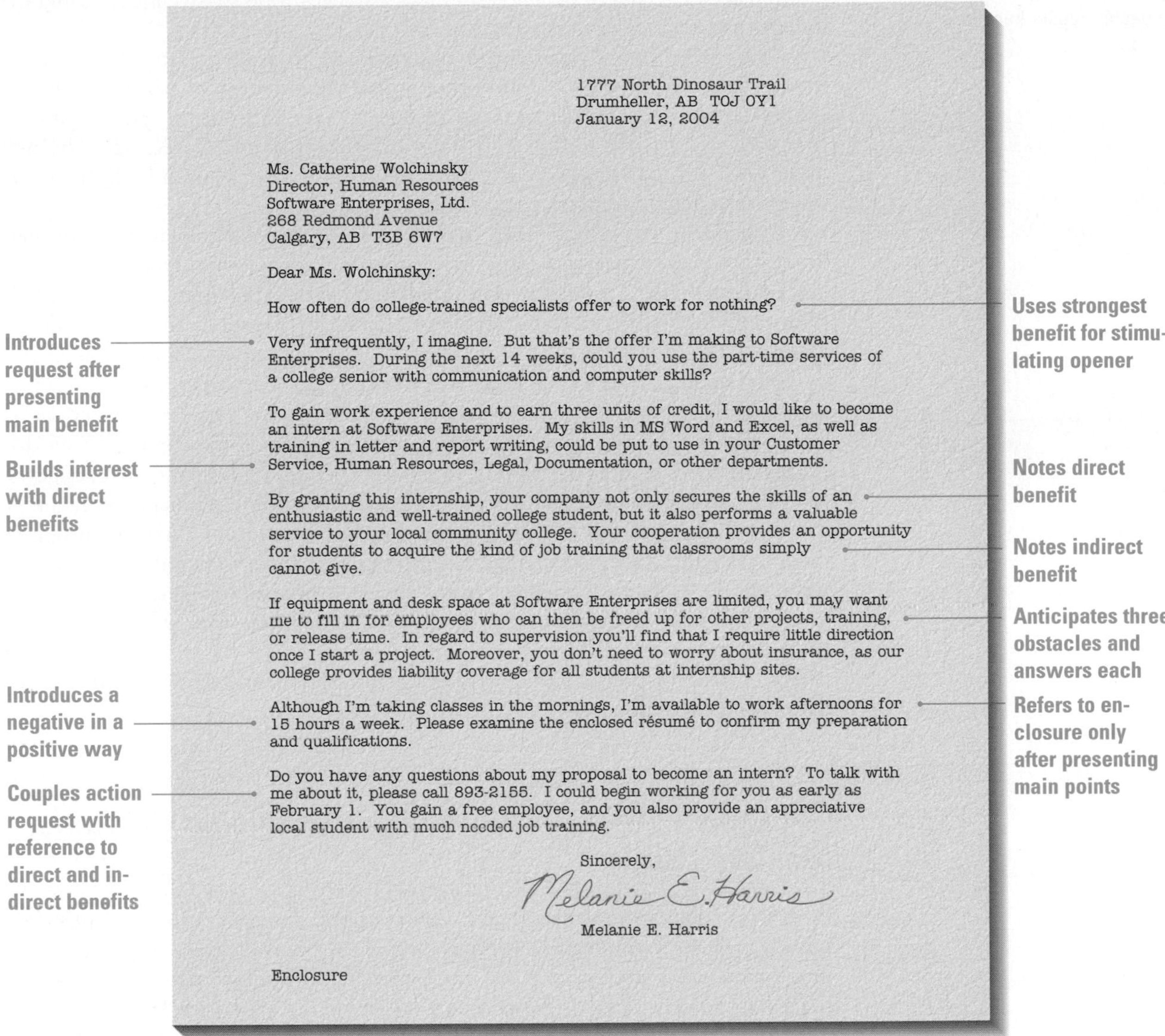
1777 North Dinosaur Trail
Drumheller, AB TOJ 0Y1
January 12, 2004

Ms. Catherine Wolchinsky
Director, Human Resources
Software Enterprises, Ltd.
268 Redmond Avenue
Calgary, AB T3B 6W7

Dear Ms. Wolchinsky:

How often do college-trained specialists offer to work for nothing?

Very infrequently, I imagine. But that's the offer I'm making to Software Enterprises. During the next 14 weeks, could you use the part-time services of a college senior with communication and computer skills?

To gain work experience and to earn three units of credit, I would like to become an intern at Software Enterprises. My skills in MS Word and Excel, as well as training in letter and report writing, could be put to use in your Customer Service, Human Resources, Legal, Documentation, or other departments.

By granting this internship, your company not only secures the skills of an enthusiastic and well-trained college student, but it also performs a valuable service to your local community college. Your cooperation provides an opportunity for students to acquire the kind of job training that classrooms simply cannot give.

If equipment and desk space at Software Enterprises are limited, you may want me to fill in for employees who can then be freed up for other projects, training, or release time. In regard to supervision you'll find that I require little direction once I start a project. Moreover, you don't need to worry about insurance, as our college provides liability coverage for all students at internship sites.

Although I'm taking classes in the mornings, I'm available to work afternoons for 15 hours a week. Please examine the enclosed résumé to confirm my preparation and qualifications.

Do you have any questions about my proposal to become an intern? To talk with me about it, please call 893-2155. I could begin working for you as early as February 1. You gain a free employee, and you also provide an appreciative local student with much needed job training.

Sincerely,

Melanie E. Harris

Melanie E. Harris

Enclosure

Uses strongest benefit for stimulating opener
Introduces request after presenting main benefit
Builds interest with direct benefits
Notes direct benefit
Notes indirect benefit
Anticipates three obstacles and answers each
Introduces a negative in a positive way
Refers to enclosure only after presenting main points
Couples action request with reference to direct and indirect benefits

vices would free up other staff members to perform more important tasks. She delays mentioning a negative (being able to work only 15 hours a week and only in the afternoon) until she builds interest and reduces resistance. And she closes confidently and motivates action with reference to both direct and indirect benefits.

Persuading Within Organizations

Instructions or directives moving downward from superiors to subordinates usually require little persuasion. Employees expect to be directed in how to perform their jobs. These messages (such as information about procedures, equipment, or customer service) follow the direct pattern, with the purpose immediately stated. However, employees are sometimes asked to perform in a capacity outside their

Internal persuasive memos present honest arguments detailing specific reader benefits.

work roles or to accept changes that are not in their best interests (such as pay cuts, job transfers, or reduced benefits). In these instances, a persuasive memo using the indirect pattern may be most effective.

The goal is not to manipulate employees or to seduce them with trickery. Rather, the goal is to present a strong but honest argument, emphasizing points that are important to the receiver. In business, honesty is not just the best policy—it's the *only* policy. Especially within your own organization, people see right through puffery and misrepresentation. For this reason, the indirect pattern is effective only when supported by accurate, honest evidence.

Evidence is also critical when subordinates submit recommendations to their bosses. "The key to making a request of a superior," advises communication consultant Patricia Buhler, "is to know your needs and have documentation [facts, figures, evidence]." Another important factor is moderation. "Going in and asking for the world right off the cuff is most likely going to elicit a negative response," she adds.[1]

The memo, in Figure 9.5, is effective. Remember that a persuasive message will typically take more space than a direct message because proving a case requires evidence. Notice that the subject line in Figure 9.5 tells the purpose of the memo without disclosing the actual request. By delaying the request until he's had a chance to describe the problem and discuss a solution, the writer prevents the reader's premature rejection.

The strength of this memo is in the clear presentation of comparison figures showing how much money can be saved by purchasing a remanufactured copier. Although the organization pattern is not obvious, the memo begins with an attention-getter (frank description of problem), builds interest (with easy-to-read facts and figures), provides benefits, and reduces resistance. Notice that the conclusion tells what action is to be taken, makes it easy to respond, and repeats the main benefit to motivate action.

Complaint Letters: Requesting Adjustments and Making Claims

5

Persuasive adjustment letters make claims about damaged products, mistaken billing, inaccurate shipments, warranty problems, return policies, insurance mix-ups, faulty merchandise, and so on. Generally, the direct pattern is best for requesting straightforward adjustments (see Chapter 7). When you feel your request is justified and will be granted, the direct strategy is most efficient. But if a past request has been refused or ignored or if you anticipate reluctance, then the indirect pattern is appropriate.

Effective complaint/adjustment letters make reasonable claims backed by solid evidence.

In a sense, an adjustment letter is a complaint letter. Someone is complaining about something that went wrong. Some complaint letters just vent anger; the writers are mad, and they want to tell someone about it. But if the goal is to change something (and why bother to write except to motivate change?), then persuasion is necessary. Effective adjustment letters make a reasonable claim, present a logical case with clear facts, and adopt a moderate tone. Anger and emotion are not effective persuaders.

You'll want to open an adjustment letter with some sincere praise, an objective statement of the problem, a point of agreement, or a quick review of what you have done to resolve the problem. Then you can explain precisely what happened or why your claim is legitimate. Be sure to enclose copies of relevant invoices, shipping orders, warranties, and payments. And close with a clear statement of what you want done: refund, replacement, credit to your account, or other action. Be sure to think through the possibilities and make your request reasonable.

FIGURE 9.5 **Persuasive Memo**

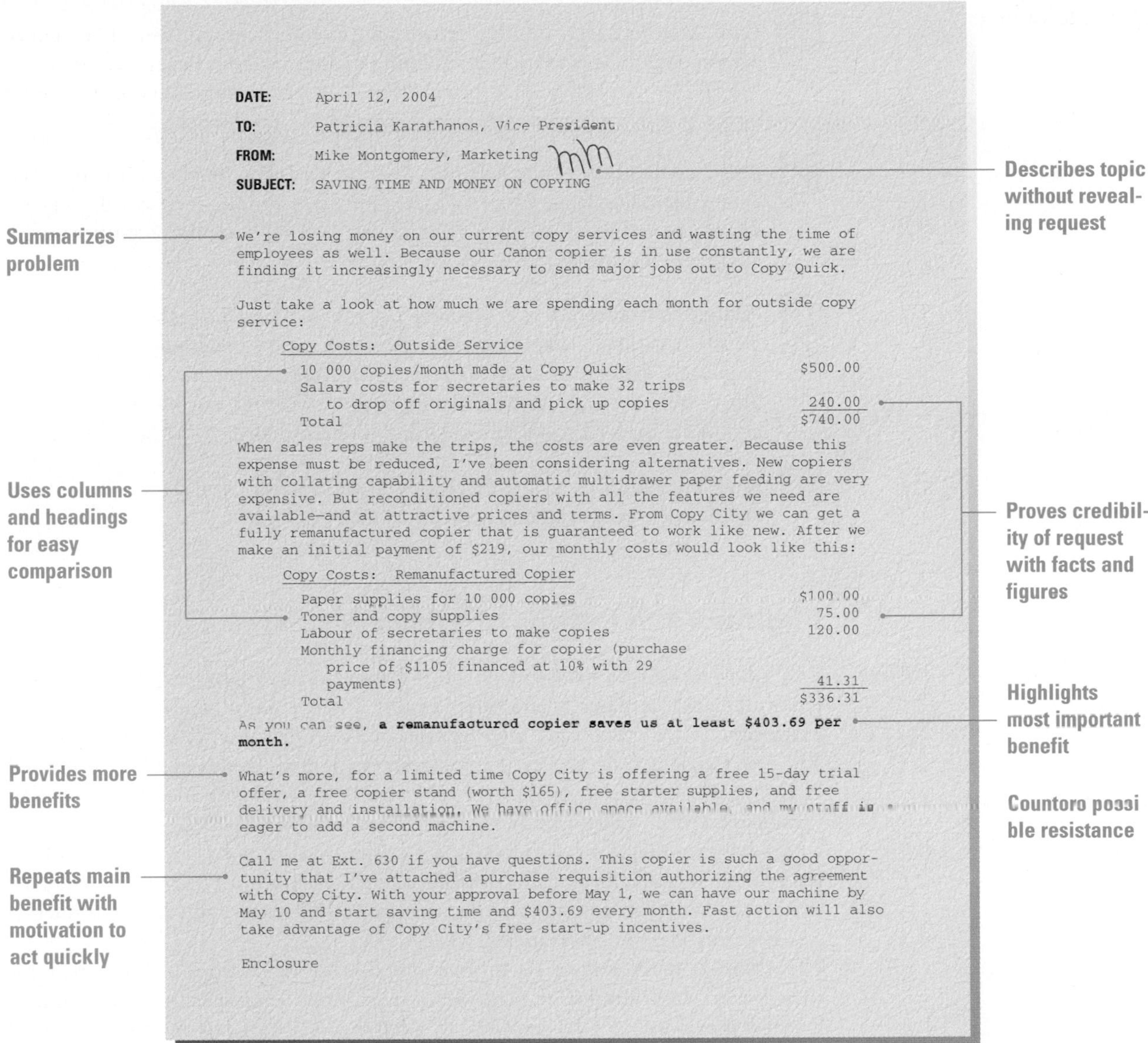

DATE: April 12, 2004

TO: Patricia Karathanos, Vice President

FROM: Mike Montgomery, Marketing MM

SUBJECT: SAVING TIME AND MONEY ON COPYING

We're losing money on our current copy services and wasting the time of employees as well. Because our Canon copier is in use constantly, we are finding it increasingly necessary to send major jobs out to Copy Quick.

Just take a look at how much we are spending each month for outside copy service:

Copy Costs: Outside Service	
10 000 copies/month made at Copy Quick	$500.00
Salary costs for secretaries to make 32 trips to drop off originals and pick up copies	240.00
Total	$740.00

When sales reps make the trips, the costs are even greater. Because this expense must be reduced, I've been considering alternatives. New copiers with collating capability and automatic multidrawer paper feeding are very expensive. But reconditioned copiers with all the features we need are available—and at attractive prices and terms. From Copy City we can get a fully remanufactured copier that is guaranteed to work like new. After we make an initial payment of $219, our monthly costs would look like this:

Copy Costs: Remanufactured Copier	
Paper supplies for 10 000 copies	$100.00
Toner and copy supplies	75.00
Labour of secretaries to make copies	120.00
Monthly financing charge for copier (purchase price of $1105 financed at 10% with 29 payments)	41.31
Total	$336.31

As you can see, **a remanufactured copier saves us at least $403.69 per month.**

What's more, for a limited time Copy City is offering a free 15-day trial offer, a free copier stand (worth $165), free starter supplies, and free delivery and installation. We have office space available, and my staff is eager to add a second machine.

Call me at Ext. 630 if you have questions. This copier is such a good opportunity that I've attached a purchase requisition authorizing the agreement with Copy City. With your approval before May 1, we can have our machine by May 10 and start saving time and $403.69 every month. Fast action will also take advantage of Copy City's free start-up incentives.

Enclosure

Summarizes problem
Uses columns and headings for easy comparison
Provides more benefits
Repeats main benefit with motivation to act quickly
Describes topic without revealing request
Proves credibility of request with facts and figures
Highlights most important benefit
Counters possible resistance

The tone of the letter is important. You should never suggest that the receiver intentionally deceived you or intentionally created the problem. Rather, appeal to the receiver's sense of responsibility and pride in its good name. Calmly express your disappointment in view of your high expectations of the product and of the company. Communicating your feelings, without rancor, is often your strongest appeal.

Adjustment requests should adopt a moderate tone, appeal to the receiver's sense of responsibility, and specify needed actions.

Janet Walker's letter, shown in Figure 9.6, follows the persuasive pattern as she seeks to return three answering machines. Notice that she uses simplified letter style (skipping the salutation and complimentary close) because she doesn't have a person's name to use in addressing the letter. Note also her positive opening, her calm, well-documented claims, and her request for specific action.

The following checklist reviews pointers for helping you make persuasive requests of all kinds.

Checklist for Making Persuasive Requests

 **Gain attention.** In requesting favours, begin with a compliment, statement of agreement, unexpected fact, stimulating question, reader benefit, summary of the problem, or candid plea for help. For claims and complaints, also consider opening with a review of action you have taken to resolve the problem.

 **Build interest.** Prove the accuracy and merit of your request with solid evidence, including facts, figures, expert opinion, examples, and details. Suggest direct and indirect benefits for the receiver. Avoid sounding high-pressured, angry, or emotional.

 **Reduce resistance.** Identify what factors will be obstacles to the receiver; offer counterarguments. Demonstrate your credibility by being knowledgeable. In requesting favours or making recommendations, show how the receiver or others will benefit. In making claims, appeal to the receiver's sense of fairness and desire for goodwill. Express your disappointment.

 **Motivate action.** Confidently ask for specific action. For favours include an end date (if appropriate) and try to repeat a key benefit.

Planning and Composing Sales Messages

Traditional direct mail marketing involves the sale of goods and services through letters, catalogues, brochures, and other messages delivered by land mail. Electronic marketing, on the other hand, involves sales messages delivered by e-mail, Web sites, and, less frequently, by fax. To some marketers, e-mail sounds like "the promised land," guaranteeing instant delivery and at only pennies per message. However, unsolicited e-mail, called "spam," has generated an incredible backlash from recipients, who want their e-mail addresses to remain private and unviolated. One of the leading direct mail marketers correctly sensed the pulse of the times when he remarked, "Nothing is more powerful than goodwill—except ill will."[2] Unsolicited e-mail seems to create enormous ill will today.

Although marketing by e-mail may one day eclipse traditional direct mail, for today's markets, traditional sales messages are still key. Sellers feel that "even with all the new media we have available today, a letter remains one of the most powerful ways to make sales, generate leads, boost retail traffic, and solicit donations."[3]

Professionals who specialize in traditional direct mail services have made a science of analyzing a market, developing an effective mailing list, studying the product, preparing a sophisticated campaign aimed at a target audience, and motivating the reader to act. You've probably received many direct mail packages, often called "junk" mail. These packages typically contain a sales letter, a brochure, a price list, illustrations of the product, testimonials, and other persuasive appeals.

We're most concerned here with the sales letter: its strategy, organization, and evidence. Because sales letters are generally written by specialists, you may never write one on the job. Why, then, learn how to write a sales letter? In many ways, every letter we create is a form of sales letter. We sell our ideas, our organizations, and ourselves. Learning the techniques of sales writing will help you be more successful in any communication that requires persuasion and promotion. Furthermore, you'll recognize sales strategies, thus enabling you to become a more perceptive consumer of ideas, products, and services.

FIGURE 9.6 **Request for Adjustment (Complaint Letter)**

Tips for Requesting Adjustments and Making Complaints

- Begin with a compliment, point of agreement, statement of the problem, or brief review of action you have taken to resolve the problem.
- Provide identifying data.
- Prove that your claim is valid; explain why the receiver is responsible.
- Enclose document copies supporting your claim.
- Appeal to the receiver's fairness, ethical and legal responsibilities, and desire for customer satisfaction.
- Describe your feelings and your disappointment.
- Avoid sounding angry, emotional, or irrational.
- Close by telling exactly what you want done.

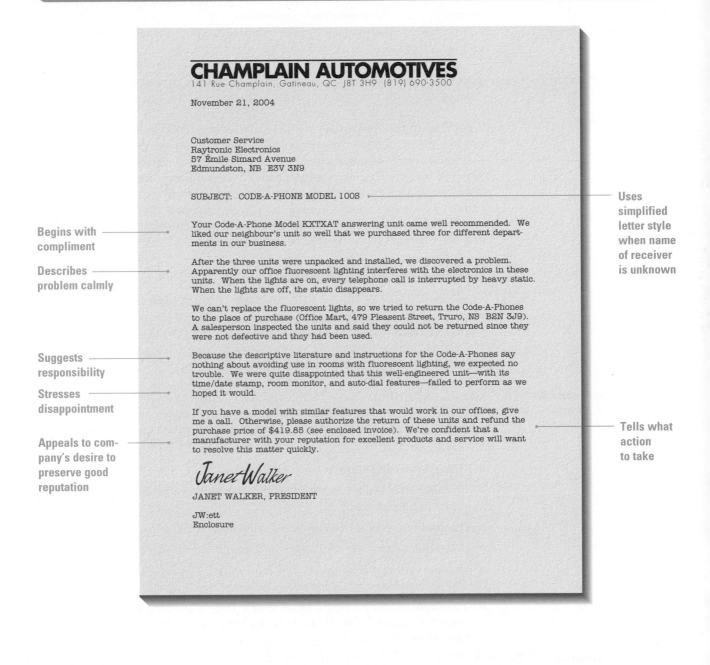

CHAMPLAIN AUTOMOTIVES
141 Rue Champlain, Gatineau, QC J8T 3H9 (819) 690-3500

November 21, 2004

Customer Service
Raytronic Electronics
57 Émile Simard Avenue
Edmundston, NB E3V 3N9

SUBJECT: CODE-A-PHONE MODEL 100S — *Uses simplified letter style when name of receiver is unknown*

Begins with compliment — Your Code-A-Phone Model KXTXAT answering unit came well recommended. We liked our neighbour's unit so well that we purchased three for different departments in our business.

Describes problem calmly — After the three units were unpacked and installed, we discovered a problem. Apparently our office fluorescent lighting interferes with the electronics in these units. When the lights are on, every telephone call is interrupted by heavy static. When the lights are off, the static disappears.

We can't replace the fluorescent lights, so we tried to return the Code-A-Phones to the place of purchase (Office Mart, 479 Pleasent Street, Truro, NS B2N 3J9). A salesperson inspected the units and said they could not be returned since they were not defective and they had been used.

Suggests responsibility — Because the descriptive literature and instructions for the Code-A-Phones say nothing about avoiding use in rooms with fluorescent lighting, we expected no trouble. *Stresses disappointment* — We were quite disappointed that this well-engineered unit—with its time/date stamp, room monitor, and auto-dial features—failed to perform as we hoped it would.

If you have a model with similar features that would work in our offices, give me a call. Otherwise, please authorize the return of these units and refund the purchase price of $419.85 (see enclosed invoice). *Tells what action to take* — *Appeals to company's desire to preserve good reputation* — We're confident that a manufacturer with your reputation for excellent products and service will want to resolve this matter quickly.

Janet Walker

JANET WALKER, PRESIDENT

JW:ett
Enclosure

Applying the 3-×-3 Writing Process to Sales Messages

Marketing professionals analyze every aspect of a sales message because consumers reject most direct mail offers. Like the experts, you'll want to pay close attention to the preparatory steps of analysis and adaptation before writing the actual message.

Analyzing the Product and Purpose. Before writing a sales letter, you should study the product carefully. What can you learn about its design, construction, raw materials, and manufacturing process? About its ease of use, efficiency, durability, and applications? Be sure to consider warranties, service, price, and special appeals. At the same time, evaluate the competition so that you can compare your product's strengths against the competitor's weaknesses.

Now you're ready to identify your central selling points. Analyzing your product and the competition helps you determine what to emphasize in your sales letter.

Another important decision in the preparatory stage involves the specific purpose of your letter. Before you write the first word of your message, know what features of the product you will emphasize and what response you want.

Adapting to the Audience. Blanket mailings sent "cold" to occupants generally produce low responses—typically only 1 to 2 percent. At the same time, 24/7 estimates the average response rate to commercial e-mail at 3 to 9 percent.[4] But the response rate can be increased dramatically by targeting the audience through selected mailing lists. By directing your message to a selected group, you can make certain assumptions about the receivers. You would expect similar interests, needs, and demographics (age, income, and other characteristics). With this knowledge you can adapt the sales letter to a specific audience.

Crafting a Winning Sales Message

Your primary goal in writing a sales message is to get someone to devote a few moments of attention to it.[5] You may be promoting a product, a service, an idea, or yourself. In each case the most effective messages will (1) gain attention, (2) build interest, (3) reduce resistance, and (4) motivate action. This is the same recipe we studied earlier, but the ingredients are different.

Openers for sales messages should be brief, honest, relevant, and provocative.

Gaining Attention. One of the most critical elements of a sales letter is its opening paragraph. This opener should be short (one to five lines), honest, relevant, and stimulating. Marketing pros have found that eye-catching typographical arrangements or provocative messages, such as the following, can hook a reader's attention:

- **Offer:** *A free trip to Hawaii is just the beginning!*
- **Promise:** *Now you can raise your sales income by 50 percent or even more with the proven techniques found in ...*
- **Question:** *Do you yearn for an honest, fulfilling relationship?*
- **Quotation or proverb:** *Necessity is the mother of invention.*
- **Product feature:** *Volvo's snazzy new convertible ensures your safety with a roll bar that pops out when the car tips 40 degrees to the side.*
- **Testimonial:** *"It's wonderful to see such a well written and informative piece of work." (Thomas J. Bata, Chairman, Bata Ltd., about* Secrets of Power Presentations*)*

- **Startling statement:** *Let the poor and hungry feed themselves! For just $100 they can.*
- **Personalized action setting:** *It's 4:30 p.m. and you've got to make a decision. You need everybody's opinion, no matter where they are. Before you pick up your phone to call them one at a time, call Bell Canada and ask for the Teleforum™ (teleconferencing) operator.*

Other openings calculated to capture attention might include a solution to a problem, an anecdote, a personalized statement using the receiver's name, or a relevant current event.

Building Interest. In this phase of your sales message, you should describe clearly the product or service. In simple language emphasize the central selling points that you identified during your prewriting analysis. Those selling points can be developed using rational or emotional appeals.

Rational appeals are associated with reason and intellect. They translate selling points into references to making or saving money, increasing efficiency, or making the best use of resources. In general, rational appeals are appropriate when a product is expensive, long-lasting, or important to health, security, and financial success. Emotional appeals relate to status, ego, and sensual feelings. Appealing to the emotions is sometimes effective when a product is inexpensive, short-lived, or nonessential. Many clever sales messages, however, combine emotional and rational strategies for a dual appeal. Consider these examples:

Rational Appeal
You can buy the things you need and want, pay household bills, pay off higher-cost loans and credit cards—as soon as you're approved and your Credit-Line account is opened.

Emotional Appeal
Leave the urban bustle behind and escape to sun-soaked Bermuda! To recharge your batteries with an injection of sun and surf, all you need is your bathing suit, a little suntan lotion, and your Credit-Line card.

Dual Appeal
New Credit-Line cardholders are immediately eligible for a $100 travel certificate and additional discounts at fun-filled resorts. Save up to 40 percent while lying on a beach in picturesque, sun-soaked Bermuda, the year-round resort island.

A physical description of your product is not enough, however. Zig Ziglar, thought by some to be America's greatest salesperson, points out that no matter how well you know your product, no one is persuaded by cold, hard facts alone. In the end, he contends, "People buy because of the product benefits."[6] Your job is to translate those cold facts into warm feelings and reader benefits.

Reducing Resistance. Marketing pros use a number of techniques to overcome resistance and build desire. When price is an obstacle, consider these suggestions:

- Delay mentioning price until after you've created a desire for the product.
- Show the price in small units, such as the price per issue of a magazine.
- Demonstrate how the reader saves money by, for instance, subscribing for two or three years.
- Compare your prices with those of a competitor.

In addition, you need to anticipate other objections and questions the receiver may have. When possible, translate these objections into selling points (*If you've never ordered software by mail, let us send you our demonstration disks at no charge*). Other techniques to overcome resistance and prove the credibility of the product include the following:

Techniques for reducing resistance include testimonials, guarantees, warranties, samples, and performance polls.

- **Testimonials:** *"I learned so much in your language courses that I began to dream in French."—Holly Franker, Woodstock, Ontario*
- **Names of satisfied users** (with permission, of course): *Enclosed is a partial list of private pilots who enthusiastically subscribe to our service.*
- **Money-back guarantee or warranty:** *We offer the longest warranties in the business—all parts and service on-site for two years!*
- **Free trial or sample:** *We're so confident that you'll like our new accounting program that we want you to try it absolutely free.*
- **Performance tests, polls, or awards:** *Last year our microwave oven won customer satisfaction polls in Canada, the U.S., the U.K., Germany, and France.*

Techniques for motivating action include offering a gift or incentive, limiting an offer, and guaranteeing satisfaction.

Motivating Action. All the effort put into a sales message is wasted if the reader fails to act. To make it easy for readers to act, you can provide a reply card, a stamped and preaddressed envelope, a toll-free telephone number, an easy Web site, or a promise of a follow-up call. Because readers often need an extra push, consider including additional motivators, such as the following:

- **Offer a gift:** *You'll receive a free calculator with your first order.*
- **Promise an incentive:** *With every new, paid subscription, we'll plant a tree in one of Canada's National Parks.*
- **Limit the offer:** *Only the first 100 customers receive free cheques.*
- **Set a deadline:** *You must act before June 1 to get these low prices.*
- **Guarantee satisfaction:** *We'll return your full payment if you're not entirely satisfied—no questions asked.*

The final paragraph of the sales letter carries the punch line. This is where you tell readers what you want done and give them reasons for doing it. Most sales letters also include postscripts because they make irresistible reading. Even readers who might skim over or bypass paragraphs are drawn to a P.S. Therefore, use a postscript to reveal your strongest motivator, to add a special inducement for a quick response, or to reemphasize a central selling point.

Because direct mail is an expensive way to advertise, messages should present complete information in a personalized tone for specific audiences.

Putting It All Together. Since Canadians purchase more than $11 billion in goods and services through direct-response marketing, including e-mail,[7] there is potential for tremendous growth in this area of marketing. Sales letters are a preferred marketing medium because they can be personalized, directed to target audiences, and filled with a more complete message than other advertising media. But direct mail is expensive. That's why the total sales message is crafted so painstakingly.

Let's examine a sales letter, shown in Figure 9.7, addressed to a target group of small-business owners. To sell the new magazine *Small Business Monthly*, the letter incorporates all four components of an effective persuasive message. Notice that the personalized action-setting opener places the reader in a familiar situation (getting into an elevator) and draws an analogy between failing to reach the top floor and failing to achieve a business goal. The writer develops a rational central selling point

FIGURE 9.7 **Sales Letter**

1 PREWRITING

Analyze: The purpose of this letter is to persuade the reader to return the reply card and subscribe to *Small Business Monthly*.

Anticipate: The targeted audience consists of small-business owners. The central selling point is providing practical business data that will help their businesses grow.

Adapt: Because readers will be reluctant, use the indirect pattern.

2 WRITING

Research: Gather facts to promote your product, including testimonials.

Organize: Gain attention by opening with a personalized action picture. Build interest with an analogy and a description of magazine features. Use a testimonial to reduce resistance. Motivate action with a free booklet and an easy-reply card.

Compose: Prepare first draft for pilot study.

3 REVISING

Revise: Use short paragraphs and short sentences. Replace words like *malfunction* with words like *glitch.*

Proofread: Indent long quotations on the left and right sides. Italicize or underscore titles of publications. Hyphenate *hard-headed* and *first-of-its-kind.*

Evaluate: Monitor the response rate to this letter to assess its effectiveness.

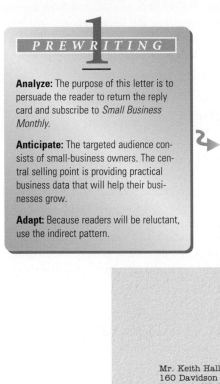

small business monthly
160 Duncan Mills Road, Toronto, ON M3B 1Z5

April 15, 2004

Mr. Keith Hall
160 Davidson Avenue North
Listowel, ON N4W 3A2

Dear Mr. Hall:

You walk into the elevator and push the button for the top floor. The elevator glides upwards. You step back and relax. [Puts reader into action setting] [Gains attention]

But the elevator never reaches the top. A glitch in its electronics prevents it from processing the information it needs to take you to your destination.

Do you see a similarity between your growing company and this elevator? You're aiming for the top, but a lack of information halts your progress. Now you can put your company into gear and propel it toward success with a new publication—*Small Business Monthly*. [Suggests analogy] [Builds interest]

This first-of-its-kind magazine brings you marketing tips, hard-headed business pointers, opportunities, and inspiration. This is the kind of savvy information you need today to be where you want to go tomorrow. One executive wrote: [Emphasizes central selling point]

> As president of a small manufacturing company, I read several top business publications, but I get my "bread and butter" from *Small Business Monthly.* I'm not interested in a lot of "pie in the sky" and theory. I find practical problems and how to solve them in *SBM.*
> —Mitchell M. Perry, Oshawa, Ontario

[Uses testimonial for credibility] [Reduces resistance]

Mr. Perry's words are the best recommendation I can offer you to try *SBM.* In less time than you might spend on an average business lunch, you learn the latest in management, operations, finance, taxes, business law, compensation, and advertising.

To evaluate *Small Business Monthly* without cost or obligation, let me send you a free issue. Just initial and return the enclosed card to start receiving a wealth of practical information that could keep your company travelling upward to its goal. [Repeats central sales pitch in last sentence] [Motivates action]

Cordially,

Richard Roberts

Richard Roberts
Vice President, Circulation

P.S. Act before May 15 and I'll send you our valuable booklet *Managing for Success*, revealing more than 100 secrets for helping small businesses grow. [Spotlights free offer in P.S. to prompt immediate reply] (a magazine that provides valuable information for a growing small business) and repeats this selling point in all the components of the letter. Notice, too, how a testimonial from a small-business executive lends support to the sales message, and how the closing pushes for action. Since the price of the magazine is not a selling feature, it's mentioned only on the reply card. This sales letter saves its strongest motivator—a free booklet—for the high-impact P.S. line.

Checklist for Writing Sales Letters

Gain attention. Offer something valuable, promise the reader a result, pose a stimulating question, describe a product feature, present a testimonial, make a startling statement, or show the reader in an action setting. Other attention-getters are a solution to a problem, an anecdote, a statement using the receiver's name, and a relevant current event.

Build interest. Describe the product in terms of what it does for the reader: save or make money, reduce effort, improve health, produce pleasure, boost status. Connect cold facts with warm feelings and needs.

Reduce resistance. Counter reluctance with testimonials, money-back guarantees, attractive warranties, trial offers, or free samples. Build credibility with results of performance tests, polls, or awards. If price is not a selling feature, describe it in small units (*only 99 cents an issue*), show it as savings, or tell how it compares favourably with the competition.

Motivate action. Close with a repetition of the central selling point and clear instructions for an easy action to be taken. Prompt the reader to act immediately with a gift, incentive, limited offer, deadline, and/or guarantee of satisfaction. Put the strongest motivator in a postscript.

Developing Persuasive Media Releases

7

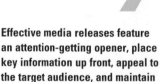

Effective media releases feature an attention-getting opener, place key information up front, appeal to the target audience, and maintain visual interest.

Media (press) releases announce information about your company to the media: new products, new managers, new facilities, participation in community projects, awards given or received, joint ventures, donations, or seminars and demonstrations. Naturally, you hope that this news will be published and provide good publicity for your company. But this kind of largely self-serving information is not always appealing to magazine and newspaper editors or to TV producers. To get them to read beyond the first sentence, try these suggestions:

- Open with an attention-getting lead or a summary of the important facts.
- Include answers to the journalistic questions (who, what, when, where, why, and how) in the article—but not all in the first sentence!
- Appeal to the audience of the target media. Emphasize reader benefits written in the style of the focus publication or newscast.
- Present the most important information early, followed by supporting information. Don't put your best ideas last because they may be chopped off or ignored.
- Make the release visually appealing. Limit the text to one or two double-spaced pages with attractive formatting.

- Look and sound credible—no typos, no imaginative spelling or punctuation, no factual errors.

The most important ingredient of a media release, of course, is news. Articles that merely plug products end up in the circular file.

Summary of Learning Objectives

1 **Apply the 3-×-3 writing process to persuasive messages.** The first step in the writing process for a persuasive message is analysis of the audience and purpose. Writers must know exactly what they want the receiver to do or think. The second step involves thinking of ways to adapt the message to the audience. Particularly important is expressing the request so that it may benefit the reader. Next, the writer must collect data and organize it into an appropriate strategy. An indirect strategy is probably best if the audience will resist the request.

2 **Explain the components of a persuasive message.** The most effective persuasive messages gain attention by opening with a problem, unexpected statement, reader benefit, compliment, related fact, stimulating question, or similar device. They build interest with facts, expert opinions, examples, details, and additional reader benefits. They reduce resistance by anticipating objections and presenting counterarguments. They conclude by motivating a specific action and making it easy for the reader to respond. Skilled communicators avoid distortion, exaggeration, and deception when making persuasive arguments.

3 **Request favours and action effectively.** When writing to ask for a favour, the indirect pattern is appropriate. This means delaying the request until after logical reasons have been presented. Such memos should emphasize, if possible, benefits to the reader. Appeals to professionalism are often a useful technique. Writers can counter any anticipated resistance with explanations and motivate action in the closing.

4 **Write convincing persuasive messages within organizations.** In writing internal messages that require persuasion, the indirect pattern is appropriate. These messages might begin with a frank discussion of a problem. They build interest by emphasizing points that are important to the readers. They support the request with accurate, honest evidence.

5 **Request adjustments and make claims successfully.** When writing about damaged products, mistaken billing, or other claims, the indirect pattern is appropriate. These messages might begin with a sincere compliment or an objective statement of the problem. They explain concisely why a claim is legitimate. Copies of relevant documents should be enclosed. The message should conclude with a clear statement of the action to be taken.

6 **Compose successful sales messages.** Before writing a sales message, it's necessary to analyze the product and purpose carefully. The letter begins with an attention-getting statement that is short, honest, relevant, and stimulating. It builds interest by describing the product or service clearly in simple language, incorporating appropriate appeals. Testimonials, a money-back guarantee, a free trial, or some other device can reduce resistance. A gift, incentive, deadline, or other device can motivate action.

7 **Describe the basic elements included in effective media releases.** Effective media releases usually open with an attention-getting lead or summary of the important facts. They attempt to answer the questions who, what, when, where, why, and how. They are written carefully to appeal to the audience of the target media. The best media releases present the most important information early, make the release visually appealing, and look and sound credible.

CHAPTER REVIEW

1. List the four steps in the indirect pattern for persuasive messages. (Objs. 1 and 2)
2. List six or more techniques for opening a persuasive request for a favour. (Obj. 3)
3. List techniques for building interest in a persuasive request for a favour. (Obj. 3)
4. Describe ways to reduce resistance in persuasive requests. (Obj. 2)
5. How should a persuasive request end? (Objs. 2 and 3)
6. When does persuasion become unethical? (Obj. 2)
7. What are the differences between direct and indirect reader benefits? Give an original example of each (other than those described). (Obj. 3)
8. When would persuasion be necessary in messages moving downward in organizations? (Obj. 4)
9. Why are persuasive messages usually longer than direct messages? (Objs. 1–7)
10. When is it necessary to use the indirect pattern in requesting adjustments or making claims? (Obj. 5)
11. What percentage of response can be expected from an untargeted direct mail campaign? (Obj. 6)
12. Name eight or more ways to attract attention in opening a sales message. (Obj. 6)
13. How do rational appeals differ from emotional appeals? Give an original example of each. (Obj. 6)
14. Name five or more ways to motivate action in closing a sales message. (Obj. 6)
15. List five or more topics that an organization might feature in a press release. (Obj. 7)

CRITICAL THINKING

1. How are requests for action and sales letters similar and how are they different? (Objs. 3 and 6)
2. What are some of the underlying motivations that prompt individuals to agree to requests that do not directly benefit themselves or their organizations? (Objs. 2–7)
3. In view of the burden that "junk" mail places on society (depleted landfills, declining timber supplies, overburdened postal system), how can "junk" mail be justified? (Obj. 6)
4. Why is it important to know your needs and have documentation when you make requests of superiors? (Obj. 5)

ACTIVITIES

9.1 Document for Analysis: Weak Persuasive Invitation (Obj. 3)

Analyze the following document. List its weaknesses. If your instructor directs, revise it.

Dear Dr. Thomas:

Because you're a local Guelph author, we thought it might not be too much trouble for you to speak at our U of G banquet May 5.

Some of us business students here at Guelph University admired your book *National Disunity,* which appeared last spring and became such a hit across the nation. One of our professors said you were now the nation's unity management guru. What exactly did you mean when you said that Canada is no longer a blend of two cultures—that it's now a "smorgasbord of multicultural expectations"?

Because we have no funds for honoraria, we have to rely on local speakers. The Reverend James R. Jones and Vice Mayor Rebecca A. Timmons were speakers in the past. Our banquets usually begin at 6:30 with a social hour, followed by dinner at 7:30 and the speaker from 8:30 until 9:00 or 9:15. We can arrange transportation for you and your wife if you need it.

We realize that you must be very busy, but we hope you'll agree. Please let our advisor, Professor Alexa North, have the favour of an early response.

9.2 Document for Analysis: Weak Persuasive Memo (Obj. 4)

Analyze the following document. List its weaknesses. If your instructor directs, revise it.

TO: Jay S. Jacobs, VP, Human Resources

Sue Simmons and I, along with other Intercontinental employees, have been eager to return to school, but we can't afford the costs of tuition and books.

Many of us were forced to go to work before we could complete our college diplomas or university degrees. We know that the continuing education divisions of some universities provide good courses that we could take at night. Sue and I—and we think many other employees as well—would like to enrol for these courses. Would Intercontinental be interested in helping us with a tuition-reimbursement program?

We've heard about other local companies (General Motors, Bell, Hydro, and others) that offer reimbursement for fees and books when employees complete approved courses with a C or higher. Sue and I have collected information, including a newspaper clipping that we're enclosing. Surveys show that tuition-reimbursement programs help improve employee morale and loyalty. They also result in higher productivity because employees develop improved skills.

We'd like a chance to talk over this worthwhile employee program with you at your convenience.

9.3 Document for Analysis: Weak Adjustment Request (Obj. 5)

Analyze the following document. List its weaknesses. If your instructor directs, revise it.

Gentlemen:

Three months ago we purchased four of your CopyMaster Model S-5 photocopiers, and we've had nothing but trouble ever since.

Our salesperson, Kevin Woo, assured us that the S-5 could easily handle our volume of 3000 copies a day. This seemed strange since the sales brochure said that the S-5 was meant for 500 copies a day. But we believed Mr. Woo. Big mistake! Our four S-5 copiers are down constantly; we can't go on like this. Because they're still under warranty, they eventually get repaired. But we're losing considerable business in downtime.

Your Mr. Woo has been less than helpful, so I telephoned the district manager, Keith Sumner. I suggested that we trade in our S-5 copiers (which we got for $2500 each) on two S-55 models (at $13 500 each). However, Mr. Sumner said he would have to charge 50-percent depreciation on our S-5 copiers. What a ripoff! I think that 20-percent depreciation is more reasonable since we've had the machines only three months. Mr. Sumner said he would get back to me, and I haven't heard from him since.

I'm writing to your headquarters because I have no faith in either Mr. Woo or Mr. Sumner, and I need action on these machines. If you understood anything about business, you would see what a sweet deal I'm offering you. I'm willing to stick with your company and purchase your most expensive model—but I can't take such a loss on the S-5 copiers. The S-5 copiers are relatively new; you should be able to sell them with no trouble. And think of all the money you'll save by not having your repair technicians making constant trips to service our S-5 copiers! Please let me hear from you immediately.

9.4 Sales Letter Analysis (Obj. 6)

Select a one- or two-page sales letter received by you or a friend. Study the letter and then answer these questions:

a. What techniques capture the reader's attention?

b. Is the opening effective? Explain.

c. What are the central selling points?

d. Does the letter use rational, emotional, or a combination of appeals? Explain.

e. What reader benefits are suggested?

f. How does the letter build interest in the product or service?

g. How is price handled?

h. How does the letter anticipate reader resistance and offer counterarguments?

i. What action is the reader to take? How is the action made easy?

j. What motivators spur the reader to act quickly?

9.5 Persuasive Favour/Action Request: Celebrity Auction (Obj. 3)

Team | **Critical Thinking**

Your professional or school organization (such as the Student Association) must find ways to raise money. The president of your group appoints a team and asks it to brainstorm for ways to meet your group's pledge to aid the United Way's battle against adult illiteracy in your community. After considering and discarding a number of silly ideas, your team comes up with the brilliant idea of a celebrity auction. At a spring function, items or services from local and other celebrities would be auctioned. Your organization approves your idea and asks your team to begin by writing a letter persuading an important person in your professional organization (or your institution president) to donate one hour of tutoring in a subject he or she chooses. If you have higher aspirations, write to a movie star or athlete of your choice (perhaps one who is part of your organization or who attended your school). Persuade the star to donate an item (perhaps a prop from a recent movie) that could be auctioned at your spring function. The campaign against adult illiteracy has targeted an estimated 10 000 people in your community who cannot read or write. As a team, decide what to request and then write an appropriate persuasive letter to secure that item.

9.6 Persuasive Favour/Action Request: Dining Gratuity Guidelines (Obj. 3)

As a server in the Tejas Grill, you have occasionally been "stiffed" by customers who left no tip. You know your service is excellent, but some customers just don't get it. They seem to think that tips are optional, a sign of appreciation. For servers, however, tips are 80 percent of their income. In a recent newspaper article, you learned that some restaurants—like the new Chez Marie in Montreal—automatically add a 15-percent tip to the bill. Meanwhile, other restaurants have a "large party" policy where parties over eight automatically have 15 percent added to their bill. Some computer programs also have a gratuity calculation feature on its terminals. This means that diners don't even have to do the math! Your fellow servers have asked you, who they know is studying business communication, to write a serious letter to Doug Young, general manager of Tejas (3150 Signal Hill Drive SW, Calgary, AB T3H 3T2), persuading him to adopt mandatory tipping guidelines. Talk with fellow servers (your classmates) to develop logical persuasive arguments. Follow the four-part plan developed in this chapter.

9.7 Persuasive Action Request: Getting Your Member of Parliament to Listen and Act (Obj. 3)

Web

Assume you are upset about an issue, and you want your member of Parliament to know your position. Choose a national issue about which you feel strongly: student loans, health care issues, human rights in other countries, federal safety regulations for employees, Aboriginal issues, environmental protection, employment equity, gun control, the federal deficit, or some other area regulated by government. Obtain your representative's address and appropriate title by visiting the Government of Canada Web site at **<www.parl.gc.ca>**. This site provides the proper courtesy titles plus land mail and e-mail addresses as available. However, although e-mail messages are quick, they don't carry as much influence as personal letters. Therefore, it's better to write a persuasive letter to your member of Parliament outlining your feelings.

For best results, consider these tips. (1) Use the proper form of address (*The Honourable John Smith, Dear Mr. Smith* or *The Right Honourable Joan Doe, Dear Ms. Doe*). (2) Identify yourself as a resident of his or her province or territory. (3) Immediately state your position (*I urge you to support/oppose ... because*). (4) Present facts and illustrations and how they affect you personally. If legislation were enacted, how would you or your organization be better off or worse off? Avoid generalities. (5) Offer to provide further information. (6) Keep the letter polite, constructive, and brief.

9.8 Persuasive Internal Request: Convincing the Boss (Obj. 4)

In your own work or organization experience, identify a situation in which persuasion is necessary. Should a procedure be altered to improve performance? Would a new or different piece of equipment help you perform your work more efficiently? Do you want to work other hours or perform other tasks? Do you deserve a promotion? Could customers be better served by changing something? Do you have a suggestion to improve profitability?

Once you have identified a situation, write a persuasive memo to your boss or organizational head. Use actual names and facts. Employ the concepts and techniques in this chapter to convince your boss that your idea should prevail. Include direct and indirect appeals, anticipate and counter objections, and emphasize reader benefits. End with a specific action to be taken.

9.9 Persuasive Internal Request: Supporting Project H.E.L.P. (Obj. 4)

E-Mail

As employee relations manager of The Prudential Insurance Company, one of your tasks is to promote Project H.E.L.P. (Higher Education Learning Program), an on-the-job learning opportunity. Project H.E.L.P. is a combined effort of major corporations and the Bruce County School Board. You must recruit 12 employees who will volunteer as instructors for 50 or more students. The students will spend four hours a week at the Prudential Bruce County facility earning an average of five units of credit a semester.

This semester the students will be serving in the Claims, Word Processing, Corporate Media Services, Marketing, Communications, Library, and Administrative Support departments. Your task is to convince employees in these departments to volunteer. They will be expected to supervise and instruct the students. In return, employees will receive two hours of release time per week to work with the students. The program has been very successful thus far. School officials, students, and employees alike express satisfaction with the experience and the outcomes. Write a persuasive memo or e-mail message with convincing appeals that will bring you 12 volunteers to work with Project H.E.L.P.

9.10 Persuasive Internal Request: Scheduling Meetings More Strategically (Obj. 4)

Can you improve the following memo? Expect the staff to be somewhat resistant because they've never before had meeting restrictions.

DATE: March 13, 2001

TO: All Managers and Employees

FROM: Lynn Wasson, CEO

SUBJECT: SCHEDULING MEETINGS

Please be reminded that travel in the greater Toronto area is time consuming. In the future we're asking that you set up meetings that

1. Are of critical importance
2. Consider travel time for the participants
3. Consider phone conferences (or video or e-mail) in lieu of face-to-face meetings
4. Meetings should be at the location where most of the participants work and at the most opportune travel times
5. Travelling together is another way to save time and resources.

We all have our traffic stories. A recent one is that a certain manager was asked to attend a one hour meeting in Guelph. This required one hour travel in advance of the meeting, one hour for the meeting, and two and a half hours of travel through Toronto afterward. This meeting was scheduled for 4 p.m. Total time consumed by the manager for the one hour meeting was four and a half hours.

Thank you for your consideration.

9.11 Persuasive Internal Request: Rapid Reviews Land Top Recruits (Obj. 5)

As Cassandra Carpenter, associate director of Human Resources at Techtronics computer consulting, you must improve company recruitment and retention rates soon. Employee turnover at the company is higher than 20 percent, and filling vacancies can take up to a year. Recruiting trends in the high-tech industry are clear. Record low unemployment rates, a burgeoning computer industry, and too few computer systems graduates have made the hiring game extremely competitive. To stay ahead, most firms have pumped up recruiting tactics, using hiring bonuses, unusually high salaries, extra vacation, and early reviews and raises to win the best employees. "I asked for a six-month review from ComputerTech," said one especially promising candidate, "and they agreed to it. They'll even offer a raise after three months if my performance is up to it."

You're certain that your boss will never agree to giving new employees salary raises after only three months on the job. However, offering reviews and pay raises at six months would enable you to snare the best hires without paying top dollar up front. Company pay scales simply don't allow for outlandish starting salaries, and reviews typically are given after 12 months. By offering early reviews for the best candidates, you could honour the internal pay scales while offering applicants the opportunity for early raises.

At a recent recruiting seminar, you learned that many companies are resorting to early reviews because they must. Nearly 30 percent of all high-tech companies offer them. Raises based on those reviews range from 2 percent to 8 percent, and a few star employees manage to gain even more. Companies using the tactic report great results. One company apparently reduced its usual 10-percent turnover to 1 percent for those who received raises. Those expecting early reviews performed well right away because they wanted the early pay raise. When they got it, they stayed on.

You are determined to make early reviews part of your hiring arsenal, and you plan to pitch the plan to your boss, Director of Public Relations Jonathon Richards, in a persuasive memo. You have checked with his assistant, and he is available for a meeting on Wednesday, November 15, at 10:30. You would like to meet with him then to discuss the issue, but your memo should precede the visit. Write a convincing memo that wins the appointment.

9.12 Claim Request: Excessive Lawyer Fees (Obj. 5)

You are the business manager for McConnell's, a producer of gourmet ice cream. McConnell's has 12 ice cream parlours in the Winnipeg area and a reputation for excellent ice cream. Your firm was approached by an independent ice cream vendor who wanted to use McConnell's name and recipes for ice cream to be distributed through grocery stores and drugstores. As business manager you worked with a law firm, Lancomb, Pereigni, and Associates, to draw up contracts regarding the use of McConnell's name and quality standards for the product. When you received the bill from Louis Lancomb, you couldn't believe it. The bill itemized 38 hours of lawyer preparation, at $300 per hour, and 55 hours of paralegal assistance, at $75 per hour. The bill also showed $415 for telephone calls, which might be accurate because Mr. Lancomb had to converse with McConnell's owners, who were living in Ireland at the time. However, you doubt that an experienced attorney would require 38 hours to draw up the contracts in question.

Perhaps some error was made in calculating the total hours. Moreover, you have checked with other businesses and found that excellent legal advice can be obtained for $150 per hour. McConnell's would like to continue using the services of Lancomb, Pereigni, and Associates for future legal business. Such future business is unlikely if an adjustment is not made on this bill. Write a persuasive request to Louis Lancomb, LL.B., Lancomb, Pereigni, and Associates, 1675 Corydon Avenue, Winnipeg, MB R3N 0J8.

9.13 Sales Letter: Fitness at Crown Pizza (Obj. 6)

Assume you are Mike Forrest, Sales Representative, Fitness Associates, 2548 Route 620 Highway, Fredericton, NB E3E 2B6. Fitness Associates sells fitness equipment and services to businesses. You need to write a letter that generates new sales, and Crown Pizza looks especially promising. Through a friend, you've learned that Crown Pizza is striving to reduce health care bills by downsizing its employee insurance plan. However, you hope to convince the company that it would benefit from an on-site fitness centre. You are targeting this area since organized weight-loss programs are more popular in Atlantic Canada than in any other region in the country.[8]

Statistics Canada reports that almost half of Canadian adults are overweight or obese, and deaths related to obesity cost the nation millions of dollars.[9] Employers and employees could save over $1000 a year for each person's medical costs if overweight employees shed their excess weight. The workout programs of Fitness Associates (FA) can help employees to do just that. With regular exercise at an on-site fitness centre, employees lose weight and improve overall health. As employee health improves, absenteeism is reduced and overall productivity increases. And employees love working out before or after work. They make the routine part of their workday, and they often have work buddies who share their fitness regimen.

Though many companies resist spending money to save money, fitness centres need not be large or expensive to be effective. Studies show that moderately sized centres coupled with motivational and training programs yield the greatest success. For just $30 000, Fitness Associates will provide exercise equipment, including stationary bikes, weight machines, and treadmills. Their fitness experts will design a fitness room, set up the fitness equipment, and design appropriate programs. Best of all, the one-time cost is usually offset by cost savings within one year of centre installation. For additional fees FA can also provide fitness consultants for employee fitness assessments. FA specialists will also train employees on proper use of equipment and clean and manage the facility—for an extra charge, of course.

Write a sales letter to Ms. Kathleen Stewart, Human Resources Vice President, Crown Pizza Company, 1546 Saint Mary's Street, Fredericton, NB E3A 8T4. Ask for an appointment to meet with her. Send her a brochure detailing the products and services that Fitness Associates provides. As an incentive, offer a free fitness assessment for all employees if Crown Pizza installs a fitness facility by December 1.

9.14 Sales Letter: Promoting Your Product or Service (Obj. 6)

Identify a situation in your current job or a previous one in which a sales letter is (was) needed. Using suggestions from this chapter, write an appropriate sales letter that promotes a product or service. Use actual names, information, and examples. If you have no work experience, imagine a business you'd like to start: word processing, student typing, pet grooming, car detailing, tutoring, specialty knitting, balloon decorating, delivery service, child care, gardening, lawn care, or something else. Write a letter selling your product or service to be distributed to your prospective customers. Be sure to tell them how to respond.

9.15 Media Release: It's New! (Obj. 7)

In a company where you now work or for an organization to which you belong, identify a product or service that could be publicized. Consider writing a press release announcing a new course at your college, a new president, new equipment, or a campaign to raise funds. Write an announcement for your local newspaper.

C.L.U.E. REVIEW 9

Edit the following sentences to correct faults in grammar, punctuation, spelling, and word use.

1. 2 loans made to Consumer products corporation must be repaid within 90 days. Or the owners will be in default.
2. One loan was for property apprised at forty thousand dollars, the other was for property estimated to be worth ten thousand dollars.
3. Our Senior Marketing Director and the sales manager are quite knowledgable about communications hardware, therefore they are traveling to the Computer show in northern California.
4. We congradulate you on winning the award, and hope that you will continue to experience simular success, in the future.
5. Mr. Salazar left three million dollars to be divided among 4 heirs; one of whom is a successful manufacture.
6. If the CEO and him had behaved more professional the chances of a practicle settlement would be considerably greater.
7. Just inside the entrance, is the desk of the receptionist and a complete directory of all departments'.
8. Every new employee must recieve their permit to park in lot 5-A or there car will be sited.
9. When we open our office in Montreal we will need at least 3 people whom are fluent in french and english.
10. Most companys can boost profits almost one hundred percent by retaining just 5% more of there permenant customers.

CHAPTER • 10 •

NEGATIVE MESSAGES

LEARNING OBJECTIVES

1 Describe the goals of business communicators in delivering bad news.

2 Identify the causes of legal problems in business writing.

3 Explain the components of a bad-news message.

4 Compare the direct and indirect patterns for breaking bad news. List situations in which the direct pattern is better.

5 Identify routine requests and describe a strategy for refusing such requests.

6 Describe a strategy for sending bad news to customers while retaining their goodwill.

7 Explain the best strategy for managing negative organization news.

8 Compare strategies for revealing bad news in different cultures.

Strategies for Breaking Bad News

Breaking bad news is a fact of business life for nearly every business communicator. Because bad news disappoints, irritates, and sometimes even angers the receiver, such messages must be written carefully. The bad feelings associated with disappointing news can be reduced if (1) the reader knows the reasons for the rejection and (2) the bad news is revealed with sensitivity. You've probably heard people say, "It wasn't so much the bad news that I resented. It was the way I was told!"

The sting of bad news can be reduced by giving reasons and communicating sensitively.

This chapter concentrates on how to use the indirect pattern in delivering negative messages. You'll apply that pattern to messages that refuse routine requests, deliver bad news to customers, and deal with negative organization news. The indirect strategy is especially appealing to relationship-oriented writers. They care about how a message will affect its receiver. The direct strategy, as you learned in earlier chapters, frontloads the main idea, even when it's bad news. The direct strategy may be more appealing to efficiency-oriented writers who don't want to waste time with efforts to soften the effects of bad news.[1] The major focus of this chapter will be on developing the indirect strategy, since it is frequently used for bad-news messages. But you'll also learn to identify instances in which the direct pattern may be preferable in announcing bad news.

Goals in Communicating Bad News

1

As a business communicator who must deliver bad news, you have many goals, the most important of which are these:

- **Acceptance.** Make sure the reader understands and accepts the bad news. The indirect pattern helps in achieving this objective.
- **Positive image.** Promote and maintain a good image of yourself and your organization. Realizing this goal assumes that you will act ethically.
- **Message clarity.** Make the message so clear that additional correspondence is unnecessary.
- **Protection.** Avoid creating legal liability or responsibility for you or your organization.

In communicating bad news, key goals include getting the receiver to accept it, maintaining goodwill, and avoiding legal liability.

These are ambitious goals, and we're not always successful in achieving them all. The patterns you're about to learn, however, provide the beginning communicator with strategies and tactics that many writers have found successful in conveying disappointing news sensitively and safely. With experience, you'll be able to vary these patterns and adapt them to your organization's specific writing tasks.

Using the Indirect Pattern to Prepare the Reader

Revealing bad news indirectly shows sensitivity to your reader. Whereas good news can be revealed quickly, bad news is generally better when broken gradually. By preparing the reader, you soften the impact. A blunt announcement of disappointing news might cause the receiver to stop reading and toss the message aside. The indirect strategy enables you to keep the reader's attention until you have been able to explain the reasons for the bad news. The most important part of a bad-news letter is the explanation, which you'll learn about shortly. The indirect plan consists of four parts, as shown in Figure 10.1:

The indirect pattern softens the impact of bad news by giving reasons and explanations first.

FIGURE 10.1 **Four-Part Indirect Pattern for Bad News**

Buffer: Open with a neutral but meaningful statement that does not mention the bad news.	➤	**Reasons:** Explain causes of the bad news before disclosing it.	➤	**Bad News:** Reveal bad news without emphasizing it. Provide alternative or compromise, if possible.	➤	**Closing:** End with a personalized, forward-looking, pleasant statement. Avoid referring to the bad news.

- **Buffer.** Offer a neutral but meaningful statement that does not mention the bad news.
- **Reasons.** Give an explanation of the causes for the bad news before disclosing it.
- **Bad news.** Provide a clear but understated announcement of the bad news that may include an alternative or compromise.
- **Close.** Include a personalized, forward-looking, pleasant statement.

Avoiding Three Causes of Legal Problems

2

Before we examine the components of a bad-news message, let's look more closely at how you can avoid exposing yourself and your employer to legal liability in writing negative messages. Although we can't always anticipate the consequences of our words, we should be alert to three causes of legal difficulties: (1) abusive language, (2) careless language, and (3) the "good-guy syndrome."

Abusive language becomes legally actionable when it is false, harmful to the person's good name, and "published."

Abusive Language. Calling people names (such as *deadbeat, crook,* or *quack*) can get you into trouble. *Defamation* is the legal term for injury to reputation. When the abusive language is written, it's called *libel*; when spoken, it's *slander.*

To be actionable (likely to result in a lawsuit), abusive language must be (1) false, (2) damaging to one's good name, and (3) "published"—that is, spoken within the presence of others or written.

You may now be prosecuted if you transmit a harassing or libelous message by e-mail on a computer bulletin board. Such electronic transmission is considered to be "published." Moreover, a company may incur liability for messages sent through its computer system by employees. That's why many companies do not allow employees to post Internet messages using the company's return address. Employees must add a "not speaking for the company" disclaimer to private messages transmitted over networks.[2]

Obviously, competent communicators avoid making unproven charges and letting their emotions prompt abusive language—in print or electronically.

Careless language includes statements that could be damaging or misinterpreted.

Careless Language. As the marketplace becomes increasingly litigious, we must be certain that our words communicate only what we intend. First, be careful in making statements that are potentially damaging or that could be misinterpreted. Be wary of explanations that convey more information than you intend. Second, be careful about what documents you save. Lawyers may demand, in pursuing a lawsuit, all company files pertaining to a case. Even documents marked "Confidential" or "Personal" may be used.

Remember, too, that e-mail messages are especially risky. You may think that a mere tap of the delete key makes a file disappear; however, messages continue to exist on backup storage devices in the files of the sender and the recipient.

The Good-Guy Syndrome. Most of us hate to have to reveal bad news—that is, to be the bad guy. To make ourselves look better, to make the receiver feel better, and to maintain good relations, we are tempted to make statements that are legally dangerous.

Avoid statements that make you feel good but may be misleading or inaccurate.

Business communicators act as agents of their organizations. Their words, decisions, and opinions are assumed to represent those of the organization. Thus, if you want to communicate your personal feelings or opinions, use your home computer or write on plain paper (rather than company letterhead) and sign your name without title or affiliation. Volunteering extra information can lead to trouble. Thus, avoid supplying data that could be misused, and avoid making promises that can't be fulfilled. Don't admit or imply responsibility for conditions that caused damage or injury. Even apologies (*We're sorry that a faulty bottle cap caused damage to your carpet*) may suggest liability.

Use organizational stationery for official business only, and beware of making promises that can't be fulfilled.

In Chapter 4, we discussed four information areas that generate the most lawsuits: investments, safety, marketing, and human resources. In this chapter we'll make specific suggestions for avoiding legal liability in writing responses to claim letters, credit letters, and personnel documents. You may find that in the most critical areas (such as collection letters or hiring/firing messages) your organization provides language guidelines and form letters approved by legal counsel. As the business environment becomes more perilous, we must be not only sensitive to receivers but also keenly aware of risks to ourselves and to the organizations we represent.

Developing Bad-News Messages

3

Legal issues aside, let's move on to the central focus of this chapter—how to deliver a bad-news message. You may use a direct method with the main idea announced immediately, as you learned in earlier chapters. Many writers, however, prefer to use an indirect strategy, which delays the bad news until after explanations have been given. In your own writing, you can use whichever strategy or medium seems most appropriate to the situation and to your organization. In this chapter you'll now learn how to develop and apply the indirect strategy. Its four components include buffer, reasons, bad news, and closing.

To reduce negative feelings, use a buffer opening for sensitive bad-news messages.

Buffering the Opening. A buffer is a device to reduce shock or pain. To buffer the pain of bad news, begin with a neutral but meaningful statement that makes the reader continue reading. The buffer should be relevant and concise and provide a natural transition to the explanation that follows. The individual situation, of course, will help determine what you should put in the buffer. Avoid trite buffers such as *Thank you for your letter.* Here are some possibilities for opening bad-news messages.

Openers can buffer the bad news with compliments, appreciation, agreement, relevant facts, and understanding.

Best News. Start with the part of the message that represents the best news.

Compliment. Praise the receiver's accomplishments, organization, or efforts. But do so with honesty and sincerity.

Appreciation. Convey thanks to the reader for doing business, for sending something, for conveying confidence in your organization, for expressing feelings, or simply for providing feedback. Avoid thanking the reader, however, for something you are about to refuse.

Agreement. Make a relevant statement with which both reader and receiver can agree.

Facts. Provide objective information that introduces the bad news.

Understanding. Show that you care about the reader. You may want to express concern.

Apology. As you learned in Chapter 7, an apology may be appropriate. A study of actual letters responding to customer complaints revealed that 67 percent carried an apology of some sort.[3] If you do apologize, do it early, briefly, and sincerely.

Good buffers avoid revealing the bad news immediately. Moreover, they do not convey a false impression that good news follows. Additionally, they provide a natural transition to the next bad-news letter component—the reasons.

Bad-news messages should explain reasons before stating the negative news.

Presenting the Reasons. The most important part of a bad-news letter is the section that explains why a negative decision is necessary. Without sound reasons for denying a request or refusing a claim, a letter will fail, no matter how cleverly it is organized or written. As part of your planning before writing, you analyzed the problem and decided to refuse a request for specific reasons. Before disclosing the bad news, try to explain those reasons. Providing an explanation reduces feelings of ill will and improves the chances that the reader will accept the bad news.

Being Cautious in Explaining. If the reasons are not confidential and if they will not create legal liability, you can be specific. Don't, however, make unrealistic or dangerous statements in an effort to be the "good guy."

Readers accept bad news more readily if they see that someone benefits.

Citing Reader or Other Benefits if Plausible. Readers are more open to bad news if in some way, even indirectly, it may help them. Readers accept bad news better if they recognize that someone or something else benefits, such as other workers or the environment.

Explaining Company Policy. Readers resent blanket policy statements prohibiting something. Instead of hiding behind company policy, gently explain why the policy makes sense. By offering explanations, you demonstrate that you care about readers and are treating them as important individuals.

Choosing Positive Words. Because the words you use can affect a reader's response, choose carefully. Remember that the objective of the indirect pattern is holding the reader's attention until you've had a chance to explain the reasons justifying the bad news. To keep the reader in a receptive mood, avoid expressions that might cause the reader to tune out. Be sensitive to negative words such as *claim, error, failure, fault, impossible, mistaken, misunderstand, never, regret, unwilling, unfortunately,* and *violate.*

Showing That the Matter Was Treated Seriously and Fairly. In explaining reasons, demonstrate to the reader that you take the matter seriously, have investigated carefully, and are making an unbiased decision. Consumers are more accepting of disappointing news when they feel that their requests have been heard and that they have been treated fairly. Avoid blaming others within your organization. Such unprofessional behaviour makes the reader lose faith in you and your company.

Cushioning the Bad News. Although you can't prevent the disappointment that bad news brings, you can reduce the pain somewhat by breaking the news sensitively. Be especially considerate when the reader will suffer personally from the bad news. A number of thoughtful techniques can cushion the blow.

Techniques for cushioning bad news include positioning it strategically, using the passive voice, implying the refusal, and suggesting alternatives or compromises.

Positioning the Bad News Strategically. Instead of spotlighting it, sandwich the bad news between other sentences, perhaps among your reasons. Don't let the refusal begin or end a paragraph—the reader's eye will linger on these high-visibility spots. Another technique that reduces shock is putting a painful idea in a subordinate clause. Subordinate clauses often begin with words like *although, as, because, if,* and *since.*

Using the Passive Voice. Passive-voice verbs enable you to depersonalize an action. Whereas the active voice focuses attention on a person, the passive voice highlights the action. Use the passive voice for the bad news. In some instances you can combine passive-voice verbs and a subordinate clause.

Accentuating the Positive. As you learned earlier, messages are far more effective when you describe what you can do instead of what you can't do.

Implying the Refusal. It's sometimes possible to avoid a direct statement of refusal. Often, your reasons and explanations leave no doubt that a request has been denied. Explicit refusals may be unnecessary and at times cruel. The danger of an implied refusal, of course, is that it is so subtle that the reader misses it. Be certain that you make the bad news clear, thus preventing the need for further correspondence.

Suggesting a Compromise or an Alternative. A refusal is not so depressing—for the sender or the receiver—if a suitable compromise, substitute, or alternative is available.

You can further reduce the impact of the bad news by refusing to dwell on it. Present it briefly (or imply it), and move on to your closing.

Closing Pleasantly. After explaining the bad news sensitively, close the message with a pleasant statement that promotes goodwill. The closing should be personalized and may include a forward look, an alternative, good wishes, freebies, resale information, or an off-the-subject remark.

Closings to bad-news messages might include a forward look, an alternative, good wishes, freebies, and resale or sales promotion information.

Forward Look. Anticipate future relations or business. A letter that refuses a contract proposal might read: *Thanks for your bid. We look forward to working with your talented staff when future projects demand your special expertise.*

Alternative. If an alternative exists, end your letter with follow-through advice. For example, in a letter rejecting a customer's demand for replacement of landscaping plants, you might say: *I will be happy to give you a free inspection and consultation. Please call 746-8112 to arrange a date for my visit.*

Good Wishes. A letter rejecting a job candidate might read: *We appreciate your interest in our company, and we extend to you our best wishes in your search to find the perfect match between your skills and job requirements.*

Freebies. When customers complain—primarily about food products or small consumer items—companies often send coupons, samples, or gifts to restore confidence and to promote future business.

Resale or Sales Promotion. When the bad news is not devastating or personal, references to resale information or promotion may be appropriate.

Avoid endings that sound canned, insincere, inappropriate, or self-serving. Don't invite further correspondence, and don't refer to the bad news.

When to Use the Direct Pattern

4 Many bad-news letters are best organized indirectly, beginning with a buffer and reasons. The direct pattern, with the bad news first, may be more effective, though, in situations such as the following:

The direct pattern is appropriate when the receiver might overlook the bad news, when directness is preferred, when firmness is necessary, or when the bad news is not damaging.

- **When the receiver may overlook the bad news.** With the crush of mail today, many readers skim messages, looking only at the opening. If they don't find substantive material, they may discard the message. Rate increases, changes in service, new policy requirements—these critical messages may require boldness to ensure attention.
- **When organization policy suggests directness.** Some companies expect all internal messages and announcements—even bad news—to be straightforward and presented without frills.
- **When the receiver prefers directness.** Busy managers may prefer directness. Such shorter messages enable the reader to get in the proper frame of mind immediately. If you suspect that the reader prefers that the facts be presented straightaway, use the direct pattern.
- **When firmness is necessary.** Messages that must demonstrate determination and strength should not use delaying techniques. For example, the last in a series of collection letters that seek payment of overdue accounts may require a direct opener.
- **When the bad news is not damaging.** If the bad news is insignificant (such as a small increase in cost) and doesn't personally affect the receiver, then the direct strategy certainly makes sense.

Rate increases represent bad news to customers. However, small increases can be announced directly. Such a letter may present the rate increase but immediately point out that other service rates remain the same or are decreasing. The letter should emphasize the "you" view throughout and close with a forward-looking thought. Clever organizations can turn bad news into an opportunity to sell their services.

Generally, writers prefer to use an indirect strategy, especially for more serious bad news. On the other hand, some researchers report that *where* the writer places the bad news is not nearly so important as the *tone* of the message.[4] Many of the techniques you've just learned will help you achieve a sensitive, personal tone in messages delivering negative news.

The 3-×-3 writing process is especially important in crafting bad-news messages because of the potential consequences of poorly written messages.

Applying the 3-×-3 Writing Process

Thinking through the entire process is especially important in bad-news letters. Not only do you want the receiver to understand and accept the message, but you want to be careful that your words say only what you intend. Thus, you'll want to apply the familiar 3-×-3 writing process to bad-news letters.

Analysis, Anticipation, and Adaptation. In Phase 1 (prewriting) you need to analyze the bad news so that you can anticipate its effect on the receiver. If the disappointment will be mild, announce it directly. If the bad news is serious or personal, consider techniques to reduce the pain. Adapt your words to protect the receiver's ego. Choose words that show you respect the reader as a responsible, valuable person.

Research, Organization, and Composition. In Phase 2 (writing) you can gather information and brainstorm for ideas. Jot down all the reasons you have that explain the bad news. If four or five reasons prompted your negative decision, concentrate on the strongest and safest ones. Avoid presenting any weak reasons; readers may seize on them to reject the entire message. After selecting your best reasons, outline the four parts of the bad-news pattern: buffer, reasons, bad news, closing. Flesh out each section as you compose your first draft.

Revision, Proofreading, and Evaluation. In Phase 3 (revising) you're ready to switch positions and put yourself into the receiver's shoes. Have you looked at the problem from the receiver's perspective? Is your message too blunt? Too subtle? Does the message make the refusal, denial, or bad-news announcement clear? Prepare the final version, and proofread for format, punctuation, and correctness.

Refusing Routine Requests

Every business communicator will occasionally have to say no to a request. Depending on how you think the receiver will react to your refusal, you can use the direct or the indirect pattern. If you have any doubt, use the indirect pattern.

Rejecting Requests for Favours, Money, Information, and Action

Most of us prefer to be let down gently when we're being refused something we want. That's why the reasons-before-refusal pattern works well when you must turn down requests for favours, money, information, action, and so forth.

Let's say you must refuse a request from Mark Stevenson, one of your managers, who wants permission to attend a conference. You can't let him go because the timing is bad; he must be present at budget planning meetings scheduled for the same two weeks. Normally, you'd try to discuss this with Mark in person. But he's been travelling among branch offices recently, and you haven't been able to catch him in. Your first inclination might be to send a quick memo, and "tell it like it is" but, you realize that this approach may hurt and have possible danger areas. Moreover, this approach misses a chance to give Mark positive feedback.

The memo, shown in Figure 10.2, starts with a buffer that delivers honest praise (*pleased with your leadership* and *your genuine professional commitment*). By the way, don't be stingy with compliments; they cost you nothing. The buffer also includes the date of the meeting, used strategically to connect the reasons that follow. You will recall from Chapter 5 that repetition of a key idea is an effective transitional device to provide smooth flow between components of a message.

Compliments can help buffer the impact of request refusals.

The middle paragraph provides reasons for the refusal. Notice that they focus on positive elements: Mark is the specialist; the company relies on his expertise; and everyone will benefit if he passes up the conference. In this section it becomes obvious that the request will be refused. The writer is not forced to say *No, you may not attend.* Although the refusal is implied, the reader gets the message.

Routine request refusals focus on explanations and praise, maintain a positive tone, and offer alternatives.

FIGURE 10.2 **Refusing a Request**

1 PREWRITING

Analyze: The purpose of this memo is to refuse a respected employee's request without damaging good relations.

Anticipate: The audience is a valued manager who wants to attend a conference.

Adapt: Because the reader will probably be hurt and disappointed at this message, the indirect pattern is best.

2 WRITING

Research: Gather necessary data, including reasons explaining the refusal.

Organize: In the buffer, praise the manager's contributions. Mention the conference date to provide a transition. In the reasons section, explain why the request cannot be granted. Imply the refusal. Close by suggesting a feasible alternative. Show appreciation.

Compose: Prepare the first draft.

3 REVISING

Revise: Respect the reader's feelings by softening the tone. Show that the refusal is in the reader's best interests. Don't apologize; you've done nothing wrong.

Proofread: Verify spelling of troublesome words. Use commas after beginning clauses and around "Mark" (direct address).

Evaluate: Will this message make the reader understand and accept the refusal?

DATE: July 2, 2004

TO: Mark Stevenson
Manager, Telecommunications

FROM: Ann Wells-Freed AWF
VP, Management Information Systems

SUBJECT: REQUEST TO ATTEND SEPTEMBER CONFERENCE

The Management Council and I are extremely pleased with the leadership you have provided in setting up live video transmission to our regional offices. Because of your genuine professional commitment, Mark, I can understand your desire to attend the conference of the Telecommunication Specialists of North America September 23 to 28 in Kelowna.

The last two weeks in September have been set aside for budget planning. As you and I know, we've only scratched the surface of our teleconferencing projects for the next five years. Since you are the specialist and we rely heavily on your expertise, we need you here for those planning sessions.

If you're able to attend a similar conference in the spring and if our work loads permit, we'll try to send you then. You're a valuable player, Mark, and I'm grateful you're on our MIS team.

Buffer: Includes sincere praise

Transition: Uses date to move smoothly from buffer to reasons

Reasons: Tells why refusal is necessary

Bad news: Implies refusal

Closing: Contains realistic alternative, praise, and appreciation

The closing suggests a qualified alternative (*If our work loads permit, we'll try to send you then*). It also ends positively with gratitude for Mark's contributions to the organization and with another compliment (*You're a valuable player*). Notice that the improved version focuses on explanations and praise rather than on refusals and apologies.

The success of this message depends on attention to the entire writing process, not just on using a buffer or scattering a few compliments throughout. Review the components of the 3-×-3 writing process and how they relate to request refusals by studying the boxes at the top of Figure 10.2.

Just as managers must refuse proposals from employees, they must also reject requests for contributions of money, time, equipment, or other support. Requests for contributions to charity are common. Most big companies receive hundreds of requests annually—from consumers as well as from employees. Although the causes may be worthy, resources are usually limited. If you were required to write frequent refusals, you might prepare a form letter, changing a few variables as needed.

Declining Invitations

When we must decline an invitation to speak or attend a program, we generally try to provide a response that says more than *I can't* or *I don't want to.* Unless the reasons are confidential or business secrets, try to explain them. Because responses to invitations are often taken personally, make a special effort to soften the refusal. In the following letter, an accountant must say no to the invitation from a friend's son to speak before the young man's college business club. The refusal is embedded in a long paragraph and de-emphasized in a subordinate clause (*Although your invitation must be declined*). The reader naturally concentrates on the main clause that follows. In this case that main clause contains an alternative that draws attention away from the refusal.

Notice that the tone of a refusal is warm, upbeat, and positive. This refusal starts with conviviality and compliments.

Dear William:

News of your leadership position in your campus business honourary club fills me with delight and pride. Your father must be proud also of your educational and extracurricular achievements.

Opens cordially with buffer statement praising reader's accomplishments

You honour me by asking me to speak to your group in the spring about codes of ethics in the accounting field. Because our firm has not yet adopted such a code, we have been investigating the codes developed by other accounting firms. I am decidedly not an expert in this area, but I have met others who are. Although your invitation must be declined, I would like to recommend Dr. Carolyn S. Marshall, who is a member of the ethics subcommittee of the Institute of Internal Auditors. Dr. Marshall is a professor who often addresses groups on the subject of ethics in accounting. I spoke with her about your club, and she indicated that she would be happy to consider your invitation.

Explains the writer's ignorance on the topic of ethics. Lessens the impact of the refusal by placing it in a subordinate clause (*Although your invitation must be declined*) using the passive voice. Concentrates attention on the alternative

It's good to learn that you are guiding your organization toward such constructive and timely program topics. Please call Dr. Marshall at (416) 389-2210 if you would like to arrange for her to address your club.

Although the direct refusal in this letter is softened by a subordinate clause, perhaps the refusal could have been avoided altogether. Notice how the following statement implies the refusal: *I'm certainly not an expert in this area, but I have met others who are. May I recommend Dr. Marshall....* If no alternative is available, focus on something positive about the situation: *Although I'm not an expert, I commend your organization for selecting this topic.*

The following checklist reviews the steps in composing a letter refusing a routine request.

Checklist for Refusing Routine Requests

 **Open indirectly with a buffer.** Pay a compliment to the reader, show appreciation for something done, or mention some mutual understanding. Avoid raising false hopes or thanking the reader for something you will refuse.

 **Provide reasons.** In the body explain why the request must be denied—without revealing the refusal. Avoid negativity (*unfortunately, unwilling,* and *impossible*) and potentially damaging statements. Show how your decision benefits the reader or others, if possible.

 **Soften the bad news.** Reduce the impact of bad news by using (1) a subordinate clause, (2) the passive voice, (3) a long sentence, or (4) a long paragraph. Consider implying the refusal, but be certain it is clear. Suggest an alternative, if a suitable one exists.

 **Close pleasantly.** Supply more information about an alternative, look forward to future relations, or offer good wishes and compliments. Maintain a bright, personal tone. Avoid referring to the refusal.

Sending Bad News to Customers

6 Messages with bad news for customers follow the same pattern as other negative messages. Customer letters, though, differ in one major way: they usually include resale or sales promotion emphasis. Customer bad-news messages typically handle problems with orders, denial of claims, or credit refusals.

Handling Problems With Orders

In handling problems with orders, the indirect pattern is appropriate unless the message has some good-news elements.

Not all orders can be filled as received. Suppliers may be able to send only part of an order or none at all. Substitutions may be necessary, or the delivery date may be delayed. Suppliers may suspect that all or part of the order is a mistake; the customer may actually want something else. In writing to customers about problem orders, it's generally wise to use the direct pattern if the message has some good-news elements. But when the message is disappointing, the indirect pattern is more appropriate.

Let's say you represent Live and Learn Toys, a large West Coast toy manufacturer, and you're scrambling for business in a slow year. A big customer, Child Land, calls in August and asks you to hold a block of your best-selling toy, the Space Station. Like most vendors, you require a deposit on large orders. September rolls

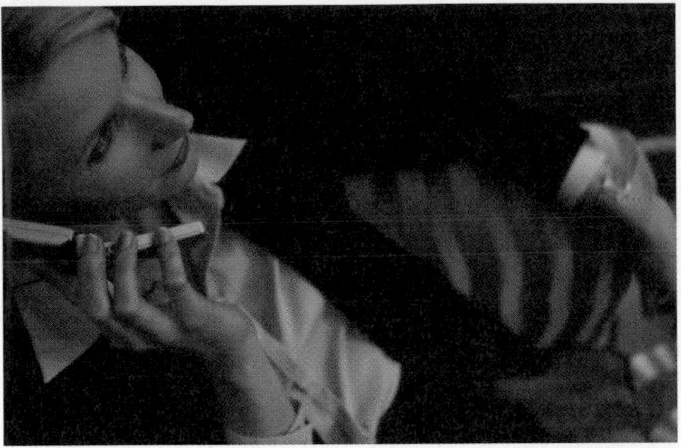

Problems with customer orders can sometimes be resolved by telephone. Large companies, though, more often rely on written messages. If the message contains any good news, begin with that. For messages that are primarily disappointing, use the indirect method, beginning with a buffer and an explanation.

around, and you still haven't received any money from Child Land. You must now write a tactful letter asking for the deposit—or else you will release the toy to other buyers. The problem, of course, is delivering the bad news without losing the customer's order and goodwill. Another challenge is making sure the reader understands the bad news. The following letter sandwiches the bad news (*Without a deposit, we must release this block to other retailers*) between resale information and sales promotion information.

 ***Effective Letter***

Dear Mr. Ronzelli:

You were smart to reserve a block of 500 Space Stations, which we have been holding for you since August. As the holidays approach, the demand for all our learning toys, including Space Station, is rapidly increasing.

Opening compliments the receiver while establishing the facts

Toy stores from St. John's to Victoria are asking us to ship these Space Stations. One reason the Space Station is moving out of our warehouses so quickly is its assortment of gizmos that children love, including a land rover vehicle, a shuttle craft, a hovercraft, astronauts, and even a robotic arm. As soon as we receive your deposit of $4000, we'll have this popular item on its way to your stores. Without a deposit by September 20, though, we must release this block to other retailers. Use the enclosed envelope to send us your cheque immediately. You can begin showing this fascinating Live and Learn toy in your stores by November 1.

Reasons justify the coming bad news. Instead of focusing on the writer's needs (*we have a full warehouse* and *we need your deposit*), the reasons concentrate on motivating the reader. After the reasons, the bad news is clearly spelled out

Please visit our Web site, which replaces our paper catalogue, for pictures, descriptions, and prices of other popular Live and Learn toys. We were voted one of the best online toy stores—with higher ratings than even FAO Schwarz and Etoys. We look forward to your cheque as well as to continuing to serve all your toy needs.

Closing promotes the company's Web site and looks ahead to future business

Denying Claims

Customers occasionally want something they're not entitled to or that you can't grant. They may misunderstand warranties or make unreasonable demands. Because these customers are often unhappy with a product or service, they are emotionally involved. Letters that say no to emotionally involved receivers will probably be your most challenging communication task.

Fortunately, the reasons-before-refusal plan helps you be empathic and artful in breaking bad news. Obviously, in denial letters you'll need to adopt the proper tone. Don't blame customers, even if they are at fault. Avoid *you* statements that sound preachy (*You would have known that cash refunds are impossible if you had read your contract*). Use neutral, objective language to explain why the claim must be refused. Consider offering resale information to rebuild the customer's confidence in your products or organization. In Figure 10.3 the writer denies a customer's claim for the difference between the price the customer paid for speakers and the price he saw advertised locally (which would have resulted in a cash refund of $151). While the catalogue service does match any advertised lower price, the price-matching policy applies *only* to exact models. This claim must be rejected because the advertisement the customer submitted showed a different, older speaker model.

The letter to Matthew Tyson opens with a buffer that agrees with a statement in the customer's letter. It repeats the key idea of product confidence as a transition to the second paragraph. Next comes an explanation of the price-matching policy. The writer does not assume that the customer is trying to pull a fast one. Nor does he suggest that the customer is a dummy who didn't read or understand the price-matching policy. The safest path is a neutral explanation of the policy along with precise distinctions between the customer's speakers and the older ones. The writer also gets a chance to resell the customer's speakers and demonstrate what a quality product they are. By the end of the third paragraph, it's evident to the reader that his claim is unjustified.

Refusing Credit

Goals when refusing credit include maintaining customer goodwill and avoiding actionable language.

As much as companies want business, they can extend credit only when payment is likely to follow. Credit applications, from individuals or from businesses, are generally approved or disapproved on the basis of the applicant's credit history. This record is supplied by a credit-reporting agency, such as Equifax. After reviewing the applicant's record, a credit manager applies the organization's guidelines and approves or disapproves the application.

If you must deny credit to prospective customers, you have four goals in conveying the refusal:

- Avoiding language that causes hard feelings
- Retaining customers on a cash basis
- Preparing for possible future credit without raising false expectations
- Avoiding disclosures that could cause a lawsuit

Because credit applicants are likely to continue to do business with an organization even if they are denied credit, you'll want to do everything possible to encourage that patronage. Thus, keep the refusal respectful, sensitive, and upbeat. To avoid possible litigation, some organizations give no explanation of the reasons for the refusal. Instead, they provide the name of the credit-reporting agency and suggest that inquiries be directed to it. Here's a credit refusal letter that uses a buffer but does not explain the reasons for the denial. Notice how the warm tone reassures the reader that she is respected and that her patronage is valued. The letter implies that her current credit condition is temporary, but it does not raise false hopes by promising future credit.

FIGURE 10.3 **Denying a Claim**

February 19, 2004

Mr. Matthew R. Tyson
177 Beech Avenue
Toronto, ON M4E 3K4

Dear Mr. Tyson:

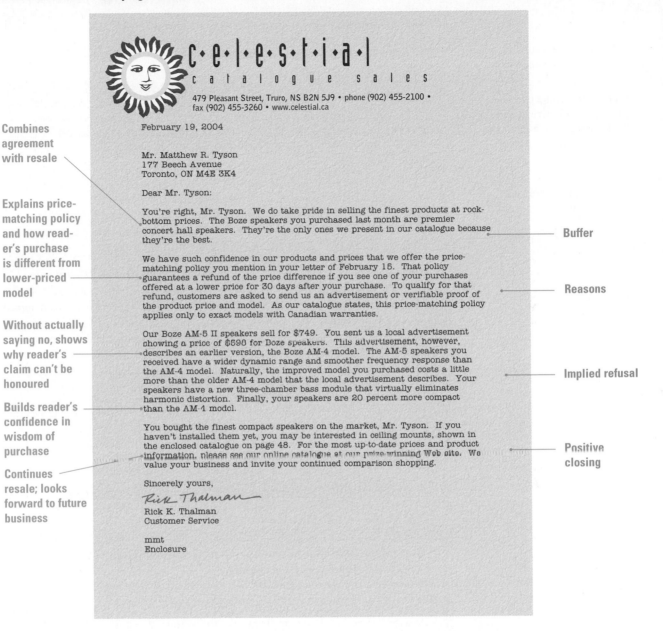

Combines agreement with resale / **Buffer**

You're right, Mr. Tyson. We do take pride in selling the finest products at rock-bottom prices. The Boze speakers you purchased last month are premier concert hall speakers. They're the only ones we present in our catalogue because they're the best.

Explains price-matching policy and how reader's purchase is different from lower-priced model / **Reasons**

We have such confidence in our products and prices that we offer the price-matching policy you mention in your letter of February 15. That policy guarantees a refund of the price difference if you see one of your purchases offered at a lower price for 30 days after your purchase. To qualify for that refund, customers are asked to send us an advertisement or verifiable proof of the product price and model. As our catalogue states, this price-matching policy applies only to exact models with Canadian warranties.

Without actually saying no, shows why reader's claim can't be honoured / **Implied refusal**

Our Boze AM-5 II speakers sell for $749. You sent us a local advertisement showing a price of $598 for Boze speakers. This advertisement, however, describes an earlier version, the Boze AM-4 model. The AM-5 speakers you received have a wider dynamic range and smoother frequency response than the AM-4 model. Naturally, the improved model you purchased costs a little more than the older AM-4 model that the local advertisement describes. Your speakers have a new three-chamber bass module that virtually eliminates harmonic distortion. Finally, your speakers are 20 percent more compact than the AM-4 model.

Builds reader's confidence in wisdom of purchase

Continues resale; looks forward to future business / **Positive closing**

You bought the finest compact speakers on the market, Mr. Tyson. If you haven't installed them yet, you may be interested in ceiling mounts, shown in the enclosed catalogue on page 48. For the most up-to-date prices and product information, please see our online catalogue at our prize-winning Web site. We value your business and invite your continued comparison shopping.

Sincerely yours,

Rick Thalman

Rick K. Thalman
Customer Service

mmt
Enclosure

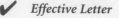

✔ *Effective Letter*

Dear Ms. Margolis:

Buffer identifies application and shows appreciation for it.

We genuinely appreciate your application of January 12 for a Fashion Express credit account.

Long sentence and passive voice de-emphasize bad news. To prevent possible litigation, offers no reason for denial

After receiving a report of your current credit record from Equifax, we find that credit cannot be extended at this time. To learn more about your record, you may call an Equifax credit counsellor at (905) 356-0922. We've arranged for you to take advantage of this service for 60 days from the date of this letter at no charge to you.

Closes cordially and looks forward to continued patronage

Thanks, Ms. Margolis, for the confidence you've shown in Fashion Express. We invite you to continue shopping at our stores, and we look forward to your reapplication in the future.

Some businesses do provide reasons explaining credit denials (*Credit cannot be granted because your firm's current and long-term credit obligations are nearly twice as great as your firm's total assets*). They may also provide alternatives, such as deferred billing or cash discounts. When the letter denies a credit application that accompanies an order, the message may contain resale information. The writer tries to convert the order from credit to cash.

Whatever form the bad-news letter takes, it's a good idea to have the message reviewed by legal counsel because of the litigation landmines awaiting unwary communicators in this area. The following checklist provides tips on how to craft effective bad-news letters.

Checklist for Delivering Bad News to Customers

Begin indirectly. Express appreciation (but don't thank the reader for requesting something you're about to refuse), show agreement on some point, review facts, or show understanding.

Provide reasons. Except in credit denials, justify the bad news with objective reasons. Use resale, if appropriate, to restore the customer's confidence. Avoid blaming the customer or hiding behind company policy. Look for reader benefits.

Present the bad news. State the bad news objectively or imply it. Although resale or sales promotion is appropriate in order letters, it may offend in claim or credit refusals.

Close pleasantly. Suggest action on an alternative, look forward to future business, offer best wishes, refer to gifts, or use resale sensitively. Don't mention the bad news.

Managing Negative Organization News

A tactful tone and a reasons-first approach help preserve friendly relations with customers. These same techniques are useful when delivering bad news to employees and when rejecting job applicants. 7

Announcing Bad News to Employees

Bad news within organizations might involve declining profits, lost contracts, harmful lawsuits, public relations controversies, and changes in policy. Whether you use a direct or an indirect pattern in delivering that news depends primarily on the anticipated reaction of the receiver. When bad news affects employees personally—such as cutbacks in pay, reduction of benefits, or relocation plans—you can generally lessen its impact and promote better relations by explaining reasons before revealing the bad news.

The bad-news memo, shown in Figure 10.4, uses the indirect pattern. Notice that it opens with a relevant, upbeat buffer regarding health care—but says nothing about increasing costs. For a smooth transition, the second paragraph begins with a key idea from the opening (*comprehensive package*). The reasons section discusses rising costs with explanations and figures. The bad news (*you will be paying $109 a month*) is clearly presented but embedded within the paragraph. Throughout, the writer strives to show the fairness of the company's position. The ending, which does not refer to the bad news, emphasizes how much the company is paying and what a wise investment it is. Notice that the entire memo demonstrates a kinder, gentler approach than that shown in the first draft. Of prime importance in breaking bad news to employees is providing clear, convincing reasons that explain the decision.

Organizations can sustain employee morale by communicating bad news openly and honestly.

Many organizations involved in a crisis (serious performance problems, major relocation, massive layoffs, management shakeup, or public controversy) prefer to communicate the news openly to employees, customers, and stockholders. Instead of letting rumours distort the truth, they explain the organization's side of the story honestly and early. Morale can be destroyed when employees learn of major events affecting their jobs through the grapevine or from news accounts—rather than from management.

Saying *No* to Job Applicants

Letters that deny applications for employment should be courteous and tactful but free of specifics that could trigger lawsuits.

Being refused a job is one of life's major rejections. The blow is intensified by tactless letters (*Unfortunately, you were not among the candidates selected for ...*).

You can reduce the receiver's disappointment somewhat by using the indirect pattern—with one important variation. In the reasons section it's wise to be vague in explaining why the candidate was not selected. First, giving concrete reasons may be painful to the receiver (*Your grade point average of 2.7 was low compared with GPAs of other candidates*). Second, and more important, providing extra information may prove fatal in a lawsuit. Hiring and firing decisions generate considerable litigation today. To avoid charges of discrimination or wrongful actions, legal advisors warn organizations to keep employment rejection letters general, simple, and short.

FIGURE 10.4 **Announcing Bad News to Employees**

1 PREWRITING

Analyze: The purpose of this memo is to tell employees that they must share with the company the increasing costs of supplementary health care benefits.

Anticipate: The audience will be employees who are unaware of health care costs and, most likely, reluctant to pay more.

Adapt: Because the readers will probably be unhappy and resentful, use the indirect pattern.

2 WRITING

Research: Collect facts and statistics that document health care costs.

Organize: Begin with a buffer describing the company's commitment to health benefits. Provide explanation of health care costs. Announce the bad news. In the closing, focus on the company's major share of the cost.

Compose: Draft the first version on a computer.

Revise: Remove negativity (*unfortunately, we can't, we were forced, inadvisable, we don't think*). Explain the increase with specifics.

Proofread: Use quotes around *defensive* to show its special sense. Spell out *percent* after 300.

Evaluate: Is there any other way to help readers accept this bad news?

DATE: November 6, 2004

TO: Fellow Employees

FROM: David P. Martin, President DPM

SUBJECT: MAINTAINING QUALITY HEALTH CARE

Supplementary health care programs have always been an important part of our commitment to employees at Midland, Inc. We're proud that our total benefits package continues to rank among the best in the country. — **Begins with positive buffer**

Offers reasons explaining why costs are rising — Such a comprehensive package does not come cheaply. In the last decade health care costs alone have risen over 300 percent. We're told that several factors fuel the cost spiral: inflation, technology improvements, increased cost of outpatient services, and "defensive" medicine practised by doctors to prevent lawsuits.

Reveals bad news clearly but embeds it in paragraph — The annual cost for supplementary health care is almost $1900 a year for family plans, which represents an increase of approximately $65 a month from the previous year. While we were able to absorb that jump without increasing your contribution last year, this year's hike forces us to ask you to share in the increase. To maintain your current health care benefits, you will be paying 10 percent more for your supplementary health care insurance premiums. The enclosed information describes the coverages and costs.

Ends positively by stressing the company's major share of the costs — Midland continues to pay the major portion of your supplementary health care program ($430 each month). We think it's a wise investment.

Enclosure

The following checklist gives tips on how to communicate bad news within an organization.

Checklist for Managing Negative Organization News

 **Start with a relevant, upbeat buffer.** Open with a small bit of good news, praise, appreciation, agreement, understanding, or a discussion of facts leading to the reasons section.

 **Discuss reasons.** Except in job refusal letters, explain what caused the decision necessitating the bad news. Use objective, nonjudgmental, and nondiscriminatory language. Show empathy and fairness.

 **Reveal the bad news.** Make the bad news clear but don't accentuate it. Avoid negative language.

 **Close harmoniously.** End on a positive, friendly note. For job refusals, extend good wishes.

Presenting Bad News in Other Cultures

To minimize disappointment, Canadians generally prefer to present negative messages indirectly. Other cultures may treat bad news differently.

In Germany, for example, business communicators occasionally use buffers but tend to present bad news directly. British writers also tend to be straightforward with bad news, seeing no reason to soften its announcement. In Latin countries the question is not how to organize negative messages but whether to present them at all. It's considered disrespectful and impolite to report bad news to superiors. Thus, reluctant employees may fail to report accurately any negative messages to their bosses.

In Asian cultures, harmony and peace are sought in all relationships. Disrupting the harmony with bad news is avoided. To prevent discord, Japanese communicators use a number of techniques to indicate *no*—without being forced to say it. In conversation they may respond with silence or with a counter question, such as "Why do you ask?" They may change the subject or tell a white lie to save face for themselves and for the questioner. Sometimes the answer sounds like a qualified *yes*: "I will do my best, but if I cannot, I hope you will understand," "Yes, but ...," or "yes" followed by an apology. All of these responses should be recognized as *no*.

Communicating bad news in other cultures may require different strategies.

In China, Westerners often have difficulty understanding the "hints" given by communicators.

"I agree" might mean "I agree with 15 percent of what you say."

"We might be able to" could mean "Not a chance."

"We will consider" could mean "WE will, but the real decision maker will not."

"That is a little too much" might equate to "That is outrageous."[5]

In Thailand the negativism represented by a refusal is completely alien; the word *no* does not exist. In many cultures negative news is offered with such subtleness or in such a positive light that it may be overlooked or misunderstood by low-context cultures. To understand the meaning of what's really being communicated, we must look beyond an individual's actual words, considering the communication style, the culture, and especially the context.

You've now studied the indirect method for revealing bad news and analyzed many examples of messages applying this method. As you observed, business writers generally try to soften the blow; however, they do eventually reveal the bad news. No effort is made to sweep it under the carpet or ignore it totally.

Summary of Learning Objectives

1 **Describe the goals of business communicators in delivering bad news.** Good communicators strive to (a) make the reader understand and accept the bad news, (b) promote and maintain a good image of themselves and their organizations, (c) make the message so clear that additional correspondence is unnecessary, and (d) avoid creating legal liability or responsibility.

2 **Identify the causes of legal problems in business writing.** Abusive language is libelous and actionable when it is false, damages a person's reputation, and is "published"—spoken within the presence of others or written. Even careless language (saying, for instance, that a manufacturing plant is "dangerous") can result in litigation. Moreover, any messages written on company stationery represent that company and can be legally binding.

3 **Explain the components of a bad-news message.** Begin with a buffer, such as a compliment, appreciation, a point of agreement, objective information, understanding, or some part of the message that represents good news. Then explain the reasons that necessitate the bad news, trying to cite benefits to the reader or others. Choose positive words, and clarify company policy if necessary. Announce the bad news strategically, mentioning a compromise or alternative if possible. Close pleasantly with a forward-looking goodwill statement.

4 **Compare the direct and indirect patterns for breaking bad news.** List situations in which the direct pattern is better. Direct messages begin by announcing the bad news immediately. Indirect messages, on the other hand, begin with a buffer, offer explanation, and then disclose the bad news. The direct pattern is most effective when (a) the receiver may overlook the bad news, (b) organization policy suggests directness, (c) the receiver prefers directness, (d) firmness is necessary, or (e) the bad news is not damaging.

5 **Identify routine requests and describe a strategy for refusing such requests.** Routine requests ask for favours, money, information, action, and other items. When the answer will be disappointing, use the reasons-before-refusal pattern. Open with a buffer; provide reasons; announce the refusal sensitively; suggest possible alternatives; and end with a positive, forward-looking comment.

6 **Describe a strategy for sending bad news to customers while retaining their goodwill.** In addition to using the indirect pattern, consider including resale information (reassuring the customer of a wise choice) or sales promotion (pushing a new product). Be especially careful of the tone of words used. Strive for a warm tone using neutral, objective language. Avoid blaming customers.

7 **Explain the best strategy for managing negative organization news.** When breaking bad news to employees, use the indirect pattern but be sure to provide clear, convincing reasons that explain the decision. In refusing job applicants, however, keep letters short, general, and tactful.

8 **Compare strategies for revealing bad news in different cultures.** North American communicators often prefer to break bad news slowly and indirectly. In other low-context cultures, such as Germany and Britain, however, bad news is revealed directly. In high-context cultures, straightforwardness is avoided. In Asian cultures negativism is avoided and hints may suggest bad news. In Latin cultures bad news may be totally suppressed. Subtle meanings must be interpreted carefully.

CHAPTER REVIEW

1. Discuss four goals of a business communicator who must deliver bad news. (Obj. 1)
2. How can business documents in an organization's files become part of a lawsuit? (Obj. 2)
3. Describe the four parts of the indirect message pattern. (Obj. 3)
4. Why should a writer give reasons before revealing bad news? (Obj. 3)
5. Name four or more ways to de-emphasize bad news when it is presented. (Obj. 3)
6. What is the most important difference between direct and indirect letters? (Obj. 4)
7. Name five situations in which the direct pattern should be used for bad news. (Obj. 4)
8. Name four kinds of routine requests that businesses must frequently refuse. (Obj. 5)
9. Why should you be especially careful in cushioning the refusal to an invitation? (Obj. 5)
10. What is the major difference between bad-news messages for customers and those for other people? (Obj. 6)
11. List four goals a writer seeks to achieve in writing messages that deny credit to prospective customers. (Obj. 6)
12. Why should a writer be somewhat vague in the reasons section of a letter rejecting a job applicant? (Obj. 7)
13. When organizations must reveal a crisis (such as the bankruptcy of Eaton's), how should they communicate the news to employees, customers, stockholders, and the public? (Obj. 7)
14. Why is the reasons-before-refusal strategy appropriate for customers who are unhappy with a product or service? (Obj. 6)
15. In Latin countries why may employees sometimes fail to accurately report any negative message to management? (Obj. 8)

CRITICAL THINKING

1. Does bad news travel faster and farther than good news? Why? What implications would this have for companies responding to unhappy customers? (Objs. 1–7)
2. Some people feel that all employee news, good or bad, should be announced directly. Do you agree or disagree? Why? (Objs. 1, 3, and 4)
3. Consider times when you have been aware that others have used the indirect pattern in writing or speaking to you. How did you react? (Objs. 1 and 3)
4. What are the legal and ethical ramifications of using company stationery to write personal letters? (Obj. 2)

ACTIVITIES

10.1 Organizational Patterns (Objs. 3–7)

Identify which organizational pattern you would use for the following messages: direct or indirect.

a. A letter refusing a request by a charitable organization asking your restaurant chain to provide refreshments for a large reception.

b. A memo from the manager denying an employee's request for computer access to the Web. Although the employee works closely with the manager on many projects, the employee's work does not require Internet access.

c. An announcement to employees that a fitness specialist has cancelled a scheduled lunchtime talk and cannot reschedule.

d. A letter from a bank refusing to fund a company's overseas expansion plan.

e. A form letter from an insurance company announcing new policy requirements that many policyholders may resent. If policyholders do not indicate the plan they prefer, they may lose their insurance coverage.

10.2 Passive-Voice Verbs (Obj. 3)

Revise the following sentences to present the bad news with passive-voice verbs.

a. We do not serve meals on any flights other than those during meal times.

b. No one is allowed to park in the yellow zone.

c. Because of our Web site, we are no longer offering a printed catalogue.

d. We are unable to grant your request for a loan.

10.3 Subordinating Bad News (Obj. 3)

Revise the following sentences to position the bad news in a subordinate clause. (Hint: Consider beginning the clause with *Although.*) Use passive-voice verbs for the bad news.

a. We cannot refund your purchase price, but we are sending you two coupons toward your next purchase.

b. We appreciate your interest in our organization. Unfortunately, we are unable to extend an employment offer to you at this time.

c. It is impossible for us to ship your complete order at this time. However, we are able to send the four oak desks now; you should receive them within five days.

d. You are able to increase the number of physician visits you make, but we find it necessary to increase the cost of your monthly health benefit contribution.

10.4 Implying Bad News (Obj. 3)

Revise the following statements to imply the bad news. Use passive-voice verbs and subordinate clauses to further de-emphasize the bad news.

a. I already have an engagement in my appointment calendar for the date you mention. Therefore, I am unable to speak to your group. However, I would like to recommend another speaker who might be able to address your organization.

b. Because of the holiday period, all our billboard space was used this month. Therefore, we are sorry to say that we could not give your charitable group free display space. However, next month, after the holidays, we hope to display your message as we promised.

c. We cannot send you a price list nor can we sell our equipment directly to customers. Our policy is to sell only through dealers, and your dealer is Stereo City, located on Yonge Street in Toronto.

10.5 Evaluating Bad-News Statements (Obj. 3)

Discuss the strengths or weaknesses of the following bad-news statements.

a. It's impossible for us to ship your order before May 1.

b. Frankly, we like your résumé, but we were hoping to hire someone a little younger who might be able to stay with us longer.

c. I'm thoroughly disgusted with this entire case, and I will never do business with shyster lawyers like you again.

d. We can assure you that on any return visit to our hotels, you will not be treated so poorly.

e. We must deny your credit application because your record shows a history of late payments, nonpayment, and irregular employment.

10.6 Negative News in Other Cultures (Obj. 8)

Interview fellow students or work colleagues who are from other cultures. How is negative news handled in their cultures? How would typical individuals refuse a request for a favour, for example? How would a business refuse credit to customers? How would an individual be turned down for a job? Is directness practised? Report your findings to the class.

10.7 Document for Analysis: Refusal of a Favour Request (Objs. 1, 3, 4, and 6)

Analyze the following letter. List its weaknesses. If your instructor directs, revise it.

Dear Mr. Waters:

Unfortunately, we cannot permit you to apply the lease payments you've been making for the past ten months toward the purchase of your Sako 600 copier.

Company policy does not allow such conversion. Have you ever wondered why we can offer such low leasing and purchase prices? Obviously, we couldn't stay in business long if we agreed to proposals such as yours.

You've had the Sako 600 copier for ten months now, Mr. Waters, and you say you like its versatility and reliability. Perhaps we could interest you in another Sako model—one that's more within your price range. Do give us a call.

10.8 Document for Analysis: Negative News for Customers (Objs. 1, 3, 4, and 6)

Analyze the following letter. List its weaknesses. If your instructor directs, revise it.

Dear Charge Customers:

This letter is being sent to you to announce the termination of in-house charge accounts at Golden West Print and Frame Shop. We are truly sorry that we can no longer offer this service.

Because some customers abused the privilege, we must eliminate local charge accounts. We regret that we must take this action, but we found that carrying our own credit had become quite costly. To continue the service would have meant raising our prices. As a small but growing business, we decided it was more logical to drop the in-house charges. As a result, we are forced to begin accepting bank credit cards, including VISA and MasterCard.

Please accept our apologies in trimming our services somewhat. We hope to see you soon when we can show you our new collection of museum-quality gilded wood frames.

10.9 Document for Analysis: Saying No to a Job Applicant (Objs. 1, 2, 3, and 7)

Analyze the following letter. List its weaknesses. If your instructor directs, revise it.

Dear Mr. Franklin:

Ms. Sievers and I wish to thank you for the pleasure of allowing us to interview you last Thursday. We were delighted to learn about your superb academic record, and we also appreciated your attentiveness in listening to our description of the operations of the Maxwell Corporation.

However, we had many well-qualified applicants who were interested in the advertised position of human resources assistant. As you may have guessed, we were particularly eager to find a minority individual who could help us fill out our employment equity goals. Although you did not fit one of our goal areas, we enjoyed talking with you. We hired a female graduate of Ryerson Polytechnic University who had most of the qualities we sought.

Although we realize that the job market is difficult at this time, you have our heartfelt wishes for good luck in finding precisely what you are looking for.

10.10 Request Refusal: The End of Free Credit Reports (Obj. 5)

Critical Thinking **Web**

You are part of the customer service team at Equifax, which was founded in 1919 and is reported to be the leading provider of information tools and knowledge-based solutions. Equifax employs more than 13 000 associates in 17 countries (including close to 1300 employees across Canada) with sales in almost 50, and has $1.8 billion in revenue. In January 2000, Equifax Canada Inc. launched a service to provide commercial reports online with access to credit information on more than 1 800 000 Canadian companies.

These reports contain comprehensive information on businesses. "Whether it's a consumer researching a contractor for home renovations or a manufacturer selling to a new customer, Equifax Internet access to commercial credit profiles offers a fast, cost-effective way to verify information about a company before committing any funds," says Veronica Maidman, president of Equifax Canada Inc.[6]

While this service is cost-effective, it is not free. Your supervisor has indicated that the company has received many requests for free information. Your task is to draft a letter refusing the requests of people who want free credit reports. Explain the reasons for this policy, as well as any exceptions. Decide whether you should tell consumers how to order a copy and how to pay for it. Consult the Equifax Web site **<www.equifax.ca>** for details. Although your letter will be used repeatedly for such requests, address your draft to Mrs. Sherry Bennett, 7024 Glover Road, Langley, BC V2Y 2R1. Sign it with your boss's name, Elizabeth Buerkle.

10.11 Request Refusal: Turning Down Software Training (Objs. 5 and 6)

As Gail Jones, Director of Marketing, Trinity Software Systems, 31 rue Prévost, Hull, QC J9A 1P1, you are confronted with the task of denying a favour to a potential customer. Ava Brown, Principal, Heritage School, 135 rue Notre-Dame, Hull, QC J8X 3T2, is interested in purchasing your educational software system, but she wants training from Trinity for 65 Heritage teachers and staff. The training costs would be extensive, but the real problem is that Trinity doesn't have the personnel for this huge task. Instead, Trinity would like to train one or two Heritage teachers as on-site trainers. These teacher-trainers then would instruct other Heritage teachers and staff. Trinity also would provide training videotapes and a training program guide.

Using teacher-trainers at other schools has kept Trinity's staff expenses low. Thus far, schools have been satisfied with the result. In fact, schools that use Trinity software enjoy having their own "experts" on hand. Because Trinity maintains an ongoing relationship with them, teacher-trainers are informed of software updates and can get help if they need it. The software is user friendly, and many local schools use it. Other software companies often provide such "hit and run" training that schools have difficulty using their software, even though all teachers supposedly have been trained. These companies offer little to the many teachers who have questions long after most training is over. Write a letter to Mrs. Brown denying her request but keeping her as a potential customer. Send her a training program guide and a training video. Offer to put her in touch with a teacher-trainer from a nearby school. She can reach you at (819) 921-1489.

10.12 Customer Bad News: The StairClimber or the LifeStep? (Obj. 6)

Critical Thinking

You are delighted to receive a large order from Kendra Coleman, Beaches Fitness Centre, 2396 Queen Street E., Toronto, ON M4E 1H4. This order includes two Lifecycle Trainers (at $1295 each), four Pro Abdominal Boards (at $295 each), three Tunturi Muscle Trainers (at $749 each), and three Dual-Action StairClimbers (at $1545 each).

You could ship immediately except for one problem. The Dual-Action StairClimber is intended for home use, not for gym or club use. Customers like it because they say it's more like scaling a mountain than climbing a flight of stairs. With each step, users exercise their arms to pull or push themselves up. And its special cylinders absorb shock so that no harmful running impact results. However, this model is not what you would recommend for gym use. You feel Ms. Coleman should order your premier stairclimber, the LifeStep (at $2395 each). This unit has sturdier construction and is meant for heavy use. Its sophisticated electronics provide a selection of customer-pleasing programs that challenge muscles progressively with a choice of workouts. It also quickly multiplies workout gains with computer-controlled interval training. Electronic monitors inform users of step height, calories burned, elapsed time, upcoming levels, and adherence to fitness goals. For gym use the LifeStep is clearly better than the StairClimber. The bad news is that the LifeStep is considerably more expensive.

You get no response when you try to telephone Ms. Coleman to discuss the problem. Should you ship what you can, or hold the entire order until you learn whether she wants the StairClimber or the LifeStep? Or perhaps you should substitute the LifeStep and send only two of them. Decide what to do and write a letter to Ms. Coleman.

10.13 Customer Bad News: Depressed Mattress (Obj. 6)

Team

The following letter was sent in response to a customer's complaint about depressions in your company's BeautyTest mattress. Your company receives enough of these kinds of letters to warrant preparation of a standard response. As an evaluation of your writing skills, your boss asks you and some other interns to come up with a better response. If your letter is better, he may begin using it to pattern similar responses. The problem seems to be that customers don't understand how the unique coil system works. And they have not read the mattress warranty. Get together with your intern team and discuss the faults in this letter before generating a new, more effective letter. Write to Mrs. Shannon Kearney, 2253 Montgomery Street, Moose Jaw, SK S6H 2X4.

Dear Mrs. Kearney:

We have received your letter of May 23 demanding repair or replacement for your newly purchased BeautyTest mattress. You say that you enjoy sleeping on it; but in the morning when you and your husband get up, you claim that the mattress has body impressions that remain all day.

Unfortunately, Mrs. Kearney, we can neither repair nor replace your mattress because those impressions are perfectly normal. If you will read your warranty carefully, you will find this statement: "Slight body impressions will appear with use and are not indicative of structural failure. The body-conforming coils and comfort cushioning materials are beginning to work for you and impressions are caused by the natural settling of these materials."

When you purchased your mattress, I'm sure your salesperson told you that the BeautyTest mattress has a unique, scientifically designed system of individually pocketed coils that provide separate support for each person occupying the bed. This unusual construction, with those hundreds of independently operating coils, reacts to every body contour, providing luxurious comfort. At the same time, this system provides firm support. It is this unique design that's causing the body impressions that you see when you get up in the morning.

Although we never repair or replace a mattress when it merely shows slight impressions, we will send our representative out to inspect your mattress, if it would make you feel better. Please call for an appointment at (800) 322-9800. Remember, on a BeautyTest mattress you get the best night's rest possible.

Cordially,

10.14 Customer Bad News: Refusing Claim to Evict Noisy Neighbour (Obj. 6)

Critical Thinking **Web**

As Arman Aryai, you must deny the request of Robert Brockway, one of the tenants in your three-storey office building. Mr. Brockway, an accountant, demands that you immediately evict a neighbouring tenant who plays loud music throughout the day, interfering with Mr. Brockway's conversations with clients and with his concentration. The noisy tenant, Ryan McInnis, seems to operate an entertainment booking agency and spends long hours in his office. You know you can't evict Mr. McInnis immediately because of his lease. Moreover, you hesitate to do anything drastic because paying tenants are hard to find. Although you need more information, you don't want to engage an expensive lawyer. On the Internet, find a site that provides information related to tenancy agreements in your area to give you some ideas about dealing with a noisy tenant. Decide on a course of action. Then write to Robert Brockway, CGA, Suite 203, 120 Wentworth Road, Hamilton, ON L9B 2F5. Deny his request but tell him how you plan to resolve the problem.

10.15 Customer Bad News: The Sports Connection (Obj. 6)

As manager of the Sports Connection, you must refuse the application of Wendy Takahashi for an extended membership in your athletic club. This is strictly a business decision. You liked Wendy very much when she applied, and she seems genuinely interested in fitness and a healthful lifestyle. However, your "extended membership" plan qualifies the member for all your testing, exercise, aerobics, and recreation programs. This multiservice program is necessarily expensive and requires a solid credit rating. To your disappointment, however, you learned that Wendy's credit rating is decidedly negative. Her credit report indicates that she is delinquent in payments to four businesses, including Holiday Health Spa, your principal competitor.

You do have other programs, including your "Drop In and Work Out" plan that offers use of available facilities on a cash basis. This plan enables a member to reserve space on the racquetball and handball courts; the member can also sign up for exercise and aerobics classes, space permitting. Since Wendy is far in debt, you would feel guilty allowing her to plunge in any more deeply. Refuse her credit application, but encourage her cash business. Suggest that she make an inquiry to the credit reporting company Equifax to learn about her credit report. She is eligible to receive a free credit report if she mentions this application. Write to Wendy Takahashi, 340 Sugar Grove Avenue, Apt. 2B, Brandon, MB R3J 7F3.

10.16 Customer Bad News: Refusing Returned Books (Obj. 6)

As the customer service manager of Kent Publishers, you must refuse most of a shipment of books returned from the Mackenzie College Bookstore. Your policy is to provide a 100-percent return on books if the books are returned prepaid in *new*, *unmarked*, and *salable* condition.

The return must be within 12 months of the original invoice date. Old editions of books must be returned within 90 days of your announcement that you will no longer be printing that edition. These conditions are published and sent with every order of books shipped. The return shipment from Mackenzie College looks as if someone was housecleaning and decided to return all unsold books to you. Fourteen books are not your titles; return them. You could have accepted the 22 copies of Donner's *Introduction to Marketing*—if they were not imprinted with "Mackenzie College," the price, and return instructions on the inside cover. The 31 copies of Heigel's *College Writing Handbook* are second editions. Since you've been selling the third edition for 14 months, you can't accept them. Five copies of Quigley's *Business Law* appear to be water damaged; they're unsalable. From the whole mess it looks as if you'll be able to give them credit for 25 copies of Miller's *The Promotable Woman* (wholesale price $31). However, since Mackenzie sent no invoice information, you'll have to tack on a 15-percent service charge to cover the effort involved in locating the order in your records.

Write a letter to Christopher Lorenze, Manager, Mackenzie College Bookstore, Peterborough, ON K9H 5Z4, that retains his goodwill. Mackenzie has been a valued customer in the past. This bookstore placed orders on time and paid on time. Tell Mr. Lorenze what is being returned and how much credit you are allowing. From the credit total, deduct $32.50 for return shipping costs.

10.17 Customer Bad News: No Credit for Cordless Phones (Obj. 6)

As Julie Abrams, sales manager, CyberSound, you are delighted to land a sizeable order for your new 25-channel cordless telephone. This great phone has speed dialling, auto scan to ensure clear conversations, caller ID, and call waiting.

The purchase order comes from High Point Electronics, a retail distributor in Regina, Saskatchewan. You send the order on to Shane Simmons, your credit manager, for approval of the credit application attached. To your disappointment, Shane tells you that High Point doesn't qualify for credit. Equifax, the credit reporting agency, reports that credit would be risky for High Point.

You decide to write to High Point with the bad news and an alternative. Suggest that High Point order a smaller number of the cordless phones. If it pays cash, it can receive a 2-percent discount. After High Point has sold these fast-moving units, it can place another cash order through your toll-free order number. With your fast delivery system, its inventory will never be depleted. High Point can get the phones it wants now and can replace its inventory almost overnight. Credit Manager Simmons tells you that your company generally reveals to credit applicants the name of the credit reporting service and encourages them to investigate their credit record. Write a credit refusal to Ryan Bardens, High Point Electronics, 1586 Albert Avenue, Regina, SK S4V 6W3.

10.18 Employee Bad News: Strikeout for Expanded Office Teams (Obj. 7)

Team **Critical Thinking**

Assume you are Hank James, vice president of Human Resources at Tissue Mills Paper Company in Kingston, Ontario. Recently several of your employees requested that their spouses or friends be allowed to participate in Tissue Mills' intramural sports teams. Although the teams play only once a week during the season, these employees claim that they can't afford more time away from friends and family. Over 100 employees currently participate in the eight coed volleyball, softball, and tennis teams, which are open to company employees only. The teams were designed to improve employee friendships and to give employees a regular occasion to have fun together.

If nonemployees were to participate, you're afraid that employee interaction would be limited. And while some team members might have fun if spouses or friends were included, you're not so sure all employees would enjoy it. You're not interested in turning intramural sports into "date night." Furthermore, the company would have to create additional teams if many nonemployees joined, and you don't want the administrative or equipment costs of more teams. Adding teams also would require changes to team rosters and game schedules, which could be a problem for some employees. You do understand the need for social time with friends and families, but guests are welcome as spectators at all intramural games. Besides, the company already sponsors a family holiday party and an annual company picnic. Write an e-mail or hard-copy memo to the staff denying the request of several employees to include nonemployees on Tissue Mills' intramural sports teams.

10.19 Employee Bad News: Refusing Christmas (Obj. 7)

In the past your office has always sponsored a Christmas party at a nice restaurant. As your company has undergone considerable downsizing and budget cuts during the past year, you know that no money is available for holiday entertaining. Moreover, as the staff becomes more diverse, you decide that it might be better to celebrate a "holiday" party instead of a Christmas event. As executive vice president, respond to the e-mail request of Dina Gillian, office manager. Dina asks permission to make restaurant reservations for this year's Christmas party. Refuse Dina, but offer some alternatives. How about a potluck dinner?

C.L.U.E. REVIEW 10

Edit the following sentences to correct all language faults, including grammar, punctuation, spelling, and word confusions.

1. Your advertisement in the June second edition of the Edmonton Sun, caught my attention; because my training and experience matches your requirements.
2. Undoubtlessly the bank is closed at this hour but it's ATM will enable you to recieve the cash you need.
3. A flow chart detailing all sales' procedures in 4 divisions were prepared by our Vice President.
4. The computer and printer was working good yesterday, and appeared to be alright this morning; when I used it for my report.
5. If I was you I would be more concerned with long term not short term returns on the invested capitol.
6. We make a conscience effort by the way to find highly-qualified individuals with up to date computer skills.
7. If your résumé had came earlier I could have showed it to Mr. Sutton and she before your interview.
8. Deborahs report summary is more easier to read then David because she used consistant headings and efficient writing techniques.
9. At McDonald's we ordered 4 big macs 3 orders of french fries, and 5 coca-colas for lunch.
10. Because the budget cuts will severely effect all programs the faculty have unanimously opposed it.

UNIT 4

REPORTS AND PROPOSALS

CHAPTER 11

Report Planning and Research

CHAPTER 12

Report Organization and Presentation

CHAPTER 13

Typical Business Reports

CHAPTER 14

Proposals and Formal Reports

CHAPTER • 11 •

REPORT PLANNING AND RESEARCH

LEARNING OBJECTIVES

1 Describe business report basics, including functions, patterns, formats, and writing styles.

2 Apply the 3-×-3 writing process to reports.

3 Conduct research by locating secondary data.

4 Generate primary data for research projects.

5 Recognize the purposes and techniques of documentation in business reports.

Understanding Report Basics

1

Reports are a fact of life in business. In a low-context culture like that of North America, our values and attitudes seem to prompt us to write reports. We analyze the pros and cons of problems, studying alternatives and assessing facts, figures, and details. We pride ourselves on being practical and logical. We solve problems by applying scientific procedures. When we must persuade management to support a project, we generally write a report laying out the case. When we look at the processes listed, it is easy to see why writing is considered to be a thinking tool.

Management decisions in many organizations are based on information submitted in the form of reports. This chapter examines categories, functions, organizational patterns, formats, and writing styles of reports. It also introduces the report-writing process and discusses methods of collecting and documenting data.

Effective business reports solve problems and answer questions systematically.

Because of their abundance and diversity, business reports are difficult to define. They may range from informal half-page trip reports to formal 200-page financial forecasts. Reports may be presented orally in front of a group or electronically on a computer screen. Some reports appear as words on paper in the form of memos and letters. Others are primarily numerical data, such as tax reports or profit-and-loss statements. Some seek to provide information only; others aim to analyze and make recommendations. Although reports vary greatly in length, content, form, and formality level, they all have one common purpose: *Business reports are systematic attempts to answer questions and solve problems.*

Functions of Reports

In terms of what they do, most of the reports just described can be placed in two broad categories: informational reports and analytical reports.

Informational reports simply present data without analysis or recommendations. Analytical reports provide data, analyses, conclusions, and, if requested, recommendations.

Informational Reports. Reports that present data without analysis or recommendations are primarily informational. Although writers collect and organize facts, they are not expected to analyze the facts for readers. A trip report describing an employee's visit to a trade show, for example, simply presents information. Other reports that present information without analysis involve routine operations, compliance with regulations, and company policies and procedures.

Analytical Reports. Reports that provide data, analyses, and conclusions are analytical. If requested, writers also supply recommendations. Analytical reports may intend to persuade readers to act or to change their beliefs. Assume you're writing a feasibility report that compares several potential locations for a workout/fitness club. After analyzing and discussing alternatives, you might recommend one site, thus attempting to persuade readers to accept this choice.

Direct and Indirect Patterns

Like letters and memos, reports may be organized directly or indirectly. The reader's expectations and the content of a report determine its pattern of development, as illustrated in Figure 11.1. In long reports, such as corporate annual reports, some parts may be developed directly while other parts are arranged indirectly.

Direct Pattern. When the purpose for writing is presented close to the beginning, the organizational pattern is direct. Informational reports, such as the letter report

FIGURE 11.1 **Audience Analysis and Report Organization**

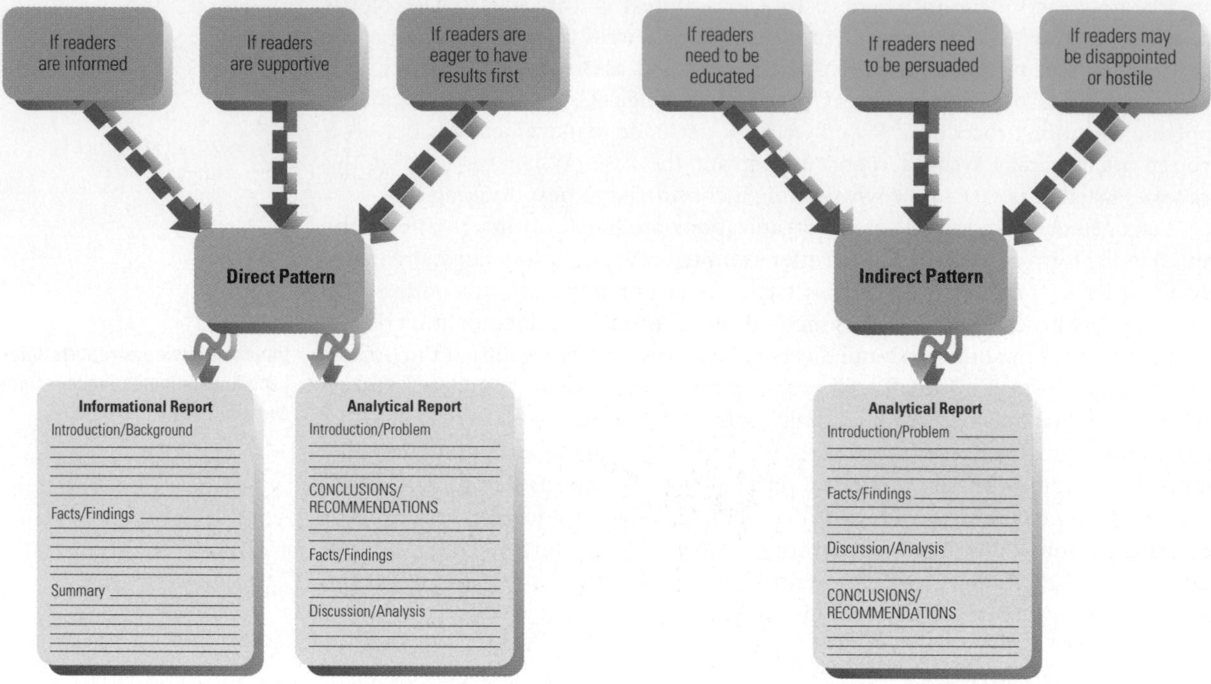

The direct pattern places conclusions and recommendations near the beginning of a report.

shown in Figure 11.2, are usually arranged directly. They open with an introduction, followed by the facts and a summary. In Figure 11.2 the writer explains a legal services plan. The letter report begins with an introduction. Then it presents the facts, which are divided into three subtopics identified by descriptive headings. The letter ends with a summary and a complimentary close.

Analytical reports may also be organized directly, especially when readers are supportive or are familiar with the topic. Many busy executives prefer this pattern because it gives them the results of the report immediately. They don't have to spend time wading through the facts, findings, discussion, and analyses to get to the two items they are most interested in—conclusions and recommendations. Figure 11.3 illustrates such an arrangement. This analytical memo report describes environmental hazards of a property that a realtor has just listed. The realtor is familiar with the investigation and eager to find out the recommendations. Therefore, the memo is organized directly.

You should be aware, though, that unless readers are familiar with the topic, they may find the direct pattern confusing. Many readers prefer the indirect pattern because it seems logical and mirrors the way we solve problems.

The indirect pattern is appropriate for analytical reports that seek to persuade or that convey bad news.

Indirect Pattern. When the conclusions and recommendations, if requested, appear at the end of the report, the organizational pattern is indirect. Such reports usually begin with an introduction or description of the problem, followed by facts and interpretation from the writer. They end with conclusions and recommendations. This pattern is helpful when readers are unfamiliar with the problem. It's also useful when readers must be persuaded or when they may be disappointed with or hostile toward the report's findings. The writer is more likely to retain the reader's

FIGURE 11.2 **Informational Report—Letter Format**

Tips for Letter Reports

- Use letter format for short informal reports sent to outsiders.
- Organize the facts section into logical divisions identified by consistent headings.
- Single-space the body.
- Double-space between paragraphs.
- Leave two blank lines above each side heading.
- Create side margins of 1 to 1¼ inches.
- Add a second-page heading, if necessary, consisting of the addressee's name, the date, and the page number.

Centre for Consumers of Legal Services
P.O. Box 260
Kitchener, ON N2K 2V5

Uses letterhead stationery for an informal report addressed to an outsider

September 8, 2004

Ms. Lisa Burgess, Secretary
Westwood Homeowners
85 Westwood Drive
Guelph, ON N1H 6Y7

Dear Ms. Burgess:

As executive director of the Centre for Consumers of Legal Services, I'm pleased to send you this information describing how your homeowners' association can sponsor a legal services plan for its members. After an introduction with background information, this report will discuss three steps necessary for your group to start its plan.

Introduction

A legal services plan promotes preventive law by letting members talk to lawyers whenever problems arise. Prompt legal advice often averts or prevents expensive litigation. Because groups can supply a flow of business to the plan's lawyers, groups can negotiate free consultation, follow-up, and discounts.

Two kinds of plans are commonly available. The first, a free plan, offers free legal consultation along with discounts for services when the participating groups are sufficiently large to generate business for the plan's lawyers. These plans actually act as a substitute for advertising for the lawyers. The second common type is the prepaid plan. Prepaid plans provide more benefits, but members must pay annual fees, usually of $200 or more a year.

Since you inquired about a free plan for your homeowners' association, the following information describes how to set up such a program.

Presents introduction and facts without analysis or recommendations

Determine the Benefits Your Group Needs

Arranges facts of report into sections with descriptive headings

The first step in establishing a free legal services plan is to meet with the members of your group to decide what benefits they want. Typical benefits include the following:

Free consultation. Members may consult a participating lawyer—by phone or in the lawyer's office—to discuss any matter. The number of consultations is unlimited, provided each is about a separate matter. Consultations are generally limited to 30 minutes, but they include substantive analysis and advice.

Emphasizes benefits in paragraph headings in boldfaced type

Free document review. Important papers—such as leases, insurance policies, and installment sales contracts—may be reviewed with legal counsel. Members may ask questions and receive an explanation of terms.

FIGURE 11.2 *(continued)*

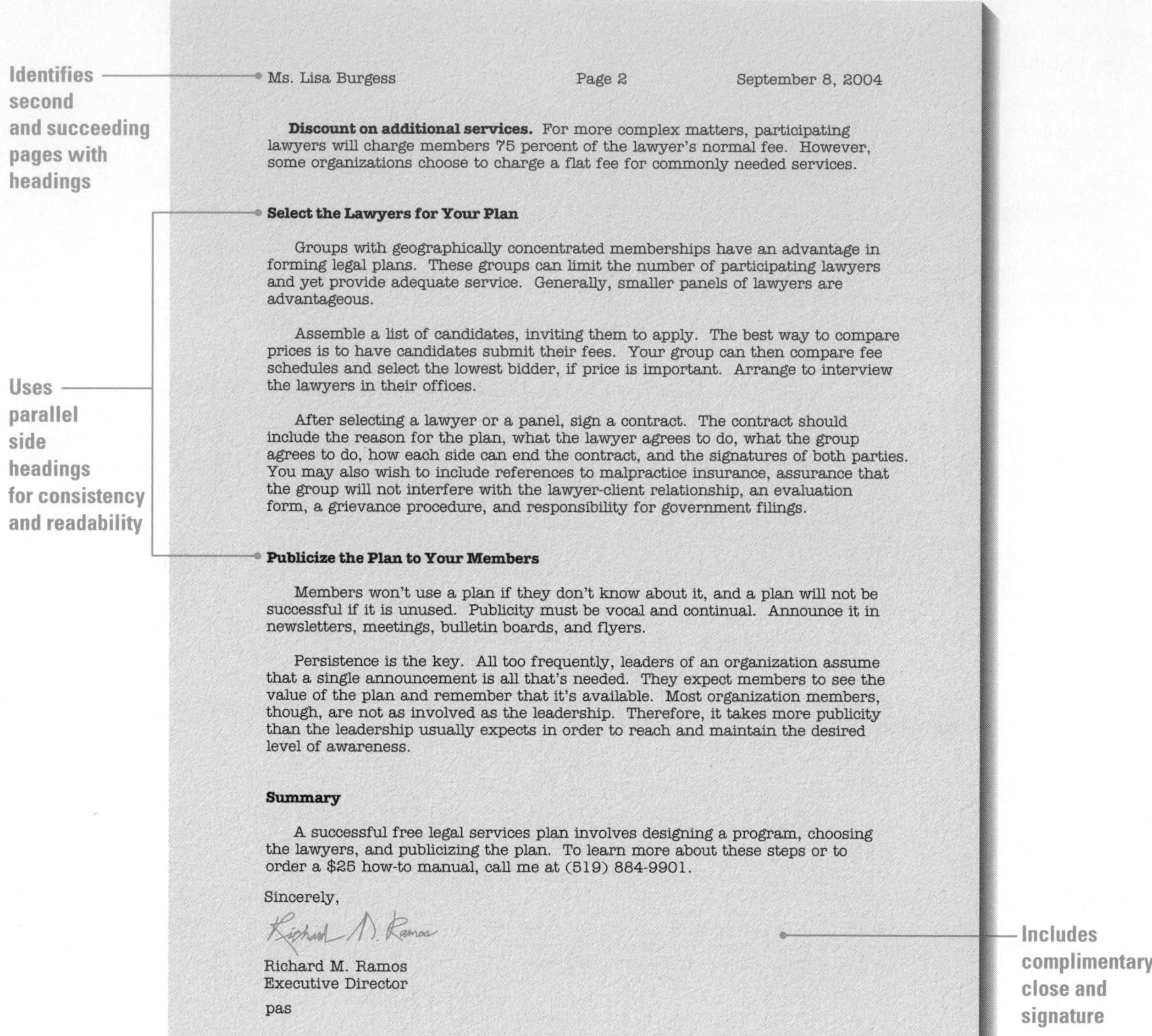
Identifies second and succeeding pages with headings
Uses parallel side headings for consistency and readability
Includes complimentary close and signature

Ms. Lisa Burgess Page 2 September 8, 2004

Discount on additional services. For more complex matters, participating lawyers will charge members 75 percent of the lawyer's normal fee. However, some organizations choose to charge a flat fee for commonly needed services.

Select the Lawyers for Your Plan

Groups with geographically concentrated memberships have an advantage in forming legal plans. These groups can limit the number of participating lawyers and yet provide adequate service. Generally, smaller panels of lawyers are advantageous.

Assemble a list of candidates, inviting them to apply. The best way to compare prices is to have candidates submit their fees. Your group can then compare fee schedules and select the lowest bidder, if price is important. Arrange to interview the lawyers in their offices.

After selecting a lawyer or a panel, sign a contract. The contract should include the reason for the plan, what the lawyer agrees to do, what the group agrees to do, how each side can end the contract, and the signatures of both parties. You may also wish to include references to malpractice insurance, assurance that the group will not interfere with the lawyer-client relationship, an evaluation form, a grievance procedure, and responsibility for government filings.

Publicize the Plan to Your Members

Members won't use a plan if they don't know about it, and a plan will not be successful if it is unused. Publicity must be vocal and continual. Announce it in newsletters, meetings, bulletin boards, and flyers.

Persistence is the key. All too frequently, leaders of an organization assume that a single announcement is all that's needed. They expect members to see the value of the plan and remember that it's available. Most organization members, though, are not as involved as the leadership. Therefore, it takes more publicity than the leadership usually expects in order to reach and maintain the desired level of awareness.

Summary

A successful free legal services plan involves designing a program, choosing the lawyers, and publicizing the plan. To learn more about these steps or to order a $25 how-to manual, call me at (519) 884-9901.

Sincerely,

Richard M. Ramos
Executive Director

pas

interest by first explaining, justifying, and analyzing the facts and then making recommendations. This pattern also seems most rational to readers because it follows the normal thought process: problem, alternatives (facts), solution.

Formats of Reports

A report's format depends on its length, audience, topic, and purpose.

The format of a report is governed by its length, topic, audience, and purpose. After considering these elements, you'll probably choose from among the following four formats:

- **Letter format.** Use letter format for short (say, ten or fewer pages) informal reports addressed outside an organization. Prepared on office stationery, a letter report contains a date, inside address, salutation, and complimentary close, as

FIGURE 11.3 **Analytical Report—Memo Format**

Tips for Memo Reports

- Use memo format for most short (10 or fewer pages) informal reports within an organization.
- Leave side margins of 1 to 1¼ inches.
- Sign your initials on the FROM line.
- Use an informal, conversational style.
- For direct analytical reports, put recommendations first.
- For indirect analytical reports, put recommendations last.

Atlantic Environmental, Inc.

Interoffice Memo

DATE: March 9, 2004

TO: Kermit Fox, President

FROM: Cynthia M. Rashid, Environmental Engineer CMR

SUBJECT: INVESTIGATION OF MOUNTAIN PARK COMMERCIAL SITE

For Laurentian Realty, Inc., I've completed a preliminary investigation of its Mountain Park property listing. The following recommendations are based on my physical inspection of the site, official records, and interviews with officials and persons knowledgeable about the site.

Recommendations

To reduce its potential environmental liability, Laurentian Realty should take the following steps in regard to its Mountain Park listing:

- Conduct an immediate asbestos survey at the site, including inspection of ceiling insulation material, floor tiles, and insulation around a gas-fired heater vent pipe at 2539 Mountain View Drive.
- Prepare an environmental audit of the generators of hazardous waste currently operating at the site, including Mountain Technology.
- Obtain lids for the dumpsters situated in the parking areas and ensure that the dumpsters are kept covered.

Findings and Analyses

My preliminary assessment of the site and its immediate vicinity revealed rooms with damaged floor tiles on the first and second floors of 2539 Mountain View Drive. Apparently, during recent remodelling, these tiles had been cracked and broken. Examination of the ceiling and attic revealed further possible contamination from asbestos. The insulation material surrounding the hot-water storage tank was in poor condition.

Located on the property is Mountain Technology, a possible hazardous waste generator. Although I could not examine its interior, this company has the potential for producing hazardous-material contamination.

In the parking area large dumpsters collect trash and debris from several businesses. These dumpsters were uncovered, thus posing a risk to the general public.

In view of the construction date of the structures on this property, asbestos-containing building materials might be present. Moreover, this property is located in an industrial part of the city, further prompting my recommendation for a thorough investigation. Laurentian Realty can act immediately to eliminate one environmental concern by covering the dumpsters in the parking area.

Applies memo format for short, informal internal report

Uses first paragraph as introduction

Presents recommendations first (direct pattern) because reader is supportive of and familiar with topic

Combines findings and analyses in short report

shown in Figure 11.2. Although they may carry information similar to that found in correspondence, letter reports usually are longer and show more careful organization than most letters. They also include headings.

- **Memo format.** For short informal reports that stay within organizations, memo format is appropriate. Memo reports begin with DATE, TO, FROM, and SUBJECT, as shown in Figure 11.3. Like letter reports, memo reports differ from regular memos in length, use of headings, and deliberate organization.
- **Manuscript format.** For longer, more formal reports, use manuscript format. These reports are usually printed on plain paper instead of letterhead stationery or memo forms. They begin with a title followed by systematically displayed headings and subheadings.
- **Printed forms.** Prepared forms are often used for repetitive data, such as monthly sales reports, performance appraisals, merchandise inventories, and personnel and financial reports. Standardized headings on these forms save time for the writer. Preprinted forms also make similar information easy to locate and ensure that all necessary information is provided.

Writing Style

Reports can be formal or informal, depending on the purpose, audience, and setting.

Like other business messages, reports can range from informal to formal, depending on their purpose, audience, and setting. Research reports from consultants to their clients tend to be rather formal. Such reports must project an impression of objectivity, authority, and impartiality. But a report to your boss describing a trip to a conference would probably be informal.

Figure 11.4, which compares characteristics of formal and informal report-writing styles, can help you decide the writing style that's appropriate for your reports.

Applying the 3-×-3 Writing Process to Reports

2

Because business reports are systematic attempts to answer questions and solve problems, the best reports are developed methodically. The same 3-×-3 writing process that guided memo and letter writing can be applied to reports. Let's channel the process into seven specific steps:

The best reports grow out of a seven-step process beginning with analysis and ending with proofreading and evaluation.

- **Step 1:** Analyze the problem and purpose.
- **Step 2:** Anticipate the audience and issues.
- **Step 3:** Prepare a work plan.
- **Step 4:** Research the data.
- **Step 5:** Organize, analyze, interpret, and illustrate the data.
- **Step 6:** Compose the first draft.
- **Step 7:** Revise, proofread, and evaluate.

How much time you spend on each step depends on your report task. A short informational report on a familiar topic might require a brief work plan, little research, and no analysis of the data. A complex analytical report, on the other hand, might demand a comprehensive work plan, extensive research, and careful analysis of the data.

FIGURE 11.4 **Report-Writing Styles**

	Formal Writing Style	Informal Writing Style
Use	Theses Research studies Controversial or complex reports (especially to outsiders)	Short, routine reports Reports for familiar audiences Noncontroversial reports Most reports for company insiders
Effect	Impression of objectivity, accuracy, professionalism, fairness Distance created between writer and reader	Feeling of warmth, personal involvement, closeness SWIF (Sincere, Warm, Interested, and Friendly)
Characteristics	Absence of first-person pronouns; use of third-person (*the researcher, the writer*) Absence of contractions (*can't, don't*) Use of passive-voice verbs (*the study was conducted*) Complex sentences; long words Absence of humour and figures of speech Reduced use of colourful adjectives and adverbs Elimination of "editorializing" (author's opinions, perceptions)	Use of first-person pronouns (*I, we, me, my, us, our*) Use of contractions Emphasis on active-voice verbs (*I conducted the study*) Shorter sentences; familiar words Occasional use of humour, metaphors Occasional use of colourful speech Acceptance of author's opinions and ideas

To illustrate the planning stages of a report, we'll watch Diane Camas develop a report she's preparing for her boss, Mike Rivers, at Mycon Pharmaceutical Laboratories. Mike asked Diane to investigate the problem of transportation for sales representatives. Currently, some Mycon reps visit customers (mostly doctors and hospitals) using company-leased cars. A few reps drive their own cars, receiving reimbursements for use. In three months Mycon's leasing agreement for 14 cars expires, and Mike is considering a major change. Diane's task is investigating the choices and reporting her findings to Mike.

Analyzing the Problem and Purpose

The first step in writing a report is understanding the problem or assignment clearly. For complex reports it's wise to prepare a written problem statement. In analyzing her report task, Diane had many questions. Is the problem that Mycon is spending too much money on leased cars? Does Mycon wish to invest in owning a fleet of cars? Is Mike unhappy with the paperwork involved in reimbursing sales reps when they use their own cars? Does he suspect that reps are submitting inflated mileage figures? Before starting research for the report, Diane talked with Mike to define the problem. She learned several dimensions of the situation and wrote the following statement to clarify the problem—both for herself and for Mike.

Before beginning a report, identify in a clear statement the problem to be solved.

Problem Statement: The leases on all company cars will be expiring in three months. Mycon must decide whether to renew them or develop a new policy regarding transportation for sales reps. Expenses and paperwork for employee-owned cars seem excessive.

Diane further defined the problem by writing a specific question that she would try to answer in her report:

Problem Question: What plan should Mycon follow in providing transportation for its sales reps?

Now Diane was ready to concentrate on the purpose of the report. Again, she had questions. Exactly what did Mike expect? Did he want a comparison of costs for buying cars and leasing cars? Should she conduct research to pinpoint exact reimbursement costs when employees drive their own cars? Did he want her to do all the legwork, present her findings in a report, and let him make a decision? Or did he want her to evaluate the choices and recommend a course of action? After talking with Mike, Diane was ready to write a simple purpose statement for this assignment.

A simple purpose statement defines the focus of a report.

Simple Statement of Purpose: To recommend a plan that provides sales reps with cars to be used in their calls.

Preparing a written purpose statement is a good idea because it defines the focus of a report and provides a standard that keeps the project on target. In writing useful purpose statements, choose active verbs telling what you intend to do: *analyze, choose, investigate, compare, justify, evaluate, explain, establish, determine,* and so on. Notice that Diane's statement begins with the active verb *recommend.*

Some reports require only a simple statement of purpose: *to investigate expanded teller hours, to select a manager from among four candidates, to describe the position of accounts supervisor.* Many assignments, though, demand additional focus to guide the project. An expanded statement of purpose considers three additional factors:

- **Scope.** What issues or elements will be investigated? To determine the scope, Diane brainstormed with Mike and others to pin down her task. She learned that Mycon currently had enough capital to consider purchasing a fleet of cars outright. Mike also told her that employee satisfaction was almost as important as cost effectiveness. Moreover, he disclosed his suspicion that employee-owned cars were costing Mycon more than leased cars. Diane had many issues to sort out in setting the boundaries of her report.
- **Significance.** Why is the topic worth investigating at this time? Some topics, after initial examination, turn out to be less important than originally thought. Others involve problems that cannot be solved, making a study useless. For Diane and Mike the problem had significance because Mycon's leasing agreement would expire shortly and decisions had to be made about a new policy for transportation of sales reps.
- **Limitations.** What conditions affect the generalizability and utility of a report's findings? In Diane's case her conclusions and recommendations might apply only to reps in her Edmonton sales district. Her findings would probably not be reliable for reps in Rimouski, Windsor, or Brandon. Another limitation for Diane is time. She must complete the report in four weeks, thus restricting the thoroughness of her research.

An expanded purpose statement considers scope, significance, and limitations.

Diane decided to expand her statement of purpose to define the scope, significance, and limitations of the report.

Expanded Statement of Purpose: The purpose of this report is to recommend a plan that provides sales reps with cars to be used in their calls. The report will compare costs for three plans: outright ownership, leasing, and compensation for employee-owned cars. It will also measure employee reaction to each plan. The report is significant because Mycon's current leasing agreement expires April 1 and an improved plan could reduce costs and paperwork. The study is limited to costs for sales reps in the Edmonton district.

After preparing a statement of purpose, Diane checked it with Mike Rivers to be sure she was on target.

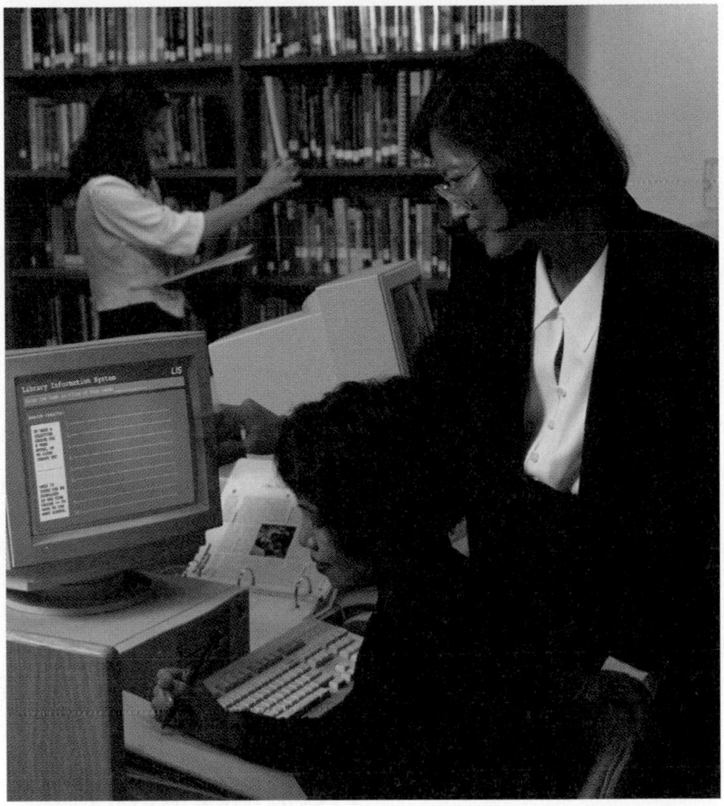

Anticipating the Audience and Issues

Once the purpose of a report is defined, a writer must think carefully about who will read the report. A major mistake is concentrating solely on a primary reader. Although one individual may have solicited the report, others within the organization may eventually read it, including upper management and people in other departments. A report to an outside client may first be read by someone who is familiar with the problem and then be distributed to others less familiar with the topic. Moreover, candid statements to one audience may be offensive to another audience. Diane could make a major blunder, for instance, if she mentioned Mike's suspicion that sales reps were padding their mileage statements. If the report were made public—as it probably would be to explain a new policy—the sales reps could feel insulted that their integrity was questioned.

Librarians use the latest cybersearch techniques to track down data. Although most librarians admit they couldn't do their job without the Internet, it is often an unpredictable tool.

As Diane considered her primary and secondary readers, she asked herself these questions:

Major report problems should be broken into subproblems—or factored—to highlight possible solutions.

- *What do my readers need to know about this topic?*
- *What do they already know?*
- *How will they react to this information?*
- *How can I make this information understandable and readable?*

Answers to these questions help writers determine how much background material to include, how much detail to add, whether to include jargon, what method of organization and presentation to follow, and what tone to use.

In the planning stages a report writer must also break the major investigative problem into subproblems. This process, sometimes called factoring, identifies issues to be investigated or possible solutions to the main problem. In this case Mycon must figure out the best way to transport sales reps. Each possible "solution" or issue that Diane considers becomes a factor or subproblem to be investigated. Diane came up with three tentative solutions to provide transportation to sales reps: (1) purchase cars outright, (2) lease cars, or (3) compensate employees for using their own cars. These three factors form the outline of Diane's study.

Diane continued to factor these main points into the following subproblems for investigation:

What plan should Mycon use to transport its sales reps?

I. Should Mycon purchase cars outright?
   A. How much capital would be required?
   B. How much would it cost to insure, operate, and maintain company-owned cars?
   C. Do employees prefer using company-owned cars?

II. Should Mycon lease cars?
   A. What is the best lease price available?
   B. How much would it cost to insure, operate, and maintain leased cars?
   C. Do employees prefer using leased cars?

III. Should Mycon compensate employees for using their own cars?
   A. How much has it cost in the past to operate employee-owned cars?
   B. How much paperwork is involved in reporting expenses?
   C. Do employees prefer being compensated for using their own cars?

Each subproblem would probably be further factored into additional subproblems. These issues may be phrased as questions, as Diane did, or as statements. In factoring a complex problem, prepare an outline showing the initial problem and its breakdown into subproblems. Make sure your divisions are consistent (don't mix issues), exclusive (don't overlap categories), and complete (don't skip significant issues). For further details on outlining, refer to the "Organizing Data" section in Chapter 5.

Preparing a Work Plan

After analyzing the problem, anticipating the audience, and factoring the problem, you're ready to prepare a work plan. Preparing a plan forces you to evaluate your resources, set priorities, outline a course of action, and establish a time schedule. Such a plan keeps you on schedule and also gives management a means of measuring your progress. A good work plan includes the following:

- Statement of the problem
- Statement of the purpose including scope, significance, and limitations
- Description of the sources and methods of collecting data
- Tentative outline
- Work schedule

A good work plan provides an overview of a project, resources, priorities, course of action, and schedule.

A work plan gives a complete picture of a project. Because the usefulness and quality of any report rest primarily on its data, you'll want to allocate plenty of time to locate sources of information. For firsthand information you might interview people, prepare a survey, or even conduct a scientific experiment. For secondary information you'll probably search printed materials such as books and magazines as well as electronic materials on the Internet and Web. Your work plan describes how you expect to generate or collect data. Since data collection is a major part of report writing, the next section of this chapter treats the topic more fully.

Figure 11.5 shows a complete work plan for a report that studies safety seals for a food company's products. This work plan is particularly useful because it outlines the issues to be investigated. Notice that considerable thought and discussion and even some preliminary research are necessary to be able to develop a useful work plan.

FIGURE 11.5 **Work Plan for a Formal Report**

Tips for Preparing a Work Plan

- Start early; allow plenty of time for brainstorming and preliminary research.
- Describe the problem motivating the report.
- Write a purpose statement that includes its scope, significance, and limitations.
- Describe data collection sources and methods.
- Divide the major problem into subproblems stated as questions to be answered.
- Develop a realistic work schedule citing dates for completion of major tasks.
- Review the work plan with whoever authorized the report.

Statement of Problem

Consumers worry that food and drug products are dangerous as a result of tampering. Our company may face loss of market share and potential liability if we don't protect our products. Many food and drug companies now offer tamper-resistant packaging, but such packaging is costly.

Statement of Purpose

The purpose of this study is to determine whether tamper-resistant packaging is necessary and/or feasible for our jams, jellies, and preserves. The study will examine published accounts of package tampering and evaluate how other companies have solved the problem. It will also measure consumers' interest in safety-seal packaging, as well as consumers' willingness to pay a slightly higher price for safety lids. We will conduct a market survey limited to a sample of 400 local consumers. Finally, the study will investigate a method for sealing our products and determine the cost for each unit we produce. This study is significant because safety seals could enhance the sales of our products and protect us from possible liability.

Defines purpose, scope, limits, and significance of report

Sources and Methods of Data Collection

Magazine and newspaper accounts of product tampering from the past 15 years will be examined. Articles describing tamper-resistant lids and other safe packaging devices for food and drug manufacturers will be studied. Moreover, our marketing staff will conduct a random telephone survey of local consumers, measuring their interest in safety seals. Finally, our production department will test various devices and determine the most cost-effective method to seal our product safely.

Describes primary and secondary data sources

Tentative Outline

I. Are consumers and producers concerned about product tampering?
   A. What incidents of tampering have been reported in the past 15 years?
   B. How did consumers react to tampering that caused harm?
   C. How did food and drug producers protect their products?
II. How do consumers react to safety seals on products today?
   A. Do consumers prefer food and drug products with safety seals?
   B. Would consumers be more likely to purchase our products if safety-sealed?
   C. Would consumers be willing to pay a few cents extra for safety seals?
III. What kind of safety seal is best for our products?
   A. What devices are other producers using—plastic "blister" packs, foil seals over bottle openings, or bands around lids?
   B. What device would work for our products?
   C. How much would each device cost per unit?
IV. Should we proceed with safety seals?

Factors problem into manageable chunks

Work Schedule

Investigate newspaper and magazine articles	Oct. 1–10
Examine safety-seal devices on the market	Oct. 8–18
Interview 400 local consumers	Oct. 8–24
Develop and test devices for our products	Oct. 15–Nov. 14
Interpret and evaluate findings	Nov. 15–17
Compose first draft of report	Nov. 18–20
Revise draft	Nov. 21–23
Submit final report	Nov. 24

Estimates time needed to complete report tasks

Although this tentative outline guides investigation, it does not determine the content or order of the final report. You may, for example, study five possible solutions to a problem. If two prove to be useless, your report may discuss only the three winners. Moreover, you will organize the report to accomplish your goal and satisfy the audience. Remember that a busy executive who is familiar with a topic may prefer to read the conclusions and recommendations before a discussion of the findings.

If the report is authorized by someone, be sure to review the work plan with that individual (your manager, client, or professor, for example) before proceeding with the project.

3

Researching Secondary Data

One of the most important steps in the process of writing a report is that of research. Because a report is only as good as its data, the remainder of this chapter describes how to find data and document it. As you analyze a report's purpose and audience, you'll assess the kinds of data needed to support your argument or explain your topic. Do you need statistics, background data, expert opinions, group opinions, or organizational data? Figure 11.6 lists five forms of data and provides questions to guide you in making your research accurate and productive.

Primary data come from firsthand experience and observation; secondary data, from reading.

Data fall into two broad categories, primary and secondary. Primary data result from firsthand experience and observation. Secondary data come from reading what others have experienced and observed. Secondary data are easier and cheaper to develop than primary data, which might involve interviewing large groups or sending out questionnaires.

We're going to discuss secondary data first because that's where nearly every research project should begin. Often, something has already been written about your topic. Reviewing secondary sources can save time and effort and prevent you from "reinventing the wheel." Most secondary material is available either in print or electronically.

Print Resources

Print sources are still the most visible part of libraries.

Although we're seeing a steady movement away from print to electronic data, print sources are still the most visible part of nearly all libraries. Much information is available only in print, and you may want to use some of the following print resources.

By the way, if you are an infrequent library user, begin your research by talking with a reference librarian about your project. These librarians won't do your research for you, but they will steer you in the right direction. And they are very accommodating. Many libraries help you understand their computer, cataloguing, and retrieval systems by providing brochures, handouts, and workshops.

Books. Although quickly outdated, books provide excellent historical, in-depth data on subjects. Books can be located through print or computer listings.

- **Card catalogue.** Some libraries still maintain card catalogues with all books indexed on 3-by-5-inch cards alphabetized by author, title, or subject.
- **Online catalogue.** Most libraries today have computerized their card catalogues. Some systems are fully automated, thus allowing users to learn not only whether a book is located in the library but also whether it is currently available.

FIGURE 11.6 **Selecting Report Data**

Form of Data	Questions to Ask
Statistical	What is the source? How were these figures derived? In what form do I need the statistics? Must they be converted? How recent are they?
Background or historical	Has this topic been explored before? What have others said about it? What sources did they use?
Expert opinion	Who are the experts? Are their opinions in print? Can they be interviewed? Do we have in-house experts?
Individual or group opinion	Do I need to interview or survey people (such as consumers, employees, or managers)? Do good questionnaires already exist? Can parts of existing test instruments be used or combined?
Organizational	What are the proper channels for obtaining in-house data? Are permissions required? How can I find data about public and private companies?

Periodicals. Magazines, pamphlets, and journals are called *periodicals* because of their recurrent or periodic publication. Journals, by the way, are compilations of scholarly articles. Articles in journals and other periodicals will be extremely useful to you because they are concise, limited in scope, current, and can supplement information in books.

- **Print indexes.** *The Readers' Guide to Periodical Literature* is a valuable index of general-interest magazine article titles. It includes such magazines as *Time, Newsweek, Maclean's,* and *The Canadian Forum.* More useful to business writers, though, will be the titles of articles appearing in business and industrial magazines (such as *Canadian Business, Canadian Banker,* and *Business Quarterly*); for an index of these publications, consult the *Business Periodicals Index.* The *Canadian Business Index* can be very useful too, listing articles from more than 200 Canadian business periodicals. Many of these indexes are also available in computerized form.
- **CD-ROM and Web-based bibliographic indexes.** Automated indexes similar to the print indexes just described are stored in CD-ROM and online databases. Many libraries now provide such bibliographic databases for computer-aided location of references and abstracts from magazines, journals, and newspapers, such as *The Globe and Mail.* When using CD-ROM and Web-based online indexes, follow the on-screen instructions or ask for assistance from a librarian. It's a good idea to begin with a subject search because it generally turns up more relevant citations

than keyword searches (especially when searching for names of people or companies). Once you locate usable references, print a copy of your findings and then check the shelf listings to see whether the publications are available.

Electronic Databases

As a writer of business reports today, you will probably begin your secondary research with electronic resources. Most writers turn to them first because they are fast, cheap, and easy to use. Some are even accessible from remote locations. This means that you can conduct detailed searches without ever leaving your office, home, or dorm room. Although some databases are still offered on CD-ROM, information is increasingly available in online databases. They have become the staple of secondary research.

Many researchers today begin by looking in electronic databases.

A database is a collection of information stored electronically so that it is accessible by computer and is digitally searchable. Databases provide both bibliographic (titles of documents and brief abstracts) and full-text documents. Most researchers today, however, prefer full-text documents. Various databases contain a rich array of magazine, newspaper, and journal articles, as well as newsletters, business reports, company profiles, government data, reviews, and directories.

Provided with this textbook is access to InfoTrac®, a Web-centred database offering nearly one million magazine and journal articles. Web-based documents are enriched with charts, graphs, bold and italic fonts, colour, and pictures. Other well-known databases are Dialog®, ABI/INFORM®, and LexisNexis.™

Although well stocked and well organized, specialized commercial databases are indeed expensive to use. Many also involve steep learning curves. While learning how to select *keywords* (or *descriptors*) and how to explore the database, you can run up quite a bill.

The Internet

The World Wide Web is a collection of hypertext pages that offer information and links.

The best-known area of the Internet is the World Wide Web. Growing at a dizzying pace, the Web includes an enormous collection of specially formatted documents called Web pages located at Web sites around the world. Web offerings include online databases, magazines, newspapers, library resources, job and résumé banks, sound and video files, and many other information resources. Creators of Web pages use a special system of codes (*HTML*, i.e., Hypertext Markup Language) to format their offerings. The crucial feature of these hypertext pages is their use of links to other Web pages. Links are identified by underlined words and phrases or, occasionally, images. When clicked, links connect you to related Web pages. These pages immediately download to your computer screen, thus creating a vast web of resources at your fingertips.

Web Opportunities and Challenges. To a business researcher, the Web offers a wide range of organizational information. You can expect to find such items as product facts, public relations material, mission statements, staff directories, press releases, current company news, government information, selected article reprints, collaborative scientific project reports, and employment information. The Web is unquestionably one of the greatest sources of information now available to anyone needing facts quickly and inexpensively. But finding that information can be frustrating and time-consuming. The constantly changing contents of the Web and its lack of organization make it more problematic for research than searching commercial databases. Moreover, Web content is uneven and often the quality is questionable. You'll learn more about evaluating Web sources shortly.

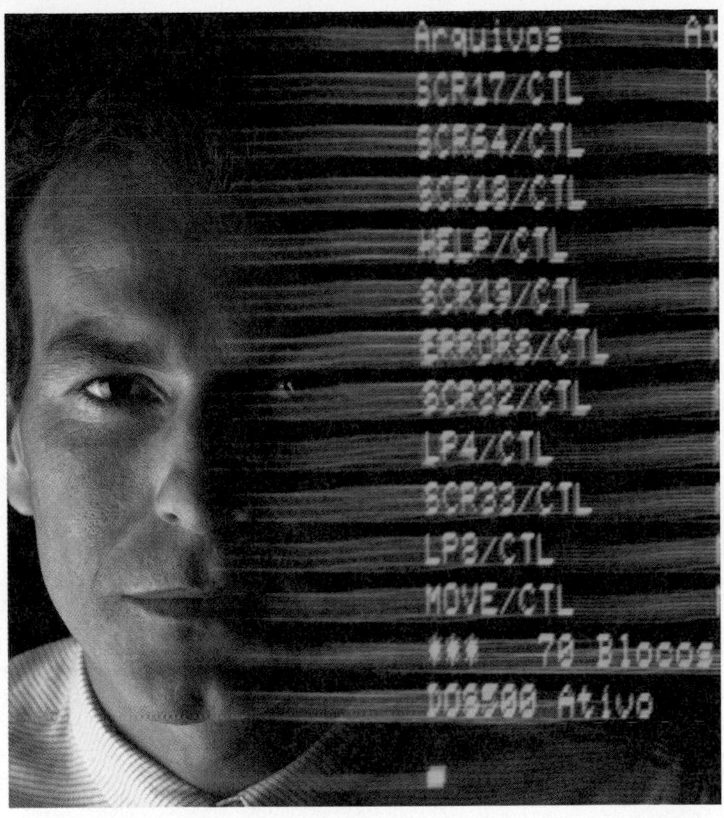

Many businesspeople recognize the value of ongoing research and reporting. It is crucial to collect data not only about the performance of your own company but also about that of the competition.

Web Browsers and URLs. Searching the Web requires a Web *browser*, such as Netscape Navigator or Microsoft Internet Explorer. Browsers are software programs that enable you to view the graphics and text, as well as access links of Web pages. To locate the Web page of a specific organization, you need its *URL (Uniform Resource Locator)*. URLs are case- and space-sensitive, so be sure to type the address exactly as it is printed. Your goal is to locate the top-level Web page of an organization's site. On this page you'll generally find an overview of the site contents or a link to a site map. If you can't guess a company's URL, you can usually find it quickly at Hoover's **<www.hoovers.com>**.

Search Tools. Finding what you are looking for on the Web is like searching for a library book without using the card catalogue. Fortunately, a number of search tools—such as Yahoo!, AltaVista, and Google—are available at specialized Web sites. These search tools can be divided into two types: search engines and directories. Search engines use automated software "spiders" that crawl through the Web to collect and index the full pages of text they find. Directories, on the other hand, rely on human editors to sift through pages, eliminating inappropriate ones and categorizing sites by subject. Hybrid search tools provide both spiders and directories. Even though search tools don't survey everything that's out there on the Web, they usually turn up more information than you want.

Like everything else about the Web, search tools are constantly evolving as developers change their features to attract more users. Figure 11.7 shows some of the best search engines and directories as ranked by *PC Magazine.*

Internet Search Tips and Techniques. Knowing how to use search engines can yield a wealth of useful information when the proper strategies are applied. Here's a summary of tips for wise Internet researchers.[1]

Web browsers are software programs that access Web pages and their links.

- **Use two or three search tools.** Different Internet search engines turn up different results. One expert wisely remarked: "Every search engine will give you good results some of the time. Every search engine will give you surprisingly bad results some of the time. No search engine will give you good results all of the time."[2]
- **Understand case sensitivity.** Generally use lowercase for your searches, unless you are searching for a term that is generally written in upper- and lowercase, such as a person's name.
- **Understand the AND/OR default and quotation marks.** When searching for a phrase, such as *cost benefit analysis*, most search tools will retrieve documents

Search tools such as Yahoo!, AltaVista, and Google help you locate specific Web sites and information.

Figure 11.7 **Search Engines and Directories: Quest for the Best**

Search Site	Features	Ease of Use	Comments
Google www.google.com	Engine/directory. Sophisticated technology returns results based on number of other sites that link to specific information at a site. Now includes Deja's Usenet discussion service with access to many browse groups.	Excellent	Returns highly relevant results; very easy to use; few advanced features, but you may not need them to find what you're looking for. Most popular search site. Clean, uncluttered home page.
AltaVista www.altavista.com	Portal. Searches news, newsgroups, audio, video, images; advanced features include Boolean queries and sorting.	Fair	Powerful engine returns high-quality results; advanced features take time to learn. Lots of clutter, but you can use its streamlined Raging.com instead.
Excite www.excite.com	Portal. Searches news, images, audio, and more; advanced features include logical queries and sorting.	Fair	Busy home page makes search engine seem like an afterthought; help section is vague; doesn't specify how many links it found.
Yahoo! www.yahoo.com	Portal. Catalogues over 500,000 sites; returns results from both directory and engine; searches audio, video, and newsgroups.	Good	Still the best portal and easier to use than most; flagship directory has fewer site descriptions than competing search tools.
Northern Light www.northernlight.com	Engine. Sorts results into folders by topic; searches fee-based databases; many advanced features, including Boolean queries.	Good	Powerful and unique, but the topic folders don't always sort results effectively; better for business searches than for fun stuff; no directory.
HotBot www.hotbot.com	Engine/directory. Advanced features include Boolean queries and much more.	Good	Good choice for serious searchers who like lots of options; basic queries may not return super-relevant results; few broken links.
LookSmart www.looksmart.com	Engine/directory. Catalogues and describes over a million sites; LookSmart Live provides advice and info from real people.	Good	Solid directory with better descriptions than Yahoo!, but it seemed slower than most in tests, with more broken links.
Lycos www.lycos.com	Portal. Searches news, audio, weather reports, and more; can restrict searches to family-friendly sites.	Fair	Lots of features, but relevance of results was erratic in tests; more broken links and duplicates than most; few advanced search options.

having all or some of the terms. This AND/OR strategy is the default of most search tools. To locate occurrences of the complete phrase, enclose it in quotation marks.

- **Prefer uncommon words.** Commonly used words make poor search keywords. For example, instead of *keeping employees*, use *employee retention*.
- **Omit articles and prepositions.** These are known as "stop words," and they do not add value to a search. Instead of *request for proposal*, use *proposal request*.
- **Use wild cards.** Most search engines support wildcards, such as asterisks. For example, the search term *cent** will retrieve cents, while *cent*** will retrieve both *centre* and *center*.

TECH TALK

UNDERSTANDING NATURAL LANGUAGE, KEYWORD, AND BOOLEAN SEARCHING

Natural language searches involve posing a search question as you would normally state it. For example, "is there a correlation between employee morale and productivity?" Using AltaVista for this search question produced nearly 5 million documents. Although the total is overwhelming, the most relevant "hits" were listed first. And the first ten items were all relevant. An increasing number of Web search engines and databases support natural language searching. It's particularly handy for vague or broad questions.

Keyword searches involve using the principal words in which you are interested. From the above question, you might choose to search on the phrase "employee morale" or "employee productivity." Omit useless words such as articles, conjunctions, and prepositions. Some search tools allow you to enclose keyword sequences (such as *employee morale*) in quotation marks to ensure that the specified words appear together and not separately.

Boolean searches involve joining keywords with "operators" (connectors) that include or exclude specific topics. For example, "employee AND morale." Using Boolean operators enables you to narrow your search and thus improve its precision. The following Boolean operators are most common:

- AND — Identifies only documents containing all of the specified words: **employee AND productivity AND morale**
- OR — Identifies documents containing at least one of the specified words: **employee OR productivity OR morale**
- NOT — Excludes documents containing the specified word: **employee productivity NOT morale**
- NEAR — Finds documents containing target words or phrases within a specified distance, for instance, within ten words: **employee NEAR productivity**

Career Application

Using a search engine that supports natural language, keyword, and Boolean searching (such as AltaVista), try an experiment. Explore the same topic using (1) a natural language question, (2) key words, and (3) Boolean operators. Which method produced the most relevant hits?

- **Know your search tool.** When connecting to a search service for the first time, always read the description of its service, including its FAQs (Frequently Asked Questions), Help, and How to Search sections.
- **Learn basic Boolean search strategies.** You can save yourself a lot of time and frustration by narrowing your search with Boolean operators, as described in the above Tech Talk box.
- **Bookmark the best.** To keep better track of your favourite Internet sites, save them on your browser as bookmarks.
- **Keep trying.** If a search produces no results, check your spelling. If you are using Boolean operators, check the syntax of your queries. Try synonyms and variations on words. Try to be less specific in your search term. If your search produces too many hits, try to be more specific. Think of words that uniquely identify what you're looking for. And use as many relevant keywords as possible.
- **Repeat your search a week later.** For the best results, return to your search a couple of days or a week later. The same keywords will probably produce additional results. That's because hundreds of thousands of new pages are being added to the Web every day.

Remember, you guide the search tools. Only through clever cybersearching can you uncover the jewels hidden on the Internet.

Evaluate the currency, authority, content, and accuracy of Web sites carefully.

Evaluating Web Sources. We have a tendency to assume that any information turned up via a search engine has somehow been evaluated as part of a valid selection process.[3] Wrong! The truth is that the Internet is rampant with unreliable sites that reside side by side with reputable sites. Anyone with a computer and an Internet connection can publish anything on the Web. Unlike library-based research, information at many sites has not undergone the editing or scrutiny of scholarly publication procedures. The information we read in journals and most reputable magazines is reviewed, authenticated, and evaluated. That's why we have learned to trust these sources as valid and authoritative. But information on the Web is much less reliable. Some sites exist to distribute propaganda; others want to sell you something. To use the Web meaningfully, you must scrutinize what you find. For comprehensive, updated information and links to guide you in evaluating Web sources, check the Guffey Web site **<buscomm.nelson.com>**. Here are specific questions to ask as you examine a site.

- **Currency.** What is the date of the Web page? When was it last updated? Is some of the information obviously out of date? If the information is time sensitive and the site has not been updated recently, the site is probably not reliable.
- **Authority.** Who publishes or sponsors this Web page? What makes the presenter an authority? Is a contact address available for the presenter? Learn to be skeptical about data and assertions from individuals whose credentials are not verifiable.
- **Content.** Is the purpose of the page to entertain, inform, convince, or sell? Who is the intended audience, based on content, tone, and style? Can you judge the overall value of the content compared with the other resources on this topic? Web presenters with a slanted point of view cannot be counted on for objective data.
- **Accuracy.** Do the facts that are presented seem reliable to you? Do you find errors in spelling, grammar, or usage? Do you see any evidence of bias? Are footnotes provided? If you find numerous errors and if facts are not referenced, you should be alert that the data may be questionable.

Generating Primary Data

4

Although you'll begin a business report by probing for secondary data, you'll probably need primary data to give a complete picture. Business reports that solve specific current problems typically rely on primary, firsthand data. Providing answers to business problems often means generating primary data through surveys, interviews, observation, or experimentation.

Primary data comes from firsthand experience.

Surveys. Surveys collect data from groups of people. When companies develop new products, for example, they often survey consumers to learn their needs. The advantages of surveys are that they gather data economically and efficiently. Mailed surveys reach big groups nearby or at great distances. Moreover, people responding to mailed surveys have time to consider their answers, thus improving the accuracy of the data.

Although mailed surveys may suffer low response rates, they are still useful in generating primary data.

Mailed questionnaires, of course, have disadvantages. Most of us rank them with junk mail, so response rates may be no higher than 10 percent. Furthermore, those who do respond may not represent an accurate sample of the overall population, thus invalidating generalizations from the group. Another problem with surveys has to do with truthfulness. Some respondents exaggerate their incomes or distort other facts, thus causing the results to be unreliable. Nevertheless, surveys may be the best way to generate data for business and student reports. Some companies are even using the Internet for gathering survey data. In preparing print or electronic surveys, consider these pointers:

- **Explain why the survey is necessary.** In a cover letter or an opening paragraph, describe the need for the survey. Suggest how someone or something other than you will benefit. If appropriate, offer to send recipients a copy of the findings.
- **Consider incentives.** If the survey is long, persuasive techniques may be necessary. Response rates can be increased by offering money, coupons, gift certificates, free books, or other gifts.
- **Limit the number of questions.** Resist the temptation to ask for too much. Request only information you will use. Don't, for example, include demographic questions (income, gender, age, and so forth) unless the information is necessary to evaluate responses.
- **Use questions that produce quantifiable answers.** Check-off, multiple-choice, yes-no, and scale (or rank-order) questions (illustrated in Figure 11.8) provide quantifiable data that are easily tabulated. Responses to open-ended questions (*What should the bookstore do about plastic bags?*) reveal interesting, but difficult-to-quantify, perceptions.[4] To obtain workable data, give interviewees a list of possible responses (as shown in items 5–8 of Figure 11.8). For scale and multiple-choice questions, try to present all the possible answer choices. To be safe, add an "Other" or "Don't know" category in case the choices seem insufficient to the respondent. Many surveys use scale questions because they capture degrees of feelings. Typical scale headings are "agree strongly," "agree somewhat," "neutral," "disagree somewhat," and "disagree strongly."

Effective surveys target appropriate samples and ask a limited number of specific questions with quantifiable answers.

- **Avoid leading or ambiguous questions.** The wording of a question can dramatically affect responses to it. Because words have different meanings for different people, you must strive to use objective language and pilot test your questions with typical respondents. Stay away from questions that suggest an answer (*Don't you agree that the salaries of CEOs are obscenely high?*). Instead, ask neutral questions (*Do CEOs earn too much, too little, or about the right amount?*). Also avoid queries that really ask two or more things (*Should the salaries of CEOs be reduced or regulated by government legislation?*). Instead, break them into separate questions (*Should the salaries of CEOs be regulated by government legislation? Should the salaries of CEOs be reduced by government legislation?*).

The way a question is stated influences its response.

- **Select the survey population carefully.** Many surveys question a small group of people (a sample) and project the findings to a larger population. To be able to generalize from a survey, you need to make the sample as large as possible. In addition, you need to determine whether the sample is like the larger population. For important surveys you will want to consult books on or experts in sampling techniques.

The larger the sample, the more accurate the resulting data is likely to be.

- **Conduct a pilot study.** Try the questionnaire with a small group so that you can remedy any problems. For example, in the survey shown in Figure 11.8, a pilot study revealed that female students generally favoured cloth book bags and were willing to pay for them. Male students opposed purchasing cloth bags. By adding a gender category, researchers could verify this finding. The pilot study also revealed the need to ensure an appropriate representation of male and female students in the survey.

Interviews. Some of the best report information, particularly on topics about which little has been written, comes from individuals. These individuals are usually

FIGURE 11.8 **Preparing a Survey**

1 PREWRITING

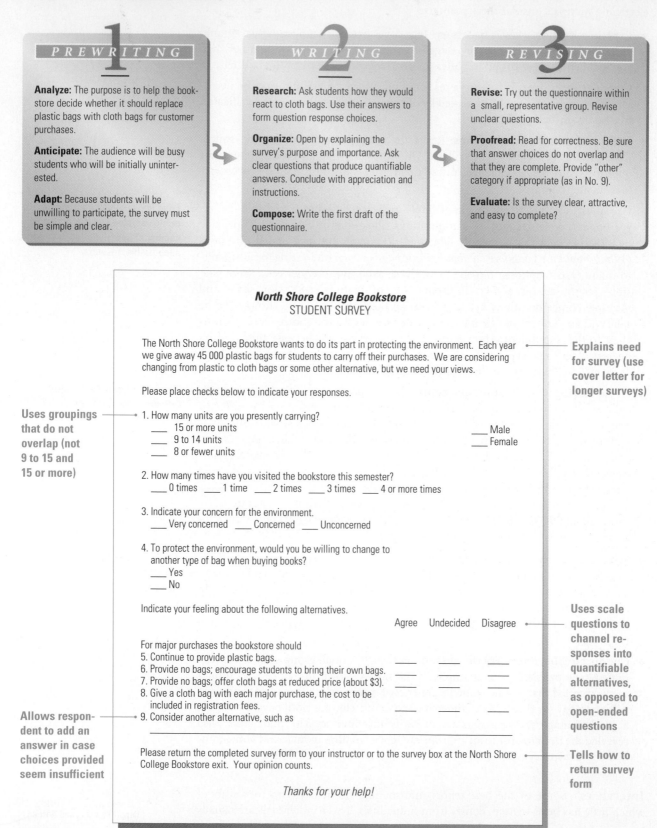

Analyze: The purpose is to help the bookstore decide whether it should replace plastic bags with cloth bags for customer purchases.

Anticipate: The audience will be busy students who will be initially uninterested.

Adapt: Because students will be unwilling to participate, the survey must be simple and clear.

2 WRITING

Research: Ask students how they would react to cloth bags. Use their answers to form question response choices.

Organize: Open by explaining the survey's purpose and importance. Ask clear questions that produce quantifiable answers. Conclude with appreciation and instructions.

Compose: Write the first draft of the questionnaire.

3 REVISING

Revise: Try out the questionnaire within a small, representative group. Revise unclear questions.

Proofread: Read for correctness. Be sure that answer choices do not overlap and that they are complete. Provide "other" category if appropriate (as in No. 9).

Evaluate: Is the survey clear, attractive, and easy to complete?

North Shore College Bookstore
STUDENT SURVEY

The North Shore College Bookstore wants to do its part in protecting the environment. Each year we give away 45 000 plastic bags for students to carry off their purchases. We are considering changing from plastic to cloth bags or some other alternative, but we need your views.

Explains need for survey (use cover letter for longer surveys)

Please place checks below to indicate your responses.

Uses groupings that do not overlap (not 9 to 15 and 15 or more)

1. How many units are you presently carrying?
   ___ 15 or more units
   ___ 9 to 14 units
   ___ 8 or fewer units

   ___ Male
   ___ Female

2. How many times have you visited the bookstore this semester?
   ___ 0 times ___ 1 time ___ 2 times ___ 3 times ___ 4 or more times

3. Indicate your concern for the environment.
   ___ Very concerned ___ Concerned ___ Unconcerned

4. To protect the environment, would you be willing to change to another type of bag when buying books?
   ___ Yes
   ___ No

Indicate your feeling about the following alternatives.

Uses scale questions to channel responses into quantifiable alternatives, as opposed to open-ended questions

For major purchases the bookstore should	Agree	Undecided	Disagree
5. Continue to provide plastic bags.	___	___	___
6. Provide no bags; encourage students to bring their own bags.	___	___	___
7. Provide no bags; offer cloth bags at reduced price (about $3).	___	___	___
8. Give a cloth bag with each major purchase, the cost to be included in registration fees.	___	___	___
9. Consider another alternative, such as			

____

Allows respondent to add an answer in case choices provided seem insufficient

Please return the completed survey form to your instructor or to the survey box at the North Shore College Bookstore exit. Your opinion counts.

Tells how to return survey form

Thanks for your help!

experts or veterans in their fields. Consider both in-house and outside experts for business reports. Tapping these sources will call for in-person or telephone interviews. To elicit the most useful data, try these techniques:

Interviews with experts yield useful report data, especially when little has been written about a topic.

- **Locate an expert.** Ask managers and individuals working in an area whom they consider to be most knowledgeable. Check membership lists of professional organizations, and consult articles about the topic or related topics. Most people enjoy being experts or at least recommending them. You could also post an inquiry to an Internet *newsgroup.*
- **Prepare for the interview.** Learn about the individual you're interviewing as well as the background and terminology of the topic. Let's say you're interviewing a corporate communication expert about producing an in-house newsletter. You ought to be familiar with terms such as *font* and software such as QuarkXpress, Adobe Pagemaker, and Ventura Publisher. In addition, be prepared by making a list of questions that pinpoint your focus on the topic. Ask the interviewee if you may record the interview.
- **Make your questions objective and friendly.** Don't get into a debating match with the interviewee. And remember that you're there to listen, not to talk! Use open-ended, rather than yes-or-no, questions to draw experts out.
- **Watch the time.** Tell interviewees in advance how much time you expect to need for the interview. Don't overstay your appointment.
- **End graciously.** Conclude the interview with a general question, such as "Is there anything you'd like to add?" Express your appreciation, and ask permission to telephone later if you need to verify points.

Some of the best report data come from firsthand observation and investigation.

Observation and Experimentation. Some kinds of primary data can be obtained only through firsthand observation and investigation. How long does a typical caller wait before a customer service rep answers the call? How is a new piece of equipment operated? Are complaints of sexual harassment being taken seriously? Observation produces rich data, but that information is especially prone to charges of subjectivity. One can interpret an observation in many ways. Thus, to make observations more objective, try to quantify them. For example, record customer telephone wait-time for 60-minute periods at different times throughout a week. Or compare the number of sexual harassment complaints made with the number of investigations undertaken and the resulting action.

Experimentation produces data suggesting causes and effects. Informal experimentation might be as simple as a pretest and post-test in a college course. Did students expand their knowledge as a result of the course? More formal experimentation is undertaken by scientists and professional researchers who control variables to test their effects. Assume, for example, that Cadbury Chocolate Canada Inc. wants to test the hypothesis (which is a tentative assumption) that chocolate lifts people out of the doldrums. An experiment testing the hypothesis would separate depressed individuals into two groups: those who ate chocolate (the experimental group) and those who did not (the control group). What effect did chocolate have? Such experiments are not done haphazardly, however. Valid experiments require sophisticated research designs and careful attention to matching the experimental and control groups.

Documenting Data

In writing business and other reports, you will often build on the ideas and words of others. In Western culture whenever you "borrow" the ideas of others, you must give credit to your information sources. This is called *documentation.*

Purposes of Documentation

Documenting data lends credibility, protects the writer from plagiarism, and aids the reader.

As a careful writer, you should take pains to properly document report data for the following reasons:

- **To strengthen your argument.** Including good data from reputable sources will convince readers of your credibility and the logic of your reasoning.
- **To protect you from charges of plagiarism.** Acknowledging your sources keeps you honest. Plagiarism, which is illegal and unethical, is the act of using others' ideas without proper documentation.
- **To instruct the reader.** Citing references enables readers to pursue a topic further and make use of the information themselves.

Academic Documentation vs. Business Documentation

In the academic world, documentation is critical. Especially in the humanities and sciences, students are taught to cite sources by using quotation marks, parenthetical citations, footnotes, and bibliographies. College term papers require full documentation to demonstrate that a student has become familiar with respected sources and can cite them properly in developing an argument. Giving credit to the author is extremely important. Students who plagiarize risk a failing grade in a class and even expulsion from school.

Business writers may not follow the same strict documentation standards as academic writers.

In the business world, however, documentation is often viewed differently. Business communicators on the job may find that much of what is written does not follow the standards they learned in school.[5] In many instances, individual authorship is unimportant. For example, employees may write for the signature of their bosses. The writer receives no credit. Similarly, team projects turn out documents written by many people, none of whom receives individual credit. Internal business reports, which often include chunks of information from previous reports, also fail to acknowledge sources or give credit. Even information from outside sources may lack proper documentation. Yet, if facts are questioned, business writers must be able to produce their source materials.

Although both internal and external business reports are not as heavily documented as school assignments or term papers, business communication students are well-advised to learn proper documentation methods. Being accused of plagiarism is a serious charge and can lead to loss of a job if ideas or words are used without giving credit. You can avoid charges of plagiarism as well as add clarity to your work by knowing what to document and developing good research habits.

Learning What to Document

When you write reports, especially in college, you are continually dealing with other people's ideas. You are expected to conduct research, synthesize ideas, and build on the work of others. But you are also expected to give proper credit for borrowed material. To avoid plagiarism, you must give credit whenever you use the following[6]:

- Another person's ideas, opinions, examples, or theory
- Any facts, statistics, graphs, and drawings that are not common knowledge
- Quotations of another person's actual spoken or written words
- Paraphrases of another person's spoken or written words

Give credit when you use another's ideas, when you borrow facts that are not common knowledge, and when you quote or paraphrase another's words.

Information that is common knowledge requires no documentation. For example, the statement *The Globe and Mail is a popular business newspaper* would require no citation. Statements that are not common knowledge, however, must be documented. For example, *The Globe and Mail is the largest daily newspaper in Canada* would require a citation because most people do not know this fact. Cite sources for proprietary information such as statistics organized and reported by a newspaper or magazine. Also use citations to document direct quotations and ideas that you summarize in your own words.

Developing Good Manual and Electronic Research Habits

Report writers who are gathering information have two methods available for recording the information they find. The time-honoured manual method of notetaking works well because information is recorded on separate cards, which can then be arranged in the order needed to develop a thesis or argument. Today, though, writers rely heavily on electronic researching. Traditional notetaking methods may seem antiquated and laborious in comparison. Let's explore both methods.

Handwritten note cards help writers identify sources and organize ideas.

Manual Notetaking. To make sure you know whose ideas you are using, train yourself to take excellent notes. If possible, know what you intend to find before you begin your research so that you won't waste time on unnecessary notes. Here are some pointers on taking good notes.

- Record all major ideas from various sources on separate note cards.
- Include all publication data along with precise quotations.
- Consider using one card colour for direct quotes and a different colour for your paraphrases and summaries.
- Put the original source material aside when you are summarizing or paraphrasing.

Set up a folder for electronic notes, but be careful not to cut-and-paste excessively in writing reports.

Electronic Notetaking. Instead of recording facts on note cards, smart researchers today take advantage of electronic tools. Beware, though, not to cut-and-paste your way into plagiarism.

- Begin your research by setting up a folder on your hard drive or on a floppy. Create subfolders for major topics, such as introduction, body, and closing.
- When you find facts on the Web or in electronic databases, highlight the material you want to record, copy it, and paste it into a document in an appropriate folder.
- Be sure to include all publication data.
- Consider archiving on a zip disk those Web pages or articles used in your research in case the data must be verified.

Paraphrasing involves putting an original passage into your own words.

Developing the Fine Art of Paraphrasing

In writing reports and using the ideas of others, you will probably rely heavily on *paraphrasing*, which means restating an original passage in your own words and in your own style. To do a good job of paraphrasing, follow these steps:

- Read the original material intently to comprehend its full meaning.
- Write your own version without looking at the original.
- Do not repeat the grammatical structure of the original, and do not merely replace words with synonyms.
- Reread the original to be sure you covered the main points but did not borrow specific language.

To better understand the difference between plagiarizing and paraphrasing, study the following passages. Notice that the writer of the plagiarized version uses the same grammatical construction as the source and often merely replaces words with synonyms. Even the acceptable version, however, requires a reference to the source author.

Source
The collapse in the cost of computing has made cellular communication economically viable. Worldwide, one in two new phone subscriptions is cellular. The digital revolution in telephony is most advanced in poorer countries because they have been able to skip an outdated technological step relying on land lines.

The plagiarized version uses the same sentence structure as the original and makes few changes other than replacing some words.

Plagiarized version
The drop in computing costs now makes cellular communication affordable around the world. In fact, one out of every two new phones is cellular. The digital revolution in cellular telephones is developing faster in poorer countries because they could skip an outdated technological process using land lines.

The acceptable paraphrase presents ideas from a different perspective and uses a different sentence structure than the original.

Acceptable paraphrase
Cellular phone use around the world is increasing rapidly as a result of decreasing computing costs. Half of all new phones are now wireless. Poorer countries are experiencing the most rapid development because they can move straight to cellular without focusing on outdated technology using land lines (Henderson 44).

Knowing When and How to Quote

On occasion you will want to use the exact words of a source. But beware of overusing quotations. Documents that contain pages of spliced-together quotations suggest that writers have few ideas of their own. Wise writers and speakers use direct quotations for three purposes only:

Use quotations only to provide background data, to cite experts, to repeat precise phrasing, or to duplicate exact wording before criticizing.

- To provide objective background data and establish the severity of a problem as seen by experts
- To repeat identical phrasing because of its precision, clarity, or aptness
- To duplicate exact wording before criticizing

When you must use a long quotation, try to summarize and introduce it in your own words. Readers want to know the gist of a quotation before they tackle it. For example, to introduce a quotation discussing the shrinking staffs of large companies, you could precede it with your words: *In predicting employment trends, Charles Waller believes the corporation of the future will depend on a small core of full-time employees.* To introduce quotations or paraphrases, use wording such as the following:

- According to Waller, ...
- Waller argues that . . . .
- In his recent study, Waller reported . . . .

Use quotation marks to enclose exact quotations, as shown in the following: "*The current image,*" says Charles Waller, "*of a big glass-and-steel corporate headquarters on landscaped grounds directing a worldwide army of tens of thousands of employees may soon be a thing of the past.*"

Using Citation Formats

You can direct readers to your sources with parenthetical notes inserted into the text and with bibliographies. The most common citation formats are those presented by the Modern Language Association (MLA) and the American Psychological Association (APA). Learn more about how to use these formats in Appendix B. For the most up-do-date citation formats for electronic references, check the Guffey Web site at <**buscomm.nelson.com**>. You will find model citation formats for online magazine, newspaper, and journal articles, as well as for Web references.

Guidelines for MLA and APA citation formats may be found in Appendix B; guidelines for electronic citations are at <buscomm.nelson.com>

Summary of Learning Objectives

1 **Describe business report basics, including functions, patterns, formats, and writing styles.** Business reports generally function either as informational reports (without analysis or recommendations) or as analytical reports (with analysis, conclusions, and possibly recommendations). Reports organized directly present the purpose immediately. This pattern is appropriate when receivers are supportive and are familiar with the topic. Reports organized indirectly provide the conclusions and recommendations last. This pattern is helpful when receivers are unfamiliar with the problem or when they may be disappointed or hostile. Reports may be formatted as letters, memos, manuscripts, or prepared forms. Reports written in a formal style use third-person constructions, avoid contractions, and include many passive-voice verbs, complex sentences, and long words. Reports written informally use first-person constructions, contractions, shorter sentences, familiar words, and active-voice verbs.

2 **Apply the 3-×-3 writing process to reports.** Report writers begin by analyzing a problem and writing a problem statement, which may include the scope, significance, and limitations of the project. Writers then analyze the audience and define major issues. They prepare a work plan, including a tentative outline and work schedule. They collect, organize, interpret, and illustrate their data. Then they compose the first draft. Finally, they revise (perhaps many times), proofread, and evaluate.

3 **Conduct research by locating secondary data.** Secondary data may be located by searching for books, periodicals, and newspapers through print or electronic indexes. Much report information today is located in electronic databases. Much information is also available on the Internet, but searching for it requires knowledge of search tools and techniques. Three popular search tools are Yahoo!, AltaVista, and Google. Information obtained on the Internet should be scrutinized for currency, authority, content, and accuracy.

4 **Generate primary data for research projects.** Researchers generate first-hand, primary data through surveys (in-person, print, and online), interviews, observation, and experimentation. Surveys are most economical and efficient for gathering information from large groups of people. Interviews are useful when working with experts in a field.

5 **Describe the purposes and techniques of documentation in business reports.** Documentation means giving credit to information sources. Careful writers document data to strengthen an argument, protect against charges of plagiarism, and instruct readers. Although documentation in business reports is less stringent than in academic reports, business writers should learn proper techniques to be able to verify their sources and to avoid charges of plagiarism. Report writers should document others' ideas, facts that are not common knowledge, quotations, and paraphrases. Good notetaking, either manual or electronic, enables writers to give accurate credit to sources. Paraphrasing involves putting another's ideas into your own words. Quotations may be used to provide objective background data, to repeat identical phrasing, and to duplicate exact wording before criticizing.

CHAPTER REVIEW

1. What purpose do most reports serve? (Obj. 1)
2. How do informational and analytical reports differ? (Obj. 1)
3. How do the direct and indirect patterns of development differ? (Obj. 1)
4. Under what circumstances would an analytical report be organized directly? Indirectly? (Obj. 1)
5. Identify four common report formats. (Obj. 1)
6. List the seven steps in the report-writing process. (Obj. 1)
7. What is factoring? (Obj. 1)
8. How do primary data differ from secondary data? Give an original example of each. (Objs. 3 and 4)
9. Should data collection for most business reports begin with primary or secondary research? Why? (Objs. 3 and 4)
10. Compare three search tools for the Web. (Objs. 3 and 4)
11. Discuss five techniques that you think are most useful in enhancing a Web search. (Obj. 3)
12. In questionnaires what kind of questions produce quantifiable answers? (Obj. 4)
13. What is documentation, and why is it necessary in reports? (Obj. 5)
14. What kind of data require no documentation? (Obj. 5)

CRITICAL THINKING

1. What kinds of reports typically flow upward in an organization? What kinds flow downward? Why? (Obj. 1)
2. Discuss this statement, made by three well-known professional business writers: "Nothing you write will be completely new."[7] (Objs. 3 and 4)
3. For long reports, why is a written work plan a wise idea? (Obj. 2)
4. Is information obtained on the Web as reliable as information obtained from journals, newspapers, and magazines? Explain your answer. (Obj. 3)

ACTIVITIES

11.1 Report Functions, Writing Styles, and Formats (Obj. 1)

For the following reports, (1) name the report's primary function (informational or analytical), (2) recommend a direct or indirect pattern of development, and (3) select a report format (memo, letter, or manuscript).

a. A persuasive proposal from a construction firm to the Ontario College of Art describing the contractor's bid to renovate and convert the school's newly purchased 1930s art deco office building into offices, studios, and classrooms.

b. A situational report submitted by a sales rep to her manager describing her attendance at a sports products trade show, including the reactions of visitors to a new noncarbonated sports drink.

c. A recommendation report from a technical specialist to the vice president, Product Development, analyzing ways to prevent piracy of the software company's latest game program. The vice president values straight talk and is familiar with the project.

d. A progress report from a location manager to a Hollywood production company describing safety, fire, and environmental precautions taken for the shooting of a stunt involving blowing up a boat off the Toronto Islands.

e. A feasibility report prepared by an outside consultant examining whether a company should invest in a health and fitness centre for its employees.

11.2 Collaborative Project: Report Portfolio (Obj. 1)

Team

In teams of four or five, collect four or more sample business reports. (Don't forget corporate annual reports.) For each report identify and discuss the following characteristics:

a. Function (informational or analytical)

b. Pattern (primarily direct or indirect)

c. Writing style (formal or informal)

d. Format (memo, letter, manuscript, preprinted form)

e. Effectiveness (clarity, accuracy, expression)

In an informational memo report to your instructor, describe your findings.

11.3 Data Forms and Questions (Obj.4)

In conducting research for the following reports, name at least one form of data you will need and the questions you should ask to determine whether that set of data is appropriate (see Figure 11.6).

a. A report evaluating the relocation of a Montreal company to Toronto. You find figures in a *Toronto Life* article showing the average cost of housing for 60 cities, including Toronto and Montreal.

b. A market research report to assess fan support for a name ("Raptors") and logo (a dinosaur holding a basketball) selected for a professional basketball team in Toronto.

c. A report examining the effectiveness of ethics codes in Canadian businesses.

11.4 Problem and Purpose Statements (Obj. 2)

The following situations require reports. For each situation write (a) a concise problem question and (b) a simple statement of purpose.

a. The Confederation Bank is losing money on its Webster branch. A number of branches are being targeted for closure. Management authorizes a report that must recommend a course of action for the Webster branch.

b. New federal regulations have changed the definitions of common terms such as *fresh, fat free, low in cholesterol,* and *light.* The Big Deal Bakery worries that it must rewrite all its package labels. Big Deal doesn't know whether to hire a laboratory or a consultant for this project.

c. Customers placing telephone orders for clothing with James River Enterprises typically order only one or two items. JRE wonders whether it can train telephone service reps to motivate customers to increase the number of items ordered per call.

11.5 Problem and Purpose Statements (Obj. 2)

Identify a problem in your current job or a previous job (such as inadequate equipment, inefficient procedures, poor customer service, poor product quality, or personnel problems). Assume your boss agrees with your criticism and asks you to prepare a report. Write (a) a two- or three-sentence statement describing the problem, (b) a problem question, and (c) a simple statement of purpose for your report.

11.6 Factoring and Outlining a Problem (Obj. 2)

Critical Thinking

Japan Airlines has asked your company, Connections International, to prepare a proposal for a training school for tour operators. JAL wants to know whether Victoria would be a good spot for its school. Victoria interests JAL but only if nearby entertainment facilities can be used for tour training. JAL also needs an advisory committee consisting, if possible, of representatives of the travel community and perhaps executives of other major airlines. The real problem is how to motivate these people to cooperate with JAL.

You've heard that CBC Studios in Victoria offers training seminars, guest speakers, and other resources for tour operators. You wonder whether Magic Mountain in Vancouver would also be willing to cooperate with the proposed school. And you remember that Griffith Park is nearby and might make a good tour training spot. Before JAL will settle on Victoria as its choice, it wants to know whether access to air travel is adequate. It's also concerned about available school building space. Moreover, JAL wants to know whether city officials in Victoria would be receptive to this tour training school proposal.

To guide your thinking and research, factor this problem into an outline with several areas to investigate. Further divide the problem into subproblems, phrasing each entry as a question. (See the tentative outline in Figure 11.5.)

11.7 Developing a Work Plan (Obj. 2)

Select a report topic from Activities 13.5–13.15, or 14.1–14.8. For that report prepare a work plan that includes the following:

- **a.** A statement of the problem
- **b.** An expanded statement of purpose (including scope, limitations, and significance)
- **c.** Sources and methods
- **d.** A tentative outline
- **e.** A work schedule (with projected completion dates)

11.8 Using Secondary Sources (Obj. 4)

Conduct research in a library. Prepare a bibliography of the most important magazines and professional journals in your major field of study. Your instructor may ask you to list the periodicals and briefly describe their content, purpose, and audience. In a cover memo to your instructor, describe your bibliography and your research sources (manual or computerized indexes, databases, CD-ROM, and so on).

11.9 Developing Primary Data: Collaborative Survey (Obj. 3)

Team

In teams of three to five, design a survey for your associated student body council. The survey seeks student feedback in addressing the parking problem on campus. Students complain bitterly about lack of parking spaces for them, distance of parking lots from classrooms, and poor condition of the lots. Some solutions have been proposed: limiting parking to full-time students, using auxiliary parking lots farther away with a shuttle bus to campus, encouraging bicycle and moped use, and reducing the number of spaces for visitors. Discuss these solutions and add at least three other possibilities. Then prepare a questionnaire to be distributed on campus. If possible, pilot test the questionnaire before submitting it to your instructor. Be sure to consider how the results will be tabulated and interpreted.

11.10 Surfing the Web for Payroll Data (Obj. 5)

Web

Alisa Robertson, compensation and payroll manager for Gulf States Paper Corporation, has been complaining for some time about its complex and outdated payroll processes. "We have over 2000 employees in nine different locations, and no set deadline for payroll submissions," she says. As a result of her urging, she has been named project manager for the company's "Human Resources/Payroll Business Information Systems Project." Her task is to learn more about payroll software programs that centralize processes, improve security, and reduce human error. As her assistant, you are to begin the research process by using the Web to see what you can turn up. Employ two or more search engines, choose keywords, and search for appropriate sites. Be sure to evaluate each site for currency, authority, content, and accuracy. Select five relevant sites and print a couple of pages of information from each site. Prepare a short memo report to Robertson naming the sites and giving her a brief summary of each.[8]

C H A P T E R • 1 2 •

REPORT ORGANIZATION AND PRESENTATION

LEARNING OBJECTIVES

1. Use tabulating and statistical techniques to sort and interpret report data.
2. Draw meaningful conclusions from report data.
3. Prepare practical report recommendations.
4. Organize report data logically.
5. Provide cues to aid report comprehension.
6. Develop graphics that create meaning and interest.
7. Incorporate graphics into reports effectively.

Interpreting Data

After collecting data for a report, you must sort it and make sense out of it. For informational reports you may organize the facts into a logical sequence, illustrate them, and present a final report. For analytical reports, though, the process is more complex. You'll also interpret the data, draw conclusions, and, if asked, make recommendations.

The data you've collected probably face you in a jumble of printouts, note cards, copies of articles, interview notes, questionnaire results, and statistics. You must sort a jumble of raw material into meaningful, usable groups. Unprocessed data become meaningful information through sorting, analysis, combination, and recombination. You'll be examining each item to see what it means by itself and what it means when connected with other data. You're looking for meanings, relationships, and answers to the research questions posed in your work plan.

Interpreting data means sorting, analyzing, combining, and recombining, to yield meaningful information.

Tabulating and Analyzing Responses 1

If you've collected considerable numerical and other information, you must tabulate and analyze it. Fortunately, several tabulating and statistical techniques can help you create order from the chaos. These techniques simplify, summarize, and classify large amounts of data into meaningful terms. From the condensed data you're more likely to be able to draw valid conclusions and make reasoned recommendations.

Tables. Numerical data from questionnaires or interviews are usually summarized and simplified in tables. Using systematic columns and rows, tables make quantitative information easier to comprehend. After assembling your data, you'll want to prepare preliminary tables to enable you to see what the information means. Sometimes data become more meaningful when cross-tabulated. This process allows analysis of two or more variables together.

Numerical data must be tabulated and analyzed statistically to bring order out of chaos.

Tables also help you compare multiple data collected from questionnaires and surveys. Figure 12.1 shows, in raw form, responses to several survey items. To convert these data into a more usable form, you need to calculate percentages for each item. Then you can arrange the responses in some rational sequence, such as largest percentage to smallest.

Once the data are displayed in a table, you can more easily draw conclusions. As Figure 12.1 shows, Midland College students apparently are not interested in public transportation or shuttle buses from satellite lots. They want to park on campus, with restricted visitor parking; and only half are willing to pay for new parking lots.

The Three Ms: Mean, Median, Mode. Tables help you organize data, and the three Ms help you describe it. These statistical terms—mean, median, and mode—are all occasionally used loosely to mean "average." To be safe, though, you should learn to apply these statistical terms precisely.

Three statistical concepts—mean, median, and mode—help you describe data.

When people say *average*, they usually intend to indicate the *mean*, or arithmetic average. The *median* represents the midpoint in a group of figures arranged from lowest to highest (or vice versa). The *mode* is simply the value that occurs most frequently. Although mode is infrequently used by researchers, knowing the mode is useful in some situations. (To remember the meaning of *mode*, think about fashion; the most frequent response, the mode, is the most fashionable.)

FIGURE 12.1 **Converting Survey Data Into Finished Tables**

Tips for Converting Raw Data

- Tabulate the responses on a copy of the survey form.
- Calculate percentages (divide the score for an item by the total for all responses to that item; for example, for item 1, divide 331 by 663).
- Round off figures to one decimal point or to whole numbers.
- Arrange items in a logical order, such as largest to smallest percentage.
- Prepare a table with a title that tells such things as who, what, when, where, and why.
- Include the total number of respondents.

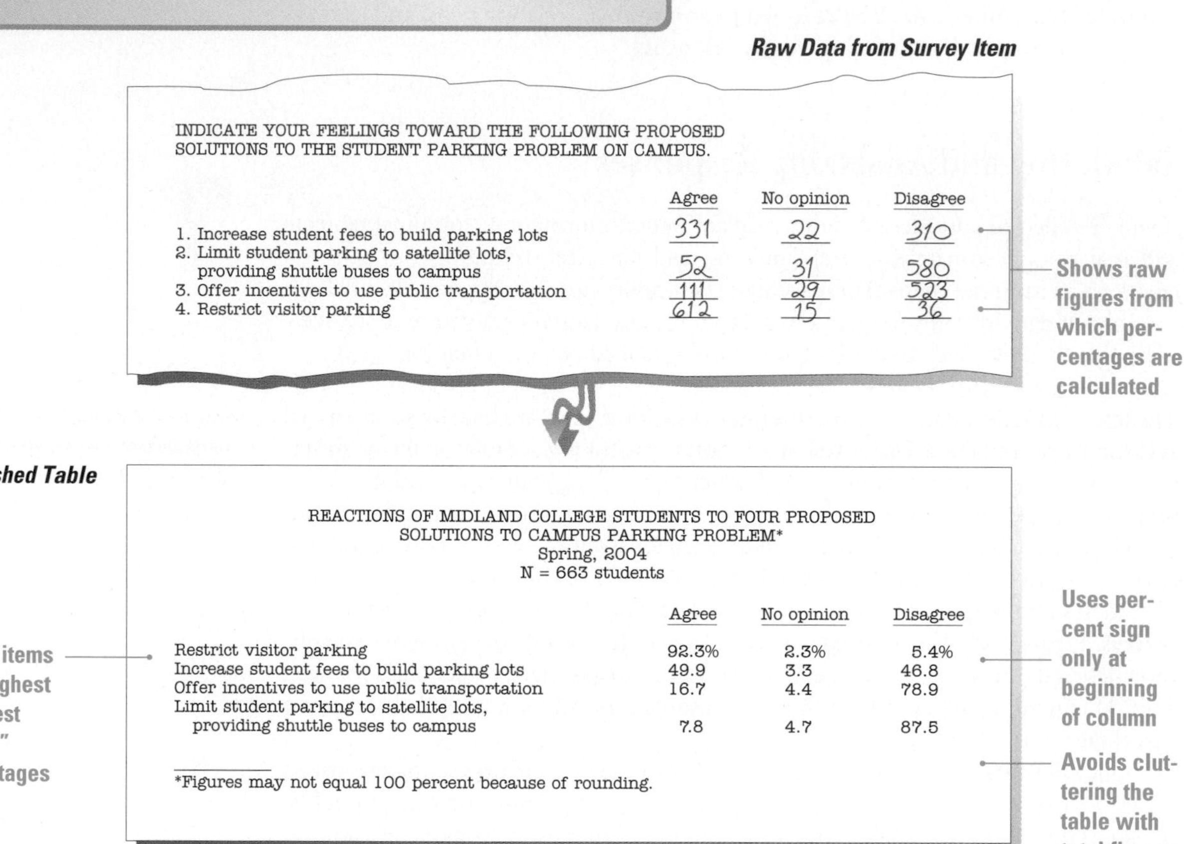

Raw Data from Survey Item

INDICATE YOUR FEELINGS TOWARD THE FOLLOWING PROPOSED SOLUTIONS TO THE STUDENT PARKING PROBLEM ON CAMPUS.

	Agree	No opinion	Disagree
1. Increase student fees to build parking lots	331	22	310
2. Limit student parking to satellite lots, providing shuttle buses to campus	52	31	580
3. Offer incentives to use public transportation	111	29	523
4. Restrict visitor parking	612	15	36

Shows raw figures from which percentages are calculated

Finished Table

REACTIONS OF MIDLAND COLLEGE STUDENTS TO FOUR PROPOSED SOLUTIONS TO CAMPUS PARKING PROBLEM*
Spring, 2004
N = 663 students

	Agree	No opinion	Disagree
Restrict visitor parking	92.3%	2.3%	5.4%
Increase student fees to build parking lots	49.9	3.3	46.8
Offer incentives to use public transportation	16.7	4.4	78.9
Limit student parking to satellite lots, providing shuttle buses to campus	7.8	4.7	87.5

*Figures may not equal 100 percent because of rounding.

Orders items from highest to lowest "Agree" percentages
Uses percent sign only at beginning of column
Avoids cluttering the table with total figures

The mean is the arithmetic average; the median is the midpoint in a group of figures; the mode is the most frequently occurring figure.

Mean, median, and mode figures are especially helpful when the range of values is also known. *Range* represents the span between the highest and lowest values. To calculate the range, you simply subtract the lowest figure from the highest. Knowing the range enables readers to put mean and median figures into perspective. This knowledge also prompts researchers to wonder why such a range exists, thus stimulating hunches and further investigation to solve problems.

Correlations. In tabulating and analyzing data, you may see relationships among two or more variables that help explain the findings.

Intuition suggests correlations that may or may not prove to be accurate. If a correlation seems to exist, can we say that one event caused the other? Although one event may not be said to cause another, the business researcher who sees a correlation begins to ask why and how the two variables are related. In this way, apparent correlations stimulate investigation and present possible problem solutions to be explored.

Correlations between variables suggest possible relationships that will explain research findings.

In reporting correlations, you should avoid suggesting that a cause-and-effect relationship exists when none can be proved. Only sophisticated research methods can statistically prove correlations. Instead, present a correlation as a possible relationship. Cautious statements followed by explanations gain you credibility and allow readers to make their own decisions.

Grids. Another technique for analyzing raw data—especially verbal data—is the grid. Complex verbal information is transformed into concise, manageable data; readers can see immediately which points are supported and opposed. Arranging data in a grid also works for projects such as feasibility studies that compare many variables.

Grids permit analysis of raw verbal data by grouping and classifying.

Drawing Conclusions in Reports

2

The most widely read portions of a report are the sections devoted to conclusions and recommendations. Knowledgeable readers go straight to the conclusions to see what the report writer thinks the data mean. Because conclusions summarize and explain the findings, they represent the heart of a report. Your value in an organization rises considerably if you can draw conclusions that analyze information logically and show how the data answer questions and solve problems.

Conclusions summarize and explain the findings in a report.

Any set of data can produce a variety of conclusions. Always bear in mind, though, that the audience for a report wants to know how these data relate to the problem being studied. What do the findings mean in terms of solving the original report problem?

For example, the Marriott Corporation recognized a serious problem among its employees. Conflicting home and work requirements seemed to be causing excessive employee turnover and decreased productivity. To learn the extent of the problem and to consider solutions, Marriott surveyed its staff.[1] It learned, among other things, that nearly 35 percent of its employees had children under age twelve, and 15 percent had children under age five. Other findings, shown in Figure 12.2, indicated that one third of its staff with young children took time off because of child-care difficulties. Moreover, many current employees left previous jobs because of work and family conflicts. The survey also showed that managers did not consider child-care or family problems to be appropriate topics for discussion at work.

A sample of possible conclusions that could be drawn from these findings is shown in Figure 12.2. Notice that each conclusion relates to the initial report problem. Although only a few possible findings and conclusions are shown here, you can see that the conclusions try to explain the causes for the home/work conflict among employees. Many report writers would expand the conclusion section by explaining each item and citing supporting evidence. Even for simplified conclusions, such as those shown in Figure 12.2, you will want to number each item separately and use parallel construction (balanced sentence structure).

Although your goal is to remain objective, drawing conclusions naturally involves a degree of subjectivity. Your goals, background, and frame of reference all colour the inferences you make. Findings will be interpreted from the writer's perspective, but they should not be manipulated to achieve a preconceived purpose.

Effective report conclusions are objective and bias-free.

You can make your report conclusions more objective if you use consistent evaluation criteria. If you evaluate each option by the same criteria, your conclusions are more likely to be bias-free.

FIGURE 12.2 **Report Conclusions and Recommendations** *(continued on the next page)*

Tips for Writing Conclusions

- Interpret and summarize the findings; tell what they mean.
- Relate the conclusions to the report problem.
- Limit the conclusions to the data presented; do not introduce new material.
- Number the conclusions and present them in parallel form.
- Be objective; avoid exaggerating or manipulating the data.
- Use consistent criteria in evaluating options.

REPORT PROBLEM

Marriott Corporation experienced employee turnover and lowered productivity resulting from conflicting home and work requirements. The hotel conducted a massive survey resulting in some of the following findings.

PARTIAL FINDINGS

Condenses significant findings in numbered statements

1. Nearly 35 percent of employees surveyed have children under age twelve.
2. Nearly 15 percent of employees have children under age five.
3. The average employee with children younger than twelve is absent four days a year and tardy five days because of child-related issues.
4. Within a one-year period, nearly 33 percent of employees who have young children take at least two days off because they can't find a replacement when their child-care plans break down.
5. Nearly 20 percent of employees left a previous employer because of work and family concerns.
6. At least 80 percent of female employees and 78 percent of male employees with young children reported job stress as a result of conflicting work and family roles.
7. Managers perceive family matters to be inappropriate issues for them to discuss at work.

From these and other findings, the following conclusions were drawn.

CONCLUSIONS

Uses conclusion to present sensible analysis without exaggerating or manipulating data

Explains what findings mean in terms of report problem

1. Home and family responsibilities directly affect job attendance and performance.
2. Time is the crucial issue to balancing work and family issues.
3. Male and female employees reported in nearly equal numbers the difficulties of managing work and family roles.
4. Problems with child-care arrangements increase the employees' level of stress and limit ability to work certain schedules or overtime.
5. A manager supportive of family and personal concerns is central to a good work environment.

You also need to avoid the temptation to sensationalize or exaggerate your findings or conclusions. Be careful of words like *many*, *most*, and *all*. Instead of *many of the respondents felt ...*, you might more accurately write *some of the respondents....* Examine your motives before drawing conclusions. Don't let preconceptions or wishful thinking colour your reasoning.

FIGURE 12.2 *(continued)*

Tips for Writing Recommendations

- Make specific suggestions for actions to solve the report problem.
- Prepare practical recommendations that will be agreeable to the audience.
- Avoid conditional words such as *maybe* and *perhaps.*
- Present each suggestion separately as a command beginning with a verb.
- Number the recommendations for improved readability.
- If requested, describe how the recommendations may be implemented.
- When possible, arrange the recommendations in an announced order, such as most important to least important.

Arranges actions to solve problems from most important to least important

RECOMMENDATIONS

1. Provide managers with training in working with personal and family matters.
2. Institute a flextime policy that allows employees to adapt their work schedules to home responsibilities.
3. Investigate opening a pilot child development centre for preschool children of employees at company headquarters.
4. Develop a child-care resource program to provide parents with professional help in locating affordable child care.
5. Offer a child-care discount program to help parents pay for services.
6. Authorize weekly payroll deductions, using tax-free dollars, to pay for child care.
7. Publish a quarterly employee newsletter devoted to family and child-care issues.

Writing Report Recommendations

3

Effective report conclusions are objective and bias-free. Effective recommendations offer specific suggestions on how to solve a problem.

Recommendations, unlike conclusions, make specific suggestions for actions that can solve the report problem. Consider the following examples:

Conclusion
Our investments are losing value because the stock market has declined. The bond market shows strength.

Recommendation
Withdraw at least half of our investment in stocks, and invest it in bonds.

Conclusion
The cost of constructing multilevel parking structures for student on-campus parking is prohibitive.

Recommendation
Explore the possibility of satellite parking lots with frequent shuttle buses to campus.

Notice that the conclusions explain what the problem is, while the recommendations tell how to solve it. Typically, readers prefer specific recommendations. They want to know exactly how to implement the suggestions. In addition to recommending satellite parking lots for campus parking, for example, the writer could have discussed sites for possible satellite lots and the cost of running shuttle buses.

Detailed recommendations are written only when the report writer is authorized to do so.

The specificity of your recommendations depends on your authorization. What are you commissioned to do, and what does the reader expect? In the planning stages of your report project, you anticipate what the reader wants in the report. Your intuition and your knowledge of the audience indicate how far your recommendations should be developed.

In the recommendations section of the Marriott employee survey, shown in Figure 12.2, many of the suggestions are summarized. In the actual report each recommendation could have been backed up with specifics and ideas for implementing them. For example, the child-care resource recommendation would be explained: it provides parents with names of agencies and professionals who specialize in locating child care across the country.

A good report provides practical recommendations that are agreeable to the audience. In the Marriott survey, for example, report researchers knew that the company wanted to help employees cope with conflicts between family and work obligations. Thus, the report's conclusions and recommendations focused on ways to resolve the conflict. If Marriott's goal had been merely to reduce employee absenteeism and save money, the recommendations would have been quite different.

If possible, make each recommendation a command. Note in Figure 12.2 that each recommendation begins with a verb. This structure sounds forceful and confident and helps the reader comprehend the information quickly. Avoid words such as *maybe* and *perhaps*; they suggest conditional statements that reduce the strength of recommendations.

Experienced writers may combine recommendations and conclusions. And in short reports, writers may omit conclusions and move straight to recommendations. The important thing about recommendations, though, is that they include practical suggestions for solving the report problem.

Organizing Data

4

After collecting sets of data, interpreting them, and drawing conclusions, you're ready to organize the parts of the report into a logical framework. Poorly organized reports lead to frustration. Readers will not understand, remember, or be persuaded. Wise writers know that reports rarely "just organize themselves." Instead, organization must be imposed on the data.

The direct pattern is appropriate for informed or receptive readers; the indirect pattern is appropriate when educating or persuading.

Informational reports typically are organized in three parts, as shown in Figure 12.3. Analytical reports typically contain four parts and may be organized directly or indirectly. For readers who know about the project, are supportive, or are eager to learn the results quickly, the direct method is appropriate. Conclusions—and recommendations, if requested—appear up front. For readers who must be educated or persuaded, the indirect method works better. Conclusions/recommendations appear last, after the findings have been presented and analyzed.

Although every report is different (you'll learn specifics for organizing informal and formal reports in Chapters 13 and 14), the overall organizational patterns described here typically hold true. The real challenge, though, lies in (1) organizing the facts/findings and discussion/analysis sections and (2) providing reader cues.

FIGURE 12.3 **Organizing Informational and Analytical Reports**

	Analytical Reports	
Informational Reports	**Direct Pattern**	**Indirect Pattern**
I. Introduction/background II. Facts/findings III. Summary/conclusion	I. Introduction/problem II. Conclusions/recommendations III. Facts/findings IV. Discussion/analysis	I. Introduction/problem II. Facts/findings III. Discussion/analysis IV. Conclusions/recommendations

Ordering Information Logically

Whether you're writing informational or analytical reports, the data you've collected must be structured coherently. Five common organizational methods are by time, component, importance, criteria, or convention. Regardless of the method you choose, be sure that it helps the reader understand the data. Reader comprehension, not writer convenience, should govern organization.

Organization by time, component, importance, criteria, or convention helps readers comprehend data.

Time. Ordering data by time means establishing a chronology of events. Agendas, minutes of meetings, progress reports, and procedures are usually organized by time. Beware of overusing time chronologies, however. Although this method is easy and often mirrors the way data are collected, chronologies—like the sales rep's trip report—tend to be boring, repetitious, and lacking in emphasis. Readers can't always pick out what's important.

Component. Especially for informational reports, data may be organized by components such as location, geography, division, product, or part. Organization by components works best when the classifications already exist.

Importance. Organization by importance involves beginning with the most important item and proceeding to the least important—or vice versa. The Marriott report describing work/family conflicts might begin by discussing child care, if the writer considered it the most important issue. Using importance to structure findings involves a value judgment. The writer must decide what is most important, always keeping in mind the readers' priorities and expectations. Busy readers appreciate seeing important points first; they may skim or skip other points. On the other hand, building to a climax by moving from least important to most important enables the writer to focus attention at the end. Thus, the reader is more likely to remember the most important item. Of course, the writer also risks losing the attention of the reader along the way.

Organizing by level of importance saves the time of busy readers and increases the odds that key information will be retained.

To evaluate choices or plans fairly, apply the same criteria to each.

Criteria. Establishing criteria by which to judge helps writers to treat topics consistently. Organizing a report around criteria helps readers make comparisons, instead of forcing them to search through the report for similar data.

Organizing by convention simplifies the organizational task and yields easy-to-follow information.

Convention. Many operational and recurring reports are structured according to convention. That is, they follow a prescribed plan that everyone understands.

Like operating reports, proposals are often organized conventionally. They might use such groupings as background, problem, proposed solution, staffing, schedule, costs, and authorization. As you might expect, reports following these conventional, prescribed structures greatly simplify the task of organization.

Providing Reader Cues

5

When you finish organizing a report, you probably see a neat outline in your mind: major points, supported by subpoints and details. However, readers don't know the material as well as you; they cannot see your outline. To guide them through the data, you need to provide the equivalent of a map and road signs. For both formal and informal reports, devices such as introductions, transitions, and headings prevent readers from getting lost.

Good openers tell readers what topics will be covered in what order and why.

Introductions. The best way to point a reader in the right direction is to provide an introduction that does three things:

- Tells the purpose of the report
- Describes the significance of the topic
- Previews the main points and the order in which they will be developed

Like highway drivers, readers can easily lose their way unless provided with road signs. To prevent your readers from wandering astray as they travel through your report, include plenty of road sign assistance in the form of introductions, transitions, and headings.

The following paragraph includes all three elements in introducing a report on computer security:

> This report examines the security of our current computer operations and presents suggestions for improving security. Lax computer security could mean loss of information, loss of business, and damage to our equipment and systems. Because many former employees, released during recent downsizing efforts, know our systems, major changes must be made. To improve security, I will present three recommendations: (1) begin using smart cards that limit access to our computer system, (2) alter sign-on and log-off procedures, (3) move central computer operations to a more secure area.

This opener tells the purpose (examining computer security), describes its significance (loss of information and business, damage to equipment and systems), and outlines how the report is organized (three recommendations). Good openers in effect set up a contract with the reader. The writer promises to cover certain topics in a specified order. Readers expect the writer to fulfil the contract. They want the topics to be developed as promised—using the same wording and presented in the order mentioned. For example, if in your introduction you state that you will discuss the use of *smart cards*, don't change the heading for that section to *access cards*. Remember that the introduction provides a map to a report; switching the names on the map will ensure that readers get lost. To maintain consistency, delay writing the introduction until after you have completed the report. Long, complex reports may require introductions for each section.

Transitions. Expressions like *on the contrary*, *at the same time*, and *however* show relationships and help reveal the logical flow of ideas in a report. These *transitional expressions* enable writers to tell readers where ideas are headed and how they relate.

Transitional expressions inform readers where ideas are headed and how they relate.

The following expressions (see Figure 5.6 for a complete list) enable you to show readers how you are developing your ideas.

To Present Additional Thoughts: additionally, again, also, moreover, furthermore

To Suggest Cause and Effect: accordingly, as a result, consequently, therefore

To Contrast Ideas: at the same time, but, however, on the contrary, though, yet

To Show Time and Order: after, before, first, finally, now, previously, then, to conclude

To Clarify Points: for example, for instance, in other words, that is, thus

In using these expressions, recognize that they don't have to sit at the head of a sentence. Listen to the rhythm of the sentence, and place the expression where a natural pause occurs. Used appropriately, transitional expressions serve readers as guides; misused or overused, they can be as distracting and frustrating as too many road signs on a highway.

Headings. Good headings are another structural cue that assists readers in comprehending the organization of a report. They highlight major ideas, allowing busy readers to see the big picture in a glance. Moreover, headings provide resting points for the mind and for the eye, breaking up large chunks of text into manageable and inviting segments.

Good headings provide organizational cues and spotlight key ideas.

Report writers may use functional or talking heads. *Functional heads* (for example, *Background*, *Findings*, *Personnel*, and *Production Costs*) describe functions or general topics. They show the outline of a report but provide little insight for readers. Functional headings are useful for routine reports. They're also appropriate for sensitive topics that might provoke emotional reactions. By keeping the headings general, experienced writers hope to minimize reader opposition or response to controversial subjects. *Talking heads* (for example, *Two Sides to Campus Parking Problem* or *Survey Shows Support for Parking Fees)* provide more information and interest. Unless carefully written, however, talking heads can fail to reveal the organization of a report. With some planning, though, headings can be both functional and talking, such as *Parking Recommendations: Shuttle and New Structures.*

Headings should be brief, parallel, and ordered in a logical hierarchy.

To create the most effective headings, follow a few basic guidelines:

- **Use appropriate heading levels.** The position and format of a heading indicate its level of importance and relationship to other points. Figure 12.4 both illustrates and discusses a commonly used heading format for business reports.
- **Capitalize and underline carefully.** Most writers use all capital letters (without underlines) for main titles, such as the report, chapter, and unit titles. For first- and second-level headings, they capitalize only the first letter of main words. For additional emphasis, they use a bold font, as shown in Figure 12.4.
- **Balance headings within levels.** All headings at a given level should be grammatically similar. For example, *Developing Quality Circles* and *Presenting Plan to*

Management are balanced, but *Development of Quality Circles* is not parallel with *Presenting Plan to Management.*

- **For short reports use first- or second-level headings.** Many business reports contain only one or two levels of headings. For such reports use first-level headings (centred, bolded) and/or second-level headings (flush left, bolded). See Figure 12.4.
- **Include at least one heading per report page.** Headings increase the readability and attractiveness of report pages. Use at least one per page to break up blocks of text.
- **Keep headings short but clear.** One-word headings are emphatic but not always clear. For example, the heading *Budget* does not adequately describe figures for a summer project involving student interns for an oil company in Alberta. Try to keep your headings brief (no more than eight words), but make sure they are understandable. Experiment with headings that concisely tell who, what, when, where, and why.

Illustrating Data With Graphics

6

After collecting information and interpreting it, you need to consider how best to present it to your audience. Whether you are delivering your report orally or in writing to company insiders or to outsiders, it will be easier to understand and remember if you include suitable graphics. Appropriate graphics make numerical data meaningful, simplify complex ideas, and provide visual interest. In contrast, readers tend to be bored and confused by text paragraphs packed with complex data and numbers. The same information summarized in a table or chart becomes clear. Tables, charts, graphs, pictures, and other graphics perform three important functions:

Effective graphics clarify numerical data and simplify complex ideas.

- They clarify data.
- They condense and simplify data.
- They emphasize data.

Because the same data can be shown in many different forms (for example, in a chart, table, or graph), you need to recognize how to match the appropriate graphic with your objective. In addition, you need to know how to incorporate graphics into your reports.

Matching Graphics and Objectives

In developing the best graphics, you must first decide what data you want to highlight. Chances are you will have many points you would like to show in a table or chart. But which graphics are most appropriate to your objectives? Tables? Bar charts? Pie charts? Line charts? Surface charts? Flow charts? Organization charts? Pictures? Figure 12.5 summarizes appropriate uses for each type of graphic; the following text discusses each visual in more detail.

Tables permit systematic presentation of large amounts of data, while charts enhance visual comparisons.

Tables. Probably the most frequently used graphic in reports is the table. Because a table presents quantitative or verbal information in systematic columns and rows, it can clarify large quantities of data in small spaces. You may have made rough tables to help you organize the raw data collected from literature, questionnaires, or interviews. In preparing tables for your readers or listeners, though, you'll need to pay more attention to clarity and emphasis. Here are tips for making good tables:

- Provide clear heads for the rows and columns.

FIGURE 12.4 **Levels of Headings in Reports**

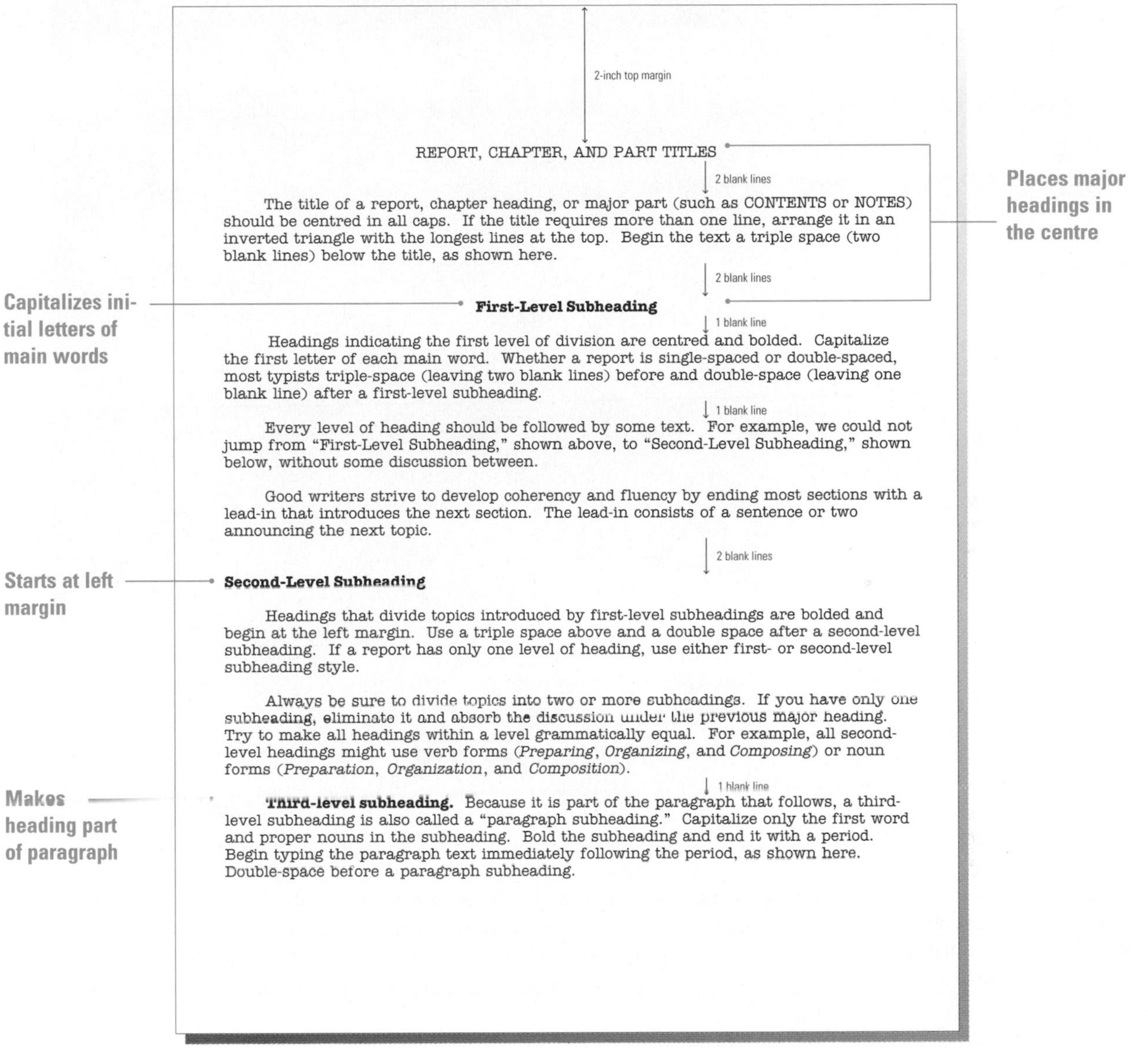

2-inch top margin

REPORT, CHAPTER, AND PART TITLES

2 blank lines

The title of a report, chapter heading, or major part (such as CONTENTS or NOTES) should be centred in all caps. If the title requires more than one line, arrange it in an inverted triangle with the longest lines at the top. Begin the text a triple space (two blank lines) below the title, as shown here.

2 blank lines

Places major headings in the centre

Capitalizes initial letters of main words

First-Level Subheading

1 blank line

Headings indicating the first level of division are centred and bolded. Capitalize the first letter of each main word. Whether a report is single-spaced or double-spaced, most typists triple-space (leaving two blank lines) before and double-space (leaving one blank line) after a first-level subheading.

1 blank line

Every level of heading should be followed by some text. For example, we could not jump from "First-Level Subheading," shown above, to "Second-Level Subheading," shown below, without some discussion between.

Good writers strive to develop coherency and fluency by ending most sections with a lead-in that introduces the next section. The lead-in consists of a sentence or two announcing the next topic.

2 blank lines

Starts at left margin

Second-Level Subheading

Headings that divide topics introduced by first-level subheadings are bolded and begin at the left margin. Use a triple space above and a double space after a second-level subheading. If a report has only one level of heading, use either first- or second-level subheading style.

Always be sure to divide topics into two or more subheadings. If you have only one subheading, eliminate it and absorb the discussion under the previous major heading. Try to make all headings within a level grammatically equal. For example, all second-level headings might use verb forms (*Preparing*, *Organizing*, and *Composing*) or noun forms (*Preparation*, *Organization*, and *Composition*).

1 blank line

Makes heading part of paragraph

Third-level subheading. Because it is part of the paragraph that follows, a third-level subheading is also called a "paragraph subheading." Capitalize only the first word and proper nouns in the subheading. Bold the subheading and end it with a period. Begin typing the paragraph text immediately following the period, as shown here. Double-space before a paragraph subheading.

- Identify the units in which figures are given (percentages, dollars, units per worker hour, and so forth) in the table title, in the column or row head, with the first item in a column, or in a note at the bottom.
- Arrange items in a logical order (alphabetical, chronological, geographical, highest to lowest) depending on what you need to emphasize.
- Use *N/A* (not available) for missing data.
- Make long tables easier to read by shading alternate lines or by leaving a blank line after groups of five.

FIGURE 12.5 **Matching Graphics to Objectives**

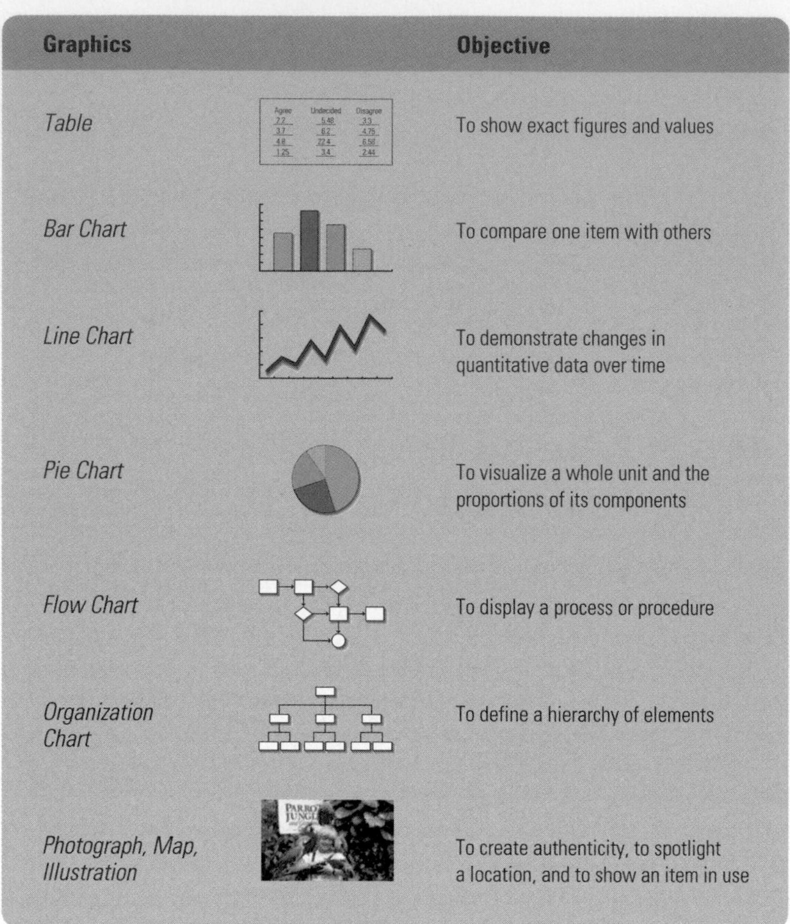

Graphics	Objective
Table	To show exact figures and values
Bar Chart	To compare one item with others
Line Chart	To demonstrate changes in quantitative data over time
Pie Chart	To visualize a whole unit and the proportions of its components
Flow Chart	To display a process or procedure
Organization Chart	To define a hierarchy of elements
Photograph, Map, Illustration	To create authenticity, to spotlight a location, and to show an item in use

Bar charts enable readers to compare related items, see changes over time, and understand how parts relate to a whole.

Bar Charts. Although they lack the precision of tables, bar charts enable you to make emphatic visual comparisons. Bar charts can be used to compare related items, illustrate changes in data over time, and show segments as part of a whole.

Many suggestions for tables also hold true for bar charts. Here are a few additional tips:

- Keep the length of each bar and segment proportional.
- Include a total figure in the middle of a bar or at its end if the figure helps the reader and does not clutter the chart.
- Start dollar or percentage amounts at zero.
- Avoid showing too much information, thus producing clutter and confusion.

Line Charts. The major advantage of line charts is that they show changes over time, thus indicating trends. They give an overview or impression of the data. Experienced report writers use tables to list exact data; they use line charts or bar charts to spotlight important points or trends.

Simple line charts show just one variable. Multiple line charts combine several variables. Segmented line charts, also called surface charts, illustrate how the components of a whole change over time. Tables don't permit such visualization.

Here are tips for preparing a line chart:

- Begin with a grid divided into squares.
- Arrange the time component (usually years) horizontally across the bottom; arrange values for the other variable vertically.
- Draw small dots at the intersections to indicate each value at a given year.
- Connect the dots and add colour if desired.
- To prepare a segmented (surface) chart, plot the first value across the bottom; add the next item to the first figures for every increment; for the third item add its value to the total of the first two items. The top line indicates the total of the three values.

Pie Charts. Pie, or circle, charts enable readers to see a whole and the proportion of its components, or wedges. Although less flexible than bar or line charts, pie charts are useful in showing percentages. Notice that a wedge can be "exploded" or popped out for special emphasis.

Pie charts are most useful in showing the proportion of parts to a whole.

For the most effective pie charts, follow these suggestions:

- Begin at the 12 o'clock position, drawing the largest wedge first. (Computer software programs don't always observe this advice, but if you're drawing your own charts, you can.)
- Include, if possible, the actual percentage or absolute value for each wedge.
- Use four to eight segments for best results; if necessary, group small portions into one wedge called "Other."
- Distinguish wedges with colour, shading, or cross-hatching.
- Keep all the labels horizontal.

Many software programs help you prepare professional-looking charts with a minimum of effort.

Flow Charts. Procedures are simplified and clarified by diagramming them in a flow chart, as shown in Figure 12.6. Whether you need to describe the procedure for handling a customer's purchase order or outline steps in solving a problem, flow charts help the reader visualize the process. Traditional flow charts use the following symbols:

- Ovals to designate the beginning and end of a process
- Diamonds to denote decision points
- Rectangles to represent major activities or steps

Organization Charts. Many large organizations are so complex that they need charts to show the chain of command, from the boss down to line managers and employees. Organization charts provide such information as who reports to whom, how many subordinates work for each manager (the span of control), and what channels of official communication exist. They may also illustrate a company's structure (by function, customer, or product, for example), the work being performed in each job, and the hierarchy of decision making.

Organization charts show the line of command and thus the flow of official communication from management to employees.

FIGURE 12.6 **Flow Chart**

Flow charts are useful to clarify procedures.

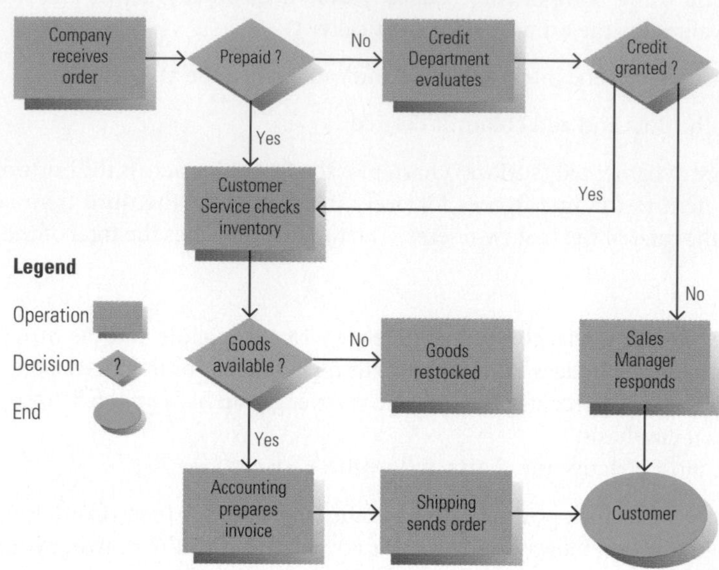

Computer technology permits photographs, maps, and illustrations to be scanned directly into a report.

Photographs, Maps, and Illustrations. Some business reports include photographs, maps, and illustrations to serve specific purposes. Photographs, for example, add authenticity and provide a visual record. With today's computer technology, photographs, maps, and illustrations can be scanned directly into business reports.

Maps enable report writers to depict activities or concentrations geographically, such as dots indicating sales reps in provinces across the country.

Illustrations and diagrams are useful in indicating how an object looks or operates.

Incorporating Graphics in Reports

7

Used appropriately, graphics make reports more interesting and easier to understand. In putting graphics into your reports, follow these suggestions for best effects.

Effective graphics are accurate and ethical, avoid overuse of colour or decorations, and include titles.

- **Evaluate the audience.** Size up your readers to determine how many graphics are appropriate. Six charts in an internal report to an executive may seem like overkill; but in a long technical report to outsiders, six may be too few.
- **Use restraint.** Don't overuse colour or decorations. Although colour can effectively distinguish bars or segments in charts, too much colour can be distracting and confusing. Remember, too, that colours themselves sometimes convey meaning: reds suggest deficits or negative values, blues suggest coolness, and oranges may mean warmth.
- **Be accurate and ethical.** Double-check all graphics for accuracy of figures and calculations. Be certain that your visuals aren't misleading—either accidentally or intentionally. Manipulation of a chart scale can make trends look steeper and more dramatic than they really are. Also, be sure to cite sources when you use someone else's facts.

- **Introduce a graphic meaningfully.** Refer to every graphic in the text, and place the graphic close to the point where it is mentioned. Most important, though, help the reader understand the significance of a graphic. You can do this by telling the reader what to look for or by summarizing the main point of a graphic. Don't assume the reader will automatically draw the same conclusions you reached from a set of data. Instead of *The findings are shown in Figure 3* tell the reader what to look for: *Two thirds of the responding employees, as shown in Figure 3, favour a flextime schedule.* The best introductions for graphics interpret them for readers.

Textual graphics should be introduced by statements that help readers interpret them.

- **Choose an appropriate caption or title style.** Like reports, graphics may use "talking" titles or generic, descriptive titles. "Talking" titles are more persuasive; they tell the reader what to think. Descriptive titles describe the facts more objectively.

Talking Title	**Descriptive Title**
Average Annual Health Care Costs per Worker Rise Steeply as Workers Grow Older	Average Annual Health Care Costs per Worker as Shown by Age Groups

Judge the style you should use by your audience and your company's preferences. Regardless of the style, make the titles consistent and specific.

Summary of Learning Objectives

1 **Use tabulating and statistical techniques to sort and interpret report data.** Report data become more meaningful when sorted into tables or when analyzed by mean (the arithmetic average), median (the midpoint in a group of figures), and mode (the most frequent response). Range represents a span between the highest and lowest figures. Grids help organize complex data into rows and columns.

2 **Draw meaningful conclusions from report data.** Conclusions tell what the survey data mean—especially in relation to the original report problem. They summarize key findings and may attempt to explain what caused the report problem. They are usually enumerated.

3 **Prepare practical report recommendations.** In reports that call for recommendations, writers make specific suggestions for actions that can solve the report problem. Recommendations should be feasible and potentially agreeable to the audience. They should all relate to the initial problem. Recommendations may be combined with conclusions.

4 **Organize report data logically.** Reports may be organized in many ways, including (1) by time (establishing a chronology or history of events), (2) by component (discussing a problem by geography, division, or product), (3) by importance (arranging data from most important to least important, or vice versa), (4) by criteria (comparing items by standards), or (5) by convention (using an already established grouping).

5 **Provide cues to aid report comprehension.** Good communicators help receivers understand a topic's organization by using introductions (to spell out topics), transitional expressions (to indicate where a topic is headed), and headings (to highlight major ideas).

6 Develop graphics that create meaning and interest. Good graphics improve reports by clarifying, simplifying, and emphasizing data. Tables organize precise data into rows and columns. Bar and line charts enable data to be compared visually. Line charts are especially helpful in showing changes over time. Pie charts show a whole and the proportion of its components. Organization charts, pictures, maps, and illustrations serve specific purposes.

7 Incorporate graphic aids into reports effectively. In choosing or crafting graphics, smart communicators evaluate their audience, purpose, topic, and budget to determine the number and kind of graphics. These communicators are accurate, ethical, and restrained in developing graphics. And they are consistent in writing "talking" titles (telling readers what to think about the graphic) or "descriptive" titles (summarizing the topic objectively).

CHAPTER REVIEW

1. Forms that use systematic columns and rows to enable you to summarize and simplify numerical data from questionnaires and interviews are called what? (Obj. 1)
2. What is cross-tabulation? Give an example. (Obj. 1)
3. Calculate the mean, median, and mode for these figures: 3, 4, 4, 4, 10. (Obj. 1)
4. How can a grid help classify material? (Obj. 1)
5. What are the two most widely read sections of a report? (Obj. 2)
6. How do conclusions differ from recommendations? (Objs. 2 and 3)
7. When reports have multiple recommendations, how should they be presented? (Obj. 3)
8. Informational reports typically are organized into what three parts? (Obj. 4)
9. Analytical reports may be organized directly or indirectly. How do the organizational patterns differ? (Obj. 4)
10. Name five methods for organizing report data. Be prepared to discuss each. (Obj. 4)
11. What three devices can report writers use to prevent readers from getting lost in the text? (Obj. 5)
12. Briefly compare the advantages and disadvantages of illustrating data with charts (bar and line) versus tables. (Obj. 6)
13. What is the major advantage of using pie charts to illustrate data? (Obj. 6)
14. What graphic is best for illustrating a process or procedure? (Obj. 6)
15. Describe two kinds of captions or titles for graphics. (Obj. 7)

CRITICAL THINKING

1. Why is audience analysis particularly important in making report recommendations? (Obj. 3)
2. Why is anticipation of the audience's response less important in an informational report than in an analytical report? (Objs. 2 and 3)
3. Should all reports be organized so that they follow the sequence of investigation—that is, describing for the reader the initial problem, analysis of issues, data collection, data analysis, and conclusions? Why or why not? (Obj. 4)
4. Why is it important for reports to contain structural cues clarifying their organization? (Obj. 5)

ACTIVITIES

12.1 Tabulation and Interpretation of Survey Results (Obj. 1)

Team | **Critical Thinking**

a. Assume your business communication class at North Shore College was asked by the college bookstore manager, Larry Krause, to conduct a survey (see Figure 11.8). Concerned about the environment, Krause wants to learn students' reactions to eliminating plastic bags, of which 45 000 are given away annually by the bookstore.

Students were questioned about a number of proposals, resulting in the following raw data. In groups of four or five, convert the data into a table (see Figure 12.1) with a descriptive title. Arrange the items in a logical sequence.

For major purchases the bookstore should	Agree	Undecided	Disagree
1. Continue to provide plastic bags	132	17	411
2. Provide no bags; encourage students to bring their own bags	414	25	121
3. Provide no bags; offer cloth bags at reduced price (about $3)	357	19	184
4. Give a cloth bag with each major purchase, the cost to be included in registration fees	63	15	482

b. How could these survey data be cross-tabulated? Would cross-tabulation serve any purpose?

c. Given the conditions of this survey, name at least three conclusions that could be drawn from the data.

d. Prepare three to five recommendations to be submitted to Mr. Krause. How could they be implemented?

12.2 Evaluating Conclusions (Obj. 2)

Team **E-Mail**

Read an in-depth article (800 or more words) in *Newsweek*, *Canadian Business*, *Maclean's*, or the *Financial Post Magazine*. What conclusions does the author draw? Are the conclusions valid, based on the evidence presented? In an e-mail message to your instructor, summarize the main points in the article and analyze the conclusions. What conclusions would you have drawn from the data?

12.3 Distinguishing Between Conclusions and Recommendations (Objs. 2 and 3)

For each of the following statements, indicate whether it could be classified as a conclusion or recommendation.

a. In times of recession, individuals spend less money on meals away from home.

b. Our restaurant should offer a menu featuring a variety of low-priced items in addition to the regular menu.

c. Absenteeism among employees with families decreases when they have adequate child care.

d. Nearly 80 percent of our business comes from only 20 percent of our customers.

e. Datatech Company should concentrate its major sales effort on its largest accounts.

12.4 Data Organization (Obj. 4)

How could the findings in the following reports be best organized? Consider these methods: time, component, importance, criteria, and convention.

a. A report comparing three sites for a company's new production plant. The report presents figures on property costs, construction costs, proximity to raw materials, provincial taxes, labour availability, and shipping distances.

b. A report describing the history of the development of dwarf and spur apple trees, starting with the first genetic dwarfs discovered about 100 years ago and progressing to today's grafted varieties on dwarfing rootstocks.

c. An informational brochure for job candidates that describes your company's areas of employment: accounting, finance, information systems, operations management, marketing, production, and computer-aided design.

d. A monthly sales report submitted to the sales manager.

e. A recommendation report, to be submitted to management, presenting four building plans to improve access to your building, in compliance with federal regulations. The plans range considerably in feasibility and cost.

12.5 Evaluating Headings and Titles (Objs. 5 and 7)

Identify the following report headings and titles as "talking" or "functional/descriptive." Discuss the usefulness and effectiveness of each.

a. Problem

b. Need for Tightening Computer ID System

c. Annual Budget

d. How to Implement Quality Circles That Work

e. Case History: Buena Vista Palace Hotel Focuses on Improving Service to Customers

12.6 Selecting Graphics (Obj. 6)

Identify the best kind of graphic to illustrate the following data.

a. Instructions for workers telling them how to distinguish between worker accidents that must be reported to provincial and federal agencies and those that need not be reported.

b. Figures showing what proportion of every provincial tax dollar is spent on education, social services, transportation, debt, and other expenses.

c. Data showing the academic, administrative, and operation divisions of a college, from the president to department chairs and division managers.

d. Figures comparing the sales of VCRs, colour TVs, and personal computers over the past ten years.

e. Figures showing the operating profit of a company for the past five years.

12.7 Evaluating Graphics (Objs. 6 and 7)

Select five graphics from newspapers or magazines. Look in *The Globe and Mail, The Economist, Canadian Business, The Financial Post* or other business news publications. In a memo to your instructor, critique each graphic based on what you have learned in this chapter.

12.8 Drawing a Bar Chart (Obj. 6)

Prepare a bar chart comparing the tax rates of eight industrial countries in the world: Canada, 34 percent; France, 42 percent; Germany, 39 percent; Japan, 26 percent; Netherlands, 48 percent; Sweden, 49 percent; United Kingdom, 37 percent; United States, 28 percent. These figures represent a percentage of the gross domestic product for each country. The sources of the figures are the International Monetary Fund and the Japanese Ministry of Finance. Arrange the entries logically. Write two titles: a talking title and a descriptive title. What conclusion might you draw from these figures? What should be emphasized in the graph and title?

12.9 Drawing a Line Chart (Obj. 6)

Prepare a line chart showing the sales of Sidekick Athletic Shoes, Inc., for these years: 2000, $6.7 million; 1999, $5.4 million; 1998, $3.2 million; 1997, $2.1 million; 1996, $2.6 million; 1995, $3.6 million. In the chart title, highlight the trend you see in the data.

12.10 Studying Graphics in Annual Reports (Objs. 6 and 7)

In a memo to your instructor, evaluate the effectiveness of graphics in three to five corporation annual reports. Critique their readability, clarity, and success in visualizing data. How were they introduced in the text? What suggestions would you make to improve them?

CHAPTER • 13 •

TYPICAL BUSINESS REPORTS

LEARNING OBJECTIVES

1 Distinguish between informational and analytical reports.

2 Prepare typical informational reports.

3 Prepare typical analytical reports.

Writing Informational Reports

1

To stay abreast of what's happening inside and outside of their firms, organizations need information, much of which will be submitted in the form of reports. This chapter examines both informational and analytical reports.

Informational reports generally deliver data and answer questions without offering recommendations or much analysis. In these reports the emphasis is on facts. Informational reports describe periodic, recurring activities (like monthly sales or weekly customer calls) as well as situational, nonrecurring events (such as trips, conferences, and progress on special projects). They also include routine operating, compliance, and investigative reports. What they have in common is delivering information to readers who do not have to be persuaded. Informational report readers usually are neutral or receptive.

Informational reports provide data on periodic and situational activities for readers who do not need to be persuaded.

You can expect to write many informational reports as an entry-level or middle-management employee. Because these reports generally deliver nonsensitive data and thus will not upset the reader, they are organized directly. Often they need little background material or introductory comments since readers are familiar with the topics. Although they're generally conversational and informal, informational reports should not be so casual that the reader struggles to find the important points. Main points must be immediately visible. Headings, lists, bulleted items, and other graphic highlighting, as well as clear organization, enable readers to grasp major ideas immediately.

Typical Informational Reports

2

Periodic Reports

Most businesses—especially larger ones—require periodic reports to keep management informed of operations. These recurring reports are written at regular intervals—weekly, monthly, yearly—so that management can monitor and, if necessary, remedy business strategies. Some periodic reports simply contain figures, such as sales volume, number and kind of customer service calls, shipments delivered, accounts payable, and personnel data. More challenging periodic reports require description and discussion of activities. In preparing a narrative description of their activities, employees writing periodic reports usually do the following:

Periodic reports keep management informed of operations and activities.

- Summarize regular activities and events performed during the reporting period.
- Describe irregular events deserving the attention of management.
- Highlight special needs and problems.

Managers naturally want to know that routine activities are progressing normally. They're often more interested, though, in what the competition is doing and in how operations may be affected by unusual events or problems. In companies with open lines of communication, managers expect to be informed of the bad news along with the good news.

The periodic report shown in Figure 13.1 uses four categories: (1) activity summary, (2) competition update, (3) product problems and comments, and (4) needs.

FIGURE 13.1 **Periodic Report**

1 PREWRITING

Analyze: The purpose of this report is to inform management of the week's activities, customer reactions, and the rep's needs.

Anticipate: The audience is a manager who wants to be able to pick out the report highlights quickly. His reaction will probably be neutral or positive.

Adapt: Introduce the report data in a direct, straightforward manner.

WRITING

Research: Verify data for the landscape judging test. Collect facts about competitors. Double-check problems and needs.

Organize: Make lists of items for each of the four report categories. Be sure to distinguish between problems and needs. Emphasize needs.

Compose: Write and print first draft on a computer.

REVISING

Revise: Look for ways to eliminate wordiness. For greater emphasis use a bulleted list for *Competition Update* and for *Needs.* Make all items parallel.

Proofread: Run spell checker. Adjust white space around headings.

Evaluate: Does this report provide significant data in an easy-to-read format?

DATE: March 15, 2004

TO: Steve Schumacher

FROM: Jim Chrisman JC

SUBJECT: Weekly Activity Report

Presents internal informational report in memo format

Activity Summary

Highlights of my activities for the week ending March 14 follow:

Sherbrooke. On Thursday and Friday I demonstrated our new Rain Stream drip systems at a vendor fair at Benbrook Farm Supply, where over 500 people walked through.

Frontenac College. Over the weekend I was a judge for the Quebec Landscape Technician test given at the college. This certification program ensures potential employers that a landscaper is properly trained. Applicants are tested in such areas as irrigation theory, repair, troubleshooting, installation, and controller programming. The event proved to be very productive. I was able to talk to my distributors and to several important contractors whose crews were taking the tests.

Condenses weekly activity report into topics requested by management

Competition Update

- Toronado can't seem to fill its open sales position in the Eastern Townships.
- RainCo tried to steal the Trinity Country Club golf course contract from us by waiting until the job was spec'd our way and then submitting a lower bid. Fortunately, the Trinity people saw through this ploy and awarded us the contract nevertheless.
- Atlas has a real warranty problem with its 500 series in this area. One distributor had over 200 controllers returned in a seven-week period.

Product Problems, Comments

A contractor in Drummondville told me that our Rain Stream No. 250 valves do not hold the adjustment screw in the throttled-down position. Are they designed to do so?

Our Remote Streamer S-100 is generating considerable excitement. Every time I mention it, people come out of the woodwork to request demos. I gave four demos last week and have three more scheduled this week. I'm not sure, though, how quickly these demos will translate into sales because contractors are waiting for our six-month special prices.

Needs

- More information on irrigation training.
- French training videos showing our products.
- Spray nozzle to service small planter areas, say 2 to 4 metres.

Summarizes needs in abbreviated, easy-to-read form

Trip, Convention, and Conference Reports.

Employees sent on business trips or to conventions and conferences typically must submit reports when they return. Organizations want to know that their money was well spent in funding the travel. These reports inform management about new procedures, equipment, and laws and supply information affecting products, operations, and service.

The hardest parts of writing these reports are selecting the most relevant material and organizing it coherently. Generally, it's best not to use chronological sequencing (in the morning we did X, at lunch we heard Y, and in the afternoon we did Z). Instead, you should focus on three to five topics in which your reader will be interested. These items become the body of the report. Then simply add an introduction and closing, and your report is organized. Here is a general outline for trip, conference, and convention reports:

- Begin by identifying the event (exact date, name, and location) and previewing the topics to be discussed.
- Summarize in the body three to five main points that might benefit the reader.
- Itemize your expenses, if requested, on a separate sheet.
- Close by expressing appreciation, suggesting action to be taken, or synthesizing the value of the trip or event.

The conference report shown in Figure 13.2 discusses three topics that the writer felt would be important to his readers.

Progress and Interim Reports.

Progress and interim reports describe ongoing projects to both internal and external readers.

Continuing projects often require progress or interim reports to describe their status. These reports may be external (advising customers regarding the headway of their projects) or internal (informing management of the status of activities). Progress reports typically follow this pattern of development:

- Specify in the opening the purpose and nature of the project.
- Provide background information if the audience requires filling in.
- Describe the work completed.
- Explain the work currently in progress, including personnel, activities, methods, and locations.
- Anticipate problems and possible remedies.
- Discuss future activities and provide the expected completion date.

Progress reports, such as the one shown in Figure 13.3, include background information to hit the high points of what has been completed, outline what the writer plans to do next, and avoid minute details.

Investigative Reports

Investigative or informational reports deliver data for a specific situation—without offering interpretation or recommendations. These nonrecurring reports are generally arranged in a direct pattern with three segments: introduction, body, and summary. The body—which includes the facts, findings, or discussion—may be organized by time, component, importance, criteria, or convention. What's important is dividing the topic into logical segments, say, three to five areas that are

FIGURE 13.2 **Conference Report**

DATE: April 22, 2004
TO: Angela Taylor
FROM: Jeff Marchant *JM*
SUBJECT: TRAINING CONFERENCE ON EMPLOYMENT INTERVIEWING

I enjoyed attending the "Interviewing People" training conference sponsored by the National Business Foundation. This one-day meeting, held in Toronto on April 19, provided excellent advice that will help us strengthen our interviewing techniques. Although the conference covered many topics, this report concentrates on three areas: structuring the interview, avoiding common mistakes, and responding to new legislation.

Identifies topic and previews how the report is organized

Structuring the Interview

Job interviews usually have three parts. The opening establishes a friendly rapport with introductions, a few polite questions, and an explanation of the purpose of the interview. The body of the interview consists of questions controlled by the interviewer. The interviewer has three goals: (a) educating the applicant about the job, (b) eliciting information about the applicant's suitability for the job, and (c) promoting goodwill about the organization. In closing, the interviewer should encourage the applicant to ask questions, summarize main points, and indicate what actions will follow.

Sets off major topics with centred headings

Avoiding Common Mistakes

Probably the most interesting and practical part of the conference centred on common mistakes made by interviewers, some of which I summarize here:

1. **Not taking notes at each interview.** Recording important facts enables you to remember the first candidate as easily as you remember the last—and all those in between.

2. **Losing control of the interview.** Keep control of the interview by digging into the candidate's answers to questions. Probe for responses of greater depth. Don't move on until a question has been satisfactorily answered.

3. **Not testing the candidate's communication skills.** To be able to evaluate a candidate's ability to express ideas, ask the individual to explain some technical jargon from his or her current position—preferably, something mentioned during the interview.

4. **Having departing employees conduct the interviews for their replacements.** Departing employees may be unreliable as interviewers because they tend to hire candidates not quite as strong as they are. Their hidden agenda may be to keep the door open in case the new job fails.

5. **Failing to check references.** As many as 15 percent of all résumés may contain falsified data. The best way to check references is to network: ask the person whose name has been given to suggest the name of another person.

Covers facts that will most interest and help reader

Angela Taylor Page 2 April 22, 2004

Responding to New Legislation

Recently enacted provisions to the Human Rights Code prohibit interviewers from asking candidates—or even their references—about candidates' disabilities. A question we frequently asked ("Do you have any physical limitations which would prevent you from performing the job for which you are applying?") would now break the law. Interviewers should also avoid asking about medical history; prescription-drug use; prior workers' compensation claims; work absenteeism due to illness; and past treatment for alcoholism, drug use, or mental illness. Questions must pertain to the job itself.

Conclusion

This conference provided me with valuable training that I would like to share with other department members at a future staff meeting. Let me know when it can be scheduled.

FIGURE 13.3 **Progress Report**

Tips for Writing Progress Reports

- Identify the purpose and the nature of the project immediately.
- Supply background information only if the reader must be educated.
- Describe the work completed.
- Discuss the work in progress, including personnel, activities, methods, and locations.
- Identify problems and possible remedies.
- Consider future activities.
- Close by telling the expected date of completion.

QuaStar Productions

Interoffice Memo

DATE: January 8, 2004

TO: Rick Willens, Executive Producer

FROM: Sheila Ryan, Location Manager *SR*

SUBJECT: Sites for "Bodega Bay" Telefilm

Identifies project and previews report

This memo describes the progress of my search for an appropriate rustic home, villa, or ranch to be used for the wine country sequences in the telefilm "Bodega Bay." Three sites will be available for you to inspect on January 22, as you requested.

Background: In preparation for this assignment, I consulted Director Dave Durslag, who gave me his preferences for the site. He suggested a picturesque ranch home situated near vineyards, preferably with a scenic background. I also consulted Producer Teresa Silva, who told me that the site must accommodate 55 to 70 production crew members for approximately three weeks of filming. Ben Waters, telefilm accountant, requested that the cost of the site not exceed $24 000 for a three-week lease.

Saves space by integrating headings into paragraphs

Work Completed: For the past eight days I have searched the Niagara Escarpment area in Southern Ontario's wine country. Possible sites include turn-of-the-century estates, Victorian mansions, and rustic farmhouses in the Welland/St. Catharines area. One exceptional site is the Country Meadow Inn, a 97-year-old farmhouse nestled among vineyards with a breathtaking view of valleys and distant hills.

Work to Be Completed: In the next five days, I'll search the Niagara countryside. Many wineries contain charming structures that may present exactly the degree of atmosphere and mystery we need. These wineries have the added advantage of easy access. I will also inspect possible structures in and around Niagara-on-the-Lake. Finally I've made an appointment with the director of provincial parks to discuss our project, use of provincial lands, restrictions, and costs.

Tells the bad news as well as the good

Anticipated Problems: You should be aware of two complications for filming in this area.

1. Property owners are very familiar with the making of films and expect to receive substantial amounts for short-term leases.
2. The trees won't have leaves again until May. You may wish to change the filming schedule somewhat.

By January 15 you'll have my final report describing the three most promising locations. Arrangements will be made for you to visit these sites January 22.

Concludes by giving completion date and describing what follows roughly equal and don't overlap. The subject matter of the report usually suggests the best way to divide and organize it.

Whether you are writing a periodic, trip, conference, progress, or investigative report, you'll want to review the suggestions found in the following checklist.

Checklist for Writing Informational Reports

Introduction

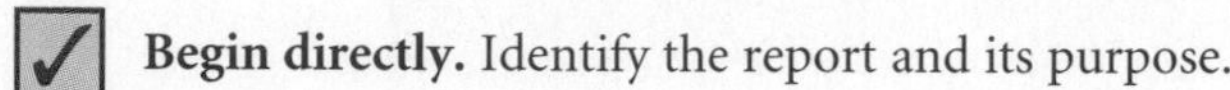
- ✓ **Begin directly.** Identify the report and its purpose.

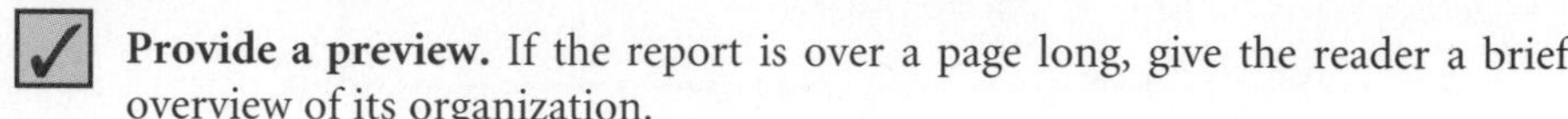
- ✓ **Provide a preview.** If the report is over a page long, give the reader a brief overview of its organization.

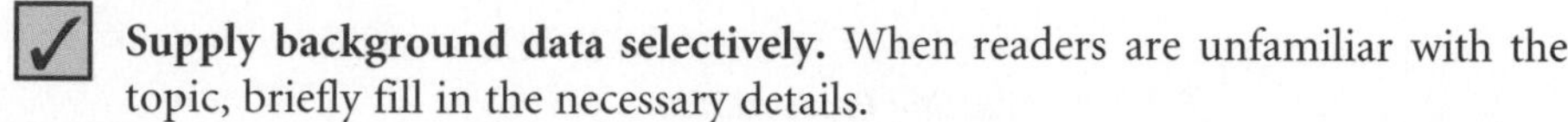
- ✓ **Supply background data selectively.** When readers are unfamiliar with the topic, briefly fill in the necessary details.

Body

- ✓ **Divide the topic.** Strive to group the facts or findings into three to five roughly equal segments that do not overlap.
- ✓ **Arrange the subtopics logically.** Consider organizing by time, component, importance, criteria, or convention.
- ✓ **Use clear headings.** Supply functional or talking heads (at least one per page) that describe each important section.
- ✓ **Determine degree of formality.** Use an informal, conversational writing style unless the audience expects a more formal tone.
- ✓ **Enhance readability with graphic highlighting.** Make liberal use of bullets, numbered and lettered lists, headings, underlined items, and white space.

Summary/Conclusion

- ✓ **When necessary, summarize the report.** Briefly review the main points and discuss what action will follow.
- ✓ **Offer a concluding thought.** If relevant, express appreciation or describe your willingness to provide further information.

Writing Analytical Reports

3

Analytical reports differ significantly from informational reports. Although both seek to collect and present data clearly, analytical reports also analyze the data and typically try to persuade the reader to accept the conclusions and act on the recommendations. Informational reports emphasize facts; analytical reports emphasize reasoning and conclusions.

For some readers analytical reports may be organized directly with the conclusions and recommendations near the beginning. Directness is appropriate when the reader has confidence in the writer, based on either experience or credentials. Front loading the recommendations also works when the topic is routine or familiar and the reader is supportive.

Directness can backfire, though. If you announce the recommendations too quickly, the reader may immediately object to a single idea, one that you had no suspicion would trigger a negative reaction. Once the reader is opposed, changing an unfavourable mindset may be difficult or impossible. A reader may also think you have oversimplified or overlooked something significant if you lay out all the recommendations before explaining how you arrived at them. When the reader must be led through the process of discovering the solution or recommendation, use the indirect method: present conclusions and recommendations last.

Most analytical reports answer questions about specific problems. Three typical analytical reports answer business questions: justification/recommendation reports, feasibility reports, and yardstick reports. Because these reports all solve problems, the categories are not mutually exclusive. What distinguishes them is their goals and organization.

Justification/Recommendation Reports

Both managers and employees must occasionally write reports that justify or recommend something, such as buying equipment, changing a procedure, hiring an employee, consolidating departments, or investing funds. Large organizations sometimes prescribe how these reports should be organized; they use forms with conventional headings. When you are free to select an organizational plan yourself, however, let your audience and topic determine your choice of direct or indirect structure.

Justification/recommendation reports follow the direct or the indirect pattern depending on the audience and the topic.

Direct Pattern. For nonsensitive topics and recommendations that will be agreeable to readers, you can organize directly according to the following sequence:

- Identify the problem or need briefly.
- Announce the recommendation, solution, or action concisely and with action verbs.
- Explain more fully the benefits of the recommendation or steps to be taken to solve the problem.
- Include a discussion of pros, cons, and costs.
- Conclude with a summary specifying the recommendation and action to be taken.

The direct pattern is appropriate for justification/recommendation reports on nonsensitive topics and for receptive audiences.

The justification/recommendation report, shown in Figure 13.4, concentrates on four separate benefits of the writer's recommendation.

Indirect Pattern. When a reader may oppose a recommendation or when circumstances suggest caution, don't be in a hurry to reveal your recommendation. Consider using the following sequence for an indirect approach to your recommendations:

The indirect pattern is appropriate for justification/recommendation reports on sensitive topics and for potentially unreceptive audiences.

- Make a general reference to the problem, not to your recommendation, in the subject line.
- Describe the problem or need your recommendation addresses. Use specific examples, supporting statistics, and authoritative quotes to lend credibility to the seriousness of the problem.
- Discuss alternative solutions, beginning with the least likely to succeed.

FIGURE 13.4 **Justification/Recommendation Report: Direct Pattern**

1 PREWRITING

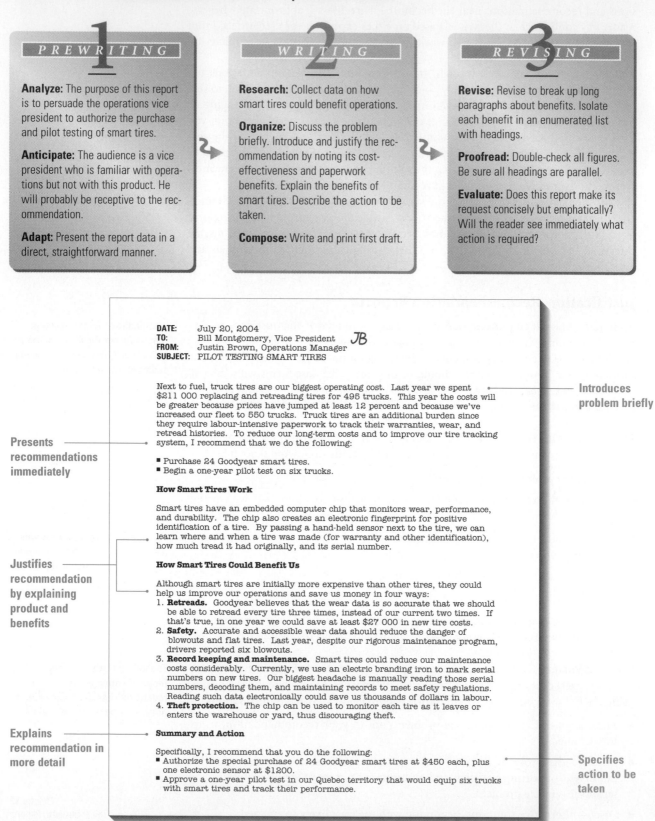

Analyze: The purpose of this report is to persuade the operations vice president to authorize the purchase and pilot testing of smart tires.

Anticipate: The audience is a vice president who is familiar with operations but not with this product. He will probably be receptive to the recommendation.

Adapt: Present the report data in a direct, straightforward manner.

2 WRITING

Research: Collect data on how smart tires could benefit operations.

Organize: Discuss the problem briefly. Introduce and justify the recommendation by noting its cost-effectiveness and paperwork benefits. Explain the benefits of smart tires. Describe the action to be taken.

Compose: Write and print first draft.

3 REVISING

Revise: Revise to break up long paragraphs about benefits. Isolate each benefit in an enumerated list with headings.

Proofread: Double-check all figures. Be sure all headings are parallel.

Evaluate: Does this report make its request concisely but emphatically? Will the reader see immediately what action is required?

DATE: July 20, 2004
TO: Bill Montgomery, Vice President
FROM: Justin Brown, Operations Manager JB
SUBJECT: PILOT TESTING SMART TIRES

Next to fuel, truck tires are our biggest operating cost. Last year we spent $211 000 replacing and retreading tires for 495 trucks. This year the costs will be greater because prices have jumped at least 12 percent and because we've increased our fleet to 550 trucks. Truck tires are an additional burden since they require labour-intensive paperwork to track their warranties, wear, and retread histories. To reduce our long-term costs and to improve our tire tracking system, I recommend that we do the following:

- Purchase 24 Goodyear smart tires.
- Begin a one-year pilot test on six trucks.

How Smart Tires Work

Smart tires have an embedded computer chip that monitors wear, performance, and durability. The chip also creates an electronic fingerprint for positive identification of a tire. By passing a hand-held sensor next to the tire, we can learn where and when a tire was made (for warranty and other identification), how much tread it had originally, and its serial number.

How Smart Tires Could Benefit Us

Although smart tires are initially more expensive than other tires, they could help us improve our operations and save us money in four ways:

1. **Retreads.** Goodyear believes that the wear data is so accurate that we should be able to retread every tire three times, instead of our current two times. If that's true, in one year we could save at least $27 000 in new tire costs.
2. **Safety.** Accurate and accessible wear data should reduce the danger of blowouts and flat tires. Last year, despite our rigorous maintenance program, drivers reported six blowouts.
3. **Record keeping and maintenance.** Smart tires could reduce our maintenance costs considerably. Currently, we use an electric branding iron to mark serial numbers on new tires. Our biggest headache is manually reading those serial numbers, decoding them, and maintaining records to meet safety regulations. Reading such data electronically could save us thousands of dollars in labour.
4. **Theft protection.** The chip can be used to monitor each tire as it leaves or enters the warehouse or yard, thus discouraging theft.

Summary and Action

Specifically, I recommend that you do the following:

- Authorize the special purchase of 24 Goodyear smart tires at $450 each, plus one electronic sensor at $1200.
- Approve a one-year pilot test in our Quebec territory that would equip six trucks with smart tires and track their performance.

Introduces problem briefly

Presents recommendations immediately

Justifies recommendation by explaining product and benefits

Explains recommendation in more detail

Specifies action to be taken

When creating a travel itinerary for a European tour, the organizer prepared a report supporting the inclusion of a greenhouse tour in the schedule. The writer argued not only that the facility was beautiful, but also that tourists can never be rained out. Persuasive justification reports explain fully all the benefits of a recommendation and also anticipate possible reader objections.

- Present the most promising alternative (your recommendation) last.
- Show how the advantages of your recommendation outweigh its disadvantages.
- Summarize your recommendation. If appropriate, specify the action it requires.
- Ask for authorization to proceed, if necessary.

The report, shown in Figure 13.5, is single spaced because that's the company's preference. Some companies prefer the readability of double spacing. Be sure to check with your organization for its preference before printing out your reports.

Feasibility Reports

Feasibility reports examine the practicality and advisability of following a course of action. They answer this question: Will this plan or proposal work? Feasibility reports typically are internal reports written to advise on matters such as consolidating departments, offering a wellness program to employees, or hiring an outside firm to handle a company's accounting or computing operations. These reports may also be written by consultants called in to investigate a problem. The focus in these reports is on the decision: stopping or proceeding with the proposal. Since your role is not to persuade the reader to accept the decision, you'll want to present the decision immediately. In writing feasibility reports, consider these suggestions:

Feasibility reports analyze whether a proposal or plan will work.

- Announce your decision immediately.
- Provide a description of the background and problem necessitating the proposal.
- Discuss the benefits of the proposal.
- Describe the problems that may result.
- Calculate the costs associated with the proposal, if appropriate.
- Show the time frame necessary for implementation of the proposal.

A typical feasibility report presents the decision, background information, benefits, problems, costs, and a schedule.

FIGURE 13.5 **Justification/Recommendation Report: Indirect Pattern** *(continued on the next page)*

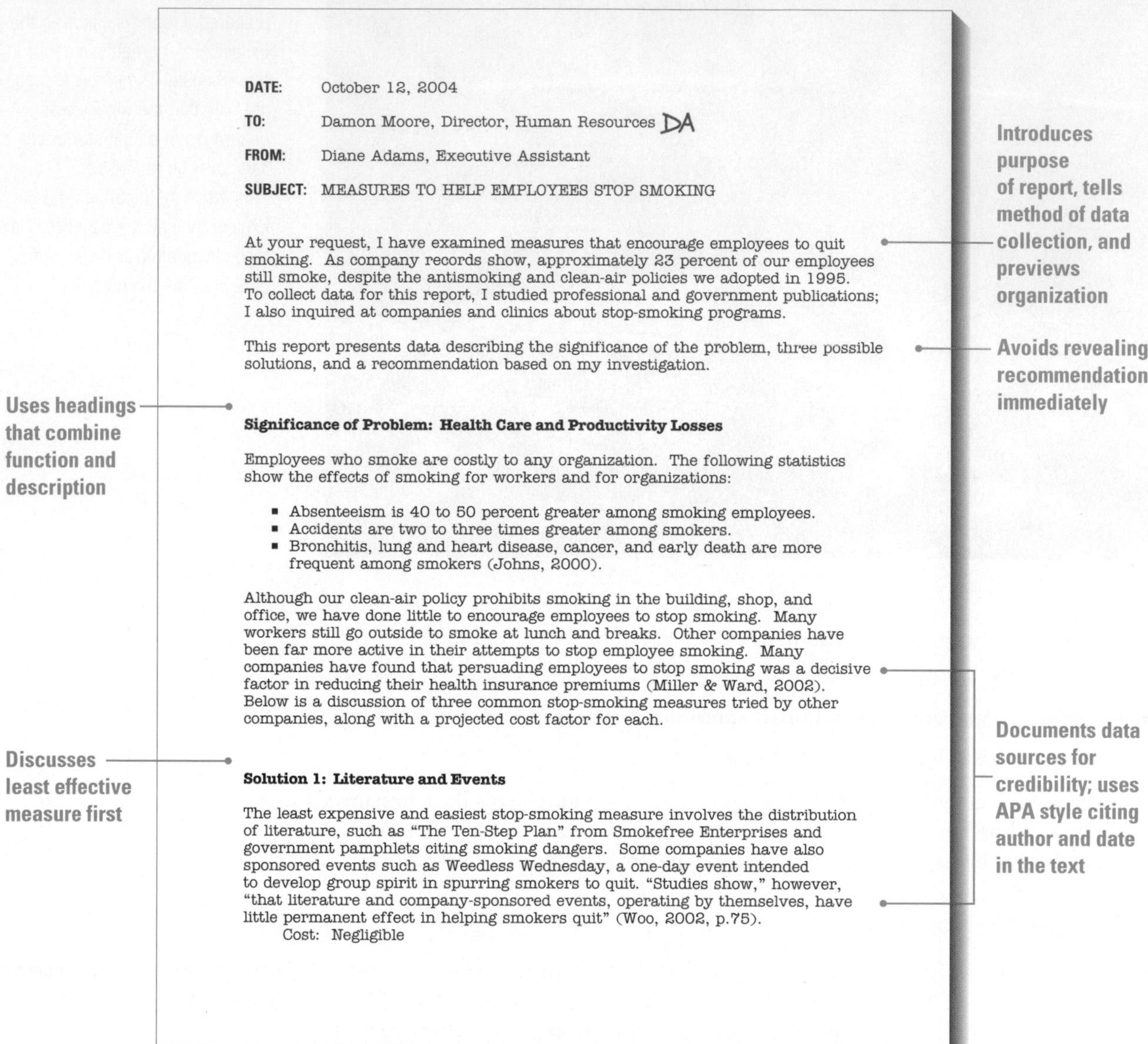

DATE: October 12, 2004

TO: Damon Moore, Director, Human Resources

FROM: Diane Adams, Executive Assistant DA

SUBJECT: MEASURES TO HELP EMPLOYEES STOP SMOKING

At your request, I have examined measures that encourage employees to quit smoking. As company records show, approximately 23 percent of our employees still smoke, despite the antismoking and clean-air policies we adopted in 1995. To collect data for this report, I studied professional and government publications; I also inquired at companies and clinics about stop-smoking programs.

This report presents data describing the significance of the problem, three possible solutions, and a recommendation based on my investigation.

Significance of Problem: Health Care and Productivity Losses

Employees who smoke are costly to any organization. The following statistics show the effects of smoking for workers and for organizations:

- Absenteeism is 40 to 50 percent greater among smoking employees.
- Accidents are two to three times greater among smokers.
- Bronchitis, lung and heart disease, cancer, and early death are more frequent among smokers (Johns, 2000).

Although our clean-air policy prohibits smoking in the building, shop, and office, we have done little to encourage employees to stop smoking. Many workers still go outside to smoke at lunch and breaks. Other companies have been far more active in their attempts to stop employee smoking. Many companies have found that persuading employees to stop smoking was a decisive factor in reducing their health insurance premiums (Miller & Ward, 2002). Below is a discussion of three common stop-smoking measures tried by other companies, along with a projected cost factor for each.

Solution 1: Literature and Events

The least expensive and easiest stop-smoking measure involves the distribution of literature, such as "The Ten-Step Plan" from Smokefree Enterprises and government pamphlets citing smoking dangers. Some companies have also sponsored events such as Weedless Wednesday, a one-day event intended to develop group spirit in spurring smokers to quit. "Studies show," however, "that literature and company-sponsored events, operating by themselves, have little permanent effect in helping smokers quit" (Woo, 2002, p.75).
Cost: Negligible

Introduces purpose of report, tells method of data collection, and previews organization
Avoids revealing recommendation immediately
Uses headings that combine function and description
Documents data sources for credibility; uses APA style citing author and date in the text
Discusses least effective measure first

The feasibility report shown in Figure 13.6 examines the feasibility of a consultant's plan and provides all necessary information: approval, background, benefits, problems, costs, and schedule.

Yardstick Reports

"Yardstick" reports examine problems with two or more solutions. To evaluate the best solution, the writer establishes criteria by which to compare the alternatives. The criteria then act as a standard against which all the alternatives are measured. This approach is effective when companies establish specifications for equipment purchases, and then compare each manufacturer's product with the established specs. The yardstick approach is also effective when exact specifications cannot be estab-

FIGURE 13.5 *(continued)*

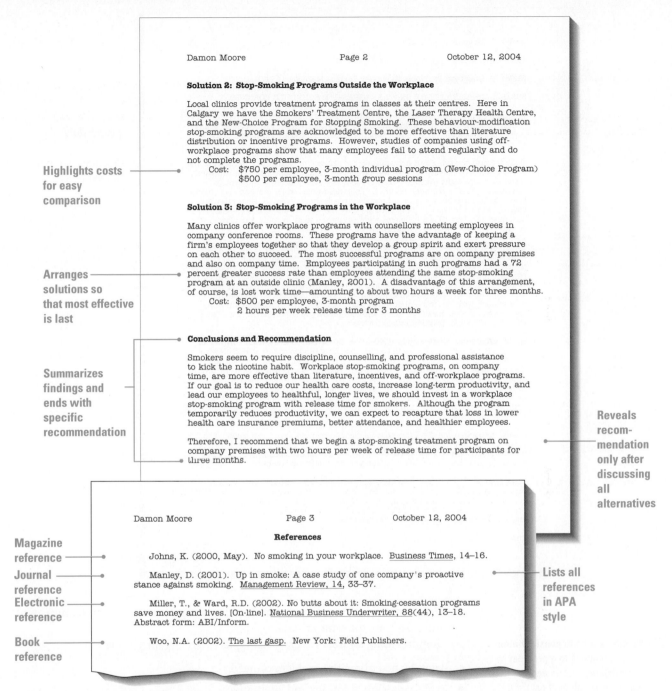

Damon Moore Page 2 October 12, 2004

Solution 2: Stop-Smoking Programs Outside the Workplace

Local clinics provide treatment programs in classes at their centres. Here in Calgary we have the Smokers' Treatment Centre, the Laser Therapy Health Centre, and the New-Choice Program for Stopping Smoking. These behaviour-modification stop-smoking programs are acknowledged to be more effective than literature distribution or incentive programs. However, studies of companies using off-workplace programs show that many employees fail to attend regularly and do not complete the programs.

Cost: $750 per employee, 3-month individual program (New-Choice Program)
$500 per employee, 3-month group sessions

Highlights costs for easy comparison

Solution 3: Stop-Smoking Programs in the Workplace

Many clinics offer workplace programs with counsellors meeting employees in company conference rooms. These programs have the advantage of keeping a firm's employees together so that they develop a group spirit and exert pressure on each other to succeed. The most successful programs are on company premises and also on company time. Employees participating in such programs had a 72 percent greater success rate than employees attending the same stop-smoking program at an outside clinic (Manley, 2001). A disadvantage of this arrangement, of course, is lost work time—amounting to about two hours a week for three months.

Cost: $500 per employee, 3-month program
2 hours per week release time for 3 months

Arranges solutions so that most effective is last

Conclusions and Recommendation

Smokers seem to require discipline, counselling, and professional assistance to kick the nicotine habit. Workplace stop-smoking programs, on company time, are more effective than literature, incentives, and off-workplace programs. If our goal is to reduce our health care costs, increase long-term productivity, and lead our employees to healthful, longer lives, we should invest in a workplace stop-smoking program with release time for smokers. Although the program temporarily reduces productivity, we can expect to recapture that loss in lower health care insurance premiums, better attendance, and healthier employees.

Therefore, I recommend that we begin a stop-smoking treatment program on company premises with two hours per week of release time for participants for three months.

Summarizes findings and ends with specific recommendation

Reveals recommendation only after discussing all alternatives

Damon Moore Page 3 October 12, 2004

References

Johns, K. (2000, May). No smoking in your workplace. Business Times, 14–16.

Manley, D. (2001). Up in smoke: A case study of one company's proactive stance against smoking. Management Review, 14, 33–37.

Miller, T., & Ward, R.D. (2002). No butts about it: Smoking-cessation programs save money and lives. [On-line]. National Business Underwriter, 88(44), 13–18. Abstract form: ABI/Inform.

Woo, N.A. (2002). The last gasp. New York: Field Publishers.

Magazine reference

Journal reference

Electronic reference

Book reference

Lists all references in APA style

FIGURE 13.6 **Feasibility Report**

DATE: November 10, 2004

TO: Shauna Clay-Taylor, Vice President

FROM: Elizabeth W. Webb, Customer Service Manager EWW

SUBJECT: FEASIBILITY OF USING PROGRESSION SCHEDULE FOR CSRs

The plan calling for a progression schedule for our customer service representatives is workable, and I think it could be fully implemented by April 1. This report discusses the background, benefits, problems, costs, and time frame involved in executing the plan.

Background: Training and Advancement Problems for CSR Reps. Because of the many insurance policies and agents we service, new customer service representatives require eight weeks of intensive training. Even after this thorough introduction, CSRs are overwhelmed. They need about eight more months before they feel competent on the job. Once they reach their potential, they often look for other positions in the company because they see few advancement possibilities in customer service. These problems were submitted to an outside consultant, who suggested a CSR progression schedule.

Benefits of Plan: Career Progression and Incremental Training. The proposed plan sets up a schedule of career progression, including these levels: (1) CSR trainee, (2) CSR Level I, (3) CSR Level II, (4) CSR Level III, (5) Senior CSR, and (6) CSR supervisor. This program, which includes salary increments with each step, provides a career ladder and incentives for increased levels of expertise and achievement. The plan also facilitates training. Instead of overloading a new trainee with an initial eight-week training program, we would train CSRs slowly with a combination of classroom and on-the-job experiences. Each level requires additional training and expertise.

Problems of Plan: Difficulty in Writing Job Descriptions and Initial Confusion. One of the biggest problems will be distinguishing the job duties at each level. However, I believe that, with the help of our consultant, we can sort out the tasks and expertise required at each level. Another problem will be determining appropriate salary differentials. Attached is a tentative schedule showing proposed wages at each level. We expect to encounter confusion and frustration in implementing this program at first, particularly in placing our current CSRs within the structure. These are small problems, though, easily outweighed by the plan's advantages.

Costs. Implementing the progression schedule involves two direct costs. The first is the salary of a trainer—about $40 000 a year. The second cost derives from increased salaries of upper-level CSRs, shown on the attached schedule. I believe, however, that the costs involved are within the estimates planned for this project.

Time Frame. Developing job descriptions should take us about three weeks. Preparing a training program will require another three weeks. Once the program is started, I expect a breaking-in period of at least three months. By April 1 the progression schedule will be fully implemented and showing positive results in improved CSR training, service, and retention.

Enclosure

Outlines organization of the report

Reveals decision immediately

Describes problem and background

Evaluates positive and negative aspects of proposal objectively

Presents costs and schedule; omits unnecessary summary

lished. The real advantage to yardstick reports is that alternatives can be measured consistently using the same criteria.

Yardstick reports consider alternative solutions to a problem by establishing criteria against which to weigh options.

Reports using a yardstick approach typically are organized this way:

- Begin by describing the problem or need.
- Explain possible solutions and alternatives.
- Establish criteria for comparing the alternatives; tell how they were selected or developed.
- Discuss and evaluate each alternative in terms of the criteria.
- Draw conclusions and make recommendations.

The report shown in Figure 13.7 compares the three outplacement agencies and recommends one of them.

FIGURE 13.7 **Yardstick Report** *(continued on the next page)*

DATE: April 28, 2004

TO: George O. Dawes, Vice President

FROM: Kelly Smythe, Benefits Administrator KS

SUBJECT: CHOICE OF OUTPLACEMENT SERVICES

Here is the report you requested April 1 investigating the possibility of CompuTech's use of outplacement services. It discusses the problem of counselling services for discharged staff and establishes criteria for selecting an outplacement agency. It then evaluates three prospective agencies and presents a recommendation based on that evaluation.

Introduces purpose and gives overview of report organization

Problem: Counselling Discharged Staff

Discusses background only briefly because readers already know the problem

In an effort to reduce costs and increase competitiveness, CompuTech will begin a program of staff reduction that will involve releasing up to 20 percent of our workforce over the next 12 to 24 months. Many of these employees have been with us for 10 or more years, and they are not being released for performance faults. These employees deserve a severance package that includes counselling and assistance in finding new careers.

Uses dual headings, giving function and description

Solution and Alternatives: Outplacement Agencies

Numerous outplacement agencies offer discharged employees counselling and assistance in locating new careers. This assistance minimizes not only the negative feelings related to job loss but also the very real possibility of litigation. Potentially expensive lawsuits have been lodged against some companies by unhappy employees who felt they were unfairly released.

In seeking an outplacement agency, we should find one that offers advice to the sponsoring company as well as to dischargees. Frankly, many of our managers need help in conducting termination sessions. A suitable outplacement agency should be selected soon so that we can learn about legal termination procedures and also have an agency immediately available when employees are discharged. Here in the metropolitan area, I have located three potential outplacement agencies appropriate to serve our needs: Gray & Associates, Right Access, and Careers Plus.

Announces solution and the alternatives it presents

Establishing Criteria for Selecting Agency

Tells how criteria were selected

In order to choose among the three agencies, I established criteria based on professional articles, discussions with officials at other companies using outplacement agencies, and interviews with agencies. Here are the four groups of criteria I used in evaluating the three agencies:

1. **Counselling services**—including job search advice, résumé help, crisis management, corporate counselling, and availability of full-time counsellors
2. **Secretarial and research assistance**—including availability of secretarial staff, librarian, and personal computers
3. **Reputation**—based on a telephone survey of former clients and listing with a professional association
4. **Costs**—for both group programs and executive services

Creates four criteria to use as yardsticks in evaluating alternatives

Checklist for Writing Analytical Reports

Introduction

Identify the purpose of the report. Explain why the report is being written. For research studies also include the significance, scope, limitations, and methodology of the investigation.

Preview the organization of the report. Especially for long reports, explain to the reader how the report will be organized.

FIGURE 13.7 *(continued on the next page)*

George Dawes Page 2 April 28, 2004

Discussion: Evaluating Agencies by Criteria

Each agency was evaluated using the four criteria just described. Data comparing the first three criteria are summarized in Table 1.

Table 1

A COMPARISON OF SERVICES AND REPUTATIONS FOR THREE LOCAL OUTPLACEMENT AGENCIES

	Gray & Associates	Right Access	Careers Plus
Counselling services			
Résumé advice	Yes	Yes	Yes
Crisis management	Yes	No	Yes
Corporate counselling	Yes	No	No
Full-time counsellors	Yes	No	Yes
Secretarial, research assistance			
Secretarial staff	Yes	Yes	Yes
Librarian, research library	Yes	No	Yes
Personal computers	Yes	No	Yes
Listed by National Association of Career Consultants	Yes	No	Yes
Reputation (telephone survey of former clients)	Excellent	Good	Excellent

Counselling Services

All three agencies offered similar basic counselling services with job-search and résumé advice. They differed, however, in three significant areas.

Right Access does not offer crisis management, a service that puts the discharged employee in contact with a counsellor the same day the employee is released. Experts in the field consider this service especially important to help the dischargee begin "bonding" with the counsellor immediately. Immediate counselling also helps the dischargee through the most traumatic moments of one of life's great disappointments and helps him or her learn how to break the news to family members. Crisis management can be instrumental in reducing lawsuits because dischargees immediately begin to focus on career planning instead of concentrating on their pain and need for revenge. Moreover, Right Access does not employ full-time counsellors; it hires part-timers according to demand. Industry authorities advise against using agencies whose staff members are inexperienced and employed on an "as-needed" basis.

In addition, neither Right Access nor Careers Plus offers regular corporate counselling, which I feel is critical in training our managers to conduct terminal interviews. Careers Plus, however, suggested that it could schedule special workshops if desired.

Secretarial and Research Assistance

Both Gray & Associates and Careers Plus offer complete secretarial services and personal computers. Dischargees have access to staff and equipment to assist them in their job searches. These agencies also provide research libraries, librarians, and databases of company information to help in securing interviews.

Places table close to spot where it is first mentioned

Summarizes complex data in table for easy reading and reference

Highlights the similarities and differences among the alternatives

Does not repeat obvious data from table

Summarize the conclusions and recommendations for receptive audiences. Use the direct pattern only if you have the confidence of the reader.

Findings

Discuss pros and cons. In recommendation/justification reports, evaluate the advantages and disadvantages of each alternative. For unreceptive audiences consider placing the recommended alternative last.

FIGURE 13.7 *(continued)*

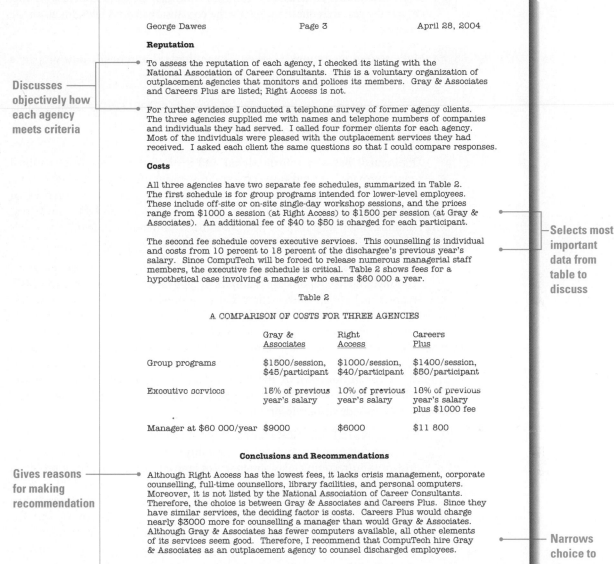

George Dawes Page 3 April 28, 2004

Reputation

To assess the reputation of each agency, I checked its listing with the National Association of Career Consultants. This is a voluntary organization of outplacement agencies that monitors and polices its members. Gray & Associates and Careers Plus are listed; Right Access is not.

For further evidence I conducted a telephone survey of former agency clients. The three agencies supplied me with names and telephone numbers of companies and individuals they had served. I called four former clients for each agency. Most of the individuals were pleased with the outplacement services they had received. I asked each client the same questions so that I could compare responses.

Discusses objectively how each agency meets criteria

Costs

All three agencies have two separate fee schedules, summarized in Table 2. The first schedule is for group programs intended for lower-level employees. These include off-site or on-site single-day workshop sessions, and the prices range from $1000 a session (at Right Access) to $1500 per session (at Gray & Associates). An additional fee of $40 to $50 is charged for each participant.

The second fee schedule covers executive services. This counselling is individual and costs from 10 percent to 18 percent of the dischargee's previous year's salary. Since CompuTech will be forced to release numerous managerial staff members, the executive fee schedule is critical. Table 2 shows fees for a hypothetical case involving a manager who earns $60 000 a year.

Selects most important data from table to discuss

Table 2

A COMPARISON OF COSTS FOR THREE AGENCIES

	Gray & Associates	Right Access	Careers Plus
Group programs	$1500/session, $45/participant	$1000/session, $40/participant	$1400/session, $50/participant
Executive services	15% of previous year's salary	10% of previous year's salary	18% of previous year's salary plus $1000 fee
Manager at $60 000/year	$9000	$6000	$11 800

Conclusions and Recommendations

Although Right Access has the lowest fees, it lacks crisis management, corporate counselling, full-time counsellors, library facilities, and personal computers. Moreover, it is not listed by the National Association of Career Consultants. Therefore, the choice is between Gray & Associates and Careers Plus. Since they have similar services, the deciding factor is costs. Careers Plus would charge nearly $3000 more for counselling a manager than would Gray & Associates. Although Gray & Associates has fewer computers available, all other elements of its services seem good. Therefore, I recommend that CompuTech hire Gray & Associates as an outplacement agency to counsel discharged employees.

Gives reasons for making recommendation

Narrows choice to one agency

✓ **Establish criteria to evaluate alternatives.** In "yardstick" studies, create criteria to use in measuring each alternative consistently.

✓ **Support the findings with evidence.** Supply facts, statistics, expert opinion, survey data, and other proof from which you can draw logical conclusions.

✓ **Organize the findings for logic and readability.** Arrange the findings around the alternatives or the reasons leading to the conclusion. Use headings, enumerations, lists, tables, and graphics to focus emphasis.

Conclusions/Recommendations

 **Draw reasonable conclusions from the findings.** Develop conclusions that answer the research question. Justify the conclusions with highlights from the findings.

 **Make recommendations, if asked.** For multiple recommendations prepare a list. Use action verbs. Explain needed action.

Summary of Learning Objectives

1 **Distinguish between informational and analytical reports.** Informational reports provide data and answer questions without offering recommendations or analysis. They may report sales, routine operations, trips, conferences, or compliance. Analytical reports organize data, draw conclusions, and often make recommendations. They may include justification/recommendation, feasibility, yardstick, and research reports.

2 **Prepare typical informational reports.** Periodic, trip, convention, progress, and investigative reports are examples of typical informational reports. Such reports include an introduction that may preview the report purpose and supply background data if necessary. The body of the report is generally divided into three to five segments that may be organized by time, component, importance, criteria, or convention. The body should include clear headings and may use an informal, conversational style unless the audience expects a more formal tone. The summary or conclusion reviews the main points and discusses what action will follow. The conclusion may offer a final thought, express appreciation, or express willingness to provide further information.

3 **Prepare typical analytical reports.** Typical analytical reports include justification/recommendation reports, feasibility reports, and yardstick reports. Justification/recommendation reports organized directly identify a problem, immediately announce a recommendation or solution, explain and discuss its merits, and summarize the action to be taken. Justification/recommendation reports organized indirectly describe a problem, discuss alternative solutions, prove the superiority of one solution, and ask for authorization to proceed with that solution. Feasibility reports study the advisability of following a course of action. They generally announce the author's proposal immediately. Then they describe the background, advantages and disadvantages, costs, and time frame for implementing the proposal. Yardstick reports compare two or more solutions to a problem by measuring each against a set of established criteria. They usually describe a problem, explain possible solutions, establish criteria for comparing alternatives, evaluate each alternative in terms of the criteria, draw conclusions, and make recommendations. The advantage to yardstick reports is consistency in comparing various alternatives.

CHAPTER REVIEW

1. Name four categories of informational reports. (Obj. 1)
2. Describe periodic reports and what they generally contain. (Obj. 2)
3. Describe situational reports and give two examples. (Obj. 2)
4. What should a progress report include? (Obj. 2)
5. How can the body of an investigative or other informational report be organized? (Obj. 2)
6. What are compliance reports? (Obj.2)
7. Informational reports emphasize facts. What do analytical reports emphasize? (Objs. 1 and 2)
8. When should an analytical report be organized directly? (Obj. 3)
9. How can directness backfire? (Obj. 3)
10. What sequence should a direct recommendation/justification report follow? (Obj. 3)
11. What sequence should an indirect recommendation/justification report follow? (Obj. 3)
12. What is a feasibility report? (Obj. 3)
13. Are feasibility reports usually intended for internal or external audiences? (Obj. 3)
14. What is a yardstick report? (Obj. 3)

CRITICAL THINKING

1. Do most reports flow upward or downward? Why? (Objs. 1–3)
2. Why are large companies more likely to require reports than smaller ones? (Objs. 1–3)
3. If you were doubtful about writing a report directly or indirectly, which pattern would be safer? Why? (Obj. 3)
4. What are the major differences between informational and analytical reports? (Objs. 1 and 3)

ACTIVITIES

13.1 Periodic Reports (Obj. 2)

In a business you know, name five situations that would require periodic reports. If you've had little business experience, imagine a large department store. What kinds of periodic reports would management require of department managers, buyers, and operations staff? Describe how one report might be organized.

13.2 Convention, Conference, and Seminar Reports (Obj. 2)

Select an article from a business publication (such as *Canadian Business, Maclean's* or *The Financial Post Magazine*) describing a convention, conference, or seminar. Imagine that you attended that meeting for your company. Outline a report to your boss describing the meeting.

13.3 Situational and Investigative Reports (Obj. 2)

For each of the following situations, suggest a report type and briefly discuss how the report would be organized.

a. The mail centre could save over $10 000 a year if the company would allow it to invest in reusable nylon mail pouches to deliver customer insurance policies to branch offices.

b. Your manager wants a quick overview of *extranets* (restricted networks that use the Internet to link a company with its customers, suppliers, and other business partners). She knows that other companies are setting up extranets, but she has little knowledge of what they are or how they work. She sees no direct need for the data immediately.

c. Home Depot is considering using shrink wrapping to secure merchandise stored on racks that range from 2 to 5 metres high. Management is concerned about the safety of employees and customers during earthquakes.

d. King Grocery must implement a worker-incentive wage program. This plan would establish standards for warehouse workers and generously reward those who exceed the standard with extra pay and time off. The current wage program pays everyone the same, causing dissension and underachievement. Other wage plans, including a union three-tier system, have drawbacks. Expect management to oppose the worker-incentive plan.

e. Your convention committee has selected a site, set up a tentative program, and is now working on keynote speakers and exhibitors. Report your progress to the organization president.

13.4 Yardstick Report Criteria (Obj. 3)

An employee assistance plan (EAP) is a supplementary benefit offered by many organizations to provide confidential counselling and/or referrals to outside agencies to employees who are facing financial/credit problems, grief, substance abuse, and other similarly personal issues. Assume you are a benefits analyst who has been assigned the task of investigating three EAPs for your company. You must recommend a plan that the company can afford and that will satisfy employees. Your company is facing a 45-percent increase in costs from its current provider. After doing some research, you find two alternatives: a plan that offers choice and is somewhat cheaper than your present carrier, and the possibility of developing your own in-house EAP service. You decide to compare the three plans using the "yardstick" approach. What criteria could you use to compare plans? How would you organize the final report?

13.5 Periodic Report: Filling in the Boss (Obj. 2)

E-Mail

Write a report of your month's accomplishments addressed to your boss. For a job that you currently hold or a previous one, describe your regular activities, discuss irregular events that management should be aware of, and highlight any special needs or problems. Use memo format.

13.6 Progress Report: Heading Toward That Degree (Obj. 2)

Assume you have made an agreement with your parents (or spouse, relative, or significant friend) that you would submit a progress report at this time describing headway toward your educational goal (such as employment, degree/diploma, or certificate). List your specific achievements, and outline what you have left to complete. Prepare a report in letter format.

13.7 Progress Report: Checking In (Obj. 2)

E-Mail

If you are preparing a long report (see Chapter 14), write a progress report informing your instructor of your work. Briefly describe the project (its purpose, scope, limitations, and methodology), work you have completed, work yet to be completed, problems encountered, future activities, and expected completion date. Address the e-mail memo report to your instructor.

13.8 Investigative Report: All You Ever Wanted to Know (Obj. 3)

Web

Investigate a company listed in *100 Best Companies to Work for in Canada* (a periodical that can be accessed through your college's library) for which you might want to work or one in which you are interested. Visit the company's Web site, look at news releases, and review its annual report. Describe its major product, service, or emphasis. Find its ranking, its current stock price (if listed), and its high and low range for the year. Include its profit-to-earnings ratio. Describe its latest marketing plan, promotion, or product. Identify its home office, major officers, and number of employees. Provide a short history of the company. Address a memo report to your professor.

13.9 Investigative Report: Marketing Abroad (Obj. 3)

You have been asked to help prepare a training program for Canadian companies doing business with (select a country other than the U.S.). Collect data from the library, the Internet, and from the country's embassy in Ottawa. Interview on-campus international students. Collect information about formats for written communication, observance of holidays, customary greetings, business ethics, and other topics of interest to businesspeople. For more information about this assignment, see Activity 3.6 in Chapter 3. Remember that your report should promote business, not tourism. Prepare a memo report addressed to Kelly Johnson, editor for the training program materials.

13.10 Investigative Report: Between the Covers (Obj. 3)

As a research assistant in an advertising agency, you must maintain data files about various magazines in which your clients may place ads. Select a business-oriented magazine and examine four to six issues. Collect information about articles (length, seriousness of topics, humour), readability (word, sentence, and paragraph length; formal or informal tone), format and design (colour, white space, glamour), and pictures and graphics. Examine the ads (advertisers, products and services, appeals). Does the magazine accept tobacco and liquor ads? At what audience is the magazine aimed (sex, education, age, income, interests)? Consider other characteristics in which your clients may be interested. Address a memo report to Judy Gold, print media coordinator.

13.11 Justification/Recommendation Report: Time for a Change (Obj. 3)

Critical Thinking

Identify a problem or a procedure that must be changed at your job (such as poor scheduling of employees, outdated equipment, slow order processing, failure to encourage employees to participate fully, restrictive rules, inadequate training, or disappointed customers). Using an indirect pattern, write a recommendation report suggesting one or more ways to solve the problem. Address the memo report to your boss.

13.12 Justification/Recommendation Report: Solving a Campus Problem (Obj. 3)

Team

In groups of three to five, investigate a problem on your campus, such as inadequate parking, slow registration, poor class schedules, inefficient bookstore, weak job-placement program, unrealistic graduation requirements, or lack of internship programs. Within your group develop a solution to the problem. After reviewing persuasive techniques discussed in Chapter 9, write a group or individual justification/recommendation report(s) addressed to the proper campus official. Decide whether to use direct or indirect patterning based on how you expect the reader to react to your recommendation. With your instructor's approval, send the report.

13.13 Feasibility Report: Improving Employee Fitness (Obj. 3)

Critical Thinking

Your company is considering ways to promote employee fitness and morale. Select a possibility that seems reasonable for your company (softball league, bowling teams, basketball league, lunchtime walks, lunchtime fitness speakers and demos, company-sponsored health club memberships, workout room, fitness centre, fitness director, and so on). Assume that your boss has tentatively agreed to one of the programs and has asked you to write a memo report investigating its feasibility.

13.14 Feasibility Report: Reducing, Reusing, and Recycling (Obj. 3)

Critical Thinking

As a management trainee for a large hotel chain, you have been asked to investigate the feasibility of saving energy and reducing waste within the hotel chain. Your task is to learn how other hotels are improving their environmental record. For example, the Bayshore Hotel in Vancouver has special guest rooms with economical fluorescent lighting, bulk shampoo and lotion, water-saving shower heads and toilets, and the option of keeping towels longer than a day. The Hotel Vancouver became the first hotel in North America to replace chlorine in swimming pools with nonstinging baking soda and salt. The Hotel Inter-Continental, with 100 hotels in 47 countries, has prepared a checklist of 134 actions to help employees "reduce, reuse, and recycle." Your task is not to present specifics on implementing a hotel environmental program, but rather to decide whether such a program is feasible. What are the benefits of environmental programs for hotels? Address your memo to Leland Jeffrey, Operations.

13.15 Yardstick Report: Evaluating Equipment (Obj. 3)

Critical Thinking

You recently complained to your boss that you were unhappy with a piece of equipment that you use (printer, computer, copier, fax, or the like). After some thought, the boss decided you were right and told you to go shopping. Compare at least three different manufacturers' models and recommend one. Since the company will be purchasing ten or more units and since several managers must approve the purchase, write a careful report documenting your findings. Establish at least five criteria for comparing the models. Submit a memo report to your boss.

CHAPTER • 14 •

PROPOSALS AND FORMAL REPORTS

LEARNING OBJECTIVES

1. Discuss the components of informal proposals.
2. Discuss the special components in formal proposals.
3. Identify the components of a formal report that precede the introduction.
4. Outline topics that might be covered in the introduction of a formal report.
5. Describe the components of a formal report that follow the introduction.
6. Specify tips that aid writers of formal reports.

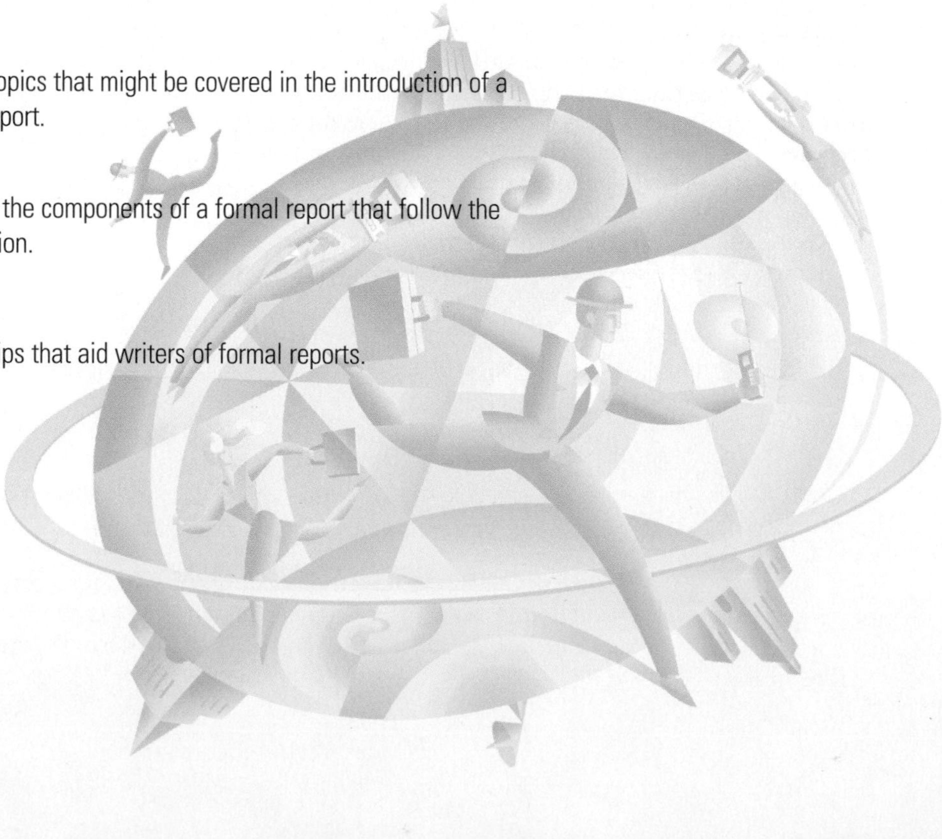

Preparing Formal and Informal Proposals

Proposals are written offers to solve problems, provide services, or sell equipment. Although some proposals are internal, often taking the form of justification and recommendation reports, most proposals are external. External proposals are an important means of generating income for many organizations.

Because proposals are vital to their success, some businesses hire consultants or maintain specialists who do nothing but write proposals. Such proposals typically tell how a problem can be solved, what procedure will be followed, who will do it, how long it will take, and how much it will cost.

Proposals are persuasive offers to solve problems, provide services, or sell equipment.

Proposals may be divided into two categories: solicited or unsolicited. When firms know exactly what they want, they prepare a request for proposal (RFP) specifying their requirements. Government agencies and large companies are likely to use RFPs to solicit competitive bids on their projects. Companies today want to be able to compare "apples with apples," and they also want the protection offered by proposals, which are legal contracts. Unsolicited proposals are written when an individual or firm sees a problem to be solved and offers a proposal to do so. Unsolicited proposals seize opportunities and capitalize on potential.

Government agencies and large companies use requests for proposals (RFPs) to solicit competitive bids on projects.

The most important point to remember about proposals—whether solicited or unsolicited—is that they are sales presentations. They must be persuasive, not merely mechanical descriptions of what you can do. Among other things, you may recall, effective persuasive sales messages (1) emphasize benefits for the reader, (2) "toot your horn" by detailing your expertise and accomplishments, and (3) make it easy for the reader to understand and respond.

Proposals may be informal or formal; they differ primarily in length and format. Notice in Figure 14.1 that formal proposals, described shortly, have many more components than informal proposals.

Components of Informal Proposals

1

Informal proposals may be presented in short (two- to four-page) letters. Sometimes called letter proposals, they may contain six principal components: introduction, background, proposal, staffing, budget, and authorization request. As you can see in Figure 14.1, both informal and formal proposals contain these six basic parts.

Informal proposals may contain an introduction, background information, the proposal, staffing requirements, a budget, and an authorization request.

Introduction. Most proposals begin by briefly explaining the reasons for the proposal and by highlighting the writer's qualifications. To make your introduction more persuasive, you need to provide a "hook" to capture the reader's interest. One proposal expert suggests these possibilities:[1]

- Hint at extraordinary results with details to be revealed shortly.
- Promise low costs or speedy results.
- Mention a remarkable resource (well-known authority, new computer program, well-trained staff) available exclusively to you.
- Identify a serious problem (worry item) and promise a solution, to be explained later.
- Specify a key issue or benefit that you feel is the heart of the proposal.

It's often a good idea to put off writing the proposal introduction until after you have completed other parts. For longer proposals the introduction also describes the scope and limitations of the project, as well as outlining the organization of the material to come.

FIGURE 14.1 **Components in Formal and Informal Proposals**

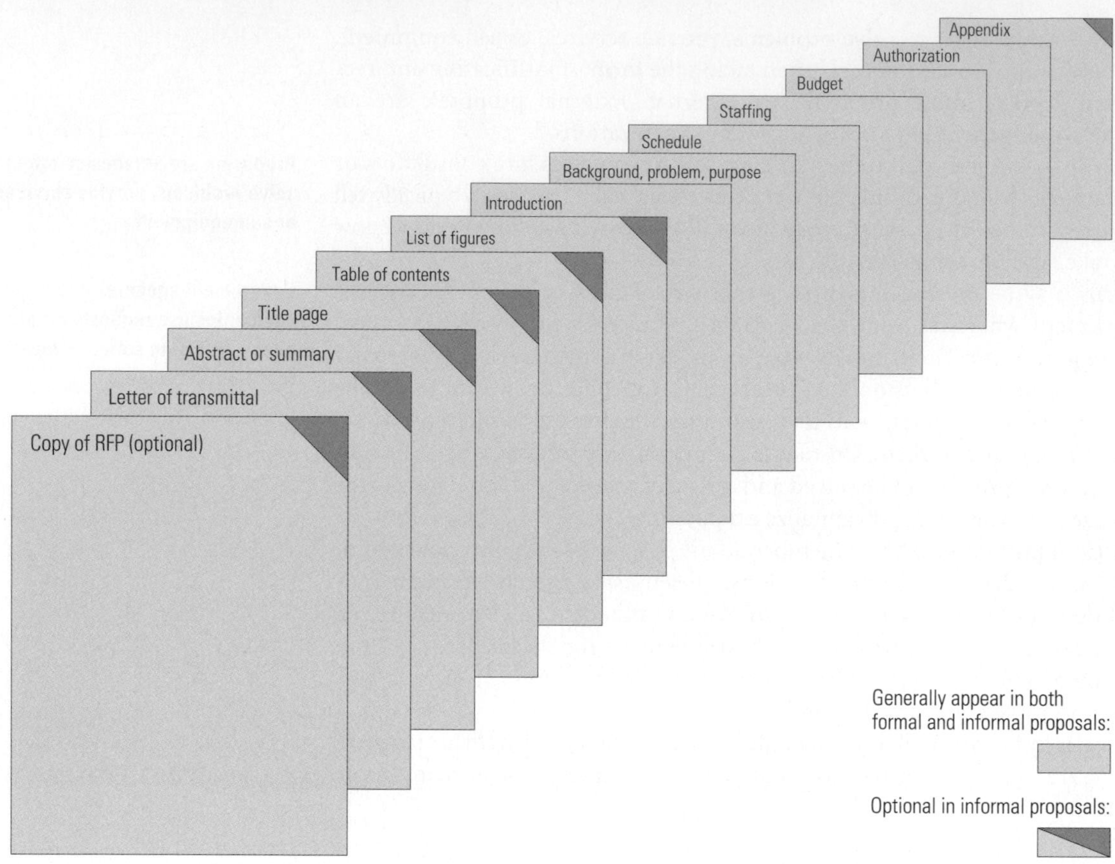

Background, Problem, Purpose. The background section identifies the problem and discusses the goals or purposes of the project. In an unsolicited proposal your goal is to convince the reader that a problem exists. Thus, you must present the problem in detail, discussing such factors as monetary losses, failure to comply with government regulations, or loss of customers. In a solicited proposal your aim is to persuade the reader that you understand the problem completely. Thus, if you are responding to an RFP, this means repeating its language.

The actual proposal section must give enough information to secure the contract but not so much detail that the services are no longer needed.

Proposal, Plan, Schedule. In the proposal section itself, you should discuss your plan for solving the problem. In some proposals this is tricky because you want to disclose enough of your plan to secure the contract without giving away so much information that your services aren't needed. Without specifics, though, your proposal has little chance, so you must decide how much to reveal. Tell what you propose to do and how it will benefit the reader. Remember, too, that a proposal is a sales presentation. Sell your methods, product, and "deliverables"—items that will be left with the client. In this section some writers specify how the project will be managed and how its progress will be audited. Most writers also include a schedule of activities or timetable showing when events take place.

Staffing. The staffing section of a proposal describes the credentials and expertise of the project leaders. It may also identify the size and qualifications of the support staff, along with other resources such as computer facilities and special programs for analyzing statistics. The staffing section is a good place to endorse and promote your staff.

Budget. A central item in most proposals is the budget, a list of proposed project costs. You need to prepare this section carefully because it represents a contract; you can't raise the price later—even if your costs increase. You can—and should—protect yourself with a deadline for acceptance. In the budget section some writers itemize hours and costs; others present a total sum only. Your analysis of the project will help you decide what kind of budget to prepare.

Because a proposal is a legal contract, the budget must be carefully researched.

Authorization Request. Informal proposals often close with a request for approval or authorization. In addition, the closing should remind the reader of key benefits and motivate action. It might also include a deadline date beyond which the offer is invalid. In some organizations, authorization to proceed is not part of the proposal. Instead, it is usually discussed after the customer has received the proposal. In this way the customer and the sales account manager are able to negotiate terms before a formal agreement is drawn.

Special Components of Formal Proposals

2

Formal proposals differ from informal proposals not only in style but also in size and format. Formal proposals respond to big projects and may range from 5 to 200 or more pages. To facilitate comprehension and reference, they are organized into many parts, as shown in Figure 14.1. In addition to the six basic components just described, formal proposals may contain some or all of the following front and end parts.

Formal proposals might also contain a copy of the RFP, a letter of transmittal, an abstract, a title page, a table of contents, a list of figures, and an appendix.

Copy of RFP. A copy of the RFP may be included in the opening parts of a formal proposal. Large organizations may have more than one RFP circulating, and identification is necessary.

Letter of Transmittal. A letter of transmittal, usually bound inside formal proposals, addresses the person who is designated to receive the proposal or who will make the final decision. The letter describes how you learned about the problem or confirms that the proposal responds to the enclosed RFP. This persuasive letter briefly presents the major features and benefits of your proposal. Here, you should assure the reader that you are authorized to make the bid and mention the time limit for which the bid stands. You may also offer to provide additional information and ask for action, if appropriate.

Abstract or Executive Summary. An abstract is a brief summary (typically one page) of a proposal's highlights intended for specialists or for technical readers. An executive summary also reviews the proposal's highlights, but it is written for managers and so should be less technically oriented. Formal proposals may contain one or both summaries.

An abstract summarizes a proposal's highlights for specialists; an executive summary does so for managers.

Title Page. The title page includes the following items, generally in this order: title of proposal, name of client organization, RFP number or other announcement, date of submission, author's name, and/or his or her organization.

Table of Contents. Because most proposals don't contain an index, the table of contents becomes quite important. Tables of contents should include all headings and their beginning page numbers. Items that appear before the contents (copy of RFP, letter of transmittal, abstract, and title page) typically are not listed in the contents. However, any appendixes should be listed.

List of Figures. Proposals with many tables and figures often contain a list of figures. This list includes each figure or table title and its page number. If you have just a few figures or tables, however, you may omit this list.

Appendix. Ancillary material of interest to some readers goes in appendixes. Appendix A might include résumés of the principal investigators or testimonial letters. Appendix B might include examples or a listing of previous projects. Other appendixes could include audit procedures, technical graphics, or professional papers cited in the body of the proposal.

Proposals in the past were always paper-based and delivered by mail or special messenger. Today, however, companies increasingly prefer *online proposals.* Receiving companies may transmit the electronic proposal to all levels of management without ever printing a page, thus appealing to many environmentally conscious organizations.

Well-written proposals win contracts and business for companies and individuals. Many companies depend entirely on proposals to generate their income, so proposal writing becomes critical. For more information about industry standards and resources, visit the Web site of the Association of Proposal Management Professionals **<www.apmp.org>**.

Another form of proposal is a business plan. Entrepreneurs who want to start a business or expand an existing business often must ask for funding. To secure financial backing, these budding businesspeople write plans to submit to potential backers. To learn more about preparing a business plan, see the accompanying Career Coach box.

Checklist for Writing Proposals

Introduction

- ✓ **Indicate the purpose.** Specify why the proposal is being made.
- ✓ **Develop a persuasive "hook."** Suggest excellent results, low costs, or exclusive resources. Identify a serious problem or name a key issue or benefit.

Background, Problem

- ✓ **Provide necessary background.** Discuss the significance of the proposal and its goals or purposes.
- ✓ **Introduce the problem.** For unsolicited proposals convince the reader that a problem exists. For solicited proposals show that you fully understand the problem and its ramifications.

Proposal, Plan

- ✓ **Explain the proposal.** Present your plan for solving the problem or meeting the need.

CAREER COACH

PREPARING AN EFFECTIVE BUSINESS PLAN

Let's say you want to start your own business. Unless you can count on the Bank of Mom and Dad, you will need financial backing (called *venture capital*). A business plan is critical for securing venture capital support. Such a plan also ensures that you have done your homework and know what you are doing in launching your business. It provides you with a detailed road map to chart a course to success. Here are suggestions for preparing an effective business plan:

- **Letter of transmittal and/or executive summary.** Explain your reason for writing. Provide your name, address, and telephone number, along with contact information for all principals. Describe your business concisely, summarize the reasons it will succeed, introduce the parts of the following plan, and ask for support.
- **Table of contents.** List the page numbers and topics included in your plan.
- **Company description.** Identify the form of your business (proprietorship, partnership, or corporation) and its business type (merchandising, manufacturing, or service). For existing companies, describe the company's founding, growth, sales, and profit. For start-ups, explain why the business will be profitable.
- **Product/service description.** In jargon-free language, explain what you are providing, how it will benefit customers, and why it is better than existing products or services.
- **Market analysis.** Discuss market characteristics, trends, projected growth, customer behaviour, complementary products and services, and barriers to entry. Identify your customers and how you will attract, hold, and increase your market share. Discuss the strengths and weaknesses of your direct and indirect competitors.
- **Operations and management.** Explain specifically how you will run your business, including location, equipment, personnel, and management. Highlight experienced and well-trained members of the management team and your advisors.
- **Financial analysis.** Outline a realistic start-up budget that includes fees for legal/professional services, occupancy, licences/permits, equipment, insurance, supplies, advertising/promotions, salaries/wages, accounting, income, and utilities. Also present an operating budget that projects costs for personnel, insurance, rent, depreciation, loan payments, salaries, taxes, repairs, and so on. Explain how much money you have, how much you will need to start up, and how much you will need to stay in business.
- **Appendixes.** Provide necessary extras such as managers' résumés, promotional materials, and product photos.

✓ **Discuss plan management and evaluation.** If appropriate, tell how the plan will be implemented and evaluated.

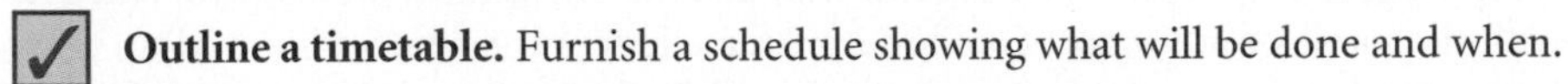

✓ **Outline a timetable.** Furnish a schedule showing what will be done and when.

Staffing

✓ **Promote the qualifications of your staff.** Explain the specific credentials and expertise of the key personnel for the project.

✓ **Mention special resources or equipment.** Show how your support staff and resources are superior to those of the competition.

Budget

 **Show project costs.** For most projects itemize costs. Remember, however, that proposals are contracts.

 **Include a deadline.** Here or in the conclusion present a date beyond which the bid figures are no longer valid.

Authorization

 **Ask for approval.** Make it easy for the reader to authorize the project (for example, *Sign and return the duplicate copy*).

Writing Formal Reports

Formal reports discuss the results of a process of thorough investigation and analysis.

Formal reports are similar to formal proposals in length, organization, and serious tone. Instead of making an offer, however, formal reports represent the end product of thorough investigation and analysis. They present ordered information to decision makers in business, industry, government, and education. In many ways formal reports are extended versions of the analytical business reports presented in Chapter 13. Figure 14.2 shows the components of typical formal reports, their normal sequence, and parts that might be omitted in informal reports.

Components of Formal Reports

A number of front and end items lengthen formal reports but enhance their professional tone and serve their multiple audiences. Formal reports may be read by many levels of managers, along with technical specialists and financial consultants. Therefore, breaking a long, formal report into small segments makes its information more accessible and easier to understand for all readers. These segments are discussed here and also illustrated in the model report shown later in the chapter (Figure 14.3). This analytical report studies the recycling program at West Coast College and makes recommendations for improving its operation.

Like proposals, formal reports are divided into many segments to make information comprehensible and accessible.

Cover. Formal reports are usually enclosed in vinyl or heavy paper binders to protect the pages and to give a professional, finished appearance. Some companies have binders imprinted with their name and logo. The title of the report may appear through a cut-out window or may be applied with an adhesive label. Good stationery and office supply stores usually stock an assortment of report binders and labels.

Title Page. A report title page, as illustrated in the Figure 14.3 model report, begins with the name of the report typed in uppercase letters (no underscore and no quotation marks). Next comes *Presented to* (or *Submitted to*) and the name, title, and organization of the individual receiving the report. Lower on the page is *Prepared by* (or *Submitted by*) and the author's name plus any necessary identification. The last item on the title page is the date of submission. All items after the title are typed in a combination of upper- and lowercase letters.

Letter or Memo of Transmittal. Generally written on organization stationery, a letter or memorandum of transmittal introduces a formal report. You will recall that

FIGURE 14.2 **Components in Formal and Informal Reports**

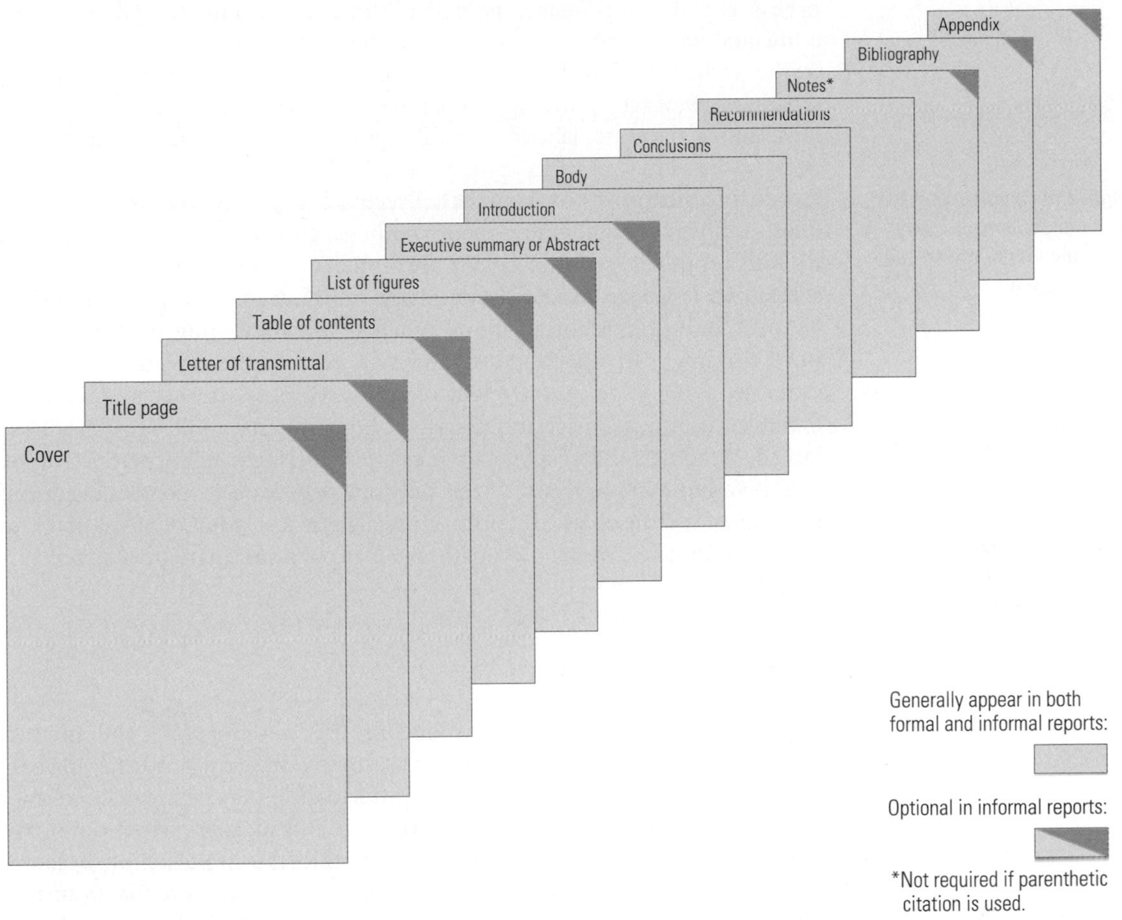

letters are sent to outsiders and memos to insiders. A transmittal letter or memo follows the direct pattern and is usually less formal than the report itself (for example, the letter or memo may use contractions and the first-person pronouns *I* and *we*). The transmittal letter or memo typically (1) announces the topic of the report and tells how it was authorized; (2) briefly describes the project; (3) highlights the report's findings, conclusions, and recommendations, if the reader is expected to be supportive; and (4) closes with appreciation for the assignment, instruction for the reader's follow-up actions, acknowledgment of help from others, or offers of assistance in answering questions. If a report is going to different readers, a special transmittal letter or memo should be prepared for each, anticipating what each reader needs to know in using the report.

A letter or memo of transmittal gives a personalized overview of a formal report.

Table of Contents. The table of contents shows the headings in a report and their initial page numbers. It gives an overview of the report topics and helps readers locate them. You should wait to prepare the table of contents until after you've completed the report. For short reports you should include all headings. For longer reports you might want to list only first- and second-level headings. Leaders (spaced or unspaced dots) help guide the eye from the heading to the page number. Items may be indented in outline form or typed flush with the left margin.

List of Figures. For reports with several figures or illustrations, you may wish to include a list of figures to help readers locate them. This list may appear on the same page as the table of contents, space permitting. For each figure or illustration, include a title and page number. Some writers distinguish between tables and all other illustrations, which are called figures. If you make this distinction, you should also prepare separate lists of tables and figures. Because the model report in Figure 14.3 has few illustrations, the writer labeled them all "figures," a method that simplifies numbering.

The length and complexity of the abstract or executive summary depend on the length of and audience for the report.

Executive Summary or Abstract. Executives and other readers appreciate a summary or abstract highlighting report findings, conclusions, and recommendations. As with proposals, report abstracts are aimed at technical experts and may contain specialized language; executive summaries concentrate on what management needs to know, omitting technical jargon. Whether you are writing an abstract or an executive summary, its length and complexity will be determined by the report. For example, a 100-page report might require a 10-page summary. A 10-page report might need only a 1-page summary—or no summary at all. Longer abstracts may include headings and graphics to adequately highlight main points. Although the executive summary in Figure 14.3 is only one page long, it includes headings to help the reader see the main divisions immediately. Let your organization's practices guide you in determining the length and form of a summary or abstract.

The Introduction

4 Formal reports begin with an introduction that sets the scene and announces the subject. Because they contain many parts serving different purposes, formal reports have a degree of redundancy. The same information may be included in the letter of transmittal, summary, and introduction. To avoid sounding repetitious, try to present the data slightly differently. But don't skip the introduction because you've included some of its information elsewhere. You can't be sure that your reader saw the information earlier. A good report introduction typically covers the following elements, although not necessarily in this order:

- **Background.** Describe events leading up to the problem or need.
- **Problem or purpose.** Explain the report topic and specify the problem or need that motivated the report.
- **Significance.** Tell why the topic is important. You may wish to quote experts or cite newspapers, journals, books, and other secondary sources to establish the importance of the topic.
- **Scope.** Clarify the boundaries of the report, defining what will be included or excluded.
- **Organization.** Launch readers by giving them a road map that previews the structure of the report.

Beyond these minimal introductory elements, consider adding any of the following information that is relevant for your readers:

- **Authorization.** Identify who commissioned the report. If no letter of transmittal is included, also tell why, when, by whom, and to whom the report was written.
- **Literature review.** Summarize what other authors and researchers have published on this topic, especially for academic and scientific reports.

- **Sources and methods.** Describe your secondary sources (periodicals, books, databases). Also explain how you collected primary data, including survey size, sample design, and statistical programs used.
- **Definitions of key terms.** Define words that may be unfamiliar to the audience. Also define terms with special meanings, such as *small business* when it specifically means businesses with fewer than 30 employees.

Components Following the Introduction

5

While the introduction provides an overview for the reader, the substance of the report is contained in the body, the conclusions, and the recommendations.

Body. The principal section in a formal report is the body. It discusses, analyzes, interprets, and evaluates the research findings or solution to the initial problem. This is where you show the evidence that justifies your conclusions. Organize the body into main categories following your original outline or using one of the patterns described earlier (such as time, component, importance, criteria, or convention).

Although we refer to this section as the *body,* it doesn't carry that heading. Instead, it contains clear headings that explain each major section. Headings may be functional or talking. Functional heads (such as *Results of the Survey, Analysis of Findings,* or *Discussion*) help readers identify the purpose of the section but don't reveal what's in it. Such headings are useful for routine reports or for sensitive topics that may upset readers. Talking heads (for example, *Recycling Habits of Campus Community*) are more informative and interesting, but they don't help readers see the organization of the report. The model report in Figure 14.3 uses functional heads for organizational sections requiring identification (*Introduction, Conclusions,* and *Recommendations*) and talking heads to divide the body.

Conclusions. This important section tells what the findings mean, particularly in terms of solving the original problem. Some writers prefer to intermix their conclusions with the analysis of the findings—instead of presenting the conclusions separately. Other writers place the conclusions before the body so that busy readers can examine the significant information immediately. Still others combine the conclusions and recommendations. Most writers, though, present the conclusions after the body because readers expect this structure. In long reports this section may include a summary of the findings. To improve comprehension, you may present the conclusions in a numbered or bulleted list.

Recommendations. When requested, you should submit recommendations that make precise suggestions for actions to solve the report problem. Recommendations are most helpful when they are practical and reasonable. Naturally, they should evolve from the findings and conclusions. Don't introduce new information in the conclusions or recommendations. As with conclusions, the position of recommendations is somewhat flexible. They may be combined with conclusions, or they may be presented before the body, especially when the audience is eager and supportive. Generally, though, in formal reports they come last.

The recommendations section of a formal report offers specific suggestions for solving a problem.

Recommendations require an appropriate introductory sentence, such as *The findings and conclusions in this study support the following recommendations.* When making many recommendations, number them and phrase each as a command, such as *Begin an employee fitness program with a workout room available five days a week.* If appropriate, add information describing how to implement each recommendation. Some reports include a timetable describing the who, what, when, where, and how for putting each recommendation into operation.

Appendix. Incidental or supporting materials belong in appendixes at the end of a formal report. These materials are relevant to some readers but not to all. Appendixes may include survey forms, copies of other reports, tables of data, computer printouts, and related correspondence. If additional appendixes are necessary, they would be named *Appendix A, Appendix B,* and so forth.

The bibliography section of a formal report identifies sources of ideas mentioned in the report.

Works Cited, References, or Bibliography. Readers look in the bibliography section to locate the sources of ideas mentioned in a report. Your method of report documentation determines how this section is developed. If you use the MLA referencing format, all citations would be listed alphabetically in the "Works Cited." If you use the APA format, your list would be called "References." With the *Chicago Manual of Style* format, you would list your references in the "Bibliography." Regardless of the format, you must include the author, title, publication, date of publication, page number, and other significant data for all ideas or quotations used in your report. For electronic references, include the preceding information plus a description of the electronic address or path leading to the citation. Also include the date on which you located the electronic reference. To see electronic and other citations, examine the list of references at the end of Figure 14.3. Appendix B contains additional documentation information.

Final Writing Tips

6

Formal reports require careful attention to all phases of the 3-×-3 writing process.

Formal reports are not undertaken lightly. They involve considerable effort in all three phases of writing, beginning with analysis of the problem and anticipation of the audience. Researching the data, organizing it into a logical presentation, and composing the first draft make up the second phase of writing. Revising, proofreading, and evaluating are the third phase. Although everyone approaches the writing process somewhat differently, the following tips offer advice in problem areas faced by most formal report writers.

Smart report writers allow themselves plenty of time, research thoroughly, draw up a useful outline, and work on a computer.

Effective formal reports maintain parallelism in verb tenses, and use the active voice.

- **Allow sufficient time to plan, outline, write and edit your report.**
- **Finish data collection before you begin writing.** For reports based on survey data, compile the tables and figures first.
- **Work from a good outline.**
- **Provide a proper writing environment.**
- **Use a computer and resave your work often.**
- **Write rapidly; revise later.**
- **Save difficult sections.** If some sections are harder to write than others, save them until you've developed confidence and rhythm working on easier topics.
- **Be consistent in verb tense.**
- **Generally avoid *I* and *we* and write in the third person.**
- **Let the first draft sit for a period of time** and return to it with the expectation of revising and improving it.

FIGURE 14.3 **Model Formal Report with MLA Citation Style**

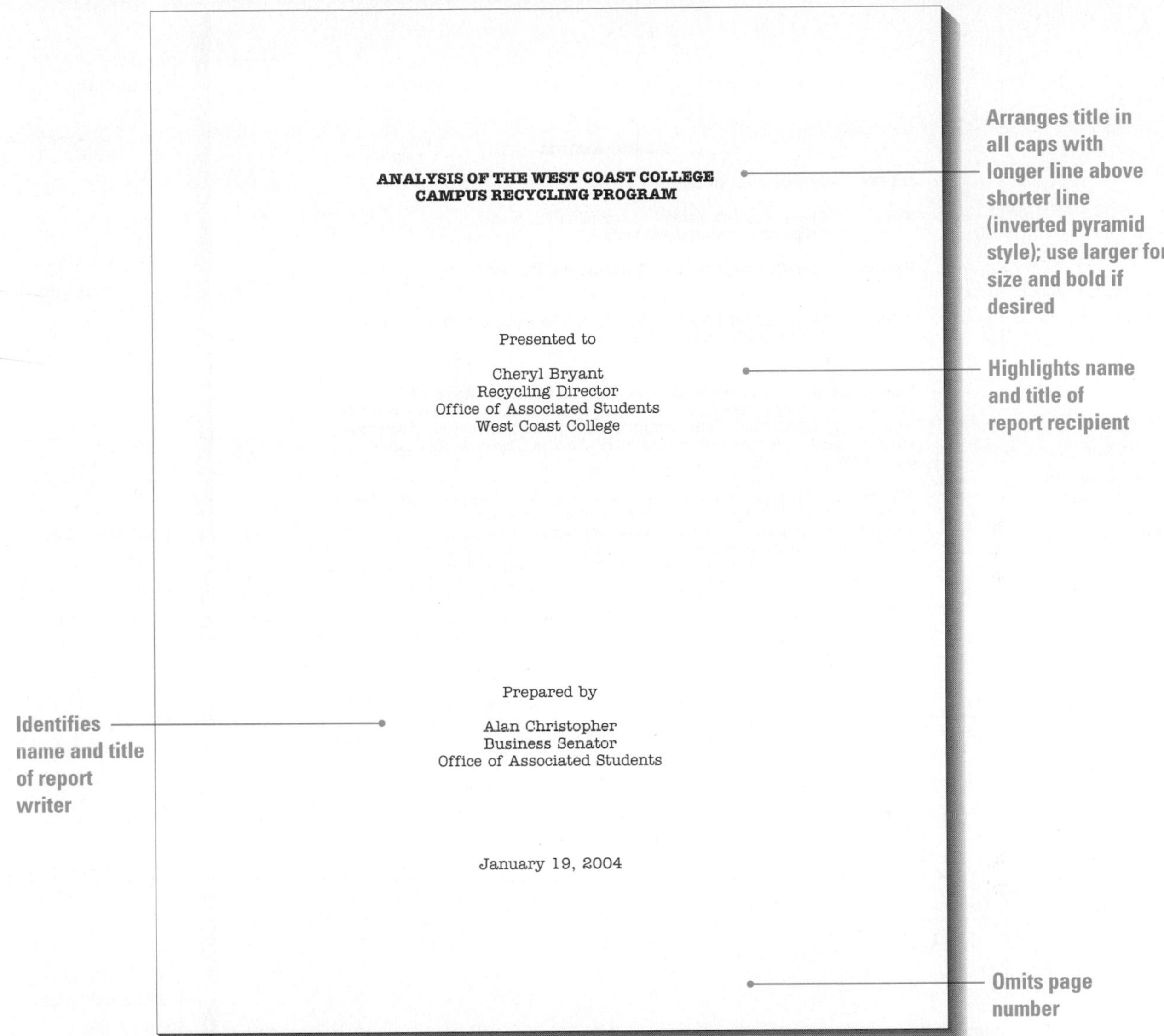

ANALYSIS OF THE WEST COAST COLLEGE
CAMPUS RECYCLING PROGRAM
Presented to
Cheryl Bryant
Recycling Director
Office of Associated Students
West Coast College
Prepared by
Alan Christopher
Business Senator
Office of Associated Students
January 19, 2004
Arranges title in all caps with longer line above shorter line (inverted pyramid style); use larger font size and bold if desired
Highlights name and title of report recipient
Identifies name and title of report writer
Omits page number

Alan arranges the title page so that the amount of space above the title is equal to the space below the date. If a report is to be bound on the left, move the left margin and centre point 1/4 inch to the right. Notice that no page number appears on the title page, although it is counted as page i.

If you use scalable fonts, word processing capability, or a laser printer to enhance your report and title page, be careful to avoid anything unprofessional (such as too many type fonts, oversized print, and inappropriate graphics).

FIGURE 14.3 *(continued)*

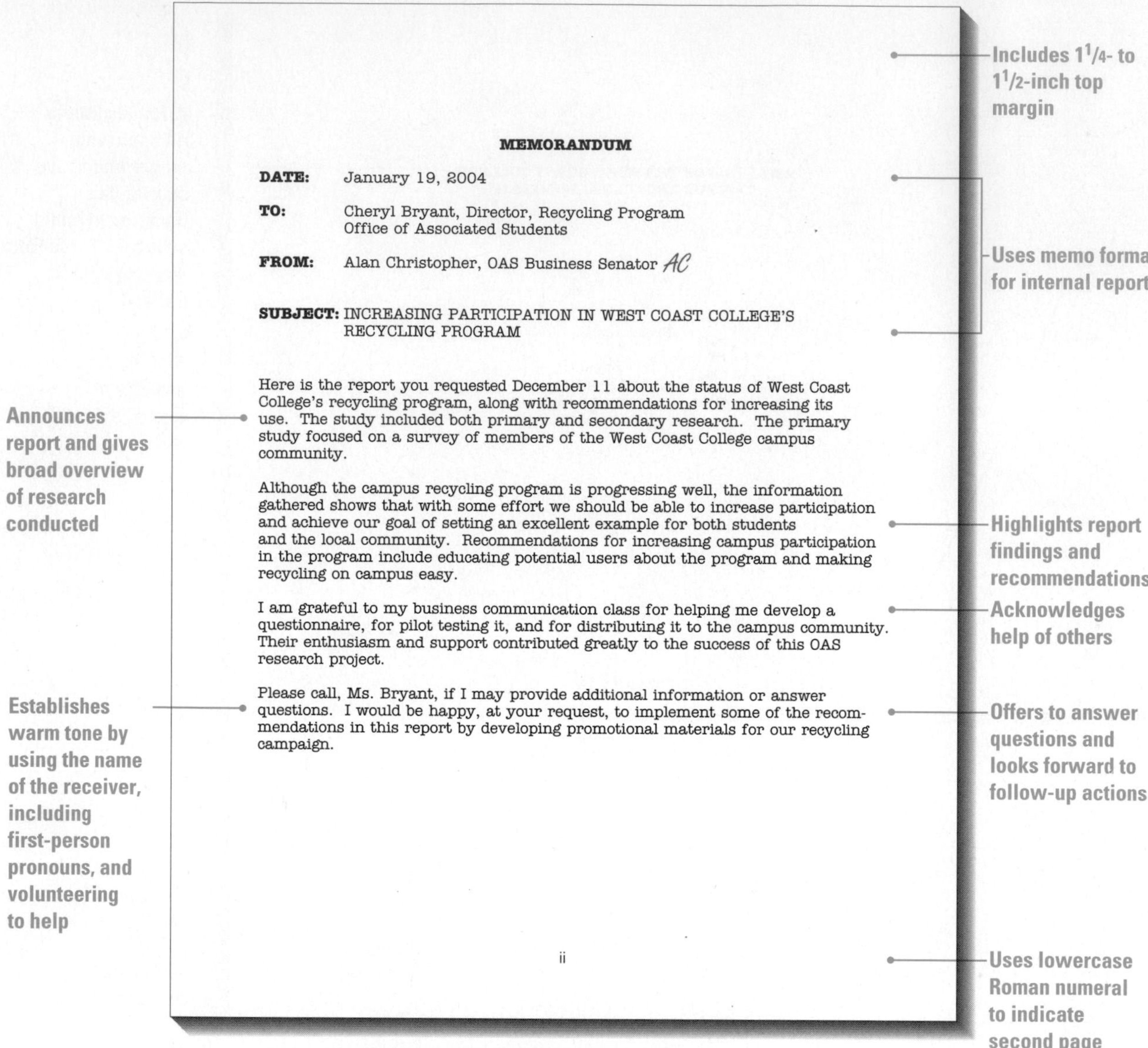

MEMORANDUM

DATE: January 19, 2004

TO: Cheryl Bryant, Director, Recycling Program
Office of Associated Students

FROM: Alan Christopher, OAS Business Senator *AC*

SUBJECT: INCREASING PARTICIPATION IN WEST COAST COLLEGE'S RECYCLING PROGRAM

Here is the report you requested December 11 about the status of West Coast College's recycling program, along with recommendations for increasing its use. The study included both primary and secondary research. The primary study focused on a survey of members of the West Coast College campus community.

Although the campus recycling program is progressing well, the information gathered shows that with some effort we should be able to increase participation and achieve our goal of setting an excellent example for both students and the local community. Recommendations for increasing campus participation in the program include educating potential users about the program and making recycling on campus easy.

I am grateful to my business communication class for helping me develop a questionnaire, for pilot testing it, and for distributing it to the campus community. Their enthusiasm and support contributed greatly to the success of this OAS research project.

Please call, Ms. Bryant, if I may provide additional information or answer questions. I would be happy, at your request, to implement some of the recommendations in this report by developing promotional materials for our recycling campaign.

ii

Includes $1^1/_4$- to $1^1/_2$-inch top margin
Uses memo format for internal report
Announces report and gives broad overview of research conducted
Highlights report findings and recommendations
Acknowledges help of others
Establishes warm tone by using the name of the receiver, including first-person pronouns, and volunteering to help
Offers to answer questions and looks forward to follow-up actions
Uses lowercase Roman numeral to indicate second page

Because this report is being submitted within his own organization, Alan uses a memorandum of transmittal. Formal organization reports submitted to outsiders would carry a letter of transmittal printed on company stationery.

The margins for the transmittal should be the same as for the report, about $1^1/_4$ inches on all sides. If a report is to be bound, add an extra $^1/_4$ inch to the left margin.

FIGURE 14.3 *(continued)*

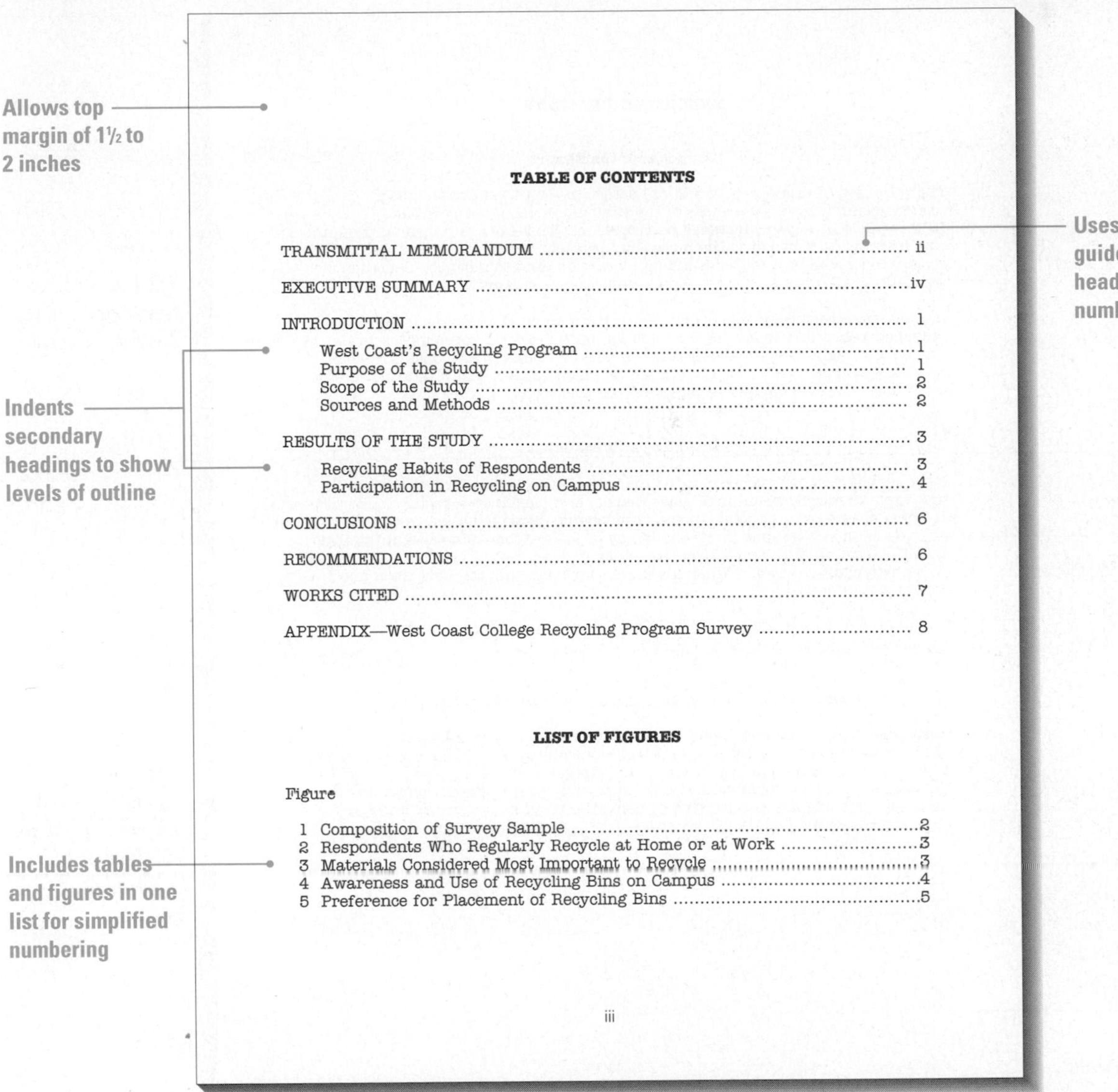

Allows top margin of 1½ to 2 inches

Uses leaders to guide eye from heading to page number

Indents secondary headings to show levels of outline

Includes tables and figures in one list for simplified numbering

TABLE OF CONTENTS

TRANSMITTAL MEMORANDUM ii

EXECUTIVE SUMMARY iv

INTRODUCTION 1

West Coast's Recycling Program 1
Purpose of the Study 1
Scope of the Study 2
Sources and Methods 2

RESULTS OF THE STUDY 3

Recycling Habits of Respondents 3
Participation in Recycling on Campus 4

CONCLUSIONS 6

RECOMMENDATIONS 6

WORKS CITED 7

APPENDIX—West Coast College Recycling Program Survey 8

LIST OF FIGURES

Figure

1 Composition of Survey Sample 2
2 Respondents Who Regularly Recycle at Home or at Work 3
3 Materials Considered Most Important to Recycle 3
4 Awareness and Use of Recycling Bins on Campus 4
5 Preference for Placement of Recycling Bins 5

iii

Because Alan's table of contents and list of figures are small, he combines them on one page. Notice that he uses all caps for the titles of major report parts and a combination of upper- and lowercase letters for first-level headings. This duplicates the style within the report.

Advanced word processing capabilities enable you to generate a table of contents automatically, with leaders and accurate page numbering—no matter how many times you revise!

FIGURE 14.3 *(continued)*

EXECUTIVE SUMMARY

Purposes of the Report

The purposes of this report are to (1) determine the West Coast College campus community's awareness of the campus recycling program and (2) recommend ways to increase participation. West Coast's recycling program was intended to respond to the increasing problem of waste disposal, to fulfil its social responsibility as an educational institution, and to meet the demands of legislation requiring individuals and organizations to recycle.

A questionnaire survey was conducted to learn about the campus community's recycling habits and to assess participation in the current recycling program. A total of 220 individuals responded to the survey. Since West Coast College's recycling program includes only aluminum, glass, paper, and plastic at this time, these were the only materials considered in this study.

Tells purpose of report and briefly describes survey

Recycling at West Coast

Summarizes findings of survey

Most survey respondents recognized the importance of recycling and stated that they do recycle aluminum, glass, paper, and plastic on a regular basis either at home or at work. However, most respondents displayed a low level of awareness and use of the on-campus program. Many of the respondents were unfamiliar with the location of the bins around campus and, therefore, had not participated in the recycling program. Other responses indicated that the bins were not conveniently located.

Draws primary conclusion

The results of this study show that more effort is needed to increase participation in the campus recycling program.

Recommendations for Increasing Recycling Participation

Recommendations for increasing participation in the program include (1) relocating the recycling bins for greater visibility, (2) developing incentive programs to gain the participation of individuals and on-campus student groups, (3) training student volunteers to give on-campus presentations explaining the need for recycling and the benefits of using the recycling program, and (4) increasing advertising about the program.

Concisely enumerates four recommendations using parallel (balanced) phrasing

Numbers pages that precede the body with lowercase Roman numerals

iv

For readers who want a quick picture of the report, the executive summary presents its most important elements. Alan has divided the summary into three sections for increased readability.

Executive summaries generally contain little jargon or complex statistics; they condense what management needs to know about a problem and the study's findings about the problem. Report abstracts, sometimes written in place of summaries, tend to be more technical and are aimed at specialists rather than management.

FIGURE 14.3 *(continued)*

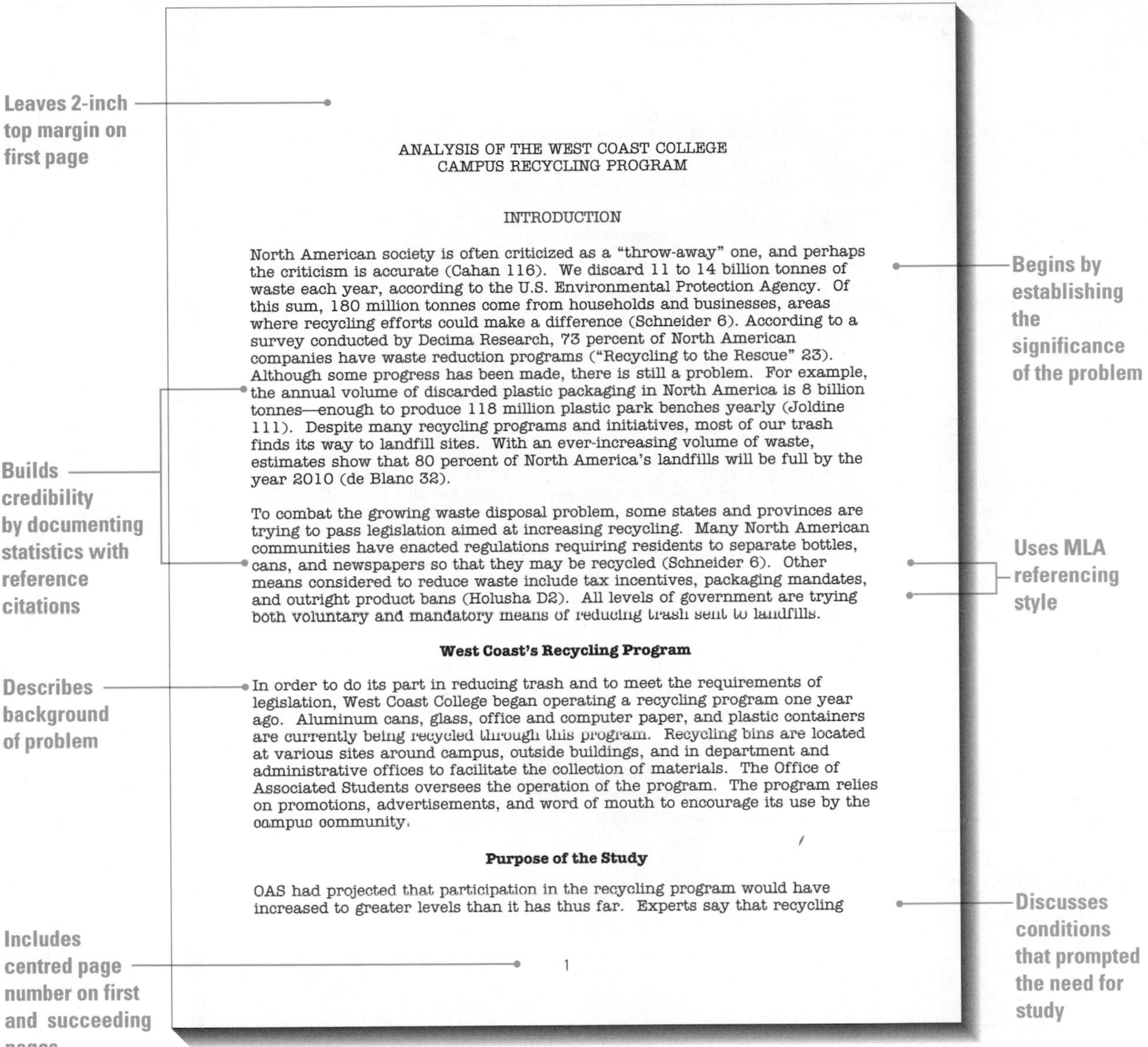

Leaves 2-inch top margin on first page
ANALYSIS OF THE WEST COAST COLLEGE
CAMPUS RECYCLING PROGRAM
INTRODUCTION
North American society is often criticized as a "throw-away" one, and perhaps the criticism is accurate (Cahan 116). We discard 11 to 14 billion tonnes of waste each year, according to the U.S. Environmental Protection Agency. Of this sum, 180 million tonnes come from households and businesses, areas where recycling efforts could make a difference (Schneider 6). According to a survey conducted by Decima Research, 73 percent of North American companies have waste reduction programs ("Recycling to the Rescue" 23). Although some progress has been made, there is still a problem. For example, the annual volume of discarded plastic packaging in North America is 8 billion tonnes—enough to produce 118 million plastic park benches yearly (Joldine 111). Despite many recycling programs and initiatives, most of our trash finds its way to landfill sites. With an ever-increasing volume of waste, estimates show that 80 percent of North America's landfills will be full by the year 2010 (de Blanc 32).
To combat the growing waste disposal problem, some states and provinces are trying to pass legislation aimed at increasing recycling. Many North American communities have enacted regulations requiring residents to separate bottles, cans, and newspapers so that they may be recycled (Schneider 6). Other means considered to reduce waste include tax incentives, packaging mandates, and outright product bans (Holusha D2). All levels of government are trying both voluntary and mandatory means of reducing trash sent to landfills.
West Coast's Recycling Program
In order to do its part in reducing trash and to meet the requirements of legislation, West Coast College began operating a recycling program one year ago. Aluminum cans, glass, office and computer paper, and plastic containers are currently being recycled through this program. Recycling bins are located at various sites around campus, outside buildings, and in department and administrative offices to facilitate the collection of materials. The Office of Associated Students oversees the operation of the program. The program relies on promotions, advertisements, and word of mouth to encourage its use by the campus community.
Purpose of the Study
OAS had projected that participation in the recycling program would have increased to greater levels than it has thus far. Experts say that recycling
1
Begins by establishing the significance of the problem
Builds credibility by documenting statistics with reference citations
Uses MLA referencing style
Describes background of problem
Discusses conditions that prompted the need for study
Includes centred page number on first and succeeding pages

The first page of a report generally contains the title printed 2 inches from the top edge. Titles for major parts of a report (such as *Introduction, Results, Conclusion,* and so forth) are centred in all caps. First-level headings are bold and printed with upper- and lowercase letters. Second-level headings begin at the side.

Notice that Alan's report is single-spaced. Many businesses prefer this space-saving format. However, some organizations prefer double-spacing, especially for preliminary drafts. Page numbers may be centred 1 inch from the top or bottom of the page or placed 1 inch from the upper right corner at the margin.

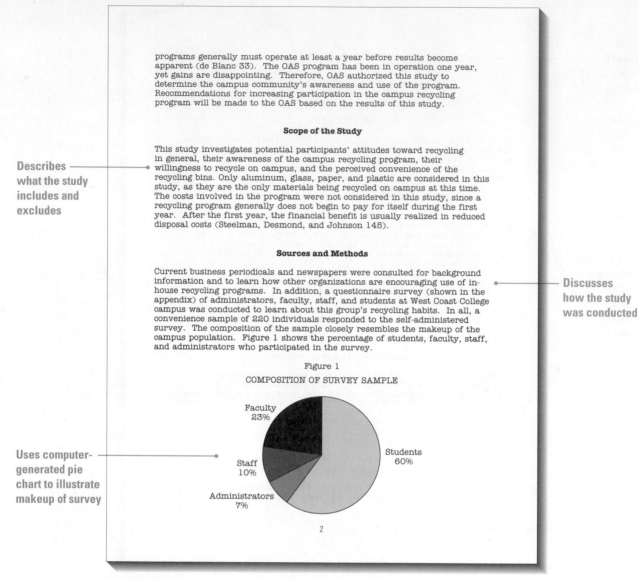

programs generally must operate at least a year before results become apparent (de Blanc 33). The OAS program has been in operation one year, yet gains are disappointing. Therefore, OAS authorized this study to determine the campus community's awareness and use of the program. Recommendations for increasing participation in the campus recycling program will be made to the OAS based on the results of this study.

Scope of the Study

Describes what the study includes and excludes

This study investigates potential participants' attitudes toward recycling in general, their awareness of the campus recycling program, their willingness to recycle on campus, and the perceived convenience of the recycling bins. Only aluminum, glass, paper, and plastic are considered in this study, as they are the only materials being recycled on campus at this time. The costs involved in the program were not considered in this study, since a recycling program generally does not begin to pay for itself during the first year. After the first year, the financial benefit is usually realized in reduced disposal costs (Steelman, Desmond, and Johnson 145).

Sources and Methods

Discusses how the study was conducted

Current business periodicals and newspapers were consulted for background information and to learn how other organizations are encouraging use of in-house recycling programs. In addition, a questionnaire survey (shown in the appendix) of administrators, faculty, staff, and students at West Coast College campus was conducted to learn about this group's recycling habits. In all, a convenience sample of 220 individuals responded to the self-administered survey. The composition of the sample closely resembles the makeup of the campus population. Figure 1 shows the percentage of students, faculty, staff, and administrators who participated in the survey.

Figure 1

COMPOSITION OF SURVEY SAMPLE

Uses computer-generated pie chart to illustrate makeup of survey

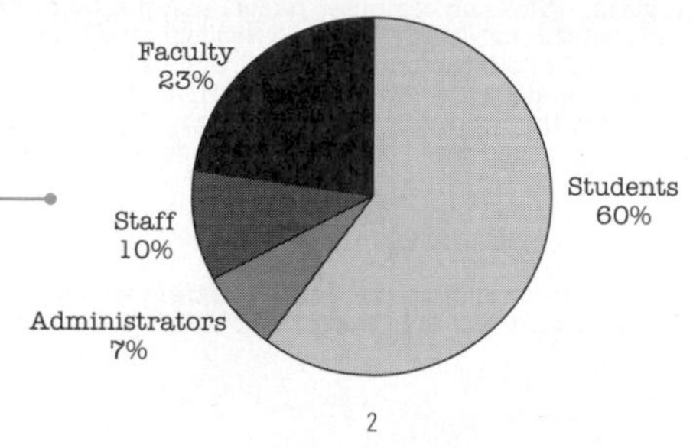

2

Because Alan wants this report to be formal in tone, he avoids *I* and *we*. Notice, too, that he uses present-tense verbs to describe his current writing (*this study investigates*), but past-tense verbs to indicate research completed in the past (*newspapers were consulted*).

If you use figures or tables, be sure to introduce them in the text. Although it's not always possible, try to place them close to the spot where they are first mentioned. If necessary to save space, you can print the title of a figure at its side.

FIGURE 14.3 *(continued)*

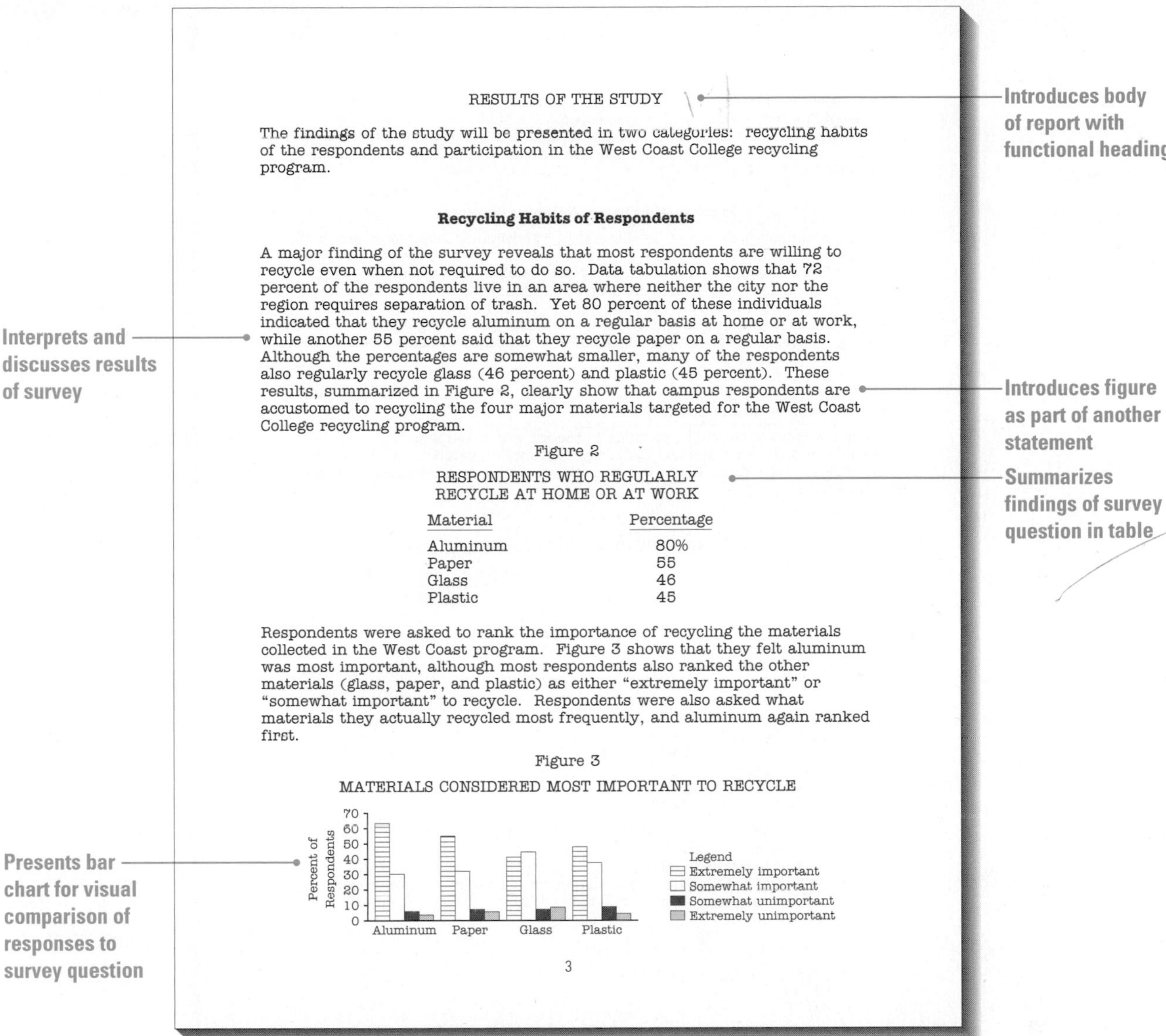

RESULTS OF THE STUDY

The findings of the study will be presented in two categories: recycling habits of the respondents and participation in the West Coast College recycling program.

Recycling Habits of Respondents

A major finding of the survey reveals that most respondents are willing to recycle even when not required to do so. Data tabulation shows that 72 percent of the respondents live in an area where neither the city nor the region requires separation of trash. Yet 80 percent of these individuals indicated that they recycle aluminum on a regular basis at home or at work, while another 55 percent said that they recycle paper on a regular basis. Although the percentages are somewhat smaller, many of the respondents also regularly recycle glass (46 percent) and plastic (45 percent). These results, summarized in Figure 2, clearly show that campus respondents are accustomed to recycling the four major materials targeted for the West Coast College recycling program.

Figure 2

RESPONDENTS WHO REGULARLY RECYCLE AT HOME OR AT WORK

Material	Percentage
Aluminum	80%
Paper	55
Glass	46
Plastic	45

Respondents were asked to rank the importance of recycling the materials collected in the West Coast program. Figure 3 shows that they felt aluminum was most important, although most respondents also ranked the other materials (glass, paper, and plastic) as either "extremely important" or "somewhat important" to recycle. Respondents were also asked what materials they actually recycled most frequently, and aluminum again ranked first.

Figure 3

MATERIALS CONSIDERED MOST IMPORTANT TO RECYCLE

70
60
50
40
30
20
10
0
Percent of Respondents
Aluminum
Paper
Glass
Plastic
Legend
Extremely important
Somewhat important
Somewhat unimportant
Extremely unimportant

3

Introduces body of report with functional heading
Interprets and discusses results of survey
Introduces figure as part of another statement
Summarizes findings of survey question in table
Presents bar chart for visual comparison of responses to survey question

Alan selects the most important survey findings to interpret and discuss for readers. Notice that he continues to use present-tense verbs (*the survey reveals* and *these results clearly show*) to discuss the current report.

Because he has few tables and charts, Alan labels them all as "Figures." Notice that he numbers them consecutively, and places the label above each figure. Report writers with a great many tables, charts, and illustrations may prefer to label and number them separately. Tables are labelled as such; everything else is generally called a figure. When tables and figures are labelled separately, tables may be labelled above the table, and figures below the figure.

Adds personal interpretation

When asked how likely they would be to go out of their way to deposit an item in a recycling bin, 29 percent of the respondents said "very likely," and 55 percent said "somewhat likely." Thus, respondents showed a willingness—at least on paper—to recycle even if it means making a special effort to locate a recycling bin.

Participation in Recycling on Campus

For any recycling program to be successful, participants must be aware of the location of recycling centres and must be trained to use them (de Blanc 33). Another important ingredient in thriving programs is convenience to users. If recycling centres are difficult for users to reach, these centres will be unsuccessful. To collect data on these topics, the survey included questions assessing awareness and use of the current bins. The survey also investigated reasons for not participating and the perceived convenience of current bin locations.

Introduces more findings and relates them to the report's purpose

Student Awareness and Use of Bins

Two of the most significant questions in the survey asked whether respondents were aware of the OAS recycling bins on campus and whether they had used the bins. Responses to both questions were disappointing, as Figure 4 illustrates.

Figure 4

AWARENESS AND USE OF RECYCLING BINS ON CAMPUS

Location	Awareness of bins at this location	Use of bins at this location
Cafeteria	38%	21%
Bookstore	29	12
Administration building	28	12
Computer labs	16	11
Library	15	7
Student union	9	5
Classrooms	8	6
Department and administrative offices	6	3
Athletic centre	5	3
Unaware of any bins; have not used any bins	20	7

Arranges responses from highest to lowest with "unaware" category placed last

Only 38 percent of the respondents, as shown in Figure 4, were aware of the bins located outside the cafeteria. Even fewer were aware of the bins outside the bookstore (29 percent) and outside the administration building (28 percent). Equally dissatisfying, only 21 percent of the respondents had used the most visible recycling bins outside the cafeteria.

Clarifies and emphasizes meaning of findings

4

In discussing the results of the survey, Alan highlights those that have significance for the purpose of the report.

As you type a report, avoid orphans and widows (ending a page with the first line of a paragraph or carrying a single line of a paragraph to a new page). Strive to start and end pages with at least two lines of a paragraph, even if a slightly larger bottom margin results.

Other recycling bin locations were even less familiar to the survey respondents and, of course, were little used. These responses plainly show that the majority of the respondents in the West Coast campus community have a low awareness of the recycling program and an even lower record of participation.

Reasons for Not Participating

Respondents offered several reasons for not participating in the campus recycling program. Forty-five percent said that the bins are not convenient to use. Thirty percent said that they did not know where the bins were located. Another 25 percent said that they are not in the habit of recycling. Although many reasons for not participating were listed, the primary one appears to centre on convenience of bin locations.

Location of Recycling Bins

When asked specifically how they would rate the location of the bins currently in use, only 13 percent of the respondents felt that the bins were extremely convenient. Another 35 percent rated the locations as somewhat convenient. Over half the respondents felt that the locations of the bins were either somewhat inconvenient or extremely inconvenient. Recycling bins are currently located outside nearly all the major campus rooms or buildings, but respondents clearly considered these locations inconvenient or inadequate.

Discusses results of other survey questions not represented in tables or charts

In indicating where they would like recycling bins placed (see Figure 5), 42 percent of the respondents felt that the most convenient locations would be inside the cafeteria. Placing more recycling bins near the student union seemed most convenient to another 33 percent of those questioned, while 15 percent stated that they would like to see the bins placed near the vending machines. Ten percent of the individuals responding to the survey did not seem to think that the locations of the bins would matter to them.

Clarifies results of another survey question with textual discussion accompanied by table

Figure 5

PREFERENCE FOR PLACEMENT OF RECYCLING BINS

Inside the cafeteria	42%
More in student union	33
Near vending machines	15
Does not matter	10

5

After completing a discussion of the survey results, Alan articulates what he considers the five most important conclusions to be drawn from this survey. Some writers combine the conclusions and recommendations, particularly when they are interrelated. Alan separated them in his study because the survey findings were quite distinct from the recommendations he would make based on them.

FIGURE 14.3 *(continued)*

CONCLUSIONS

Based on the findings of the recycling survey of members of the West Coast College campus community, the following conclusions are drawn:

1. Most members of the campus community are already recycling at home or at work without being required to do so.
2. Over half of the respondents recycle aluminum and paper on a regular basis; most recycle glass and plastic to some degree.
3. Most of the surveyed individuals expressed a willingness to participate in a recycling program. Many, however, seem unwilling to travel very far to participate; 42 percent would like more recycling bins to be located inside the cafeteria.
4. Awareness and use of the current campus recycling program are low. Only a little over one-third of the respondents knew of any recycling bin locations on campus, and only one-fifth had actually used them.
5. Respondents considered the locations of the campus bins inconvenient. This perceived inconvenience was given as the principal reason for not participating in the campus recycling program.

Draws conclusions based on survey findings; summarizes previous discussion

RECOMMENDATIONS

Supported by the findings and conclusions of this study, the following recommendations are offered in an effort to improve the operations and success of the West Coast recycling program:

1. Increase on-campus awareness and visibility by designing an eye-catching logo that represents the campus recycling program for use in promotions.
2. Enhance comprehension of recycling procedures by teaching users how to recycle. Use posters to explain the recycling program and to inform users of recycling bin locations. Label each bin clearly as to what materials may be deposited.
3. Add bins in several new locations, particularly more in the food service and vending machine areas.
4. Recruit student leaders to promote participation in the recycling program by giving educational talks to classes and other campus groups, informing them of the importance of recycling.
5. Develop an incentive program for student organizations. Offer incentives for meeting recycling goals as determined by OAS. On-campus groups could compete in recycling drives designed to raise money for the group, the college, or a charity. Money from the proceeds of the recycling program could be used to fund the incentive program.

Lists specific actions to help solve report problem; suggests practical ways to implement recommendations

6

The most important parts of a report are its conclusions and recommendations. To make them especially clear, Alan enumerated each conclusion and recommendation. Notice that each recommendation starts with a verb and is stated as a command for emphasis and readability.

Report recommendations are most helpful to readers when they not only make suggestions to solve the original research problem but also describe specific actions to be taken. Notice that this report goes beyond merely listing ideas; instead, it makes practical suggestions for ways to implement the recommendations.

FIGURE 14.3 *(continued)*

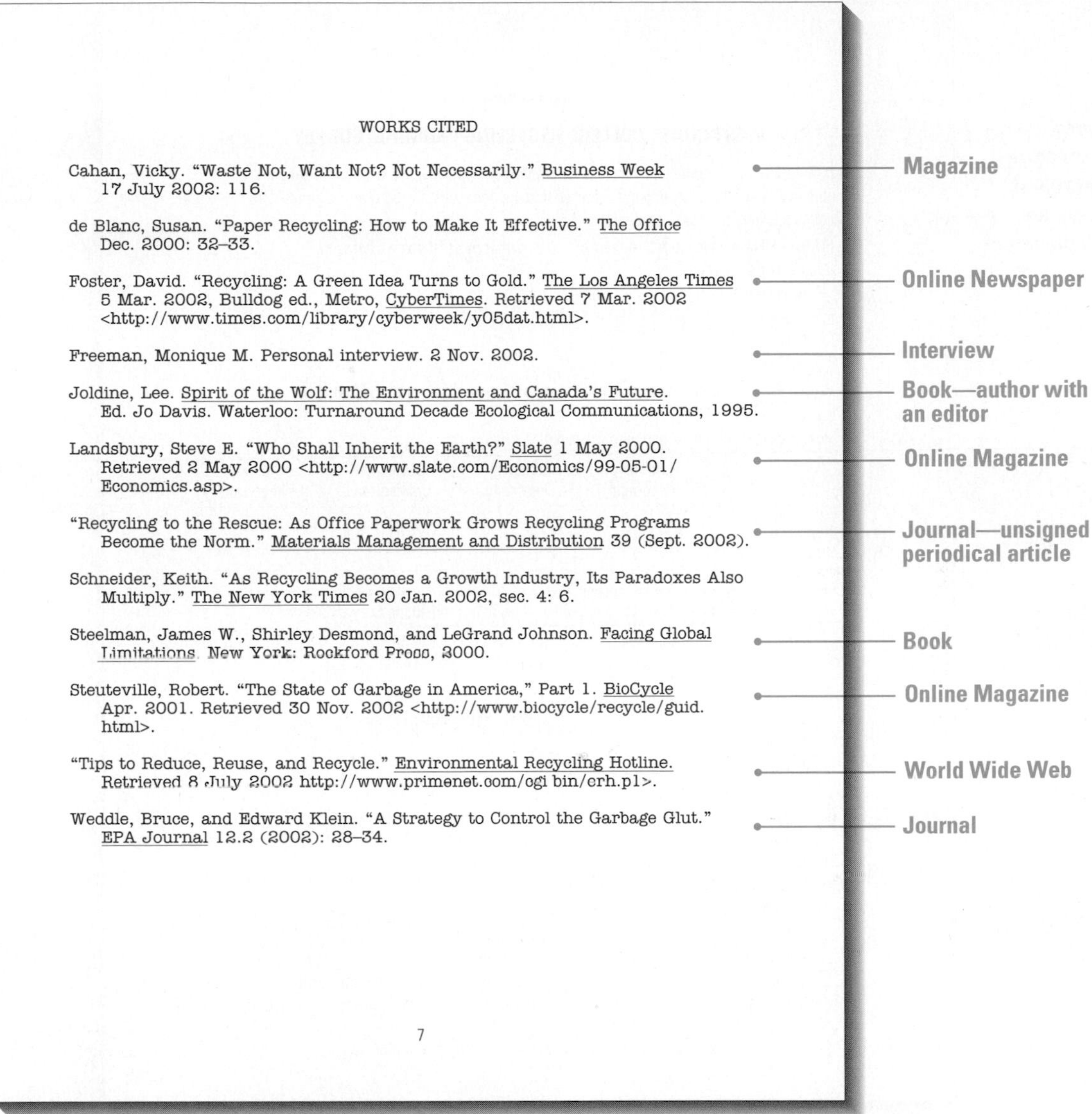

WORKS CITED

Cahan, Vicky. "Waste Not, Want Not? Not Necessarily." Business Week 17 July 2002: 116.

de Blanc, Susan. "Paper Recycling: How to Make It Effective." The Office Dec. 2000: 32–33.

Foster, David. "Recycling: A Green Idea Turns to Gold." The Los Angeles Times 5 Mar. 2002, Bulldog ed., Metro, CyberTimes. Retrieved 7 Mar. 2002 <http://www.times.com/library/cyberweek/y05dat.html>.

Freeman, Monique M. Personal interview. 2 Nov. 2002.

Joldine, Lee. Spirit of the Wolf: The Environment and Canada's Future. Ed. Jo Davis. Waterloo: Turnaround Decade Ecological Communications, 1995.

Landsbury, Steve E. "Who Shall Inherit the Earth?" Slate 1 May 2000. Retrieved 2 May 2000 <http://www.slate.com/Economics/99-05-01/Economics.asp>.

"Recycling to the Rescue: As Office Paperwork Grows Recycling Programs Become the Norm." Materials Management and Distribution 39 (Sept. 2002).

Schneider, Keith. "As Recycling Becomes a Growth Industry, Its Paradoxes Also Multiply." The New York Times 20 Jan. 2002, sec. 4: 6.

Steelman, James W., Shirley Desmond, and LeGrand Johnson. Facing Global Limitations. New York: Rockford Press, 2000.

Steuteville, Robert. "The State of Garbage in America," Part 1. BioCycle Apr. 2001. Retrieved 30 Nov. 2002 <http://www.biocycle/recycle/guid.html>.

"Tips to Reduce, Reuse, and Recycle." Environmental Recycling Hotline. Retrieved 8 July 2002 http://www.primenet.com/cgi bin/crh.pl>.

Weddle, Bruce, and Edward Klein. "A Strategy to Control the Garbage Glut." EPA Journal 12.2 (2002): 28–34.

7

On this page Alan lists all the references cited in the text as well as others that he examined during his research. (Some authors list only those works cited in the report.) Alan formats his citations following the MLA referencing style. Notice that all entries are arranged alphabetically. He underlines book and periodical titles, but italics could be used. When referring to online items, he shows the full name of the citation and then identifies the path leading to that reference as well as the date on which he accessed the electronic reference.

Most word processing software today automatically updates the numbering of references within the text and prints a complete list for you. For more information about documentation styles, see Chapter 11 and Appendix B.

FIGURE 14.3 *(continued)*

Includes copy of survey questionnaire so that report readers can see actual questions

APPENDIX

WEST COAST COLLEGE RECYCLING PROGRAM SURVEY

West Coast College recently implemented a recycling program on campus. Please take a few minutes to answer the following questions so that we can make this program as convenient and helpful as possible for you to use.

Explains why survey is necessary, emphasizing "you" view

1. Please indicate which items you recycle on a regular basis at home or at work. (Check *all* that apply.)
   - ☐ Aluminum
   - ☐ Glass
   - ☐ Paper
   - ☐ Plastic
2. Do you live in an area where the city/municipality requires separation of waste?
   ☐ Yes ☐ No
3. How important is it to you to recycle each of the following:

	Extremely Important	Somewhat Important	Somewhat Unimportant	Extremely Unimportant
Aluminum				
Glass				
Paper				
Plastic				

Provides range of answers that will be easy to tabulate

4. How likely would it be for you to go out of your way to put something in a recycling bin?

Very Likely	Somewhat Likely	Somewhat Unlikely	Very Unlikely

5. Which of the following items do you recycle *most* often? (Choose *one* item only.)
   - ☐ Aluminum
   - ☐ Glass
   - ☐ Paper
   - ☐ Plastic
   - ☐ Other
6. The following are locations of the recycling bins on campus. (Check *all* those of which you are aware.)
   - ☐ Administration building
   - ☐ Bookstore
   - ☐ Athletic centre
   - ☐ Computer labs
   - ☐ Cafeteria
   - ☐ Library
   - ☐ Classrooms
   - ☐ Student union
   - ☐ Department and administrative offices
   - ☐ I'm unaware of any of these recycling bins.

8

Alan had space to add the word "Appendix" to the top of the survey questionnaire. If space were not available, he could have typed a separate page with that title on it. If more than one item were included, he would have named them Appendix A, Appendix B, and so on.

Notice that the appendix continues the report's pagination.

FIGURE 14.3 *(continued)*

7. Which of the following recycling bins have you actually used? (Check *all* that you have used.)
   - ☐ Administration building
   - ☐ Bookstore
   - ☐ Athletic centre
   - ☐ Computer labs
   - ☐ Cafeteria
   - ☐ Library
   - ☐ Classrooms
   - ☐ Student union
   - ☐ Department and administrative offices
   - ☐ I've not used any of these recycling bins.
8. If you don't recycle on campus, why don't you participate?
   - ☐ I'm not in the habit of recycling.
   - ☐ I don't know where the bins are.
   - ☐ The bins aren't convenient to me.
   - ☐ Other ______________________
9. How do you rate the convenience of the bins' locations?
   - ☐ Extremely convenient
   - ☐ Somewhat convenient
   - ☐ Somewhat inconvenient
   - ☐ Extremely inconvenient
10. Which of the following possible recycling bin locations would be most convenient for you to use? (Check *one* only.)
    - ☐ Outside each building
    - ☐ Near the food service facilities
    - ☐ Near the vending machines
    - ☐ Does not matter
    - ☐ Other ______________________
11. Please indicate:
    - ☐ Student
    - ☐ Faculty
    - ☐ Administrator
    - ☐ Staff

COMMENTS:

Thank you for your responses! Please return the questionnaire in the enclosed, stamped envelope to West Coast College, School of Business, Rm. 321. If you have any questions, please call (555) 450-2391.

9

Anticipates responses but also supplies "Other" category

Uses scale questions to capture degrees of feeling

Requests little demographic data to keep survey short

Offers comment section for explanations and remarks

Concludes with appreciation and instructions

- **Revise for clarity, coherence, and conciseness.**
- **Proofread the final copy three times** to check for word meanings and content, spelling, punctuation, grammar, other mechanical errors and formatting consistency.

Putting It All Together

Formal reports in business generally aim to study problems and recommend solutions. Alan Christopher, business senator to the Office of Associated Students (OAS) at West Coast College, was given a campus problem to study, resulting in the formal report shown in Figure 14.3.

The campus recycling program, under the direction of Cheryl Bryant and supported by the OAS, was not attracting the anticipated level of participation. Committee members wondered whether campus community members were sufficiently aware of the program and how participation could be increased.

Alan's report illustrates many of the points discussed in this chapter. Although it's a good example of typical report format and style, it should not be viewed as the only way to present a report. Wide variation exists in reports.

The following checklist summarizes the report process and report components in one handy list.

Checklist for Preparing Formal Reports

Report Process

☑ **Analyze the report problem and purpose.** Develop a problem question (*Is sexual harassment affecting employees at DataTech?*) and a purpose statement (*The purpose of this report is to investigate sexual harassment at DataTech and recommend remedies*).

☑ **Anticipate the audience and issues.** Consider primary and secondary audiences. What do they already know? What do they need to know? Divide the major problem into subproblems for investigation.

☑ **Prepare a work plan.** Include problem and purpose statements, as well as a description of the sources and methods of collecting data. Prepare a tentative project outline and a work schedule with anticipated dates of completion for all segments of the project.

☑ **Collect data.** Begin by searching secondary sources (electronic databases, books, magazines, journals, newspapers) for information on your topic. Then, if necessary, gather primary data by surveying, interviewing, observing, and experimenting.

☑ **Document data sources.** Prepare note cards or separate sheets of paper citing all references (author, date, source, page, and quotation). Select a documentation format and use it consistently.

☑ **Interpret and organize the data.** Arrange the collected information in tables, grids, or outlines to help you visualize relationships and interpret meanings. Organize the data into an outline.

Prepare graphics. Make tables, charts, graphs, and illustrations—but *only* if they serve a function. Use graphics to help clarify, condense, simplify, or emphasize your data.

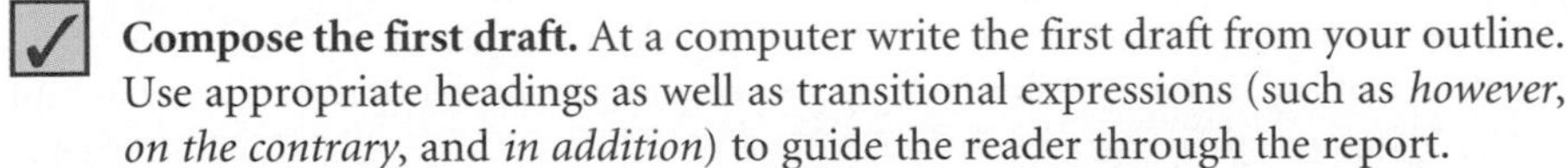

Compose the first draft. At a computer write the first draft from your outline. Use appropriate headings as well as transitional expressions (such as *however, on the contrary,* and *in addition*) to guide the reader through the report.

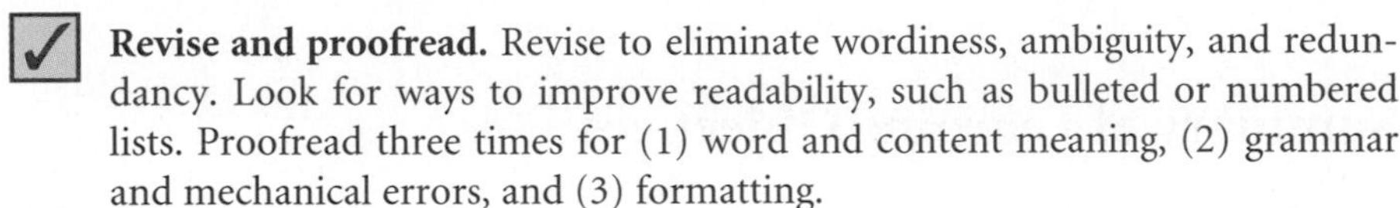

Revise and proofread. Revise to eliminate wordiness, ambiguity, and redundancy. Look for ways to improve readability, such as bulleted or numbered lists. Proofread three times for (1) word and content meaning, (2) grammar and mechanical errors, and (3) formatting.

Evaluate the product. Examine the final report. Will it achieve its purpose? Encourage feedback so that you can learn how to improve future reports.

Report Components

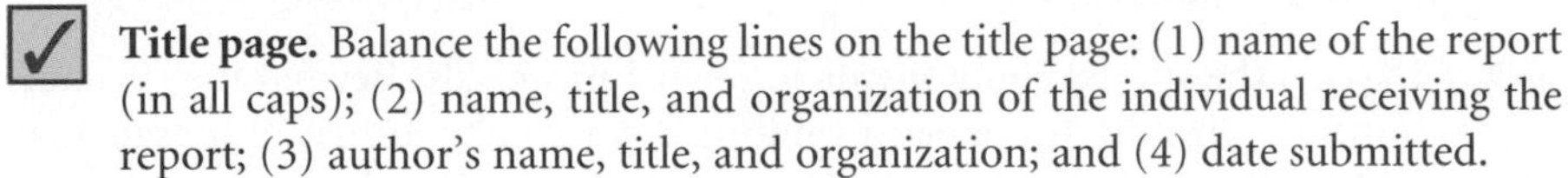

Title page. Balance the following lines on the title page: (1) name of the report (in all caps); (2) name, title, and organization of the individual receiving the report; (3) author's name, title, and organization; and (4) date submitted.

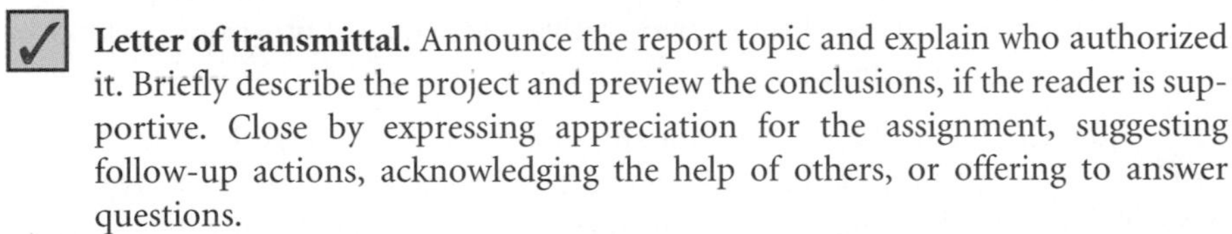

Letter of transmittal. Announce the report topic and explain who authorized it. Briefly describe the project and preview the conclusions, if the reader is supportive. Close by expressing appreciation for the assignment, suggesting follow-up actions, acknowledging the help of others, or offering to answer questions.

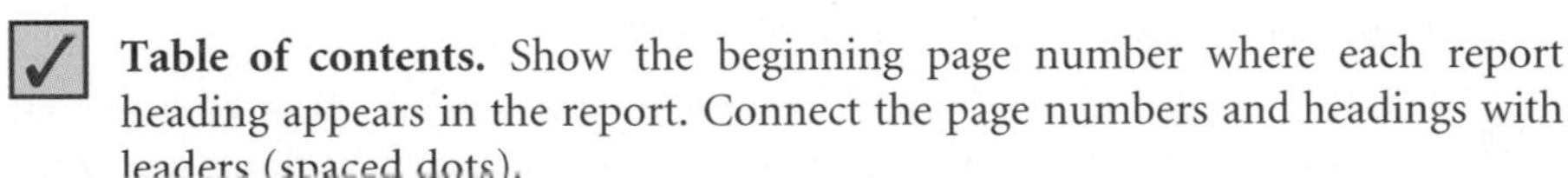

Table of contents. Show the beginning page number where each report heading appears in the report. Connect the page numbers and headings with leaders (spaced dots).

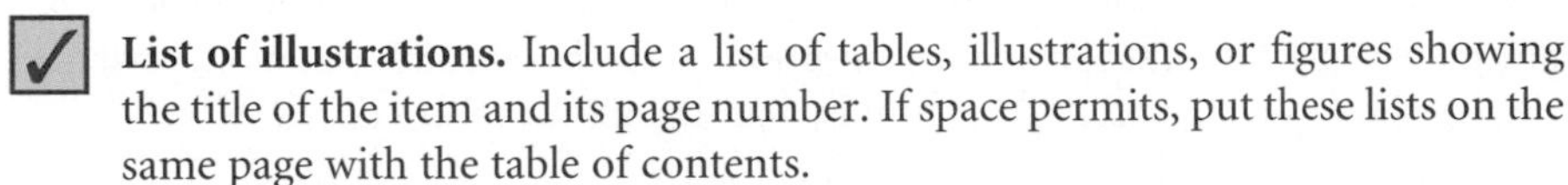

List of illustrations. Include a list of tables, illustrations, or figures showing the title of the item and its page number. If space permits, put these lists on the same page with the table of contents.

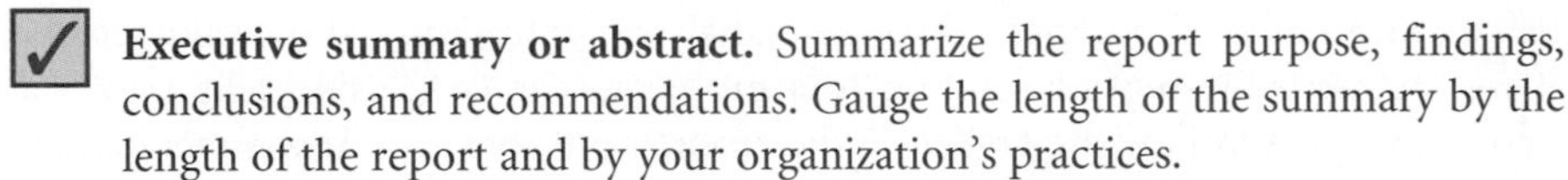

Executive summary or abstract. Summarize the report purpose, findings, conclusions, and recommendations. Gauge the length of the summary by the length of the report and by your organization's practices.

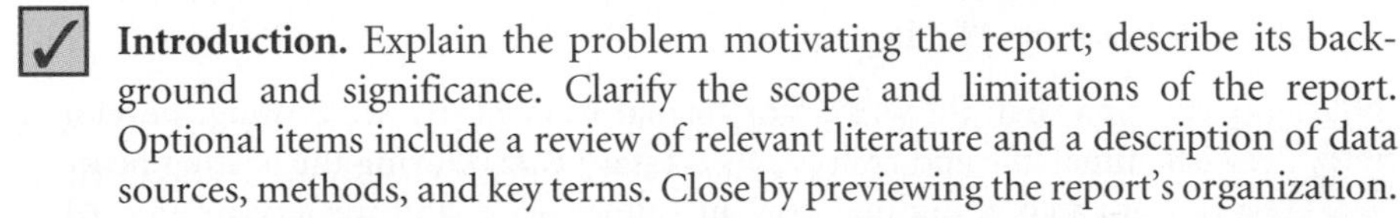

Introduction. Explain the problem motivating the report; describe its background and significance. Clarify the scope and limitations of the report. Optional items include a review of relevant literature and a description of data sources, methods, and key terms. Close by previewing the report's organization.

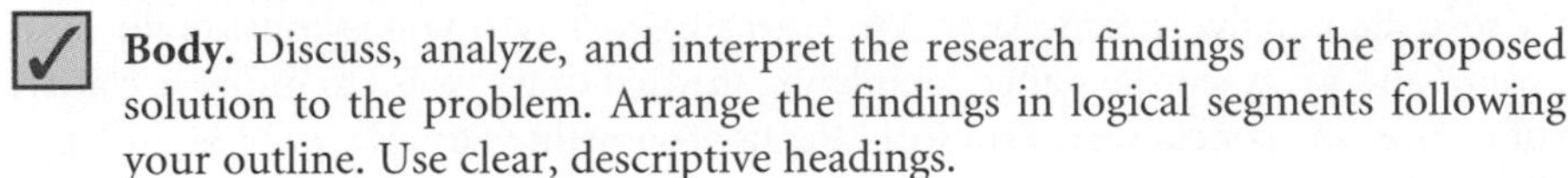

Body. Discuss, analyze, and interpret the research findings or the proposed solution to the problem. Arrange the findings in logical segments following your outline. Use clear, descriptive headings.

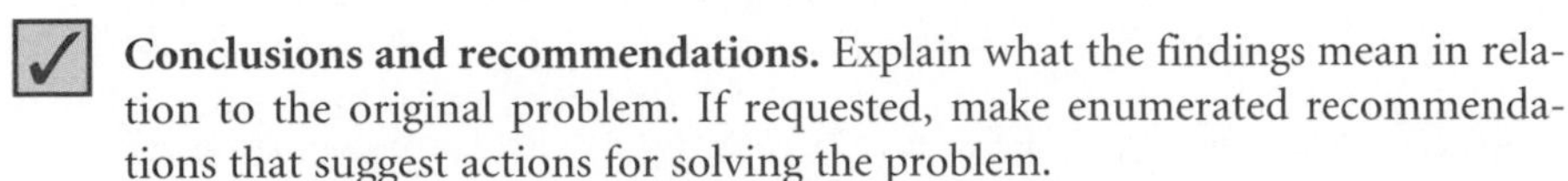

Conclusions and recommendations. Explain what the findings mean in relation to the original problem. If requested, make enumerated recommendations that suggest actions for solving the problem.

 **Appendix.** Include items of interest to some, but not all, readers, such as a data questionnaire or computer printouts.

 **References and bibliography.** If footnotes are not provided in the text, list all references in a section called "Endnotes," "Works Cited," or "References." As an option, include a bibliography showing all the works cited (and perhaps all those consulted) arranged alphabetically.

Summary of Learning Objectives

1 **Discuss the components of informal proposals.** Most informal proposals contain (1) a persuasive introduction that explains the purpose of the proposal and qualifies the writer; (2) background material identifying the problem and project goals; (3) a proposal, plan, or schedule outlining the project; (4) a section describing staff qualifications; (5) a budget showing expected costs; and (6) a request for approval or authorization.

2 **Discuss the special components in formal proposals.** Beyond the six components generally contained in informal proposals, formal proposals may include these additional parts: (1) copy of the RFP (request for proposal), (2) letter of transmittal, (3) abstract or executive summary, (4) title page, (5) table of contents, (6) list of illustrations, and (7) appendix.

3 **Identify formal report components that precede its introduction**. Formal reports may include these beginning components: (1) vinyl or heavy paper cover, (2) title page, (3) letter of transmittal, (4) table of contents, (5) list of illustrations, and (6) executive summary or abstract.

4 **Outline topics that might be covered in the introduction of a formal report.** The introduction to a formal report sets the scene by discussing some or all of the following topics: background material, problem or purpose, significance of the topic, scope and organization of the report, authorization, review of relevant literature, sources and methods, and definitions of key terms.

5 **Describe the components of a formal report that follow the introduction.** The body of a report discusses, analyzes, interprets, and evaluates the research findings or solution to a problem. The conclusion tells what the findings mean and how they relate to the report's purpose. The recommendations tell how to solve the report problem. The last portions of a formal report are the appendix, references, and bibliography.

6 **Specify tips that aid writers of formal reports**. Before writing, develop a realistic timetable and collect all necessary data. During the writing process, work from a good outline, work in a quiet place, and use a computer. Also, try to write rapidly, revising later. While writing, use verb tenses consistently, and avoid *I* and *we.* A few days after completing the first draft, revise to improve clarity, coherence, and conciseness. Proofread the final copy three times.

CHAPTER REVIEW

1. Proposals are written offers to do what? (Obj. 1)
2. What is an RFP? (Objs. 1 and 2)
3. What are the six principal parts of a letter proposal? (Obj. 1)
4. What is a "worry item" in a proposal? (Obj. 1)
5. Why should a proposal budget be prepared very carefully? (Obj. 1)
6. What is generally contained in a letter of transmittal accompanying a formal report? (Obj. 3)
7. What label can a report writer use to describe all illustrations and tables? (Obj. 3)
8. How is an abstract different from an executive summary? (Objs. 2 and 3)
9. What does *scope* mean in relation to a formal report? (Obj. 4)
10. Should the body of a report include the heading *Body*? (Obj. 5)
11. What are the advantages of functional headings? Of talking headings? (Obj. 5)
12. In a formal report where do most writers place the conclusions? (Obj. 5)
13. What materials go in an appendix? (Obj. 5)
14. What environment enhances writing? (Obj. 6)
15. How should a formal report be proofread? (Obj. 6)

CRITICAL THINKING

1. Why are proposals important to many businesses? (Obj. 1)
2. How do formal reports differ from informal reports? (Objs. 1 and 2)
3. Why do some parts of formal reports tend to be redundant? (Objs. 4 and 5)
4. Discuss the three phases of the writing process in relation to formal reports. What activities take place in each phase? (Objs. 3–6)

ACTIVITIES

Consult your instructor to determine the length, format, and emphasis for the following report projects. Some require additional research; others do not.

14.1 Proposal: Outsourcing (Objs. 1 and 2)

Critical Thinking

Businesses today are doing more "outsourcing" than ever before. This means that they are going outside to find specialists to handle some aspect of their business, such as billing, shipping, or advertising. They're also hiring experts with special training and equipment to solve problems for which they lack the necessary talent and staff. For a business where you have worked or an organization you know, select a problem. Here are some possibilities: poor handling of customer orders, inefficient payroll practices, inadequate computer equipment or software, unsatisfactory inventory control, poor use of sales staff, bad scheduling of employees, poorly trained employees, sexual harassment on the job, Internet misuse, and poor telephone techniques. Assume the boss has asked you as a consultant to either solve the problem or study it and tell the organization what to do. Prepare an informal proposal describing your plan to solve the problem or perform a service. Decide how much you will charge and what staff you will need. Send your letter proposal to your boss.

14.2 Proposal: Don't Give Up Your Day Job (Objs. 1 and 2)

Critical Thinking

As a struggling student, single parent, or budding entrepreneur, you decide to start your own part-time word-processing business in your home. Select a company or professional in your city that might need your services. Often, businesses, medical centres, lawyers, and other professionals have overload transcribing or word processing to farm out to a service. Assess your expertise and equipment. Check out the competition. What do other word-processing services offer, and what do they charge? Although many apply a flat hourly rate, you may decide to charge more for items that require heavy editing. Find out what a particular company needs. Prepare a letter proposal addressed to a specific individual outlining your plan to offer your services.

14.3 Research Report: Work Teams (Objs. 3–6)

Web

Research shows that 60 percent of Fortune 500 firms either have implemented or are experimenting with different types of employee involvement programs, such as work teams, quality circles, and workplace democracy councils. In large and small firms these programs are thought to reap many benefits—from increasing production to boosting morale. Mike Rivera, vice president of operations at DataTech, which employs about 80 electronics assemblers and 30 supporting employees, wants to learn more about these programs. He asks you, his executive assistant, to prepare a report that investigates how other companies have used them. He's particularly interested in safety applications. Could quality circles or work teams improve DataTech's safety record? How are such programs operated at other companies? Collect secondary data, including research on the Web. Start by using the search terms "work teams" and "quality circles." Analyze your findings, draw conclusions, and make recommendations in a letter report to Mike Rivera.

14.4 Formal Report: Entrepreneurial Women (Objs. 3–6)

By the year 2005, 40 to 50 percent of all businesses will be owned by women. As an intern at the Canadian Association of Women in Business, you have been asked to collect information for a booklet to be distributed to women who inquire about starting businesses. Specifically, you have been asked to find articles describing three or four women who have started their own businesses. Examine why they started their businesses, how they did it, and how successful they were. In your report draw conclusions about what kinds of women start businesses, why they do it, what kinds of businesses they are likely to start, and what difficulties they face. Speculate on the dramatic increase in the number of female business owners. Make recommendations to women about starting businesses. Use your research skills to prepare a report for Rochelle Robinson, director, Canadian Association of Women in Business.

14.5 Formal Report: Lending a Helping Hand to the Student Council (Objs. 3–6)

Team

Volunteer your class to conduct research aimed at a specific problem facing your campus student council. Ask the council president to visit your class to discuss a problem that requires research. Most student councils want to learn what students think about their activities, projects, and use of resources, but generally lack the expertise and staff needed to gather reliable data. Question the president to isolate the issues to be investigated. For example, the student council may want students to prioritize activities deserving support. With a limited budget, what activities should the council fund: concerts, lectures, intramural sports, movies, a craft store, or something else? Other questions may face the leadership: Should the student council undertake a recycling centre? Should it sponsor an adult literacy volunteer program? How should these programs be implemented?

Once a problem for investigation has been selected, divide into groups of three to five to develop a survey questionnaire. Evaluate each group's questionnaire in class, and select the best one. Pilot test the questionnaire. Administer the revised questionnaire to a targeted student group. Tabulate the findings. In teams of three to five or individually, write a report to the student council president discussing your findings, conclusions, and recommendations.

14.6 Formal Report: Fast-Food Checkup (Objs. 3–6)

Select a fast-food franchise in your area. Assume that the national franchising headquarters has received complaints about the service, quality, and cleanliness of the unit. You have been sent to inspect and to report on what you see. Visit on two or more occasions. Make notes on how many customers were served, how quickly they received their food, and how courteously they were treated. Observe the number of employees and supervisors working. Note the cleanliness of observable parts of the restaurant. Inspect the restroom as well as the exterior and surrounding grounds. Sample the food. Your boss is a stickler for details; he has no use for general statements like *The restroom was not clean.* Be specific. Draw conclusions. Are the complaints justified? If improvements are necessary, make recommendations. Address your report to Lawrence C. Kelsey, president.

14.7 Formal Reports Requiring Secondary Research (Objs. 3–6)

Select one of the following topics for a report. Discuss with your instructor its purpose, scope, length, format, audience, and data sources. For each topic analyze your findings, draw conclusions, and make logical recommendations. Your instructor may ask teams to complete the secondary research.

- **a.** How does the compensation of Canadian executives compare with that of Japanese executives?
- **b.** How are corporations managing employee drug and alcohol abuse?
- **c.** Are corporate fitness programs worth their costs?
- **d.** Has the image of women in advertisements today changed from that shown 15 years ago?
- **e.** How are businesses dealing with computer fraud and malice?
- **f.** Should McDonald's expand its company-owned and franchise restaurants in Latin America and Asia?
- **g.** Should you invest in an event-planning franchise that specializes in children's parties?
- **h.** What is the best way for you to invest $100 000?
- **i.** Should environmentalists engage in junk-mail promotions to advertise their causes?
- **j.** Of three locations, which is the best for a new McDonald's (or Dairy Queen, Subway, or franchise of your choice)?
- **k.** What magazines represent the best advertising choice for Reebok (or a product with which you are familiar)?

l. What effects do aromas have on the senses, and how can aromas be used to advantage in the workplace?

14.8 Formal Reports Requiring Primary Research (Objs. 3–6)

Select one of the following topics for a report. Discuss with your instructor its purpose, scope, length, format, audience, and data sources. For each topic analyze your findings, draw conclusions, and make logical recommendations. Your instructor may ask teams to complete the primary research.

a. How can your community improve its image and attract new businesses?

b. How can your community improve its recycling efforts?

c. Does your campus need to add or improve a student computer lab?

d. How can the student association (or a club of your choice) increase its membership and support on this campus?

e. Can the registration process at your college or university be improved?

f. Are the requirements for a degree or diploma in your major realistic and relevant?

g. How can drug and alcohol abuse be reduced in your community?

h. What is a significant student problem on your campus, and how can it be solved?

i. What does an analysis of local and national newspapers reveal about employment possibilities for college graduates?

j. What demographic characteristics (age, gender, income, major, socioeconomic status, family, employment, interests, and so forth) does the typical student have on your campus?

UNIT 5
PRESENTATIONS

CHAPTER 15
Speaking Skills

CHAPTER 16
Employment Communication

CHAPTER • 15 •

SPEAKING SKILLS

LEARNING OBJECTIVES

1. Discuss two important first steps in preparing an effective oral presentation.
2. Explain the major elements in the introduction, body, and conclusion of an oral presentation and discuss the importance of verbal signposts.
3. Identify appropriate visual aids and handouts for a presentation.
4. Review techniques for designing an electronic presentation.
5. Specify delivery techniques for use before, during, and after a presentation.
6. Discuss effective techniques for adapting oral presentations to cross-cultural audiences.
7. List techniques for improving telephone and voice-mail effectiveness.

Preparing an Effective Oral Presentation

1

Many businesspeople must make presentations as part of their careers.

According to Canadian speaker and author Peter Urs Bender, the greatest fear of most people is not death, but public speaking.[1] While this may seem extreme, most of us feel great stress when faced with making a speech. The physiological responses that you experience are much like those triggered by a car accident or a narrow escape from a dangerous situation.[2] Regardless, at some point everyone in business has to sell an idea, and such persuasion is often done in person.

Many future businesspeople fail to take advantage of opportunities in college to develop speaking skills. Yet, such skills often play an important role in a successful career. You might, for example, need to describe your company's expansion plans to your banker, or you might need to persuade management to support your proposed marketing strategy. You might have to make a sales pitch before customers or speak to a professional gathering. This chapter develops speaking skills in making oral presentations and in using the telephone and voice mail to advantage.

For any presentation, you can reduce your fears and lay the foundation for a professional performance by focusing on four areas: preparation, organization, visual aids, and delivery.

Knowing Your Purpose

The most important part of your preparation is deciding what you want to accomplish. Whether your goal is to persuade or to inform, you must have a clear idea of where you are going. At the end of your presentation, what do you want your listeners to remember or do?

Eric Evans, a loan officer at Dominion Trust, faced such questions as he planned a talk for a class in small business management. Eric's former business professor had asked him to return to campus and give the class advice about borrowing money from banks in order to start new businesses. Because Eric knew so much about this topic, he found it difficult to extract a specific purpose statement for his presentation. After much thought he narrowed his purpose to this: *To inform potential entrepreneurs about three important factors that loan officers consider before granting start-up loans to launch small businesses.* His entire presentation focused on ensuring that the class members understood and remembered three principal ideas.

Knowing Your Audience

Audience analysis issues include number of people, age, gender, experience, attitude, and expectations.

A second key element in preparation is analyzing your audience, anticipating its reactions, and making appropriate adaptations. Many factors influence a presentation. A large audience, for example, usually requires a more formal and less personalized approach. Other elements, such as age, gender, education, experience, and attitude toward the subject, will also affect your style and message content. Analyze these factors to determine your strategy, vocabulary, illustrations, and level of detail. Here are specific questions to consider:

- *How will this topic appeal to this audience?*
- *How can I relate this information to their needs?*
- *How can I earn respect so that they accept my message?*
- *Which of the following would be most effective in making my point? Statistics? Graphic illustrations? Demonstrations? Case histories? Analogies? Cost figures?*
- *What measures must I take to ensure that this audience remembers my main points?*

Organizing the Content

2

Once you have determined your purpose and analyzed the audience, you're ready to collect information and organize it logically. Good organization and conscious repetition are the two most powerful keys to audience comprehension and retention. In fact, many speech experts recommend the following admittedly repetitious, but effective, plan:

- **Step 1:** Tell them what you're going to say.
- **Step 2:** Say it.
- **Step 3:** Tell them what you've just said.

In other words, repeat your main points in the introduction, body, and conclusion of your presentation. Although it sounds deadly, this strategy works surprisingly well. Let's examine how to construct the three parts of a presentation and add appropriate verbal signposts to ensure that listeners understand and remember.

Introduction

The opening of your presentation should strive to accomplish three specific goals:

- Capture listeners' attention and get them involved.
- Identify yourself and establish your credibility.
- Preview your main points.

If you're able to appeal to listeners and involve them in your presentation right from the start, you're more likely to hold their attention until the finish. Consider some of the same techniques that you used to open sales letters: a question, a startling fact, a joke, a story, or a quotation. Some speakers achieve involvement by opening with a question or command that requires audience members to raise their hands or stand up. Additional techniques to gain and keep audience attention are presented in the accompanying Career Coach box.

To establish your credibility, you need to describe your position, knowledge, or experience—whatever qualifies you to speak. Try also to connect with your audience. Listeners are particularly drawn to speakers who reveal something of themselves and identify with them. A consultant addressing office workers might reminisce about how she started as a clerk-typist; a CEO might tell a funny story in which the joke is on himself.

After capturing attention and establishing yourself, you'll want to preview the main points of your topic, perhaps with a visual aid. You may wish to put off actually writing your introduction, however, until after you have organized the rest of the presentation and crystallized your principal ideas.

Take a look at Eric Evans' introduction, shown in Figure 15.1, to see how he integrated all the elements necessary for a good opening.

Body

The best oral presentations focus on a few key ideas.

The biggest problem with most oral presentations is a failure to focus on a few principal ideas. Thus, the body of your short presentation (20 or fewer minutes) should include a limited number of main points, say, two to four. Develop each main point with adequate, but not excessive, explanation and details. Too many details can obscure the main message, so keep your presentation simple and logical. Remember, listeners have no pages to leaf back through should they become confused.

CAREER COACH

NINE TECHNIQUES FOR GAINING AND KEEPING AUDIENCE ATTENTION

Experienced speakers know how to capture the attention of an audience and how to maintain that attention during a presentation. Here are nine proven techniques.

- **A promise.** Begin with a promise that keeps the audience expectant (for example, "By the end of this presentation I will show you how you can increase your sales by 50 percent").
- **Drama.** Open by telling an emotionally moving story or by describing a serious problem that involves the audience. Throughout your talk include other dramatic elements, such as a long pause after a key statement. Change your vocal tone or pitch. Professionals use high-intensity emotions such as anger, joy, sadness, and excitement.
- **Eye contact.** As you begin, command attention by surveying the entire audience to take in all listeners. Take two to five seconds to make eye contact with as many people as possible.
- **Movement.** Leave the lectern area whenever possible. Walk around the conference table or between the aisles of your audience. Try to move toward your audience, especially at the beginning and end of your talk.
- **Questions.** Keep listeners active and involved with rhetorical questions. Ask for a show of hands to get each listener thinking. The response will also give you a quick gauge of audience attention.
- **Demonstrations.** Include a member of the audience in a demonstration (for example, "I'm going to show you exactly how to implement our four-step customer courtesy process, but I need a volunteer from the audience to help me").
- **Samples/gimmicks.** If you're promoting a product, consider using items to toss out to the audience or to award as prizes to volunteer participants. You can also pass around product samples or promotional literature. Be careful, though, to maintain control.
- **Visuals.** Give your audience something to look at besides yourself. Use a variety of visual aids in a single session. Also consider writing the concerns expressed by your listeners on a flipchart or on the board as you go along.
- **Self-interest.** Review your entire presentation to ensure that it meets the critical "What's-in-it-for-me?" audience test. Remember that people are most interested in things that benefit them.

When Eric Evans began planning his presentation, he realized immediately that he could talk for hours on his topic. He also knew that listeners are not good at separating major and minor points. Thus, instead of submerging his listeners in a sea of information, he sorted out a few principal ideas. In the mortgage business, loan officers generally ask the following three questions of each applicant for a small business loan: (1) Are you ready to "hit the ground running" in starting your business? (2) Have you done your homework? and (3) Have you made realistic projections of potential sales, cash flow, and equity investment? These questions would become his main points, but Eric wanted to streamline them further so that his audience would be sure to remember them. He capsulated the questions in three words: *experience*, *preparation*, and *projection*. As you can see in Figure 15.1, Eric prepared a sentence outline showing these three main ideas. Each is supported by examples and explanations.

Main ideas can be organized according to time, component, importance, criteria, or conventional groupings.

How to organize and sequence main ideas may not be immediately obvious when you begin working on a presentation. Let's review the five organizational methods employed for written reports in Chapter 12, because those methods are equally appropriate for oral presentations. You could structure your ideas by the following elements:

- **Time.** Example: A presentation describing the history of a problem, organized from the first sign of trouble to the present.
- **Component.** Example: A sales report organized by divisions or products.
- **Importance.** Example: A report describing operating problems arranged from the most important to the least.
- **Criteria.** Example: A presentation evaluating equipment by comparing each model against a set of specifications.
- **Conventional groupings.** Example: A report comparing asset size, fees charged, and yields of mutual funds arranged by these existing categories.

In his presentation Eric arranged the main points by importance, placing the most important point last where it had maximum effect.

In organizing any presentation, prepare a little more material than you think you will actually need. Engaging speakers always have something useful in reserve (such as an extra handout, transparency, or idea)—just in case they finish early. To help you visualize the organization of your presentation, consider using the outline feature of a software presentation program. You'll learn more about preparing electronic presentations shortly.

Conclusion

Effective conclusions summarize main points and focus on a goal.

You should prepare the conclusion carefully because this is your last chance to drive home your main points. Don't end limply with comments like "I guess that's about all I have to say." Skilled speakers use the conclusion to review the main themes of the presentation and focus on a goal. They concentrate on what they want the audience to do, think, or remember. Even though they were mentioned earlier, important ideas must be repeated. Notice how Eric Evans, in the conclusion shown in Figure 15.1, summarized his three main points and provided a final focus to listeners.

When they finish, most speakers encourage questions. If silence ensues, you can prime the pump with "One question that I'm frequently asked is ...." You can also remark that you will be happy to answer questions individually after the presentation is completed.

Verbal Signposts

Knowledgeable speakers provide verbal signposts to spotlight organization and key ideas.

Speakers must remember that listeners, unlike readers of a report, cannot control the rate of presentation or flip back through pages to review main points. As a result, listeners get lost easily. Knowledgeable speakers help the audience recognize the organization and main points in an oral message with verbal signposts. They keep listeners on track by including helpful previews, summaries, and transitions, such as these:

To Preview
The next segment of my talk presents three reasons for ...
Let's now consider the causes of ...

To Summarize
Let me review with you the major problems I've just discussed ...
You see, then, that the most significant factors are ...

To Switch Directions
Thus far we've talked solely about ...; now let's move to ...
I've argued that ... and ..., but an alternate view holds that ...

FIGURE 15.1 **Oral Presentation Outline**

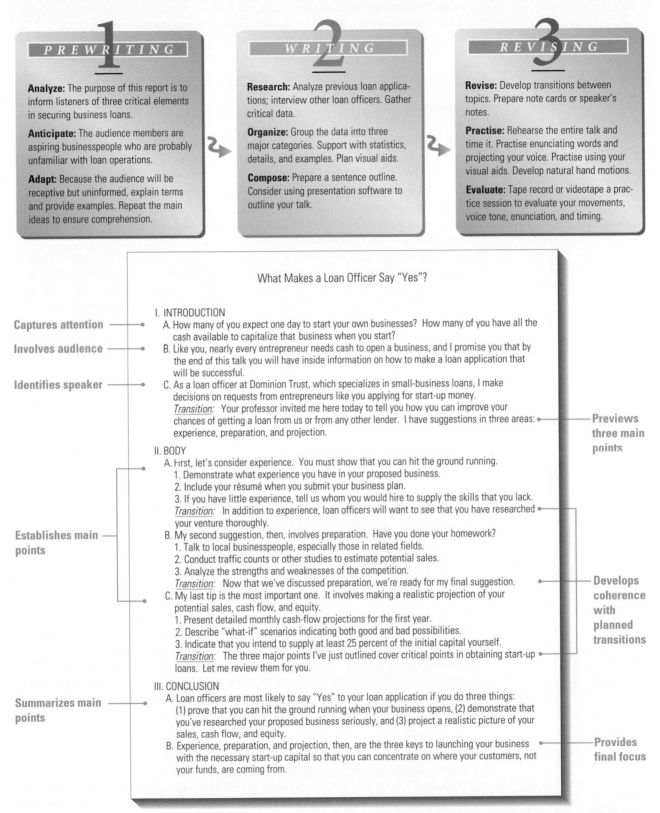

1 PREWRITING

Analyze: The purpose of this report is to inform listeners of three critical elements in securing business loans.

Anticipate: The audience members are aspiring businesspeople who are probably unfamiliar with loan operations.

Adapt: Because the audience will be receptive but uninformed, explain terms and provide examples. Repeat the main ideas to ensure comprehension.

2 WRITING

Research: Analyze previous loan applications; interview other loan officers. Gather critical data.

Organize: Group the data into three major categories. Support with statistics, details, and examples. Plan visual aids.

Compose: Prepare a sentence outline. Consider using presentation software to outline your talk.

3 REVISING

Revise: Develop transitions between topics. Prepare note cards or speaker's notes.

Practise: Rehearse the entire talk and time it. Practise enunciating words and projecting your voice. Practise using your visual aids. Develop natural hand motions.

Evaluate: Tape record or videotape a practice session to evaluate your movements, voice tone, enunciation, and timing.

What Makes a Loan Officer Say "Yes"?

I. INTRODUCTION

A. How many of you expect one day to start your own businesses? How many of you have all the cash available to capitalize that business when you start? — **Captures attention**

B. Like you, nearly every entrepreneur needs cash to open a business, and I promise you that by the end of this talk you will have inside information on how to make a loan application that will be successful. — **Involves audience**

C. As a loan officer at Dominion Trust, which specializes in small-business loans, I make decisions on requests from entrepreneurs like you applying for start-up money. — **Identifies speaker**

Transition: Your professor invited me here today to tell you how you can improve your chances of getting a loan from us or from any other lender. I have suggestions in three areas: experience, preparation, and projection. — **Previews three main points**

II. BODY (**Establishes main points**)

A. First, let's consider experience. You must show that you can hit the ground running.
1. Demonstrate what experience you have in your proposed business.
2. Include your résumé when you submit your business plan.
3. If you have little experience, tell us whom you would hire to supply the skills that you lack.

Transition: In addition to experience, loan officers will want to see that you have researched your venture thoroughly.

B. My second suggestion, then, involves preparation. Have you done your homework?
1. Talk to local businesspeople, especially those in related fields.
2. Conduct traffic counts or other studies to estimate potential sales.
3. Analyze the strengths and weaknesses of the competition.

Transition: Now that we've discussed preparation, we're ready for my final suggestion.

C. My last tip is the most important one. It involves making a realistic projection of your potential sales, cash flow, and equity.
1. Present detailed monthly cash-flow projections for the first year.
2. Describe "what-if" scenarios indicating both good and bad possibilities.
3. Indicate that you intend to supply at least 25 percent of the initial capital yourself.

Transition: The three major points I've just outlined cover critical points in obtaining start-up loans. Let me review them for you.

(**Develops coherence with planned transitions**)

III. CONCLUSION

A. Loan officers are most likely to say "Yes" to your loan application if you do three things: (1) prove that you can hit the ground running when your business opens, (2) demonstrate that you've researched your proposed business seriously, and (3) project a realistic picture of your sales, cash flow, and equity. — **Summarizes main points**

B. Experience, preparation, and projection, then, are the three keys to launching your business with the necessary start-up capital so that you can concentrate on where your customers, not your funds, are coming from. — **Provides final focus**

You can further improve any oral presentation by including appropriate transitional expressions such as *first, second, next, then, therefore, moreover, on the other hand, on the contrary,* and *in conclusion.* These expressions lend emphasis and tell listeners where you are headed. Notice in Eric Evans' outline, in Figure 15.1, the specific transitional elements designed to help listeners recognize each new principal point.

Planning Visual Aids and Handouts

3

Visual aids clarify points, improve comprehension, and aid retention.

Before you make a business presentation, consider this wise Chinese proverb: "Tell me, I forget. Show me, I remember. Involve me, I understand." Because your goals as a speaker are to make listeners understand, remember, and act on your ideas, include visual aids to get them interested and involved. Some authorities suggest that we acquire 85 percent of all our knowledge visually. Therefore, an oral presentation that incorporates visual aids is far more likely to be understood and retained than one lacking visual enhancement.

Good visual aids have many purposes. They emphasize and clarify main points, thus improving comprehension and retention. They increase audience interest, and they make the presenter appear more professional, better prepared, and more persuasive. Furthermore, research shows that the use of visual aids actually shortens meetings.[3] Visual aids are particularly helpful for inexperienced speakers because the audience concentrates on the aid rather than on the speaker. Good visuals also serve to jog the memory of a speaker, thus improving self-confidence, poise, and delivery.

Fortunately for today's speakers, many forms of visual media are available to enhance a presentation. Figure 15.2 describes a number of visual aids and compares their cost, degree of formality, and other considerations. Three of the most popular visuals are overhead transparencies, handouts, and computer visuals.

Overhead Transparencies

Student and professional speakers alike rely on the overhead projector for many reasons. Most meeting areas are equipped with projectors and screens. Moreover, acetate transparencies for the overhead are cheap, easily prepared on a computer or copier, and simple to use. And, because rooms need not be darkened, a speaker using transparencies can maintain eye contact with the audience. A word of caution, though: stand to the side of the projector so that you don't obstruct the audience's view.

Handouts

You can enhance and complement your presentations by distributing pictures, outlines, brochures, articles, charts, summaries, or other supplements. Speakers who use computer presentation programs often prepare a set of their slides along with notes to hand out to viewers. Timing the distribution of any handout, though, is tricky. If given out during a presentation, your handouts tend to distract the audience, causing you to lose control. Thus, it's probably best to discuss most handouts during the presentation but delay distributing them until after you finish.

Computer Visuals

With today's excellent software programs you can create dynamic, colourful presentations with your PC. The output from these programs is generally shown on a PC monitor, a TV monitor, an LCD (liquid crystal display) panel, or a screen. With a

FIGURE 15.2 **Presentation Enhancers**

Medium	Cost	Audience Size	Formality Level	Advantages and Disadvantages
Overhead projector	Low	2–200	Formal or informal	✓ Transparencies are easy and inexpensive to produce. Speaker keeps contact with audience.
Flipchart	Low	2–200	Informal	✓ Easels and charts are readily available and portable. Speaker can prepare the display in advance or on the spot.
Write-and-wipe board	Medium	2–200	Informal	✓ Porcelain-on-steel surface replaces messy chalkboard. Speaker can wipe clean with cloth.
Slide projector	Medium	2–500	Formal	✓ Slides provide excellent graphic images. ✘ Darkened room may put audience to sleep. Slides demand expertise, time, and equipment to produce.
Video monitor	Medium	2–100	Formal or informal	✓ A VCR display features motion and sound. ✘ Videos require skill, time, and equipment to prepare.
Computer slides	Low	2–200	Formal or informal	✓ Computers generate slides, transparencies, or multimedia visuals. Presentation software programs are easy to use, and they create dazzling results.
Handouts	Varies	Unlimited	Formal or informal	✓ Audience appreciates take-home items such as outlines, tables, charts, reports, brochures, or summaries. ✘ Handouts can divert attention from speaker.

little expertise and advanced equipment, you can create a multimedia presentation that includes stereo sound, videos, and hyperlinks, as described in the following discussion of electronic presentations.

Designing an Electronic Presentation

The content of most presentations today hasn't changed, but the medium certainly has. At meetings and conferences smart speakers now use computer programs, such as PowerPoint, to present, defend, and sell their ideas most effectively. Business speakers have switched to computer presentations because they are economical, flexible, and easy to prepare. Changes can be made right up to the last minute. Most important, though, such presentations make even amateurs look like real pros.

4

Computer-aided presentations are economical, flexible, professional, and easy to prepare.

Using Templates

Many novice presenters begin by using one of the professionally designed templates that come with a software program such as PowerPoint. These templates combine harmonious colours, borders, and fonts for pleasing visual effects. Templates also provide guidance in laying out each slide. You can select a layout for a title page, a bulleted list, a bar chart, a double-column list, an organization chart, and so on.

Working With Colour

Background and text colours depend on lightness of room.

You don't need training in colour theory to create presentation images that impress your audience rather than confuse them. You can use the colour schemes from the design templates that come with your presentation program or you can alter them. Generally, you're smart to use a colour palette of five or fewer colours for an entire presentation. Use warm colours—reds, oranges, and yellows—to highlight important elements. Use the same colour for like elements. For example, all slide titles should be the same colour. The colour for backgrounds and text depends on where the presentation will be given. Use light text on a dark background for presentations in darkened rooms. Use dark text on a light background for computer presentations in lighted rooms and for projecting transparencies.

Building Bullet Points

When you prepare your slides, translate the major headings in your presentation outline into titles for slides. For example, Alan Christopher prepared a PowerPoint presentation based on his research report featured in Figure 14.3 in Chapter 14. Part of his presentation slides are shown in Figure 15.3. Notice that the major topics from his outline became the titles of slides. Then he developed bulleted items for major subpoints. As you learned earlier, bulleted items must be constructed in parallel form. They should be phrases or key words, not complete sentences.

One of the best features about electronic presentation programs is the "build" capability. You can focus the viewer's attention on each specific item as you add bullet points line by line. The bulleted items may "fly" in from the left, right, top, or bottom. They can also build or dissolve from the centre. As each new bullet point is added, leave the previous ones on the slide but show them in lightened text. In building bulleted points or in moving from one slide to the next, you can use *slide transition* elements, such as "wipe outs," glitter, ripple, liquid, and vortex effects. But don't overdo it. Experts suggest choosing one transition effect and applying it consistently.[4]

For the most readable slides, apply the *Rule of Seven*. Each slide should include no more than seven words in a line, no more than seven total lines, and no more than 7 × 7 or 49 total words. And remember that presentation slides summarize; they don't tell the whole story. That's the job of the presenter.

Adding Multimedia and Other Effects

Multimedia elements include sound, animation, and video features.

Many presentation programs also provide libraries of multimedia features to enhance your content. These include sound, animation, and video elements. For example, you could use sound effects to "reward" correct answers from your audience. But using the sound of screeching tires in a Transport Canada presentation is probably unwise. Similarly, video clips—when used judiciously—can add excitement and depth to a presentation. You might use video to capture attention in a stimulating introduction, to show the benefits of a product in use, or to bring the personality of a distant expert or satisfied customer right into the meeting room.

Another way to enliven a presentation is with real-life photographic images, which are now easy to obtain thanks to the prevalence of new low-cost scanners and digital cameras. Some programs are also capable of generating hyperlinks ("hot" spots on the screen) that allow you to instantly jump to relevant data or multimedia content.

Producing Speaker's Notes and Handouts

Most electronic presentation programs offer a variety of presentation options. In addition to printouts of your slides, you can make speaker's notes. These are won-

FIGURE 15.3 **Making a PowerPoint™ Presentation**

Tips for Preparing and Using Slides

- Use colour effectively.
- Keep all visuals simple; spotlight major points only.
- Use the same font size and style for similar headings.
- Apply the Rule of Seven: No more than seven words on a line, seven total lines, and 7 × 7 or 49 total words.
- Be sure that everyone in the audience can see the slides.
- Show a slide, allow audience to read it, then paraphrase it. Do NOT read from a slide.
- Rehearse by practising talking to the audience, not to the slides.
- Bring back-up transparencies in case of equipment failure.

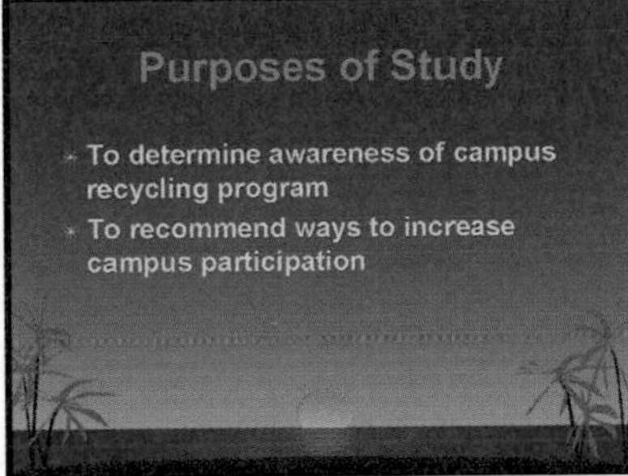

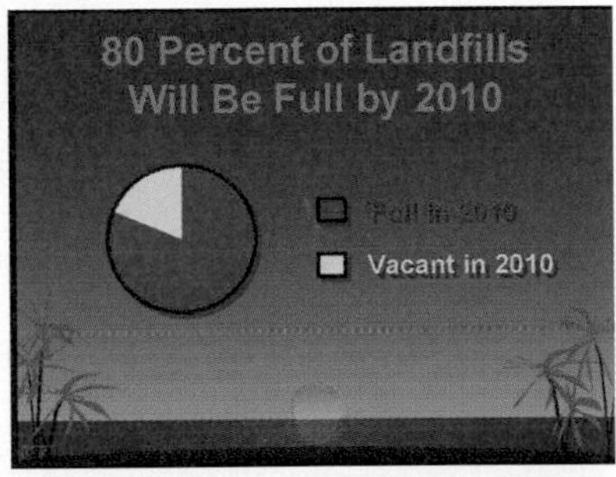

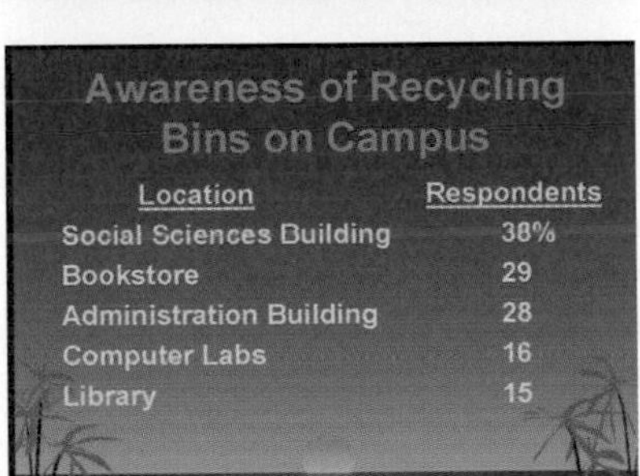

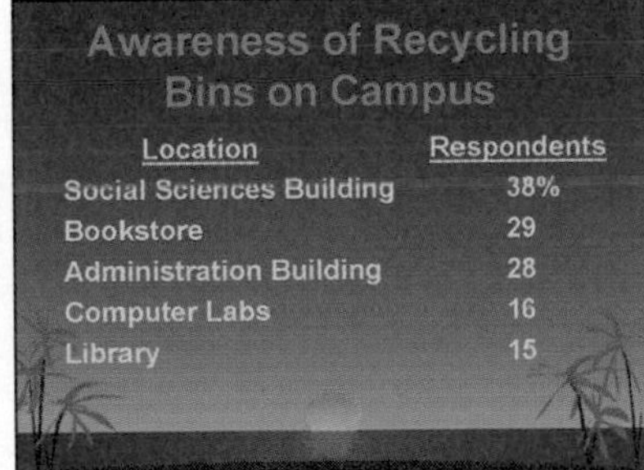

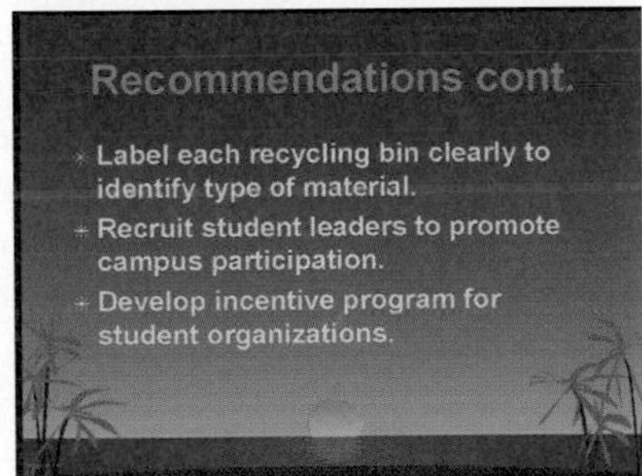

derful aids for practising your talk; they remind you of the supporting comments for the abbreviated material in your slides. Many programs allow you to print miniature versions of your slides with numerous slides to a page, if you wish. These miniatures are handy if you want to preview your talk to a sponsoring organization or if you wish to supply the audience with a summary of your presentation.

Developing Web-Based Presentations and Electronic Handouts

Because of recent technological improvements, you can now give a talk without even travelling off-site. In other words, you can put your slides "on the road." Web presentations with slides, narration, and speaker control are emerging as a less expensive alternative to videoconferencing, which was discussed in Chapter 2. Web-based presentations have many applications, including providing access to updated training or sales data whenever needed.[5] Larry Magid, computer expert and noted speaker, suggests still another way that speakers can use the Web. He recommends posting your slides on the Web even if you are giving a face-to-face presentation. Attendees appreciate these electronic handouts because they don't have to lug them home.[6]

Avoiding Being Upstaged by Your Slides

In developing a presentation, don't expect your slides to carry the show. They merely summarize important points. As the speaker, you must explain the analyses leading up to the major points. You must explain what the major points mean. Slides provide you with talking points. For each slide you should have one or more paragraphs of narration to present to your audience. Make use of the speaker's notes feature to capture your supporting ideas while you make the slides. And don't let a PowerPoint presentation "steal your thunder." Elizabeth Hunt warns, "At the end of the day, it won't be a fancy computer generated presentation that will persuade or move an audience to action. For even if you pull out all the technological stops, it's up to you to win your audience over."[7] You must maintain control of the presentation rather than allowing the electronics to take over.

5

Polishing Your Delivery

Once you've organized your presentation and prepared visuals, you're ready to practise delivering it. Here are suggestions for selecting a delivery method, along with specific techniques to use before, during, and after your presentation.

Delivery Method

Inexperienced speakers often feel that they must memorize an entire presentation to be effective. Unless you're an experienced performer, however, you will sound wooden and unnatural. Moreover, forgetting your place can be disastrous! Therefore, memorizing an entire oral presentation is not recommended. However, memorizing significant parts—the introduction, the conclusion, and perhaps a meaningful quotation—can be dramatic and impressive.

If memorizing won't work, is reading your presentation the best plan? Definitely not! Reading to an audience is boring and ineffective. Because reading suggests that you don't know your topic very well, the audience loses confidence in your expertise. Reading also prevents you from maintaining eye contact. You can't see audience reactions; consequently, you can't benefit from feedback.

Neither the memorizing nor the reading method creates very convincing presentations. The best plan, by far, is a "notes" method. Plan your presentation carefully and talk from note cards or an outline containing key sentences and major ideas. By preparing and then practising with your notes, you can talk to your audience in a conversational manner. Your notes should be neither entire paragraphs nor single words. Instead, they should contain a complete sentence or two to introduce each major idea. Below the topic sentence(s), outline subpoints and illustrations. Note cards will keep you on track and prompt your memory, but only if you have rehearsed the presentation thoroughly.

Delivery Techniques

Nearly everyone experiences some degree of stage fright when speaking before a group. A University of Manitoba study found that a third of respondents reported excessive anxiety when speaking to crowds. Showing signs of anxiety, having their

CAREER COACH

HOW TO AVOID STAGE FRIGHT

Ever get nervous before giving a speech? Everyone does! And it's not all in your head, either. When you face something threatening or challenging, your body reacts in what psychologists call the *fight-or-flight response.* This response provides your body with increased energy to deal with threatening situations. It also creates those sensations—dry mouth, sweaty hands, increased heartbeat, and stomach butterflies—that we associate with stage fright. The fight-or-flight response arouses your body for action—in this case, giving a speech.

Since everyone feels some form of apprehension before speaking, it's impossible to eliminate the physiological symptoms altogether. But you can help reduce their effects with the following techniques:

- Use deep breathing to ease your fight-or-flight symptoms. Inhale to a count of ten, hold this breath to a count of ten, and exhale to a count of ten. Concentrate on your counting and your breathing; both activities reduce your stress.
- Don't view your sweaty palms and dry mouth as evidence of fear. Interpret them as symptoms of exuberance, excitement, and enthusiasm to share your ideas.
- Feel confident about your topic. Select a topic that you know well and that is relevant to your audience.
- Use positive self-talk. Remind yourself that you know your topic and are prepared. Tell yourself that the audience is on your side—because it is!
- Shift the spotlight to your visuals. At least some of the time the audience will be focusing on your slides, transparencies, handouts, or whatever you have prepared—and not on you.
- Ignore any stumbles. Don't apologize or confess your nervousness. If you keep going, the audience will forget any mistakes quickly.

When you're finished, you'll be surprised at how good you feel. You can take pride in what you've accomplished, and your audience will reward you with applause and congratulations. And, of course, your body will call off the fight-or-flight response and return to normal!

minds go blank, or doing something embarrassing were fears of the respondents.[8] Being afraid is quite natural and results from actual physiological changes occurring in your body. Faced with a frightening situation, your body responds with the fight-or-flight response, discussed more fully in the Career Coach box above. You can learn to control and reduce stage fright, as well as to incorporate techniques for effective speaking, by using the following strategies and techniques before, during, and after your presentation.

Stage fright is both natural and controllable.

Before Your Presentation

Thorough preparation, extensive rehearsal, and stress-reduction techniques can lessen stage fright.

- **Prepare thoroughly.** One of the most effective strategies for reducing stage fright is knowing your subject thoroughly. Research your topic diligently and prepare a careful sentence outline. Those who try to "wing it" usually suffer the worst butterflies—and make the worst presentations.
- **Rehearse repeatedly.** When you rehearse, practise your entire presentation, not just the first half. Place your outline sentences on separate cards. You may also wish to include transitional sentences to help you move to the next topic. Use

these cards as you practise, and include your visual aids in your rehearsal. Record your rehearsal on audio- or videotape so that you can evaluate your effectiveness.

- **Time yourself.** Most audiences tend to get restless during longer talks. Thus, try to complete your presentation in no more than 20 minutes. Set a timer during your rehearsal to measure your speaking time.
- **Request a lectern.** Every beginning speaker needs the security of a high desk or lectern from which to deliver a presentation. It serves as a note holder and a convenient place to rest wandering hands and arms.
- **Check the room.** Before you talk, make sure that a lectern has been provided. If you are using sound equipment or a projector, be certain they are operational. Check electrical outlets and the position of the viewing screen. Ensure that the seating arrangement is appropriate to your needs.
- **Practise stress reduction.** If you feel tension and fear while you are waiting your turn to speak, use stress reduction techniques, such as deep breathing. Additional techniques to help you conquer stage fright are presented in the accompanying Career Coach box.

During Your Presentation

Eye contact, a moderate tone of voice, and natural movements enhance a presentation.

- **Begin with a pause.** When you first approach the audience, take a moment to adjust your notes and make yourself comfortable. Establish your control of the situation.
- **Present your first sentence from memory.** By memorizing your opening, you can immediately establish rapport with the audience through eye contact. You'll also sound confident and knowledgeable.
- **Maintain eye contact.** If the size of the audience overwhelms you, pick out two individuals on the right and two on the left. Talk directly to these people.
- **Control your voice and vocabulary.** This means speaking in moderated tones but loudly enough to be heard. Eliminate verbal static, such as *ah, er, you know*, and *um*. Silence is preferable to meaningless fillers when you are thinking of your next idea.
- **Put the brakes on.** Many novice speakers talk too rapidly, displaying their nervousness and making it very difficult for audience members to understand their ideas. Slow down and listen to what you are saying.
- **Move naturally.** You can use the lectern to hold your notes so that you are free to move about casually and naturally. Avoid fidgeting with your notes, your clothing, or items in your pockets. Learn to use your body to express a point.
- **Use visual aids effectively.** You should discuss and interpret each visual aid for the audience. Move aside as you describe it so that it can be seen fully. Use a pointer if necessary.
- **Avoid digressions.** Stick to your outline and notes. Don't suddenly include clever little anecdotes or digressions that occur to you on the spot. If it's not part of your rehearsed material, leave it out so that you can finish on time. Remember, too, that your audience may not be as enthralled with your topic as you are.
- **Summarize your main points.** Conclude your presentation by reiterating your main points or by emphasizing what you want the audience to think or do. Once you have announced your conclusion, proceed to it directly. Don't irritate the audience by talking for five or ten more minutes.

After Your Presentation

- **Distribute handouts.** If you prepared handouts with data the audience will need, pass them out when you finish.
- **Encourage questions.** If the situation permits a question-and-answer period, announce it at the beginning of your presentation. Then, when you finish, ask for questions. Set a time limit for questions and answers.
- **Repeat questions.** Although the speaker may hear the question, audience members often do not. Begin each answer with a repetition of the question. This also gives you thinking time. Then, direct your answer to the entire audience.
- **Reinforce your main points.** You can use your answers to restate your primary ideas ("I'm glad you brought that up because it gives me a chance to elaborate on ..."). In answering questions, avoid becoming defensive or debating the questioner.
- **Keep control.** Don't allow one individual to take over. Keep the entire audience involved.
- **End with a summary and appreciation.** To signal the end of the session before you take the last question, say something like "We have time for just one more question." As you answer the last question, try to work it into a summary of your main points. Then, express appreciation to the audience for the opportunity to talk with them.

The time to answer questions, distribute handouts, and reiterate main points is after a presentation.

Preparing and organizing an oral presentation, as summarized in the concluding checklist, requires attention to content and strategy. Along with the care you devote to developing your talk, consider also its ethics.

Adapting to International and Cross-Cultural Audiences

Every good speaker adapts to the audience, and cross-cultural presentations call for special adjustments and sensitivity. When working with an interpreter or speaking before individuals whose English is limited, you'll need to be very careful about your language.

Beyond these basic language adaptations, however, more fundamental sensitivity is often necessary. In organizing a presentation for a cross-cultural audience, think twice about delivering your main idea up front. Many people (notably those in Japanese, Latin American, and Arabic cultures) consider such directness to be brash and inappropriate. Remember that not all cultures appreciate straightforwardness.

Also consider breaking your presentation into short, discrete segments. In the Middle East, for example, Arab speakers "mix circuitous, irrelevant (by North American standards) conversations with short dashes of information that go directly to the point." Presenters who are patient, tolerant, and "mature" (in the eyes of the audience) will make the sale or win the contract.[9]

Remember, too, that some cultures prefer greater formality than Westerners exercise. Writing on a flipchart or transparency seems natural and spontaneous in this country. Abroad, though, such informal techniques may suggest that the speaker does not value the audience enough to prepare proper visual aids in advance.[10]

This caution aside, you'll still want to use visual aids to communicate your message. These visuals should be written in both languages, so that you and your audience understand them. Never use numbers without writing them out for all to see. If possible, say numbers in both languages. Distribute translated handouts, summarizing your important information, when you finish. Finally, be careful of your body language. Looking people in the eye suggests intimacy and self-confidence in this country, but in other cultures, such eye contact may be considered disrespectful.

Checklist for Preparing and Organizing Oral Presentations

Getting Ready to Speak

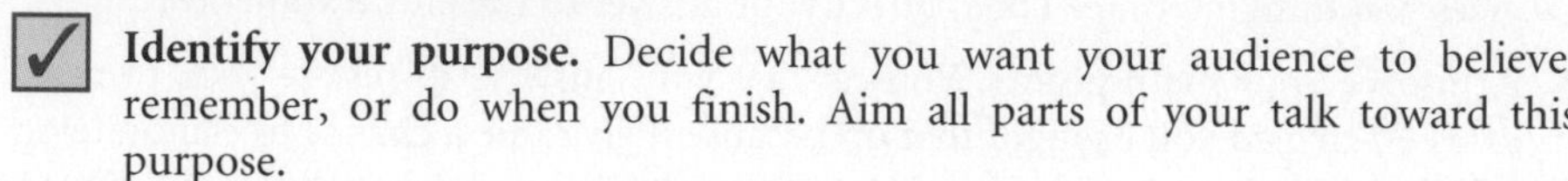

- ✓ **Identify your purpose.** Decide what you want your audience to believe, remember, or do when you finish. Aim all parts of your talk toward this purpose.
- ✓ **Analyze the audience.** Consider how to adapt your message (its organization, appeals, and examples) to your audience's knowledge and needs.

Organizing the Introduction

- ✓ **Get the audience involved.** Capture the audience's attention by opening with a promise, story, startling fact, question, quote, relevant problem, or self-effacing joke.
- ✓ **Establish yourself.** Demonstrate your credibility by identifying your position, expertise, knowledge, or qualifications.
- ✓ **Preview your main points.** Introduce your topic and summarize its principal parts.

Organizing the Body

- ✓ **Develop two to four main points.** Streamline your topic so that you can concentrate on its major issues.
- ✓ **Arrange the points logically.** Sequence your points chronologically, from most important to least important, by comparison and contrast, or by some other strategy.
- ✓ **Prepare transitions.** Between each major point write "bridge" statements that connect the previous item to the next one. Use transitional expressions as verbal signposts (*first, second, then, however, consequently, on the contrary,* and so forth).
- ✓ **Have extra material ready.** Be prepared with more information and visuals in case you have additional time to fill.

Organizing the Conclusion

- ✓ **Review your main points.** Emphasize your main ideas in your closing so that your audience will remember them.
- ✓ **Provide a final focus.** Tell how your listeners can use this information, why you have spoken, or what you want them to do.

Designing Visual Aids

☑ **Select your medium carefully.** Consider the size of your audience, degree of formality desired, cost and ease of preparation, and potential effectiveness.

☑ **Highlight main ideas.** Use visual aids to illustrate major concepts only. Keep them brief and simple.

☑ **Use aids skillfully.** Talk to the audience, not to the visuals. Paraphrase their contents.

Developing Electronic Presentations

☑ **Learn to use your software program.** Study template and slide layout designs to see how you can adapt them to your purposes.

☑ **Select a pleasing colour palette.** Work with five or fewer colours for your entire presentation.

☑ **Use bulleted points for major headings.** Make sure your points are all parallel and observe the Rule of Seven.

☑ **Make speaker's notes.** Jot down the narrative supporting each slide and use these notes to practise your presentation.

☑ **Maintain control.** Don't let your slides upstage you. Use a laser pointer to connect you to the slides and your audience.

Telephones and Voice Mail

7

The telephone is the most universal—and, some would say, one of the most important—pieces of equipment in offices today.[11] And with the addition of today's wireless technology, it doesn't matter whether you are in or out of the office. As a business communicator, you can be most effective by following these suggestions for making and receiving telephone calls and for using voice mail.

Making Productive Telephone Calls

Before making a telephone call, decide whether the intended call is really necessary. Could you find the information yourself? If you wait a while, would the problem resolve itself? Perhaps your message could be delivered more efficiently by some other means. One West Coast company found that telephone interruptions consumed about 18 percent of staff members' workdays. Another study found that two thirds of all calls were less important than the work they interrupted.[12] Alternatives to telephone calls include e-mail, memos, or calls to voice-mail systems. If a telephone call must be made, consider using the following suggestions to make it fully productive.

- **Plan a mini-agenda.** Have you ever been embarrassed when you had to make a second telephone call because you forgot an important item the first time? Before placing a call, jot down notes regarding all the topics you need to discuss. Following an agenda guarantees not only a complete call but also a quick one. You'll be less likely to wander from the business at hand while rummaging through your mind trying to remember everything.

Making productive telephone calls means planning an agenda, identifying the purpose, being courteous and cheerful, and avoiding rambling.

- **Use a three-point introduction.** When placing a call, immediately (1) name the person you are calling, (2) identify yourself and your affiliation, and (3) give a brief explanation of your reason for calling.
- **Be cheerful and accurate.** Let your voice show the same kind of animation that you radiate when you greet people in person. In your mind try to envision the individual answering the telephone. A smile can certainly affect the tone of your voice, so smile at that person. Moreover, be accurate about what you say. "Hang on a second; I'll be right back" rarely is true. Better to say, "It may take me two or three minutes to get that information. Would you prefer to hold or have me call you back?"
- **Bring it to a close.** The responsibility for ending a call lies with the caller. This is sometimes difficult to do if the other person rambles on. You may need to use suggestive closing language, such as "I've certainly enjoyed talking with you," "I've learned what I needed to know, and now I can proceed with my work," "Thanks for your help," or "I must go now, but may I call you again in the future if I need ...?"
- **Avoid telephone tag.** If you call someone who's not in, ask when it would be best for you to call again. State that you will call at a specific time—and do it. If you ask a person to call you, give a time when you can be reached—and then be sure you are in at that time.
- **Leave complete voice-mail messages.** Remember that there's no rush when you leave a voice-mail message. Always enunciate clearly. And be sure to provide a complete message, including your name, telephone number, and the time and date of your call. Explain your purpose so that the receiver can be ready with the required information when returning your call.

Receiving Productive Telephone Calls

With a little forethought you can make your telephone a productive, efficient work tool. Developing good telephone manners also reflects well on you and on your organization.

- **Identify yourself immediately.** In answering your telephone or someone else's, provide your name, title or affiliation, and, possibly, a greeting. Force yourself to speak clearly and slowly. Remember that the caller may be unfamiliar with what you are saying and fail to recognize slurred syllables.
- **Be responsive and helpful.** If you are in a support role, be sympathetic to callers' needs. Instead of "I don't know," try "That's a good question; let me investigate." Instead of "We can't do that," try "That's a tough one; let's see what we can do." Avoid "No" at the beginning of a sentence. It sounds especially abrasive and displeasing because it suggests total rejection.
- **Be cautious when answering calls for others.** Be courteous and helpful, but don't give out confidential information. Better to say, "She's away from her desk" or "He's out of the office" than to report a colleague's exact whereabouts.
- **Take messages carefully.** Few things are as frustrating as receiving a potentially important phone message that is illegible. Repeat the spelling of names and verify telephone numbers. Write messages legibly and record their time and date. Promise to give the messages to intended recipients, but don't guarantee return calls.
- **Explain what you're doing when transferring calls.** Give a reason for transferring, and identify the extension to which you are directing the call in case the caller is disconnected.

Making the Best Use of Voice Mail

Voice mail links a telephone system to a computer that digitizes and stores incoming messages. Some systems also provide functions such as automated attendant menus, allowing callers to reach any associated extension by pushing specific buttons on a touch-tone telephone. "Direct access" interactive utilities provide users with a wide range of opportunities. Telephone banking has expanded to giving consumers the opportunity to check balances, pay bills, and review past transactions. Movie theatres and other entertainment facilities permit users to access up-to-date information without ever talking to someone at the end of the line.

Voice mail eliminates telephone tag, inaccurate message-taking, and time-zone barriers; it also allows communicators to focus on essentials.

Voice mail serves many functions, but the most important is message storage. Because as many as half of all business calls require no discussion or feedback, the messaging capabilities of voice mail can mean huge savings for businesses. Incoming information is delivered without interrupting potential receivers and without all the niceties that most two-way conversations require. Stripped of superfluous chit-chat, voice-mail messages allow communicators to focus on essentials. Voice mail also eliminates telephone tag, inaccurate message-taking, and time-zone barriers. Critics complain, nevertheless, that automated systems seem cold and impersonal and are sometimes confusing and irritating. In any event, here are some ways that you can make voice mail work more effectively for you.

- **Announce your voice mail.** If you rely principally on a voice-mail message system, identify it on your business stationery and cards. Then, when people call, they will be ready to leave a message.
- **Prepare a warm and informative greeting.** Make your mechanical greeting sound warm and inviting, both in tone and content. Identify yourself and your organization so that callers know they have reached the right number. Thank the caller and briefly explain that you are unavailable and when you will return. Invite the caller to leave a message or, if appropriate, call back.
- **Be reachable "live."** Tell the caller how to access a "real person." For example, "To speak to someone directly, please press zero." Provide options to the sender; in other words, give callers an "out."
- **Test your message.** Call your number and assess your message. Does it sound inviting? Sincere? Understandable? Are you pleased with your tone? If not, says one consultant, have someone else, perhaps a professional, record a message for you.
- **Use group broadcasts wisely.** Group broadcasts are messages sent to everyone in a particular group or to an entire organization. They are, therefore, very general informational messages. When using group broadcasts, carefully consider who will need the message. Remember the importance of audience analysis.

Finally, keep these ideas in mind when you are leaving messages on someone's voice-mail system:

- **Speak naturally.** Use a tone that encourages people to return your call.
- **Speak clearly.** Enunciate well and don't rush the message.
- **Include all details.** Leave complete, detailed messages; specify the action that you want and how you can be reached.
- **Avoid small talk.** If the receiver has 20 voice-mail messages to be cleared, important details are what matter.

Summary of Learning Objectives

1 **Discuss two important first steps in preparing an effective oral presentation.** First, identify what your purpose is and what you want the audience to believe or do so that you can aim the entire presentation toward your goal. Second, know your audience so that you can adjust your message and style to its knowledge and needs.

2 **Explain the major elements in the introduction, body, and conclusion of an oral presentation and discuss the importance of verbal signposts.** The introduction of a good presentation should capture the listener's attention, identify the speaker, establish credibility, and preview the main points. The body should discuss two to four main points, with appropriate explanations, details, and verbal signposts to guide listeners. The conclusion should review the main points and provide a final focus. Good speakers provide verbal signposts to preview, summarize, and switch directions.

3 **Identify appropriate visual aids and handouts for a presentation.** Use simple, easily understood visual aids to emphasize and clarify main points. Choose transparencies, flipcharts, slides, or other visuals depending on audience size, degree of formality desired, and budget. Generally, it's best to distribute handouts after a presentation.

4 **Review techniques for designing an electronic presentation.** Speakers employing a program such as Microsoft PowerPoint™ use templates, layout designs, and bullet points to produce effective slides. A presentation may be enhanced with slide transitions, sound, animation, and video elements. Speaker's notes and handouts may be generated from slides. Web-based presentations allow speakers to narrate and show slides without leaving their home bases. Increasing numbers of speakers are using the Web to provide copies of their slides as electronic handouts.

5 **Specify delivery techniques for use before, during, and after a presentation.** Before your talk prepare a sentence outline on note cards or speaker's notes and rehearse repeatedly. Check the room, lectern, and equipment. During the presentation consider beginning with a pause and presenting your first sentence from memory. Make eye contact, control your voice, speak and move naturally, and avoid digressions. After your talk distribute handouts and answer questions. End gracefully and express appreciation.

6 **Discuss effective techniques for adapting oral presentations to cross-cultural audiences.** In presentations before groups whose English is limited, speak slowly, use simple English, avoid jargon and clichés, and use short sentences. Consider building up to your main idea rather than announcing it immediately. Also consider breaking the presentation into short segments to allow participants to ask questions and digest small parts separately. Beware of appearing too spontaneous and informal. Use visual aids to help communicate your message, but also distribute translated handouts summarizing the most important information.

7 **List techniques for improving telephone and voice-mail effectiveness.** You can improve your telephone calls by planning a mini-agenda and using a three-point introduction (name, affiliation, and purpose). Be cheerful and responsive, and use closing language to end a conversation. Avoid telephone tag by leaving complete messages. In answering calls, identify yourself immediately, avoid giving out confidential information when answering for others, and take careful

messages. In setting up an automated-attendance voice-mail menu, limit the number of choices. For your own message prepare a warm and informative greeting. Tell when you will be available. Evaluate your message by calling it yourself.

CHAPTER REVIEW

1. The planning of an oral presentation should begin with serious thinking about what two factors? (Obj. 1)
2. Name three goals to be achieved in the introduction of an oral presentation. (Obj. 2)
3. For a 20-minute presentation, how many main points should be developed? (Obj. 2)
4. What should the conclusion to an oral presentation include? (Obj. 2)
5. Name three ways for a speaker to use verbal signposts in a presentation. Illustrate each. (Obj. 2)
6. Why are visual aids particularly useful to inexperienced speakers? (Obj. 3)
7. Why are transparencies a favourite visual aid? (Obj. 3)
8. Name three specific advantages of electronic presentation software. (Obj. 4)
9. What is a *template* and how is it useful? (Obj. 4)
10. How is the Rule of Seven applied in preparing bulleted points? (Obj. 4)
11. What delivery method is most effective for speakers? (Obj. 5)
12. Why should speakers deliver the first sentence from memory? (Obj. 5)
13. How might presentations before international or cross-cultural audiences be altered to be most effective? (Obj. 6)
14. What is a three-point introduction for a telephone call? (Obj. 7)
15. What is voice mail? (Obj. 7)

CRITICAL THINKING

1. Why is it necessary to repeat key points in an oral presentation? (Objs. 2 and 5)
2. How can a speaker make the most effective use of visual aids? (Obj. 3)
3. How can speakers prevent electronic presentation software from stealing their thunder? (Obj. 4)
4. Discuss effective techniques for reducing stage fright. (Obj. 5)

ACTIVITIES

15.1 Outlining an Oral Presentation (Objs. 1 and 2)

One of the hardest parts of preparing an oral presentation is developing the outline. Select an oral presentation topic from the list in Activity 15.4 or suggest an original topic. Prepare an outline for your presentation using the following format.

Title	
Purpose	
	I. INTRODUCTION
Gain attention of audience	A.
Involve audience	B.
Establish credibility	C.
Preview main points	D.
Transition	
	II. BODY
Main point	A.
Illustrate, clarify, contrast	1.
	2.
	3.
Transition	
Main point	B.
Illustrate, clarify, contrast	1.
	2.
	3.
Transition	
Main point	C.
Illustrate, clarify, contrast	1.
	2.
	3.
Transition	
	III. CONCLUSION
Summarize main points	A.
Provide final focus	B.
Encourage questions	C.

15.2 Overcoming Stage Fright (Obj. 5)

In a class discussion develop a list of reasons for being fearful when making a presentation before class. What makes you nervous? Being tongue-tied? Fearing all eyes on you? Messing up? Forgetting your ideas and looking silly? Then, in groups of three or four discuss ways to overcome these fears. Your instructor may ask you to write a memo (individual or collective) summarizing your suggestions, or you may break out of your small groups and report your best ideas to the entire class.

15.3 Discovering Presentation Tips on the Internet (Objs. 2–5)

Web

Using your favourite search engine and the search term "presentation tips," visit at least three Web sites that provide suggestions for giving presentations. If possible, print the most relevant findings. Select at least eight good tips or techniques that you did not learn from this chapter. Your instructor may ask you to bring them to class for discussion or submit a short memo report outlining your tips.

15.4 Choosing a Topic for an Oral Presentation (Objs. 1–6)

Select a topic from the list below or from the report topics in Activities 14.7 and 14.8 for a five- to ten-minute oral presentation. Consider yourself an expert who has been called in to explain some aspect of the topic before a group of interested people. Since your time is limited, prepare a concise yet forceful presentation with effective visual aids.

a. What kinds of employment advertisements are legal, and what kinds are potentially illegal?

b. How can the Internet be used to find a job?

c. What graphics package should your fellow students use to prepare visual aids for reports?

d. What is the employment outlook in three career areas of interest to you?

e. What is telecommuting, and for what kind of workers is it an appropriate work alternative?

f. How much choice should parents have in selecting schools for their young children (parochial, private, and public)?

g. What travel location would you recommend for postsecondary students in December (or another school break)?

h. What is the economic outlook for a given product (such as domestic cars, laptop computers, economy cameras, fitness equipment, or a product of your choice)?

i. How can your organization or institution improve its image?

j. Why should people invest in a company or scheme of your choice?

CHAPTER • 16 •

EMPLOYMENT COMMUNICATION

LEARNING OBJECTIVES

1 Prepare for employment by identifying your interests, evaluating your assets, recognizing the changing nature of jobs, choosing a career path, and studying traditional and electronic job search techniques.

2 Compare and contrast chronological, functional, and combination résumés.

3 Organize, format, and produce a persuasive résumé.

4 Identify techniques that prepare a résumé for computer scanning, posting at a Web site, faxing, and e-mailing.

5 Write a persuasive letter of application to accompany your résumé.

6 Write effective employment follow-up letters and other messages.

7 Evaluate successful job interview strategies.

FIGURE 16.1 **The Employment Search**

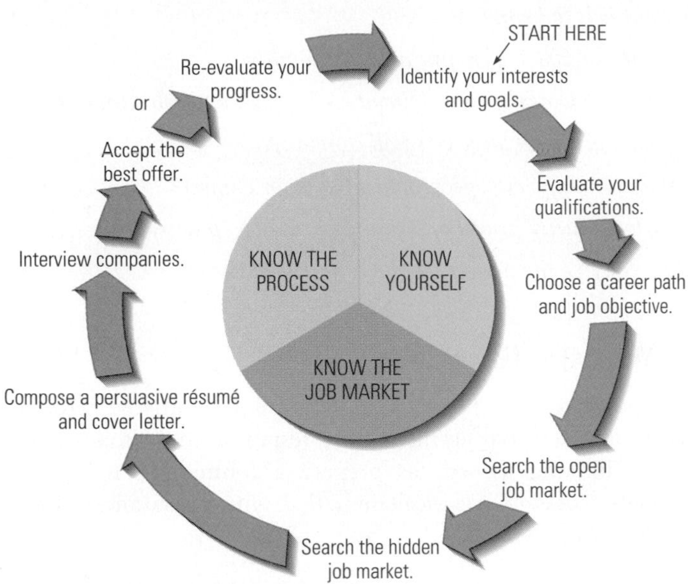

Preparing for Employment

1

Finding a satisfying career means learning about yourself, the job market, and the employment process.

One day you may be sending your résumé to a recruiting specialist who reads thousands of such résumés annually. What can you do to make your résumé and cover letter stand out? This chapter provides many tips for writing dynamite résumés and cover letters, as well as suggestions for successful interviewing. But the job search process actually begins long before you are ready to write a résumé. Whether you are looking for an internship, applying for a full-time position, searching for a part-time job, competing for a promotion, or changing careers, you must invest time and effort preparing yourself. You can't hope to find the position of your dreams without first (1) knowing yourself, (2) knowing the job market, and (3) knowing the employment process.

One of the first things you should do is obtain career information and choose a specific job objective. At the same time, you should be studying the job market and becoming aware of substantial changes in the nature of work. You'll want to understand how to use the latest Internet resources in your job search. Finally, you'll need to design a persuasive résumé and letter of application appropriate for small businesses as well as for larger organizations that may be using résumé-scanning programs. Following these steps, summarized in Figure 16.1 and described in this chapter, gives you a master plan for landing a job you really want.

Identifying Your Interests

The employment process begins with introspection. This means looking inside yourself to analyze what you like and dislike so that you can make good employment choices. For guidance in choosing a field that eventually proves to be satisfying, answer the following questions. If you have already chosen a field, think carefully about how your answers relate to that choice.

- *Do I enjoy working with people, data, or things?*
- *How important is it to be my own boss?*
- *How important are salary, benefits, and job stability?*
- *How important are working environment, colleagues, and job stimulation?*
- *Would I rather work for a large or small company?*
- *Must I work in a specific city, geographical area, or climate?*
- *Am I looking for security, travel opportunities, money, power, or prestige?*
- *How would I describe the perfect job, boss, and coworkers?*

Evaluating Your Qualifications

In addition to your interests, assess your qualifications. Employers today want to know what assets you have to offer them. Your responses to the following questions will target your thinking as well as prepare a foundation for your résumé. Remember, though, that employers seek more than empty assurances; they will want proof of your qualifications.

- *What computer skills can I offer?* Employers are often interested in specific software programs.
- *What other skills have I acquired in school, on the job, or through activities? How can I demonstrate these skills?*
- *Do I work well with people? What proof can I offer?* Consider extracurricular activities, clubs, and jobs.
- *Am I a leader, self-starter, or manager? What evidence can I offer?*
- *Do I speak, write, or understand another language?*
- *Do I learn quickly? Am I creative? How can I demonstrate these characteristics?*
- *Do I communicate well in speech and in writing? How can I verify these talents?*

Recognizing the Changing Nature of Jobs

As you learned in Chapter 1, the nature of the workplace is changing. One of the most significant changes involves the concept of the "job." Following the downsizing in the early years of the 1990s and the movement toward flattened organizations, fewer people are employed in permanent positions. Many employees are feeling less job security although they are doing more work.

People feel less job security after downsizing and movement to flatter organizations.

Workplaces are becoming more flexible and big companies are no longer the main employers. People seem to be working for smaller companies, or they are becoming consultants or specialists who work on tasks or projects under arrangements too fluid to be called "jobs." And because new technologies can spring up overnight making today's skills obsolete, employers are less willing to hire people into jobs with narrow descriptions.

"Jobs" are becoming more flexible and less permanent.

What do these changes mean for you? For one thing, you should probably no longer think in terms of a lifelong career with a single company. In fact, you can't even expect reasonably permanent employment for work well done. This social contract between employer and employee is no longer a given. And predictable career paths within companies have largely disappeared. Career advancement is in your own hands.[1] In the new workplace you can expect to work for multiple employers on flexible job assignments associated with teams and projects. Finally, never become complacent about your position or job skills. Be prepared for constant retraining and updating of your skills. People who learn quickly and adapt to change are "high-value-added" individuals who will always be in demand even in a climate of surging change.

Choosing a Career Path

The employment picture today is much different from that of a decade or two ago. You can expect to have eight to ten jobs in as many as three different careers during your lifetime.[2] Some of you probably have not yet settled on your first career choice; others are returning to college to retrain for a new career. Although you may be changing jobs in the future, you still need to train for a specific career area now. In choosing an area, you'll make the best decisions when you can match your interests and qualifications with the requirements and rewards in specific careers. But where can you find career data? Here are some suggestions:

- **Visit your campus career centre.**
- **Search the Web.**
- **Use your library.**
- **Take a summer job, internship, or part-time position in your field.**
- **Interview someone in your chosen field.**
- **Monitor the classified ads.**
- **Join professional organizations in your field.**

Summer and part-time jobs and internships are good opportunities to learn about different careers.

Using Traditional Job Search Techniques

Finding the perfect job requires an early start and a determined effort. Whether you use traditional or online job search techniques, you should be prepared to launch an aggressive campaign. And you can't start too early. Here are some traditional steps that job candidates take:

- **Check classified ads in local and national newspapers.**
- **Check announcements in publications of professional organizations.**
- **Contact companies in which you're interested, even if you know of no current opening.**
- **Sign up for campus interviews with visiting company representatives.**
- **Attend career and job fairs.**
- **Ask for advice from your professors.**
- **Develop your own network of contacts.**

Using Electronic Job Search Techniques

Just as the Internet has changed the way the world works, it's also changing the nature of the job search. Increasing numbers of employers are listing their job openings at special Web sites that are similar to newspaper classified ads. Companies are also listing job openings at their own Web sites, providing a more direct connection to employment opportunities. Although we will describe six Internet job sites here, you can find a more extensive and continuously updated list with clickable hot links at the Guffey student Web site **<buscomm.nelson.com>**. Our site includes many job lists for recent postsecondary graduates and entry-level positions.

An electronic job-search campaign includes searching career and company Web sites for job listings.

- **Canada WorkInfoNet** **<www.canworknet.ca>** is sponsored by Human Resources Development Canada and provides over 2000 Canadian Web sites. It describes itself as "the primary source of career, education, and labour market information for Canadians." This collaborative venture developed by public, private, and not-for-profit sectors is a great place to start. There are valuable links to provincial and territorial partner sites.
- **Globecareers.com**, combined with Workopolis, calls itself "Canada's biggest job site." This Canada-only database provides more than 7000 available jobs and has a Career Alert feature that will e-mail listings to you that match your profile.
- **Human Resources Development Canada** **<www.hrdc-drhc.gc.ca>** provides a variety of resources such as career counselling information and a national job bank. Its most unique feature is the Electronic Labour Exchange. A database of available jobs is compared to the candidate's skill profile. With a match, the profile is forwarded to the potential employer.
- **CACEE WorkWeb** **<www.cacee.com>** is dedicated to helping students and recent graduates find "meaningful" employment. Its WorkWeb (created by the Canadian Association of Career Educators and Employers) provides job-search advice, links to employers, and access to government and professional home pages. It even includes information about the rights of the job seeker.
- **Monster Board** offers access to information on more than 50 000 jobs worldwide. It will find job listings that match your profile and e-mail them to you once a week. Although most of its jobs are aimed at experienced candidates, it also has plenty of entry-level positions. Its much smaller Canadian site **<www.monster.ca>** offers the same features.

Perhaps even better are the job openings listed at company Web sites. Check out your favourite companies to see what positions are open. What's the fastest way to find a company's Web address? We recommend Hoover's **<www.hoovers.com>** for quick company information and Web site links. If that fails, use your favourite search engine to see whether a company has its own Web site. Some companies even have online résumé forms that encourage job candidates to submit their qualifications immediately.

Many jobs are posted on the Internet, but most jobs are still found through networking.

Hundreds of job sites now flood the Internet, and increasing numbers of companies offer online recruiting. In fact, some companies will only accept electronic résumés. However, the harsh reality is that landing a job still depends largely on personal contacts.

The Persuasive Résumé

2

After using both traditional and online resources to learn about the employment market and to develop job leads, you'll focus on writing a persuasive résumé. Such a résumé does more than merely list your qualifications. It packages your assets into a convincing advertisement that sells you for a specific job. The goal of a persuasive résumé is winning an interview. Even if you are not in the job market at this moment, preparing a résumé now has advantages. Having a current résumé makes you look well organized and professional should an unexpected employment opportunity arise. Moreover, preparing a résumé early helps you recognize weak qualifications and gives you two or three years in which to bolster them.

Choosing a Résumé Style

Your qualifications and career goal will help you choose from among three résumé styles: chronological, functional, and combination.

Chronological résumés focus on past employment; functional résumés focus on skills.

Chronological. Most popular with recruiters is the chronological résumé, shown in Figure 16.2. It lists work history job by job, starting with the most recent position. Recruiters favour the chronological style because such résumés quickly reveal a candidate's education and experience record. The chronological style works well for candidates who have experience in their field of employment and for those who show steady career growth. But for many college students and others who lack extensive experience, the functional résumé format may be preferable.

Functional. The functional résumé, shown in Figure 16.3, focuses attention on a candidate's skills rather than on past employment. Like a chronological résumé, the functional résumé begins with the candidate's name, address, telephone number, job objective, and education. Instead of listing jobs, though, the functional résumé groups skills and accomplishments in special categories, such as *Supervisory and Management Skills* or *Retailing and Marketing Experience.* This résumé style highlights accomplishments and can de-emphasize a negative employment history. People who have changed jobs frequently or who have gaps in their employment records may prefer the functional résumé. Recent graduates with little employment experience often find the functional résumé useful.

Functional résumés are also called *skill* résumés. Although the functional résumé of Donald Vinton shown in Figure 16.3 concentrates on skills, it does include a short employment section because recruiters expect it. Notice that Donald breaks his skills into three categories. An alternative—and easier—method is to make one large list, perhaps with a title such as *Areas of Accomplishment, Summary of Qualifications,* or *Areas of Expertise and Ability.*

Combination. The combination résumé style, shown in Figure 16.4, draws on the best features of the chronological and functional résumés. It emphasizes a candidate's capabilities while also including a complete job history. For recent graduates the combination résumé is a good choice because it enables them to profile what they can do for a prospective employer. If the writer has a specific job in mind, the items should be targeted to that job description.

Arranging the Parts

3

The parts of résumés must be arranged with the most important qualifications first.

Although résumés have standard parts, their arrangement and content should be strategically planned. The most persuasive résumés emphasize skills and achievements aimed at a particular job or company. They show a candidate's most important qualifications first, and they de-emphasize any weaknesses. In arranging the parts, try to create as few headings as possible; more than six generally looks cluttered. No two résumés are ever exactly alike, but most writers consider the following parts.

FIGURE 16.2 **Chronological Résumé**

1 PREWRITING

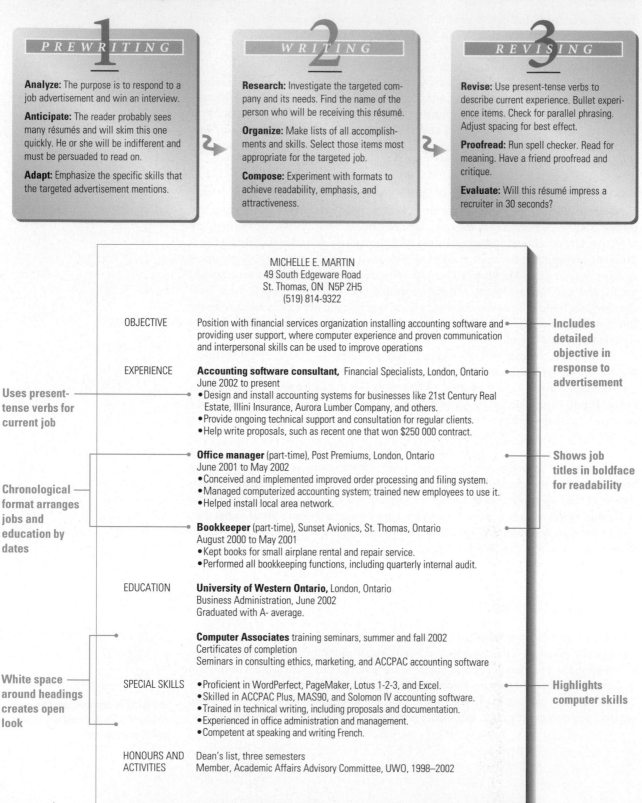

Analyze: The purpose is to respond to a job advertisement and win an interview.

Anticipate: The reader probably sees many résumés and will skim this one quickly. He or she will be indifferent and must be persuaded to read on.

Adapt: Emphasize the specific skills that the targeted advertisement mentions.

2 WRITING

Research: Investigate the targeted company and its needs. Find the name of the person who will be receiving this résumé.

Organize: Make lists of all accomplishments and skills. Select those items most appropriate for the targeted job.

Compose: Experiment with formats to achieve readability, emphasis, and attractiveness.

3 REVISING

Revise: Use present-tense verbs to describe current experience. Bullet experience items. Check for parallel phrasing. Adjust spacing for best effect.

Proofread: Run spell checker. Read for meaning. Have a friend proofread and critique.

Evaluate: Will this résumé impress a recruiter in 30 seconds?

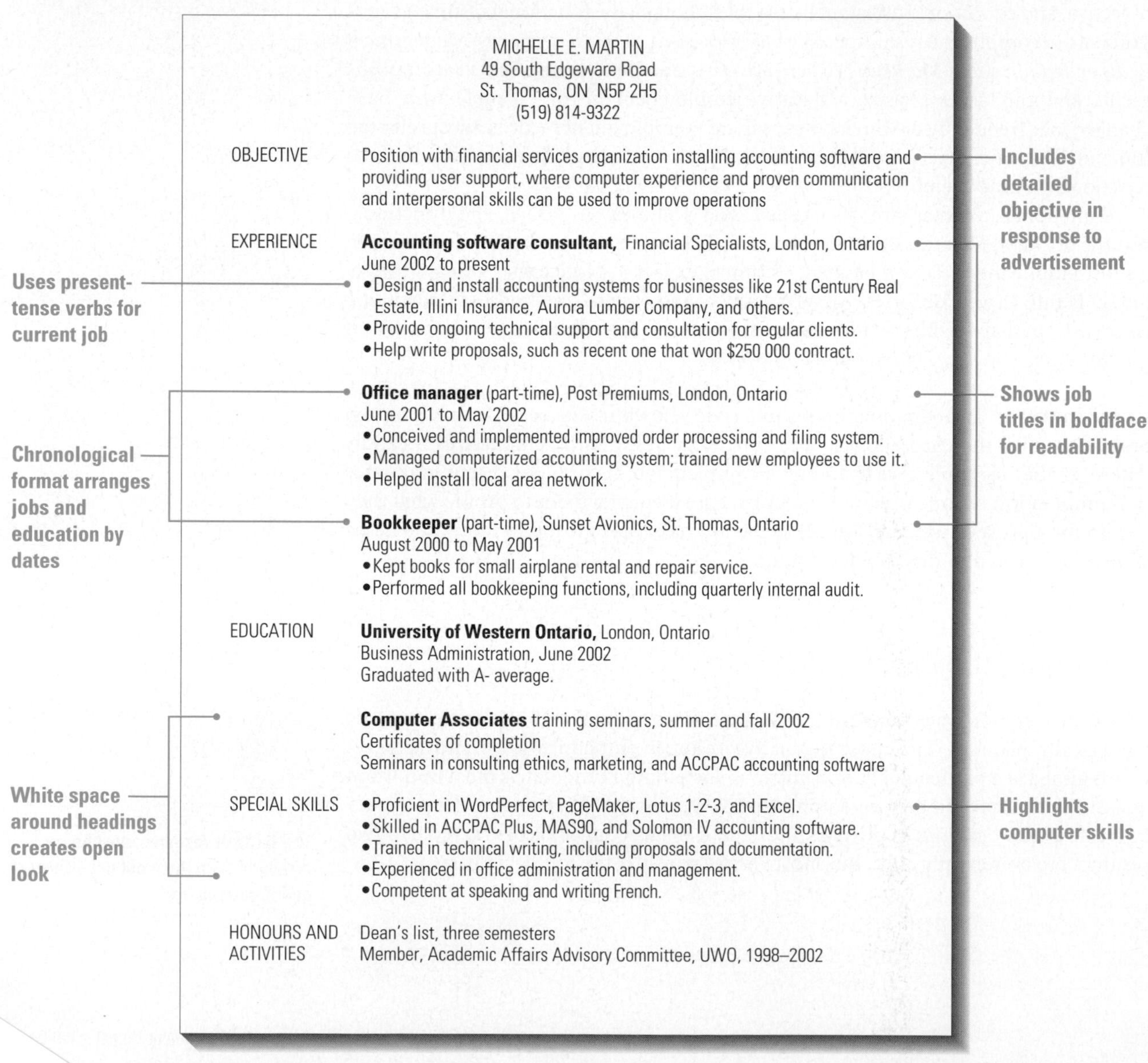

MICHELLE E. MARTIN
49 South Edgeware Road
St. Thomas, ON N5P 2H5
(519) 814-9322

OBJECTIVE
Position with financial services organization installing accounting software and providing user support, where computer experience and proven communication and interpersonal skills can be used to improve operations

EXPERIENCE
Accounting software consultant, Financial Specialists, London, Ontario
June 2002 to present
- Design and install accounting systems for businesses like 21st Century Real Estate, Illini Insurance, Aurora Lumber Company, and others.
- Provide ongoing technical support and consultation for regular clients.
- Help write proposals, such as recent one that won $250 000 contract.

Office manager (part-time), Post Premiums, London, Ontario
June 2001 to May 2002
- Conceived and implemented improved order processing and filing system.
- Managed computerized accounting system; trained new employees to use it.
- Helped install local area network.

Bookkeeper (part-time), Sunset Avionics, St. Thomas, Ontario
August 2000 to May 2001
- Kept books for small airplane rental and repair service.
- Performed all bookkeeping functions, including quarterly internal audit.

EDUCATION
University of Western Ontario, London, Ontario
Business Administration, June 2002
Graduated with A- average.

Computer Associates training seminars, summer and fall 2002
Certificates of completion
Seminars in consulting ethics, marketing, and ACCPAC accounting software

SPECIAL SKILLS
- Proficient in WordPerfect, PageMaker, Lotus 1-2-3, and Excel.
- Skilled in ACCPAC Plus, MAS90, and Solomon IV accounting software.
- Trained in technical writing, including proposals and documentation.
- Experienced in office administration and management.
- Competent at speaking and writing French.

HONOURS AND ACTIVITIES
Dean's list, three semesters
Member, Academic Affairs Advisory Committee, UWO, 1998–2002

Includes detailed objective in response to advertisement
Uses present-tense verbs for current job
Shows job titles in boldface for readability
Chronological format arranges jobs and education by dates
White space around headings creates open look
Highlights computer skills

FIGURE 16.3 **Functional Résumé**

Donald, a recent graduate, chose the functional format to de-emphasize his limited work experience and emphasize his potential in sales and marketing. He included an employment section to satisfy recruiters.

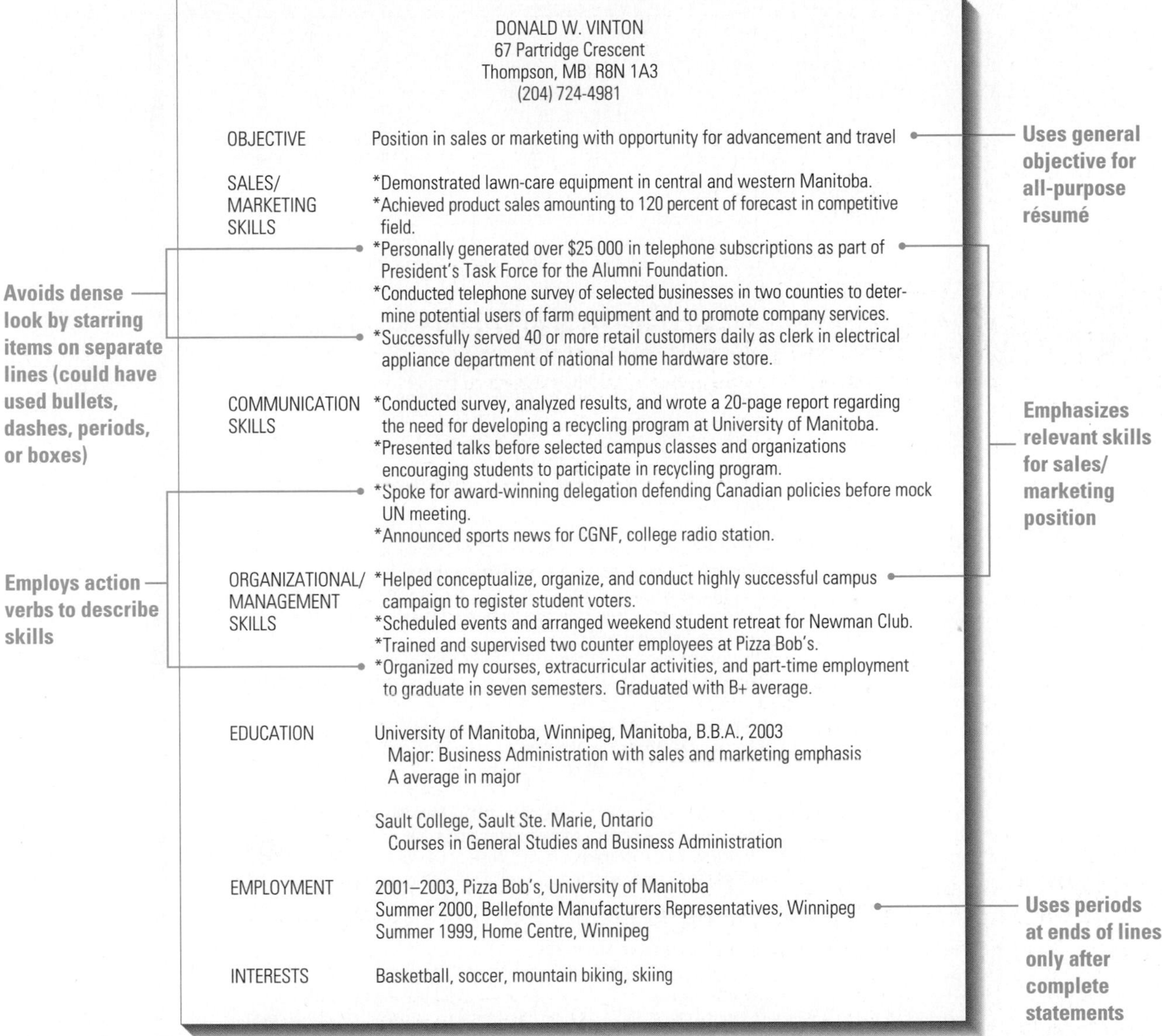
DONALD W. VINTON
67 Partridge Crescent
Thompson, MB R8N 1A3
(204) 724-4981

OBJECTIVE	Position in sales or marketing with opportunity for advancement and travel
SALES/ MARKETING SKILLS	*Demonstrated lawn-care equipment in central and western Manitoba. *Achieved product sales amounting to 120 percent of forecast in competitive field. *Personally generated over $25 000 in telephone subscriptions as part of President's Task Force for the Alumni Foundation. *Conducted telephone survey of selected businesses in two counties to determine potential users of farm equipment and to promote company services. *Successfully served 40 or more retail customers daily as clerk in electrical appliance department of national home hardware store.
COMMUNICATION SKILLS	*Conducted survey, analyzed results, and wrote a 20-page report regarding the need for developing a recycling program at University of Manitoba. *Presented talks before selected campus classes and organizations encouraging students to participate in recycling program. *Spoke for award-winning delegation defending Canadian policies before mock UN meeting. *Announced sports news for CGNF, college radio station.
ORGANIZATIONAL/ MANAGEMENT SKILLS	*Helped conceptualize, organize, and conduct highly successful campus campaign to register student voters. *Scheduled events and arranged weekend student retreat for Newman Club. *Trained and supervised two counter employees at Pizza Bob's. *Organized my courses, extracurricular activities, and part-time employment to graduate in seven semesters. Graduated with B+ average.
EDUCATION	University of Manitoba, Winnipeg, Manitoba, B.B.A., 2003 Major: Business Administration with sales and marketing emphasis A average in major Sault College, Sault Ste. Marie, Ontario Courses in General Studies and Business Administration
EMPLOYMENT	2001–2003, Pizza Bob's, University of Manitoba Summer 2000, Bellefonte Manufacturers Representatives, Winnipeg Summer 1999, Home Centre, Winnipeg
INTERESTS	Basketball, soccer, mountain biking, skiing

Uses general objective for all-purpose résumé
Avoids dense look by starring items on separate lines (could have used bullets, dashes, periods, or boxes)
Emphasizes relevant skills for sales/ marketing position
Employs action verbs to describe skills
Uses periods at ends of lines only after complete statements

Main Heading. Your résumé should always begin with your name, address, telephone number, and e-mail address. If possible, include a number where messages may be left for you. Prospective employers tend to call the next applicant when no one answers. Avoid showing both permanent and temporary addresses; some specialists say that dual addresses immediately identify about-to-graduate college students. Keep the main heading as uncluttered and simple as possible. And don't include the word *résumé*; it's like putting the word *letter* above correspondence.

Résumés targeted to specific positions have the best chance of being read.

FIGURE 16.4 **Combination Résumé**

Because Susan wanted to highlight her skills and capabilities along with her experience, she combined the best features of functional and traditional résumés. This résumé style is becoming increasingly popular.

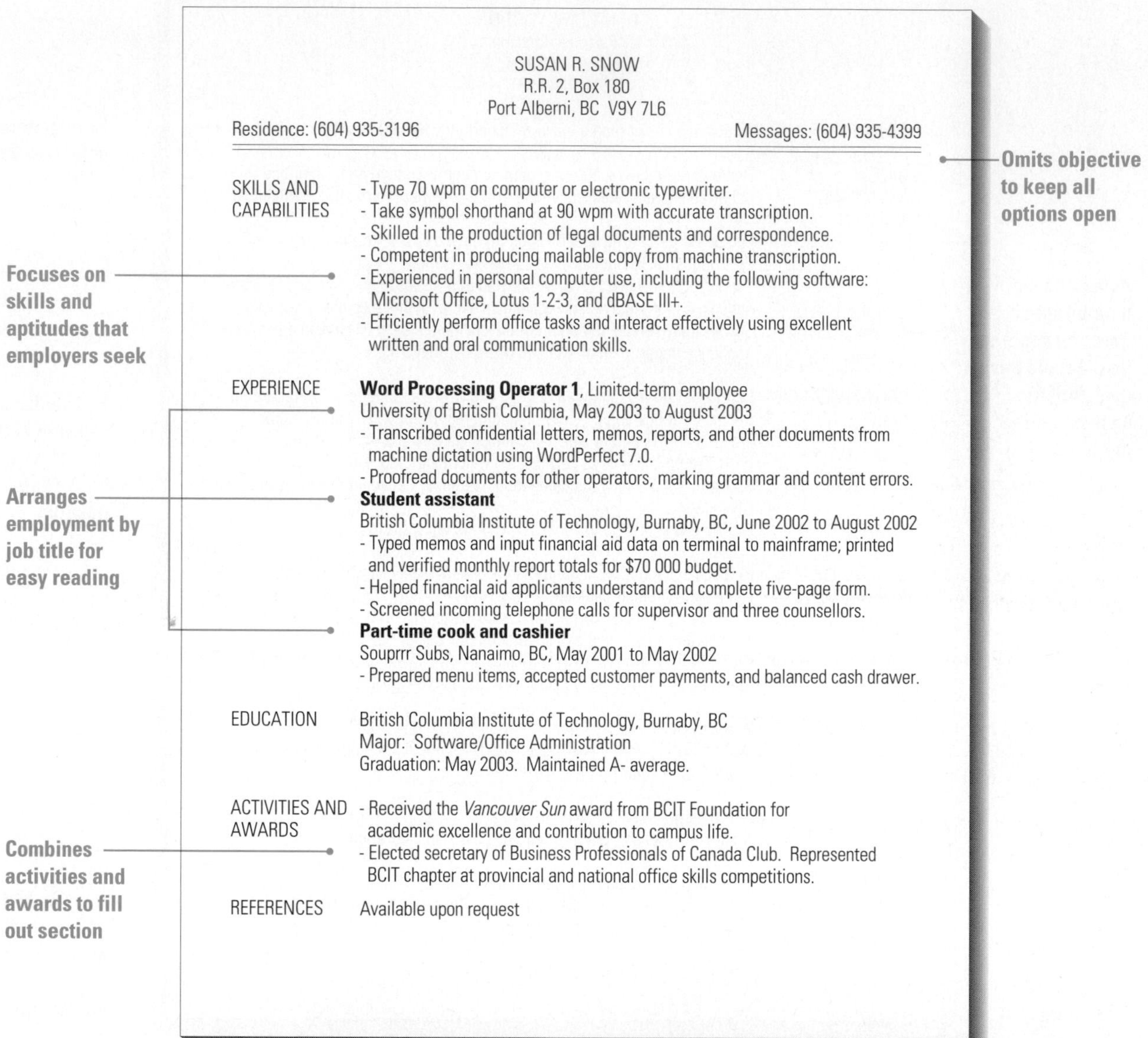

SUSAN R. SNOW
R.R. 2, Box 180
Port Alberni, BC V9Y 7L6

Residence: (604) 935-3196 Messages: (604) 935-4399

SKILLS AND CAPABILITIES
- Type 70 wpm on computer or electronic typewriter.
- Take symbol shorthand at 90 wpm with accurate transcription.
- Skilled in the production of legal documents and correspondence.
- Competent in producing mailable copy from machine transcription.
- Experienced in personal computer use, including the following software: Microsoft Office, Lotus 1-2-3, and dBASE III+.
- Efficiently perform office tasks and interact effectively using excellent written and oral communication skills.

EXPERIENCE

Word Processing Operator 1, Limited-term employee
University of British Columbia, May 2003 to August 2003
- Transcribed confidential letters, memos, reports, and other documents from machine dictation using WordPerfect 7.0.
- Proofread documents for other operators, marking grammar and content errors.

Student assistant
British Columbia Institute of Technology, Burnaby, BC, June 2002 to August 2002
- Typed memos and input financial aid data on terminal to mainframe; printed and verified monthly report totals for $70 000 budget.
- Helped financial aid applicants understand and complete five-page form.
- Screened incoming telephone calls for supervisor and three counsellors.

Part-time cook and cashier
Souprrr Subs, Nanaimo, BC, May 2001 to May 2002
- Prepared menu items, accepted customer payments, and balanced cash drawer.

EDUCATION
British Columbia Institute of Technology, Burnaby, BC
Major: Software/Office Administration
Graduation: May 2003. Maintained A- average.

ACTIVITIES AND AWARDS
- Received the *Vancouver Sun* award from BCIT Foundation for academic excellence and contribution to campus life.
- Elected secretary of Business Professionals of Canada Club. Represented BCIT chapter at provincial and national office skills competitions.

REFERENCES
Available upon request

Omits objective to keep all options open
Focuses on skills and aptitudes that employers seek
Arranges employment by job title for easy reading
Combines activities and awards to fill out section

Career Objective. Opinion is divided on the effect of including a career objective on a résumé. Recruiters think such statements indicate that a candidate has made a commitment to a career. Moreover, career objectives make the recruiter's life easier by quickly classifying the résumé.

You have four choices regarding career objectives. One option is to include a career objective when applying for a specific, targeted position. For example, the following responds to an advertised position: *Objective: To work in the health care industry as a human resources trainee with exposure to recruiting, training, and benefit adminis-*

tration. A second choice—one that makes sense if you are preparing an all-purpose résumé—is to omit the career objective. A third possibility involves using a general statement, such as *Objective: Challenging position in urban planning* or *Job Goal: Position in sales/marketing.* A fourth possibility is omitting an objective on the résumé but including it in the cover letter, where it can be tailored to a specific position.[3]

Some consultants warn against using the words *entry-level* in your objective, as these words emphasize lack of experience. Many aggressive job applicants today prepare individual résumés that are targeted for each company or position sought. Thanks to word processing, the task is easy.

Education. The next component is your education—if it is more noteworthy than your work experience. In this section you should include the name and location of schools, dates of attendance, major fields of study, and diplomas or degrees received. Your grade-point average and/or class ranking are important to prospective employers. One way to enhance your GPA is to calculate it in your major courses only (for example, *3.6/4.0 in major*). By the way, it is not unethical to showcase your GPA in your major—so long as you clearly indicate what you are doing. Some applicants want to list all their courses, but such a list makes for very dull reading. Refer to courses only if you can relate them to the position sought. When relevant, include certificates earned, seminars attended, and workshops completed. Because employers are interested in your degree of self-sufficiency, you might wish to indicate the percentage of your education for which you paid. If your education is incomplete, include such statements as *B.Sc. degree expected 6/02* or *80 units completed in 120-unit program.* Entitle this section *Education, Academic Preparation,* or *Professional Training.*

The work experience section of a résumé should list specifics and quantify achievements.

Work Experience or Employment History. If your work experience is significant and relevant to the position sought, this information should appear before education. List your most recent employment first and work backwards, including only those jobs that you think will help you win the targeted position. A job application form may demand a full employment history, but your résumé may be selective. (Be aware, though, that time gaps in your employment history will probably be questioned in the interview.) For each position show the following:

- Employer's name, city, and province
- Dates of employment
- Most important job title
- Significant duties, activities, accomplishments, and promotions

Describe your employment achievements concisely but concretely. Avoid generalities like *Worked with customers.* Be more specific, with statements such as *Served 40 or more retail customers a day*; *Successfully resolved problems about custom stationery orders;* or *Acted as intermediary among customers, printers, and suppliers.* If possible, quantify your accomplishments, such as *Conducted study of equipment needs of 100 small businesses in Halifax; Personally generated orders for sales of $90 000 annually; Keyboarded all the production models for a 250-page employee procedures manual;* or *Assisted editor in layout, design, and news writing for 12 issues of division newsletter.*

In addition to technical skills, employers seek individuals with communication, management, and interpersonal capabilities. This means you'll want to select work experiences and achievements that illustrate your initiative, dependability, responsibility, resourcefulness, and leadership. Employers also want people who can work together in teams. Thus, include statements like *Collaborated with interdepartmental*

FIGURE 16.5 **Action Verbs for Persuasive Résumés***

Management Skills	Communication Skills	Research Skills	Technical Skills	Teaching Skills
administered	addressed	clarified	assembled	adapted
analyzed	arbitrated	collected	built	advised
consolidated	arranged	critiqued	calculated	clarified
coordinated	collaborated	diagnosed	computed	coached
delegated	convinced	evaluated	designed	communicated
developed	developed	examined	devised	coordinated
directed	drafted	extracted	engineered	developed
evaluated	edited	identified	executed	enabled
improved	explained	inspected	fabricated	encouraged
increased	formulated	interpreted	maintained	evaluated
organized	interpreted	interviewed	operated	explained
oversaw	negotiated	investigated	overhauled	facilitated
planned	persuaded	organized	programmed	guided
prioritized	promoted	summarized	remodeled	informed
recommended	publicized	surveyed	repaired	instructed
scheduled	recruited	systematized	solved	persuaded
strengthened	translated		upgraded	set goals
supervised	wrote			trained

*The underlined words are especially good for pointing out **accomplishments.**

task force in developing 10-page handbook for temporary workers and *Headed student government team that conducted most successful voter registration in campus history.*

Statements describing your work experience can be made forceful and persuasive by using action verbs, such as those listed in Figure 16.5 and demonstrated in Figure 16.6.

Emphasize the skills and aptitudes that recommend you for a specific position.

Capabilities and Skills. Recruiters want to know specifically what you can do for their companies. Therefore, list your special skills, such as *Proficient in preparing correspondence and reports using Word.* Include your ability to use computer programs, office equipment, foreign languages, or sign language. Describe proficiencies you have acquired through training and experience, such as *Trained in computer accounting, including general ledger, accounts receivable, accounts payable, and payroll.* Use expressions like *competent in, skilled in, proficient with, experienced in,* and *ability to;* for example, *Competent in typing, editing, and/or proofreading reports, tables, letters, memos, manuscripts, and business forms.*

You'll also want to highlight exceptional aptitudes, such as working well under stress and learning computer programs quickly. If possible, provide details and evidence that back up your assertions; for example, *Mastered PhotoShop in 25 hours with little instruction.* Search for examples of your writing, speaking, management, organizational, and interpersonal skills—particularly those talents that are relevant to your targeted job.

For recent graduates, this section can be used to give recruiters evidence of your potential. Instead of *Capabilities,* the section might be called *Skills and Abilities.*

FIGURE 16.5 *(continued)*

Financial Skills	Creative Skills	Helping Skills	Clerical or Detail Skills	More Verbs for Accomplishments
administered	acted	assessed	approved	achieved
allocated	conceptualized	assisted	catalogued	expanded
analyzed	created	clarified	classified	improved
appraised	customized	coached	collected	pioneered
audited	designed	counselled	compiled	reduced (losses)
balanced	developed	demonstrated	generated	resolved (problems)
budgeted	directed	diagnosed	inspected	restored
calculated	established	educated	monitored	spearheaded
computed	founded	expedited	operated	transformed
developed	illustrated	facilitated	organized	
forecasted	initiated	familiarized	prepared	
managed	instituted	guided	processed	
marketed	introduced	motivated	purchased	
planned	invented	referred	recorded	
projected	originated	represented	screened	
researched	performed		specified	
	planned		systematized	
	revitalized		tabulated	

Source: Adapted from Yana Parker, *The Damn Good Résumé Guide* (Berkeley, CA: Ten Speed Press, 1996). Reprinted with permission.

Awards, Honours, and Activities. If you have three or more awards or honours, highlight them by listing them under a separate heading. If not, put them with activities. Include awards, scholarships (financial and other), fellowships, honours, recognition, commendations, and certificates. Be sure to identify items clearly. Your reader may be unfamiliar, for example, with the honours and awards given out by professional organizations; tell what they mean. Instead of saying *Recipient of Star award,* give more details: *Recipient of Star award given by Mount Allison University to outstanding graduates who combine academic excellence and extracurricular activities.*

Awards, honours, and activities are appropriate for résumés; most personal information is not.

It's also appropriate to include school, community, and professional activities. Employers are interested in evidence that you are a well-rounded person. This section provides an opportunity to demonstrate leadership and interpersonal skills. Strive to use action statements. For example, instead of saying *Treasurer of business club,* explain more fully: *Collected dues, kept financial records, and paid bills while serving as treasurer of 35-member business management club.*

Personal Data. Today's résumés omit personal data, such as birth date, marital status, height, weight, and religious affiliation. Such information doesn't relate to genuine occupational qualifications, and recruiters are legally barred from asking for such information. Some job seekers do, however, include hobbies or interests (such as skiing or photography) that might grab the recruiter's attention or serve as conversation starters. Naturally, you wouldn't mention dangerous pastimes (such as bungee jumping or sports car racing) or time-consuming interests. But you should indicate your willingness to travel or to relocate, since many companies will be interested.

Omit personal data not related to job qualifications.

FIGURE 16.6 **Using Action Verbs to Strengthen Your Résumé**

Identified weaknesses in internship program and **researched** five alternative programs.

Reduced delivery delays by an average of three days per order.

Streamlined filing system, thus reducing 400-item backlog to 0.

Organized holiday awards program for 1200 attendees and 140 awardees.

Created a 12-point checklist for managers to use when requesting temporary workers.

Designed five posters announcing new employee suggestion program.

Calculated shipping charges for overseas deliveries and **recommended** most economical rates.

Managed 24-station computer network linking data and employees in three departments.

Distributed and **explained** voter registration forms to over 500 prospective student voters.

Praised by top management for enthusiastic teamwork and achievement.

Secured national recognition from Communities in Bloom for neighbourhood beautification project.

References are unnecessary for the résumé, but they should be available for the interview.

References. Listing references on a résumé is favoured by some recruiters and opposed by others.[4] Such a list takes up valuable space. Moreover, it is not normally instrumental in securing an interview—few companies check references before the interview. Instead, they prefer that a candidate bring to the interview a list of individuals willing to discuss her or his qualifications. If you do list them, use parallel form. For example, if you show a title for one person (*Professor, Dr., Mrs.*), show titles for all. Include addresses and telephone numbers. On the other hand, if your references include individuals who are well known in their professions or communities, it could be to your advantage to include these.

Whether or not you include references on your résumé, you should have their names available when you begin your job search. Ask three to five instructors or previous employers whether they will be willing to answer inquiries regarding your qualifications for employment. Be sure, however, to provide them with an opportunity to refuse. Not having a reference is better than having a negative one. Do not include personal or character references, such as friends or neighbours, because recruiters rarely consult them. Companies are more interested in the opinions of objective individuals.

Although many employers advise not to include references on the résumé, some still expect to see a statement indicating "References Available on Request."[5]

Preparing for Computer Scanning

4

Thus far we've aimed our résumé advice at human readers. However, the first reader of your résumé may well be a computer. An increasing number of companies are now using electronic applicant-tracking (also called résumé management systems) to reduce costs of hiring, make résumé information more accessible, and rank candidates. These systems scan incoming résumés.

Applicant-tracking programs scan incoming résumés and store the information for future hiring.

Making Your Résumé Computer Friendly

Before you send your résumé, you should learn whether the recipient uses scanning software. One simple solution is to call any company where you plan to apply. Ask whether it scans résumés electronically. What if you can't get a clear answer? If you have even the slightest suspicion that your résumé might be read electronically, you'll be smart to prepare a plain, scannable version. A scannable résumé must sacrifice many of the graphic possibilities that wise writers employ. Computers aren't impressed by graphics. Computers prefer "vanilla" résumés—free of graphics and fancy fonts. To make a computer-friendly "vanilla" résumé, you'll want to apply the following suggestions about its physical appearance.

Computer-friendly résumés are free of graphics and fancy fonts.

- **Avoid unusual typefaces, underlining, and italics.** Moreover, don't use boxing, shading, or other graphics to highlight text. These features don't scan well. Most applicant-tracking programs, however, can accurately read bold print, solid bullets, and asterisks.
- **Use 10- to 14-point type.** Because touching letters or unusual fonts are likely to be misread, it's safest to use a large, well-known font, such as 12-point Times Roman or Helvetica. This may mean that your résumé will require two pages. After printing, inspect your résumé to see whether any letters touch—especially in your name.
- **Use smooth white paper, black ink, and quality printing.** Avoid coloured and textured papers as well as dot-matrix printing.
- **Be sure that your name is the first line on the page.** Don't use fancy layouts that may confuse a scanner.
- **Provide white space.** To ensure separation of words and categories, leave plenty of white space. For example, instead of using parentheses to enclose a telephone area code, insert blank spaces, such as 613 799-2415. Leave blank lines around headings.
- **Avoid double columns.** When listing job duties, skills, computer programs, and so forth, don't tabulate items into two- or three-column lists. Scanners read across and may convert tables into gobbledygook.
- **Don't fold or staple your résumé.** Send it in a large envelope so that you can avoid folds. Words that appear on folds may not be scanned correctly. Avoid staples because the indentions left after they are removed may cause pages to stick.
- **Use abbreviations carefully.** Minimize unfamiliar abbreviations, but maximize easily recognized abbreviations—especially those within your field, such as CAD, COBRA, or JIT. When in doubt, though, spell out! Computers are less addled by whole words.
- **Include all your addresses and telephone numbers.** Be sure your résumé contains your electronic mail address, as well as your home address, telephone numbers, and fax number, if available.
- **Be prepared to send your résumé in ASCII.** Pronounced "AS-kee," this format offers text only and is immediately readable by all computer programs. It eliminates italics, bold, underlining, and unusual keyboard characters.

Emphasizing Keywords

Keywords are usually nouns that describe specific candidate traits or job requirements.

In addition to paying attention to the physical appearance of your résumé, you must also be concerned with keywords. These are usually nouns that describe what an employer wants.

Joyce Lain Kennedy, nationally syndicated career columnist and author of *Electronic Résumé Revolution*,[6] suggests using a *keyword* summary. On your résumé this list of keyword descriptors immediately follows your name and address.

A keyword summary should contain your targeted job title and alternative labels, as well as previous job titles, skills, software programs, and selected jargon known in your field. It concentrates on nouns rather than on verbs or adjectives.

To construct your summary, go through your core résumé and mark all relevant nouns. Also try to imagine what eight to ten words an employer might use to describe the job you want. Then select the 25 best words for your summary. Because interpersonal traits are often requested by employers, consult Figure 16.7. It shows the most frequently requested interpersonal traits, as reported by Resumix, one of the leaders in résumé-scanning software.

You may entitle your list "Keyword Summary," "Keyword Profile," or "Keyword Index." Here's an example of a possible keyword summary for a junior accountant:

A computer-friendly résumé may contain a keyword summary filled with words (usually nouns) that describe the job or candidate.

Keyword Summary

Accountant: Public. Junior. Staff. Dipl. Conestoga College—Business Administration. B.A., University of Waterloo—Accounting. Payables. Receivables. Payroll Experience. Quarterly Reports. Unemployment Reports. Communication Skills. Computer Skills. Excel. Word 2000. PCs. Mainframes. Internet. Web. Networks. J. D. Edwards Software. Ability to learn software. Accurate. Dean's List. Award of Merit. Team player. Willing to travel. Relocate.

After an introductory keyword summary, your résumé should contain the standard parts discussed in this chapter. Remember that the keyword section merely helps ensure that your résumé will be selected for inspection. Then human eyes take over. Therefore, you'll want to observe the other writing tips you've learned to make your résumé attractive and forceful. Notice that the scannable résumé in Figure 16.8 is not drastically different from other resume types. It does, however, include a keyword summary.

Preparing an Online, Hypertext Résumé

To give your résumé life and make it stand out from others, you might wish to prepare an online résumé. This is actually an HTML (Hypertext Markup Language) document located at a Web site. Posting an online résumé has some distinct advantages—and a few disadvantages.

An online résumé contains hypertext links to work samples or a portfolio of additional information.

On the plus side, merely preparing an online résumé suggests that you have exceptional technical skill. (You would, of course, give credit for any borrowed graphics or code.) An online résumé can be viewed whenever it is convenient for an employer, and it can be seen by many individuals in an organization without circulating a paper copy. But the real reason for preparing an online résumé is that it can become an electronic portfolio with links to examples of your work.

You could include clickable links to reports you have written, summaries of projects completed, a complete list of your coursework, letters of recommendation (with permissions from your recommenders), and extra information about your work experience. An advanced portfolio might include links to electronic copies of your artwork, film projects, blueprints, and photographs of classwork that might otherwise be difficult to share with potential employers. Moreover, you can include dazzling effects such as colour, animation, sound, and graphics. An online résumé provides ample opportunity to show off your creative talents, but only if the position calls for creativity.

On the minus side, online résumés must be more generic than print résumés. They cannot be easily altered if you apply for different positions. Moreover, they present a security problem unless password protected. You may wish to include only an e-mail address instead of offering your address and telephone number.

Because of the changing standards and requirements of today's world of work, corporate Web sites and those that provide information on job search startegies,

FIGURE 16.7 **Interpersonal Keywords Most Requested by Employers Using Résumé-Scanning Software***

Ability to delegate	Creative	Leadership	Self-accountable
Ability to implement	Customer oriented	Multitasking	Self-managing
Ability to plan	Detail minded	Open communication	Setting priorities
Ability to train	Ethical	Open minded	Supportive
Accurate	Flexible	Oral communication	Takes initiative
Adaptable	Follow instructions	Organizational skills	Team building
Aggressive worker	Follow through	Persuasive	Team player
Analytical ability	Follow up	Problem solving	Tenacious
Assertive	High energy	Public speaking	Willing to travel
Communication skills	Industrious	Results oriented	
Competitive	Innovative	Safety conscious	

*Reported by Resumix, a leading producer of résumé-scanning software.

Source: Joyce Lain Kennedy and Thomas J. Morrow, *Electronic Résumé Revolution* (New York: John Wiley & Sons, 1994), 70. Reprinted by permission of John Wiley & Sons, Inc.

including preparing online and HTML résumés, are being created and updated regularly. To find out more about the electronic job search, refer to a search engine such as Google **<www.google.ca>**.

Applying the Final Touches

Because your résumé is probably the most important message you will ever write, you'll revise it many times. With so much information in concentrated form and with so much riding on its outcome, your résumé demands careful polishing, proofreading, and critiquing.

As you revise, be certain to verify all the facts, particularly those involving your previous employment and education. Don't be caught in a mistake, or worse, distortion of previous jobs and dates of employment. These items likely will be checked. And the consequences of puffing up a résumé with deception or flat-out lies are simply not worth the risk. Other ethical traps you'll want to avoid are described in the accompanying Ethical Insights box.

As you continue revising, look for other ways to improve your résumé. For example, consider consolidating headings. By condensing your information into as few headings as possible, you'll produce a clean, professional-looking document. Study other résumés for valuable formatting ideas. Ask yourself what graphic highlighting techniques you can use to improve readability: capitalization, underlining, indenting, and bulleting. Experiment with headings and styles to achieve a pleasing, easy-to-read message. Moreover, look for ways to eliminate wordiness. For example, instead of *Supervised two employees who worked at the counter*, try *Supervised two counter employees.* Review Chapter 6 for more tips.

Above all, make your résumé look professional. Avoid anything humorous or "cute," such as a help-wanted poster with your name or picture inside. Eliminate the personal pronoun *I.* The abbreviated, objective style of a résumé precludes the use of personal pronouns. Use white, off-white, or buff-coloured heavy bond paper (24-pound) and a first-rate printer.

FIGURE 16.8 **Computer-Friendly Résumé**

Cassandra prepared this "vanilla" résumé (free of graphics and fancy formatting) so that it would scan well if read by a computer. Notice that she begins with a keyword summary that contains job titles, skills, traits, and other descriptive words. She hopes that some of these keywords will match those submitted by an employer. To improve accurate scanning, she avoids italics, vertical and horizontal lines, and double columns.

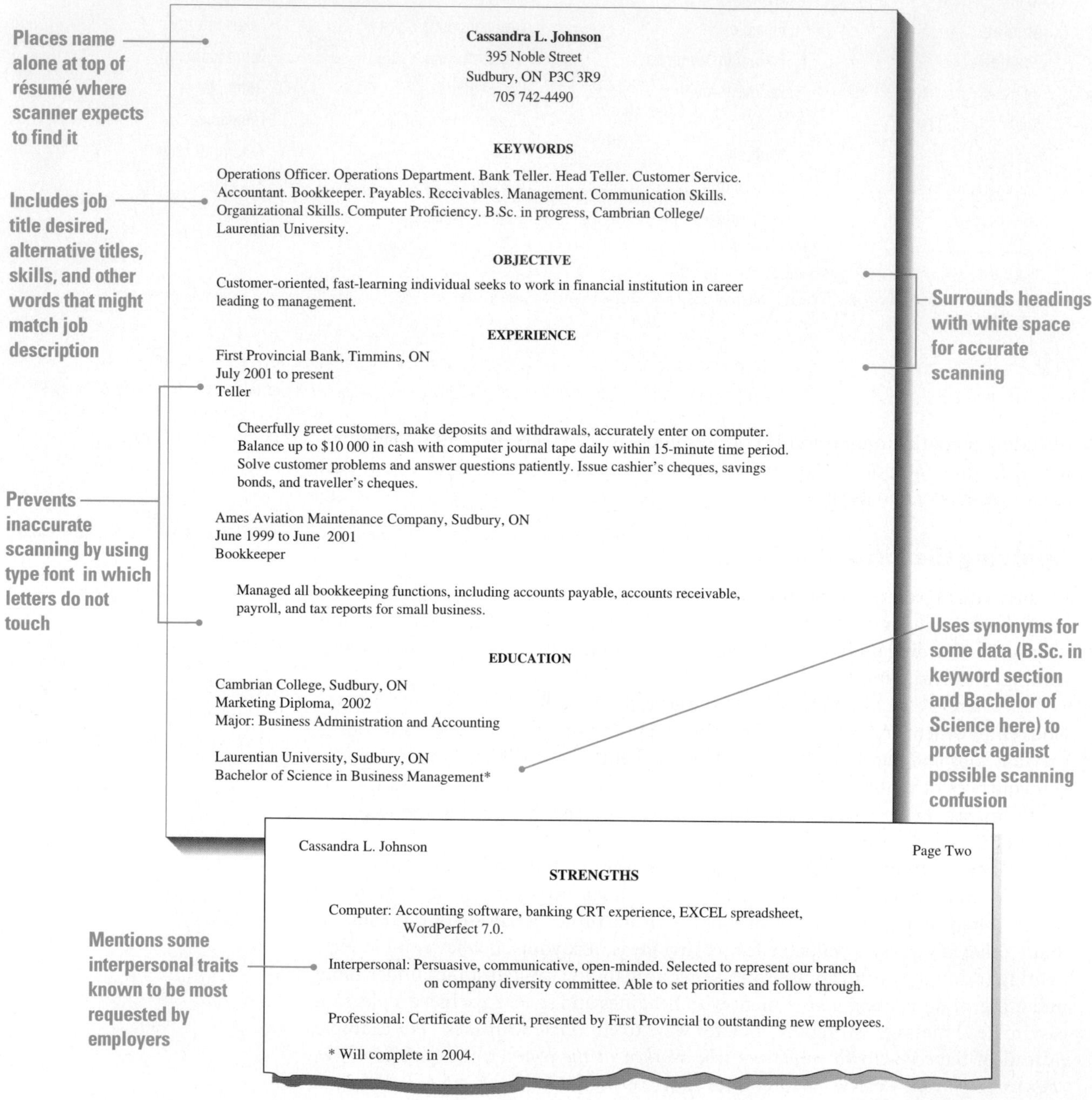

Places name alone at top of résumé where scanner expects to find it
Includes job title desired, alternative titles, skills, and other words that might match job description
Surrounds headings with white space for accurate scanning
Prevents inaccurate scanning by using type font in which letters do not touch
Uses synonyms for some data (B.Sc. in keyword section and Bachelor of Science here) to protect against possible scanning confusion
Mentions some interpersonal traits known to be most requested by employers

Cassandra L. Johnson
395 Noble Street
Sudbury, ON P3C 3R9
705 742-4490

KEYWORDS

Operations Officer. Operations Department. Bank Teller. Head Teller. Customer Service. Accountant. Bookkeeper. Payables. Receivables. Management. Communication Skills. Organizational Skills. Computer Proficiency. B.Sc. in progress, Cambrian College/ Laurentian University.

OBJECTIVE

Customer-oriented, fast-learning individual seeks to work in financial institution in career leading to management.

EXPERIENCE

First Provincial Bank, Timmins, ON
July 2001 to present
Teller

Cheerfully greet customers, make deposits and withdrawals, accurately enter on computer. Balance up to $10 000 in cash with computer journal tape daily within 15-minute time period. Solve customer problems and answer questions patiently. Issue cashier's cheques, savings bonds, and traveller's cheques.

Ames Aviation Maintenance Company, Sudbury, ON
June 1999 to June 2001
Bookkeeper

Managed all bookkeeping functions, including accounts payable, accounts receivable, payroll, and tax reports for small business.

EDUCATION

Cambrian College, Sudbury, ON
Marketing Diploma, 2002
Major: Business Administration and Accounting

Laurentian University, Sudbury, ON
Bachelor of Science in Business Management*

Cassandra L. Johnson — Page Two

STRENGTHS

Computer: Accounting software, banking CRT experience, EXCEL spreadsheet, WordPerfect 7.0.

Interpersonal: Persuasive, communicative, open-minded. Selected to represent our branch on company diversity committee. Able to set priorities and follow through.

Professional: Certificate of Merit, presented by First Provincial to outstanding new employees.

* Will complete in 2004.

After revising, proofread, proofread, and proofread again: for spelling and mechanics, for content, and for format. Then, have a knowledgeable friend or relative proofread it again. This is one document that must be perfect.

Because résumés must be perfect, they should be proofread many times.

By now you may be thinking that you'd like to hire someone to write your résumé. Don't. First, you know yourself better than anyone else could know you. Second, you'll end up with either a generic or a one-time résumé. A generic résumé in today's highly competitive job market will lose out to a targeted résumé nine times out of ten. Equally useless is a one-time résumé aimed at a single job. What if you don't get that job? Because you will need to revise your résumé many times as you seek a variety of jobs, be prepared to write (and rewrite) it yourself.

A final word about résumé-writing services. Some tend to produce eye-catching, elaborate documents with lofty language, fancy borders, and fuzzy thinking. Here's an example of empty writing: "Seeking a position which will utilize academic achievements and hands-on experience while providing for career-development opportunities."[7] Save your money and buy a good interview suit instead.

Faxing or E-Mailing Your Résumé

In this hurry-up world, employers increasingly want information immediately. If you must fax or e-mail your résumé, take a second look at it. The key to success is SPACE. Without it, letters and character blur. Underlines blend with the words above, and bold print may look like an ink blot.[8] How can you improve your chances of making a good impression when you must fax or e-mail your résumé?

Résumés to be faxed should have ample space between letters, be printed in 12-point or larger font, and avoid underlines.

If you are faxing your printed résumé, select a font with adequate space between each character. Thinner fonts—such as Times, Palatino, New Century Schoolbook, Courier, and Bookman—are clearer than thicker ones. Use a 12-point or larger font, and avoid underlines, which may look broken or choppy when faxed. To be safe, get a transmission report to ensure that all pages were transmitted satisfactorily. Finally, follow up with your polished, printed résumé.

If you are e-mailing your résumé, you may wish to prepare an ASCII version (text only). It will eliminate bold, italics, underlining, tabulated indentions, and unusual characters. To prevent lines from wrapping at awkward spots, keep your line length to 65 characters or less. You can, of course, transmit a fully formatted, attractive résumé if you send it as an attachment and your receiver is using a compatible e-mail program.

Résumés that are sent by e-mail transmit best as ASCII (text-only) files without tabs, underlines, italics, bold, or unusual characters.

As you prepare to write your current résumé, consult the following checklist to review the job search process and important résumé-writing techniques.

Checklist for Writing a Persuasive Résumé

Preparation

Research the job market. Learn about available jobs, common qualifications, and potential employers. The best résumés are targeted for specific jobs with specific companies.

Analyze your strengths. Determine what aspects of your education, experience, and personal characteristics will be assets to prospective employers.

ETHICAL INSIGHTS

ARE INFLATED RÉSUMÉS WORTH THE RISK?

A résumé is expected to showcase a candidate's strengths and minimize weaknesses. For this reason, recruiters expect a certain degree of self-promotion. But some résumé writers step over the line that separates honest self-marketing from deceptive half-truths and flat-out lies. Distorting facts on a résumé is unethical; lying is illegal. And either practice can destroy a career.

Although recruiters can't check everything, most will verify previous employment and education before hiring candidates. Over half will require official transcripts. And after hiring, the checking process may continue. At one of North America's top accounting firms, the human resources director described the posthiring routine: "If we find a discrepancy in GPA or prior experience due to an honest mistake, we meet with the new hire to hear an explanation. But if it wasn't a mistake, we terminate the person immediately. Unfortunately, we've had to do that too often."[9]

No job seeker wants to be in the unhappy position of explaining résumé errors or defending misrepresentation. Avoiding the following common problems can keep you off the hot seat:

- **Inflated education, grades, or honours.** Some job candidates claim degrees from colleges or universities when in fact they merely attended classes. Others increase their grade-point averages or claim fictitious honours. Any such dishonest reporting is grounds for dismissal when discovered.

- **Enhanced job titles.** Wishing to elevate their status, some applicants misrepresent their titles. For example, one technician called himself a "programmer" when he had actually programmed only one project for his boss. A mail clerk who assumed added responsibilities conferred upon herself the title of "supervisor." Even when the description seems accurate, it's unethical to list any title not officially granted.

- **Puffed-up accomplishments.** Some job seekers inflate their employment experience or achievements. One clerk, eager to make her photocopying duties sound more important, said that she *assisted the vice president in communicating and distributing employee directives.* A graduate who spent the better part of six months watching rented videos on his VCR described the activity as *Independent Film Study.* The latter statement may have helped win an interview, but it lost him the job.[10] In addition to avoiding puffery, guard against taking sole credit for achievements that required many people. When recruiters suspect dubious claims on résumés, they nail applicants with specific—and often embarrassing—questions during their interviews.[11]

- **Altered employment dates.** Some candidates extend the dates of employment to hide unimpressive jobs or to cover up periods of unemployment and illness. Let's say that several years ago Cindy was unemployed for fourteen months between working for Company A and being hired by Company B. To make her employment history look better, she adds seven months to her tenure with Company A and seven months to Company B. Now her employment history has no gaps, but her résumé is dishonest and represents a potential landmine for her.

The employment process can easily lure you into ethical traps, such as those described in Chapter 1. Beware of these specific temptations:

- **The relative-filth trap:** "A little fudging on my GPA is nothing compared with the degrees that some people buy in degree mills."
- **The rationalization trap:** "I deserve to call myself 'manager' because that's what I really did."
- **The self-deception trap:** "Giving myself a certificate from the institute is OK because I really intended to finish the program, but I got sick."

Falling into these ethical traps risks your entire employment future. If your honest qualifications aren't good enough to get you the job you want, start working now to improve them.

 **Study models.** Look at other résumés for formatting and element placement ideas. Experiment with headings and styles to achieve an artistic, readable product.

Heading and Objective

 **Identify yourself.** List your name, address, and telephone number. Skip the word *résumé.*

 **Include a career objective for a targeted job.** If this résumé is intended for a specific job, include a statement tailored to it (*Objective: Cost accounting position in the petroleum industry*).

Education

 **Name your diploma or degree, date of graduation, and institution.** Emphasize your education if your experience is limited.

 **List your major and GPA.** Give information about your studies, but don't inventory all your courses.

Work Experience

 **Itemize your jobs.** Start with your most recent job. Give the employer's name and city, dates of employment (month, year), and most significant job title.

 **Describe your experience.** Use action verbs to summarize achievements and skills relevant to your targeted job.

 **Present nontechnical skills.** Give evidence of communication, management, and interpersonal talents. Employers want more than empty assurances; try to quantify your skills and accomplishments (*Collaborated with six-member task force in producing 20-page mission statement*).

Special Skills, Achievements, and Awards

 **Highlight computer skills.** Remember that nearly all employers seek employees who are proficient in using the Internet, e-mail, word processing, databases, and spreadsheets.

 **List your languages.** Because Canada has two official languages, your skills as a bilingual employee may be needed. In addition, a culturally diverse workplace may require employees to communicate in a variety of languages.

 **Show that you are a well-rounded individual.** List awards, experiences, and extracurricular activities—particularly if they demonstrate leadership, teamwork, reliability, loyalty, industry, initiative, efficiency, and self-sufficiency.

Final Tips

 **Consider omitting references.** Have a list of references available for the interview, but don't include them or refer to them unless you have a specific reason to do so.

 **Look for ways to condense your data.** Omit all street addresses except your own. Consolidate your headings. Study models and experiment with formats to find the most readable and efficient groupings.

 **Double-check for parallel phrasing.** Be sure that all entries have balanced construction, such as similar verb forms (*Organized files, trained assistants, scheduled events*).

 **Make your résumé scannable.** If there's a chance it will be read by a computer, add a keyword summary, use a common font, and remove graphics.

 **Project professionalism and quality.** Avoid personal pronouns and humour. Use 24-pound bond paper and a high-quality printer.

 **Proofread, proofread, proofread.** Make this document perfect by proofreading at least three times.

The Persuasive Letter of Application

Letters of application introduce résumés, relate writer strengths to reader benefits, and seek an interview.

To accompany your résumé, you'll need a persuasive letter of application (also called a *cover letter*). The letter of application has three purposes: (1) introducing the résumé, (2) highlighting your strengths in terms of benefits to the reader, and (3) gaining an interview. In many ways your letter of application is a sales letter; it sells your talents and tries to beat the competition. It will, accordingly, include many of the techniques you learned for sales presentations (Chapter 9).

Personnel professionals disagree on how long to make the letter of application. Many prefer short letters with no more than four paragraphs; instead of concentrating on the letter, these readers focus on the résumé. Others desire longer letters that supply more information, thus giving them a better opportunity to evaluate a candidate's qualifications.

Regardless of its length, a letter of application should have three primary parts: (1) an opening that gains attention, (2) a body that builds interest and reduces resistance, and (3) a closing that motivates action.

Gaining Attention in the Opening

The opening in a letter of application gains attention by addressing the receiver by name.

The first step in gaining the interest of your reader is addressing that individual by name. Rather than sending your letter to the "Personnel Manager" or "Human Resources Department," try to identify the name of the appropriate individual. Make it a rule to call the organization for the correct spelling and the complete address. This personal touch distinguishes your letter and demonstrates your serious interest.

How you open your letter of application depends largely on whether the application is solicited or unsolicited. If an employment position has been announced and applicants are being solicited, you can use a direct approach. If you do not know whether a position is open and you are prospecting for a job, use an indirect approach. Whether direct or indirect, the opening should attract the attention of the reader. Strive for openings that are more imaginative than *Please consider this letter an application for the position of ...* or *I would like to apply for ...*

Openings for Solicited Jobs. Here are some of the best techniques to open a letter of application for a job that has been announced:

- **Refer to the name of an employee in the company.** Remember that employers always hope to hire known quantities rather than complete strangers:

  At the suggestion of Ms. Jennifer Larson of your Human Resources Department, I submit my qualifications for the position of staffing coordinator.

- **Refer to the source of your information precisely.** If you are answering an advertisement, include the exact position advertised and the name and date of the publication. For large organizations it's also wise to mention the section of the newspaper where the ad appeared:

  Your advertisement in Section C-3 of the June 1 *Daily News* for an accounting administrator greatly appeals to me. With my accounting training and computer experience, I believe I could serve Quad Graphics well.

  Susan Butler, placement director at Durham College, told me that DataTech has an opening for a technical writer with knowledge of Web design and graphics.

- **Refer to the job title and describe how your qualifications fit the requirements.** Personnel directors are looking for a match between an applicant's credentials and the job needs:

  Because of my specialized training in computerized accounting at the University of Regina, I feel confident that I have the qualifications you described in your advertisement for a cost accountant trainee.

Openings for solicited jobs refer to the source of the information, the job title, and qualifications for the position.

Openings for Unsolicited Jobs. If you are unsure whether a position actually exists, you may wish to use a more persuasive opening. Since your goal is to convince this person to read on, try one of the following techniques:

Openings for unsolicited jobs show interest in and knowledge of the company, as well as spotlighting reader benefits.

- **Demonstrate interest in and knowledge of the reader's business.** Show the personnel director that you have done your research and that this organization is more than a mere name to you:

  Since Signa HealthNet, Inc., is organizing a new information management team for its recently established group insurance division, could you use the services of a well-trained information systems graduate who seeks to become a professional systems analyst?

- **Show how your special talents and background will benefit the company.** Personnel directors need to be convinced that you can do something for them:

  Could your rapidly expanding publications division use the services of an editorial assistant who offers exceptional language skills, an honours degree from the University of Prince Edward Island, and two years' experience in producing a campus literary publication?

In applying for an advertised job, Nancy Sullivan James wrote the solicited letter of application shown in Figure 16.9. Notice that her opening identifies the position and the newspaper completely so that the reader knows exactly to which advertisement Nancy is referring. More challenging are unsolicited letters of application, such as Donald Vinton's, shown in Figure 16.10. Because he hopes to discover or create a job, his opening must grab the reader's attention immediately. To do that, he capitalizes on company information appearing in the newspaper. Notice, too, that

Donald purposely kept his cover letter short and to the point because he anticipated that a busy executive would be unwilling to read a long, detailed letter.

Donald's unsolicited letter "prospects" for a job. Some job candidates feel that such letters may be even more productive than efforts to secure advertised jobs, since "prospecting" candidates face less competition.

Building Interest in the Body

The body of a letter of application should build interest, reduce resistance, and discuss relevant personal traits.

Once you have captured the attention of the reader, you can use the body of the letter to build interest and reduce resistance. Keep in mind that your résumé emphasizes what you *have done*; your application letter stresses what you *can do* for the employer.

Your first goal is to relate your remarks to a specific position. If you are responding to an advertisement, you'll want to explain how your preparation and experience fill the stated requirements. If you are prospecting for a job, you may not know the exact requirements. Your employment research and knowledge of your field, however, should give you a reasonably good idea of what is expected for this position.

It's also important to emphasize reader benefits. In other words, you should describe your strong points in relation to the needs of the employer. In one employment survey many personnel professionals expressed the same view: "I want you to tell me what you can do for my organization. This is much more important to me than telling me what courses you took in college or what 'duties' you performed on your previous jobs."[12] Instead of *I have completed courses in business communication, report writing, and technical writing,* try this:

Spotlighting reader benefits means matching personal strengths to employer needs.

> Courses in business communication, report writing, and technical writing have helped me develop the research and writing skills required of your technical writers.

Choose your strongest qualifications and show how they fit the targeted job. And remember, students with little experience are better off spotlighting their education and its practical applications, as these candidates did:

> Successfully transcribing over 100 letters and memos in my college transcription class gave me experience in converting the spoken word into the written word, an exacting communication skill demanded of your administrative assistants.

The body of a letter of application may describe such traits as taking responsibility, showing initiative, and learning easily.

In the body of your letter, you'll also want to discuss relevant personal traits. Employers are looking for candidates who, among other things, are team players, take responsibility, show initiative, and learn easily. Notice how the following paragraph uses action verbs to paint a picture of a promising candidate:

> In addition to developing technical and academic skills at Dalhousie University, I have gained interpersonal, leadership, and organizational skills. As vice president of the business students' organization, I helped organize and supervise two successful fundraising events. These activities involved conceptualizing the tasks, motivating others to help, scheduling work sessions, and coordinating the efforts of 35 diverse students in reaching our goal. I enjoyed my success with these activities and look forward to applying such experience in your management trainee program.

Finally, in this section or the next, you should refer the reader to your résumé. Do so directly or as part of another statement, as shown here:

> Please refer to the attached résumé for additional information regarding my education, experience, and references.

FIGURE 16.9 **Solicited Letter of Application**

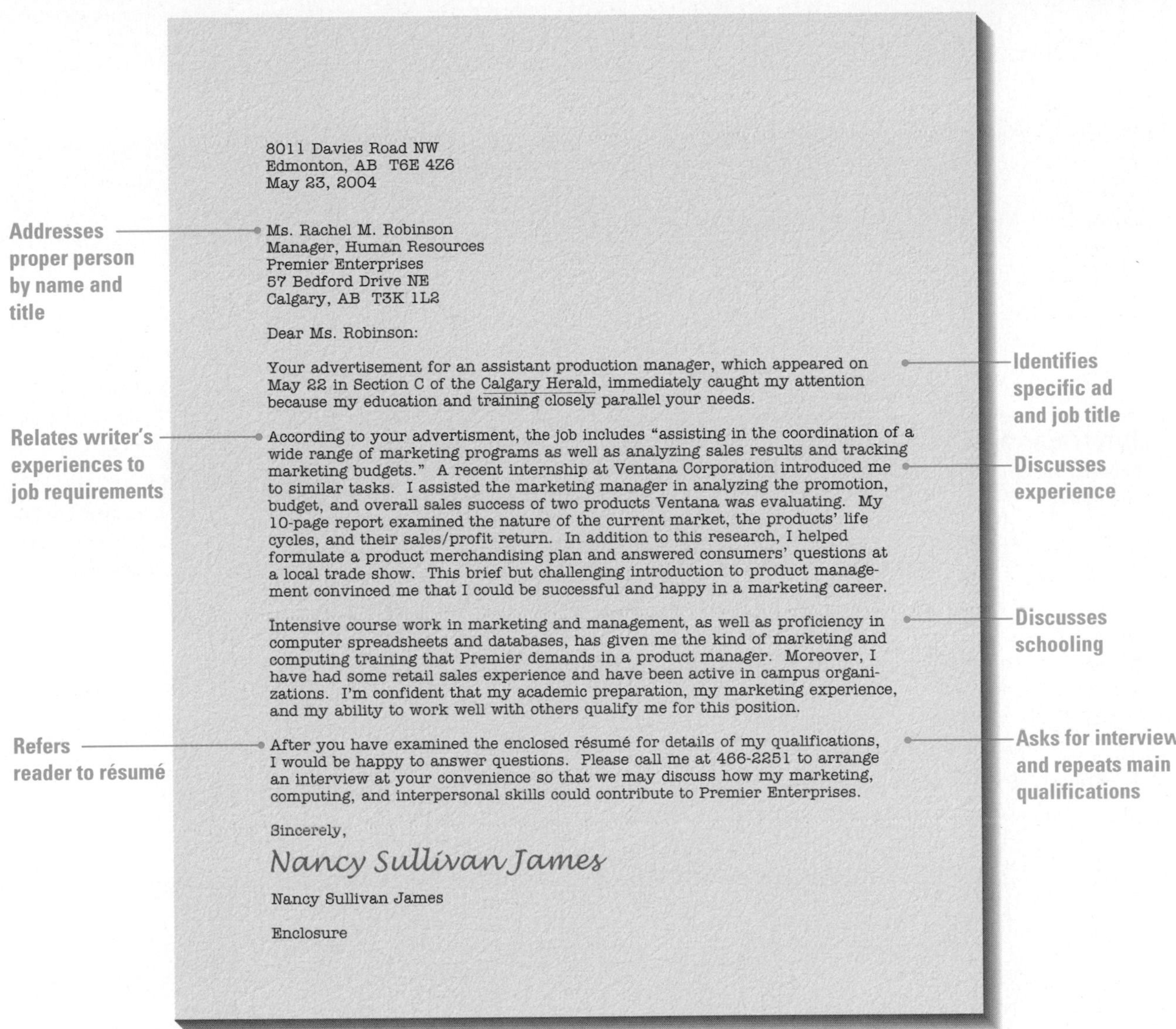

8011 Davies Road NW
Edmonton, AB T6E 4Z6
May 23, 2004

Ms. Rachel M. Robinson
Manager, Human Resources
Premier Enterprises
57 Bedford Drive NE
Calgary, AB T3K 1L2

Dear Ms. Robinson:

Your advertisement for an assistant production manager, which appeared on May 22 in Section C of the Calgary Herald, immediately caught my attention because my education and training closely parallel your needs.

According to your advertisment, the job includes "assisting in the coordination of a wide range of marketing programs as well as analyzing sales results and tracking marketing budgets." A recent internship at Ventana Corporation introduced me to similar tasks. I assisted the marketing manager in analyzing the promotion, budget, and overall sales success of two products Ventana was evaluating. My 10-page report examined the nature of the current market, the products' life cycles, and their sales/profit return. In addition to this research, I helped formulate a product merchandising plan and answered consumers' questions at a local trade show. This brief but challenging introduction to product management convinced me that I could be successful and happy in a marketing career.

Intensive course work in marketing and management, as well as proficiency in computer spreadsheets and databases, has given me the kind of marketing and computing training that Premier demands in a product manager. Moreover, I have had some retail sales experience and have been active in campus organizations. I'm confident that my academic preparation, my marketing experience, and my ability to work well with others qualify me for this position.

After you have examined the enclosed résumé for details of my qualifications, I would be happy to answer questions. Please call me at 466-2251 to arrange an interview at your convenience so that we may discuss how my marketing, computing, and interpersonal skills could contribute to Premier Enterprises.

Sincerely,

Nancy Sullivan James

Nancy Sullivan James

Enclosure

Addresses proper person by name and title
Identifies specific ad and job title
Relates writer's experiences to job requirements
Discusses experience
Discusses schooling
Refers reader to résumé
Asks for interview and repeats main qualifications

Motivating Action in the Closing

The closing of a letter of application should include a request for an interview.

After presenting your case, you should conclude with a spur to action. This is where you ask for an interview. If you live in a distant city, you may request an employment application or an opportunity to be interviewed by the organization's nearest representative. However, never ask for the job. To do so would be presumptuous and naive. In requesting an interview, suggest reader benefits or review your strongest points. Sound sincere and appreciative. Remember to make it easy for the reader to agree by supplying your telephone number and best times to call you. And keep in mind that some personnel directors prefer that you take the initiative to call them. Here are possible endings:

> To add to your staff an industrious, well-trained administrative assistant with proven word processing and communication skills, call me at (604) 492-1433 to

FIGURE 16.10 **Unsolicited Letter of Application**

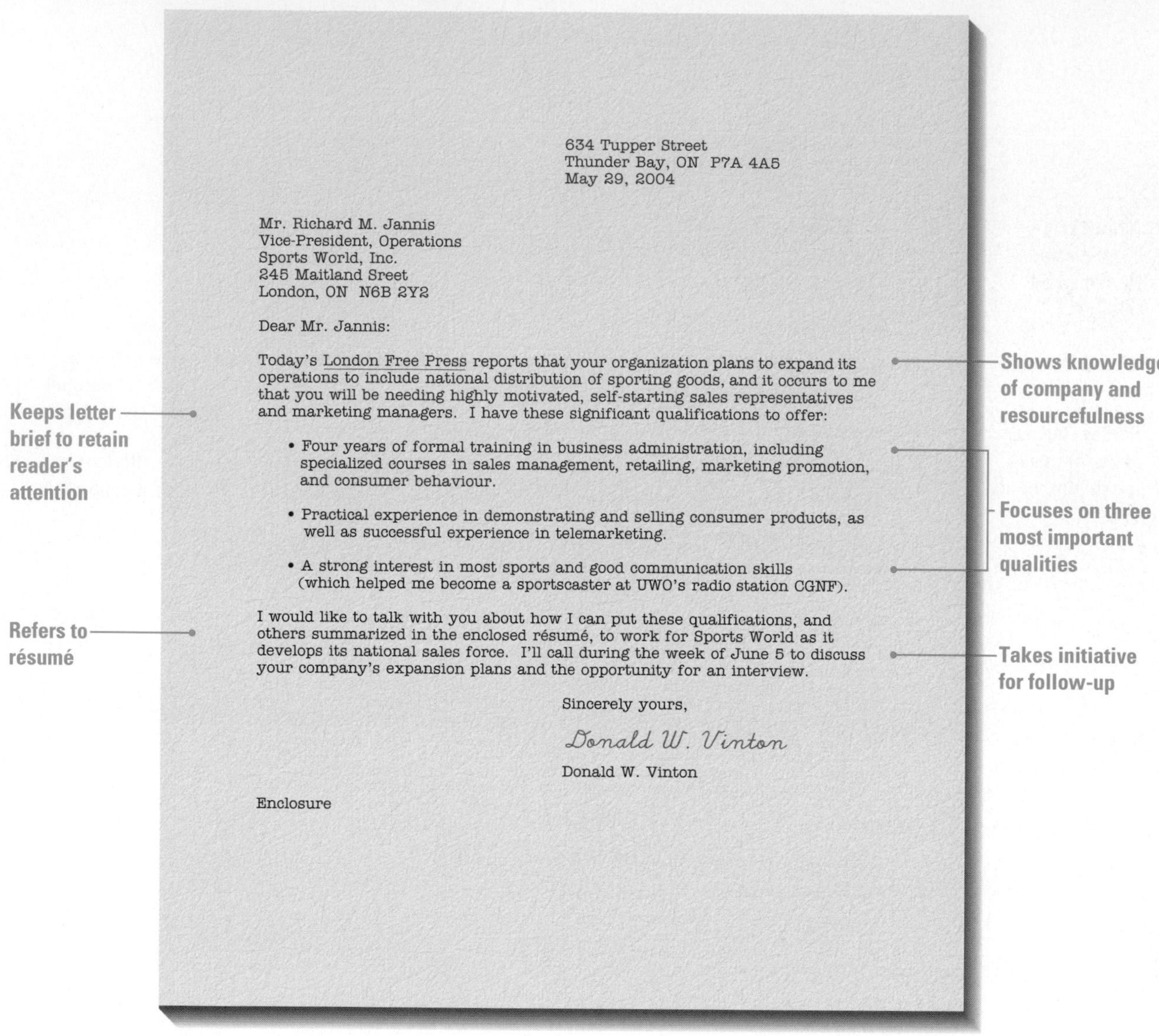

634 Tupper Street
Thunder Bay, ON P7A 4A5
May 29, 2004

Mr. Richard M. Jannis
Vice-President, Operations
Sports World, Inc.
245 Maitland Sreet
London, ON N6B 2Y2

Dear Mr. Jannis:

Today's London Free Press reports that your organization plans to expand its operations to include national distribution of sporting goods, and it occurs to me that you will be needing highly motivated, self-starting sales representatives and marketing managers. I have these significant qualifications to offer:

- Four years of formal training in business administration, including specialized courses in sales management, retailing, marketing promotion, and consumer behaviour.
- Practical experience in demonstrating and selling consumer products, as well as successful experience in telemarketing.
- A strong interest in most sports and good communication skills (which helped me become a sportscaster at UWO's radio station CGNF).

I would like to talk with you about how I can put these qualifications, and others summarized in the enclosed résumé, to work for Sports World as it develops its national sales force. I'll call during the week of June 5 to discuss your company's expansion plans and the opportunity for an interview.

Sincerely yours,

Donald W. Vinton

Donald W. Vinton

Enclosure

Keeps letter brief to retain reader's attention
Refers to résumé
Shows knowledge of company and resourcefulness
Focuses on three most important qualities
Takes initiative for follow-up

arrange an interview. I can meet with you at any time convenient to your schedule.

Next week, after you have examined the attached résumé, I will call you to discuss the possibility of arranging an interview.

Final Tips

As you revise your letter of application, notice how many sentences begin with *I.* Although it's impossible to talk about yourself without using *I,* you can reduce "I" domination with this writing technique. Make activities and outcomes, and not yourself, the subjects of sentences. For example, rather than *I took classes in business communication and computer applications,* say *Classes in business communication and computer applications prepared me to ...* Instead of *I enjoyed helping customers,* say *Helping customers was a real pleasure.*

Like the résumé, your letter of application must look professional and suggest quality. This means using a traditional letter style, such as block or modified block. Also, be sure to print it on the same bond paper as your résumé. And, as with your résumé, proofread it several times yourself; then, have a friend read it for content and mechanics. The following checklist provides a quick summary of suggestions to review when you compose and proofread your cover letter.

Checklist for Writing a Persuasive Letter of Application

Opening

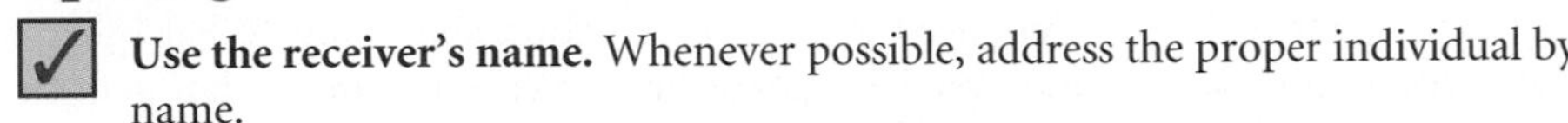
✓ **Use the receiver's name.** Whenever possible, address the proper individual by name.

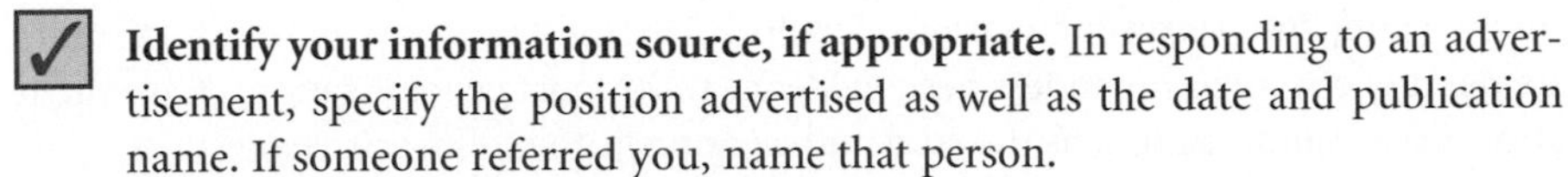
✓ **Identify your information source, if appropriate.** In responding to an advertisement, specify the position advertised as well as the date and publication name. If someone referred you, name that person.

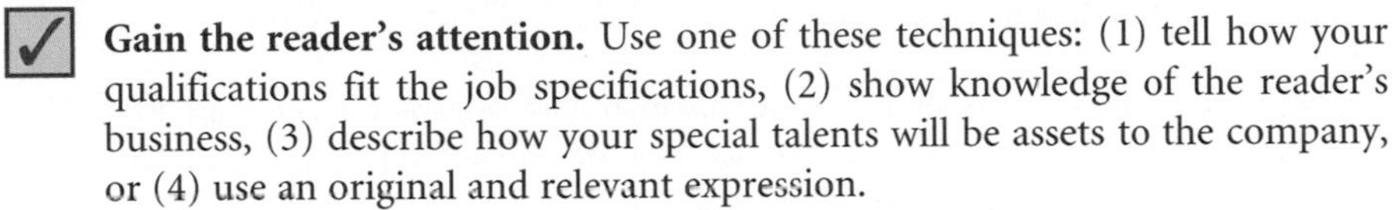
✓ **Gain the reader's attention.** Use one of these techniques: (1) tell how your qualifications fit the job specifications, (2) show knowledge of the reader's business, (3) describe how your special talents will be assets to the company, or (4) use an original and relevant expression.

Body

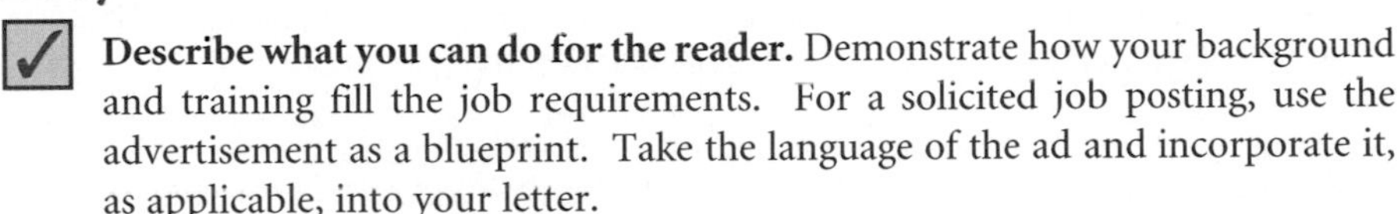
✓ **Describe what you can do for the reader.** Demonstrate how your background and training fill the job requirements. For a solicited job posting, use the advertisement as a blueprint. Take the language of the ad and incorporate it, as applicable, into your letter.

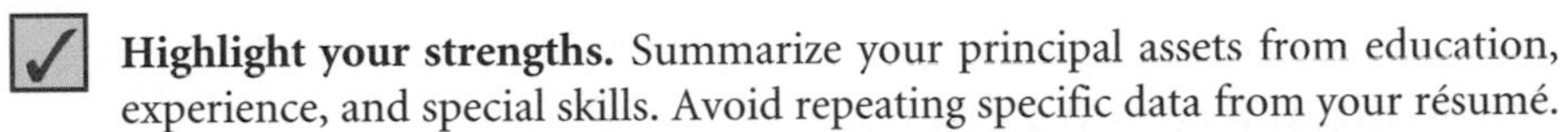
✓ **Highlight your strengths.** Summarize your principal assets from education, experience, and special skills. Avoid repeating specific data from your résumé.

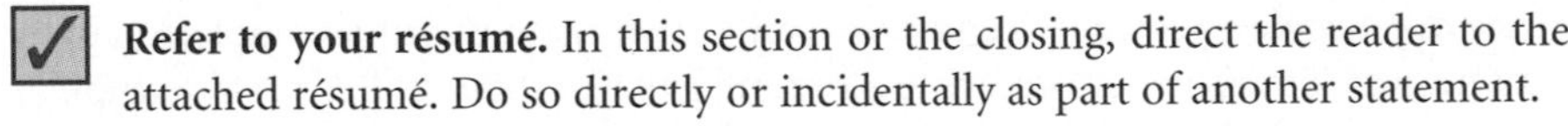
✓ **Refer to your résumé.** In this section or the closing, direct the reader to the attached résumé. Do so directly or incidentally as part of another statement.

Closing

✓ **Ask for an interview.** Also consider reviewing your strongest points or suggesting how your assets will benefit the company.

✓ **Make it easy to respond.** Tell when you can be reached during office hours or announce when you will call the reader. Note that some recruiters prefer that you call them.

Follow-Up Letters and Other Employment Documents

Although the résumé and letter of application are your major tasks, other important letters and documents are often required during the employment process. You may need to make requests, write follow-up letters, or fill out employment applications.

Because each of these tasks reveals something about you and your communication skills, you'll want to put your best foot forward. These documents often subtly influence company officials to extend an interview or offer a job.

Reference Request

To get good letters of recommendation, find willing people and provide ample data about yourself.

Most employers expect job candidates at some point to submit names of individuals who are willing to discuss the candidates' qualifications. Before you list anyone as a reference, however, be sure to ask permission. Try to do this in person. Ask an instructor, for example, if he or she would be willing and has the time to act as your recommender. If you detect any sign of reluctance, don't force the issue. Your goal is to find willing individuals who think well of you.

What your recommenders need most is information about you. What should they stress to prospective employers? To get the best letter of recommendation from your references, help them out. Write a letter explaining the position, its requirements, and the recommendation deadline. Include a copy of your résumé. Remember that recommenders need evidence to support generalizations. Give them appropriate ammunition, as the student has done in the following request:

Dear Professor Smith:

Identify the target position and company. Tell immediately why you are writing.

Recently I applied for the position of administrative assistant in the Human Resources Department of Host International. Because you kindly agreed to help me, I am now asking you to write a letter of recommendation to Host.

Specify the job requirements so that the recommender knows what to stress in the letter. Also, supply data to jog the memory of the writer.

The position calls for good organizational, interpersonal, and writing skills, as well as computer experience. To help you review my skills and training, I enclose my résumé. As you may recall, I earned an A in your business communication class, and you commended my long report for its clarity and organization.

Provide a stamped, addressed envelope.

Please send your letter before July 1 in the enclosed stamped, addressed envelope. I'm grateful for your support, and I promise to let you know the results of my job search.

Application Request Letter

Some organizations consider candidates only when they submit a completed application form. To secure a form, write a routine letter of request. But provide enough information about yourself, as shown in the following example, to assure the reader that you are a serious applicant:

Because you expect a positive response, announce your request immediately.

Dear Mr. Adams:

Please send me an application form for work in your Human Resources Department. In June I will be completing my studies in psychology and communications at Sir Wilfrid Laurier University in Waterloo, Ontario. My program included courses in public relations, psychology, and communications.

Supply an end date, if it seems appropriate. End on a forward-looking note.

I would appreciate receiving this application by May 15 so that I may complete it before making a visit to your city in June. I'm looking forward to beginning a career in personnel management.

Application or Résumé Follow-Up Letter

If your letter or application generates no response within a reasonable time, you may decide to send a short follow-up letter like the one below. Doing so (1) jogs the memory of the personnel officer, (2) demonstrates your serious interest, and (3) allows you to emphasize your qualifications or to add new information.

Dear Ms. Lopez:

Please know I am still interested in becoming an administrative support specialist with Quad, Inc.

Open by reminding the reader of your interest.

Since I submitted an application in May, I have completed my schooling and have been employed as a summer replacement for office workers in several downtown offices. This experience has honed my word processing and communication skills. It has also introduced me to a wide range of office procedures.

Substitute *letter* or *résumé* if appropriate. Use this opportunity to review your strengths or to add new qualifications.

Please keep my application in your active file and let me know when I may put my formal training, technical skills, and practical experience to work for you.

Close by looking forward positively; avoid accusations that make the reader defensive.

Interview Follow-Up Letter

After a job interview you should always send a brief letter of thanks. This courtesy sets you apart from other applicants (most of whom will not bother). Your letter also reminds the interviewer of your visit as well as suggesting your good manners and genuine enthusiasm for the job.

Follow-up letters are most effective if sent immediately after the interview. In your letter refer to the date of the interview, the exact job title for which you were interviewed, and specific topics discussed. Avoid worn-out phrases, such as *Thank you for taking the time to interview me.* Be careful, too, about overusing *I*, especially to begin sentences. Most important, show that you really want the job and that you are qualified for it. Notice how the following letter conveys enthusiasm and confidence:

Dear Ms. Cogan:

Talking with you Thursday, May 23, about the graphic designer position was both informative and interesting.

Mention the interview date and specific position.

Thanks for describing the position in such detail and for introducing me to Ms. Thomas, the senior designer. Her current project designing the annual report in four colours on a Macintosh sounds fascinating as well as quite challenging.

Show appreciation, good manners, and perseverance—traits that recruiters value.

Now that I've learned in greater detail the specific tasks of your graphic designers, I'm more than ever convinced that my computer and creative skills can make a genuine contribution to your graphic productions. My training in Macintosh design and layout ensures that I could be immediately productive on your staff.

Personalize your letter by mentioning topics discussed in the interview. Highlight a specific skill you have for the job.

You will find me an enthusiastic and hard-working member of any team effort. I'm eager to join the graphics staff at your Kitchener headquarters, and I look forward to hearing from you soon.

Remind the reader of your interpersonal skills as well as your enthusiasm and eagerness for this job.

Rejection Follow-Up Letter

If you didn't get the job and you think it was perfect for you, don't give up. In a rejection follow-up letter, it's okay to admit you're disappointed. Be sure to add, however, that you're still interested and will contact them again in a month in case a job opens up. Then follow through for a couple of months—but don't overdo it. Here's an example of an effective rejection follow-up letter:

Dear Mr. Crenshaw:

Subordinate your disappointment to your appreciation at being notified promptly and courteously.

Although I'm disappointed that someone else was selected for your accounting position, I appreciate your promptness and courtesy in notifying me.

Emphasize your continuing interest. Express confidence in meeting the job requirements.

Because I firmly believe that I have the technical and interpersonal skills needed to work in your fast-paced environment, I hope you will keep my résumé in your active file. My desire to become a productive member of your Trillium staff remains strong.

Refer to specifics of your interview. If possible, tell how you are improving your skills.

I enjoyed our interview, and I especially appreciate the time you and Mr. Samson spent describing your company's expansion into international markets. To enhance my qualifications, I've enrolled in a course in International Accounting at NBU.

Take the initiative; tell when you will call for an update.

Should you have an opening for which I am qualified, you may reach me at (506) 719-3901. In the meantime, I will call you in a month to discuss employment possibilities.

Application Form

Some organizations require job candidates to fill out job application forms instead of submitting résumés. This practice permits them to gather and store standardized data about each applicant. Here are some tips for filling out such forms:

- Carry a card summarizing those vital statistics not included on your résumé. If you are asked to fill out an application form in an employer's office, you will need a handy reference to the following data: social insurance number, graduation dates, beginning and ending dates of all employment; salary history; full names, titles, and present work addresses of former supervisors; and full names, occupational titles, occupational addresses, and telephone numbers of persons who have agreed to serve as references.
- Look over all the questions before starting. Fill out the form neatly, printing if your handwriting is poor.
- Answer all questions. Write *Not applicable* if appropriate.
- Be prepared for a salary question. Unless you know what comparable employees are earning in the company, the best strategy is to suggest a salary range or to write in *Negotiable* or *Open*.
- Ask whether you may submit your résumé in addition to the application form.

7 Interviewing for Employment

Job interviews, for most of us, are intimidating; no one enjoys being judged and, possibly, rejected. You can overcome your fear of the interview process by knowing how it works and how to prepare for it.

Trained recruiters generally structure the interview in three separate activities: (1) establishing a cordial relationship, (2) eliciting information about the candidate, and (3) giving information about the job and company. During the interview its participants have opposing goals. The interviewer tries to uncover any negative information that would eliminate a candidate. The candidate, of course, tries to minimize faults and emphasize strengths to avoid being eliminated.

You can become a more skillful player in the interview game if you know what to do before, during, and after the interview.

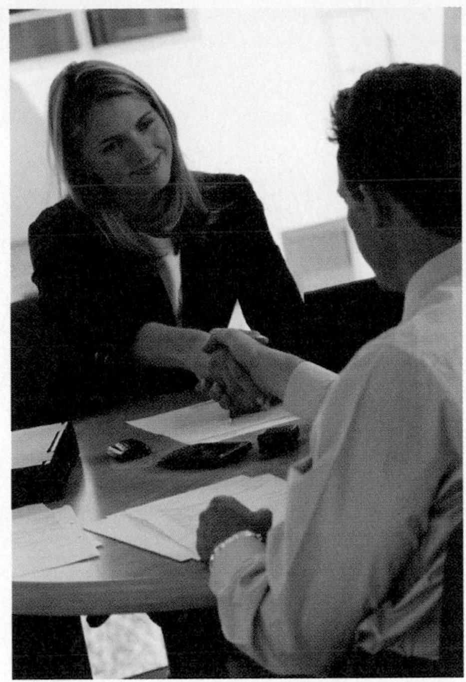

A job interview gives you a chance to explain your résumé and sell your technical expertise as well as your communication and interpersonal skills. But the interview also allows the recruiter to promote his company and explain the duties of the position. Be prepared to ask meaningful questions.

Before the Interview

- **Research the organization.** Never enter an interview cold. Visit the library or use your computer to search for information about the target company or its field, service, or product. Visit the company's Web site and read everything. Call the company to request annual reports, catalogues, or brochures. Ask about the organization and possibly the interviewer. Learn something about the company's size, number of employees, competitors, reputation, and strengths and weaknesses.
- **Learn about the position.** Obtain as much specific information as possible. What are the functions of an individual in this position? What is the typical salary range? What career paths are generally open to this individual? What did the last person in this position do right or wrong?
- **Plan to sell yourself.** Identify three to five of your major selling points regarding skills, training, personal characteristics, and specialized experience. Memorize them; then in the interview be certain to find a place to insert them.
- **Prepare answers to possible questions.** Imagine the kinds of questions you may be asked and work out sample answers. Although you can't anticipate precise questions, you can expect to be asked about your education, skills, experience, and availability. The accompanying Career Coach box shows ten of the most common questions and suggests responses.
- **Prepare success stories.** Rehearse two or three incidents that you can relate about your accomplishments. These may focus on problems you have solved, promotions you have earned, or recognition or praise you have received.
- **Arrive early.** Get to the interview five or ten minutes early. If you are unfamiliar with the area where the interview is to be held, you might visit it before the scheduled day. Locate the building, parking facilities, and office. Time yourself.
- **Dress appropriately.** Don't overdo perfume, jewellery, or aftershave lotion. Avoid loud colours; strive for a coordinated, natural appearance. Favourite "power" colours for interviews are gray and dark blue. It's not a bad idea to check your appearance in a restroom before entering the office.

Prior to an interview, applicants should research the organization and plan answers to potential questions.

During the Interview

- **Establish the relationship.** Shake hands firmly. Don't be afraid to offer your hand first. Address the interviewer formally ("Hello, Mrs. Jones"). Allow the interviewer to put you at ease with small talk.

CAREER COACH

ANSWERING TEN FREQUENTLY ASKED INTERVIEW QUESTIONS

Interviewers want to learn about your job experiences and education so that they can evaluate who you are and predict how you might perform on the job. Study each of the following frequently asked interview questions and the strategies for answering them successfully.

- **Why do you want to work for us?** Questions like this illustrate the need for you to research an organization thoroughly before the interview. Go to the company's Web site, read its annual report, conduct library research, ask friends, and read the company's advertisements and other printed materials to gather data. Describe your desire to work for them not only from your perspective but also from their point of view. What have you to offer them?

- **Why should we hire you?** Here is an opportunity for you to sell your strong points in relation to this specific position. Describe your skills, academic preparation, and relevant experience. If you have little experience, don't apologize—the interviewer has read your résumé. Emphasize strengths as demonstrated in your education, such as initiative and persistence in completing assignments, ability to learn quickly, self-sufficiency, and excellent attendance.

- **What can you tell me about yourself?** Use this chance to promote yourself. Stick to professional or business-related strengths; avoid personal or humorous references. Be ready with at least three success stories illustrating characteristics important to this job. Demonstrate responsibility you have been given; describe how you contributed as a team player.

- **What are your strongest (or weakest) personal qualities?** Stress your strengths, such as "I believe I am conscientious, reliable, tolerant, patient, and thorough." Add examples that illustrate these qualities: "My supervisor said that my research was exceptionally thorough." If pressed for a weakness, give a strength disguised as a weakness: "Perhaps my greatest fault is being too painstaking with details." Or, "I am impatient when tasks are not completed on time." Don't admit weaknesses, not even to sound human. You'll be hired for your strengths, not your weaknesses.

- **What do you expect to be doing ten years from now?** Formulate a realistic plan with respect to your present age and situation. The important thing is to be prepared for this question.

- **Do you prefer working with others or by yourself?** This question can be tricky. Provide a middle-of-the-road answer that not only suggests your interpersonal qualities but also reflects an ability to make independent decisions and work without supervision.

- **Have you ever changed your major during your education? Why?** Another tricky question. Don't admit weaknesses or failures. In explaining changes, suggest career potential and new aspirations awakened by your expanding education, experience, or maturity.

- **What have been your most rewarding or disappointing work (or school) experiences?** If possible, concentrate on positive experiences such as technical and interpersonal skills you acquired. Avoid dwelling on negative or unhappy topics. Never criticize former employers. If you worked for an ungrateful, penny-pinching slave driver in a dead-end position, say that you learned all you could from that job. Move the conversation to the prospective position and what attracts you to it.

- **Have you established any new goals lately?** Watch out here. If you reveal new goals, you may inadvertently admit deficiencies. Instead of "I've resolved to finally learn something about graphic design," try "Although I'm familiar with simple graphics programs, I decided to get serious about graphic design by mastering the tools of Adobe PhotoShop and Illustrator."

- **What are your long- and short-term goals?** Suggest realistic goals that you have consciously worked out before the interview. Know what you want to do with your future. To admit to an interviewer that you're not sure what you want to do is a sign of immaturity, weakness, and indecision.

- **Act confident but natural.** Establish and maintain eye contact, but don't get into a staring contest. Sit up straight, facing the interviewer. Don't manipulate objects, like a pencil or keys, during the interview. Try to remain natural and at ease.

During an interview, applicants should act confident, focus on their strengths, and sell themselves.

- **Don't criticize.** Avoid making negative comments about previous employers, instructors, or others. Such criticism may be taken to indicate a negative personality. Employers are not eager to hire complainers. Moreover, such criticism may suggest that you would do the same to this organization.
- **Stay focused on your strengths.** If the interviewer asks a question that does not help you promote your strongest qualifications, answer briefly. Alternatively, try to turn your response into a positive selling point.
- **Find out about the job early.** Because your time will be short, try to learn all you can about the target job early in the interview. Ask about its responsibilities and the kinds of people who have done well in the position before. Inquiring about the company's culture will help you decide whether your personality fits with this organization.

Asking questions about the job helps applicants learn whether this position is right for them.

- **Prepare for salary questions.** Remember that nearly all salaries are negotiable, depending on your qualifications. Knowing the typical salary range for the target position helps. The recruiter can tell you the salary ranges—but you will have to ask. If you've had little experience, you will probably be offered a salary somewhere between the low point and the midpoint in the range. With more experience you can negotiate for a higher figure. A word of caution, though. One personnel manager warns that candidates who emphasize money are suspect because they may leave if offered a few thousand dollars more elsewhere.
- **Be ready for inappropriate questions.** If you are asked a question that you think is illegal, politely ask the interviewer how that question is related to this job. Ask the purpose of the question. Perhaps valid reasons exist that are not obvious.
- **Ask your own questions.** Often, the interviewer concludes an interview with "Do you have any questions about the position?" Inquire about career paths, orientation or training for new employees, or the company's promotion policies. Have a list of relevant questions prepared. If the interview has gone well, ask the recruiter about his or her career in the company.
- **Conclude positively.** Summarize your strongest qualifications, show your enthusiasm for obtaining this position, and thank the interviewer for a constructive interview. Be sure you understand the next step in the employment process.

After the Interview

- **Make notes on the interview.** While the events are fresh in your mind, jot down the key points—good and bad.

Keeping notes of the meeting helps candidates remember what happened.

- **Write a thank-you letter.** Immediately write a letter thanking the interviewer for a pleasant and enlightening discussion. Be sure to spell his or her name correctly.

Summary of Learning Objectives

1 **Prepare for employment by identifying your interests, evaluating your assets, recognizing the changing nature of jobs, choosing a career path, and studying traditional and electronic job search techniques.** The employment process begins with an analysis of your likes and your qualifications. Because the nature of jobs is changing, your future work may include flexible work assignments, multiple employers, and constant retraining. You can learn more about career opportunities through your campus career centre, the Web, your library, internships, part-time jobs, interviews, classified ads, and professional organizations. Traditional job search techniques range from newspaper ads to developing your own network of friends and relatives. Electronic job search techniques include visiting Internet job sites and company Web sites.

2 **Compare and contrast chronological, functional, and combination résumés.** Chronological résumés, listing work and education by dates, rank highest with recruiters. Functional résumés, highlighting skills instead of jobs, appeal to people changing careers or those having negative employment histories. Combination résumés, including a complete job history along with skill areas, are increasingly popular.

3 **Organize, format, and produce a persuasive résumé.** Target your résumé for a specific job. Study models to arrange most effectively your main heading, career objective (optional), education, work experience, capabilities, awards and activities, personal data, and references (optional). Use action verbs to show how your assets will help the target organization.

4 **Identify techniques that prepare a résumé for computer scanning, posting at a Web site, faxing, and e-mailing.** Computer-friendly résumés avoid unusual typefaces, underlining, and italics. They use 10- to 14-point type, smooth white paper, and quality printing. The applicant's name appears on the first line. The résumé includes ample white space, avoids double columns, and is not folded or stapled. It emphasizes keywords, which are nouns that an employer might use to describe the position and skills desired. Résumés posted at Web sites must be prepared in HTML (Hypertext Markup Language). They may include links to résumé extras such as work samples and letters of recommendation. Faxed résumés must avoid small fonts and underlining. E-mailed résumés should probably be sent in ASCII (text-only format). Follow up faxed and e-mail résumés with polished copies.

5 **Write a persuasive letter of application to accompany your résumé.** Gain attention in the opening by mentioning the job or a person who referred you. Build interest in the body by stressing what you can do for the targeted company. Refer to your résumé, request an interview, and motivate action in the closing.

6 **Write effective employment follow-up letters and other messages.** Follow up all your employment activities with appropriate messages. After submitting your résumé or after an interview, even after being rejected, follow up with letters that express your appreciation and continuing interest.

7 **Evaluate successful job interview strategies.** Learn about the job and the organization. Prepare answers to possible questions and be ready with success stories. Act confident and natural. Be prepared to ask or answer salary questions. Have a list of your own questions, summarize your key strengths, and stay focused on your strong points. Afterwards, send a thank-you letter.

CHAPTER REVIEW

1. Name at least five questions that you should ask yourself to identify your employment interests. (Obj. 1)
2. List five sources of career information. (Obj. 1)
3. How are most jobs likely to be found? Through classified ads? The Internet? Employment agencies? Networking? (Obj. 1)
4. What is the goal of your résumé? (Obj. 2)
5. Describe a chronological résumé and discuss its advantages. (Obj. 2)
6. Describe a functional résumé and discuss its advantages. (Obj. 2)
7. What are the disadvantages of a functional résumé? (Obj. 2)
8. When does it make sense to include a career objective on your résumé? (Obj. 3)
9. What information should you include for the jobs you list on a chronological résumé? (Objs. 2 and 3)
10. In addition to technical skills, what traits and characteristics do employers seek? (Objs. 2 and 3)
11. What changes must be made in a typical résumé to make it effective for computer scanning? (Obj. 4)
12. What are the three purposes of a letter of application? (Obj. 5)
13. How can you make it easy for a recruiter to reach you? (Obj. 5)
14. Other than a letter of application, name five kinds of letters you might need to write in the employment process. (Obj. 6)
15. What information should a candidate gather in preparing for a job interview? (Obj. 7)

CRITICAL THINKING

1. How has the concept of the "job" changed, and how will it affect your employment search? (Obj. 1)
2. How is a résumé different from a company employment application? (Objs. 1 and 2)
3. Some job candidates think that applying for unsolicited jobs can be more fruitful than applying for advertised openings. Discuss the advantages and disadvantages of letters that "prospect" for jobs. (Obj. 5)
4. How do the interviewer and interviewee play opposing roles during job interviews? What strategies should the interviewee prepare in advance? (Obj. 7)

ACTIVITIES

16.1 Identifying Your Employment Interests (Obj. 1)

In a memo addressed to your instructor, answer the questions in the "Identifying Your Interests" section at the beginning of the chapter. Draw a conclusion from your answers. What kind of career, company, position, and location seem to fit your self-analysis?

16.2 Evaluating Your Qualifications (Objs. 1, 2, and 3)

Prepare five worksheets that inventory your qualifications in these areas: employment, education, capabilities and skills, honours and activities, and volunteer activities. Use active verbs when appropriate.

a. *Employment.* Begin with your most recent job or internship. For each position list the following information: employer, job title, dates of employment, and three to five duties, activities, or accomplishments. Emphasize activities related to your job goal. Strive to quantify your achievements.

b. *Education.* List degrees and/or diplomas, certificates, and training accomplishments. Include courses, seminars, or skills that are relevant to your job goal. Calculate your grade-point average in your major.

c. *Capabilities and skills.* List all capabilities and skills that recommend you for the job you seek. Use words like *skilled, competent, trained, experienced,* and *ability to.* Also list five or more qualities or interpersonal skills necessary for a successful individual in your chosen field. Write action statements demonstrating that you possess some of these qualities. Empty assurances aren't good enough; try to show evidence (*Developed teamwork skills by working with a committee of eight to produce a ...*).

d. *Awards, honours, and activities.* Explain any awards so that the reader will understand them. List campus, community, and professional activities that suggest you are a well-rounded individual or possess traits relevant to your target job.

e. *Volunteer activities.* If you have been involved as a volunteer, you may be able to point out your organization and communication skills along with your sense of community spirit.

16.3 Choosing a Career Path (Obj. 1)

Visit your college library, local library, or campus career centre. Consult the National Occupational Classification (NOC) binder and guide, published by Employment and Immigration Canada, or the latest release of Job Futures

<www.hrdc-drhc.gc.ca/JobFutures>. From either of the two sources, photocopy or print the pages that describe employment in the area in which you are interested. If your instructor directs, attach these copies to the letter of application you will write in Activity 16.10.

16.4 Searching the Job Market (Obj. 1)

Clip a job advertisement from the classified section of a newspaper or print one from a career site on the Web. Select an ad describing the kind of employment you are seeking now or plan to seek when you graduate. Save this advertisement to attach to the résumé you will write in Activity 16.9.

16.5 Posting a Résumé on the Web (Obj. 4)

Web

Prepare a list of at least three Web sites where you could post your résumé. Describe the procedure involved and the advantages for each site.

16.6 Researching a Company: Preparing a Company Data Sheet (Objs. 1 and 7)

Prepare a template that can be used for all of the companies to which you may wish to apply, or for which you have an interview. Considering your employment interests and needs, create a list of questions that are relevant to you in your job search. Your instructor may ask you to submit a template or a company data sheet of a company in which you are interested. Consult a minimum of three sources to access relevant information on the company you have selected.

16.7 Draft Document: Résumé (Objs. 2 and 3)

Analyze the following résumé. Discuss its strengths and weaknesses. Your instructor may ask you to revise sections of this résumé before showing you an improved version.

Wendy Lee Cox
9 Franklin Terrace
Timmins, ON
Phone: (d) (705) 834-4583 (n) (705) 594-2985

Seeking to be hired at Mead Products as an intern in Accounting

SKILLS: Accounting, Internet, Windows 98, Excel, PowerPoint, Freelance Graphics

EDUCATION
Now working on diploma in Business Administration. Major, Management and Accounting; GPA is 3.5. Expect to graduate in June, 2004.

EXPERIENCE:
Assistant Accountant, 1999 to present. March and McLennan, Inc., Bookkeeping/Tax Service, Timmins. I keep accounting records for several small businesses accurately. I prepare 150 to 200 individual income tax returns each year. For Hill and Hill Truck Line I maintain accurate and up-to-date A/R records. And I prepare payroll records for 16 employees at three firms.

Peterson Controls Inc., Timmins. Data Processing Internship, 2003 to present. I design and maintain spreadsheets and also process weekly and monthly information for production uptime and downtime. I prepare graphs to illustrate uptime and downtime data.

Timmins Country Club. Accounts Payable Internship, 2002 to 2003. Took care of accounts payable including filing system for the club. Responsible for processing monthly adjusting entries for general ledger. Worked closely with treasurer to give the Board budget/disbursement figures regularly.

Northern College, Timmins. I marketed the VITA program to Northern students and organized volunteers and supplies. Official title: Coordinator of Volunteer Income Tax Assistance Project.

COMMUNITY SERVICE: March of Dimes Drive, Central Park High School; All Souls Unitarian Church, coordinator for Children's Choir

16.8 Draft Document: Letter of Application (Obj. 5)

Analyze each section of the following letter of application written by an accounting major about to graduate.

Dear Human Resources Director:

Please consider this letter as an application for the position of staff accountant that I saw advertised in the *Whig Standard*. Although I have had no paid work experience in this field, accounting has been my major in college and I'm sure I could be an asset to your company.

For four years I have studied accounting, and I am fully trained for full-charge bookkeeping as well as electronic accounting. I have taken 36 units of college accounting and courses in business law, economics, statistics, finance, management, and marketing.

In addition to my course work, during the tax season I have been a student volunteer for VITA. This is a project to help individuals in the community prepare their income tax returns, and I learned a lot from this experience. I have also received some experience in office work and working with figures when I was employed as an office assistant for Copy Quick, Inc.

I am a competent and responsible person who gets along pretty well with others. I have been a member of some college and social organizations and have even held elective office.

I feel that I have a strong foundation in accounting as a result of my course work and my experience. Along with my personal qualities and my desire to succeed, I hope that you will agree that I qualify for the position of staff accountant with your company.

Sincerely,

16.9 Résumé (Objs. 2 and 3)

Using the data you developed in Activity 16.2, write your résumé. Aim it at a full-time job, part-time position, or internship. Attach a job listing for a specific position (from Activity 16.4). Use a computer. Revise your résumé until it is perfect.

16.10 Letter of Application (Obj. 5)

Write a cover letter introducing your résumé. Again, use a computer. Revise your cover letter until it is perfect.

16.11 Interview Follow-Up Letter (Obj. 6)

Assume you were interviewed for the position you seek. Write a follow-up thank-you letter.

16.12 Reference Request (Obj. 6)

Your favourite professor has agreed to recommend you. Write to the professor and request that he or she send a letter of recommendation to a company where you are applying for a job. Provide data about the job description and about yourself so that the professor can target its content.

16.13 Résumé Follow-Up Letter (Obj. 6)

A month has passed since you sent your résumé and letter of application in response to a job advertisement. Write a follow-up letter that doesn't offend the reader or damage your chances of employment.

16.14 Application Request (Obj. 6)

Select a company for which you'd like to work. Write a letter requesting an employment application, which the company requires for all job seekers.

16.15 Rejection Follow-Up Letter (Obj. 6)

Assume you didn't get the job. Although someone else was selected, you hope that other jobs may become available. Write a follow-up letter that keeps the door open.

APPENDIX **A**

C.L.U.E. Competent Language Usage Essentials

A Business Communicator's Guide

In the business world, people are often judged by the way they speak and write. Using the language competently can mean the difference between individual success and failure. Often a speaker sounds accomplished; but when that same individual puts ideas in print, errors in language usage destroy his or her credibility.

What C.L.U.E. Is

This appendix provides a condensed guide to competency in language usage essentials (C.L.U.E.). Fifty guidelines review sentence structure, grammar, usage, punctuation, capitalization, and number style. These guidelines focus on the most frequently used—and abused—language elements. Presented from a business communicator's perspective, the guidelines also include realistic tips for application. And frequent checkpoint exercises enable you to try out your skills immediately.

The concentrated materials in this guide will help novice business communicators focus on the major areas of language use, but are not meant to teach or review *all* the principles of English grammar and punctuation.

How to Use C.L.U.E.

Two kinds of exercises are available for your practice. (1) *Checkpoints,* located in this appendix, focus on a small group of language guidelines. Use them to test your comprehension as you complete each section. (2) *Review exercises,* located in Chapters 1 through 10, cover all guidelines, spelling words, and confusing words. Use the review exercises to reinforce your language skills at the same time you are learning about the processes and products of business communication.

Guidelines: Competent Language Usage Essentials

Sentence Structure

GUIDE 1: Express ideas in complete sentences. You can recognize a complete sentence because it (a) includes a subject (a noun or pronoun that interacts with a verb), (b) includes a verb (a word expressing action or describing a condition), and (c) makes sense (comes to a closure). A complete sentence is an independent clause. One of the most serious errors a writer can make is punctuating a fragment as if it were a complete sentence. A fragment is a broken-off part of a sentence.

Fragment	**Improved**
Because 90 percent of all business transactions involve written messages. Good writing skills are critical.	Because 90 percent of all business transactions involve written messages, good writing skills are critical.
The recruiter requested a writing sample. Even though the candidate seemed to communicate well.	The recruiter requested a writing sample, even though the candidate seemed to communicate well.

Tip. Fragments often can be identified by the words that introduce them—words like *although, as, because, even, except, for example, if, instead of, since, so, such as, that, which,* and *when.* These words introduce dependent clauses. Make sure such clauses are always connected to independent clauses.

DEPENDENT CLAUSE — INDEPENDENT CLAUSE

Since she became supervisor, she had to write more memos and reports.

GUIDE 2: Avoid run-on (fused) sentences. A sentence with two independent clauses must be joined by a coordinating conjunction (*and, or, nor, but*) or by a semicolon (;). Without a conjunction or a semicolon, a run-on sentence results.

Run-on	**Improved**
Robin visited resorts of the rich and the famous he also dropped in on luxury spas.	Robin visited resorts of the rich and famous, and he also dropped in on luxury spas.
	Robin visited resorts of the rich and famous; he also dropped in on luxury spas.

GUIDE 3: Avoid comma-splice sentences. A comma splice results when a writer joins (splices together) two independent clauses—without using a coordinating conjunction (*and, or, nor, but*).

Comma Splice	**Improved**
Disney World operates in Orlando, EuroDisney serves Paris.	Disney World operates in Orlando; EuroDisney serves Paris.
	Disney World operates in Orlando, and EuroDisney serves Paris.
Visitors wanted a resort vacation, however they were disappointed.	Visitors wanted a resort vacation; however, they were disappointed.

Tip. In joining independent clauses, beware of using a comma and words like *consequently, furthermore, however, therefore, then, thus,* and so on. These conjunctive adverbs require semicolons.

✓ Checkpoint

Revise the following to rectify sentence fragments, comma splices, and run-ons.

1. When McDonald's tested pizza, Pizza Hut fought back. With aggressive ads ridiculing McPizza.
2. Aggressive ads can backfire, consequently, marketing directors consider them carefully.
3. Corporations study the legality of attack advertisements they also retaliate with counterattacks.
4. Although Pizza Hut is the country's number one pizza chain. Domino's Pizza leads in deliveries.
5. About half of the 6600 outlets make deliveries, the others concentrate on walk-in customers.

For all the Checkpoint sentences, compare your responses with the answers at the end of Appendix A (page A-22).

Grammar

Verb Tense

GUIDE 4: Use present tense, past tense, and past participle verb forms correctly.

Present Tense (Today I ______)	Past Tense (Yesterday I ______)	Past Participle (I have ______)
am	was	been
begin	began	begun
break	broke	broken
bring	brought	brought
choose	chose	chosen
come	came	come
do	did	done
give	gave	given
go	went	gone
know	knew	known
pay	paid	paid
see	saw	seen
steal	stole	stolen
take	took	taken
write	wrote	written

The package *came* yesterday, and Kevin *knew* what it contained.

If I *had seen* the shipper's bill, I *would have paid* it immediately.

I *know* the answer now; I wish I *had known* it yesterday.

Tip. Probably the most frequent mistake in tenses results from substituting the past participle form for the past tense. Notice that the past participle tense requires auxiliary verbs such as *has, had, have, would have,* and *could have.*

Faulty	**Correct**
When he *come* over last night, he *brung* pizza.	When he *came* over last night, he *brought* pizza.
If he *had came* earlier, we *could have saw* the video.	If he *had come* earlier, we *could have seen* the video.

Verb Mood

GUIDE 5: Use the subjunctive mood to express hypothetical (untrue) ideas. The most frequent misuse of the subjunctive mood involves using *was* instead of *were* in clauses introduced by *if* and *as though* or containing *wish.*

If I *were* (not *was*) you, I would take a business writing course.

Sometimes I wish I *were* (not *was*) the manager of this department.

He acts as though he *were* (not *was*) in charge of this department.

Tip. If the statement could possibly be true, use *was.*

If I *was* to blame, I accept the consequences.

Checkpoint

Correct faults in verb tenses and mood.

6. If I was in your position, I would have wrote the manager a letter.
7. You could have wrote a better résumé if you have read the chapter first.
8. When Trevor seen the want ad, he immediately contacted the company.
9. I wish I was able to operate a computer so that I could have went to work there.
10. Because she had took many computer courses, Maria was able to chose a good job.

Verb Voice

For a discussion of active- and passive-voice verbs, see page 101 in Chapter 5.

Verb Agreement

GUIDE 6: Make subjects agree with verbs despite intervening phrases and clauses. Become a detective in locating *true* subjects. Don't be deceived by prepositional phrases and parenthetic words that often disguise the true subject.

Our study of annual budgets, five-year plans, and sales proposals *is* (not *are*) progressing on schedule. (The true subject is *study.*)

The budgeted item, despite additions proposed yesterday, *remains* (not *remain*) as submitted. (The true subject is *item.*)

A salesperson's evaluation of the prospects for a sale, together with plans for follow-up action, *is* (not *are*) what we need. (The true subject is *evaluation.*)

Tip. Subjects are nouns or pronouns that control verbs. To find subjects, cross out prepositional phrases beginning with words like *about, at, by, for, from, of,* and *to.* Subjects of verbs are not found in prepositional phrases. Also, don't be tricked by expressions introduced by *together with, in addition to,* and *along with.*

GUIDE 7: Subjects joined by *and* require plural verbs. Watch for true subjects joined by the conjunction *and.* They require plural verbs.

The CEO and one of his assistants *have* (not *has*) ordered a limo.

Considerable time and money *were* (not *was*) spent on remodeling.

Exercising in the gym and jogging every day *are* (not *is*) how he keeps fit.

GUIDE 8: Subjects joined by *or* or *nor* may require singular or plural verbs. The verb should agree with the closest subject.

Either the software or the printer *is* (not *are*) causing the glitch. (The verb is controlled by closer subject, *printer.*)

Neither Montreal nor Calgary *has* (not *have*) a chance of winning. (The verb is controlled by *Calgary.*)

Tip. In joining singular and plural subjects with *or* or *nor,* place the plural subject closer to the verb. Then, the plural verb sounds natural. For example, *Either the manufacturer or the distributors are responsible.*

GUIDE 9: Use singular verbs for most indefinite pronouns. For example: *anyone, anybody, anything, each, either, every, everyone, everybody, everything, neither, nobody, nothing, someone, somebody,* and *something* all take singular verbs.

Everyone in both offices *was* (not *were*) given a bonus.

Each of the employees *is* (not *are*) being interviewed.

GUIDE 10: Use singular or plural verbs for collective nouns, depending on whether the members of the group are operating as a unit or individually. Words like *faculty, administration, class, crowd,* and *committee* are considered *collective* nouns. If the members of the collective are acting as a unit, treat them as singular subjects. If they are acting individually, it's usually better to add the word *members* and use a plural verb.

Correct
The Finance Committee *is* working harmoniously. (*Committee* is singular because its action is unified.)

The Planning Committee *are* having difficulty agreeing. (*Committee* is plural because its members are acting individually.)

Improved
The Planning Committee members *are* having difficulty agreeing. (Add the word *members* if a plural meaning is intended.)

Tip. In North America collective nouns are generally considered singular. In Britain these collective nouns are generally considered plural.

✓ Checkpoint

Correct the errors in subject–verb agreement.

11. A manager's time and energy has to be focused on important issues.
12. Promotion of women, despite managerial training programs and networking efforts, are disappointingly small.
13. We're not sure whether Mr. Murphy or Ms. Wagner are in charge of the program.
14. Each of the Fortune 500 companies are being sent a survey regarding women in management.
15. Our CEO, like other good executives, know how to be totally informed without being totally involved.

Pronoun Case

GUIDE 11: Learn the three cases of pronouns and how each is used. Pronouns are substitutes for nouns. Every business writer must know the following pronoun cases.

Nominative or Subjective Case	**Objective Case**	**Possessive Case**
(used for subjects of verbs and subject complements)	(used for objects of prepositions and objects of verbs)	(used to show possession)
I	me	my, mine
we	us	our, ours

Nominative or Subjective Case	**Objective Case**	**Possessive Case**
you	you	your, yours
he	him	his
she	her	her, hers
it	it	its
they	them	their, theirs
who, whoever	whom, whomever	whose

GUIDE 12: Use nominative case pronouns as subjects of verbs and as complements. Complements are words that follow linking verbs (such as *am, is, are, was, were, be, being,* and *been*) and rename the words to which they refer.

She and *I* (not *her* and *me*) prefer easy-riding mountain bikes. (Use nominative case pronouns as the subjects of the verb *prefer.*)

We think that *she* and *he* (not *her* and *him*) will win the race. (Use nominative case pronouns as the subjects of the verb *will win.*)

It must have been *she* (not *her*) who called last night. (Use a nominative case pronoun as a subject complement.)

Tip. If you feel awkward using nominative pronouns after linking verbs, rephrase the sentence to avoid the dilemma. Instead of *It is she who is the boss,* say *She is the boss.*

GUIDE 13: Use objective case pronouns as objects of prepositions and verbs.

Please order stationery for *her* and *me* (not *she* and *I*). (The pronouns *her* and *me* are objects of the preposition *for.*)

The CEO appointed *him* (not *he*) to the position. (The pronoun *him* is the object of the verb *appointed.*)

Tip. When a pronoun appears in combination with a noun or another pronoun, ignore the extra noun or pronoun and its conjunction. Then, the case of the pronoun becomes more obvious.

Jason asked Jennifer and *me* (not *I*) to lunch. (Ignore *Jennifer and.*)

The waiter didn't know whether to give the bill to Jason or *her* (not *she*). (Ignore *Jason or.*)

Tip. Be especially alert to the following prepositions: *except, between, but,* and *like.* Be sure to use objective pronouns as their objects.

Just between you and *me* (not *I*), that mineral water comes from the tap.

Computer grammar checkers work well for writers like Lee and *him* (not *he*).

GUIDE 14: Use possessive case pronouns to show ownership. Possessive pronouns (such as *hers, yours, whose, ours, theirs,* and *its*) require no apostrophes.

All reports except *yours* (not *your's*) have to be rewritten.

The printer and *its* (not *it's*) fonts produce exceptional copy.

Tip. Don't confuse possessive pronouns and contractions. Contractions are shortened forms of subject–verb phrases (such as *it's* for *it is, there's* for *there is, who's* for *who is,* and *they're* for *they are*).

 **Checkpoint**

Correct errors in pronoun case.

16. Although my friend and myself are interested in this computer, it's price seems high.

17. Letters addressed to he and I were delivered to you and Ann in error.

18. Just between you and I, the mail room and its procedures need improvement.

19. Several applications were lost; your's and her's were the only ones delivered.

20. It could have been her who sent the program update to you and I.

GUIDE 15: Use *self*-ending pronouns only when they refer to previously mentioned nouns or pronouns.

The president *himself* ate all the M & Ms.

Send the package to Marcus or *me* (not *myself*).

Tip. Trying to sound less egocentric, some radio and TV announcers incorrectly substitute *myself* when they should use *I*. For example, "Jerry and *myself* (should be *I*) are cohosting the telethon."

GUIDE 16: Use *who* or *whoever* for nominative case constructions and *whom* or *whomever* for objective case constructions. In determining the correct choice, it's helpful to substitute *he* for *who* or *whoever* and *him* for *whom* or *whomever.*

For *whom* was this software ordered? (The software was ordered for *him.*)

Who did you say called? (You did say *he* called?)

Give the supplies to *whoever* asked for them. (In this sentence the clause *whoever asked for them* functions as the object of the preposition *to.* Within the clause, *whoever* is the subject of the verb *asked.* Again, try substituting *he: he asked for them.*)

✓ Checkpoint

Correct any errors in the use of *self*-ending pronouns and *who/whom.*

21. The boss herself is willing to call whoever we nominate for the position.
22. Who would you like to see nominated?
23. These supplies are for whomever ordered them.
24. The meeting is set for Tuesday; however, Jeff and myself cannot attend.
25. Incident reports are to be written by whomever experiences a sales problem.

Pronoun Reference

GUIDE 17: Make pronouns agree in number and gender with the words to which they refer (their antecedents). When the gender of the antecedent is obvious, pronoun references are simple.

One of the boys lost *his* (not *their*) new tennis shoes. (The singular pronoun *his* refers to the singular *One.*)

Each of the female nurses was escorted to *her car* (not *their cars*). (The singular pronoun *her* and singular noun *car* are necessary because they refer to the singular subject *Each.*)

Somebody on the girls' team left *her* (not *their*) headlights on.

When the gender of the antecedent could be male or female, sensitive writers today have a number of options.

Faulty

Every employee should receive *their* cheque Friday. (The plural pronoun *their* does not agree with its singular antecedent *employee.*)

Improved

All employees should receive *their* cheques Friday. (Make the subject plural so that the plural pronoun *their* is acceptable. This option is preferred by many writers today.)

All employees should receive cheques Friday. (Omit the possessive pronoun entirely.)

Every employee should receive *a* cheque Friday. (Substitute *a* for a pronoun.)

Every employee should receive *his or her* cheque Friday. (Use the combination *his or her.* However, this option is wordy and should be avoided.)

GUIDE 18: Be sure that pronouns such as *it, which, this,* and *that* refer to clear antecedents. Vague pronouns confuse the reader because they have no clear single antecedent. The most troublesome are *it, which, this,* and *that.* Replace vaguc pronouns with concrete nouns, or provide these pronouns with clear antecedents.

Faulty

Our office recycles as much paper as possible because *it* helps the environment. (Does *it* refer to *paper, recycling,* or *office*?)

Ihe disadvantages of local area networks can offset their advantages, *which* merits further evaluation. (What merits evaluation: advantages, disadvantages, or offsetting of one by the other?)

Improved

Our office recycles as much paper as possible because *such efforts* help the environment. (Replace *it* with *such efforts.*)

The disadvantages of local area networks can offset their advantages, a *fact* which merits further evaluation. (*Fact* supplies a clear antecedent for *which.*)

Faulty

Negotiators announced an expanded health care plan, reductions in dental coverage, and a proposal of on-site child care facilities. *This* caused employee protests. (What exactly caused employee protests?)

Improved

Negotiators announced an expanded health care plan, reductions in dental coverage, and a proposal of on-site child care facilities. *This* reduction in dental coverage caused employee protests. (The pronoun *This* now has a clear reference.)

Tip. Whenever you use the words *this, that, these,* and *those* by themselves, a red flag should pop up. These words are dangerous when they stand alone. Inexperienced writers often use them to refer to an entire previous idea, rather than to a specific antecedent, as shown in the preceding example. You can often solve the problem by adding another idea to the pronoun (such as *this announcement*).

✓ Checkpoint

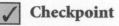

Correct the faulty and vague pronoun references in the following sentences. Numerous remedies exist.

26. Every employee is entitled to have their tuition reimbursed.

27. Flexible working hours may mean slower career advancement, but it appeals to me anyway.

28. Any subscriber may cancel their subscription at any time.

29. Every voter must have their name and address verified at the polling place.

30. Obtaining agreement on job standards, listening to coworkers, and encouraging employee suggestions all helped to open lines of communication. This is particularly important in team projects.

Adjectives and Adverbs

GUIDE 19: Use adverbs, not adjectives, to describe or limit the action of verbs.

Andrew said he did *well* (not *good*) on the exam.

After its tune-up, the engine is running *smoothly* (not *smooth*).

Don't take the manager's criticism *personally* (not *personal*).

GUIDE 20: Hyphenate two or more adjectives that are joined to create a compound modifier before a noun.

Follow the *step-by-step* instructions to construct the *low-cost* bookshelves.

A *well-designed* keyboard is part of their *state-of-the-art* equipment.

Tip. Don't confuse adverbs ending in *-ly* with compound adjectives: *newly enacted* law and *highly regarded* CEO would not be hyphenated.

Checkpoint

Correct any problems in the use of pronouns, adjectives, and adverbs.

31. My manager and myself prepared a point by point analysis of the proposal.

32. Because we completed the work so quick, we were able to visit the recently-opened snack bar.

33. If I do good on the placement exam, I qualify for many part time jobs and a few full time positions.

34. The vice president told him and I not to take the announcement personal.

35. In the not too distant future, we may enjoy interactive television.

Punctuation

GUIDE 21: Use commas to separate three or more items (words, phrases, or short clauses) in a series.

> Downward communication delivers job instructions, procedures, and appraisals.
>
> In preparing your résumé, try to keep it brief, make it easy to read, and include only job-related information.
>
> The new ice cream flavours include cookie dough, chocolate raspberry truffle, cappuccino, and almond amaretto.

Tip. Some professional writers omit the comma before *and.* However, most business writers prefer to retain that comma because it prevents misreading the last two items as one item. Notice in the previous example how the final two ice cream flavours could have been misread if the comma had been omitted.

GUIDE 22: Use commas to separate introductory clauses and certain phrases from independent clauses. This guideline describes the comma most often omitted by business writers. Sentences that open with dependent clauses (often introduced by words such as *since, when, if, as, although,* and *because*) require commas to separate them from the main idea. The comma helps readers recognize where the introduction ends and the big idea begins. Introductory phrases of more than five words or phrases containing verbal elements also require commas.

> If you recognize introductory clauses, you will have no trouble placing the comma. (Comma separates introductory dependent clause from main clause.)
>
> When you have mastered this rule, half the battle with commas will be won.
>
> As expected, additional explanations are necessary. (Use a comma even if the introductory clause omits the understood subject: *As we expected.*)
>
> In the spring of last year, we opened our franchise. (Use a comma after a phrase containing five or more words.)
>
> Having considered several alternatives, we decided to invest. (Use a comma after an introductory verbal phrase.)
>
> To invest, we needed $100 000. (Use a comma after an introductory verbal phrase, regardless of its length.)

Tip. Short introductory prepositional phrases (four or fewer words) require no commas. Don't clutter your writing with unnecessary commas after introductory phrases such as *by 2000, in the fall,* or *at this time.*

GUIDE 23: Use a comma before the coordinating conjunction in a compound sentence. The most common coordinating conjunctions are *and, or, nor,* and *but.* Occasionally, *for, so,* and *yet* may also function as coordinating conjunctions. When coordinating conjunctions join two independent clauses, commas are needed.

> The investment sounded too good to be true, *and* many investors were dubious. (Use a comma before the coordinating conjunction *and* in a compound sentence.)
>
> Niagara Falls is the honeymoon capital of the world, *but* some newlyweds prefer to go to more exotic destinations.

Tip. Before inserting a comma, test the two clauses. Can each of them stand alone as a complete sentence? If either is incomplete, skip the comma.

Promoters said the investment offer was for a limited time and couldn't be extended even one day. (Omit a comma before *and* because the second part of the sentence is not a complete independent clause.)

Home is a place you grow up wanting to leave but grow old wanting to return to. (Omit a comma before *but* because the second half of the sentence is not a complete clause.)

✓ Checkpoint

Add appropriate commas.

36. Before he entered this class Jeff used to sprinkle his writing with commas semicolons and dashes.

37. After studying punctuation he learned to use commas more carefully and to reduce his reliance on dashes.

38. At this time Jeff is engaged in a strenuous body-building program but he also finds time to enlighten his mind.

39. Next spring Jeff may enroll in accounting and business law or he may work for a semester to earn money.

40. When he completes his degree he plans to apply for employment in Montreal, Toronto or Ottawa.

GUIDE 24: Use commas appropriately in dates, addresses, geographical names, degrees, and long numbers.

September 30, 1963, is her birthday. (For dates use commas before and after the year.)

Send the application to James Kirby, 3405 120th Ave. N.W., Edmonton, AB T5W 1M3, as soon as possible. (For addresses use commas to separate all units except the two-letter province abbreviation and the postal code.)

She expects to move from Salmon Arm, British Columbia, to Mississauga, Ontario, next fall. (For geographical areas use commas to enclose the second element.)

Karen Munson, CPA, and Richard B. Larsen, Ph.D., were the speakers. (For professional designations and academic degrees following names, use commas to enclose each item.)

The latest census figures show the city's population to be 342 000. (In figures use commas to separate every three digits, counting from the right. The metric system, as used in this book, uses a narrow space instead of a comma.)

GUIDE 25: Use commas to set off internal sentence interrupters. Sentence interrupters may be verbal phrases, dependent clauses, contrasting elements, or parenthetical expressions (also called transitional phrases). These interrupters often provide information that is not grammatically essential.

Medical researchers, working steadily for 18 months, developed a new cancer therapy. (Use commas to set off an interrupting verbal phrase.)

The new therapy, which applies a genetically engineered virus, raises hopes among cancer specialists. (Use commas to set off nonessential dependent clauses.)

Dr. James C. Morrison, who is one of the researchers, made the announcement. (Use commas to set off nonessential dependent clauses.)

It was Dr. Morrison, not Dr. Arturo, who led the team effort. (Use commas to set off a contrasting element.)

This new therapy, by the way, was developed from a herpes virus. (Use commas to set off a parenthetical expression.)

Tip. Parenthetical (transitional) expressions are helpful words that guide the reader from one thought to the next. Here are representative parenthetical expressions that require commas:

as a matter of fact	in addition	of course
as a result	in the meantime	on the other hand
consequently	nevertheless	therefore
for example		

Tip. Always use *two* commas to set off an interrupter, unless it begins or ends a sentence.

 Checkpoint

Insert necessary commas.

41. Sue listed 222 George Henry Blvd. Toronto ON M2J 1E6 as her forwarding address.

42. The personnel director felt nevertheless that the applicant should be given an interview.

43. Employment of paralegals which is expected to increase 32 percent next year is growing rapidly because of the expanding legal services industry.

44. The contract was signed April 1 1999 and remained in effect until January 1 2003.

45. As a matter of fact the average North American drinks enough coffee to require 12 pounds of coffee beans annually.

GUIDE 26: Avoid unnecessary commas. Do not use commas between sentence elements that belong together. Don't automatically insert commas before every *and* or at points where your voice might drop if you were saying the sentence out loud.

Faulty

Growth will be spurred by the increasing complexity of business operations, and by large employment gains in trade and services. (A comma unnecessarily precedes *and*.)

All students with high grades, are eligible for the honour society. (A comma unnecessarily separates the subject and verb.)

One of the reasons for the success of the business honour society is, that it is very active. (A comma unnecessarily separates the verb and its complement.)

Our honour society has, at this time, over 50 members. (Commas unnecessarily separate a prepositional phrase from the sentence.)

 **Checkpoint**

Remove unnecessary commas. Add necessary ones.

46. Businesspeople from all over the world, gathered in Windsor for the meeting.

47. When shopping for computer equipment consider buying products that have been on the market for at least a year.

48. The trouble with talking fast is, that you sometimes say something before you've thought of it.

49. We think on the other hand, that we must develop management talent pools with the aim of promoting women minorities and people with disabilities.

50. A powerful reason for mail-order purchasing is, that customers make big savings.

Semicolons, Colons

GUIDE 27: Use a semicolon to join closely related independent clauses. Mature writers use semicolons to show readers that two thoughts are closely associated. If the ideas are not related, they should be expressed as separate sentences. Often, but not always, the second independent clause contains a conjunctive adverb (such as *however, consequently, therefore,* or *furthermore*) to show the relation between the two clauses.

Learning history is easy; learning its lessons is almost impossible.

He was determined to complete his degree; consequently, he studied diligently.

Most people want to be delivered from temptation; they would like, however, to keep in touch.

Tip. Don't use a semicolon unless each clause is truly independent. Try the sentence test. Omit the semicolon if each clause could not stand alone as a complete sentence.

Faulty	**Improved**
There's no point in speaking; unless you can improve on silence. (The second half of the sentence is a dependent clause. It could not stand alone as a sentence.)	There's no point in speaking unless you can improve on silence.
Although I cannot change the direction of the wind; I can adjust my sails to reach my destination. (The first clause could not stand alone.)	Although I cannot change the direction of the wind, I can adjust my sails to reach my destination.

GUIDE 28: Use a semicolon to separate items in a series when one or more of the items contains internal commas.

Representatives from as far away as Longueil, Quebec; Vancouver, British Columbia; and Whitehorse, Yukon Territory, attended the conference.

Stories circulated about Henry Ford, founder, Ford Motor Company; Lee Iacocca, CEO, Chrysler Motor Company; and Shoichiro Toyoda, chief, Toyota Motor Company.

GUIDE 29: Use a colon after a complete thought that introduces a list of items. Words such as *these, the following,* and *as follows* may introduce the list or they may be implied.

The following cities are on the tour: Toronto, Ottawa, and Montreal.

An alternate tour includes several western cities: Calgary, Saskatoon, and Edmonton.

Tip. Be sure that the statement before a colon is grammatically complete. An introductory statement that ends with a preposition (such as *by, for, at,* and *to*) or a verb (such as *is, are,* or *were*) is incomplete. The list following a preposition or a verb actually functions as an object or as a complement to finish the sentence.

Faulty	**Improved**
Three Big Macs were ordered by: Pam, Jim, and Lee. (Do not use a colon after an incomplete statement.)	Three Big Macs were ordered by Pam, Jim, and Lee.
Other items that they ordered were: fries, Cokes, and salads. (Do not use a colon after an incomplete statement.)	Other items that they ordered were fries, Cokes, and salads.

GUIDE 30: Use a colon after business letter salutations and to introducc long quotations.

Dear Mr. Duran: Dear Lisa:

The Asian consultant bluntly said: "North Americans tend to be too blabby, too impatient, and too informal for Asian tastes. To succeed in trade with Pacific Rim countries, North Americans must become more willing to adapt to native cultures."

Tip. Use a comma to introduce short quotations. Use a colon to introduce long one-sentence quotations and quotations of two or more sentences.

✓ Checkpoint

Add appropriate semicolons and colons.

51. My short-term goal is an entry-level job my long-term goal however is a management position.

52. Reebok interviewed the following candidates Joni Sims Simon Fraser University James Jones Wilfrid Laurier University and Madonna Farr Ryerson Polytechnic University.

53. The recruiter was looking for three qualities initiative versatility and enthusiasm.

54. Reebok seeks experienced individuals however it will hire recent graduates who have excellent records.

55. Mississauga is an expanding area therefore many business opportunities are available.

Apostrophe

GUIDE 31: Add an apostrophe plus *s* to an ownership word that does not end in an *s* sound.

We hope to show a profit in one year's time. (Add *'s* because the ownership word *year* does not end in an *s*.)

The company's assets rose in value. (Add *'s* because the ownership word *company* does not end in *s*.)

All the women's votes were counted. (Add *'s* because the ownership word *women* does not end in *s*.)

GUIDE 32: Add only an apostrophe to an ownership word that ends in an *s* sound—unless an extra syllable can be pronounced easily.

Some workers' benefits will cost more. (Add only an apostrophe because the ownership word *workers* ends in an *s*.)

Several months' rent are now due. (Add only an apostrophe because the ownership word *months* ends in an *s*.)

The boss's son got the job. (Add *'s* because an extra syllable can be pronounced easily.)

Tip. To determine whether an ownership word ends in an *s*, use it in an *of* phrase. For example, *one month's salary* becomes *the salary of one month.* By isolating the ownership word without its apostrophe, you can decide whether it ends in an *s*.

GUIDE 33: Use *'s* to make a noun possessive when it precedes a gerund, a verb form used as a noun.

We all protested *Laura's* (not *Laura*) smoking.

His (not *Him*) talking interfered with the movie.

I appreciate *your* (not *you*) answering the telephone while I was gone.

✓ Checkpoint

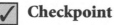

Correct erroneous possessives.

56. Both companies presidents received huge salaries, even when profits were falling.

57. Within one months time we were able to verify all members names and addresses.

58. Bryans supporters worry that there's little chance of him being elected.

59. The position requires five years experience in waste management.

60. Ms. Jackson car is serviced every six months.

GUIDE 34: Use a period to end a statement, command, indirect question, or polite request.

Everyone must row with the oars that he or she has. (Statement)

Send the completed report to me by June 1. (Command)

Stacy asked whether she could use the car next weekend. (Indirect question)

Will you please send me an employment application. (Polite request)

Tip. Polite requests often sound like questions. To determine the punctuation, apply the action test. If the request prompts an action, use a period. If it prompts a verbal response, use a question mark.

Faulty	**Improved**
Could you please correct the balance on my next statement? (This polite request prompts an action rather than a verbal response.)	Could you please correct the balance on my next statement.

GUIDE 35: Use a question mark after a direct question and after statements with questions appended.

Is it illegal to duplicate training videotapes?

Most of their training is in-house, isn't it?

GUIDE 36: Use a dash to (a) set off parenthetical elements containing internal commas, (b) emphasize a sentence interruption, or (c) separate an introductory list from a summarizing statement. The dash has legitimate uses. However, some writers use it whenever they know that punctuation is necessary, but they're not sure exactly what. The dash can be very effective, if not misused.

Three top students—Gene Engle, Donna Hersh, and Mika Sato—won awards. (Use dashes to set off elements with internal commas.)

Executives at IBM—despite rampant rumours in the stock market—remained quiet regarding dividend earnings. (Use dashes to emphasize a sentence interruption.)

Dell, Compaq, and Apple—these were the three leading computer manufacturers. (Use a dash to separate an introductory list from a summarizing statement.)

GUIDE 37: Use parentheses to set off nonessential sentence elements, such as explanations, directions, questions, or references.

Researchers find that the office grapevine (see Chapter 1 for more discussion) carries surprisingly accurate information.

Only two dates (February 15 and March 1) are suitable for the meeting.

Tip. Careful writers use parentheses to de-emphasize and the dash to emphasize parenthetical information. One expert said, "Dashes shout the news; parentheses whisper it."

GUIDE 38: Use quotation marks to (a) enclose the exact words of a speaker or writer; (b) distinguish words used in a special sense, such as slang; or (c) enclose titles of articles, chapters, or other short works.

"If you make your job important," said the consultant, "it's quite likely to return the favour."

The recruiter said that she was looking for candidates with good communication skills. (Omit quotation marks because the exact words of the speaker are not quoted.)

This office discourages "rad" hair styles and clothing. (Use quotes for slang.)

In *Business Week* I saw an article entitled "Communication for Global Markets." (Use quotation marks around the title of an article; use all caps, underlines, or italics for the name of the publication.)

Tip. Never use quotation marks arbitrarily, as in *Our "spring" sale starts April 1.*

 Checkpoint

Add appropriate punctuation.

61. Will you please send me your latest catalogue as soon as possible

62. (Direct quote) The only thing you get in a hurry said the professor is trouble

63. (De-emphasize) Two kinds of batteries see page 16 of the instruction booklet may be used in this camera.

64. (Emphasize) The first three colours that we tested red, yellow, and orange were selected.

65. All letters with erroneous addresses were reprinted weren't they

Capitalization

GUIDE 39: Capitalize proper nouns and proper adjectives. Capitalize the *specific* names of persons, places, institutions, buildings, religions, holidays, months, organizations, laws, races, languages, and so forth. Don't capitalize common nouns that make *general* references.

Proper Nouns	**Common Nouns**
Michelle DeLuca	the manufacturer's rep
Algonquin Provincial Park	the wilderness park
College of the Rockies	the community college
CN Tower	the downtown building
Department of the Environment	the federal agency
Persian, Armenian, Hindi	modern foreign languages

Proper Adjectives

French markets (but *francophone*)	Italian dressing
Xerox copy	Japanese executives
Swiss chocolates	Red River economics

GUIDE 40: Capitalize only specific academic courses and degrees.

Professor Jane Mangrum, Ph.D., will teach Accounting 121 next spring.

James Barker, who holds bachelor's and master's degrees, teaches marketing.

Jessica enrolled in classes in management, English, and business law.

GUIDE 41: Capitalize courtesy, professional, religious, government, family, and business titles when they precede names.

Mr. Jameson, Mrs. Alvarez, and Ms. Robinson (Courtesy titles)
Professor Andrews, Dr. Lee (Professional titles)
Rabbi Cohen, Pastor Williams, Pope John (Religious titles)
Prime Minister Trudeau, Mayor Drapeau (Government titles)
Uncle Edward, Mother Teresa, Cousin Vinney (Family titles)
Vice President Morris, Budget Director Lopez (Business titles)

Do not capitalize a title when it is followed by an appositive (that is, when the title is followed by a noun that renames or explains it).

Only one professor, Jonathan Marcus, favoured a tuition hike.

Local candidates counted on their premier, Ralph Klein, to raise funds.

Do not capitalize titles following names unless they are part of an address:

Mark Yoder, president of Yoder Enterprises, hired all employees.

Paula Beech, director of Human Resources, interviewed all candidates.

Send the package to Amanda Harr, Advertising Manager, Cambridge Publishers, 20 Park Plaza, Saint John, NB E2L 1G2.

Generally, do not capitalize a title that replaces a person's name.

Only the president, his chief of staff, and one senator made the trip.

The director of marketing and the sales manager will meet at 1 p.m.

Do not capitalize family titles used with possessive pronouns.

my mother, his father, your cousin

GUIDE 42: Capitalize the principal words in the titles of books, magazines, newspapers, articles, movies, plays, songs, poems, and reports. Do *not* capitalize articles (*a, an, the*) and prepositions of fewer than four letters (*in, to, by, for*) unless they begin or end the title.

I enjoyed the book *A Customer Is More Than a Name.*

Did you read the article entitled "Companies in Europe Seeking Executives With Multinational Skills"?

We liked the article entitled "Advice From a Pro: How to Say It With Pictures."

(Note that the titles of books are underlined or italicized while the titles of articles are enclosed in quotation marks.)

GUIDE 43: Capitalize *north, south, east, west,* and their derivatives only when they represent specific geographical regions.

from the Pacific Northwest	heading northwest on the highway
living in the East	east of the city
Maritimers	western Quebec, southern Ontario

GUIDE 44: Capitalize the names of departments, divisions, or committees within your own organization. Outside your organization capitalize only *specific* department, division, or committee names.

Lawyers in our Legal Assistance Department handle numerous cases.

Samsung offers TVs in its Consumer Electronics Division.

We volunteered for the Employee Social Responsibility Committee.

You might send an application to their personnel department.

GUIDE 45: Capitalize product names only when they refer to trademarked items. Don't capitalize the common names following manufacturers' names.

Sony portable television	Skippy peanut butter	NordicTrack treadmill
Eveready Energizer	Gillette razor	Kodak colour copier
Coca-Cola	Apple computer	Big Mac sandwich

GUIDE 46: Capitalize most nouns followed by numbers or letters (except in page, paragraph, line, and verse references).

Room 14	Exhibit A	Flight 12, Gate 43
Figure 2.1	Plan No. 1	Model Z2010

 **Checkpoint**

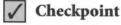

Capitalize all appropriate words.

66. vice president ellis bought a toshiba computer for use on her trips to europe.

67. our director of research brought plan no. 1 with him to the meeting in our engineering research department.

68. proceed west on highway 10 until you reach the mt. vernon exit.

69. you are booked on air canada flight 164 leaving from gate 5 at mirabel airport.

70. to improve their english, many new canadians purchased the book entitled *the power of language is yours.*

Number Usage

GUIDE 47: Use word form to express (a) numbers *ten* and under and (b) numbers beginning sentences. General references to numbers *ten* and under should be expressed in word form. Also use word form for numbers that begin sentences. If the resulting number involves more than two words, however, the sentence should be recast so that the number does not fall at the beginning.

We answered *six* telephone calls for the *four* sales reps.

Fifteen customers responded to the *three* advertisements today.

A total of 155 cameras were awarded as prizes. (Avoid beginning the sentence with a long number such as *one hundred fifty-five.*)

GUIDE 48: Use words to express general references to ages, small fractions, and periods of time.

When she reached *twenty-one,* she received *one half* of the estate.

James owns a *one-third* interest in the electronics business. (Note that fractions are hyphenated only when they function as adjectives.)

That business was founded *thirty-five* years ago.

Tip. Exact ages and specific business terms may be expressed in figures.

Both Meredith Jones, *55,* and Jack Jones, *57,* appeared in the article.

The note is payable in *60* days.

GUIDE 49: Use figures to express most references to numbers *11* and over.

Over *150* people from *53* companies attended the two-day workshop.

A four-ounce serving of Häagen-Dazs toffee crunch ice cream contains *300* calories and *19* grams of fat.

GUIDE 50: Use figures to express money, dates, clock time, decimals, and percents. Use a combination of words and figures to express sums of 1 million and over.

One item cost only *$1.95*; most, however, were priced between *$10* and *$35.* (Omit the decimals and zeros in even sums of money.)

A total of *3700* employees approved the contract *May 12* at *3 p.m.*

When sales dropped *4.7* percent, net income fell *9.8* percent. (Use the word *percent* instead of the *%* symbol.)

Orion lost *$62.9 million* in the latest fiscal year on revenues of *$584 million.* (Use a combination of words and figures for sums 1 million and over.)

Tip. To ease your memory load, concentrate on the numbers normally expressed in words: numbers *ten* and under, numbers at the beginning of a sentence, and small fractions. Nearly everything else in business is generally written with figures.

Checkpoint

Correct any inappropriate expression of numbers.

71. McDonald's former McLean Deluxe, priced at one dollar and fifty-nine cents, had only three hundred ten calories and nine percent fat.

72. 175 employees will attend the meeting January tenth at one p.m.

73. The Nordstrom family, which owns forty percent of the company's stock, recently added four co-presidents.

74. Our three branch offices, with a total of ninety-six workers, needs to add six computers and nine printers.

75. On March eighth we paid thirty-two dollars a share to acquire one third of the stocks.

Key to C.L.U.E. Checkpoint Exercises in Appendix A

This key shows all corrections. If you marked anything else, double-check the appropriate guideline.

1. Pizza Hut fought back with
2. backfire; consequently,
3. advertisements; they
4. chain, Domino's
5. deliveries; the
6. If I *were* … I would have *written*
7. could have *written* … if you *had* read
8. When Trevor *saw*
9. I wish I *were* … could have *gone*
10. she had *taken* … able to *choose*
11. energy *have*
12. efforts, *is* disappointingly
13. Ms. Wagner *is* in charge
14. companies *is* being
15. *knows* how
16. my friend and *I* … *its* price
17. to *him* and *me*
18. between you and *me*
19. *yours* and *hers*
20. could have been *she* … to you and *me*
21. *whomever* we nominate
22. *Whom* would you
23. *whoever* ordered
24. Jeff and *I*
25. by *whoever* experiences
26. to have *his or her* tuition; to have *the* tuition; *all employees are entitled to have their tuition reimbursed*
27. but *this advancement plan* appeals (*Revise to avoid vague pronoun* it.)
28. may cancel *his or her* subscription; may cancel *the* subscription; *subscribers* may cancel *their* subscriptions
29. *his or her* name and address; *all voters must have their names and addresses*
30. *These activities are* particularly important (*Revise to avoid the vague pronoun* this.)
31. my manager and *I* … point-by-point
32. completed the work so *quickly* … recently opened (*Omit hyphen.*)
33. If I do *well* … part-time … full-time
34. told him and *me* … *personally*
35. *not-too-distant* future

36. class, Jeff ... commas, semicolons, and
37. punctuation, (*No comma before* and!)
38. program, but
39. business law, or
40. degree, he ... Montreal, Toronto, or
41. 222 George Henry Blvd., Toronto, ON M2J 1E6, as her
42. felt, nevertheless,
43. paralegals, which ... year,
44. April 1, 1999, ... January 1, 2003.
45. As a matter of fact,
46. (*Remove comma.*)
47. equipment,
48. (*Remove comma.*)
49. think, on the other hand, ... women, minorities, and
50. (*Remove comma.*)
51. entry-level job; my ... goal, however,
52. candidates: Joni Sims, Simon Fraser University; James Jones, Wilfrid Laurier University; and Madonna Farr, Ryerson Polytechnic University.
53. qualities: initiative, versatility, and
54. individuals; however,
55. area; therefore,
56. companies'
57. one month's time ... members'
58. Bryan's ... *his* being elected
59. years' experience
60. Jackson's car
61. possible.
62. "The only thing you get in a hurry," said the professor, "is trouble."
63. batteries (see page 16 of the instruction booklet) may be
64. tested—red, yellow, and orange—were selected.
65. reprinted, weren't they?
66. Vice President Ellis ... Toshiba computer ...Europe
67. Our ... Plan No. 1 ... Engineering Research Department
68. Proceed ... Highway 10 ... Mt. Vernon exit.
69. You ... Air Canada Flight 164 ... Gate 5 at Mirabel Airport.
70. To improve their English, many new Canadians ... *The Power of Language Is Yours.*
71. priced at $1.59, had only 310 calories and 9 percent fat.
72. A total of 175 employees ... January 10 at 1 p.m.
73. 40 percent
74. 96 workers
75. March 8 ... $32

APPENDIX **B**

Documentation Formats

For many reasons business writers are careful to properly document report data. Citing sources strengthens a writer's argument, as you learned in Chapter 11. Acknowledging sources also shields writers from charges of plagiarism. Moreover, good references help readers pursue further research.

Source notes identify quotations or paraphrased ideas in the text, and they direct readers to a complete list of references (a bibliography) at the end of your report. Researchers have struggled for years to develop the perfect documentation system, one that is efficient for the writer and crystal clear to the reader. As a result, many systems exist, each with its advantages. The important thing for you is to adopt one system and use it consistently.

Students frequently ask, "But what documentation system is most used in business?" Actually, no one method dominates. Many businesses have developed their own hybrid systems. These companies generally supply guidelines illustrating their in-house style to employees. Before starting any research project on the job, you'll want to inquire about your organization's preferred documentation style. You can also look in the files for examples of previous reports.

References are usually cited in two places: (1) a brief citation appears in the text, and (2) a complete citation appears in a bibliography at the end of the report. The two most common formats for citations and bibliographies are those of the Modern Language Association (MLA) and the American Psychological Association (APA). Each has its own style for textual references and bibliography lists.

Modern Language Association Format

Writers in the humanities frequently use the MLA format, as illustrated in Figure B.1. In parentheses close to the textual reference appears the author's name and page cited. If no author is known, a shortened version of the source title is used. At the end of the report, the writer lists alphabetically all references in a bibliography called "Works Cited." To see a long report illustrating MLA documentation, turn to Figure 14.3 in Chapter 14. For more information consult Joseph Gibaldi, *MLA Handbook for Writers of Research Papers,* Fifth Edition (New York: The Modern Language Association of America, 1999).

MLA In-Text Format. In-text citations generally appear close to the point where the reference is mentioned or at the end of the sentence inside the closing period. Follow these guidelines:

- Include the last name of the author(s) and the page number. Omit a comma, as (Smith 310).

FIGURE B.1 **Portions of MLA Text Page and Bibliography**

Peanut butter was first delivered to the world by a St. Louis physician in 1890. As discussed at the Peanut Advisory Board's Web site, peanut butter was originally promoted as a protein substitute for elderly patients ("History," screen 2). However, it was the 1905 Universal Exposition in St. Louis that truly launched peanut butter. Since then, annual peanut butter consumption has zoomed to 3.3 pounds a person in the United States (Barrons 46). America's farmers produce 1.6 million tons of peanuts annually, about half of which is used for oil, nuts, and candy. Lisa Gibbons, executive secretary of the Peanut Advisory Board, says that "peanuts in some form are in the top four candies: Snickers, Reese's Peanut Butter Cups, Peanut M & Ms, and Butterfingers" (Meadows 32).

Works Cited

Barrons, Elizabeth Ruth. "A Comparison of Domestic and International Consumption of Legumes." *Journal of Economic Agriculture* 23 (1998): 45–49.

"History of Peanut Butter." *Peanut Advisory Board.* Retrieved 19 Jan. 2003 <http://www.peanutbutterlovers.com/History/index.html>.

Meadows, Mark Allen. "Peanut Crop Is Anything but Peanuts at Home and Overseas." *Business Monthly*, 30 Sept. 2002, 31–34.

- If the author's name is mentioned in the text, cite only the page number in parentheses. Do not include either the word *page* or the abbreviations *p.* or *pp.*
- If no author is known, refer to the document title or a shortened version of it, as (Facts at Fingertips 102).

MLA Bibliographic Format. The "Works Cited" bibliography lists all references cited in a report. Some writers include all works consulted. A portion of an MLA bibliography is shown in Figure B.1. A more complete list of model references appears in Figure B.2. Following are selected guidelines summarizing important points regarding MLA bibliographic format:

- Use italics or underscores for the titles of books, magazines, newspapers, and journals. Check with your organization or instructor for guidance. Capitalize all important words.
- Enclose the titles of magazine, newspaper, and journal articles in quotation marks. Include volume and issue numbers for journals only.
- For Internet citations, include a retrival date. Although MLA format does not include the words "Retrieved" or "Accessed," such wording helps distinguish the retrieval date from the document date.

American Psychological Association Format

Popular in the social and physical sciences, the American Psychological Association (APA) documentation style uses parenthetic citations. That is, each author reference is shown in parentheses when cited in the text, as shown in Figure B.3. At the end

FIGURE B.2 **MLA Bibliography Sample References**

Works Cited

Air Canada. *2002 Annual Report*. Dorval, QC.	Annual report
Berss, Marcia. "Protein Man." *Forbes 24* Oct. 2001: 65–66.	Magazine article
Connors, H. Lee. "Saturn's Orbit Still High With Consumers." *Marketing News Online*. 31 Aug. 2002. Retrieved 1 Sept. 2002 <http://www.marketingnews.com/08-31-02.htm>.	Magazine article, online
"Globalization Often Means That the Fast Track Leads Overseas." *The Financial Post* 17 June 2002: A10.	Newspaper article, no author
Lancaster, Hal. "When Taking a Tip From a Job Network, Proceed With Caution." *The Wall Street Journal* 7 Feb. 2001: B1.	Newspaper article, one author
Markoff, John. "Voluntary Rules Proposed to Help Insure Privacy for Internet Users." *New York Times* on the Web 5 June 2002. Retrieved 9 June 2002 <http://www.nytimes.com/library/tech/02/05/biztech/articles/05privacy.html>.	Newspaper article, online
Pinkerton Investigation Services. *The Employer's Guide to Investigation Services*, 2nd ed. Atlanta: Pinkerton Information Center, 2002.	Brochure
Rivers, Frank. Personal interview. 16 May 2003.	Interview
Rose, Richard C., and Echo Montgomery Garrett. *How to Make a Buck and Still Be a Decent Human Being*. New York: HarperCollins, 2001.	Book, two authors
"Spam: How to Eliminate It From Your Workplace." *SmartPros*. 8 Aug. 1997. Retrieved 12 Sept. 2002 <http://accounting.smartpros.com/x10434.xml>.	Internet document, no author
Statistics Canada. *A Portrait of Persons with Disabilities: Target Groups Project*. Ottawa: Ministry of Industry, Science and Technology, 2001.	Government publication
Wetherbee, James C., Nicholas P. Vitalari, and Andrew Milner. "Key Trends in Systems Development in Europe and North America." *Journal of Global Information Management* 3.2 (2001): 5–20. ["3.2" signifies volume 3, issue 2]	Journal article with volume and issue numbers
Wilson, Craig M. "E-Mail Bill May Fail to Curtail Spamming." *eWeek*. 9 July 2001: 49. Retrieved 26 Aug 2002 from Infotrac College Edition database, Article No. A76563183.	Article from online database
Yeller, Martin. "E-commerce challenges and victories" [Msg. 4]. Online posting 4 Dec 2002 to Google Group biz—ecommerce. Retrieved 14 Jan. 2003 from <http://groups.google.com/groups?h1-en@safe=off&group=biz.eco>.	Message from online forum or discussion group

Note: If a printed document is viewed electronically and you have no reason to believe the electronic version is different from the print version, use the same format as for the print citation.

of the report, all references are listed alphabetically in a bibliography called "References." For more information about APA formats, see the *Publication Manual of the American Psychological Association*, Fifth Edition (Washington, DC: American Psychological Association, 2001).

APA In-Text Format. Within the text, document each specific textual source with a short description in parentheses. Following are selected guidelines summarizing important elements of APA style:

FIGURE B.3 **Portions of APA Text Page and Bibliography**

Peanut butter was first delivered to the world by a St. Louis physician in 1890. As discussed at the Peanut Advisory Board's Web site, peanut butter was originally promoted as a protein substitute for elderly patients (History, n.d.). However, it was the 1905 Universal Exposition in St. Louis that truly launched peanut butter. Since then, annual peanut butter consumption has zoomed to 3.3 pounds a person in the United States (Barrons, 1998, p. 46). America's farmers produce 1.6 million tons of peanuts annually, about half of which is used for oil, nuts, and candy. Lisa Gibbons, executive secretary of the Peanut Advisory Board, says that "peanuts in some form are in the top four candies: Snickers, Reese's Peanut Butter Cups, Peanut M & Ms, and Butterfingers" (Meadows, 2002, p. 32).

References

Barrons, E. (1998, November). A comparison of domestic and international consumption of legumes. *Journal of Economic Agriculture*, 23(3), 45–49.

Meadows, M. (2002, September 30). Peanut crop is anything but peanuts at home and overseas. *Business Monthly*, 14, 31–34.

History of peanut butter (n.d.). Peanut Advisory Board. Retrieved January 17, 2002, from http://www.peanutbutterlovers.com/History/index.html

- Include the last name of the author(s), date of publication, and page number, as (Jones, 2002, p. 36). Use "n.d." if no date is available.
- If no author is known, refer to the first few words of the reference list entry and the year, as (Computer Privacy, 2003, p. 59).
- Omit page numbers for general references, but always include page numbers for direct quotations.

APA Bibliographic Format. List all citations alphabetically in a section called "References." A portion of an APA bibliography is shown in Figure B.3. A more complete list of model references appears in Figure B.4. APA style requires specific capitalization and sequencing guidelines, some of which are summarized here:

- Include an author's name with the last name first followed by initials, such as *Smith, M. A.* First and middle names are not used.
- Show the date of publication in parentheses immediately after the author's name, as *Smith M. A. (2002).*
- Italicize the titles of books. Use "sentence-style" capitalization. This means that only the first word of a title, proper nouns, and the first word after an internal colon is capitalized.
- Do not italicize or underscore the titles of magazine and journal articles. Use sentence-style capitalization for article titles.
- Italicize the names of magazines and journals. Capitalize the initial letters of all important words.

FIGURE B.4 **Model APA Bibliography Sample References**

References

Air Canada. (2002). *2002 Annual Report*. Dorval, QC. — **Annual report**

Atamian, R. M., & Ferranto, M. (2000). *Driving market forces*. New York: HarperCollins. — **Book, two authors**

Berss, M. (2001, October 24). Protein man. *Forbes*, 154, 64–66. — **Magazine article**

Cantrell, M. R., & Watson, H. (2001, January 10). Violence in today's workplace [Electronic version]. *Office Review*, 26(1), 24–29. — **Magazine article, viewed electronically**

Globalization often means that the fast track leads overseas. (2002, June 16). *The Financial Post*, p. A10. — **Newspaper article, no author**

Lancaster, H. (2002, February 7). When taking a tip from a job network, proceed with caution. *The Wall Street Journal*, p. B1. — **Newspaper article, one author**

Lang, R. T. (2001, March 2). Most people fail to identify nonverbal signs. *The New York Times*. Retrieved November 15, 2001, from http://www.nytimes.com — **Newspaper article, online**

Moon, J. (1999). Solid waste disposal. *Microsoft Encarta 2000* [CD-ROM]. Redmond, WA: Microsoft. — **CD-ROM encyclopedia article**

Pinkerton Investigation Services. (2001). *The employer's guide to investigation services* (3rd ed.) [Brochure]. Atlanta: Pinkerton Information Center. — **Brochure**

Wetherbee, J. C., Vitalari, N. P., & Milner, A. (2001, May). Key trends in systems development in Europe and North America. *Journal of Global Information Management*, 3(2), 5–20. ["3(2)" signifies volume 3, series or issue 2] — **Journal article with volume and issue numbers**

Wilson, G. & Simmons, P. (2001). *Plagiarism: What it is, and how to avoid it*. Retrieved July 4, 2001, from Biology Program Guide 2001/2002 at the University of British Columbia Web site: http://www.zoology.ubc/ca/bpg/plagiarism.htm — **World Wide Web document with author and date**

WWW user survey reveals consumer trends. (n.d.). Retrieved August 2, 2002, from http://www.cc.gatech.edu/gvu/user_surveys/survey-2001-10/ — **World Wide Web document, no author, no date**

Yudkin, M. (2001, July 4). The marketing minute: Truth is always in season [Msg. ID:ruf6kt0 aiu5eui6523qsrofhu70h21evoj@4ax.com]. Message posted to news://biz.ecommerce — **Message to online forum or discussion group**

Citing Electronic Sources

Standards for researchers using electronic sources are still emerging. When citing electronic media, you should hold the same goals as for print sources. That is, you try to give credit to the authors and to allow others to easily locate the same or updated information. However, traditional formats for identifying authors, publication dates, and page numbers become confusing when applied to sources on the Internet. Strive to give correct credit for electronic sources by including the author's name (when available), document title, Web page title, Web address, and retrieval date. Formats for some electronic sources are shown here.

Key to C.L.U.E. Exercises

Chapter 1

1. After he checked many statements, our accountant found the error in Column 2 of the balance sheet.
2. Because Mr. Lockwood's business owned considerable property, we were surprised by its lack of liquid assets.
3. The mortgage company checked all property titles separately; however, it found no discrepancies.
4. When Ms. Diaz finished the audit, she wrote three letters to apprise the owners of her findings.
5. Just between you and me, who do you think could have ordered all this stationery?
6. Assets and liabilities are what the four buyers want to see; consequently, we are preparing this year's statements.
7. Next spring my brother and I plan to enroll in the following courses: marketing, English, and history.
8. Dan felt that he had done well on the exam, but he wants to do even better when it's given again next fall.
9. Our records show that your end-of-the-month balance was $96.30.
10. When the principal in the account grows too large, we must make annual withdrawals.

Chapter 2

1. If swimming is especially good for your figure, how do you explain whales?
2. Although you may be on the right track, you can get run over if you just sit there.
3. Ellen and I examined all similar accounts on a case-by-case basis.
4. Although both reports were written by Jeff and me, they carried the boss's signature.
5. The vice president said, "Meetings are places where minutes may be kept, but hours are lost."
6. At least 14 patients were admitted after the accident; however, only 4 required treatment.
7. If the company is sold, about 150 employees will be out of work.
8. The meeting is scheduled for 4 p.m.; consequently, Melissa and I may be a little late.
9. Did you know that 45 percent of Canadians have visited Disneyland or Disney World?
10. I have already checked the Web, but I visited only one government site.

Chapter 3

1. To avoid embarrassing any employee, the personnel manager and I have decided to talk personally to each individual.
2. Three assistants were sent on a search-and-destroy mission in a conscious effort to remove at least 15 000 old documents from the files.
3. Electronic mail, now used by three fourths of Canada's largest companies, transmits messages quickly and cheaply.

4. An article entitled "What's New With Managers" appeared in *Maclean's*, which is read by millions of Canadians.
5. Your account is now 60 days overdue; consequently, we have only one alternative left.
6. The marketing manager's itinerary listed the following three destinations: Moncton, Thunder Bay, and Calgary.
7. Each of the beautifully printed books available at Pickwick Book Company has been reduced to $30.
8. We recommend, therefore, that a committee study our mail procedures for a three-week period and submit a report of its findings.
9. They're going to visit their relatives in Lethbridge, Alberta, over the Victoria Day holiday.
10. The hotel can accommodate 300 convention guests, but it has parking facilities for only 100 cars.

Chapter 4

1. If I were you, I would schedule the conference for one of these cities: Ottawa, Kingston, or Montreal.
2. The committee's next meeting is scheduled for May 5 at 3 p.m. and should last about two hours.
3. We're not asking you to alter the figures; we are asking you to check their accuracy.
4. Will you please fax me a list of our independent contractors' names and addresses.
5. The vacation calendar fills up quickly for the summer months; therefore, you should make your plans early.
6. After the inspector issues the waiver, we will be able to proceed with the architect's plan.
7. If we can't give out necessary information, what is the point in our answering the telephone?
8. All new employees will receive their orientation packets and be told about their parking privileges.
9. About 85 percent of all new entrants into the workforce in the 2000s are expected to be women, minorities, and immigrants.
10. Our vice president in the Human Resources Development Department asked the manager and me to come to her office at 3:30 p.m.

Chapter 5

1. Although we formerly used a neighbourhood printer for all our print jobs, we are now saving almost $500 a month by using desktop publishing.
2. Powerful software, however, cannot guarantee a good final product.
3. To develop a better sense of design, we collected desirable samples from books, magazines, brochures, and newsletters.
4. We noticed that poorly designed projects often were filled with cluttered layouts, incompatible typefaces, and too many typefaces.
5. Our layout design is usually formal, but occasionally we use an informal layout design, which is shown in Figure 6.
6. We usually prefer a black-and-white design because colour printing is much more costly.
7. Expensive colour printing jobs are sent to foreign countries; for example, China, Italy, and Japan.
8. Jeffrey's article, which he entitled "The Shaping of a Corporate Image," was accepted for publication in *The Journal of Communication.*
9. Every employee will personally receive a copy of his or her performance evaluation, which the president said will be the principal basis for promotion.
10. We will print 350 copies of the newsletter to be sent to whoever is currently listed in our database.

Chapter 6

1. Business documents must be written clearly to ensure that readers comprehend the message quickly.
2. We expect Mayor Wilson to visit the premier in an attempt to increase the city's share of provincial funding.
3. The caller could have been he, but we don't know for sure since he didn't leave his name.
4. The survey was cited in an article entitled "What's New in Software"; however, I can't locate it now.
5. All three of our company's auditors—Jim Lucus, Doreen Delgado, and Brad Kirby—criticized their accounting procedures.
6. Any one of the auditors is authorized to proceed with an independent action; however, only a member of the management council can alter policy.

7. Because our printer has been broken every day this week, we're looking at new models.
8. Have you already ordered the following: a dictionary, a reference manual, and a style book?
9. In the morning Mrs. Williams ordinarily opens the office; in the evening Mr. Williams usually closes it.
10. When you travel in England and Ireland, I advise you to charge purchases to your Visa credit card.

Chapter 7

1. The extraordinary increase in sales is related to our placing the staff on a commission basis, and the increase also affected our stock value.
2. She acts as if she were the only person who ever received a compliment about his or her business writing. [OR omit **his or her**.]
3. Karen is interested in working for the Department of Foreign Affairs since she is hoping to travel.
4. Major Hawkins, who I think will be elected, has already served three consecutive terms as a member of the Oshawa City Council.
5. After Mr. Freeman and he returned from lunch, the customers were handled more quickly.
6. Our new employees' cafeteria, which opened six months ago, has a salad bar that everyone definitely likes.
7. On Tuesday Ms. Adams can see you at 2 p.m.; on Wednesday she has a full schedule.
8. His determination, courage, and sincerity could not be denied; however, his methods were often questioned.
9. After you have checked the matter further, report to the CEO and me.
10. Mr. Garcia and she advised me not to desert my employer at this time, although they were quite sympathetic to my personal problems.

Chapter 8

1. Mr. Krikorian always tries, however, to wear a tie and shirt that have complementary colours.
2. The House of Commons Committee on Trade and Commerce is holding hearings in 21 cities.
3. Consumer buying and spending for the past five years are being studied by a federal team of analysts.
4. Because we recommend that students bring their own supplies, the total expense for the trip should be a minor amount.
5. Wasn't it Mr. Cohen, not Ms. Lyons, who asked for a tuition waiver?
6. As soon as we can verify the figures, either my sales manager or I will call you; nevertheless, you must continue to disburse payroll funds.
7. Our Human Resources Department, which was formerly in Room 35, has moved its offices to Room 5.
8. We have arranged interviews on the following dates: Wednesday at 3:30 p.m., Thursday at 10:30 a.m., and Friday at 4:15 p.m.
9. The *Bay News*, our local newspaper, featured as its principal article a story entitled "Smarter E-Mail Is Here."
10. Everyone on the payroll, which includes all dispatchers and supervisors, was cautioned to maintain careful records every day.

Chapter 9

1. Two loans made to Consumer Products Corporation must be repaid within 90 days, or the owners will be in default.
2. One loan was for property appraised at $40 000; the other was for property estimated to be worth $10 000.
3. Our senior marketing director and the sales manager are quite knowledgeable about communications hardware; therefore, they are travelling to the computer show in northern California.
4. We congratulate you on winning the award and hope that you will continue to experience similar success in the future.
5. Mr. Salazar left $3 million to be divided among four heirs, one of whom is a successful manufacturer.
6. If the CEO and he had behaved more professionally, the chances of a practical settlement would be considerably greater.
7. Just inside the entrance are the desk of the receptionist and a complete directory of all departments.

8. All new employees must receive their permits to park in Lot 5-A, or their cars will be cited. OR Every new employee must submit a permit to park in Lot 5-A, or his or her car will be cited.
9. When we open our office in Montreal, we will need at least three people who are fluent in French and English.
10. Most companies can boost profits almost 100 percent by retaining just 5 percent more of their permanent customers.

Chapter 10

1. Your advertisement in the June 2 edition of the *Edmonton Sun* caught my attention because my training and experience match your requirements.
2. Doubtlessly, the bank is closed at this hour, but its ATM will enable you to receive the cash you need.
3. A flow chart detailing all sales procedures in four divisions was prepared by our vice president.
4. The computer and printer were working well yesterday and appeared to be all right this morning when I used them for my report.
5. If I were you, I would be more concerned with long-term, not short-term, returns on the invested capital.
6. We make a conscious effort, by the way, to find highly qualified individuals with up-to-date computer skills.
7. If your résumé had come earlier, I could have showed it to Mr. Sutton and her before your interview.
8. Deborah's report summary is easier to read than David's because she used consistent headings and efficient writing techniques.
9. At McDonald's we ordered four Big Macs, three orders of french fries, and five Coca-Colas for lunch.
10. Because the budget cuts will severely affect all programs, the faculty has unanimously opposed it.

Endnotes

CHAPTER 1

1. Hal Lancaster, "Learning to Manage in a Global Workplace," *The Wall Street Journal,* 2 June 1998, B1.
2. Paula Jacobs, "Strong Writing Skills Essential for Success, Even in IT," *Infoworld,* 6 July 1998, 86.
3. Kirk Johnson, "Limits on the Work-at-Home Life," *The New York Times,* 17 December 1997, A20.
4. Hal Lancaster, "Hiring a Full Staff May Be the Next Fad in Management," *The Wall Street Journal,* 4 April 1998, B1.
5. Andrew Denka, "New Office Etiquette Dilemmas," *CPA Journal,* August 1996, 13.
6. Paul Paquet, "Reaching Out to Ethnic Audiences: How to Hit a Target You Can't Afford to Miss," <www. web.net/cornerstore/ethnic. htm> (Retreived 12 April 2000).
7. G. A. Marken, "New Approach to Moving Up the Corporate Ladder," *Public Relations Quarterly,* Winter 1996, 47.
8. Jerry Sullivan, Naoki Darmeda, and Tatsuo Nobu, "Bypassing in Managerial Communication," *Business Horizons,* January/February 1991, 72.
9. Peter Drucker, *Managing the Non-Profit Organization: Practices and Principles* (New York: HarperCollins, 1990), 46.
10. Mitch Betts and Tim Ouellette, "Taming the E-mail Shrew," *Computerworld,* 6 November 1995, 1, 32.
11. Leslie Walker, as quoted in "Coping With Communication Overload," *Association Management,* October 1997, 32–33.
12. Marken, "New Approach to Moving Up the Corporate Ladder."
13. Thomas J. Hackett, "Giving Teams a Tune-Up: Reviving Work Teams," *HR Focus,* November 1997.
14. Stephanie Zimmermann, Beverly Davenport, and John W. Haas, "A Communication Metamyth in the Workplace: The Assumption That More Is Better," *Journal of Business Communication,* April 1996, 185–204.
15. Bob Nelson, "How to Energize Everyone in the Company," *Bottom Line/Business,* October 1997, 3.
16. Ellen Roseman, "Force Firms to Disclose Ethics, Report Urges," *Toronto Star,* 31 January 2002, C1.
17. Max M. Thomas, "Classroom Conundrum: Profits + Ethics = ?" *Business Month,* February 1990, 6.
18. Tina Kelley, "Charting a Course to Ethical Profits," *The New York Times,* 8 February 1998, BU1.
19. "The Values Added Banker Brings Ethics to Investing," *National Post,* 4 March 2000, E4.
20. Based on Michael Josephson's remarks reported in Alison Bell, "What Price Ethics?" *Entrepreneurial Woman,* January/February 1991, 68.
21. "Making Ethical Decisions—Common Rationalizations" <www.josephinstitute/org/MED/ Medrationalizations.htm> (Retrieved 10 July 2000).

CHAPTER 2

1. Patricia Buhler, "Managing in the 90s: Creating Flexibility in Today's Workplace," *Supervision,* January 1996, 24–26.
2. Harvey Schacter, "Workers of the World, Retire!" *Canadian Economic Outlook,* 12 February 1999, 44–46.
3. John R. Katzenbach and Douglas K. Smith, *The Wisdom of Teams* (New York: HarperBusiness and Harvard Business School Press, 1994), 19.
4. Dana Wilson and Dave Redekopp, "Worker, Manage Thyself! Future Skills: Self-Management in the 21st Century," *Edmonton Sun,* 5 December 1998, 64.
5. Charles Parnell, "Teamwork: Not a New Idea, But It's Transforming the Workplace," *Executive Speeches,* December 1997/January 1998, 35–40.
6. Harvey Robbins and Michael Finley, *Why Teams Don't Work: What Went Wrong and How to Make It Right* (Princeton, NJ: Peterson's/Pacesetter Books, 1995), 11–12.
7. The discussion of Tuckman's model is adapted from Robbins and Finley, *Why Teams Don't Work,* Chapter 22. See also Jane Henderson-Loney, "Tuckman and Tears: Developing Teams During Profound Organizational Change," *Supervision,* May 1996, 3–5.
8. Allen C. Amason, Wayne A. Hochwarter, Kenneth R. Thompson, and Allison W. Harrison, "Conflict: An Important Dimenson in Successful Management Teams," *Organizational Dynamics,* Autumn 1995, 1.
9. Parnell, "Teamwork: Not a New Idea," 36–40.
10. Katzenbach and Smith, *Wisdom of Teams,* 45.
11. Jon Hanke, "Presenting as a Team," *Presentations,* January 1998, 74–82.

12. Robbins and Finley, *Why Teams Don't Work*, 123.
13. Cynthia MacDermid. "Top Tip to Listening is Stop Talking," *New Glasgow Evening News*, Nova Scotia, 19 January 2002, Canadian Newspaper Service.
14. "Effective Communication," *Training Tomorrow*, November 1994, 32–33.
15. Ray Birdwhistel, *Kinesics and Context* (Philadelphia: University of Pennsylvania Press, 1970).
16. Hal Lancaster, "Learning Some Ways to Make Meetings Slightly Less Awful," *The Wall Street Journal*, 26 May 1998, B1.
17. John C. Bruening, "There's Good News About Meetings," *Managing Office Technology*, July 1996, 24–25.
18. Kirsten Schabacker, "A Short, Snappy Guide to Meaningful Meetings," *Working Women*, June 1991, 73.
19. J. Keith Cook, "Try These Eight Guidelines for More Effective Meetings," *Communication Briefings Bonus Item*, April 1995, 8a. See also Morey Strettner, "How to Manage a Corporate Motormouth," *Investor's Business Daily*, 8 October 1998, A1.
20. Mary Munter, "Meeting Technology: From Low-Tech to High-Tech," *Business Communication Quarterly*, June 1998, 84–85.
21. "Taking Us to the Talkies: As the Price of Videoconferencing Falls, Collaboration Becomes a Necessity Rather Than a Luxury" *Canadian Computer Reseller*, 4 August 1998, 33–36.

CHAPTER 3

1. Joseph B. White, "There Are No German or U.S. Companies, Only Successful Ones," *The Wall Street Journal*, 17 May 1998, A1.
2. Raju Narisetti, "Can Rubbermaid Crack Foreign Markets?" *The Wall Street Journal*, 20 June 1996, B1.
3. E. S. Browning, "In Pursuit of the Elusive Euroconsumer," *The Wall Street Journal*, 23 April 1992, B1.
4. Mary O'Hara-Devereaux and Robert Johansen, *GlobalWork: Bridging Distance, Culture and Time* (San Francisco: Jossey-Bass Publishers, 1994), 245.
5. Sari Kalin, "The Importance of Being Multiculturally Correct," *Computerworld*, 6 October 1997, G16–G17.
6. Mark Wegierski, "Canada's Civil War," *The World and I*, vol. 2, Electric Library Canada, 1 September 1997, 112.
7. "Facts on Canada," *Canada Information Office* <www.cio.bic.gc.ca/facts/multi_e.html> (Retrieved 8 April 2000).
8. Andrew Pollack, "Barbie's Journey in Japan," *The New York Times*, 22 December 1996, E3.
9. Lennie Copeland and Lewis Griggs, *Going International* (New York: Plume Books, 1985), 14.
10. Guy Rocher, "Culture," *1998 Canadian Encyclopedia*, Electric Library Canada, 6 September 1997.
11. Michael Adams, *Sex in the Snow: Canadian Social Values at the End of the Millennium* (Toronto: Viking, 1997), 195.
12. Chris Wood, "The Vanishing Border," *Maclean's*, 20 December 1999, 21.
13. "Canada Business, Business Culture," *Canada Business*, Electric Library Canada, 30 June 1997.
14. Edward T. Hall and Mildred Reed Hall, *Understanding Cultural Differences* (Yarmouth, ME: Intercultural Press, 1987), 183–84.
15. Nicholas Keung, "Learning the Signs of Communication," *Toronto Star*, 22 May 1999, L1–L2.
16. Vivienne Luk, Mumtaz Patel, and Kathryn White, "Personal Attributes of American and Chinese Business Associates," *The Bulletin of the Association for Business Communication*, December 1990, 67.
17. "Canada Business, Business Culture."
18. "Canada Business, Business Culture."
19. T. Morrison, Wayne Conaway, and George Borden, *Kiss, Bow, or Shake Hands: How to Do Business in Sixty Countries* (Holbrook, MA: Bob Adams Inc., 1994), 44.
20. Susan S. Jarvis, "Preparing Employees to Work South of the Border," *Personnel*, June 1990, 763.
21. Gallois and Callan, *Communication and Culture*, 29.
22. Copeland and Griggs, *Going International*, 94.
23. Copeland and Griggs, *Going International*, 108.
24. "Canada Business, Business Culture."
25. Copeland and Griggs, *Going International*, 12.
26. T. Morrison et al., *Kiss, Bow, or Shake Hands*, 44.
27. Keung, "Learning the Signs of Communication."
28. Keung, "Learning the Signs of Communication."
29. Keung, "Learning the Signs of Communication."
30. Guo-Ming Chen and William J. Starosta, *Foundations of Intercultural Communication* (Boston: Allyn and Bacon, 1998), 40.
31. Iris Varner and Linda Beamer, *Intercultural Communication in the Global Workplace* (Boston: Irwin McGraw-Hill, 1995), 15.
32. Lillian H. Chaney and Jeanette S. Martin, *Intercultural Business Communication* (Englewood Cliffs, NJ: Prentice Hall Career and Technology, 1995), 67.
33. *Do's and Taboos Around the World*, 2nd ed. (New York: Wiley, 1990), 71.
34. Robert McGarvey, "Foreign Exchange," *USAir Magazine*, June 1992, 64.
35. "Latest Employment News from Statistics Canada Released: March 10, 2000," *Canada NewsWire Career Monitor*, 10 March 2000, <www.newswire.ca/releases/March2000/10/>.
36. "Business Discovers Financial Link with Cultural Diversity," *Government of Alberta News Release*, 30 November 1995.

37. Will Harvie, "J. P. Bryan Whacks Management, Calls for Leadership," *Oilweek*, 4 December 1995, 1.
38. Dana Flavelle, "Glass Ceiling More Visible in U.S.," *Toronto Star*, 31 January 2002, C1, C11.
39. Rae Andre, "Diversity Stress as Morality Stress," *Journal of Business Ethics*, June 1995, 489–96.
40. George Simons and Darlene Dunham, "Making Inclusion Happen," *Managing Diversity*, December 1995 <www.jalmc.org/mkincl.htm> (Retrieved 9 August 1996).
41. Michele Wucker, "Keep on Trekking," *Working Woman*, December/January 1998, 32–36.
42. Karl Schoenberger, "Motorola Bets Big on China," *Fortune*, 27 May 1996, 116–24.
43. Based on Rose Knotts and Mary S. Thibodeaux, "Verbal Skills in Cross-Culture Managerial Communication," *European Business Review* 92, no. 2 (1992): v–vii.
44. Joel Makower, "Managing Diversity in the Workplace," *Business and Society Review*, Winter 1995, 48–54.
45. Jayne Tear, "They Just Don't Understand Gender Dynamics," *The Wall Street Journal*, 20 November 1995, A1; Anne Roiphe, "Talking Trouble," *Working Woman*, October 1994, 28–31; Cristina Stuart, "Why Can't a Woman Be More Like a Man?" *Training Tomorrow*, February 1994, 22–24; and Alan Wolfe, "Talking From 9 to 5: How Women's and Men's Conversational Styles Affect Who Gets Heard, Who Gets Credit, and What Gets Done at Work," *New Republic*, 12 December 1994.

CHAPTER 4

1. Earl N. Harbert, "Knowing Your Audience," in *The Handbook of Executive Communication*, ed. John L. DiGaetani (Homewood, IL: Dow Jones/Irwin, 1986), 3.
2. Mark Bacon, quoted in "Business Writing: One-on-One Speaks Best to the Masses," *Training*, April 1988, 95. See also Elizabeth Danziger, "Communicate Up," *Journal of Accountancy*, February 1998, 67.
3. For more information see Marilyn Schwartz, *Guidelines for Bias-Free Writing* (Bloomington, IN: Indiana University Press, 1994).
4. Leslie Matthies, as mentioned in Carl Heyel, "Policy and Procedure Manuals," in *The Handbook of Executive Communication*, 212.
5. Parts of this section are based on Kristin R. Woolever's "Corporate Language and the Law: Avoiding Liability in Corporate Communications," *IEE Transactions on Professional Communication*, 2 June 1990, 95–98.
6. "Effects of Product Liability Laws on Small Business: An Introduction to International Exposure Through a Comparison of U.S. and Canadian Law," *Journal of Small Business Management*, 7 January 1998, 72.
7. Lewis N. Klar, "Torts," *The 1998 Canadian Encyclopedia*, Electric Library Canada, 9 June 1997.
8. Klar, "Torts."
9. Lisa Jenner, "Develop Communication and Training With Literacy in Mind," *HR Focus*, March 1994, 14.
10. 1996 Minister of Public Works and Government Services and the WWLIA, "Misleading Advertising Under the Federal Competition Act," <www.wwlia.org/ca-comp1.htm> (Retrieved 18 April 2000).
11. Woolever, "Corporate Language," 96.
12. Lisa Jenner, "Employment-at-Will Liability: How Protected Are You?" *HR Focus*, March 1994, 11.
13. Judy E. Pickens, "Communication: Terms of Equality: A Guide to Bias-Free Language," *Personnel Journal*, August 1985, 5.

CHAPTER 5

1. Kimberly Paterson, "The Writing Process," *Rough Notes*, April 1998, 59–60.
2. Andrew Fluegelman and Jeremy Joan Hewes, "The Word Processor and the Writing Process, in Kevin J. Harty, *Strategies for Business and Technical Writing*, 4th ed. (San Diego: Harcourt Brace Jovanovich, 1989), 43. See also Lynn Quitman Troyka, *Simon & Schuster Handbook for Writers*, 4th ed. (Upper Saddle River, NJ: Prentice Hall, 1996), 49.
3. Maryann V. Piotrowski, *Effective Business Writing* (New York: HarperPerennial, 1996), 12.
4. Robert W. Goddard, "Communication: Use Language Effectively," *Personnel Journal*, April 1989, 32.
5. Frederick Crews, *The Random House Handbook*, 4th ed. (New York: Random House, 1991), 152.
6. "Creating the Right Environment." *National Post* Joint Venture Supplement with the Conference Board of Canada, 27 April 1999, CB1, CB3.

CHAPTER 6

1. Peter Elbow, *Writing With Power: Techniques for Mastering the Writing Process* (Oxford: Oxford University Press, 1998), 30.
2. Sonia Von Matt Stoddard, "Proofreading for Perfection," *Legal Assistant Today*, March/April 1997, 84–85.
3. Ralph Brown, "Add Some Informal Polish to Your Writing," *Management*, March 1998, 12.
4. Carol Ann Wilson, "Be on the Cutting Edge: Learn These Seven Plain Language Principles Now!" <www.wwlia.org/plainlan.htm> (Retrieved 20 April 2000).
5. Richard E. Neff, "CEOs Want Information, Not Just Words," *Communication World*, April/May 1997, 22–25.
6. William Power and Michael Siconolfi, "Memo to: Mr. Ball, RE: Your Messages, Sir: They're Weird," *The Wall Street Journal*, 30 November 1990, 1; Brown, "Add Some Informal Polish to Your Writing."

7. Wilson, "Be on the Cutting Edge."
8. *The Canadian Style: A Guide to Writing and Editing* (Toronto: Dundurn Press Limited, 1985).
9. Laurie Bildfell, "Standard Time: The Canadian Style? Versatile and Not Pushy," *Quill and Quire*, December 1994, 12–13.
10. *The Canadian Style: A Guide to Writing and Editing.*

CHAPTER 7

1. Hugh Hay-Roe, "The Secret of Excess," *Executive Excellence*, January 1995, 20.
2. Dennis Chambers, *Writing to Get Action* (Bristol, VT: Velocity Business Publishing, 1998), 12.
3. *Business Week*, 6 July 1981, 107.
4. Robert Beauchemin, "How to Help Customers Look After Customers: Comprehensive Relationship Management Solution," *Computing Canada*, 13 October 1998, 31.
5. "New Company Raises $6.25 Million to Improve Customer Experience Online and Off," *Business Wire*, 5 January 2000.
6. Stephen B. Knouse, "Confidentiality and the Letter of Recommendation: A New Approach," *The Bulletin of the Association for Business Communication*, September 1987, 7.
7. Steven N. Spertz and Glenda S. Spertz, *The Rule of Law: Canadian Business Law*, 2nd ed. (Toronto: Copp Clark Ltd., 1995), 289.
8. Robert Klara, "Press 1 to Gripe," *Restaurant Business*, 15 May 1998, 96–102.
9. Stephanie Armour, "Companies Grapple With Gripes Posted on Web," *USA Today*, 16 September 1998, O5B.
10. Marcia Mascolini, "Another Look at Teaching the External Negative Message," *The Bulletin of the Association for Business Communication*, June 1994, 46; Robert J. Aalberts and Lorraine A. Krajewski, "Claim and Adjustment Letters," *The Bulletin of the Association for Business Communication*, September 1987, 2.
11. Elizabeth Blackburn Brockman and Kelly Belanger, "You-Attitude and Positive Emphasis: Testing Received Wisdom in Business Communication," *The Bulletin of the Association for Business Communication*, June 1993, 1–5; C. Goodwin and I. Ross, "Consumer Evaluations of Responses to Complaints: What's Fair and Why," *Journal of Consumer Marketing* 7 (1990): 39–47; Mascolini, "Another Look at Teaching the External Negative Message," 46.
12. Pamela Gilbert, "Two Words That Can Help a Business Thrive," *The Wall Street Journal*, 30 December 1996, A12.

CHAPTER 8

1. Hollie Shaw, "E-Mail is Eating Into our Letter-writing Habits," *Toronto Star*, 18 February 1999, E7.
2. "Canada Post Launched in Cyberspace," *Canadian Press*, 30 November 1999.
3. Barb Cole-Gomolski, "E-Mail Traffic, Costs Hit High-Speed Lane," *Computerworld*, 14 April 1997.
4. Sana Reynolds, "Composing Effective E-Mail Messages," *Communication World*, July 1997, 8–9.
5. Reynolds, "Composing Effective E-Mail," 8.
6. Paula Jacobs, "Strong Writing Skills Essential for Success, Even in IT," *InfoWorld*, 6 July 1998, 86.
7. John Fielden, "Clear Writing Is Not Enough," *Management Review*, April 1989, 51.
8. Based on Maggie Jackson, "Casual Day a Bad Fit?" *Los Angeles Times Careers*, 19 January 1998, 27–28.
9. George D. Webster, "Internal Communications Issues," *Association Management*, May 1995, 150–53.

CHAPTER 9

1. "How to Ask For—And Get—What You Want!" *Supervision*, February 1990, 11.
2. Rob Yogel, "Sending Your Message Electronically," *Target Marketing*, June 1998, 77–78.
3. Dean Riek, "Great Letters and Why They Work," *Direct Marketing*, June 1998, 20–24.
4. David Carr, "The Limits of E-Mail," *Marketing Magazine*, 24 April 2000, 13–14.
5. Dennis Chambers, *The Agile Manager's Guide to Writing to Get Action* (Bristol, VT: Velocity Press, 1998), 86.
6. Kevin McLaughlin, "Words of Wisdom," *Entrepreneur*, October 1990, 101.
7. "Canadian Bacon," *Marketing Tools*, May 1998, 14.
8. "'Uh Oh Canada': National Survey Finds Canadians Overweight and Confused About it," Canada News Wire, 1 December 1999, <www.pollara.ca/new/Library/surveys/news1201.htm> (Retrieved 19 September 2000).
9. "Almost Half of Canadians Overweight," Canadian Press, 20 August 1999, <www.canoe.ca/Health9908/20_weight.html> (Retrieved 19 September 2000).

CHAPTER 10

1. Mohan R. Limaye, "Further Conceptualization of Explanations in Negative Messages," *Business Communication Quarterly*, June 1997, 46.
2. Robert Mirguet, information security manager, Eastman Kodak Co., Rochester, New York, quoted in *Computerworld*, cited in "Telecommunicating," *Boardroom Reports*, 1 March 1995, 15; Sandy Sampson, "Wild Wild Web: Legal Exposure on the Internet," *Software Magazine*, November 1997, 75–78.
3. Marcia Mascolini, "Another Look at Teaching the External Negative Message," *The Bulletin of the Association for Business Communication*, June 1994, 47.
4. Carol David and Margaret Ann Baker, "Rereading Bad News:

Compliance-Gaining Features in Management Memos," *The Journal of Business Communication* 31, no. 4: 268.
5. Jeanette W. Gilsdorf, "Metacommunication Effects on International Business Negotiating in China," *Business Communication Quarterly*, June 1997, 27.
6. Equifax Canada Inc. <www.equifax.ca>. (Reviewed 17 July 2000).

CHAPTER 11

1. Based on Konnie G. Kustron, "Searching the World Wide Web," *Records Management Quarterly*, July 1997, 8–12.
2. Susan Feldman quoted in Annette Skov, "Internet Quality," *Database*, August/September 1998.
3. M. Theodore Farries, II, Jeanne D. Maes, and Ulla K. Bunz, "References and Bibliography: Citing the Internet," *Journal of Applied Business Research*, Summer 1998, 33–36.
4. Christopher Velotta, "How to Design and Implement a Questionnaire," *Technical Communication*, fall 1991.
5. Daphne A. Jameson, "The Ethics of Plagiarism: How Genre Affects Writers' Use of Source Materials," *The Bulletin of the Association for Business Communication*, June 1993, 18.
6. Writing Tutorial Services, Indiana University, " 'Plagiarism' What It Is and How To Recognize and Avoid It,"<www.indiana.edu/~wts/wts/plagiarism.html> (Retrieved 22 August 2001).
7. Gerald J. Alred, Walter E. Oliu, and Charles T. Brusaw, *The Professional Writer* (New York: St. Martin's Press, 1991), 78.
8. "Gulf States Centralizes HR/Payroll Functions," *Workforce*, December 1998, 70.

CHAPTER 12

1. "Charlene Marmer Solomon, "Marriott's Family Matters," *Personnel Journal*, October 1991, 40–42; Jennifer Laabs, "They Want More Support—Inside and Outside of Work," *Workforce*, November 1998, 54–56.

CHAPTER 14

1. Herman Holtz, *The Consultant's Guide to Proposal Writing* (New York: John Wiley, 1990), 188.

CHAPTER 15

1. Peter Urs Bender, *Secrets of Power Presentations* (Toronto: The Achievement Group, 1991).
2. Rod Plotnik, *Introduction to Psychology* (Pacific Grove, CA: Brooks/Cole, 1993), 484.
3. Wharton Applied Research Center, "A Study of the Effects of the Use of Overhead Transparencies on Business Meetings, Final Report" cited in "Short, Snappy Guide to Meaningful Presentations," *Working Woman*, June 1991, 73.
4. Jim Endicott, "For Better Presentations, Avoid PowerPoint Pitfalls," *Presentations*, June 1998, 36–37.
5. Victoria Hall Smith, "Gigs by the Gigabyte," *Working Woman*, May 1998, 114.
6. Smith, "Gigs," 115.
7. Hunt, "Picture This,." *CMA Magazine*, October 1998, 11.
8. "Addressing Fears," *Psychology Today*, May/June 1996, 11.
9. Ronald E. Dulek, John S. Fielden, and John S. Hill, "International Communication: An Executive Primer," *Business Horizons*, January/February 1991, 23.
10. Dulek, Fielden, and Hill, "International Communication," 22.
11. Patricia A. LaRosa, "Voice Messaging Is Quality 'Lip Service,'" *The Office*, May 1992, 10.
12. "Did You Know That …," *Boardroom Reports*, 15 August 1992, 15.

CHAPTER 16

1. George B. Weathersby, "Responding to Change," *Management Review*, October 1998, 5.
2. Sharon Voros, "Managing Your Career: The New Realities," *Communication World*, February 1997, 28–30.
3. Natalie Bortoli, "Resumes in the Right: New Rules Make Writing a Winner Easy," *Manage*, August 1997, 20.
4. Robert Lorentz, James W. Carland, and Jo Ann Carland, "The Résumé: What Value Is There in References?" *Journal of Technical Writing and Communication*, Fall 1993, 371.
5. Susan Toop, "Employers' Views on Résumés," *Career Options*, 1997–1998 (published by the Canadian Association of Career Educators and Employers [CACEE]) 34–35.
6. Joyce Lain Kennedy and Thomas J. Morrow, *Electronic Résumé Revolution* (New York: John Wiley & Sons, 1994), Chapter 3.
7. Marc Silver, "Selling the Perfect You," *U.S. News & World Report*, 5 February 1990, 70–72.
8. Rhonda D. Findling, "The Résumé Fax-periment," *Résumé Pro Newsletter*, Fall 1994, 10.
9. Diane Cole, "Ethics: Companies Crack Down on Dishonesty," *The Wall Street Journal*, Managing Your Career supplement, Spring 1991, 8.
10. "Managing Your Career," *National Business Employment Weekly*, Fall 1989, 29.
11. Joan E. Rigdon, "Deceptive Résumés Can Be Door-Openers but Can Become an Employee's Undoing," *The Wall Street Journal*, 17 June 1992, B1. See also Barbara Solomon, "Too Good to Be True?" *Management Review*, April 1998, 28.
12. Harriett M. Augustin, "The Written Job Search: A Comparison of the Traditional and a Nontraditional Approach," *The Bulletin of the Association for Business Communication*, September 1991, 13.

Acknowledgments

Text, Figures, Captions

pp. 25–28: Discussion of four phases of team development, role of conflict, and characteristics of successful teams based on Jon R. Katzenbach and Douglas K. Smith, *The Wisdom of Teams* (New York: HarperCollins, 1994); Jon R. Katzenbach, *Teams at the Top* (Boston: Harvard Business School Press, 1997); Laurel Kieffer, "Building a Team," *Nonprofit World*, July/August 1997, 39–41; Stephanie Reynolds, "Managing Conflict Through a Team Intervention and Training Strategy," *Employee Relations Today*, Winter 1998, 57–64; Odette Pollar, "Sticking Together," *Successful Meetings*, January 1997, 87–90; Kathleen M. Eisenhardt, "How Management Teams Can Have a Good Fight," *Harvard Business Review*, July/August 1997, 77–85; Charles Parnell, "Teamwork: Not a New Idea, But It's Transforming the Workplace," *Executive Speeches*, December 1997/January 1998, 38–40; Patricia Buhler, "Managing in the 90s: Creating Flexibility in Today's Workplace," *Supervision*, January 1996, 24–26; Erich Brockmann, "Removing the Paradox of Conflict from Group Decisions," *Academy of Management Executive*, May 1996, 61–62; Peter Jackson, "Getting the Group to Work," *CA Magazine*, January/February 1998, 41–43; Judith Bogert and David Butt, "Opportunities Lost, Challenges Met: Understanding and Applying Group Dynamics in Writing Projects," *The Bulletin*, June 1990, 51–58; Sandra J. Nelson and Douglas C. Smith, "Maximizing Cohesion and Minimizing Conflict in Collaborative Writing Groups," *The Bulletin*, June 1990, 59–62; Allen C. Amason, Wayne A. Hochwarter, Kenneth R. Thompson, and Allison W. Harrison, "Conflict: An Important Dimension in Successful Management Teams," *Organizational Dynamics*, Autumn 1995, 20–35; Allen C. Amason, "Distinguishing the Effects of Functional and Dysfunctional Conflict on Strategic Decision Making: Resolving a Paradox for Top Management Teams," *Academy of Management Journal*, February 1996, 123–48; Kathleen M. Eisenhardt, Jean L. Kahwajy, and L. J. Bourgeois, III, "Conflict and Strategic Choice: How Top Management Teams Disagree," *California Management Review*, Winter 1997, 42–62; Jane Henderson-Loney, "Tuckman and Tears: Developing Teams During Profound Organizational Change," *Supervision*, May 1996, 3–5; Christopher P. Neck and Charles C. Manz, "From Groupthink to Team-think: Toward the Creation of Constructive Thought Patterns in Self-Managing Work Teams," *Human Relations*, August 1994, 929–52; Shaila M. Miranda and Carol Saunders, "Group Support Systems: An Organization Development Intervention to Combat Groupthink," *Public Administration Quarterly*, Summer 1995, 193–216; Christopher P. Neck and Gregory Moorhead, "Groupthink Remodeled: The Importance of Leadership, Time Pressure, and Methodical Decision-Making Procedures," *Human Relations*, May 1995, 537–57.

p. 29: Portions of discussion for organizing effective written and oral team presentations based on Frank Jossi, "Putting It All Together: Creating Presentations as a Team," *Presentations*, July 1996, 18–26; Jon Rosen, "10 Ways to Make Your Next Team Presentation a Winner," *Presentations*, August 1997, 31; Jon Hanke, "Presenting as a Team," Presentations, January 1998, 74–82.

p. 32: Portions of discussion on tips for better team listening based on Hal Lancaster, "It's Time to Stop Promoting Yourself and Start Listening," *The Wall Street Journal*, 10 June 1997, B1; "Good Ideas Go Unheard," *Management Review*, February 1998, 7; Morey Stettner, "Angry? Slow Down and Listen to Others," *Investor's Business Daily*, 19 January 1998, A1; "Effective Communication," *Training Tomorrow*, November 1994, 32–33; John W. Haas and Christa L. Arnold, "An Examination of the Role of Listening in Judgments of Communication," *Journal of Business Communication*, April 1995, 123–39; Richard L. Papiernik, "Diversity Demands New Understanding," *Nation's Restaurant News*, 30 October 1995, 54, 84; and Kenneth Kaye, "The Art of Listening," *HR Focus*, October 1994, 24.

p. 35: Atlanta Committee for the Olympic Games as presented by Sam Ward, "The Olympic Don'ts of Gestures," USA Today (Thursday, March 14, 1996), p. 7C.

pp. 38–42: Portions of discussion based on Hal Lancaster, "Learning Some Ways to Make Meetings Slightly Less Awful," *The Wall Street Journal*, 26 May 1998, B1; Melinda Ligos, "Why Your Meetings Are a Total Bore," *Sales & Marketing Management*, May 1998, 84; Jana M. Kemp, "The Writing's on the Wall," *Successful Meetings*, August 1996, 74; Charles R. McConnell, "The Chairperson's Guide to Effective Meetings," *Health Care Supervisor*, March 1997, 1–9; John C. Bruening, "There's Good News About Meetings," *Managing Office Technology*, July 1996,

24–25; Tom McDonald, "Minimizing Meetings," *Successful Meetings*, June 1996, 24; Robert E. Levasseur, "Breaking the Silence," *Successful Meetings*, December 1995, 61–63; Sharon M. Lippincott, "Better Meetings," *Bottom Line/Business*, 15 August 1995, 3; Carol M. Barnum, "Here's How to Manage Your Meetings Effectively," *Communication Briefings* Bonus Item, April 1994, 8a–b; J. Keith Cook, "Try These Eight Guidelines for More Effective Meetings," *Communication Briefings* Bonus Item, April 1995, 8a–b; Larry D. Lauer, "A New Way to Look at Meetings," *Nonprofit World*, March/April 1995, 55–58.

pp. 43–44: Portions of discussion based on Mary Munter, "Meeting Technology: From Low-Tech to High-Tech," *Business Communication Quarterly*, June 1998, 80–87; Jon Hanke, "Presenting as a Team," *Presentations*, January 1998, 74–82; Sacha Cohen, "@ Work," *Predictions*, April 1998, 18–19; Michelle Mitterer, "Taming the Waves," *Successful Meetings*, March 1998, 112; Mary E. Thyfault, "Videoconferencing Boost," *Informationweek*, 4 May 1998, 148; Thomas Love, "A High-Tech Way to Save Time and Money," *Nation's Business*, June 1998; Phil Jones, *Official Netscape Communicator 4 Book* (Research Triangle Park, NC: Ventana, 1997), Chapter 11; Bryan Pfaffenberger, *Official Microsoft Internet Explorer 4 Book* (Redmond, WA: Microsoft Press, 1997), Chapter 17; William R. Pape, "A Meeting of Minds," *Inc*, Technology Supplement, 16 September 1997, 29–30; Jon Rosen, "10 Ways to Make Your Next Team Presentation a Winner," *Presentations*, August 1997, 31; Heath Row, "Real-time Collaboration Tools," CIO, 1 April 1997, 90–99; Larry Tuck, "Brave New Meetings," *Presentations*, September 1996, 30–36; Michael C. Brandon, "From Need to Know to Need to Know," *Communication World*, October/November, 1996, 18–19; Nancy R. Daly, "Reaching Board Decisions Online," *Association Management*, January 1996, L53–L56+; Leonard M. Jessup and David Van Over, "When a System Must Be All Things to All People: The Functions, Components and Costs of a Multi-purpose Group Support System Facility," *Journal of Systems Management*, July/August 1996, 14–21; Frank Jossi, "Putting It All Together: Creating Presentations as a Team," *Presentations*, July 1996, 18–26; Jim Clark and Richard Koonce, "Meetings Go High-Tech," *Training & Development*, November 1995, 32–38; Paul Dishman and Kregg Aytes, "Exploring Group Support Systems in Sales Management Applications," *Journal of Personal Selling & Sales Management*, Winter 1996, 65–77; Barbara Langham, "Mediated Meetings," *Successful Meetings*, January 1995, 75–76; M. Suzanne C. Berry, "Conducting Conference Calls," *Association Management*, January 1995, L-58 to L-60.

p. 52: Tech Talk box based on Sari Kalin, "The Importance of Being Multiculturally Correct," *Computerworld*, 6 October 1997, G16–17; B. G. Yovovich, "Making Sense of all the Web's Numbers," *Editor & Publisher*, Mediainfo.com Supplement, November 1998, 30–31; Laura Morelli, "Writing for a Global Audience on the Web," *Marketing News*, 17 August 1998, 16.

p. 56: Figure 3.1 based on J. Chung's analysis appearing in Guo-Ming Chen and William J. Starosta, *Foundations of Intercultural Communication* (Boston: Allyn and Bacon, 1998), 51; and Mary O'Hara-Devereaux and Robert Johansen, *Globalwork: Bridging Distance, Culture, and Time* (San Francisco: Jossey-Bass, 1994), 55.

p. 144: Raptors logo and letterhead reprinted by permission of the Toronto Raptors and NBA.

pp. 146–49: Discussion on claim and adjustment letters based on Jeffry J. Roth, "When the Customer's Got a Beef," *ABA Banking Journal*, July 1998, 24–29; Geoffrey Brewer, "The Customer Stops Here," *Sales & Marketing Management*, March 1998, 30–36; Bill Knapp, "Communication Breakdown," *World Wastes*, February 1998, 16; Stephen S. Tax, Stephen W. Brown, and Murali Chandrashekaran, "Customer Evaluations of Service Complaint Experiences: Implications for Relationship Marketing," *Journal of Marketing*, April 1998, 60–76; Edmund S. Fine, "Are You Listening to Your Customers?" *Quality Progress*, January 1998, 120; Robert Klara, "Press 1 to Gripe," *Restaurant Business*, 15 May 1998, 96–102; "Foiling the Rogues: 'Anti' Web Sites Are Great for Angry Customers, But Now Companies Are Trying to Fight Back," *Newsweek*, 27 October 1997, 80; Roberta Furger, "Don't Get Mad, Get Online," *PC World*, October 1997, 37; Gary Hren, "The Sales Behind the Scowl," *American Demographics*, Marketing Tools Supplement, March/April 1996, 14–17; Gwendolyn N. Smith, Rebecca F. Nolan, and Young Dai, "Job-Refusal Letters: Readers' Affective Responses to Direct and Indirect Organizational Plans," *Business Communication Quarterly*, March 1996, 67–73; Carol David and Margaret Ann Baker, "Rereading Bad News: Compliance-Gaining Features in Management Memos," *The Journal of Business Communications*, October 1994, 267–90; "Grove's Internet Apology," *Computer Reseller News*, 5 December 1994, 313; Denise T. Smart and Charles L. Martin, "Consumers Who Correspond With Business: A Profile and Measure of Satisfaction With Responses," *Journal of Applied Business Research*, Spring 1993, 30–42; Gary L. Clark, Peter F. Kaminski, and David R. Rink, "Consumer Complaints: Advice on How Companies Should Respond Based on an Empirical Study," *Journal of Services Marketing*, Winter 1992, 41–50; "How to Turn Complaints Into Business," *Agency Sales Magazine*, August 1990, 41–45; and Robert J. Aalberts and Lorraine A. Krajewski, "Claim and Adjustment Letters: Theory Versus Practice and Legal Implications," *The Bulletin of the Association of Business Communication*, September 1987, 1–5.

pp. 167–70: Text discussion based on "Surviving Information Glut," *Communication Briefings*, September

1998, 2; Margaret Boles and Brenda Paik Sunoo, "Don't Let E-Mail Botch Your Career," *Workforce*, February 1998, 21; Brenda Paik Sunoo, "What if Your E-Mail Ends Up in Court?" *Workforce*, July 1998, 36–41; G. A. Marken, "Think Before You Click," *Office Systems*, March 1998, 44–46; Hubert B. Van Hoof and Marja J. Verbeeten, "E-Mail, Web Site Most Commonly Used Internet Tools," *Hotel & Motel Management*, 15 June 1998, 34; Howard Millman, "Easy EDI for Everyone," *InfoWorld*, 17 August 1998, 38–39; Joe Dysart, "Establishing an Internet Policy," *Credit Union Executive*, May/June 1998, 18–22; "Do's and Don'ts for E-Mail Use," *CA Magazine*, June/July 1998, 40; Sana Reynolds, "Composing Effective E-Mail Messages," *Communication World*, July 1997, 8–9; Laura K. Romei, "ee cummings was a punk!" *Managing Office Technology*, February 1997, 9; Jenny C. McCune, "Get the Message," *Management Review*, January 1997, 10–11; John Edwards, "The Six Most Common Mistakes in Sending E-Mail," *Bottom Line/Business*, October 1997, 8; Mark Gibbs, "Where Do You Want Your E-Mail To Go Today?" *Network World*, 28 April 1997, 74; Barb Cole-Gomolski, "E-Mail Traffic, Costs Hit High-Speed Lane," *Computerworld*, 14 April 1997, 14; Marianne Kolbasuk McGee, "E-Mail Study Shows Few Constraints," *Informationweek*, 9 December 1996, 103–5; Elizabeth J. Hunt, "A Matter of 'Netiquette,'" *Business Quarterly*, Winter 1996, 13–14.

pp. 188–89: Career Coach box based on Michael E. Hattersley and Linda McJannet, *Management Communication* (New York: McGraw-Hill, 1996), 78–84; David W. Ewing, "Strategies of Persuasion," *Writing for Results* (New York: Wiley, 1979); and Joseph Mancuso, *Winning With the Power of Persuasion* (Dearborn, MI: Enterprise, 1993).

pp. 241–42: Figure 11.2 based on William A. Bolger, "How to Start a Free Legal Services Plan for Your Group" (Gloucester, VA: National Resource Center for Consumers of Legal Services, 1987).

p. 254: Figure 11.7 based on "Search Engines and Directories: The Quest for the Best," *PC Magazine*, September 2000, 131.

pp. 272–73: Figure 12.2 based on Charlene Marmer Solomon, "Marriott's Family Matters," *Personnel Journal*, October 1991, 40–42; Suzanne Gordon, "Helping Corporations Care," *Working Woman*, January 1993, 30.

p. 279: Figure 12.4 based on James Clark and Lyn Clark, *A Handbook for Office Workers*, 8e (Cincinnati: South-Western, 1998), 358–59.

p. 343: Career Coach box based on Bert Decker, "Successful Presentations: Simple and Practical," *HR Focus*, February 1992, 19; Lawrence Stevens, "The Proof Is in the Presentation," *Nation's Business*, July 1991, 33; Hal Lancaster, "Practice and Coaching Can Help You Improve Um, Y'Know, Speeches," *The Wall Street Journal*, 9 January 1996, B1.

pp. 347–350: Based on Scott Heimes, "Add Some Visual Thunder to Your Presentations," *Presentations*, March 1998, 11–12; Stuart Kahan, "Capturing Clients Through High-Powered Presentations," *Practical Accountant*, February 1997, 39–42; Nancy Ferris, "Brief the Boss, Dazzle the Audience," *Government Executive*, February 1998, 61–62; David Fine, "Chart a Clear Course for Better Financial Graphics," *Presentations*, June 1998, 40–41; "How to Put Together a Great Presentation," *Supervisory Management*, November 1995, 6; Jim Endicott, "For Better Presentations, Avoid PowerPoint Pitfalls," *Presentations*, June 1998, 36–37; Victoria Hall Smith, "Gigs by the Gigabyte," *Working Woman*, May 1998, 114–15.

pp. 365–66: Discussion on electronic job searching based on Rebecca Quick, "Your CyberCareer: Using the Internet to Find a Job," *The Wall Street Journal*, 5 March 1998, B7; Michele Pepe, "Online Job-Search Sites Flourish, Prosper," *Computer Reseller* News, 18 May 1998, 169; "Beyond Company Web Sites," *InfoWorld*, 22 June 1998, 103.

p. 372–373: Figure 16.5 adapted and reprinted with permission from *The Damn Good Resume Guide* by Yana Parker. Copyright © 1996 by Yana Parker, Ten Speed Press, Berkeley, CA 94707, www.tenspeed.com.

p. 377: Figure 16.7 from *Electronic Resume Revolution* by Joyce Lain Kennedy and Thomas J. Morrow, © 1994, John Wiley & Sons, Inc. This material is used by permission of John Wiley & Sons, Inc.

Photo Credits

p. 5: Superstock
p. 33: Superstock
p. 64: Superstock
p. 120: Dick Hemingway
p. 165: Dick Hemingway
p. 223: Photodisc
p. 247: John A. Rizzo/Photodisc
p. 253: Milton Montenegro/Photodisc
p. 276: Canadian Press – 95036
p. 297: Craig Brener/Photodisc
p. 391: Photodisc

Index

A

Abbreviations, 61, 375
Abstract, 311, 316
Academic courses, A-18
Academic degrees, A-18
Acronyms, 61
Action, in listening process, 32
Active voice, 101, 174
Adams, Michael, 55
Adaptation
 chronological résumé, 368
 customer reply letter, 143
 direct request letter, 137
 favour request, 194
 graphics, 282
 information e-mail message, 168
 justification/recommendation report, 296
 legal responsibilities, 84–85
 oral presentation, 345, 353
 periodic report, 290
 persuasive letter, 189
 positive tone, 78
 sales letter, 200, 203
 survey, 258
 task and audience, 78
 thank-you letter, 153
Adjectives, A-10, A-18
Adjustment letters
 apology, 149
 checklist, 150–151
 closing, 149, 196
 customer goodwill, 146
 explanation of problem, 148
 goals, 146
 opening, 148, 196
 sample, 151
 tone, 197
 writing tips, 199
Adverbs, A-10
Age
 avoiding bias, 81
 references, A-21
Alphanumeric outline, 94
AltaVista search site, 254
Ambiguous expressions, 61
American Psychological Association (APA) format
 in-text format, B-3 to B-4, B-5
 parenthetic citations, B-2 to B-3
 references, 318, B-4 to B-5
Analytical reports
 checklist, 300–304
 feasibility reports, 297–298, 300
 functions, 239
 justification/recommendation reports, 295–299
 organization, 240, 274, 275, 295
 yardstick reports, 298, 300, 301
Antecedents
 gender, A-8 to A-10
 it, which, this, that, A-9
 this, that, these, those, A-10
Anticipation
 customer reply letter, 143
 direct request letter, 137
 favour request, 194
 information e-mail message, 168
 sales letter, 203
 thank-you letter, 153
 See also Audience
Apologies, 149, 216
Apostrophe, A-16
Appearance
 application letter, 387
 dress and grooming, 37
 job interview, 391
 résumés, 375, 377, 379
 and silent messages, 37–38
 sloppy e-mail messages, 167, 169
Appendixes, 312, 313, 318, 330–331
Application form, 390
Application letter
 appearance, 387
 body, 384
 motivating action, 385–386
 opening, 382–384
 revision, 386
Application request letter, 388
Arithmetic average, 269
ASCII, 375, 379
Association of Proposal Management Professionals, 312
Attachments, 170
Attention-gaining techniques, 190–191, 200–201, 343
Audience
 building interest of, 190, 191, 201
 motivating action, 190, 191–192, 202
 profile, 77–78
 receiver-focused messages, 78–80
 receptive audience, 97–99, 188
 reducing resistance, 190, 191, 201–202
 secondary audience, 77–78
 tone and, 78
 unreceptive audience, 99, 188, 189
Authorization, of report, 316
Authorization request, 311
Awards, as marketing tool, 202
Axtell, Roger, 61

B

Background data, 251
Bad news. *See* Negative messages
Bar charts, 280
Beamer, Linda, 58–59
Bender, Peter Urs, 341
Benefits
 indirect, 193, 195
 positive effects, 216
 and reader's attention, 190
 and reader's interest, 191, 384
Bias-free language, 80–81, A-8 to A-9
Bibliography
 bibliographic indexes, 251
 style format, 318, 329, B-1, B-2, B-3, B-4 to B-5
Blame, 217
Blanket mailings, 200
Block style, 132, 133
Body language. *See* Posture and gestures
Bold type, 118
Bookmarking, 255

Boolean searches, 255
Brainstorming, 92
Browser, Web, 253
Bryan, J.P., 63
Buffer, 214, 215–216
Buhler, Patricia, 196
Bullet points, 84, 118, 348
  See also Highlighting
Business plan, 313
Business titles, A-19
Bypassing, 7, 9

C

CACEE WorkWeb, 366
Canada WorkInfoNet, 366
Canadian spelling, 120, 121
Canadian Style, The, 121
Capitalization
  academic courses and degrees, A-18
  departments, divisions, commit tees, A-20
  geographical names, A-19
  for highlighting, 118
  and netiquette, 170
  nouns followed by numbers or letters, A-20
  product names, A-20
  proper nouns and proper adjec tives, A-18
  titles of literary works, A-19
  titles preceding names, A-19
Captions, 283
Card catalogue, 250
Cause-and-effect
  paragraphs, 103
  relationship, 271
Cell phones, 11
  etiquette, 12
Central selling point, 201, 202, 204
Chambers, Kevin, 62
Channels
  appropriate communication channel, 76–77
  communication channel, 7–8
  formal channels, 13–15
  informal channels, 15–16
Charts, 280–282
Chernia, Ruth, 121
Chicago Manual of Style, 318
Chronological-functional résumés, 367
Chronological résumés, 367, 368
Chronology, 275, 344
Churchill, Winston, 114
Citation formats. *See* Documentation formats
Claim letters, 138–139, 140, 196–197
  See also Adjustment letters
Claims, denying, 223–224
Clause, 100
Clothing, 37
Cluster diagramming, 93, 94
Coherence, paragraphs, 104
Collective nouns, A-5
Colon, A-15
Comma
  comma splice, A-2
  coordinating conjunction, A-11 to A-12
  dates, addresses, geographical names, degrees, long numbers, A-12
  internal sentence interrupters, A-12 to A-13
  introductory clauses and phrases, A-11
  series, A-11
  unnecessary use, A-13 to A-14
  usage, A-11 to A-14
Common knowledge, 251
Communication
  in age of knowledge, 5
  communication process, 7–9
  cross-cultural communication, 59–61
  in diverse workplace, 5
  ethical behaviour, 16–18
  global competition and, 3
  nonverbal communication, 34–38
  objectivity, 17
  oral communication, 11
  organizational communication, 3–4, 10–16
  successful communication, 10
  written communication, 11–12
  See also Miscommunication
Communication coaches/trainers, 15, 18
Communication skills
  skills assessment, 21
  tactful disagreement, 27
Complaints. *See* Adjustment letters; Claim letters
Complimentary close, 132, 133
Compliments, 190, 215, 219, 220
Compound modifiers, A-10
Compound prepositions, 115
Compton, Linda, 16
Computer visuals. *See* Electronic presentations
Conclusions, 271–273, 317, 327–328
Condolences. *See* Sympathy, messages of
Conference reports, 291, 292
Confidentiality, 147
Confirmation memos and e-mail messages, 176–177
Conflict
  and creative thinking, 29
  divided loyalties, 17
  self-interest, 15
  task-oriented confrontation, 27
  in team development, 25–26
Congratulatory messages, answering, 154, 155
Conjunctive adverbs, A-3
Contrast and comparison, in paragraphs, 103
Convention reports, 291
Conversation, face-to-face, 76
Correlations, 270–271
Courtesy titles, A-19
Cover letter. *See* Application letter
Covers, 314
Credibility
  acquiring credibility, 188, 342
  offsetting audience resistance, 191
  and persuasion, 187
Credit, refusing, 224, 226
Critical thinking, procedure, 6
Cross-cultural communication
  bad-news messages, 229–230
  nonverbal communication, 35, 59–60
  oral messages, 60–61
  oral presentation, 354–355
  training, 65
  written messages, 61–62, 170
  See also Bias-free language; Multicultural sensitivity
Culture
  characteristics, 54
  communication style, 57
  context, 55
  dimensions, 54–57
  formality, 56
  individualism, 55–56
  learned behaviour, 54
  time orientation, 57

D

Daimler-Benz, 51
Dangling modifiers, 100
Dash, A-17
Data collection. *See* Research
Dateline, 132, 133

Date, references, A-21
Deadline
for acceptance, 311
as marketing tool, 202
Deception, 17
Decimal outline, 94
Decimal, references, A-21
Decoding, message, 8
Defamation lawsuits, 85, 214
Demonstrations, 343
Dependent clause, 100
Digressions, 352
Direct mail marketing, 198
Direct opening, 134, 174
Direct organizational plan
advantages, 98
analytical reports, 295
direct reply letter, 140
direct request letters, 135
investigative reports, 291, 294
justification/recommendation reports, 295
negative messages, 213
negative news, 213
paragraph plan, 102–103
possible negative outcome, 295
receptive audience, 97–99, 188
reports, 239–240
request and reply e-mail and memos, 173–176
straightforward claims, 138
Directories, online, 253
Direct reply letters
3-×-3 writing process, 143
adjustment letters, 146–151
arrangement of information, 142
body, 145, 148–149
closings, 142, 145–146, 149
complying with requests, 140–146
granting claims and making adjust ments, 146–151
illustration, 142, 143
letters of recommendation, 145–146, 147
openings, 140, 142, 145, 148
treating mixed messages, 142–143
Direct request letters
3-×-3 writing process, 137
application request, 388
checklist, 139
clarifying requests, 135–136
closings, 136, 139
information and action, 135–136, 137
openings, 135, 136, 138
placing orders, 136–137
reference request, 388
showing appreciation, 136
straightforward claims, 138–139
Disability bias, avoiding, 81
Discrimination, 64–65
Distorted messages
length of communication lines, 14
personal biases, 17
Distractions, 8, 10
barriers to listening, 33
Diversity
advantages of, 63–64
in business organizations, 64
and delivery of goods and services, 63
divisiveness of, 64
in teams, 27, 63–64
in workforce, 52–53
in workplace, 5
Doctrine-of-relative-filth trap, 16, 380
Documentation
academic writing, 260
business writing, 260
conventions, 260–261
ethical behaviour, 17, 282
purposes, 260
Documentation formats, 263
APA format, B2 to B5
Chicago style, 318
electronic sources, B5
in-house styles, B-1
MLA format, B1 to B2
Document format, 120
business letters, 131–133
e-mail, 170–172
formal report, 319–332
hard-copy memos, 175
letter reports, 241–242, 243
manuscript reports, 244
memo reports, 244
reports on preprinted forms, 244
Dovetailing, of sentences, 104
Downward flow, 13–14
Drafting
composing off-line, 168
customer reply letter, 143
favour request, 194
first draft, 99–102
formal report, 318
paragraphs, 102–105
questionnaire, 258
sales letter, 203
sentences, 100–101
sprint writing, 99–100
Drama, in oral presentations, 343
Drucker, Peter, 10

E

Editing, team writing, 30
Editing Canadian English, 121
Electronic applicant-tracking, 374
Electronic databases, 251, 252
Electronic Labour Exchange, 366
Electronic marketing, 198
Electronic notetaking, 261
Electronic presentation
bullet points, 348
colour schemes, 348
computer visuals, 346–347
multimedia features, 348
speaker's notes, 348–349
templates, 347
Web-based presentations, 349
See also Oral presentation
Electronic research, 91
Electronic sources, citing, B-2, B-5
E-mail and memos
3-×-3 writing process, 164–165, 168
analysis, 165
body, 166–167, 172
checklist, 176–178
closing lines, 172
closings, 167, 191–192
communication channel, 76
conciseness, 163, 169
confirmation, messages of, 176–178
e-mail formatting, 170–172
e-mail meetings, 44
formatting hard-copy memos, 175
graphic highlighting, 164
guideword headings, 163, 170, 172
inappropriate content and use, 169, 170
informational memos, 92, 172–173
information management, 14
marketing by e-mail, 198
openings, 166, 173, 174
organization, 166–167
procedure messages, 172–173
request and reply messages, 173–176
routine messages, 163–165
salutation, 172
smart e-mail practices, 167–172
tone, 163, 169, 172
Emoticons, 167
Emotional appeals, 201
Emotional outbursts, 169, 196
Empathy, 78, 80
Employee handbooks, 85
Employment
applicant's interests, 363

career path, 365
job search, 365–366
prospecting, 384
qualifications, 364
Employment rejection, 227
Empty words, 115–116
Enclosure notation, 132
Encoding, message, 7
Ends-justify-the-means trap, 17
Errors
apologies for, 149
sidestepping the issue, 148
Ethics
common ethical traps, 16–17
ethical behaviour, 16, 17–18, 282
goals of business communication, 17
letters of recommendation, 145
and persuasion, 192–193
résumé information, 371, 377, 380
Ethnocentrism, 58
Etiquette
cell phone, 12
cross-cultural communication, 61
culture and, 56
e-mail, 169–170
telephone calls, 356
Evaluation
customer reply letter, 143
direct request letter, 137
e-mail and memos, 165, 168
favour request, 194
final document, 30, 122
information e-mail message, 168
justification/recommendation report, 296
in letters of recommendation, 145–146
in listening process, 32
oral presentation, 345
periodic report, 290
questionnaire, 258
résumés, 368
sales letter, 203
thank-you letter, 153
Web sources, 256
Executive summary, 311, 316, 322
Experimentation, 91, 259
Expert opinion, 251
Explanation, in bad-news messages, 216–217
Explicit refusal, 217
Eye contact, 35–36, 343, 350, 352, 354

F

Face-saving, concept of, 58
Facial expression, 36
Facts, 17, 188–189, 190–191
False necessity trap, 16
Family titles, A-19
Favour requests, 193–195
Fax, 76
Feasibility reports, 297–298, 300
Feedback, 9, 13, 27
anonymous feedback, 15
cross-cultural communication, 61
listener feedback, 32
Fight-or-flight response, 351
Figures
clarity, 61
See also Numbers
Fireman, Paul, 65
Flipchart, 347
Flow charts, 281, 282
Fog index, 119
Follow-up letters
to application/résumé letter, 389
to interview letter, 389, 393
to rejection letter, 390
Formal reports. *See* Reports
Format. *See* Document format
Forming, 25
Form letters, 221
Fraction, references, A-21
Fragments, sentence, A-2
Frames of reference, miscommunication, 9
Freebies, 218
Free trials, 202
Frontloading. *See* Direct organizational plan
Functional heads, 277, 317
Functional résumés, 367, 369
Fused sentences, A-2

G

Gender bias, avoiding, 80–81, A-8 to A-9
General Agreement on Tariffs and Trade (GATT), 51
Generalizations, 59
Generic résumé, 379
George, Usha, 55, 58
Gestures. *See* Posture and gestures
Gibaldi, Joseph, B-1
Glass ceiling, 64
Globecareers.com, 366
Good-news openers, 174
Goodwill, 131, 139, 146
Goodwill messages
3-×-3 writing process, 153
characteristics, 151–152
checklist, 155–156
response to goodwill message, 154, 155
sympathy, 154–155
thank-you letter, 152–153
Google search site, 254, 377
Government titles, A-19
Grammar
correct usage, 62
mood, A-4
pronouns, A-6 to A-10
proofreading, 120
subject–verb agreement, A-4 to A-5
tenses, A-3 to A-4
verb voice, 101, 174, 217
Grapevine, 15–16
Graphics
captions, 283
colour in, 282
functions, 278
incorporation, 282–283, 324–325
objectives, 278–282
symbols, 281
Grids, 271
Group broadcasts, 357
Groupthink, 29, 65
Groupware, 43–44
Guarantee, as marketing tool, 202
Guffey Web site, 256, 263, 365
Guideword headings, 163, 170, 172
Gulf Canada Resources, 64
Gunning, Robert, 119

H

Hall, Edward T., 36, 55
Hall, Mildred Reed, 53
Handouts, 346, 347, 353
Hard-copy memos, 175
Headings, 84, 118, 277–278, 279, 315, 323
High-context cultures, 55–56
Highlighting
e-mail messages, 164, 167
headings, 118, 277–278
memos, 175, 176
techniques, 84, 117–119
Historical data, 251
Hoover's Online, 366
Horizontal flow, 15
HotBot search site, 254
HTML (Hypertext Markup Language), 252, 276
Human Resources Development Canada, 366
Human resources information, 84–85

Humour
in cross-cultural communication, 61
and e-mail messages, 169
jokes, 65
Hunt, Elizabeth, 350
Hyperlinks, 348
Hyphenation, compound modifiers, A-10

I

Ideas
cluster diagramming, 93, 94
emphasizing, 100–101
highlighting, 118
idea generation, 91–93
in message, 7
ordering, 93–97
organizational patterns, 97–99
outlining, 94–97
in paragraphs, 102–104
as supporting evidence, 188
Idioms, 60, 61
Illustrations, 282, 346–350
Implied contracts, 85
Implied refusal, 217
Incident reports. *See* Confirmation memos and e-mail messages
Indefinite pronouns, A-5
Independent clause, 100
Indexes, periodical, 251
Indirect opening, 134
Indirect organizational pattern
four-part indirect pattern, 189–192
justification/recommendation reports, 295, 297
negative news, 213–214
paragraph plan, 103–104
persuasive requests, 196
reports, 240, 242
unreceptive audiences, 99
Indirect questions, A-16 to A-17
Informational reports
checklist, 294
functions, 239
investigative reports, 291, 294
letter format, 241–242
memo format, 290
organization, 274, 275
periodic reports, 289–290
progress reports, 291, 293
trip, convention, conference reports, 291, 292
Information e-mail messages, 168, 172–173
Information overload, 12–13
InfoTrac®, 252
Inside address, 132, 133
Interactive technologies
forms of communication, 11
groupware, 43–44
impact of, 4
Interim reports, 291
Internet. *See* Online search; Online sources
Interpretation
frame of reference, 9
in listening process, 31–32
nonverbal cues, 34–38
Interruptions, and listening, 33, 61
Interview
common questions, 392
confidence, 393
data collection, 92
follow-up letter, 389, 393
interviewing techniques, 257, 259
job candidate, 390–393
preparation, 391
Intranet, 52
Investigative reports, 291, 294
Investment information, 84
Invitations, declining, 221–222
Italics, 118, 375, B-2, B-4

J

Jargon, 60, 61, 82–83
Job market, 364–365
Job search
online techniques, 365–366, 377
traditional techniques, 365
Jokes, 61, 65
Justification/recommendation reports, 295–299

K

Kallen, Martin, 114
Kennedy, Joyce Lain, 375
Keywords
definitions, 317
electronic résumés, 375–375, 377
interpersonal keywords, 377
keyword searches, 255

L

Lag time, in listening, 31, 33
Lawsuits
abusive language and, 84–85, 214
admission of liability, 148
careless language and, 214–215
defamation, 85
"good-guy syndrome," 215
hiring and firing decisions, 227
Leaders, dot, 315
Leadership
shared, 28
team leader, 25–26
Letterhead, 132, 133
Letter proposals, 309–311
Letter reports, 241
Letters (alphabet), for itemizing, 118
Letters (correspondence)
3-×-3 writing process, 135
analysis, 135
clarity, 131
communication channel, 76
direct reply letters, 140–151
direct request letters, 135–139
follow-up letters, 61
form, 131–133
good news, 148
goodwill messages, 151–156
mixed-news messages, 142, 144
organization, 132, 134
tone, 131
See also Persuasion
Line charts, 280–281
Line endings, 132
Lipton, Jeffery, 63
Listening process
action, 32
evaluation, 32
interpretation, 31–32
perception, 31
Listening skills, 9, 10
active involvement, 33
checklist, 34
clarifying questions, 33
identifying important facts, 33
increased understanding, 33, 34
team context, 31–34
Listing
in e-mail messages, 166–167
figures, 312
lettered lists, 118
numbered lists, 118
in purchase orders, 136, 138
scratch lists, 93
Literature review, 316
Loaded words, 81
Logical fallacies, 192
LookSmart search site, 254
Love, Richard, 188
Low-context cultures, 55
Lycos search site, 254

M

Magid, Larry, 349
Manual notetaking, 261
Manual research, 91
Maps, 282
Margins
  letter reports, 241
  memos, 175
  modified block style, 132
Marketing, 198, 202
  marketing information, 84–85
  proposals, 309, 310
McDonald's, 52
Mean, 269
Median, 269
Meetings
  agenda and time schedule, 41, 43
  checklists, 42–43
  closure, 42, 43
  communication channel, 76
  dealing with conflict, 42
  deciding to call a meeting, 39, 42
  distributing advance information, 40–41
  following up activity, 42
  preliminaries, 41
  purpose, 38–39
  recorder, 41
  selecting participants, 39–40
Memo reports, 243, 244, 290
Memorized presentation, 350
Memos. *See* E-mail and memos
Method, note on, 317
Minutes, of meeting, 41, 42
Miscommunication
  barriers to listening, 31
  distorted information, 14
  interpersonal barriers, 9–10
  job insecurity and, 14–15
  office politics and, 15
Misleading advertising, 85
Misplaced modifiers, 100–101
Mistakes. *See* Errors
Mixed-news messages, 142, 144
MLA Handbook for Writers of Research Papers, B-1
Mode, 269
Modern Language Association (MLA) format, B-1 to B-2
Modified block style, 131–132
Money, references, A-21
Monsanto Europe, 114
Monster Board, 366
Mood, verb, A-4
Morse, Wing, 57, 58
Movement, in oral presentation, 343, 352
Multicultural sensitivity, 57–59
  avoiding ethnocentrism, 58
  inclusive orientation, 66
  jokes, 61, 65
  nonverbal communication, 60
  patience, 58
  saving face, concept of, 58
  tips, 61–62
  tolerance, 58
  written messages, 62
  See also Bias-free language; Cross-cultural communication
Multiple line charts, 280

N

Names, spelling, 120
Negative messages
  3-×-3 writing process, 218–219, 220
  checklists, 222, 226, 228
  communication goals, 213
  declining invitations, 221–222
  denying claims, 223–224, 225
  direct pattern, 213, 218
  employee bad news, 227
  employment rejection, 227
  loaded words, 81
  organization news, 227–229
  problems with orders, 222–223
  reasons-before-refusal pattern, 213–214, 219–221
  refusing credit, 224, 226
  rejecting requests for favours, money, information, and action, 219–221
  tone, 218
  word choice, 216
Nelson Canadian Dictionary of the English Language, 121
Netiquette, 169–170
Networking, 365
Newby, Judy, 52
Noise, channel, 8
Nominative case pronouns, A-6, A-8
Nonverbal communication
  appearance of business documents, 37
  checklist, 38
  cross-cultural communication, 35, 59–60, 354–355
  eye contact, 35–36, 343, 350, 352, 354
  facial expression, 36
  influence of cues, 34–35
  interpersonal space, 36–37
  personal appearance, 37
  posture and gestures, 36
  sincerity and warmth, 80
  spatial arrangement and, 36
  time use, 36
Norming, 25
North American Free Trade Agreement, 51
Northern Light search site, 254
Notes, 34, 261, 350, 393
Nouns
  capitalization, A-18
  collective nouns, A-5
  wordiness, 116
NOVA Corporation, 63
Numbers
  checking for accuracy, 120
  sequencing, 118
  style conventions, A-20 to A-21

O

Objective case pronouns, A-7, A-8
Observation, 257
Offer, as marketing tool, 200, 202
Ombudsman programs, 15
Online resources, 91
  electronic databases, 251, 252
  World Wide Web, 252
Online résumés, 376–377
Online search
  library catalogue, 250
  search tools, 253–256
  tips and techniques, 253–256
Opening
  action-setting opener, 202, 203
  attention-gaining techniques, 200–201
  buffers, 215–216
  fillers, 114
  good-news openers, 174
  indirect opening, 134
  oral presentation, 352
  report introduction, 276–277
  for solicited jobs, 382–383
  for unsolicited jobs, 383–384
Opinions, 17, 188, 251
Oral communication, 11
  cross-cultural communication, 60–61
  face-to-face conversation, 76
  tone, 80
Oral presentation
  addressing questions, 353
  audience comprehension and retention, 342, 344, 346, 353

body, 342–344
checklist, 354–355
conclusion, 344
cross-cultural audiences, 353
ending, 353
introduction, 342
main ideas, 343
rehearsals, 31, 345, 351–352
team guidelines, 29–31
transitions, 30, 344
verbal signposts, 344, 346
See also Electronic presentation; Speaking skills; Written communication
Orders. *See* Purchase orders
Organization
chronological order, 275, 344
chronological résumé, 368
classification, 275, 344
comparison, 344
conventional grouping, 275–276, 344
customer reply letter, 143
data, 94–97, 274–277
direct request letter, 137
e-mail and memos, 166–167, 168
favour request, 194
justification/recommendation report, 296
listing, 93
oral presentation, 342–344, 345, 353
outlining, 94–97
periodic report, 290
primary goals, 93
relative importance, 275, 344
sales letter, 203
survey, 258
thank-you letter, 154
See also Direct organizational plan; Indirect organizational pattern
Organizational communication
downward flow, 13–14
external functions, 11
flattened hierarchies, 3–4
grapevine information, 15–16
horizontal flow, 15
internal functions, 10–11
managing negative news, 227–229
persuasive requests, 195–196
upward flow, 14–15
Organizational data, 251
Organization charts, 281
Orphans, 326
Outlining, 94–97
reports, 247–248
Overhead transparencies, 346, 347

P

Pagination, 323, 330
Paragraphs
alignment, 132
checklist, 106
coherence, 104
defined, 102
direct paragraph plan, 102–103
drafting, 102–105
indirect paragraph plan, 103–104
main idea, 102
pivoting paragraph plan, 103
short paragraphs, 105
Parallelism, 117
Paraphrasing, 33, 261–262
Parentheses, A-17
Parenthetical expressions. *See* Transitions
Passive voice, 101, 217
Past participles, A-3
Past tense, A-3 to A-4
Percent, references, A-21
Perception, in listening process, 31
Performance tests, 202
Performing, 25
Period, A-16 to A-17
Periodicals, 251
titles, B-2, B-4
Periodic reports, 289, 290
Personalized action statement, 201
Personalized closings, 217–218
proposals, 309
Persuasion
3-×-3 writing process, 187, 189–190
adjustments and claims, 196–198, 199
application letter, 382–387
checklist, 198
components, 190–192
credibility, 187, 188, 191
and ethics, 192–193
favours and actions, 193–195
four-part indirect pattern, 189–192
media releases, 204–205
within organizations, 195–196
purpose, 187
rational and emotional appeals, 201
sales messages, 198–204
supporting evidence, 188
Persuasive résumés
ASCII version, 375, 379
awards, honours, activities, 373
capabilities and skills, 372
career objective, 370–371
checklist, 379, 381–382
education, 370–371
e-mailing and faxing, 379
goal, 366
main heading, 369
online version, 376–377
parts, 367–374
personal data, 373
references, 374
scannable version, 374–375, 378
style and layout, 365, 375
work experience/employment history, 371–372
Photographs, 282
Phrases, 100
trite phrases, 116–117
Pie charts, 281
Pilot study, 257
Pivoting paragraph plan, 103
Plagiarism, 17, 260, 262
Plain English, 17
Polite command, 135, 174, A-17
Polls, as marketing tool, 202
Possessive case pronouns, A-7
Posture and gestures, 36, 60, 352, 354
Prejudice, 59
Prepositions, prepositional phrases, 115
Prewriting
adaptation, 78–83
analysis, 75–77
anticipation, 77–78
in writing process, 73
Primary research, 256–259
Primary sources, 91
Problem description, 190
Procedure e-mail messages, 172–173
Procter & Gamble, 51
Product feature, 200
Product liability, 84
Professional titles, A-19
Progress reports, 291, 393
Promise
as attention-keeping technique, 343
as marketing tool, 200, 202
Pronouns
case, A-6 to A-8
demonstrative pronouns, 104
indefinite pronouns, A-5
and paragraph coherence, 104
reference, A-8 to A-10
self-ending pronouns, A-7 to A-8
Proofreading, 74
customer reply letters, 143
direct request letters, 137
e-mail and memos, 165, 168
favour requests, 194
formal reports, 332

justification/recommendation reports, 296
periodic reports, 290
problems to watch, 120–121
questionnaires, 258
résumés, 368, 379
routine documents, 121–122
routine letters, 135
sales letters, 203
standard marks, 121
thank-you letters, 153
Proposals, 76
abstract, 311
appendix, 312, 313
authorization rcqucst, 311
background, problem, purpose, 310
budget, 311
business plan, 313
checklist, 312–314
formal proposals, 311–312
informal proposals, 309–311
introduction, 309
letter of transmittal, 311, 313
list of figures, 312
proposal, plan, schedule, 310–311
RPF, 309, 311
staffing, 311
table of contents, 312, 313
title page, 311
Proprietary information, 261
Prospecting, 384
Prototypes, 59
Proverbs, 201
Pseudolistening, 31
Publication Manual of the American Psychological Association, B-3
Punctuality
cultural value, 57
meetings, 41
silent messages, 36
Punctuation
apostrophe, A-16
capitalization, A-18 to A-20
checking for, 120
colon, A-15
comma, A-11 to A-14
dash, A-17
open style, 133
parentheses, A-17
period, A-16 to A-17
question mark, A-17
quotation marks, A-17 to A-18
semicolon, A-14 to A-15
Puns, 60
Purchase orders, 136–137
problems with, 222–223
Purpose, statement of, 246–247

Q

Question mark, A-17
Questions
clarifying questions, 27, 33
inappropriate questions, 393
interview, 392
as marketing tool, 200
open-ended questions, 93, 136, 257
primary questions, 91
question-and-answer period, 344, 353
rhetorical questions, 343
salary, 393
secondary questions, 91
stimulating questions, 191
survey, 257
Quotation marks, A-17–A-18
Quotations, 201, 261, 262–263

R

Racial/ethnic bias, avoiding, 81
Range, of values, 270
Rational appeals, 201
Rationalization trap, 16, 380
Reasons-before-refusal pattern
bad news, 214, 217
buffer, 214, 215–216
closing, 214, 217–218
explanation, 214, 216–217
Receiver-focused messages, 78–80
Recommendation
direct pattern, 295
letters of, 144-146, 147
reports, 273–274, 317–318, 327–328
Redundancies, 115
Reebok, 65
Reference initials, 132
Reference librarians, 250
Reference request, 388
References (professional), 374
References (sources). *See* Documentation; Documentation format
Rejection follow-up letter, 390
Relative-filth trap. *See* Doctrine-of-relative-filth trap
Religious titles, A-19
Remedy, to claims, 138, 139
Repetition, and coherence, 104
Reply memos. *See* Request and reply memos
Reports, 76
3-×-3 writing process, 244–245
analytical reports, 239, 240, 274, 275, 294–304
body, 317
checklist, 332–334
conclusions, 271–273
cover, 314
executive summary/abstract, 316, 322
format, 242, 244, 319–332
functions, 239
informational reports, 239, 241, 274, 275, 289–294
introduction, 276–277, 316–317
list of figures, 316
organizational patterns, 239–240, 242
outlining, 247–248
pagination, 323, 330
problem statement, 245–246
recommendations, 273–274, 317–318
statement of purpose, 246–247
table of contents, 315, 321
title page, 314, 319
transmittal letter/memo, 314–315, 320
work plan, 248–250
writing styles, 244, 245
Request and reply memos, 173–176
See also Direct reply letters; Direct request letters
Request for proposal (RFP), 309, 311
Research
chronological résumé, 368
customer reply letter, 143
direct request letter, 137
favour request, 194
formal methods, 91, 93
informal techniques, 92, 93
information e-mail message, 168
on the job, 91–92
primary research techniques, 256–259
sales letter, 203
thank-you letter, 153
Resistance-reducing techniques, 190, 191, 201–202
Résumé follow-up letter, 389
Résumés. *See* Persuasive résumés
Résumé-writing services, 379
Revision
application letter, 387
clarity, 113
conciseness, 114–116

customer reply letter, 143
direct request letter, 137
e-mail and memos, 163, 168
favour request, 194
formal report, 332
information e-mail messages, 168
justification/recommendation report, 296
oral presentation, 345
periodic report, 290
questionnaire, 258
readability, 117–120
résumés, 368, 377
sales letter, 203
thank-you letter, 153
tone, 114
vigour and directness, 116–117
in writing process, 73, 74
Robert's Rules of Order, 41
Rubbermaid, 51
Rumours. *See* Grapevine
Run-on sentences, A-2

S

Safety information, 84
Salary questions, 393
Sales letter, 198–204
3-×-3 writing process, 200, 203
building interest, 201
central selling point, 201, 202, 204
gaining attention, 200–201
motivating action, 202
reducing resistance, 201–202
Salutation, 132, 133, 146, 172, A-15
Samples
as attention-holding technique, 343
as marketing tool, 202
Sampling, 257
Saving face, concept of, 58
Scratch lists, 93
Scripted presentation, 350
Search engines, 253, 377
Secondary sources, 250–256
Segmented line (surface) charts, 280, 281
Self-deception trap, 16, 380
Self-ending pronouns, A-7 to A-8
Self-identity, culture and, 54
Self-talk, 351
Semicolon, A-3, A-14 to A-15
Sentences
checklist, 105
comma-splice sentences, A-2
dovetailing, 104
drafting, 100–102
elements, 100
fragments, A-2
length, 100
limiting sentences, 102–103
main sentences, 102–104
run-on sentences, A-2
structure, A-1 to A-3
supporting sentences, 102–104
Sexual harassment, 64
Signature, 132
Signature block, 132, 133
Simple line charts, 280
Slang, 60, 61
Slide projectors, 347
Slides. *See* Electronic presentation
Sony Music Entertainment, Inc., 52
Sources
books, 250
electronic databases, 252
note on, 317
online resources, 252–256
periodicals, 251–252
print resources, 250–252
research sources, 91–92
secondary sources, 250–256
Space, and nonverbal cues, 36
Spam, 198
Speaking skills
anxiety-reducing techniques, 350–351
attention-holding techniques, 353
delivery method, 350
presentation, 352
rehearsal, 351–352
slides as talking points, 350
speaking from notes, 350
See also Electronic presentation; Oral presentation
Spelling
Canadian style, 121
proofreading for, 120
Spiders, 253
Sprint writing, 99–100
Stage fright, avoiding, 351
Startling statement, 201
Statistical data, 251, 269–271
Stereotyping, 58–59, 65
"Stop words," 254
Storming, 25–26, 42
Subject line, 132, 133, 140, 166, 169
Subject–verb agreement, A-5 to A-6
Subjunctive mood, A-4
Summary, 295, 297, 352
executive summary, 311, 316, 322
keyword summary, 375–376
oral presentation, 352
Surveys
design, 257
informal survey, 92
mailed questionnaires, 256
Sympathy, messages of, 154–155

T

Table of contents, 312, 313, 315, 321
Tables, 269, 278–279
Talking heads, 277, 317
Targeted résumé, 379
Team-based management, 4
Team listening, 31–34
Teams
optimum size, 27
as primary performance unit, 25
procedures, 27
successful teams, 27–28
team development, 25–26
typical problems, 26
Teamware, 43–44
Teamwork
checklist, 28
collaboration, 27, 75–76
common purpose, 27
horizontal communication, 15
information sharing, 27
shared leadership, 28
skills, 44
Team writing
assigning tasks, 30
collecting information, 30
deadlines, 30
drafting, 30
generating ideas, 29, 30
ground rules, 29
guidelines, 29–31
planning the document, 30–31
roles of members, 29
Teleconferencing, 43
Telephone
cell phones, 11, 12
communication channel, 76
making calls, 355–356
receiving calls, 356
telephone tag, 356, 357
voice mail, 76, 356, 357
Tense, A-3 to A-4
Territory, and interpersonal space, 36–37
Testimonials, 200, 202, 203, 204
Thank-you letter, 152–153, 155, 393
Time
chronology, 275
clock time references, A-21

culture and, 57
personal structuring and use of, 36
time period references, A-21
Title page
formal proposal, 311
formal report, 314, 319
To-file reports. *See* Confirmation memos and e-mail messages
Tolerance, 58
Tone
adjustment letters, 197
belligerent tone, 139, 141
conversational tone, 114, 163
courteous tone, 82, 135, 136
cross-cultural communication, 62
formal tone, 318, 324
goodwill, 131
language and, 82–83, 172–173
negative words, 81
positive tone, 78, 81–82, 216, 217, 221
procedure and informational memos, 172–173
professional tone, 114
pushy tone, 192
sincerity and warmth, 80
timid tone, 192
voice and, 352, 356
Transitions
oral presentations, 30, 344, 346
reader cues, 277
transitional expressions, 104–105, 346, A-12 to A-13
Transmittal letter/memo, 311, 313, 314–315, 320
Trip reports, 291
Trite phrases, 116–117
Trudeau, Pierre, 55
Tuckman, B.A., 25
Two-sided strategy, 188

U

Underlining, 118, 375, 379
Unexpected statement, 190
Unilever, 51
Unknown recipient
adjustment letter, 199
letter of recommendation, 145
Upward flow, 14–15
URL (Uniform Resource Locator), 253
Usage
apostrophe and words ending in *s* sound, A-16
bias-free language, 80–81, A-8 to A-9
denoting slang and special words, A-17 to A-18
geographical names, A-19
indirect questions, A-16–A-17
names of organizational units, A-20
numbers, A-20–A-21
polite commands, A-16–A-17
product names, A-20
title of persons, A-19
title of works, A-19
who/whom, A-8
See also Grammar; Punctuation

V

Vanilla résumés, 374–375, 378
Varner, Iris, 58–59
Verbal static, 352
Verbs, A-3 to A-6
mood, A-4
for persuasive résumés, 372–374
subject–verb agreement, A-5 to A-6
tense, A-3 to A-4
Videoconferencing, 43–44, 76
Video monitor, 347
Visual aids, 343, 346–347, 353
Voice mail, 76, 356, 357
Voice, verb. *See* Active voice; Passive voice

W

Warranty, as marketing tool, 202
Web browsers, 253
Web sites
Association of Proposal Management Professionals, 312
disgruntled customers, 146
employment sites, 365–366
evaluation, 256
multilingual presence, 52
See also Online search; Online sources
Widows, 326
Wild cards, 254
Wordiness
empty words, 115–116
long-winded openers, 174
noun phrases, 116
opening fillers, 114
prepositional phrases, 115
redundancies, 115
trite phrases, 116–117
Word processing, 75
Workopolis, 366
Work plan, 248–250
Works Cited, bibliography, 318, 329, B-1, B-2
Write-and-wipe board, 347
Writer's printed name. *See* Signature block
Writing process. *See* Written communication
Written communication, 11–12
3-×-3 writing process, 73–74
basics, 73
bias-free language, 80–81
clarity, 61–62, 73, 84, 113–119
conciseness, 73, 113, 114–116
correct grammar usage, 62
highlighting techniques, 84
plain English, 17
prewriting, 77–85
purpose, 75–76
tone, 62, 78, 82–83, 114
word choice, 61, 81, 82, 85
See also Drafting; Revision

Y

Yahoo! search site, 254
Yardstick reports, 298, 300, 301